Fodor's 2013

LONDON

P9-AZX-253

Fodor's Travel Publications · New York, Toronto, London, Sydney, Auckland

www.fodors.com

FODOR'S LONDON 2013

Editors: Stephen Brewer, Robert I. C. Fisher

Editorial Contributors: Julius Honnor, Jack Jewers, James O'Neill, Ellin Stein, Alex Wijeratna

Production Editor: Evangelos Vasilakis
Maps & Illustrations: Mark Stroud, David Lindroth, *cartographers;* Rebecca Baer, *map editor;* William Wu, *information graphics*
Design: Fabrizio La Rocca, *creative director;* Tina Malaney, Chie Ushio, Jessica Walsh, *designers;* Melanie Marin, *associate director of photography;* Jennifer Romains, *photo research*
Cover Photo: BildagenturHuber/Picture Finders/Fototeca 9x12
Production Manager: Angela L. McLean

ISBN 978-0-307-92930-3

ISSN 0149-631X

SPECIAL SALES

This book is available at special discounts for bulk purchases for sales promotions or premiums. Special editions, including personalized covers, excerpts of existing books, and corporate imprints, can be created in large quantities for special needs. For more information, write to Special Markets/Premium Sales, 1745 Broadway, MD 3-1, New York, NY 10019, or e-mail specialmarkets@randomhouse.com.

AN IMPORTANT TIP & AN INVITATION

Although all prices, opening times, and other details in this book are based on information supplied to us at press time, changes occur all the time in the travel world, and Fodor's cannot accept responsibility for facts that become outdated or for inadvertent errors or omissions. So **always confirm information when it matters,** especially if you're making a detour to visit a specific place. Your experiences—positive and negative— matter to us. If we have missed or misstated something, **please write to us.** Share your opinion instantly through our online feedback center at fodors.com/contact-us.

PRINTED IN SINGAPORE

10 9 8 7 6 5 4 3 2 1

CONTENTS

MAPS

ABOUT THIS GUIDE

Fodor's Ratings

Everything in this guide is worth doing—we don't cover what isn't—but exceptional sights, hotels, and restaurants are recognized with additional accolades. **Fodor's Choice** ★ indicates our top recommendations; ★ highlights places we deem **Highly Recommended**; and **Best Bets** call attention to notable hotels and restaurants in various categories. Care to nominate a new place? Visit Fodors.com/contact-us.

Trip Costs

We list prices wherever possible to help you budget well. Hotel and restaurant price categories from **$** to **$$$$** are noted alongside each recommendation. For hotels, we include the lowest cost of a standard double room in high season. For restaurants, we cite the average price of a main course at dinner or, if dinner isn't served, at lunch. For attractions, we always list adult admission fees; discounts are usually available for children, students, and senior citizens.

Hotels

Our local writers vet every hotel to recommend the best overnights in each price category, from budget to expensive. Unless otherwise specified, you can expect private bath, phone, and TV in your room. For expanded hotel reviews, facilities, and deals visit Fodors.com.

TripAdvisor 🔘🔘

Our expert hotel picks are reinforced by high ratings on TripAdvisor. Look for representative quotes in this guide, and the latest TripAdvisor ratings and feedback at Fodors.com.

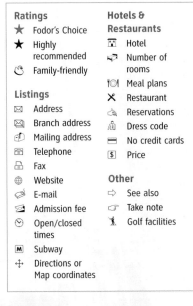

Ratings

★	Fodor's Choice
★	Highly recommended
ⓒ	Family-friendly

Listings

⊠	Address
⊠	Branch address
⌖	Mailing address
☎	Telephone
⎙	Fax
⊕	Website
✉	E-mail
🎫	Admission fee
⊙	Open/closed times
Ⓜ	Subway
⊹	Directions or Map coordinates

Hotels & Restaurants

🏨	Hotel
⇨	Number of rooms
❧◎	Meal plans
✕	Restaurant
⌑	Reservations
🏛	Dress code
⊟	No credit cards
💲	Price

Other

⇨	See also
☞	Take note
🏌	Golf facilities

Restaurants

Unless we state otherwise, restaurants are open for lunch and dinner daily. We mention dress code only when there's a specific requirement and reservations only when they're essential or not accepted. To make restaurant reservations, visit Fodors.com.

Credit Cards

The hotels and restaurants in this guide typically accept credit cards. If not, we'll say so.

Experience
London

LONDON TODAY

If London contained only its landmarks—Buckingham Palace, Big Ben, the Tower of London—it would still rank as one of the world's top destinations. But England's capital is much more.

It is a bevy of British bobbies, an ocean of black umbrellas, and an unconquered continuance of more than 2,000 years of history.

A city that loves to be explored, London beckons with great museums, royal pageantry, and 1,001 historic delights. Rain, crowds, high prices aside—just what is it that makes London such a great place to be?

The World Comes to Town

Londoners are among the least xenophobic in Europe, and with one-third of its residents born outside England, London is perhaps the most culturally diverse city on Earth.

It's part indifference and part adaptability (heavily sprinkled with tolerance), but Londoners pay precious little attention to outsiders.

This is undeniably part of London's charm: without the attentions of strangers, you can lose yourself here like in no other city.

With more than 300 languages spoken on its streets—from the hybrid multicultural London English to Pashto—the city is a terrific tangle of tongues.

And as one of Europe's largest cities—whether it's cuisine, music, theater, poetry, or fashion—the outside world converges on London to leave its mark.

A City of Ideas

The capital of England's knowledge economy, London is foremost a city of ideas and creativity.

From literati to glitterati, London is a vibrantly experimental capital and one of the destinations of choice for global culture hounds.

Whether it's experimental drama, offbeat literature, street fashion, street performers, sparkling West End productions, cutting-edge art, urban music, or left-field public sculpture, the city is a refreshing haven for the inventive, innovative, and independent-minded.

Scores of theaters in the West End make London a powerful magnet for drama enthusiasts, while the city's top-drawer museums embrace an almanac of human wisdom.

DID YOU KNOW?

With nearly 8 million residents, London is the most populous city in Europe—and the most cosmopolitan, with more than 300 different languages spoken.

■ A penthouse in Hyde Park sold for £135 million (about $200 million) in 2011, making it the world's most expensive apartment.

■ Westminster, home to many of London's top attractions, is technically a separate city. Long since absorbed by London, it survives in name only—"City of Westminster" is written on every street sign.

■ The River Thames is a treasure trove. Everything from Roman jewels to medieval swords wash up on its shores, though you're more likely to find Victorian clay pipes or rusted coins if you hunt along the South Bank at low tide.

Stormy Weather

The rough seas of the global financial crisis have crashed down pretty hard on London over the past couple of years.

Some assigned part of the blame for the riots that gripped the capital in the summer of 2011 on a perception that The City (the confusingly named financial district) had been let off lightly for their part in the recession, while the poor were hit hard.

Meanwhile, Britain became embroiled in bitter rows with France and Germany over whether London—which, since 2009, has been the world's preeminent financial center, ahead of New York—should avoid undue penalization during the desperate efforts to save the ailing euro and shore up troubled European economies.

This has once more raised questions about how Britain sees itself in the world, and nowhere are these arguments had more fiercely than in its staunchly internationalist capital.

Is London more a thriving European city or the beating heart of an island nation? The future is unwritten.

Have and Have-Nots

For the people who live here, money is what makes London's cogs go around.

The credit crunch may have pierced its bubble of prosperity, but London's housing market enjoys its own economic microclimate, with prices still rising as they fall elsewhere.

Elegant areas such as Kensington and Knightsbridge are in a different world, with gravity-defying prices fed by waves of overseas investors and tycoons.

Today, The City contributes about 2.5% of the country's GDP, which highlights the pivotal role it plays in the country's economy.

But while its Kazakh oligarchs, Saudi playboys, and cash-splashing freewheelers suggest a city endlessly flaunting its wealth, income disparities are colossal.

London remains a reasonably safe city but it pays to keep your wits about you; gang culture and incidents of knife and gun crime conspire to make some neighborhoods a grittier and disadvantaged flip side to the city's flashier boroughs. But, happily, most of the city is safe, sound, and one of the most sublimely civilized places in the world.

The Museum of London offers a free identification service.

■ The Middle Temple, Covent Garden, is where many of the capital's attorneys matriculate. They'd better be handy with a sword, though; by ancient custom a suit of armor is kept by the front door for lawyers to don in case of attack.

■ The Tube (the London Underground) is the world's oldest subway system, dating from 1863. With more than 253 miles of track, it now covers more ground than systems in New York, Paris, and Tokyo.

■ London manners they never warn you about: Brits drive on the left, and they scurry on the left, too. You must stand to the right on escalators to avoid sharp words from a local trying to pass in a hurry.

WHAT'S WHERE

The following numbers refer to chapters.

2 Westminster and Royal London. This is the place to embrace the "tourist" label. Snap pictures of the mounted Horse Guards, watch kids clambering onto the lions in Trafalgar Square, and visit stacks of art in the fantastic national galleries. Do brave the crowds to peruse historic Westminster Abbey and its ancient narrative in stone.

3 St. James's and Mayfair. You might not have the wallet for London's most prestigious district, but remember window-shopping in Mayfair is free. St. James's is the ultimate enclave of old money and gentlemen's London. Here you'll find the noted private members' clubs of Pall Mall, and the starched shirts and cigars of Jermyn Street, where you can shop like the Duke of Windsor.

4 Soho and Covent Garden. More sophisticated than seedy these days, the heart of London puts Theaterland, strip joints, Chinatown, and the trendiest of film studios side by side. Nearby Charing Cross Road is a bibliophile's dream, but steer clear of the hectic hordes in Leicester Square, London's crowd-packed answer to Times Square. Covent Garden's piazza is one of the busiest, most raffishly enjoyable parts of the city.

5 Bloomsbury and Holborn. Once the intellectual center of London, elegant Bloomsbury is now mostly a business district—albeit with the mother lode of museums at its heart. The British Museum has enough to keep you busy for a week; otherwise offerings are limited, though the Law Courts and University of London are worth a passing glance.

6 The City. London's Wall Street might be the oldest part of the capital, but thanks to futuristic skyscrapers and a sleek Millennium Bridge, it looks like the newest. Fans of history won't be short-changed, however: head for the baroque dome of St. Paul's Cathedral; the Victorian iconography of Tower Bridge; and the grisly medieval terrors of the Tower of London.

7 The East End. Once famed for the 19th-century slums immortalized by Charles Dickens, today the area has become the razor-sharp cutting edge of London's contemporary art scene. For spit-and-sawdust sensations of market London on the weekend, dive headfirst into the wares at Spitalfields, Petticoat Lane, Brick Lane (popular for curry houses and bagel bakeries), and Columbia Road's much-loved flower market.

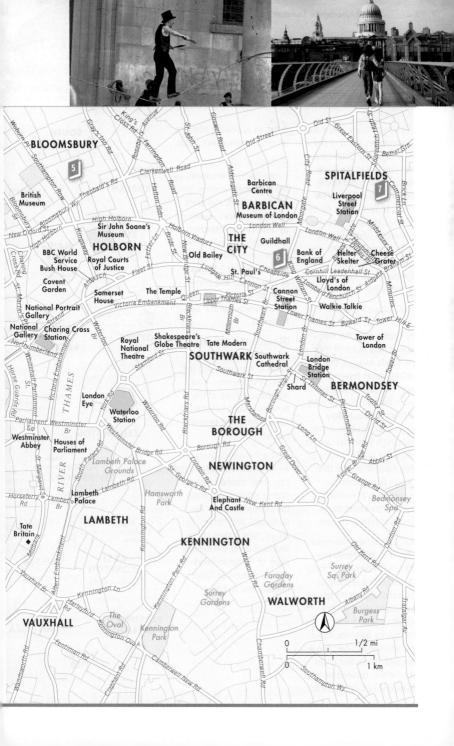

WHAT'S WHERE

8 The South Bank. Die-hard culture vultures could spend a lifetime here. The Southbank Centre—including the Royal National Theatre and Royal Festival Hall, the British Film Institute, Shakespeare's Globe, the Design Museum, and the Tate Modern—showcase the capital's crowning artistic glories. Or put it all in sweeping perspective from high up on the London Eye.

9 Kensington, Chelsea, and Knightsbridge. Although the many boutiques of the King's Road have lost much of their heady 1960s swagger, the museums are as awe-inspiring as ever. The playful Science Museum and the magnificently overblown Natural History Museum are crucial must-sees for kids. High Street Kensington ("High Street Ken" to locals) is slightly more affordable than the King's Road; otherwise, flash your cash at London's snazziest department stores, Harrods and Harvey Nichols.

10 Notting Hill and Bayswater. For that effortlessly hip North London demeanor, hang out in its coolest residential postal code. Around Portobello Road, Notting Hill Gate is a trendsetting square mile of multiethnicity, galleries, bijous shops, and see-and-be-seen-in restaurants. Bayswater mixes eclectic ethnic fashions and fresh-food shops. Some think it has an appealing edginess, others a nouveau-riche élan.

11 Regent's Park and Hampstead. Surrounded by the supremely elegant "terraces"—in truth, mansions as big as palaces—designed by 19th-century starchitect John Nash, Regent's Park is a Regency extravaganza, and the nearby "villages" of Hampstead and Primrose Hill attract residents like Gwyneth Paltrow and Madonna.

12 Greenwich. The Royal Observatory, Christopher Wren architecture, and the Greenwich Meridian Line all add up to one of the best excursions beyond the cut-and-thrust of central London.

13 The Thames Upstream. As an idyllic retreat from the city, stroll around London's stately gardens and enjoy the stately homes of Kew, Richmond, and Putney. Better yet, take a river cruise and land up at the famous maze of Hampton Court Palace, a vision of Tudor majesty and ambition.

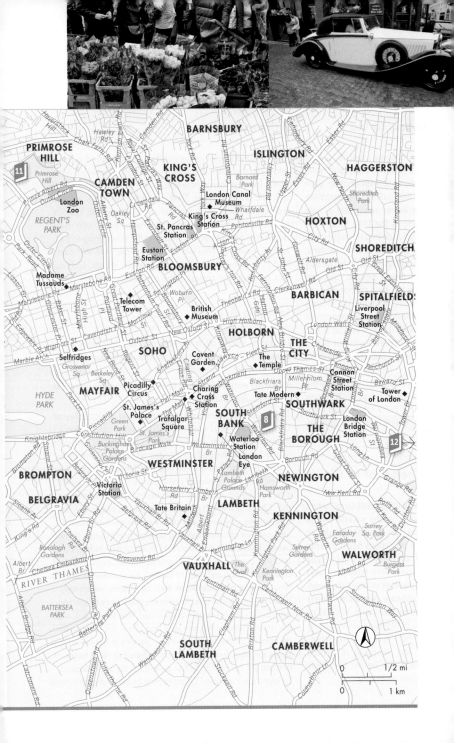

LONDON PLANNER

When to Go

The heaviest tourist season runs mid-April through mid-September, with another peak around Christmas—though the tide never really ebbs. Late spring is the time to see the countryside and the royal parks and gardens at their freshest; fall brings autumnal beauty and fewer people. Summer gives the best chance of good weather, although the crowds are most intense. Winter can be dismal—the sun sets at 4 and it's pitch dark by 5—but all the theaters, concerts, and exhibitions go full speed ahead, and festive Christmas lights bring a touch of magic to the busy streets. For a schedule of festivals, check ⊕ www.visitbritain.com.

When Not to Go

The October "half-term," when schools in the capital take a break for a week, results in most attractions being overrun by children. The start of August can be a very busy time, and hot weather makes Tube travel a nightmare. Air-conditioning is far from the norm in London, even in hotels; so while it rarely tops 90°F, it can feel much hotter. And shopping in central London just before Christmas borders on insane.

Addresses

Central London and its surrounding districts are divided into 32 boroughs—33, counting the City of London. More useful for navigating, however, are the subdivisions of London into postal districts. Throughout the guide we've given the abbreviated postal code for most listings. The first one or two letters give the location: N means north, NW means northwest, and so on. Don't expect the numbering to be logical, however. (You won't, for example, find W2 next to W3.) The general rule is that the lower numbers, such as W1 or SW1, are closest to the city center.

Getting Around

London is, above all, a walker's city, and will repay every moment you spend exploring on foot. But if you're in a rush, here are other options.

By far the easiest and most practical way to get around is on the Underground, or "Tube."

Trains run daily from early morning to late at night. Buy an Oyster card for £5, which will allow you to use London's transport at a lower cost than using paper tickets. The plastic card can be topped up as often as you want, and your £5 will be reimbursed when you hand the card back. Alternatively, buy a Travelcard pass (from £7 per day), which offers unlimited use of the Tube, buses, and the commuter rail. Check ⊕ www.tfl.gov.uk for details on ongoing Tube renovations. The commuter rail system is an over-ground network that connects outlying districts and suburbs to the center. Prices are comparable to those of the Underground, and you can easily transfer between the Underground and other connecting rail lines at many Tube stations. Buses crisscross London and often have their own lanes, which only buses and taxis can use. They are a great way to see London, but routes are more complicated than the Tube's; scan the route posted at the bus stop and check the number and destination on the front of the bus. Service is frequent; most buses run from 5 am to midnight, others are night buses or operate 24 hours. *For further details on transport around London, see the Travel Smart section at the end of this book.*

London Hours

The usual shop hours are Monday–Saturday 9–5:30 and Sunday noon–5. Around Oxford Street, High Street Kensington, and Knightsbridge, hours are 9:30–6, with late-night hours (until 7:30 or 8) on Wednesday or Thursday.

Many businesses are closed on Sunday and national ("bank") holidays, except in the center, where most open 10–4.

Banks are open weekdays 9:30–4:30; offices are generally open 9–5:30.

The major national museums and galleries are open daily, with shorter hours on weekends than weekdays. Often they are open late one night a week.

Deal or No Deal?

There's no getting around it: London can be as expensive as New York, Paris, or any other large city. But it's much better to accept this fact in advance and factor it into your vacation planning, tailoring outings and trips that will reflect your interests—and your budget.

Often, booking in advance, harnessing low-season deals, and taking advantage of Internet specials for flights and hotel rooms can cut down on costs. London is also great at offering things for free, and the quality of the culture, entertainment, relaxation, and fun to be had in the city means that if you target your spending wisely, you'll go home penny-pinched but satisfied.

How's the Weather?

It's a standard joke that Londoners—and English people in general—chat obsessively about meteorology. The London drizzle generates a fatalism that kicks off any conversation with a long-suffering nod to the weather. Winter is usually dreary and wet (with occasional snow), spring is colorful and fair, June to August can be anything from a total washout to a long, hot Indian summer and anything in between, while autumn is cool and mild. Come prepared for anything: layers and an umbrella are your best friends. One thing is sure: it's virtually impossible to forecast London weather, but you can be fairly certain that it will *not* be what you expect.

The following are the average daily maximum and minimum temperatures for London.

What It Costs

	IN LONDON	IN NEW YORK
Pair of theater tickets	£30–£70	$70–$250
Museum admission	Usually free; sometimes £4–£10	Usually $5–$25; rarely free
Fast-food value meal	£4	$4
Tall latte	£2.50	$3.50
Pint of beer in a pub	£3 and up	$6 and up
1-mile taxi ride before tips	£5	$5
Subway ride within city center	£4.50 without Oyster or Travelcard	$2.25

AVERAGE LONDON
TEMPERATURES

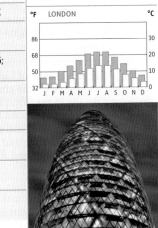

LONDON
TOP ATTRACTIONS

Westminster Abbey

(A) Steeped in history and tradition, the pillars of this great Christian edifice stand around the final resting place of the men and women who built Britain. Not only an iconic monument, the abbey continues to play an active role in the life of the nation, from the coronation of sovereigns to royal weddings and state funerals.

Buckingham Palace

(B) Not the largest or prettiest royal residence, the palace at the center of London is nonetheless a must-see for the glimpse it affords into the life of the Royal Family. The opulence of the state rooms open to the public are jaw dropping, and don't forget the collection of china and carriages at the Queen's Gallery and Royal Mews (stables) next door.

Tower of London

(C) The Tower is London at its majestic, historic best. This is truly the heart of the kingdom—with foundations dating back nine centuries, every brick tells a story, and the ax-blows and fortunes that have risen and fallen within this turreted mini-city provide an inexhaustible supply of intrigue.

St. Paul's Cathedral

(D) No matter how many times you have been here before, Sir Christopher Wren's masterpiece never fails to take the breath away. Climb the enormous dome, one of the world's largest, to experience the freaky acoustics of the Whispering Gallery, and higher still to the Golden Gallery for far-reaching views across London.

British Museum

(E) One of the world's greatest cultural institutions has been wowing visitors to London since 1753. Its collection spans virtually all recorded history, including the Elgin Marbles, the Rosetta Stone, and the treasures of Sutton Hoo.

Shakespeare's Globe Theatre

(F) You can catch a Shakespeare play almost every night of the year in London. But standing in the yard on a floor of leaves and sawdust in a scrupulously re-created version of the Tudor theater for which he wrote is a genuine thrill.

Tate Modern

(G) More of an event than the average museum visit, Tate Modern, housed in the striking 1940s Bankside Power Station, is a hip and immensely successful feature of London's artistic landscape. Passing judgment on the latest controversial temporary exhibit inside the giant turbine hall has become almost a civic duty among art-loving Londoners.

London's Central Parks

(H) A whopping 25% of London is parkland, so it seems churlish to pick out just one in the middle of it all. But if you must choose: pick St. James's Park for fairy-tale views; Green Park for hillocks and wide boulevards; Regent's Park for its open-air theater and the zoo; and Hyde Park for rowing on the Serpentine Lido.

Hampton Court Palace

(I) This idyllic palace on the banks of the Thames so captivated Henry VIII that it became the main seat of the British monarchy and remained so for centuries. Its Tudor charm, augmented by Wren's touch, and a picturesque location make it a great day out—not even dour Oliver Cromwell, who moved here in 1653, could resist its charms.

National Gallery

(J) Whatever the collective noun is for a set of old masters—a palette? a canvas?— there are enough here to have the most casual art enthusiast drooling with admiration. When you've finished, pause by the raised front door for one of London's great photo ops—Big Ben and Nelson's column are framed by pedestrianized Trafalgar Square.

LONDON
ROYAL LEGACY

Don't know your House of York from your Houses of Parliament? Here's the lowdown (or high-up) to the most famous kings and queens that have influenced London, and where you can still see their mark.

Queen Mary I

(A) "Bloody Mary" (r. 1553–58, House of Tudor), the Roman Catholic daughter of Henry VIII and his first wife, Catherine of Aragon, persecuted Protestants in an attempt to reverse the Reformation and return England to Catholicism. She imprisoned her half-sister, Elizabeth—daughter of Anne Boleyn—in the Tower, suspecting her of a plot against her, but there was no evidence and Elizabeth came to the throne after her death.

Edward the Confessor

(B) Edward (r. 1042–66) came to the throne in 1042 and ordered the construction of the original Westminster Abbey, which was consecrated in 1065, just a week before he died.

William the Conqueror

(C) The Battle of 1066 was won by William (r. 1066–87, House of Normandy) when he shot the then-king Harold through the eye with an arrow at the battle of Hastings. He is credited with starting the building of the White Tower in the Tower of London, though it wasn't completed until after his death.

Queen Elizabeth I

(D) The "Virgin Queen" (r. 1558–1603, House of Tudor) never married—perhaps because she thought that any man would try to wrest control from her (though she did move Robert Dudley, Earl of Leicester, into rooms close to her own at Hampton Court). She oversaw and supported a golden age of playwriting and poetry and famously inspired her troops as they prepared to battle the Spanish Armada.

Henry VIII

(E) A true Renaissance man, Henry (r. 1509–47, House of Tudor) was keen to bring new ideas to the Royal Court. All of Henry's six wives lived at Hampton Court Palace. Henry was desperate for a male heir—the main reason for having two of his wives executed: Anne Boleyn and Catherine Howard.

George III

(F) His frequent bouts of irrational behavior led to the nickname "The Mad One," but George (r. 1760–1820, House of Hanover) is now thought to have suffered from an inherited metabolic illness and often secluded himself at Kew Palace. With the Declaration of Independence in 1776, he lost the American colonies. One of the most cultured monarchs, George donated 65,000 of his books to the British Museum.

Duke and Duchess of Cambridge

(G) It's exciting to catch the Windsors on a royal walkabout—so go to ⊕ www.royal. gov.uk and search for the Diary of Events to catch Prince William and his new wife at a public event.

Charles I

(H) "The Martyr" (r. 1625–49, House of Stuart) is famous for losing the English Civil War, and was beheaded at Banqueting House—a twist of fate as Charles had commissioned the palace to be decorated with paintings showing a monarch being received into heaven.

Queen Victoria

(I) Famous for the longest reign so far in British history, 63 years, Victoria (r. 1837–1901, House of Hanover) was born in, and spent her childhood at, Kensington Palace, where she learned she would become queen. The Albert memorial is a monument to her beloved husband and the British Empire.

GIVE THE SPORTS SCENE A GO

London may have hosted the 2012 Olympic Games, but don't expect to see many residents practicing their javelin throws in Hyde Park or going for a synchronized swim across the Thames.

Sport in the capital comes into its own when it's watched, rather than participated in. You'll most easily witness London's fervent sporting passions in front of a screen in a pub with a pint in hand. And those passions run deep.

If you're lucky enough to score a ticket for a big football match, you'll experience a seething, jeering mass of mockery and rude chants, especially if the opposition happens to be another London team.

Amid all the aggression you might also catch a glimpse of why the excitement of English football makes it world sport's hottest media property.

And sport does mainly mean football (refer to it as "soccer" at your mortal peril). A generation of footballers lives the high life in London, their status somewhere between sporting rock stars and royalty.

Cricket, rugby, and tennis briefly impinge on Londoners' sporting horizons at certain times of year, but you're unlikely to see grown men crying at the outcome of matches at Wimbledon, or beating each other up about the Ashes.

Football

The English may not be the world's best when it comes to football (they last won the World Cup in 1966), but they invented the modern game and the sport is *the* national obsession.

London's top teams—Chelsea, Arsenal, Tottenham Hotspur, and West Ham—are world class (especially the first two),

however, and regularly progress in the European Champions League.

It's unlikely you'll be able to get tickets for anything except the least popular Premier League games during the August–May season, despite absurdly high ticket prices (as much as £50 for a standard seat).

You'll have a better chance of seeing a match if you avoid the top-tier teams. And a quick tip on conversation: locals love to talk football, but if you're going to join in the banter it is imperative to know your way around the big teams.

Arsenal. Arsenal (aka the Gunners) is historically London's most successful club. Under the managerial reign of Arsene Wenger they have shed their boring image to become proponents of attractive, free-flowing football—while hardly ever employing any English players. ⊠ *Emirates Stadium, Dayton Park* ☏ *020/7704–4040* ⊕ *www.arsenal.com* Ⓜ *Arsenal.*

Chelsea. Chief rivals of Manchester United in the Premier League, Champions League finalists in 2008, and Premier League title and FA Cup winners in 2009 and 2010, Chelsea (aka the Blues) is owned by one of Russia's richest men.

In recent years the team has been forged into a formidable and ruthless footballing machine. ⊠ *Stamford Bridge, Fulham Rd., Fulham* ☏ *0871/984–1905* ⊕ *www.chelseafc.com* Ⓜ *Fulham Broadway.*

Tottenham Hotspur. Tottenham Hotspur (aka Spurs)—bitter North London rivals of Arsenal—has underperformed for many years but there are strong hints of a revival with a bevy of England national team regulars. ⊠ *White Hart La., 748 High Rd.* ☏ *0844/499–5000* ⊕ *www. tottenhamhotspur.com* Ⓜ *National Rail: White Hart La.*

West Ham. West Ham, despite the name, is the team of the East End. After a long period of failing to match their past success, the Hammers have created a more consistent team, but one unlikely to claim too many trophies. ⊠ *Boleyn Ground, Green St., Upton Park* ☎ *0871/222–2700* ⊕ *www.whufc.com* Ⓜ *Upton Park.*

Cricket

At its best, cricket can be a slow-build of smoldering tension and excitement. At its worst, it can be too slow for the casual observer, as five-day games crawl toward a draw, or as the English weather interferes and rain stops play.

Lord's. Lord's has been hallowed cricketing turf since 1811. Tickets for major matches are hard to come by: obtain an application form and enter the ballot (lottery) to purchase them.

Forms are sent out in early December or you can apply online. Test Match tickets cost between £25 and £95. County matches (Middlesex plays here) can usually be seen by standing in line on match day. ⊠ *St. John's Wood Rd., St. John's Wood* ☎ *020/7432–1000* ⊕ *www.lords. org* Ⓜ *St. John's Wood.*

Horse Racing

Derby Day. Derby Day, usually held on the first Saturday in June, is the second-biggest social event of the racing calendar. It's also one of the world's greatest horse races, first run in 1780. Tickets are between £20 and £100. ⊠ *The Grandstand, Epsom Downs, Surrey* ☎ *0844/579–3004* ⊕ *www.epsomderby. co.uk.*

Royal Ascot. The Queen attends Royal Ascot in mid-June, driving from Windsor in an open carriage for a procession before the plebs.

Grandstand tickets, which go on sale in November, cost £50–£70, although some tickets can usually be bought on the day of the race (generally on Tuesday or Wednesday) for under £20. The real spectacle is the crowd itself, and those who arrive dressed inappropriately (jeans, shorts, sneakers) will be turned away from their grandstand seats. ⊠ *Grand Stand, Ascot, Berkshire* ☎ *0870/727–1234* ⊕ *www. ascot.co.uk.*

Tennis

Wimbledon Lawn Tennis Championships. The Wimbledon Lawn Tennis Championships are famous for the green grass of Centre Court and an old-fashioned insistence on players wearing white.

Rain, a perennial hazard even in the last-week-of-June–first-week-of-July timing, has been banished on Centre Court by the addition of a retractable roof.

Whether you can get grandstand tickets is literally down to the luck of the draw, because there's a ballot system (lottery) for advance purchase. For more information, see their website.

You can also buy entry to roam matches on the outside courts, where even the top-seeded players compete early.

Get to Southfields or Wimbledon Tube station as early as possible and get in line.

Five hundred show court tickets are also sold, but these usually go to those prepared to stand in line all night. ⊠ *Ticket Office, All England Lawn Tennis & Croquet Club, Box 98, Church Rd., Wimbledon* ☎ *020/8944–1066* ⊕ *www. wimbledon.org.*

FREE (AND ALMOST FREE) THINGS TO DO

The exchange rate may vary, but there's one conversion that'll never change: £0 = $0. Here are our picks for the top free things to do in London.

MUSEUMS AND GALLERIES

Many of London's biggest and best cultural attractions are free to enter, and the number of museums offering free entry is staggering. Donations are often more than welcome, and special exhibits usually cost extra.

Major Museums
British Museum
Imperial War Museum London
Museum of London
National Gallery
National Maritime Museum, Queen's House, and Royal Observatory
National Portrait Gallery
Natural History Museum
Science Museum
Tate Britain
Tate Modern
Victoria & Albert Museum

Smaller Museums and Galleries
Courtauld Institute Gallery (Permanent Exhibition free on Monday only)
Geffrye Museum
Hogarth's House
Horniman Museum
Houses of Parliament
Institute of Contemporary Arts (ICA) Gallery
Museum of London Docklands
Saatchi Gallery
Serpentine Gallery
Sir John Soane's Museum
V&A Museum of Childhood
Wallace Collection

CONCERTS

St. Martin-in-the-Fields, St. Stephen Walbrook, and St. James's Church have regular lunchtime concerts, as does St. George Bloomsbury on Sunday, Hyde Park Chapel on Thursday, and St. Giles in the Fields on Friday. There are regular organ recitals at Westminster Abbey.

Of the music colleges, the Royal Academy of Music, the Royal College of Music, the Guildhall, the Trinity College of Music and the Royal Opera House have regular free recitals.

For contemporary ears, the area outside the National Theatre on the South Bank (known as the Djanogly Concert Pitch) reverberates to an eclectic range of music weekdays at 5:45 pm, and on Saturday at 1 pm and 5:45 pm and Sunday at 1:45 pm. St. Olave's Church (Hart Street, EC3) has lunchtime recitals on Wednesday and Thursday at 1 pm. You can often catch some pretty good musicians busking on the Tube—they're licensed and have to pass an audition first.

Free jazz and classical evenings (sometimes there's a charge) are held on Thursday to Saturday (plus two Sundays per month at the excellent Dysart Arms (☎ 0208/940–8005 ⊕ www.thedysartarms.co.uk) in Richmond. Live Jazz also comes to the central and ancient Lamb and Flag (✉ 33 Rose St., WC2 ☎ 0207/497–9504) on Sunday from 7:30 pm. For regular doses of free blues, down a drink at the Ain't Nothing But Blues Bar (✉ 20 Kingly St. ☎ 020/7287–0514). One of Camden's most celebrated pubs, the Dublin Castle (✉ 94 Parkway ☎ 020/7485–1773) has long been one of the best places in London to catch big and soon-to-be-big Indie acts for about the price of two beers.

FILM, THEATER, AND OPERA

If all seats have been sold, the Royal National Theatre sells standing tickets for £5 each. Check at the box office.

Standing-only tickets with obstructed views at the Royal Opera House are between £4 and £14.

"Groundling" standing-only tickets are a traditional way to experience the Globe Theatre from £5.

Sloane Square's Royal Court Theatre, one of the United Kingdom's best venues for new playwriting, has restricted-view, standing-room-only tickets at the downstairs Jerwood Theatre for 10 pence (yes, £0.10), available one hour before the performance.

Under 30? Becoming an "access all arias" member of the English National Opera is free, and allows you to buy tickets for just £10.

OFFBEAT EXPERIENCES

Take a walk down the Greenwich Foot Tunnel. Claustrophobics steer clear, but for those looking for a quirky journey, take the old lift or the spiral stairs down and stroll under the Thames from the Isle of Dogs to the *Cutty Sark* in Greenwich.

There are free spectacles throughout the year, but one of the most warmly enjoyed is Guy Fawkes' Night (November 5), when parks throughout the country hold spectacular fireworks displays.

On New Year's Eve thousands of revelers descend on Trafalgar Square and the South Bank to watch more free fireworks. The Underground usually runs for free well into the small hours.

Finally, set aside so╌╌der. London is a gre╌╌ to explore on foot because so many of its real treasures are unsung: tiny alleyways barely visible on the map, garden squares, churchyards, shop windows, sudden vistas of skyline or park. With comfortable, weatherproof shoes and an umbrella, walking might well become your favorite activity here.

Barclays Cycle Hire. Barclays Cycle Hire has 330 docking stations housing 5,000 bicycles around central London. The first 30 minutes is free, but then it's £1 for the first hour and £4 for 90 minutes; you need a £45 yearly membership to get a card (you can also pay for casual use by credit card at any docking station). Remember to cycle on the left! ☏ 0645/026–3630.

SIGHTSEEING ON THE CHEAP

Join real Londoners on the top deck of a double-decker bus for a ride through some of the most scenic parts of the city. Routes 9 and 15 also operate shortened Heritage routes on the traditional Routemaster buses. You can use your Oyster card or buy tickets from machines at the bus stops for the following routes:

Bus 11: King's Road, Sloane Square, Victoria station, Westminster Abbey, Houses of Parliament and Big Ben, Whitehall, Trafalgar Square, the Strand, Fleet Street, and St. Paul's Cathedral.

Bus 12: Bayswater, Marble Arch, Oxford Street, Piccadilly Circus, Trafalgar Square, Horse Guards, Whitehall, Houses of Parliament and Big Ben, Westminster Bridge.

Bus 19: Sloane Square, Knightsbridge, Hyde Park Corner, Green Park, Piccadilly Circus, Shaftsbury Avenue, Oxford Street, Bloomsbury, Islington.

LONDON HISTORIC PUB CRAWL

An excellent and beery way to see London and its backstreets is on a "pub crawl" — this walk takes you through some of the city's most historically textured neighborhoods and pops you in and out of a string of cheerful and ancient pubs. Remember to settle back several times with a pint and drink in all the history.

The South Bank

Like Chaucer's *Canterbury Tales* pilgrims, we start in Southwark. Head down Borough High Street to the **George Inn**, a long black-and-white affair with wonky galleries, warped beams, and smoothed stairs. First chronicled in 1542, the pub is mentioned in Dickens's *Little Dorrit*. Cross Borough High Street and take the Stoney Street entrance to **Borough Market;** at the arched entrance to Green Market, turn left and walk along Cathedral Street, with **Southwark Cathedral** on your right. At the fork head left to the **Golden Hind** and then walk along Pickfords Wharf to reach the **Anchor**. Although recently renovated, this historic pub proudly declares it was built in 1615; head up to the roof terrace for sterling views of the river and **St. Paul's.** It is thought that writer Samuel Pepys stood here as he observed the 1666 fire of London.

Across the Thames

Cross Southwark Bridge to The City. On the corner of Bow Lane, **Ye Olde Watling** was originally built just before the Great Fire, and promptly torched. Rebuilt around 1668, again in 1901, and then again after the Blitz, it is named after Watling Street, the Roman Road on which it sits.

Head west along Watling Street to St. Paul's Cathedral and take a left down Creed Lane from Ludgate Hill. Wind your way down to Queen Victoria Street and turn right to the **Black Friar** at No 174.

The spectacular Arts and Crafts interior is all marble and brass bas-reliefs of friars interspersed with aphorisms and quotes.

Head up New Bridge Street and turn left onto Fleet Street to dig out the **Ye Olde Cheshire Cheese** in a minute alley called Wine Office Court. Dr. Johnson, author of the first dictionary, used to have a tipple or two here, as did Dickens, Mark Twain, and Theodore Roosevelt.

Bloomsbury

Wander west along Fleet Street, then walk north along Fetter Lane to the **Ye Olde Mitre,** which has served up brews since 1546 and was rebuilt around 1772. Find the preserved trunk of a cherry tree that Elizabeth I supposedly once danced around.

Walk north up Gray's Inn Road, then left onto Theobalds Road before turning right onto Lamb's Conduit Street, to find the **Lamb,** notable for its wooden horseshoe bar with etched-glass "snob screens" to shield the "pillars of society" when drinking with "women of dubious distinction." Head West along Great Ormond Street to the far side of Queen Square and the **Queen's Larder,** where Queen Charlotte reputedly rented out the cellar. Just north is the Russell Square Tube station, or you can continue to the British Museum, which is opposite the Museum Tavern, where Karl Marx would loosen his neck-tie and take time off from researching *Das Kapital*.

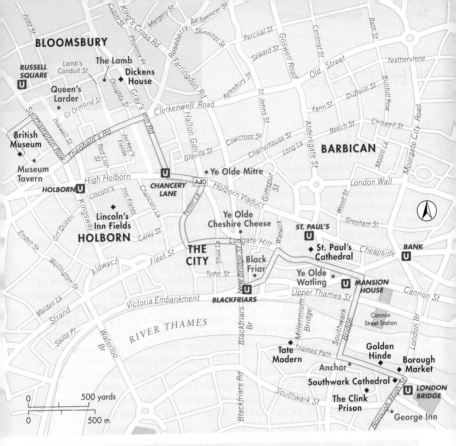

Where to Start:	On the South Bank at the London Bridge Tube/rail station.
Length:	4 miles (about 1.5 hours without stopping). Just part of this walk will give you a taste of the oldest part of London.
Where to Stop:	Russell Square Tube station or Tottenham Court Road.
Best Time to Go:	Weekday afternoons (most pubs open late in the morning). Some of these pubs are shut on weekends.
Worst Time to Go:	Busy summer weekends may be too crowded.
Eating and Drinking:	All the pubs will serve food at lunchtime. Stop when you're hungry or pick up some tasty morsels in Borough Market and stop in either Gray's Inn Fields or Lincoln's Inn Fields for a picnic.
Diversions:	From the Anchor, consider continuing along the riverside to the Tate Modern, before crossing over the River Thames to ferret out Ye Olde Watling or the Black Friar.
Pub Highlights:	The Anchor, Black Friar, George Inn, the Lamb, Ye Olde Cheshire Cheese, Ye Old Watling, Ye Olde Mitre.

WHAT'S NEW

The Changing Face

"London," so a local saying goes "will be nice when it's finished." You'll soon get the joke— it's hard to turn a corner in the city center without finding some work-in-progress crater so vast you can only imagine what was there before. This latest wave of development started in the 1990s and was accelerated by the 2012 Olympics. Meanwhile, new neighborhoods are brought into the limelight— currently, a visit to Hoxton or Shoreditch should provide you with your quotient of London hipness—and the creative fervor that has always swirled through London like fog shows up in art galleries, designer boutiques, and theaters.

Getting Around

More than £17 billion were earmarked for transport development in the run-up to the 2012 Games in this city that sees 20 million trips daily on the transport system. Served by five airports, London has the world's second-largest (and oldest) underground system, and recent years have seen the extension of the East London line and the Docklands Light Railway, and the upgrading and modernization of all Underground stations. Happily, the Congestion Charge, imposing a fee of £10 per day on vehicles entering central London, has reduced both traffic and pollution.

London under Construction

London seized upon the occasion of the 2012 Olympics to showcase some sparkling new architecture. With the exceptions of Canary Wharf, the Swiss Re Headquarters (the "Gherkin"), the Lloyd's of London building, and the London Eye, London's skyline has traditionally been low-key, with little of the brash swagger of, say, Shanghai or Manhattan.

But a spectacular crop of new architecture—the 945-foot "Helter-Skelter" Bishopsgate Tower, 740-foot Leadenhall Building "Cheese Grater," and 1,020-foot "Shard of Glass"—is injecting fresh adrenaline into London's otherwise staid streetscapes and revitalizing its skyline.

Some laud the boldness of these brand new steel-and-glass skyscrapers, and Londoners tend to give a thumbs-up to the bulbous 30 St. Mary Axe ("the Gherkin"). Others lament the desecration of historic vistas and despair at designs such as the proposed Tate Modern extension, which resembles a giant pyramid folding in on itself. The verdict is still out on the Shard at London Bridge—designed by Enzo Piano, this irregular triangle of glass is the tallest building in Europe. Whatever critics and those who must look at these structures every day may say, London will never be quite the same again.

The Remains of the Games

The gorgeous **Aquatics Centre,** a curvilinear £303-million piece of eye candy, was the centerpiece of London's Olympics display. Designed by Iraqi architect Zaha Hadid, the center's wavelike form is impressive and inspirational, rising above the East London neighborhood of Stratford. The center will continue to serve as London's main venue for aquatic sports. The design of the nearby **Olympic Stadium** has been received with divided opinion, with critics making unfavorable comparisons with Beijing's iconic Bird's Nest. Supporters point to the 80,000-capacity stadium's ongoing use for football matches and other events, but for many the stadium's major plus point is its ability to be dismantled.

AFTERNOON TEA

So, what is Afternoon Tea, exactly? Well, it means real tea (Earl Grey, English Breakfast, Ceylon, Darjeeling, or Assam) brewed in a china pot, and served with china cups and saucers, milk, lemon, and silver spoons, between 3 and 5:30 pm.

For the full experience there should be elegant finger foods on a three-tiered cake stand: crustless sandwiches on the bottom; fruit scones with Devonshire clotted cream and strawberry jam in the middle; and rich cakes, shortbread, patisseries, macaroons, and fancies on top.

Tea-goers dress smartly (though not ostentatiously) and a certain level of decorum is, of course, expected.

The Savoy. Hands down, this superglamorous hotel offers the most beautiful setting for tea: the Thames Foyer, a symphony of grays and golds centered around a "winter garden" wrought-iron gazebo, just the place for the house pianist to accompany you as you enjoy the award-winning house teas along with finger sandwiches, homemade scones, and yumptious pastries. Don't forget to stop in the adjacent Chinoiserie Vestibule—a gloriously chic black-and-white chintz-covered room—to make some purchases in the Savoy Tea Boutique. ⊠ *Strand, Covent Garden* ☎ *020/7836–4343* ⊗ *Served daily 3 to 5* Ⓜ *Covent Garden, Charing Cross.*

Claridge's. The hallowed tradition is given a sophisticated, contemporary twist at Claridge's, where your teatime companions are more likely to be film stars and supermodels than aristocrats. Afternoon tea is £38 and Champagne tea is £49. ⊠ *Brook St., Mayfair* ☎ *020/7629–8860* ⊗ *Served daily 3, 3:30, 5, and 5:30* Ⓜ *Bond St.*

The Dorchester. Amid a maze of marble and gold leaf, tea in the Promenade is best taken on comfy sofas and to the sound of the resident pianist. Afternoon tea is £38.50, Champagne tea is £46.50. Book well ahead. ⊠ *53 Park La.* ☎ *020/7629–8888* ⚑ *Reservations essential* ⊗ *Served daily 2:30 and 4:45* Ⓜ *Hyde Park Corner.*

Fortnum & Mason. Upstairs at the venerable 300-year-old store (grocer to the Queen), three set teas are ceremoniously served: afternoon tea (£35), old-fashioned high tea (a traditional light meal, £37), and Champagne tea (priced according to Champagne). Unfortunately, the tea parlor decor is tired and stained while many of the edibles served are shockingly inedible. ⊠ *St. James's Restaurant, 4th fl., 181 Piccadilly, St. James's* ☎ *020/7734–8040* ⊗ *Served Mon.–Sat. 2–7, Sun. noon–4:30* Ⓜ *Green Park.*

The Ritz. At the Ritz tea is served in the impressive Palm Court, with marble tables and Louis XIV chaises complete with musical accompaniment, providing a taste of "Edwardian London" in the 21st century. Afternoon tea is £52 and Champagne tea £54. Reserve two to three months ahead and remember to wear a jacket and tie. ⊠ *150 Piccadilly, St. James's* ☎ *020/7300–2309* ⚑ *Reservations essential* ⊗ *Served daily 11:30, 1:30, 3:30, 5:30, 7:30* Ⓜ *Green Park.*

The Wolseley. The sumptuous dining room at the Wolseley has barely changed since the 1920s, and it remains as fashionable a hangout as it was in its roaring heyday. Afternoon tea is £21 and Champagne tea £30. ⊠ *160 Piccadilly, St. James's* ☎ *020/7499–6996* ⊗ *Served weekdays 3–6:30, Sat. 3:30–5, Sun. 3:30–6:30* Ⓜ *Green Park.*

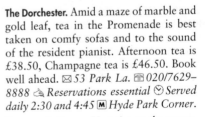

LONDON WITH KIDS

Education Without Yawns

London Dungeon. Gore galore (did you ever see a disembowelment?) plunges you into murky depths of history, with gruesome rides and special effects scary enough to frighten the coolest of kids. And if you're coming at Christmas, dare you enter "Satan's Grotto?" We didn't!

London Zoo. City? What city? Disappear into the animal kingdom among the enclosures, complete with sessions for kids afraid of spiders (even bird-eating ones!), in this popular animal retreat set in Regent's Park.

Kew Gardens. If the sun penetrates the London clouds, Kew Gardens is great for kids, with family activities, the "climbers and creepers" play zone, zip wires, scramble slides, and children's trails; free for children.

Natural History Museum. It doesn't get much more awe-inspiring than bloodsucking bats, fake earthquakes, and a life-size blue whale. Just make sure you know your diplodocus from your dodo.

Science Museum. Special effects, virtual voyages, interactive galleries, puzzles, and mysteries from the world of science can keep kids effortlessly amused all day.

Tower of London. Perfect for playing princess in front of the crown jewels. Not so perfect for imagining what becomes of the fairy tale—watch your royal necks.

Performances

Applaud street performers. You can't beat the cacophony of jugglers, fire-eaters, unicyclists, and the human statues tantalizing crowds in Covent Garden.

Enjoy Regent's Park Open Air Theatre. Welcome to the land of fairy dust and magic. Don't miss an evening performance under the stars of *A Midsummer Night's Dream* in summer.

Sing along to musicals. Move over, Broadway: you can't beat a song-and-dance number from London's West End.

Activities

Ride the London Eye. Europe's biggest observation wheel looks like a giant fairground ride, and you can see for what seems like half the world from the top.

Pose with a Queen's Guard. There's always a soldier, dressed in full traditional regalia, standing watch by the entrance to Horse Guards on the Trafalgar Square end of Whitehall. They don't mind you posing for pictures, but they're not allowed to smile . . . which some kids see as a challenge.

Ice-skating at the Natural History Museum. Send your kids whizzing, arms whirling, across ice from November to January at this fantastic ice rink right outside the museum.

Night at the Museum. Find out what the dinosaurs really do when the lights go out at the monthly Dino Snores sleepover (minimum of one adult and five kids per group).

Paddle on the Serpentine. Pack a picnic and take a rowboat out into the middle of Hyde Park's famed lake; settle back and tuck in to lunch.

Lose your kids at Hampton Court. The greenery might be more than 300 years old, but the quest to reach the middle of the world-famous hedge maze remains as challenging as ever.

Little Angel Theatre. Entertaining children since 1961, this Islington puppet theater (⊠ *14 Dagmar Passage* ☎ *0207/226–1787* ⊕ *www.littleangeltheatre.com*) also has drama classes for young thespians.

Millennium Bridge and St. Paul's Cathedral.

THE BUILDING OF LONDON

The past is knit into the very fabric of the lives of Londoners: they live in Regency townhouses, worship in Baroque churches, and chill out in Edwardian-era parks. Unfolding like a gigantic historical pop-up book, London reveals—building by building—the pageant of a nation's history. To make sense of it all, here's a quick architectural tour through time.

Despite invading tribes, an epic fire, and 20th-century bombing, London has always survived, and a surprising amount of yesterday remains visible in its streets today. Starting with remnants of Londinium, the early Roman city contained by a defensive wall some 2,000 years ago, you can trace the city's beginnings. Only pieces of the wall remain, but the name of each entrance to the city has been preserved: Aldgate, Newgate, Bishopsgate, Cripplegate, Aldersgate, and Ludgate.

As commerce grew the city over the centuries, London expanded between two centers of power, Westminster in the west and the Tower in the east. Following both the Great Fire and World War II destruction, the need to rebuild outweighed the desire for sensible street layouts, and often any aesthetic considerations. In fact, London as a whole has rarely been planned, and the financial center is still roughly in the shape of that original Roman wall. London's haphazard streets and alleys are filled with diverse architectural styles side-by-side, each representing a piece of the city's history.

(top left) Statue of the Roman Emperor Trajan (r. AD 98-117) outside the largest remaining section of the Roman wall at Tower Hill. (right) Tower of London; (left) Carausius coin struck circa 288-290 AD at the Londinium mint.

Roman Londinium

Pre–410

As the Roman Empire expanded, Britain was conquered and the first city where London now stands began to develop along the Thames. Among many building projects, the Romans enclosed Londinium with a wall to protect against invading tribes after the Celtic warrior queen Boudicca razed the city. Today chunks of the ancient barrier remain in the City, and at the Guildhall art gallery you can see a partial Roman amphitheatre from this time.

■ Visit: Guildhall (Ch. 6), London Wall at Tower Hill Tube station (Ch. 6), Museum of London (Ch. 5)

Saxon and Medieval London

410–1485

Little is known of the 250 years after the Romans left London. Following these "Dark Ages," most medieval houses and bridges were built of timber or wattle and daub and the perishable materials didn't last in the changing city.

England's royalty began building heavily in the capital as a sign of strength and power, focusing on defensive structures. In 1042, the Saxon King Edward the Confessor moved his court and began a church on the site of the current Westminster Abbey, where almost all the monarchs of England have been crowned since. From

across the English Channel, William the Conqueror brought Norman architectural styles with him. William built the White Tower; later expanded, the solid castle became the heart of the Tower of London complex. His son and heir William II saw the construction of Westminster Hall, the oldest part of the Palace of Westminster (today's Houses of Parliament). St. Bartholomew's Hospital, founded in 1123, and the Guildhall, a center of commerce from the early 15th century, are among the few buildings that survived the later Great Fire.

■ Visit: Guildhall (Ch. 6), St. Bartholomew's Hospital (Ch. 6), Tower of London (Ch. 6)

1066 William the Conqueror becomes King of England	1240 Parliament sits at Westminster for the first time	1348 The Black Death	1605 Guy Fawkes's Gunpowder Plot uncovered 1534 Dissolution of the Monasteries	1642–51 Civil War 1666 Great Fire
1000	1250		1500	1750

1

IN FOCUS THE BUILDING OF LONDON

(top left) Painted ceiling of Banqueting House by Peter Paul Rubens; (top right) *The Great Fire of London, with Ludgate and old St Paul's;* (bottom right) St. Paul's Cathedral, built 1675–1708, designed by Christopher Wren

Tudor and Stuart London

1485–1700

As London grew, the Tudor royals influenced the architecture of London not only by creating, but also by destroying. Henry VII continued the expansion of Westminster Abbey and his successor, Henry VIII, resided at Hampton Court. The arts flourished under Elizabeth I, and the original Globe Theatre was built in 1599. Yet many fine medieval churches were torn down as England separated from the Roman Catholic Church.

Architects brought continental ideas to London, notably the influential Italian Palladian style introduced by Inigo Jones. You can see this classical style with it's mathematical proportions and balanced lines at the Queen's House in Greenwich and at Banqueting House, where Charles I was executed following the civil war. Eleven years later, Charles II was restored to the throne, returning from exile in France.

The Great Fire of 1666 destroyed five-sixths of London, but it also wiped out the plague that had ravaged the impoverished and overcrowded population the year before. Sir Christopher Wren was given the Herculean charge of rebuilding London. He wanted to map out a more organized grid for the city, but it was rebuilt on the old haphazard lines. It took Wren 35 years to build his baroque masterpiece, St. Paul's Cathedral. Wren also designed 50 other churches (only 23 still stand, including St. Bride's and St. Stephen Walbrook) and Monument to commemorate the fire. Nicholas Hawksmoor assisted Wren and designed his own highly original churches including the splendid Christ Church in Spitalfields.

■ Visit: Banqueting House (Ch. 2), Christ Church, Spitalfields (Ch. 7), Shakespeare's Globe Theatre (Ch. 8), Queen's House, Greenwich (Ch. 12), St. Bride's (Ch. 6), St. Paul's Cathedral (Ch. 6), St. Stephen Walbrook (Ch. 6), Hampton Court (Ch. 13)

(top left) Courtyard of Neo-classical Somerset House, built for George III. (right) The Rotunda of the Victoria and Albert (V&A) Museum with modern Chihuly sculpture; (bottom left) St Martin-in-the-Fields on Trafalgar Square.

Georgian Era

1700–1836

By the beginning of the 18th century, London was the biggest city in Europe and a center of world trade. This growth led to changes in politics, as power moved to a parliamentary system. Increased wealth led to an explosion of art and architecture.

Many different styles flourished—rococo, neo-classical, regency, and gothic revival. The predominant neo-classical, based on the styles of ancient Greece, can be seen in many stately homes. You can admire the elegant Regency terraces around John Nash's Regent's Park.

■ Visit: Regent's Park (Ch. 11), Somerset House (Ch. 4), St. Martin-in-the-Fields (Ch. 2)

Victorian Age

1837–1901

Queen Victoria ruled the British Empire for 63 years. London experienced the growth of wealth, industrialization, and philanthropy; this was also a period of desperate poverty, as depicted in Charles Dickens's novels. At the start of the 19th century the population of the city was over a million; by the end of Victoria's reign it was six million.

This rapid growth required many building programs, from worker housing to even bigger projects such as the bridges, government buildings, and the first subway system in the world. Businessmen, artists, and architects helped create many institutions that still exist

today from the Tate Britain to the Ragged Schools and Foundling hospitals.

The clean, classical lines of the previous era gave way to more elaborate styles— which were considered more "English"—such as the Gothic Revival Houses of Parliament. Other Victorian projects included covered markets, canal locks, arcades, palaces, memorials, museums, theaters, and parks. So much building took place during this period that it's hard to miss the style: look for elaborate, highly decorated architecture.

■ Visit: Burlington Arcade (Ch. 3), Houses of Parliament (Ch. 2), Leadenhall Market in The City (Ch. 6), V&A and Natural History Museum (Ch. 9)

1851 Great Exhibition held in Hyde Park	1901 Death of Queen Victoria	1939–1945 WWII	1951 Festival of Britain
1863 Underground opens		1914–1918 WWI	
1870	1900	1930	1960

1

IN FOCUS THE BUILDING OF LONDON

(left) Theatregoers at The National Theatre on the South Bank of the Thames River; (right) Tower block at Barbican Centre, a 1980s complex of art venues and apartments.

20th-century building

1901–1979

The turn of the 20th century saw wealthy Westminster widening its streets to accommodate the arrival of motor cars and department stores. Even after the First World War, a "live for today" attitude continued among the upper classes, while the poorest Londoners suffered increasing prices and low wages. While modernism—a cultural movement embracing the future and rejecting anything associated with the past—was gathering pace in 1920s Europe, conservative British architecture continued to hark back to traditional influences of ancient Greece and the middle ages.

The WWII devastation of the Blitz bombings changed this and an enormous amount of post-war building was needed quickly. Émigrés such as Hungarian Ernö Goldfinger and Russian-born Berthold Lubetkin brought the modernist architectural movement to London with their high-rise buildings—a solution to the desperate housing shortage. One of the most exciting post-war projects was the 1951 Festival of Britain, celebrating the great inventions of the century. Out of a host of new architecture at the South Bank for this event, only the Royal Festival Hall remains.

Mass-produced concrete, steel, and glass ushered in the brutalist style in the '60s. This outgrowth of modernism can be seen in the Hayward Gallery and National Theatre. It was not a popular style, partly because the use of raw concrete—pioneered in the sunny south of France— looked gray, ugly, and even sinister against the backdrop of wet and windy London.

London's powers-that-be haven't always embraced modernist architecture, and many examples have been torn down. Today some iconic buildings are protected and the massive concrete Barbican Centre finally brought modernism right into the conservative City.

■ Visit: The Barbican Centre (Ch. 6), Hayward Gallery (Ch. 8), National Theatre (Ch. 8), Royal Festival Hall (Ch. 8)

(left) Lloyd's of London by the Richard Rogers Pertnership, completed in 1986. (top right) Current design of the London Aquatics Centre by Zaha Hadid. (bottom right) The 2000 Great Court at the British Museum by Sir Norman Foster.

1980–Present

Modern and Millennium London

While the sun may have set on the British empire, London remains a global city, perhaps more now than ever before. The '80s saw changes in economic policy and ambitious building projects, including the Jubilee Line extension to the Underground system. Great business and banking centers reached higher into the sky as London's importance in financial markets increased. London's disused Docklands area got a revitalizing boost with the Canary Wharf development and the DLR (Docklands Light Railway).

Internationally-known architects began to make their mark on the city with creative projects. Known as Tower 42, the NatWest Tower opened in 1980 as the tallest skyscraper in the city—for a great view, head to its bar on the 42nd floor. The Richard Rogers Partnership designed the fabulous 1986 Lloyd's of London building. Sir Norman Foster and his associates have designed the Sackler Galleries at the Royal Academy of Arts, the British Museum's Great Court, City Hall, and the Swiss Re Headquarters (known as the Gherkin).

Building projects to celebrate the Millennium are now so beloved it's hard to imagine London without the pedestrian-only Millennium Bridge and the London Eye.

The "Helter Skelter" Bishopsgate Tower is to be completed in 2012, followed by the Richard Rogers Partnership's "Cheese Grater." Beijing's Olympic Games are a tough act to follow, but the eyes of the world will be on London as the 2012 host city. Everyone's waiting for the curvaceous Aquatics Center designed by world-renowned Zaha Hadid and the 1,016-foot "Shard of Glass" designed by Italian Renzo Piano—it will be the tallest building in the EU by 2012; but for future buildings...the sky's the limit.

■ Visit: Canary Wharf (Ch. 12), Lloyd's of London (Ch. 6), Swiss Re (Ch. 6)

Westminster and Royal London

WORD OF MOUTH

"I really, really recommend taking a verger's tour at Westminster Abbey—our guide really made history come alive. If you get to the Abbey when it opens, just sign up for the first tour of the day or you can sign up in advance the previous day."

—azzure

GETTING ORIENTED

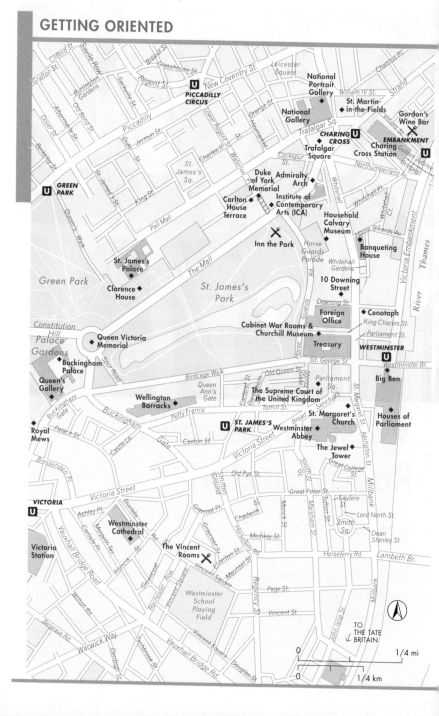

TOP REASONS TO GO

Steep yourself in history in Westminster Abbey: This sublime Gothic church was not only the site of Prince William's 2011 marriage but has also seen 38 hallowed coronations, starting with William the Conqueror in 1066.

Experience Royal London at Buckingham Palace: Even if you miss the palace's summer opening, keep pace with the marching soldiers and bands as they enact the time-honored ceremony of the "Changing the Guard" in front of the residence of Her Majesty.

Enjoy the company of Leonardo da Vinci: Raphael, Van Eyck, Rembrandt, Rubens, and other old masters are shown off in the splendor of gorgeously renovated rooms at the National Gallery.

Relive Britain's "Finest Hour" in the Cabinet War Rooms: Listen to Churchill's radio addresses to the British people as you explore this cavernous underground wartime hideout.

Hear Big Ben's chimes: As the Eiffel Tower is to Paris, so is Big Ben to London—just follow your ears from Trafalgar Square to see the 320-foot-high Clock Tower.

FEELING PECKISH?

Gordon's Wine Bar. Gordon's Wine Bar, established in 1890 and the oldest in London, is hidden below ground among vaulted brick arches and bathed in candlelight. A range of bottles will suit any budget, and the buffet offerings include excellent beef. ⊠ *47 Villiers St.* ☎ *020/7930–1408* ⊕ *www. gordonswinebar.com.*

Inn the Park. Great food, drink, and location—what more could you want? Inn the Park is the perfect place to while away an hour or three, especially on the terrace in the summer. ⊠ *St. James's Park* ☎ *020/7451–9999* ⊕ *www. innthepark.com.*

GETTING THERE

Trafalgar Square—easy to access and smack-dab in the center of the action—is the perfect place to start.

Take the Tube to Embankment (Northern, Bakerloo, District, and Circle lines) and walk north until you cross the Strand, or alight at the Charing Cross (Bakerloo and Northern lines) Northumberland Avenue exit. Buses are another great option, as almost all roads lead to Trafalgar Square.

MAKING THE MOST OF YOUR TIME

A lifetime of exploring may still be insufficient to cover this historically rich part of London. But don't fret: More practically, two to three days can take in the highlights.

For royal pageantry begin with Buckingham Palace, Westminster Abbey, the Queen's Gallery, and the Guards Museum. For more constitutional sightseeing, there's the Houses of Parliament. For art, the National Gallery and the Tate Britain head anyone's list.

NEAREST PUBLIC RESTROOMS

If you get caught short in Westminster Abbey, paid loos (150p) are across the street at the bottom of Victoria Street. Banqueting House and the Queen's Gallery have very elegant restrooms.

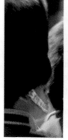

Sightseeing
★★★★★
Nightlife
★★
Dining
★★★
Lodging
★
Shopping
★★

This is postcard London at its best. Crammed with historic churches, grand state buildings, and major art collections, Royal London and Westminster unites politics, high culture, and religion. (Oh, and the Queen lives here, too.) The places you'll want to explore are grouped into three distinct areas—Trafalgar Square, Whitehall, and Buckingham Palace—each occupying a corner of triangular St. James's Park. Happily, there is as much history in these few acres as in many whole cities, so pace yourself—this is concentrated sightseeing.

Updated by
James O'Neill

Trafalgar Square is the official center of London, but what will bring you here are the two magnificent museums on the northern edge of the square, the **National Gallery** and the **National Portrait Gallery.** From the square two boulevards lead to the seats of different ideas of governance. **Whitehall** drops south to the neo-Gothic **Houses of Parliament,** where members of both Houses (Commons and Lords) hold debates and vote on pending legislation, and, just opposite, **Westminster Abbey,** a monument to the nation's history and for centuries the scene of daily worship, coronations, and royal weddings. Poets, political leaders, and 17 monarchs are buried in the 13th-century Gothic building. Halfway down Whitehall, **No. 10 Downing Street** is both the residence and the office of the prime minister. One of the most celebrated occupants, Winston Churchill, is commemorated in the **Churchill War Rooms,** his underground wartime headquarters off Whitehall. Just down the road is the **Cenotaph,** which acts as a focal point for the annual remembrance of those lost in war.

The **Mall,** a wide, pink avenue beyond the stone curtain of **Admiralty Arch,** heads southwest from Trafalgar Square toward the **Queen Victoria Memorial** and **Buckingham Palace,** the sovereign's official residence. The building is open to the public only in summer, but you can see much of the royal art collection in the Queen's Gallery and spectacular ceremonial

A BRIEF HISTORY OF WESTMINSTER

The Romans may have gunned for The City, but England's royals went for Westminster. London's future home of democracy started out as Edward the Confessor's palace, when he moved his cramped court west in the 11th century. He founded Westminster Abbey in 1050, where every British monarch has been crowned since. Under the Normans, the palace of Westminster was an elaborate and French-speaking affair. The politicos finally got their hands on it in 1529 (when Henry VII and his court shifted up to the roomier Whitehall Palace), but nearly lost it forever with the Gunpowder Plot of 1605, when Catholic militants attempted to blow the prototypical Parliament to smithereens.

Inigo Jones's magnificent Banqueting House is the only surviving building of Whitehall Palace, and was the setting for the 1649 beheading of Charles I. The Westminster we see today took shape during the Georgian and Victorian periods, as Britain reached the zenith of its imperial power. Grand architecture sprang up, and Buckingham Palace became the principal royal residence in 1837, when Victoria acceded to the throne. Trafalgar Square and Nelson's Column were built in 1843, to commemorate Britain's most famous naval victory, and the Houses of Parliament were rebuilt in 1858 in the trendy neo-Gothic style of the time. The illustrious Clarence House, built in 1825 for the Duke of Clarence (later William IV), is now the home of Prince Charles and Camilla Parker Bowles, Duchess of Cornwall.

coaches in the **Royal Mews,** both open all year. Farther south toward Pimlico, **Tate Britain** focuses on prominent British artists from 1500 to today.

TOP ATTRACTIONS

Banqueting House. James I commissioned Inigo Jones, one of England's great architects, to undertake a grand building on the site of the original Tudor Palace of Whitehall, which was (according to one foreign visitor) "ill-built, and nothing but a heap of houses." Influenced during a sojourn in Italy by Andrea Palladio's work, Jones brought Palladian sophistication and purity back to London with him. The resulting graceful and disciplined classical style of Banqueting House, completed in 1622, must have stunned its early occupants. In the quiet vaults beneath, James would escape the stresses of being a sovereign with a glass or two. His son Charles I enhanced the interior by employing the Flemish painter Peter Paul Rubens to glorify his father and the Stuart dynasty in vibrant painted ceiling panels. As it turned out, these allegorical paintings, depicting a wise monarch being received into heaven, were the last thing Charles saw before he was beheaded by Cromwell's Parliamentarians in 1649. But his son, Charles II, was able to celebrate the restoration of the monarchy in this same place 20 years later. Banqueting House is also the setting for lunchtime classical concerts, held 1–2 pm. Call, or check the website for details. ⊠ *Whitehall, Westminster* ☎ *020/3166–6154, 020/3166–6155, 020/3166–6153* concert information ⊕ *www.hrp. org.uk* ✉ *£5, includes audio guide, concerts from £20* ⊙ *Mon.–Sat. 10–5, last admission 4:30. Closed Christmas wk. Liable to close at short notice for events so calling first is advisable* Ⓜ *Charing Cross, Embankment, Westminster.*

Fodor's Choice **Buckingham Palace.**
★ *See the highlighted listing in this chapter.*

Ⓒ **Cabinet War Rooms and Churchill Museum.** It was from this small war-
★ ren of underground rooms—beneath the vast government buildings of the Treasury—that Winston Churchill and his team directed troops in World War II. Designed to be bombproof, the whole complex has been preserved almost exactly as it was when the last light was turned off at the end of the war. Every clock shows almost 5 pm, and the furniture, fittings, and paraphernalia of a busy, round-the-clock war office are in situ, down to the colored map pins.

During air raids, the leading government ministers met here, and the Cabinet Room is still arranged as if a meeting were about to convene. In the Map Room, the Allied campaign is charted on wall-to-wall maps with a rash of pinholes showing the movements of convoys. In the hub of the room, a bank of different-color phones known as the "Beauty Chorus" linked the War Rooms to control rooms around the nation. The Prime Minister's Room holds the desk from which Churchill made his morale-boosting broadcasts; the Telephone Room (a converted broom cupboard) has his hotline to FDR. You can also see the restored suite of rooms that the PM used for dining and sleeping. Telephonists and clerks who worked 16-hour shifts slept in lesser quarters in unenviable conditions; it would not have been unusual for a secretary in pajamas to scurry past a field marshal en route to a meeting.

An absorbing addition to the Cabinet War Rooms is the Churchill Museum, a tribute to the stirring politician and defiant wartime icon. Different zones explore his life and achievements—and failures, too—through objects and documents, many of which, such as his personal papers, had never previously been made public. Central to the exhibition is an interactive timeline, with layers of facts, figures, and tales. ⊠ *Clive Steps, King Charles St., Westminster* ☎ *020/7930–6961* ⊕ *www.iwm. org.uk* ✉ *£15.95, includes audio tour* ⊙ *Daily 9:30–6; last admission 5; disabled access* Ⓜ *Westminster.*

Clarence House. The London home of Queen Elizabeth the Queen Mother for nearly 50 years, Clarence House is now the Prince of Wales's and the Duchess of Cornwall's residence. The Regency mansion was built by John Nash for the Duke of Clarence, who found living in St. James's Palace quite unsuitable. Since then it has remained a royal home for princesses, dukes, and duchesses, including the present monarch, Queen Elizabeth, as a newlywed before her coronation. The rooms

A classic photo op: cavalry from the Queen's Life Guard at Buckingham Palace.

have been sensitively preserved to reflect the Queen Mother's taste, with the addition of many works of art from the Royal Collection, including works by Winterhalter, Augustus John, and Sickert. You'll find it less palace and more home (for the Prince and his sons William and Harry), with informal family pictures and comfortable sofas. The tour (by timed ticket entry only) is of the ground-floor rooms and includes the Lancaster Room, so called because of the marble chimneypiece presented by Lancaster County to the newly married Princess Elizabeth and the Duke of Edinburgh. Like Buckingham Palace, Clarence House is usually open only in August and September and tickets must be booked in advance. ⊠ *Clarence House, St. James's Palace, St. James's* ☏ *020/7766–7303* ⊕ *www.royalcollection.org.uk* ✉ *Check website* ☺ *Aug. and Sept.* Ⓜ *Green Park.*

★ **Houses of Parliament.**
See the highlighted listing in this chapter.

☺ **National Gallery.**

Fodor's Choice
★ *See the highlighted listing in this chapter.*

☺ **National Portrait Gallery.** The National Portrait Gallery was founded in

Fodor's Choice
★ 1856 with a single aim: to gather together portraits of famous British men and women. Over 150 years and 160,000 portraits later, this museum is an essential stop for all history and literature buffs. The spacious, bright galleries make it a pleasant place to visit, and you can choose to take in a little or a lot. Pop into Portrait Explorer in the IT Gallery for computer-aided exploration. At the summit, the Portrait Restaurant (open an hour after gallery closing times on Thursday and

Continued on page 44.

BUCKINGHAM PALACE

✉ Buckingham Palace Rd., St. James ☎ 020/7766–7300 ⊕ www.royalcollection.org.uk 🎟 £18 🕑 Aug.–late Sept., daily 9:45–6 (last admission 3:45); times subject to change; book ahead for disabled access; check website before visiting Ⓜ Victoria, St. James's Park, Green Park.

TIPS

■ If bought directly from the palace ticket office, tickets are valid for a repeat visit over the course of 12 months from the first visit.

■ Admission is by timed ticket with entry every 15 minutes throughout the day. Allow up to two hours.

■ A Royal Day Out ticket, available August and September, gives you the triple whammy of the Royal Mews, the Queen's Gallery, and the State Rooms, and is valid throughout the day. Tickets cost £31.95.

■ Get there by 10:30 to grab a spot for the Changing the Guard (www.changing-the-guard.com), daily at 11:30 from May until the end of July and on alternate days for the rest of the year, weather permitting.

■ New for 2013: in honor of the Queen's Jubilee, special evening "Champagne" tours of the palace are offered in the summer months. Cost is £65.00 per person.

It's rare to get a chance to see how the other half—well, other minute fraction—lives and works. But when the Queen heads off to Scotland on her annual summer holiday (you can tell because the Union Jack flies above the palace instead of the Royal Standard), the palace's 19 State Rooms open up to visitors (although the north wing's private apartments remain behind closed doors). With fabulous gilt moldings and walls adorned with masterpieces by Rembrandt, Rubens, and other old masters, the State Rooms are the grandest of the palace's 775 rooms.

HIGHLIGHTS

The **Grand Hall,** followed by the **Grand Staircase** and **Guard Room,** give a taste of the marble, gold leaf galore, and massive, twinkling chandeliers that embellish the palace. Don't miss the theatrical **Throne Room,** with the original 1953 coronation throne, or the sword in **the Ballroom,** used by the Queen to bestow knighthoods and other honors. Royal portraits line the **State Dining Room,** and the **Blue Drawing Room** is splendor in overdrive. The bow-shape **Music Room** features lapis lazuli columns between arched floor-to-ceiling windows, and the alabaster-and-gold plasterwork of the **White Drawing Room** is a dramatic crescendo. Spend some time ambling around the splendid gardens, a gorgeous epilogue to the visit.

The **Changing the Guard,** also known as **Guard Mounting,** remains one of London's best free shows and culminates in front of the palace. Marching to live bands, the old guard proceeds up the Mall from St. James's Palace to Buckingham Palace. Shortly afterward, the new guard approaches from Wellington Barracks. Then within the forecourt, the captains of the old and new guards symbolically transfer the keys to the palace.

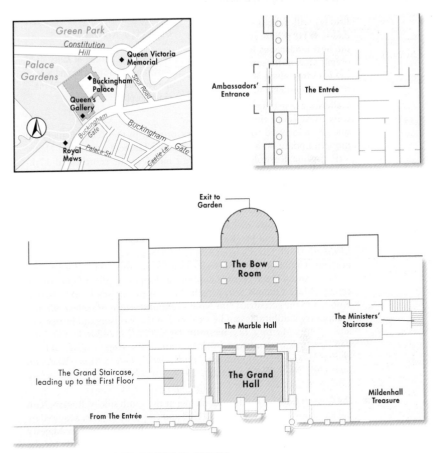

BUCKINGHAM PALACE: GROUND FLOOR

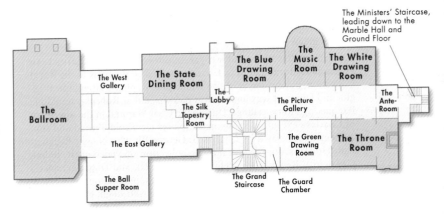

BUCKINGHAM PALACE: FIRST FLOOR

Friday) will delight skyline aficio-nados. ■ TIP→ Here you'll see one of the best landscapes for real: a pan-oramic view of Nelson's Column and the backdrop along Whitehall to the Houses of Parliament.

Galleries are arranged chronologi-cally from Tudor times on the sec-ond floor forward to contemporary Britain. In the Tudor Gallery—a modern update on a Tudor long hall—is a Holbein cartoon of Henry VIII. Joshua Reynolds's self-portrait hangs in the refurbished 17th-century rooms; portraits of notables, including Shakespeare, the Brontë sisters, Jane Austen, and the Queen are always on display. Other faces are more obscure and will be just as unknown to you if you're English, because the portraits outlasted their sitters' fame—not so surprising when the portraitists are such greats as Reynolds, Gainsborough, Law-rence, Romney, and Hockney. Look for the four Andy Warhol *Queen Elizabeth II* silk screens from 1985 and Maggi Hambling's surreal self-portrait. Contemporary portraits range from the iconic (*Julian with T-shirt*—an LCD screen on a continuous loop—by Julian Opie) to the creepy (Marc Quinn's *Self*, a realization of the artist's head in frozen blood) and the eccentric (Tim Noble's ghoulish *Head of Isabella Blow*). Temporary exhibitions can be explored in the Wolfson and Porter gal-leries. ⊠ *St. Martin's Pl., Westminster* ☎ *020/7312–2463, 020/730–0555 recorded switchboard information* ⊕ *www.npg.org.uk* ◳ *Free, charge for special exhibitions; £3 audiovisual guide* ⊗ *Mon.–Wed. and weekends 10–6, Thurs. and Fri. 10–9, last admission 45 mins before closing* Ⓜ *Charing Cross, Leicester Sq.*

★ **The Queen's Gallery.** The former chapel at the south side of Buckingham Palace is now a temple of art and rare and exquisite objects, acquired by kings and queens over the centuries. Technically speaking, Her Majesty doesn't "own" these treasures but merely holds them in trust for the nation—and what treasures they are! Only a selection from the Royal Collection is on view at any one time, presented in themed exhibitions. Whatever the exhibition happens to be, let the excellent audio guide take you through the elegant, spacious galleries filled with some of the world's greatest art works.

A rough timeline of the major royal collectors starts with Charles I. An avid appreciator of painters, Charles established the basis of the Royal Collection, purchasing works by Mantegna, Raphael, Titian, Caravag-gio, and Dürer (it was under royal patronage that Rubens painted the Banqueting House ceiling). During the Civil War and in the aftermath of Charles's execution, many masterpieces were sold abroad and sub-sequently repatriated by Charles II. George III, who bought Bucking-ham House, scooped up a notable collection of Venetian (including Canaletto), Renaissance (Bellini and Raphael), and Dutch (Vermeer) art, and a large number of baroque drawings, in addition to patroniz-ing English contemporary artists such as Gainsborough, Hoppner, and Beechey. He also took a liking to American artist Benjamin West. The Prince Regent, George IV, transformed his father's house into a palace,

HOUSES OF PARLIAMENT

✉ *St. Stephen's Entrance,
St. Margaret St., Westmin-
ster* ☎ *020/7219–4272 or
0844/847–1672* ⊕ *www.
parliament.uk/visiting* 🎫 *Free;
£15 tours (must book ahead)*
🕑 *Call to confirm hrs for
Visitors Galleries. Tours: Aug.,
Mon., Tues., Fri., Sat. 9:15–4:30,
Wed. and Thurs. 1:15–4:30;
Sept., Mon., Fri., Sat. 9:15–4:30,
Tues., Wed., Thurs. 1:15–4:30*
Ⓜ *Westminster.*

TIPS

■ The only guided tour non-residents can go on is the paid-for (£14) tour offered on Saturday or during August and September (book through www.ticketmaster.co.uk).

■ Nonresidents are able to watch debates when Parliament is in session if they wait in line for tickets. Embassies and High Commissions often have a quota of tickets available to their citizens, which can help avoid long queues.

■ If you're pressed for time, queues for the House of Lords are often shorter than for the House of Commons. The easiest time to get into the Commons is during an evening session—Parliament is still sitting if the top of the Clock Tower is illuminated.

■ The most romantic view of the Houses is from the opposite (south) bank, across Lambeth Bridge. It is especially dramatic at night when floodlighted green and gold.

If you want to understand some of the centuries-old traditions and arcane idiosyncrasies that make up constitutionless British parliamentary democracy, the Palace of Westminster, as the complex is still properly called, is the place to come. The architecture in this 1,100-room labyrinth impresses, but the real excitement lies in stalking the corridors of power. A palace was first established on this site by Edward the Confessor in the 11th century. William II started building a new palace in 1087, and this gradually became the seat of English administrative power. However, fire destroyed most of the palace in 1834, and the current complex dates largely from the middle of the 19th century.

HIGHLIGHTS

Visitors aren't allowed to snoop too much, but the **Visitors' Galleries** of the House of Commons do afford a view of democracy in process when the banks of green-leather benches are filled by opposing MPs (members of Parliament). When they speak, it's not directly to each other but through the Speaker, who also decides who will get time on the floor. Elaborate procedures notwithstanding, debate is often drowned out by raucous jeers. When MPs vote, they exit by the "Aye" or the "No" corridor, thus being counted by the party "tellers."

Westminster Hall, with its remarkable hammer-beam roof, was the work of William the Conqueror's son William Rufus. It's one of the largest remaining Norman halls in Europe, and its dramatic interior was the scene of the trial of Charles I. After the 1834 fire, the **Clock Tower** was completed in 1858, and contains the 13-ton bell known as **Big Ben.** At the southwest end of the main Parliament building is the 323-foot-high Victoria Tower.

2

filling it with fine art from paintings to porcelain. In particular, he had a good eye for Rembrandt, contemporary equestrian works by Stubbs, and lavish portraits by Lawrence. Queen Victoria had a penchant for Landseer animals and landscapes, Frith's contemporary scenes, and portraits by Winterhalter. Finally, Edward VII indulged Queen Alex-

andra's love of Fabergé, and many royal tours around the empire produced gifts of gorgeous caliber, such as the Cullinan diamond from South Africa and an emerald-studded belt from India.

More than 3,000 other objects from the Royal Collection reside in museums and galleries in the United Kingdom and abroad: check out the National Gallery, the Victoria & Albert Museum, the Museum of London, and the British Museum. ■ TIP→ The E-gallery provides an interactive electronic version of the collection, allowing the user to open lockets, remove a sword from its scabbard, or take apart the tulip vases. It's probably the closest you could get to eyeing practically every diamond in the sovereign's glittering diadem. ⊠ *Buckingham Palace, Buckingham Palace Rd., St. James's* ☎ *020/7766–7301* ⊕ *www.royal.gov.uk* ✉ *£9.25 with free audio guide, joint ticket with Royal Mews £15.75* ☉ *Daily 10–5:30; last admission 4:30* Ⓜ *Victoria, St. James's Park, Green Park.*

○ **St. James's Park.** With three palaces at its borders (the Palace of Westmin-
Fodor'sChoice ster, the Tudor **St. James's Palace,** and Buckingham Palace), St. James's
★ Park is acclaimed as the most royal of the royal parks. It's London's smallest, most ornamental park, as well as the oldest; once marshy water meadows, the land was acquired by Henry VIII in 1532 as a royal deer-hunting park (with dueling and sword fights forbidden); the public was always allowed access. James I improved the land and installed an aviary and zoo (complete with crocodiles). Charles II (after his exile in France, where he admired Louis XIV's formal Versailles Palace landscapes) had formal gardens laid out, with avenues, fruit orchards, and a canal. Lawns were grazed by goats, sheep, and deer, and in the 18th century the park became a different kind of hunting ground, for wealthy lotharios looking to pick up nighttime escorts. In the early 19th century John Nash redesigned the landscape in a more naturalistic, romantic style, and if you gaze down the lake toward Buckingham Palace, you can believe you are on a country estate.

A large population of waterfowl—including pelicans, geese, ducks, and swans (which belong to the Queen)—breed on and around Duck Island at the east end of the lake, while well-fed squirrels hop about on the grass. From April to September, the deck chairs (charge levied) come out for the longer days, crammed with office workers lunching while being serenaded by music from the bandstands. One of the best times to stroll the leafy walkways is after dark, with Westminster Abbey and the Houses of Parliament rising above the floodlighted lake. The popular Inn the Park restaurant is a wood-and-glass pavilion with a turf roof that blends in beautifully with the surrounding landscape; it's a good stopping place for a meal or a snack on a nice day. ✉ *The Mall or Horse Guards approach, or Birdcage Walk, St. James's* 🌐 *www.royalparks.gov.uk* 🕐 *Daily 5 am–midnight* Ⓜ *St. James's Park, Westminster.*

Supreme Court. The Supreme Court, the highest court of appeal in the United Kingdom, is housed in the carefully restored Middlesex Guildhall. Visitors are welcome to pop in (for free) and look at the three courtrooms, including the impressive Court Room 1, on the second floor, with its magnificent carved wood ceiling. There is a café downstairs. ✉ *Parliament Square, Westminster* ☎ *0207/960–1500* 🌐 *www. supremecourt.gov.uk* 🎟 *Free* 🕐 *Weekdays 9:30–4:30* Ⓜ *Westminster.*

🕐
Fodor's Choice
★

Tate Britain. The stately neoclassical institution may not be as ambitious as its sibling Tate Modern on the South Bank, but Tate Britain's bright galleries lure only a fraction of the Modern's crowds and are a great place to explore British art from 1500 to the present. First opened in 1897, funded by the sugar magnate Sir Henry Tate, the museum includes the Linbury Galleries on the lower floors, which stage temporary (and often popular) exhibitions, whereas the upper floors show the permanent collection. Pictures are regularly rehung and whatever is on view, you can find classic works by John Constable, Thomas Gainsborough, George Stubbs, David Wilkie, Francis Bacon, Duncan Grant, Barbara Hepworth, and Ben Nicholson and an outstanding display from J.M.W. Turner in the Clore Gallery, including many later vaporous and light-infused works such as *Sunrise with Sea Monsters*. Sumptuous Pre-Raphaelite pieces are a major drawcard while the Contemporary British Art galleries bring you face to face with Damien Hirst's *Away from the Flock* and other recent conceptions. The Tate Britain also hosts the annual Turner Prize exhibition, with its accompanying furor over the state of contemporary art, from about October to January each year.

Craving more art? Head down the river on the Tate-to-Tate shuttle boat to the Thames Modern, running between the two museums every 40 minutes. A River Roamer ticket permits additional stops at the London Eye and the Tower of London. ✉ *Millbank, Westminster* ☎ *020/7887–8888* 🌐 *www.tate.org.uk/britain* 🎟 *Free, special exhibitions £9–£15; Tate-to-Tate shuttle £5 each way; River Roamer ticket £12.60* 🕐 *Sat.–Thurs. 10–6 (last entry at 5.15), Fri. 10–10 (last entry at 9:15)* Ⓜ *Pimlico (signposted 5-min walk).*

NEED A BREAK?

Rather than search for a suitable place in Pimlico or Victoria, you can eat well right at the Tate. The Rex Whistler Restaurant, in the Tate Britain, is almost a destination in itself, with its celebrated Rex Whistler murals and a daily fixed-price three-course lunch menu (around £20) and à la carte choices. Ingredients celebrate British produce, such as Cornish crab, Welsh lamb, organic smoked salmon, and Stilton cheese. Children's portions

Continued on page 51.

NATIONAL GALLERY

✉ *Trafalgar Square, Westminster* ☎ *020/7747-2885* ⊕ *www.nationalgallery.org.uk* 🎟 *Free; charge for special exhibitions; audio guide £3.50* ⊙ *Sun.–Thurs. 10–6, Fri. 10–9* Ⓜ *Charing Cross, Embankment, Leicester Square.*

TIPS

■ Color coding throughout the galleries helps you keep track of the period you're immersed in.

■ Begin at an "Art Start" terminal in the Sainsbury Wing or East Wing Espresso Bar. The interactive screens give you access to information on all of the museum's holdings; you can choose your favorites, and print out a free personal tour map.

■ Want some stimulation? Try a free weekday lunchtime lecture, or Ten Minute Talk, which illuminates the story behind a key work of art. One-hour free, guided tours start at the Sainsbury Wing daily at 11:30 and 2:30.

■ Pick up a themed audio guide, which takes in about 20 paintings.

■ There are free Family Sundays with special talks for children and their parents. Check the website for other one-off events.

Standing proudly on the north side of Trafalgar Square is one of the world's supreme art collections, with more than 2,300 masterpieces on show. Picasso, van Gogh, Michelangelo, Leonardo, Monet, Turner, and more—all for free.

HIGHLIGHTS

In chronological order: (1) **Van Eyck** (circa 1395–1441), *The Arnolfini Portrait*—a solemn couple holds hands, the fish-eye mirror behind them mysteriously illuminating what can't be seen from the front view. (2) **Holbein** (1497–1543), *The Ambassadors*—two wealthy visitors from France stand surrounded by what were considered luxury goods at the time. Note the elongated skull at the bottom of the painting, which takes shape when viewed from an angle. (3) **Leonardo da Vinci** (1452–1519), *The Virgin and Child*—this exquisite black-chalk "Burlington Cartoon" depicts the master's most haunting Mary. (4) **Titian** (1490–1576), *Diana and Callisto*—a great mythological scene inspired by Ovid and purchased in 2012 for more than $70 million. (5) **Velazquez** (1599–1660), *Christ in the House of Martha and Mary*—in this enigmatic masterpiece the Spaniard plays with perspective and the role of the viewer. (6) **Caravaggio** (1573–1610), *The Supper at Emmaus* —a cinematically lightened, freshly resurrected Christ blesses bread in an astonishingly domestic vision from the master of chiaroscuro. (7) **Turner** (1775–1851), *Rain, Steam and Speed: The Great Western Railway* — the whirl of rain, mist, steam, and locomotion is nothing short of astonishing (spot the hare). (8) **Van Gogh** (1853–1890), *Sunflowers* — painted during his sojourn with Gauguin in Arles, this is quintessential Van Gogh. (9) **Seurat** (1859–91), *Bathers at Asnières*—a pointillist stunner.

are available. It's open for lunch daily from 11:30 to 3; for afternoon tea daily from 2:30 to 5; breakfast is served on weekends from 10 to 11:30. ⊠ *Westminster.*

Tate Britain Café. The Tate Britain Café has drinks, sandwiches, and cakes and is open daily from 10 am to 5:30 pm. ⊠ *Westminster.*

Trafalgar Square. This is literally the center of London: a plaque on the corner of the Strand and Charing Cross Road marks the spot from which distances on U.K. signposts are measured. **Nelson's Column** stands at the heart of the square

BEARSKIN, NOT BUSBY
While on duty, guardsmen take their job very, very seriously. They don't speak, don't acknowledge anyone (even those tourists trying in vain to make them laugh), don't even swat away troublesome flies from their noses. Worse: They're not even allowed to keel over under the weight of their enormous, saunalike hats. Called "bearskins," the headdress was originally worn by the French Imperial Guard defeated in the Battle of Waterloo in 1815.

(which is named after the great admiral's most important victory), guarded by haughty lions designed by Sir Edwin Landseer and flanked by statues of two generals who helped establish the British Empire in India, **Charles Napier** and **Henry Havelock.** The fourth plinth is given over to rotating works by contemporary sculptors. Great events, such as New Year's Eve celebrations, political protests, and sporting triumphs always see the crowds gathering in the city's most famous square. Although Trafalgar Square is known to Chinese tourists as Pigeon Square, feeding the birds is now banned and the gray flocks have flown.

The commanding open space is built on the grand scale demanded by its central position. From the 13th century, the site housed the royal hawks and falcons until 1530, when these buildings were replaced by stabling for royal horses. This "Great Mews" was demolished in 1830 as part of John Nash's Charing Cross Improvement Scheme. Nash, who envisioned the square as a cultural space open to the public, exploited its natural north–south incline to create a succession of high points from which to look down imposing carriageways toward the Thames, the Houses of Parliament, and Buckingham Palace. Upon Nash's death, the design baton was passed to Sir Charles Barry and then to Sir Edwin Lutyens, and the square was finally completed in 1850.

At the southern point of the square, en route to Whitehall, is the **equestrian statue of Charles I.** After the Civil War and the king's execution, Oliver Cromwell, then the leader of the "Commonwealth," commissioned a scrap dealer, brazier John Rivett, to melt the statue. The story goes that Rivett buried it in his garden and made a fortune peddling knickknacks wrought, he claimed, from its metal, only to produce the statue miraculously unscathed after the restoration of the monarchy— and to make more cash reselling it to the authorities. In 1767 Charles II had it placed where it stands today, near the spot where his father was executed in 1649. Each year, on January 30, the day of the king's death,

The Tate Britain showcases British art from the last 500 years, including contemporary works.

the Royal Stuart Society lays a wreath at the foot of the statue. ✉ *Trafalgar Sq., Westminster* Ⓜ *Charing Cross.*

Fodor's Choice **Westminster Abbey.**
★   *See the highlighted listing in this chapter.*

WORTH NOTING

Admiralty Arch. A stately and bombastic gateway to the Mall, this is one of the city's finest set pieces. On the southwest corner of Trafalgar Square, the arch, which was named after the adjacent Royal Navy headquarters, was designed in 1908–11 by Sir Aston Webb as a two-part memorial to Queen Victoria, along the ceremonial route to Buckingham Palace; the second part is the Victoria Memorial just outside the palace. Passing under one of its five arches—two for pedestrians, two for traffic, and a central arch, opened only for state occasions—one enters the Mall (rhymes with the American pronunciation of shall). A quirky feature of the arch is its curious "nose": about 7 feet up, on the inside wall of the most northerly arch is a noselike protrusion, said to be based on the proboscis of either Wellington or Napoléon. ✉ *The Mall, Cockspur St., Trafalgar Sq., Westminster* Ⓜ *Charing Cross.*

Carlton House Terrace. Architect John Nash designed Carlton House, a glorious example of the Regency style, between 1812 and 1830, under the patronage of George IV (Prince Regent until George III's death in 1820). Nash was the architect of the grand scheme for Regent Street, which started here and ended with the sweep of neoclassical houses encircling Regent's Park, where the Prince Regent, who lived at Carlton

ROYALTY WATCHING

You've seen Big Ben, the Tower, and Westminster Abbey. But somehow you feel something is missing: a close encounter with Britain's most famous attraction—Her actual Majesty, Elizabeth II. The Queen and the Royal Family attend hundreds of functions a year, and if you want to know what they are doing on any given date, turn to the Court Circular, printed in the major London dailies, or check out the Royal Family website, www.royal.gov.uk, for the latest events on the Royal Diary. Trooping the Colour is usually held on the second Saturday in June, to celebrate the Queen's official birthday. This spectacular parade begins when she leaves Buckingham Palace in her carriage and rides down the Mall to arrive at Horse Guards Parade at 11 exactly. To watch, just line up along the Mall with your binoculars!

Another time you can catch the Queen in all her regalia is when she and the Duke of Edinburgh ride in state to open the Houses of Parliament. The famous gilded black, gilt-trimmed Irish State Coach travels from Buckingham Palace—on a clear day, it's to be hoped, for this ceremony takes place in late October or early November. The Gold State Coach, an icon of fairy-tale glamour, is used for coronations and jubilees only.

But perhaps the most relaxed, least formal time to see the Queen is during Royal Ascot, held at the racetrack near Windsor Castle—a short train ride out of London—usually during the third week of June (Tuesday–Friday). The Queen and members of the Royal Family are driven down the track to the Royal Box in an open carriage, giving spectators a chance to see them. After several races, the famously horse-loving Queen invariably walks down to the paddock, greeting race goers as she proceeds. If you meet her, remember to address her as "Your Majesty."

House, had plans to build a country villa. Even though Carlton House was considered a most extravagant building for its time, it was demolished after the prince's accession to the throne, and Nash built Carlton House Terrace, no less imposing, with white-stucco facades and massive Corinthian columns, in its place. Carlton Terrace was a smart address and one that prime ministers Gladstone (1856) and Palmerston (1857–75) enjoyed. Today Carlton House Terrace houses the Royal College of Pathologists (No. 2), the Royal Society (No. 6–9), whose members have included Isaac Newton and Charles Darwin, and the Turf Club (No. 5). ⊠ *The Mall, St. James's* Ⓜ *Charing Cross.*

Downing Street. Looking like an unassuming alley but for the iron gates at both its Whitehall and Horse Guards Road approaches, this is the location of the famous **No. 10,** London's modest equivalent of the White House. The Georgian entrance is deceptive, though, since the old house now leads to a large mansion behind it, overlooking the Horse Guards Parade. Only three houses remain of the terrace built circa 1680 by Sir George Downing, who spent enough of his youth in America to graduate from Harvard—the second man ever to do so. **No. 11** is traditionally the residence of the chancellor of the exchequer (secretary of the treasury), and **No. 12** is the party whips' office. No. 10 has officially housed the prime minister since 1732. Just south of Downing Street, in the middle of Whitehall, you'll see the **Cenotaph**, a stark white monolith designed in 1920 by Edwin Lutyens to commemorate the 1918 armistice. On Remembrance Day (the Sunday nearest November 11, Armistice Day) it's strewn with red poppy wreaths to honor the dead of both world wars and all British and Commonwealth soldiers killed in action since; the first wreath is laid by the Queen or the senior member of the Royal Family present, and there's a march-past by war veterans, who salute their fallen comrades. ⊠ *Whitehall* Ⓜ *Westminster.*

PHOTO OP

The best place for a photo opportunity alongside one of the Queen's guardsmen is at St. James's Palace, or try to keep up alongside them during the morning Changing the Guard. They leave St. James's at about 10:50 am, for Buckingham Palace. Failing that, shuffle up to the mounted horse guards on the Whitehall side, there until 4 pm.

Horse Guards Parade. Once the tiltyard of Whitehall Palace, where jousting tournaments were held, the Horse Guards Parade is now notable mainly for the annual Trooping the Colour ceremony, in which the Queen takes the salute, her official birthday tribute, on the second Saturday in June. (Like Paddington Bear, the Queen has two birthdays; her real one is on April 21.) There is pageantry galore, with marching bands and throngs of onlookers, and the ceremony is televised. Throughout the rest of the year the changing of two mounted sentries known as the **Queen's Life Guard** at the Whitehall facade of Horse Guards provides what may be London's most popular photo opportunity. The ceremony last about half an hour. ⊠ *Whitehall* ☏ *020/7930–4832* ⊙ *Changing of the Queen's Life Guard at 11 am Mon.–Sat. and 10 am Sun.; inspection of the Queen's Life Guard daily at 4 pm* Ⓜ *Westminster.*

Household Cavalry Museum. Horse lovers can see working horses belonging to the British Army's two senior regiments, the Life Guards and the Blues and Royals, being tended to in their stable block behind a glass wall. Located in the cavalry's original 17th-century stables, the museum has displays of uniforms and weapons going back to 1661 as well as interactive exhibits on the regiments' current operational roles. In the tack room you can handle saddles and bridles, and try on a trooper's uniform, including its distinctive brass helmet with horsehair plume. ⊠ *Horse Guards, Whitehall* ☏ *020/7930–3070* ⊕ *www.householdcavalrymuseum.org.uk* ☏ *£6* ⊙ *Mar.–Sept., daily 10–6; Oct.–Feb., daily 10–5* Ⓜ *Charing Cross, Westminster.*

QUICK BITES

Notes Music and Coffee. Next door to the London Coliseum (home of the English National Opera), this spacious, hip café serves some of the best sandwiches, salads, and coffee in town. Check out the music and DVD shop in the basement. ⊠ *31 St. Martin's La., Westminster* ☏ *020/7240–0424* ⊕ *www.notesmusiccoffee.com.*

Institute of Contemporary Arts (ICA). You would never suspect that behind the stately white-stucco facade in the heart of Establishment London is to be found that champion of the avant-garde, the ICA. Since 1947, the ICA has been pushing boundaries in the visual arts, performance, theater, dance, and music. There are two cinemas, a theater, three galleries, a highbrow bookshop, reading room, a café and a hip bar. ⊠ *The Mall, St. James's* ☎ *020/7930–3647* ⊕ *www. ica.org.uk* ⌑ *Free; £10 for screenings* ☉ *Wed. and Fri.–Sun. noon–7; Thurs. noon–9* Ⓜ *Charing Cross, Piccadilly Circus.*

> **QUIRKY LONDON**
>
> Commemorated in the stained glass of the west window of St Margaret's, Sir Walter Raleigh is among the notables buried at the church, only without his head. This had been removed at Old Palace Yard, Westminster, and kept by his wife, who was said to be fond of asking visitors, "Have you met Sir Walter?" as she produced it from a velvet bag.

QUICK BITES

ICA Bar and Café. The ICA Bar and Café has a Modern British menu and windows overlooking the Mall—it's popular at lunchtime, so come early. Open Wednesday–Sunday from noon.

The Mall. This stately, 115-foot-wide processional route sweeping from Admiralty Arch to the Queen Victoria Memorial at Buckingham Palace is an updated 1904 version of a promenade laid out around 1660 for the game of *paille-maille* (a type of croquet crossed with golf), which also gave the parallel road Pall Mall its name. The **Duke of York Memorial** up the steps toward Carlton House Terrace is a towering column dedicated to George III's second son, further immortalized in the English nursery rhyme "The Grand old Duke of York." Sadly the internal spiral steps are inaccessible. ■TIP→ Be sure to stroll along the Mall on Sunday when the road is closed to traffic, or catch the bands and troops of the Household Division on their way from St. James's Palace to Buckingham Palace for the Changing the Guard. ⊠ *The Mall, St. James's* Ⓜ *Charing Cross, Green Park.*

Royal Mews. Fairy-tale gold-and-glass coaches and sleek Rolls-Royce state cars emanate from the Royal Mews, next door to the Queen's Gallery. The John Nash–designed Mews serves as the headquarters for Her Majesty's travel department (so beware of closures for state visits), complete with the Queen's own special breed of horses, ridden by wigged postilions decked in red-and-gold regalia. Between the stables and riding school arena are exhibits of polished saddlery and riding tack. The highlight of the Mews is the splendid Gold State Coach, not unlike an art gallery on wheels, with its sculpted tritons and sea gods. Mews were originally falcons' quarters (the name comes from their "mewing," or feather shedding), but the horses gradually eclipsed the birds. Royal Collection staff guide tours. ⊠ *Buckingham Palace Rd., St. James's* ☎ *020/7766–7302* ⊕ *www.royalcollection.org.uk* ⌑ *£8; joint ticket with Queen's Gallery £15.50* ☉ *Feb., Mar., and Nov.–Dec. 21, Mon.–Sat. 10–4 (last admission 3:15); Apr.–Oct., daily 10–5 (last admission 4:15); no guided tours* Ⓜ *Victoria, St. James's Park.*

St. James's Palace. With its solitary sentry posted at the gate, this surprisingly small palace of Tudor brick was once a home for many British sovereigns, including the first Elizabeth and Charles I, who spent his last night here before his execution. Today it's the working office of another Charles—the Prince of Wales. The front door actually opens right onto the street, but His Royal Highness always uses a back entrance. Matters to ponder as you look (you can't go in): the palace was named after a hospital for women lepers that stood here during the 11th century; Henry VIII had it built; foreign ambassadors to Britain are still accredited to the Court of St. James's even though it has rarely been a primary royal residence; the present Queen made her first speech here; and after the death of a monarch, the accession of the new sovereign is announced by the Garter King of Arms from the Proclamation Gallery overlooking Friary Court. Friary Court out front is a splendid setting for Trooping the Colour, part of the Queen's official birthday celebrations. Everyone loves to take a snapshot of the scarlet-coated guardsman standing sentry outside the imposing Tudor gateway. Note that the Changing the Guard ceremony at St. James's Palace occurs only on days when the guard at Buckingham Palace is changed. *See entry for Buckingham Palace for details.* ⊠ *Friary Court, St. James's* ⊕ *www.royal.gov.uk* Ⓜ *Green Park.*

> ## ST. MARTIN'S CONCERTS
>
> Classical concerts (some in candlelight) are held every Thursday to Saturday (and some Tuesdays) at 7:30 pm with evening jazz concerts in the crypt every Wednesday at 8 pm. Tickets are available from the box office in the crypt. Free (donation appreciated) lunchtime concerts take place Monday, Tuesday, and Friday, 1–2 pm.

St. Margaret's Church. Dwarfed by its neighbor, Westminster Abbey, St. Margaret's was founded in the 11th century and rebuilt between 1488 and 1523. As the unofficial parish church of the House of Commons, St. Margaret's is much sought after for weddings and memorial services. Samuel Pepys, Chaucer, and John Milton worshiped here, and Winston Churchill tied the knot here in 1908. Since 1681, a pew off the south aisle has been set aside for the Speaker of the House (look for the carved portcullis). The stained glass in the north windows is classically Victorian, facing abstract glass from John Piper in the south, replacing the originals, which were ruined in WWII. ⊠ *St. Margaret's St., Parliament Sq., Westminster* ☎ *020/7654–4840* ⊕ *www.westminster-abbey. org/st-margarets* ☉ *Weekdays 9:30–3:30, Sat. 9–1:30, Sun. 2–5 (entry via east door). Church may close on short notice for services, so call ahead* Ⓜ *Westminster.*

Ⓒ **St. Martin-in-the-Fields.** One of London's best-loved and most welcoming of churches is more than just a place of worship. Named after the saint who helped beggars, St Martin's has long been a welcome sight for the homeless, who have sought soup and shelter at the church since 1914. The church is also a haven for music lovers; the internationally known Academy of St. Martin-in-the-Fields was founded here, and a popular program of concerts continues today. (Although the interior is a wonderful setting, the wooden benches can make it hard to give your undivided attention to the music.) The crypt is a hive of activity, with a café and shop, plus the **London Brass-Rubbing Centre**, where you can make your own life-size souvenir knight, lady, or monarch from replica tomb brasses, with metallic waxes, paper, and instructions from about £5.

For the historical details, take the worthwhile audio tour. St. Martin's is often called the royal parish church, partly because Charles II was christened here: The small medieval chapel that once stood here, probably used by the monks of Westminster Abbey, gave way to a grand rebuilding, completed in 1726, and James Gibbs's classical temple-with-spire design also became a familiar pattern for churches in early colonial America. Though it has to compete for attention with Trafalgar Square's many prominent structures, its spire is slightly taller than Nelson's Column. ⊠ *Trafalgar Sq., Covent Garden* ☎ *020/7766–1100, 020/7839–8362 brass rubbings, 020/7766–1122 evening-concert credit-card bookings* ⊕ *www.smitf.org* ✉ *Concerts £7–£22; audio tour £4* ⊙ *Mon.–Sat. 8–6, Sun. 8–6 for worship; café Mon. and Tues. 8–8, Wed. 8–7, Thurs.–Sat. 8–9, Sun. 11–6* Ⓜ *Charing Cross, Leicester Sq.*

QUICK
BITES

The atmospheric St. Martin's Café in the Crypt, with its magnificent high-arched brick vault and gravestone floor, serves full English and continental breakfasts, sandwiches, salads, snacks, afternoon tea, and wine. Lunch and dinner options include vegetarian meals and the setting, at the heart of London, is superb.

☾ **Wellington Barracks.** These are the headquarters of the Guards Division, the Queen's five regiments of elite foot guards (Grenadier, Coldstream, Scots, Irish, and Welsh) who protect the sovereign and, dressed in tunics of gold-purled scarlet and tall bearskin caps, patrol her palaces. Guardsmen alternate these ceremonial postings with serving in current conflicts, for which they wear more practical uniforms. If you want to learn more about the guards, visit the **Guards Museum,** which has displays on all aspects of a guardsman's life in conflicts dating back to 1642; the entrance is next to the Guards Chapel. Next door is the **Guards Toy Soldier Centre,** a great place for a souvenir. ⊠ *Wellington Barracks, Birdcage Walk, Westminster* ☎ *020/7414–3428* ⊕ *www.theguardsmuseum. com* ✉ *£5* ⊙ *Daily 10–4; last admission 3:30* Ⓜ *St. James's Park.*

Westminster Cathedral. Amid the concrete jungle of Victoria Street lies this remarkable neo-Byzantine find, seat of the Archbishop of Westminster, head of the Roman Catholic Church in Britain. Faced with the daunting proximity of Westminster Abbey, architect John Francis Bentley flew in the face of fashion by rejecting neo-Gothic in favor of the Byzantine idiom, which still provides maximum contrast today. The asymmetrical redbrick Byzantine edifice, dating from 1903, is banded with stripes of Portland stone and abutted by a 273-foot-high bell tower containing Big Edward at the northwest corner, ascendable by elevator for sterling views. The interior remains incomplete and is unusual for the unfinished overhead brickwork of the ceiling, which lends the church a dark, brooding intensity. Several side chapels—such as the eastern-Roman styled Chapel of the Blessed Sacrament and the Holy Souls

Continued on page 64

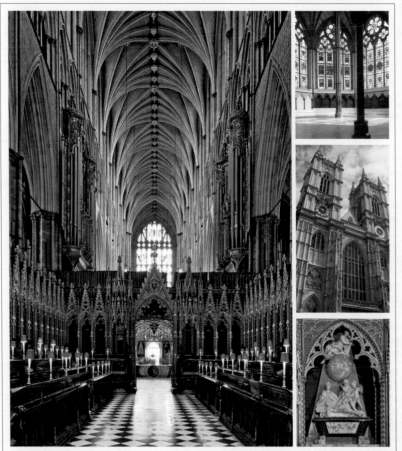

WESTMINSTER ABBEY

A monument to the rich—and often bloody and scandalous—history of Great Britain, Westminster Abbey rises on the Thames skyline as one of the most iconic sites in London.

The mysterious gloom of the lofty medieval interior is home to more than 600 monuments and memorial statues. About 3,300 people, from kings to composers to wordsmiths, are buried in the abbey. It has been the scene of 14 royal weddings and no less than 38 coronations—the first in 1066, when William the Conqueror was made king here.

TOURING THE ABBEY

There's only one way around the abbey, and as there will almost certainly be a long stream of shuffling tourists at your heels, you'll need to be alert to catch the highlights. Enter by the north door.

When you enter the church, turn around and look up to see the ❶ painted-glass rose window, the largest of its kind.

The ❷ Coronation Chair, at the foot of the Henry VII Chapel, has been briefly graced by nearly every regal posterior since Edward I ordered it in 1301. Look for the graffiti on the back of the Coronation chair. It's the work of 18th- and 19th-century visitors and Westminster schoolboys who carved their names there.

The ❸ Henry VII's Lady Chapel contains the tombs of Henry VII and his queen, Elizabeth of York. Close by are monuments to the young daughters of James I, and an urn purported to hold the remains of the so-called Princes in the Tower—Edward V and Richard. Interestingly, arch enemies Elizabeth I and her half-sister Mary Tudor share a tomb here. Begun in 1503, the chapel is famed for its ceiling—a dazzling fan-vaulted roof with carved pendants—and the heraldic banners of living knights that hang above its oak stalls.

In front of the ❹ High Altar, which was used for the funerals of Princess Diana and

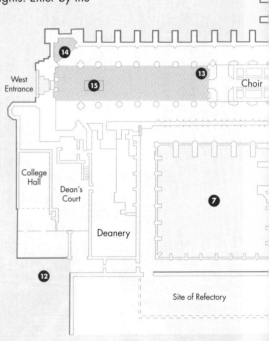

the Queen Mother, is a black-and-white marble pavement laid in 1268. The intricate Italian Cosmati work contains three Latin inscriptions, one of which states that the world will last for 19,683 years.

The ❺ Shrine of St. Edward the Confessor contains the shrine to the pre-Norman king. Because of its great age, you must join a tour with the verger to be admitted to the chapel. (Details are available at the

admission desk; there is a small extra charge.)

Geoffrey Chaucer was the first poet to be buried in ❻ Poets' Corner in 1400. Other memorials include: William Shakespeare, William Blake, John Milton, Jane Austen, Samuel Taylor Coleridge, William Wordsworth, and Charles Dickens.

A door from the south transept and south choir aisle leads to the calm of the ❼ Great Cloisters.

North Entrance

❶ North Transept

North Ambulatory

❷

❸

Sanctuary ❻

❹ ❺

South Ambulatory

South Transept

❻

❽

❾

❿

⓫

and actual clothing of Charles II and Admiral Lord Nelson (complete with eye patch).

The ❿ **Little Cloister** is a quiet haven, and just beyond, the ⓫ **College Garden** is a delightful diversion. Filled with medicinal herbs, it has been tended by monks for more than 900 years.

The ⓬ **Dean's Yard** is the best spot for a fine view of the massive flying buttresses above.

The medieval ❽ **Chapter House** is adorned with 14th-century frescoes. The King's Council met here between 1257 and 1547. Be sure to look at the floor, one of the finest surviving tiled floors in the country.

The ❾ **Abbey Museum** includes a collection of deliciously macabre effigies made from the death masks

In the choir screen, north of the entrance to the choir, is a marble ⓭ **monument to Sir Isaac Newton.**

⓮ **A plaque to Franklin D. Roosevelt** is one of the Abbey's very few tributes to a foreigner.

The ⓯ **Grave of the Unknown Warrior,** in memory of the soldiers who lost their lives in both world wars, is near the exit of the abbey.

QUIRKY LONDON

Near the Henry VII chapel, keep an eye open for St. Wilgefortis, who was so concerned to protect her chastity that she prayed to God for help and woke up one morning with a full growth of beard.

A BRIEF HISTORY

960 AD Benedictine monastery founded on the site by King Edward and King Dunstan.

1045–65 King Edward the Confessor enlarges the original monastery, erecting a stone church in honor of St. Paul the Apostle. Named "west minster" to distinguish from "east minster" (St. Paul's Cathedral).

1065 The church is consecrated on December 28. Edward doesn't live to see the ceremony.

1161 Following Edward's canonization, his body is moved by Henry III to a more elaborate resting place behind the High Altar. Other medieval kings are later buried around his tomb.

1245–54 Henry III pulls down the abbey and starts again with a new Gothic style influenced by his travels in France. Master mason Henry de Reyns ("of Rheims") constructs the transepts, north front, and rose windows, as well as part of the cloisters and Chapter House.

1269 The new abbey is consecrated and the choir is completed.

1350s Richard II resumes Henry III's plan to rebuild the monastery. Henry V and Henry VII continue as benefactors.

1503 The Lady Chapel is demolished and the foundation stone of Henry VII's Chapel is laid on the site.

1540 The abbey ceases to be used as a monastery.

1560 Elizabeth I refounds the abbey as a Collegiate Church. From this point on it is a "Royal Peculiar," exempt from the jurisdiction of bishops.

1745 The western towers, left unfinished from medieval times, are finally completed, based on a design by Sir Christopher Wren.

1995 Following a 25-year restoration program, saints and allegorical figures are added to the niches on the western towers and around the Great West Door.

PLANNING YOUR DAY

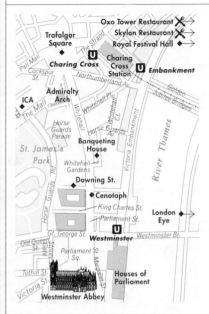

GETTING HERE: The closest Tube stop is Westminster. When you exit the station, walk west along Great George Street, away from the river. Turn left on St. Margaret Street.

CONTACT INFO: ✉ Broad Sanctuary, Westminster SW1 P3PA ☎ 020/7222-5152 ⊕ www.westminster-abbey.org.

ADMISSION: Adults: Abbey and museum £15. **Family tickets:** 2 adults and 1 child, £32, 2 adults and 2 children, £38. **Children under 11:** free.

HOURS: The abbey is a house of worship. Services may cause changes to the visiting hours on any given day, so be sure to call ahead.
Abbey: Weekdays 9:30–3:30; Sat. 9:30–2:30; (last admission 1:30); Sun, worship only.
Museum: Mon.–Sat. 10:30–4.
Cloisters: Daily 8–6
College Garden: Tues.–Thurs. 10–6
Chapter House: Mon.–Sat. 10–4

WHAT'S NEARBY: To make the most of your day, arrive at the abbey early (doors open at 9:30), then make an afternoon visit to the Parliament buildings and finish with a sunset ride on the **London Eye.** Post-flight, take a walk along the fairy-lit South Bank and have dinner (or a drink in the bar) with a view, at the **Oxo Tower Restaurant** (☎ 020/7803–3888) or the Royal Festival Hall's **Skylon Restaurant** (☎ 020/7654–7800).

Please note that overseas visitors can no longer visit the **Houses of Parliament** during session. However, tours of the buildings are available in August and September. For more information and booking call ☎ 0870/906–3773. Also, it's advisable to prebook tickets for the London Eye. Do this online at www.londoneye.com, or call 0870/990–8883.

IN A HURRY?

If you're pressed for time, concentrate on the following four highlights: the Coronation Chair; Chapter House; Poets' Corner; and Grave of the Unknown Warrior.

THINGS TO KNOW

■ Photography and filming are not permitted anywhere in the abbey.

■ In winter the interior of the abbey can get quite cold; dress accordingly.

■ For an animated history of the Abbey, join one of the verger-led tours (90 minutes) that depart from the North Door: Apr.–Sept.: Mon.–Fri. 10, 10:30, 11, 2, 2:30, Sat. 10, 10:30, 11; Oct.–Mar.: Mon.–Fri. 10:30, 11, 2, 2:30, Sat. 10:30, 11. Ask at information desk, £3 per person (in addition to entrance charge).

■ Touring the abbey can take half a day, especially in summer, when lines are long.

■ To avoid the crowds, make sure you arrive early. If you're first in line you can enjoy parts of the abbey in relative calm before the mad rush descends.

■ If you want to study up before you go, visit www.westminster-abbey.org, which includes an in-depth history and self-guided tour of the abbey. Otherwise pick up a free leaflet from the information desk.

■ On Sundays the abbey is not open to visitors. Join a service instead. Check the Web site for service times, as well as details of concerts, organ recitals, and special events.

Chapel—are beautifully finished in glittering mosaics. The lovely Lady Chapel—dedicated to the Virgin Mary—is also sumptuously decorated. In front of the chapel, a small stone statue of Jesus's mother attracts particular veneration. Look out for the Stations of the Cross (stopping points for prayer or contemplation) by Eric Gill and the striking baldachin—the enormous stone canopy standing over the altar and giant cross suspended in front of it. The nave, the widest in the country, is constructed in green marble, which also has a Byzantine connection—it was cut from the same place as the 6th-century St. Sophia's in Istanbul, and was almost confiscated by warring Turks as it traveled west. All told, more than 200 different types of marble can be found within the cathedral's interior. Just inside the main entrance is the tomb of Cardinal Basil Hume, head of the Catholic Church in the United Kingdom for more than 25 years. There's a café in the crypt. ⊠ *Ashley Pl., Westminster* ☎ *020/7798-9055* ⊕ *www.westminstercathedral.org.uk* ✉ *Bell Tower and viewing gallery £5; Treasures of the Cathedral exhibition £5 (exhibition opening hrs weekdays 9:30–5 pm, weekends 9:30–6); joint ticket for both Bell Tower and exhibition £8* ☉ *Weekdays 7–6, weekends 8–7* Ⓜ *Victoria.*

St. James's and Mayfair

WORD OF MOUTH

"We really liked being based in Mayfair, a very upscale area with many embassies and gorgeous town homes. The kids were impressed at the number of Bentleys, Aston Martins, and Ferraris. It's a short walk to Hyde Park or Green Park, and there are many restaurants and pubs to choose from."

—BelTib

GETTING ORIENTED

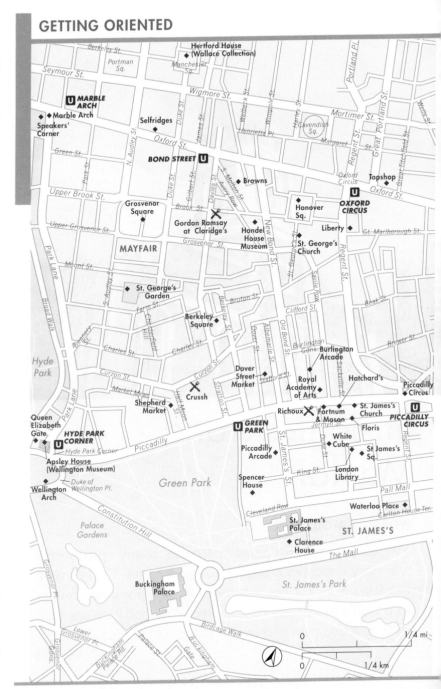

3

TOP REASONS TO GO

Call on the Duke of Wellington: His Apsley House—known as No. 1, London—is filled with splendid salons nearly wallpapered with grand old master paintings.

Get a passion for fashion: The shopping on Bond and Mount streets will keep your credit card occupied at McQueen and McCartney, and don't forget stylish, gigantic Selfridges.

Go for Baroque at St. James's: Designed by Sir Christopher Wren—top architect of 17th-century London—this beautiful church was the site of poet William Blake's baptism.

Visit Spencer House: Tour the ancestral house of Princess Diana, restored by Lord Rothschild, and the only great aristocratic family mansion extant in London.

Dress to impress at Claridge's: Afternoon tea at this sumptuous art deco gem is the perfect end to a shopping spree in Mayfair.

FEELING PECKISH?

Crussh. Eating healthfully can be a challenge in London but here you'll find excellent juices, smoothies, soups, sandwiches, salads, and wraps; take them across to nearby Green Park and snag a deck chair. ⊠ *1 Curzon St., Mayfair* ☎ *020/7629–2554.*

Gordon Ramsay at Claridge's. The foul-mouthed master of the kitchen takes fine dining to exquisite heights of elegance; it's the perfect marriage of art deco beauty and culinary genius. ⊠ *55 Brook St., Mayfair* ☎ *020/7499–0099* ⊕ *www. gordonramsay.com/claridges.*

Richoux. Since 1909, Richoux has been an affordable refuge from busy Piccadilly; enjoy simple but well-executed French bistro food and great afternoon teas. ⊠ *172 Piccadilly, Mayfair* ☎ *020/7493–2204* ⊕ *www.richoux.co.uk.*

GETTING THERE

Three Tube stops on the Central line will leave you smack in the center of these neighborhoods: Marble Arch, Bond Street (also Jubilee line), and Oxford Circus (also Victoria and Bakerloo lines).

You can also take the Piccadilly or Bakerloo line to the Piccadilly Circus Tube station, the Piccadilly to the Hyde Park Corner station, or the Piccadilly, Victoria, or Jubilee line to the Green Park station.

The best buses are the 8, which takes in Green Park, Berkeley Square, and New Bond Street, and the 9, one of the few routes that still use the traditional double-decker Routemaster model, which runs along Piccadilly.

MAKING THE MOST OF YOUR TIME

Reserve at least a day to experience St. James's and Mayfair. Leave enough time for shopping and also to wander casually through the streets and squares.

The only areas to avoid are the Tube stations at rush hour, and Oxford Street if you don't like crowds.

At all costs, stay away from Oxford Circus around 5 pm, when the commuter rush can, at times, resemble an East African wildebeest migration—but without the charm.

The area becomes as quiet as a tomb at night—so plan to party elsewhere.

Sightseeing
★★★★★

Nightlife
★★★

Dining
★★★★

Lodging
★★★★

Shopping
★★★★

Updated by
James O'Neill

St. James's and Mayfair form the core of London's West End, the city's smartest central area. These neighborhoods epitomize the stately flavor that is peculiarly London's—the sense of being in a great, rich, powerful city is almost palpable as you wander along the posh and polished streets.

Neither district is stuffed with must-sees, though there is no shortage of history and gorgeous architecture, but they are custom-built for window-shopping, expansive strolling, and getting a peek into the lifestyles of London's rich and famous, 18th-and-21st-century versions. St. James's is found to the south of Piccadilly and north of the Mall, while Mayfair is located to the north of Piccadilly and south of Oxford Street.

Although many will say Mayfair is only a state of mind, the heart of Mayfair has shifted from the 19th-century's Park Lane to beautiful Carlos Place and Mount Street. Even if you head to adjacent Bond Street to bid on a letter at Sotheby's signed by one of the Brontë sisters, or stop in a Graff to price a weighty diamond, the window-shopping is next best to the real thing and is free. Mayfair is primarily residential, so its homes are off-limits except for two satisfyingly grand houses: Apsley House, the Duke of Wellington's home, built by Robert Adam in 1771, and once known as No. 1, London, and Spencer House, ancestral digs of Princess Diana. The district of St. James—named after the centuries-old palace that lies at its center—remains the ultimate enclave of old-fashioned gentleman's London, with the great clubs on Pall Mall along with famed shops for the sartorial peacock.

Despite being bounded by four of the busiest streets in London—bustling budget-shopping mecca Oxford Street to the north, traffic artery Park Lane with Hyde Park beyond to the west, and elegant boulevards Regent Street and Piccadilly to the east and south respectively—Mayfair itself is remarkably traffic-free and a delight to explore. Starting at **Selfridges** on Oxford Street, a southward stroll will take you through quiet residential streets lined with Georgian town houses (the area was largely developed in the 17th and 18th centuries) and, with a bit of artful navigating, to four lovely greenswards: **Grosvenor Square, Berkeley Square, Hanover Square**, with its splendid **St. George's Church** where

A BRIEF HISTORY

The name Mayfair derives from the 15-day May fair that was once held in the charming warren of small streets known as Shepherd Market.

But in the 18th century, the residents of this now-fashionable neighborhood felt the fair was lowering the tone and so put a stop to it.

The area was mostly fields and farms belonging to families whose names are commemorated in the surrounding streets—Grosvenor, Burlington,

and Berkeley—until it was developed in the early 1700s.

The beautiful St. James's Park, meanwhile, stands as an idyllic emblem of this elite past.

It's the oldest royal park in London and all that remains of the royal hunting grounds that once traversed the city to Islington, Marylebone, and Hampstead.

Henry VIII acquired the land in 1532 for a deer park.

Handel worshipped, and the quiet St. George's Gardens, bounded by a maze of atmospheric streets and mews. Mayfair is also London's most exclusive shopping destination, with such enclaves as **Mount Street, Bruton Street, Savile Row,** and the **Burlington Arcade.** At the western end of Mayfair at Hyde Park corner are two memorials to England's great hero the Duke of Wellington: **Wellington Arch** and the duke's restored London residence, **Apsley House.**

The **Royal Academy of Arts** is at the southern fringe of Mayfair on Picadilly, and just across the road begins more sedate St. James's, with its old-money galleries, restaurants, and gentlemen's clubs that embody the history and privilege of traditional London. You'll get the best sense of the neighborhood just to the south on **St. James's Square** and **Pall Mall,** with its private clubs tucked away in 18th- and 19th-century patrician buildings.

TOP ATTRACTIONS

Fodor'sChoice **Apsley House (Wellington Museum).** The mansion built by Robert Adam and presented to the Duke of Wellington in thanks for his victory over Napoléon at the Battle of Waterloo in 1815 was long celebrated as the best address in town. Once popularly known as Number 1, London, because it was the first and grandest house at the old tollgate from Knightsbridge village, the mansion was the residence of the Duke of Wellington from 1817 until his death in 1852. The years of war against the French made the "Iron Duke"—born in Ireland as Arthur Wellesley—the greatest soldier and statesman in the land, so much so that the house's location at Hyde Park Corner was soon nicknamed "hero's corner" (in the nearby subway, beneath the turmoil of traffic, the Duke of Wellington's heroic exploits are retold in murals). Opposite the house is the 1828 ⇨ *Wellington Arch,* designed by Decimus Burton, with the four-horse chariot of peace at its pinnacle (open to the public as an exhibition area and viewing platform); the **Achilles** statue (legendarily naked and cast from captured French guns) points the way

Piccadilly Circus is London's "Times Square."

with thrusting shield to the ducal mansion from the edge of Hyde Park, entered through an elaborate gateway designed and built by Burton at the same time as the arch.

The duke's former residence shows off his uniforms, weapons, a fine collection of paintings (partially looted from his war campaigns), and his porcelain and plate collections acquired as a result of his military success, such as a Sévres dessert service commissioned by Napoléon for his empress, Josephine. Wellington's extensive art collection, much of it presented to him by admirers, includes works by Brueghel, Van Dyck, and Rubens, as well as the famous Veláquez portrait of Pope Innocent X and a portrait of the duke on horseback by Goya. A gigantic Canova statue of a nude (fig-leafed) Napoléon presides over the grand staircase that leads to the many elegant reception rooms. The sculptor chose to present his subject, at the time the most powerful man in Europe, as Mars the Peacemaker, depicting the short and stocky emperor as a classical god more than 11 feet tall with a perfect physique. Napoléon wasn't happy with the nudity or the athleticism of Canova's approach and ordered the marble statue to be hidden behind a screen.

The free audio guide highlights the most significant works and the superb decor, most notably the stunning Waterloo Gallery, where an annual banquet for officers who fought beside Wellington was held beneath the sculpted and gilded ceiling and old-master paintings on red damask walls. Special events take place on the annual Waterloo weekend and occasionally on Waterloo Day (June 18) itself, in addition to other special events throughout the year. Call or check the website for details. Limited disabled access. ⊠ *149 Piccadilly, Hyde Park Corner,*

Regent Street, home to Liberty department store and Hamleys toyshop, decorated for the holidays

Mayfair ☎ *020/7499–5676* ⊕ *www.english-heritage.org.uk* ✉ *£6.50; check wWeb site for joint ticket with Wellington Arch* ☯ *Mar.–Oct., Wed.–Sun. and bank holiday Mon. 11–5; Nov.–Feb., weekendsSat.– Sun. 11–4* Ⓜ *Hyde Park Corner.*

Bond Street. This world-class shopping haunt is divided into northern "New" (1710) and southern "Old" (1690) halves. You can spot the juncture by a bronzed bench on which Franklin D. Roosevelt sits companionably next to Winston Churchill. On New Bond Street you'll find **Sotheby's,** the world-famous auction house, at No. 35, as well as upscale retailers like Asprey's, Burberry, Louis Vuitton, Georg Jensen, and Church's. You'll find even more opportunities to flirt with financial ruin on Old Bond Street: flagship boutiques of top-end designers like Chanel, Gucci, and Yves St. Laurent; an array of fine jewelers including Tiffany's; and art dealers Colnaghi, Spink Leger, and Agnew's. **Cork Street,** which parallels the top half of Old Bond Street, is where London's top dealers in contemporary art have their galleries. ⊠ *Bond St., Mayfair* Ⓜ *Bond St., Green Park.*

Burlington Arcade. Perhaps the finest of Mayfair's enchanting covered shopping alleys is the second oldest in London, built in 1819 for Lord Cavendish, to stop hoi polloi from jettisoning rubbish (oyster shells in particular) into his garden at Burlington House, behind the arcade. Top-hatted watchmen called Beadles—the world's smallest private police force—still patrol, preserving decorum by preventing you from singing, running, or carrying an open umbrella. The arcade is also the main link between the Royal Academy of Arts and its extended galleries at 6 Burlington Gardens. ⊠ *Piccadilly, Mayfair* ⊕ *www.burlington-arcade.*

co.uk ⊙ M *Weekdays on.–Fri. 10–7, Sat. 9–6:.30, Sun. 11–5; opening times of shops within the arcade vary* M *Green Park, Piccadilly Circus.*

Several of London's most storied and stylish hotels are in Mayfair. Even if you're not staying at one, sample the high life by popping into their glamorous bars for a cocktail or some afternoon tea. **Claridge's Bar** takes its cue from art deco, as do the Ritz's intimate **Rivoli Bar** and the eponymous **Connaught Bar**; the bar at **Brown's Hotel** is modernist.

Marble Arch. John Nash's 1827 arch, moved here from Buckingham Palace in 1851, stands amid the traffic whirlpool where Bayswater Road segues into Oxford Street, at the top of Park Lane. The arch actually contains three small chambers, which served as a police station until the mid-20th century. Search the sidewalk on the traffic island opposite the cinema for the stone plaque recalling the Tyburn Tree, an elaborately designed gallows that stood here for 400 years, until 1783. The condemned would be conveyed here in their finest clothes from Newgate Prison in The City, and were expected to affect a casual indifference or face a merciless heckling from the crowds. Towering across the grass from the arch towards Tyburn Way is a vast patina-green statue of a horse's head called *Horse at Water* by sculptor Nic Fiddian. Cross over (or under) to the northeastern corner of Hyde Park for Speakers' Corner. ⊠ *Park La., Mayfair* M *Marble Arch.*

Piccadilly Circus. The origins of the name "Piccadilly" relate to a humble 17th-century tailor from the Strand named Robert Baker who sold picadils—a stiff ruffled collar all the rage in courtly circles—and built a house with the proceeds. Snobs dubbed his new-money mansion Piccadilly Hall, and the name stuck.

Pride of place in the circus—a circular junction until the construction of Shaftesbury Avenue in 1886—belongs to London's favorite statue, **Eros** (actually, the 1893 work is a representation of Eros' brother Anteros, the Greek God of requited love). The creation of young sculptor Alfred Gilbert is a memorial to the selflessness of the philanthropic Earl of Shaftesbury (the god's bow and arrow are an allusion to the earl's name). Gilbert cast the statue he called his "missile of kindness" in the then-novel medium of aluminum. Unfortunately, he spent most of his £8,000 fee ensuring the bronze fountain beneath was cast to his specifications. Already in debt, Gilbert eventually went bankrupt and fled the country. (In the end he was redeemed with a knighthood.)

ROYALTY IN AISLE 9

Shoppers and historians alike will enjoy **Fortnum & Mason** at 181 Piccadilly. This old-fashioned fine-foods store seems to have been lifted from another century, with ornate murals decorating the walls, glass cabinets, and brass fixtures casting a dazzling glow all around. The store is especially famous for its loose-leaf tea and luxury picnic hampers (a wise purchase with St. James' Park just a stone's throw away). Built in 1788, Fortnum & Mason sent hams to the Duke of Wellington's army and baskets of treats to Florence Nightingale in the Crimea. (It also happens to be the Queen's grocery store.)

Marble Arch was originally a gateway to Buckingham Palace before it was moved to the corner of Hyde Park.

Beneath the modern bank of neon advertisements surrounding the circus are some of the most elegant Edwardian-era buildings in London. ⊠ *St. James's* Ⓜ *Piccadilly Circus.*

☾ **Ripley's Believe It Or Not!.** Ripley's contains five floors of curiosities: natural mutations (an albino alligator), cultural artifacts (Eucadorian shrunken heads), and historic memorabilia (a piece of the Berlin Wall). ⊠ *1 Piccadilly Circus, Mayfair* ☎ *020/3238–0022* ⊕ *www.ripleyslondon.com* 🎫 *£25.95* ☾ *Daily 10–midnight* Ⓜ *Piccadilly Circus.*

Fodor's Choice **Royal Academy of Arts.** Burlington House was originally built in 1664, ★ with later Palladian additions for the 3rd Earl of Burlington in 1720. The piazza in front is a later conception from 1873, when the Renaissance-style buildings around the courtyard were designed by Banks and Barry to house a gaggle of noble scientific societies, including the Royal Society of Chemistry, the Linnean Society of London, and the Royal Astronomical Society.

Burlington House itself houses the draw-card tenant, the Royal Academy of Arts. The statue of the academy's first president, Sir Joshua Reynolds, palette in hand, is prominent in the piazza of light stone with fountains by Sir Phillip King. Within the house and up the stairs are statues of creative giants J.W.M. Turner and Thomas Gainsborough. Free tours show off part of the RA collection, some of it housed in the John Madejski Fine Rooms, and the RA hosts excellent temporary exhibitions. Every June for the past 240 years, the RA has put on its Summer Exhibition, a huge and always surprising collection of art by living Royal Academicians and a plethora of other contemporary artists. ⊠ *Burlington House, Piccadilly, Mayfair* ☎ *020/7300–8000,*

Don't miss the globe-spanning Food Hall in the basement of Selfridges.

0207/300–5839 lectures, 0207/300–5995 family programs ⊕ *www.royalacademy.org.uk* ✉ *From £12; prices vary with exhibition* ⊗ *Sat.–Thurs. 10–6, Fri. 10–10; tours Tues. 1, Wed.–Fri. 1, and 3, Sat. 11:30* Ⓜ *Piccadilly Circus, Green Park.*

QUICK
BITES

Royal Academy Restaurant. The Royal Academy Restaurant, with its walls covered in Gilbert Spencer murals, is almost as beautiful as the art hanging in the galleries. The accent is on flexibility: you can linger over a three-course meal, order tapas-style, or just pop in for a quick, delicious bite. Open Sunday–Thursday 10–6, Fri. and Sat. 9–11. ☎ *020/7300–5608.*

For something a little less substantial, have a snack at the Gallery Café, which offers a range of muffins, sandwiches, and pastries. Outdoor tables are available in the summer.

★ **Selfridges.** With its row of massive Ionic columns, this huge store was opened three years after Harry Gordon Selfridge came to London from Chicago in 1906. Now Selfridges is comparable to Harrods in size and scope, and, since investing in major face-lift operations, to Harvey Nichols in designer cachet. ✉ *400 Oxford St., Mayfair* ☎ *0800/123-400* ⊕ *www.selfridges.com* ⊗ *Mon.–Sat. 9:30–9, Sun. 11:30–6:15* Ⓜ *Marble Arch, Bond Street.*

St. James's Church. Blitzed by the German Luftwaffe in 1940 and not restored under 1954, this was one of the last of Sir Christopher Wren's London churches—and his favorite. Completed in 1684, it envelops one of Grinling Gibbon's finest works, an ornate lime-wood reredos (the screen behind the altar), and the organ was brought here in 1691 from Whitehall Palace. The church is a lively place, with all manner of lectures and (some free) concerts. A café enjoys a fine location right alongside the church, while a small, sedate garden is tucked away at the rear. The market out front is full of surprises, hosting antiques on Tuesday, and arts and crafts from Wednesday to Saturday. ⊠ *197 Piccadilly, St. James's* ☎ *020/7734–4511, 020/7381–0441 concert program and tickets* ⊕ *www.st-james-piccadilly.org* Ⓜ *Piccadilly Circus, Green Park.*

Wellington Arch. Opposite the Duke of Wellington's mansion, Apsley House, this majestic stone arch surveys the busy traffic rushing around Hyde Park Corner. Designed by Decimus Burton and built in 1828, it was created as a grand entrance to the west side of London and echoes the design of that other landmark gate, ⇨ *Marble Arch.* Both were triumphal arches commemorating Britain's victory against France in the Napoleonic Wars. The exterior of the arch was intended to be much more ornate but King George IV was going vastly over budget with his refurbishment of Buckingham Palace and cutbacks had to be made elsewhere. Atop the building, the Angel of Peace descends on the quadriga, or four-horse chariot of war. This replaced the Duke of Wellington on his horse, which was considered too large and moved to an army barracks in Aldershot. Inside the arch, three floors of exhibits reveal the history of the building and explore other great arches around the world. Best of all is the platform at the top of the arch, where you can enjoy brilliant panoramas over Hyde Park and peer into the private gardens of Buckingham Palace. ⊠ *Hyde Park Corner, Mayfair* ☎ *020/7930–2726* ⊕ *www.english-heritage.org.uk* ⌖ *£3.50* ⊗ *Check w Web site for opening hours* Ⓜ *Hyde Park Corner.*

WORTH NOTING

Grosvenor Square. Leafy Grosvenor Square (pronounced *Grove*-na) was laid out in 1725–31 and is as desirable an address today as it was then. Americans have certainly always thought so—from John Adams, the second president, who as ambassador lived at No. 38, to Dwight D. Eisenhower, whose wartime headquarters was at No. 20. Now the massive 1960s block of the U.S. Embassy occupies the entire west side, and a British memorial to Franklin D. Roosevelt stands in the center. There is also a classically styled memorial to those who died in New York on September 11, 2001. Little brick Grosvenor Chapel, completed in 1730 and used by Eisenhower's men during World War II, stands a couple of blocks south of the square on South Audley Street, with the entrance to pretty **St. George's Gardens** to its left. Across the gardens is the headquarters of the English Jesuits as well as the society-wedding favorite, the mid-19th-century Church of the Immaculate Conception, known as Farm Street Church because of its location. A Barclays Cycle Hire docking station is immediately northeast of the square. ⊠ *Mayfair* Ⓜ *Bond St.*

★ **Handel House Museum.** The former home of the composer, where he lived for more than 30 years until his death in 1759, is a celebration of his genius. It's the first museum in London solely dedicated to one composer. In rooms decorated in fine Georgian style you can linger over original manuscripts (there are more to be seen in the British Library) and gaze at portraits—accompanied by live music if the adjoining music rooms are being used by musicians in rehearsal. Some of the composer's most famous pieces were created here, including *Messiah* and *Music for the Royal Fireworks.* To hear a live concert here—there are Thursday evening performances, mostly of baroque music—is to imagine the atmosphere of rehearsals and "salon" music in its day. Handel House makes a perfect cultural pit stop after shopping on nearby Bond and Oxford streets, and if you come on Saturday, there is free admission for kids. The museum occupies both No. 25 and the adjoining house, where life in Georgian London is displayed, and where another musical star, Jimi Hendrix, lived for a brief time in the 1960s, as a blue plaque outside the house indicates—also look for the petite exhibition of Hendrix photos. Tours of his flat, currently administrative offices and not usually open to the public, are offered twice a year. Phone or check the website for details. ⊠ *25 Brook St., entrance in Lancashire Court, Mayfair* ☎ *020/7495–1685* ⊕ *www.handelhouse.org* 🎫 *£5* ⊙ *Tues.–Sat. 10–6, Thurs. 10–8, Sun. noon–6* Ⓜ *Bond St.*

★ **Spencer House.** Ancestral abode of the Spencers—Diana, Princess of Wales's family—this is perhaps the finest example of an elegant 18th-century town house extant in London. Reflecting his passion for the Grand Tour and classical antiquities, the first Earl Spencer commissioned architect John Vardy to adapt designs from ancient Rome for a magnificent private palace. Vardy was responsible for the external elevation, including the gorgeous west-facing Palladian facade, its pediment adorned with classical statues, and the ground-floor interiors, notably the lavish Palm Room, which boasts a spectacular screen of columns covered in gilded carvings that resemble gold palm trees. The purpose of the bling-tastic decor was not only to attest to Spencer's power and wealth but also to celebrate his marriage, a love match then rare in aristocratic circles (the palms are a symbol of marital fertility). Midway through construction—the house was built between 1756 and 1766—Spencer changed architects and hired James "Athenian" Stuart, whose designs were based on a classical Greek aesthetic, to decorate the gilded State Rooms on the first floor. These include the Painted Room, the first completely neoclassical room in Europe. In recent years the house was superlatively restored by Lord Rothschild (to impress close friend, Princess Diana), but in 2010 the Spencer family scandalously decided to sell off all the house's best furnishings and paintings at Christie's so that today's viewers see a decidedly denuded house, alas. The garden, of

Gentlemen's shops in St. James's specialize in high-quality, handmade goods.

Henry Holland design, has also been replanted in the 18th- and 19th-century fashion. The house is open only on Sunday (closed January and August), and only to guided tours. The garden is open some Sundays in summer. Check the website for details. ⊠ *27 St. James's Pl., St. James's* ☎ *020/7499–8620* ⊕ *www.spencerhouse.co.uk* ✉ *£9* ⊗ *Sept.–Dec. and Feb.–July, Sun. 10:30–5:45, last tour 4:45* Ⓜ *Green Park.*

St. James's Square. One of London's oldest and leafiest squares was also the most snobbish address of all when it was laid out around 1670, with 14 resident dukes and earls installed by 1720. Since 1841, No. 14—one of the several 18th-century residences spared by World War II bombs—has housed the **London Library,** founded by Thomas Carlyle. With its million or so volumes, this is the world's largest independent lending library and is also considered the best private humanities library in the land. The workplace of literary luminaries from T.S. Eliot to Bruce Chatwin, Kingsley Amis, Winston Churchill, John Betjeman, and Charles Dickens, the library invites you to read famous authors' complaints in the comments book—but you'll need a £15 day or £50 week membership to peruse the collection (bring ID and proof of address), although these have to be booked in advance. Other notable institutions around the square include the East India Club at No. 16, the Naval and Military Club (known as the "In and Out" after the signage on its gateposts) at No. 4, as well as Chatham House, a think tank on international affairs. A small epitaph to WPC Yvonne Fletcher—shot by a Libyan gunman—can be found on the sidewalk around the square. ⊠ *St. James's* ⊕ *www.londonlibrary.co.uk* ⊗ *Mon.–Wed. 9:30–9, Thurs.–Sat. 9:30–5:30;, closed Sun.* Ⓜ *Piccadilly Circus.*

Soho and Covent Garden

WORD OF MOUTH

"If you accept the consensus that Mayfair and Soho aren't 'real' neighborhoods, you're mostly left with tourist ghettoes like Bloomsbury, Earl's Court, Gloucester Rd, Covent Garden, Bayswater, and Victoria, where hotelization and foreigners' London pads have driven full-time residents out."

—Flanneruk

GETTING ORIENTED

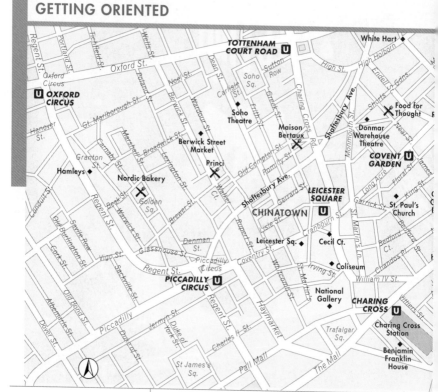

GETTING THERE

Almost all Tube lines cross the Covent Garden and Soho areas, so it's easy to hop off for a dinner or show in the hippest area of London. For Soho, take any train to Piccadilly Circus, or Leicester Square, Oxford Circus, or Tottenham Court Road. For Covent Garden, get off at the Covent Garden station on the Piccadilly line. It might be easier to exit the Tube at Leicester Square or Holborn and walk. Thirty buses connect to the Covent Garden area from all over London; check out the area's website, www.coventgarden. uk.com.

TOP REASONS TO GO

Find tomorrow's look in the Newburgh Quarter: Head to this adorable, cobblestoned warren of streets for a ultra-hip array of specialist boutiques, edgy stores, and young indy upstarts.

Gourmet Country: London has fallen in love with its tummy and Soho is home to many of the most talked-about restaurants in town.

Delight in the Covent Garden Piazza: Eliza Doolittle's former stamping ground has been taken over by fun boutiques and performers (who play to the crowds at night).

The Royal Opera House: Even if you're not going to the opera or ballet, take in the beautiful architecture and sense of history.

See a West End hit in Theatreland: Shaftesbury Avenue is the heart of Theatreland, where almost 50 West End theaters are a stand-in Mecca for those who love Shakespeare, Maggie Smith, and the Phantom.

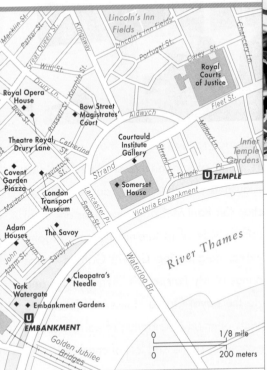

4

MAKING THE MOST OF YOUR TIME

You can comfortably tour all the sights around Soho and Covent Garden in a day. Visit the small but perfect Courtauld Gallery on Monday before 2 pm, when entry is free. That leaves plenty of time to watch some street entertainment or shop at the food and souvenir and stalls around Covent Garden Piazza or in the fashion boutiques of Soho. Save some energy for a night on the town (or "on the tiles," as the British say) in Soho.

FEELING PECKISH?

Although they may set out a few tables, the coffee shops and snack bars along the Covent Garden market buildings can be overpriced and of poor quality. It's usually best to head for Soho when the munchies strike.

Food for Thought. Food for Thought is always crowded, with hungry customers queuing outside for a delicious range of vegetarian dishes. Be prepared to share a table. ✉ *31 Neal St., Covent Garden* ☎ *020/7836–9072.*

Kulu Kulu. Kulu Kulu offers fresh, good-value sushi. Dishes trundle around on a conveyor belt—ideal if you're pressed for time. ✉ *51–53 Shelton St., Covent Garden* ☎ *020/7240–5687.*

Maison Bertaux. Maison Bertaux has been around since the end of the 19th century. Decor is spartan, but fab French cakes, tarts, and savory quiches more than make up for that. Nobody's mother ever baked this well. ✉ *28 Greek St., Soho* ☎ *020/7437–6007.*

GAY LONDON

Old Compton Street in Soho is the epicenter of London's affluent, stylish gay scene. There are some smart nightclubs in the area, with crowds forming in Soho Square, south of Oxford Street.

Madame Jo Jo's. Madame Jo Jo's has been around for 50 years. The club's **Kitsch Cabaret,** performed every Saturday evening, is so popular (with straights as well as gays) that it's usually booked weeks in advance. ✉ *8–10 Brewer St.* ☎ *020/7734–3040* ⊕ *www. madamejojos.com.*

Sightseeing
★★★
Nightlife
★★★★
Dining
★★★★
Lodging
★★
Shopping
★★★

Once a red-light district, today's Soho is more stylish than seedy and offers some of London's best nightclubs, live music venues, restaurants, and theaters. By day, this hotbed of media production (Sir Paul McCartney's offices are here) reverts to the business side of its late-night scene. If Soho is all about showbiz, neighboring Covent Garden—once the stomping grounds of *My Fair Lady*'s Eliza Doolittle and landmark home to the Royal Opera House—is devoted to culture. Both districts offer an abundance of narrow streets packed with one-of-a-kind shops and lots of character.

Updated by Julius Honnor

The narrow, winding streets of Soho lie to the east of Regent Street and to the south of Oxford Street and are unabashedly devoted to pleasure. Wardour Street bisects the neighborhood, with lots of interesting boutiques and some of London's best-value restaurants to the west (especially around Foubert's Place and on Brewer and Lexington streets), and nightlife central to the east, including London's gay mecca, Old Compton Street, and beyond that, the city's densest collection of theaters on Shaftesbury Avenue. London's compact Chinatown is wedged between Soho and **Leicester Square**. A bit of erudition surfaces on Charing Cross Road, to the east of the square, famous for its secondhand bookshops, and on tiny **Cecil Court**, a pedestrianized passage lined with small antiquarian booksellers.

To the east of Charing Cross Road lies Covent Garden, the famous marketplace turned shopping mall. Although boutiques and haute fashion shops line the surrounding streets, many Londoners come to Convent Garden for its two outposts of culture: the **Royal Opera House** and the **Donmar Warehouse**, one of London's best and most innovative theaters. The area becomes more sedate just to the north, at the end of Wellington Street, where semicircular Aldwych is lined with grand buildings, and from there the Strand leads to the huge, stately piazza of **Somerset House**, which contains the many masterpieces on view at the **Courtauld Institute**

DID YOU KNOW

Covent Garden was a convent garden for 300 years before it was Britain's first planned public square with a fruit and vegetable market. The greengrocers are gone but the 1840 market building and the courtyard still teem with shoppers.

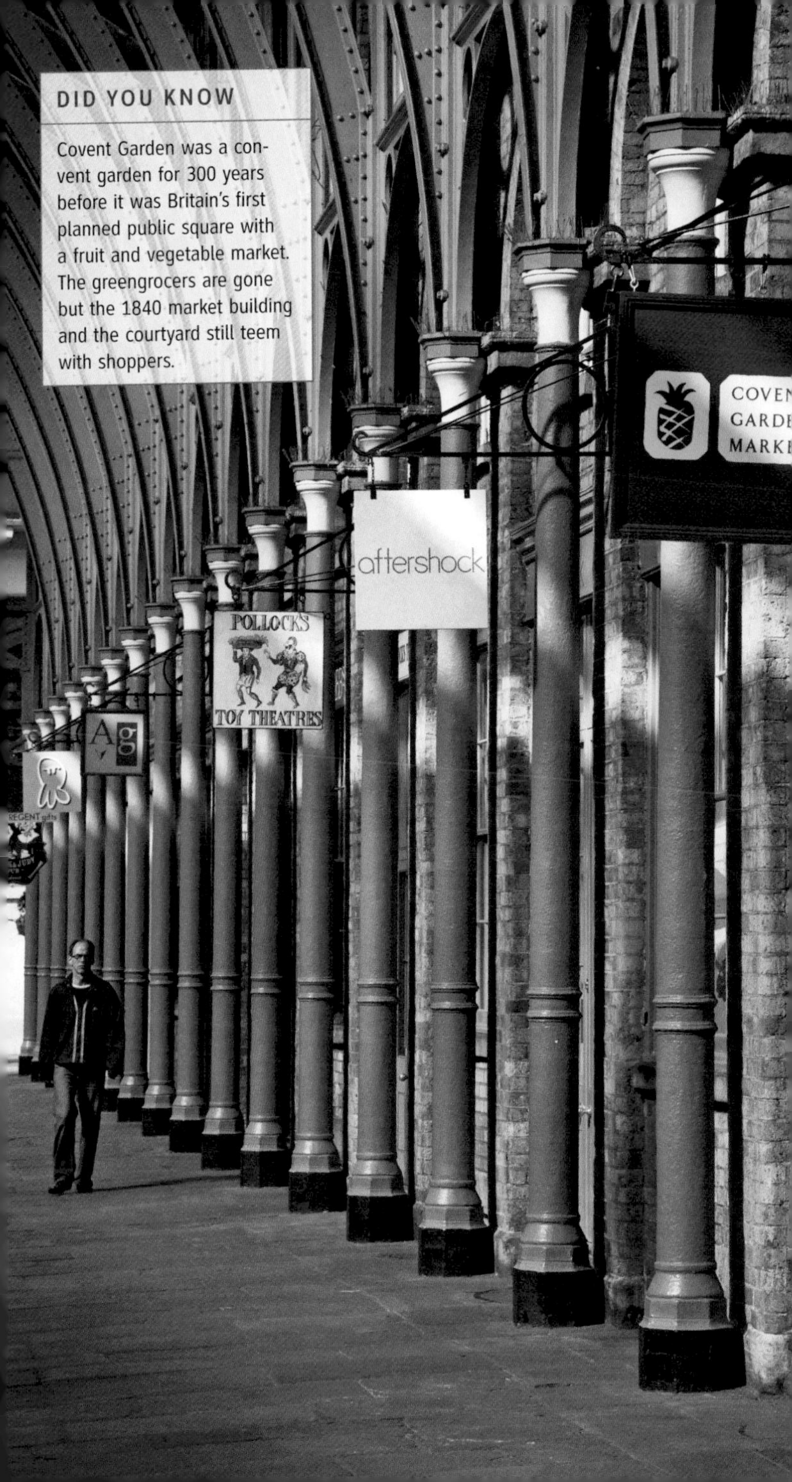
COVEN
GARDE
MARKE
aftershock
POLLOCKS
TOY THEATRES
Ag

You can't miss the buskers performing in the streets of Soho and Covent Garden.

Gallery. You'll get a sense of old-fashioned London just behind the Strand, where small lanes are little changed since the 18th century. On the way to the verdant **Embankment Gardens** bordering the Thames, you may pass the **Adam Houses, the remnants of a grand 18th-century riverside housing development,** and the **Benjamin Franklin House,** where the noted statesman lived in the years leading up to the American Revolution.

TOP ATTRACTIONS

Courtauld Institute Gallery. One of London's most beloved art collections, the Courtauld is to your right as you pass through the archway into the grounds of the beautifully restored, grand 18th-century neoclassical **Somerset House.** Founded in 1931 by the textile magnate Samuel Courtauld to house his remarkable private collection, this is one of the world's finest Impressionist and post-Impressionist galleries, with artists ranging from Bonnard to van Gogh. A déjà-vu moment with Cézanne, Degas, Seurat, or Monet awaits on every wall (Manet's *Bar at the Folies-Bergère* and *Le Dejjeuner sur L'Herbe* are two of the stars). Botticelli, Brueghel, Tiepolo, and Rubens are also represented, thanks to the exquisite bequest of Count Antoine Seilern's Princes Gate collection. German Renaissance paintings, bequeathed in 1947, include the colorful and delightfully wicked *Adam and Eve* by Lucas Cranach the Elder. The second floor has a more provocative, experimental feel, with masterpieces such as Modigliani's iconic *Female Nude*. Don't miss the little café downstairs, a perfect place for a spot of tea. ⊠ *Somerset House, Strand, Covent Garden* ☎ *020/7848–2526* ⊕ *www.courtauld.*

A BRIEF HISTORY

Almost as soon as a 17th-century housing development covered what had been a royal park and hunting ground, Soho earned a reputation for entertainment, bohemianism, and cosmopolitan tolerance. When the authorities introduced zero tolerance of soliciting in 1991 (the most recent of several attempts to end Soho's sex trade), they cracked down on an old neighborhood tradition that still resurfaces from time to time.

Successive waves of refugees, from French Huguenots in the 1680s followed by Germans, Russians, Poles, Greeks, Italians, and Chinese, settled and brought their ethnic cuisines with them. So when dining out became fashionable after World War I, Soho was the natural place for restaurants to flourish.

In the 1950s and '60s, Soho was London's artists' quarter and the place to find the top jazz clubs and art galleries. Among the luminaries who have made their home here are landscape painter John Constable; Casanova, the famous Lothario; Canaletto, the great painter of Venice; poet William Blake; and the revolutionary Karl Marx.

Present-day Covent Garden took shape in the 1630s, when Inigo Jones turned what had been agricultural land into Britain's first planned public square. After the Great Fire of 1666, it became the site of England's largest fruit-and-vegetable market (the flower market arrived in the 19th century). This, along with the district's many theaters and taverns, gave the area a somewhat dubious reputation, and after the produce market relocated in 1973, the surviving buildings were scheduled for demolition. A local campaign saved them, and the restored market opened in 1980.

4

ac.uk ⊠ £6, free Mon. 10–2, except bank holidays ⊘ Daily 10–6; last admission 5:30 Ⓜ Covent Garden, Holborn, Temple.

★ **Covent Garden Piazza.** Once home to London's main flower market, and former stomping ground of *My Fair Lady's* Eliza Doolittle, the square around which Covent Garden pivots is known as the Piazza. In the center, a building houses market stalls and shops selling higher-class clothing, plus several restaurants and cafés and knickknack stores that are good for gifts. One particular gem is Benjamin Pollock's Toyshop at No. 44 in the market. Established in the 1880s, it sells delightful toy theaters. The superior **Apple Market** has good crafts stalls on most days, too. On the south side of the Piazza, the indoor **Jubilee Market,** with its stalls of clothing, army-surplus gear, and more crafts and knickknacks, has a distinct flea-market feel. In summer it may seem that everyone you see around the Piazza (and the crowds are legion) is a fellow tourist, but there's still plenty of office life in the area. Londoners who shop here tend to head for Neal Street and the area to the north of Covent Garden Tube station rather than the touristy market itself. In the Piazza, performers—from global musicians to jugglers and mimes—play to the crowds, as they have done since the first English Punch and Judy Show, staged here in the 17th century. ⊠ Covent Garden Ⓜ Covent Garden.

DID YOU KNOW?

Somerset House was lapped by the River Thames before the Victoria Embankment was built in the 19th century. The neoclassical building's grand courtyard is home to ice skating in winter and dancing fountains in summer.

London Transport Museum. Housed in the old flower market at the south-east corner of Covent Garden, this stimulating museum is filled with impressive poster, photograph, and vehicle collections. As you watch the crowds drive a Tube-train simulation and gawk at the horse-drawn trams (and the piles of detritus that remained behind) and steam locomotives, it's unclear who's enjoying it more, children or adults. Best of all, the kid-friendly (under 16 admitted free) museum has a multilevel approach to education, including information for the youngest visitor to the most advanced transit aficionado. Food and drink are available at the Upper Deck café and the shop has lots of good options for gift-buying. ⊠ *Covent Garden Piazza* ☎ *020/7565–7298* ⊕ *www.ltmuseum.co.uk* ⊠ *£13.50* ⊗ *Sat.–Thurs. 10–6 (last admission 5:15), Fri. 11–6 (last admission 5:15)* Ⓜ *Leicester Sq., Covent Garden.*

Newburgh Quarter. Want to see the hip style of today's London? Find it just one block east of Carnaby Street—where the look of the '60s "Swinging London" was born and publicized—in an adorable warren of cobblestoned streets now lined with specialist boutiques, edgy stores, young indy upstarts, and concept stores (for biggies like Barbour and Levi's). Here, just two blocks west of roaring Regent Street, the future of England's fashion is being incubated in stores such as Lucy in Disguise and Sweaty Betty. A check of the ingredients reveals one part '60s London, one part Futuristic Fetishism, one part Dickensian charm, and one part British street swagger. The Nouveau Boho look flourishes best in shops like Peckham Rye, a tiny boutique crowded with rockers and fashion plates who adore its grunge–meets–Brideshead Revisted vibe. Or continue down Newburgh Street to Beyond the Valley, an art-school showcase whose designers have successfully paired graphic art-prints with kitschy outfits. ⊠ *Newburgh St., Foubert's Pl., Ganton St., and Carnaby St., Soho* ⊕ *Carnaby.co.uk.*

Royal Opera House. London's premier opera and ballet venue was designed in 1858 by E.M. Barry, son of Sir Charles, the House of Commons architect, and is the third theater on the site. The first theater opened in 1732 and burned down in 1808; the second opened a year later, only to succumb to fire in 1856. The entire building, which has been given a spectacular overhaul, retains the magic of the grand Victorian theater (but is now more accessible). The glass-and-steel Floral Hall is the most wonderful feature; you can wander around and drink in (literally, in the foyer café) the interior. The same is true of the

Amphitheatre Bar and Piazza concourse, where you can have lunch while looking out at a splendid panorama across the city. There are free lunchtime chamber concerts and lectures, as well as tea dances and occasional free jazz concerts, which go a long way to making this venue a great space for the common people. ⊠ *Bow St., Covent Garden* ☎ *020/7240–1200* ⊕ *www.roh.org.uk* Ⓜ *Covent Garden.*

☽ **Somerset House.** In recent years this huge complex—the work of Sir William Chambers (1726–96), built during the reign of George III to house offices of the Navy—has completed its transformation from dusty government offices to one

Fodor's Choice
★

of the capital's most buzzing centers of culture and the arts, hosting several interesting exhibitions at any one time. The cobbled Italianate courtyard, where Admiral Nelson used to walk, makes a great setting for 55 playful fountains and is transformed into a romantic ice rink in winter; the grand space is the venue for music and outdoor cinema screenings in summer. The Courtauld Institute Gallery occupies most of the north building, facing the busy Strand. Across the courtyard are the Embankment Galleries, with a vibrant calendar of design, fashion, architecture, and photography exhibitions. The East Wing has another fine exhibition space and events are sometimes also held in the atmospherically gloomy cellars below the Fountain Court. Tom's Kitchen offers fine dining and the Deli has mouthwatering cakes and pastries. In summer eating and drinking spills out onto the large terrace next to the Thames. ⊠ *The Strand, Covent Garden* ☎ *020/7845–4600* ⊕ *www.somersethouse.org.uk* ✉ *Embankment Galleries £5, Courtauld Gallery £6, other areas free* ☉ *Daily 10–6; last admission 5:30* Ⓜ *Charing Cross, Waterloo, Blackfriars.*

WORTH NOTING

The Adam Houses. Only a few structures remain of what was once a regal riverfront row of houses on a 3-acre site, but such is their quality that they are worth a detour off the Strand to see. The work of 18th-century Scottish architects and interior designers (John, Robert, James, and William Adam, known collectively as the Adam brothers), the original development was damaged in the 19th century during the building of the embankment, and mostly demolished in 1936 to be replaced by an art deco tower. The original houses still standing are protected, and give a glimpse of their former grandeur. Nos. 1–4 Robert Street and Nos. 7 and 10 Adam Street are the best.

Leicester Square is home to many cinemas and a half-price theater ticket booth.

Royal Society of Arts. At the Royal Society of Arts, you can see a suite of Adam rooms; no reservations are required. ✉ *8 John Adam St.* ☎ *020/7930–5115* ⊕ *www.thersa.org* 🗺 *Free* ⊙ *1st Sun. of month, 10–1* ✉ *The Strand, Covent Garden* ⊙ *Closed weekends* Ⓜ *Charing Cross, Embankment.*

Benjamin Franklin House. This architecturally significant 1730 house is the only surviving residence of American statesman, scientist, writer, and inventor Benjamin Franklin, who lived and worked here for 16 years preceding the American Revolution. The restored Georgian town house has been left unfurnished, the better to show off the original features—18th-century paneling, stoves, beams, bricks, and windows. Older children (under 16 admitted free) particularly enjoy the Student Science Centre, an interactive display of scientific experiments that contrasts historical and modern knowledge. There's also a glass harmonica (which Franklin invented while living there) and a scholarship center with a complete collection of Franklin's papers. On Monday you can take a guided tour focusing on the architectural details of the building. ✉ *36 Craven St., Covent Garden* ☎ *020/7839–2006, 020/7925–1405 booking line* ⊕ *www.benjaminfranklinhouse.org* 🗺 *£7* ⊙ *Wed.–Sun. noon–5* Ⓜ *Charing Cross, Embankment.*

Leicester Square. Looking at the neon of the major movie houses, the fast-food outlets, and the disco entrances, you'd never guess that this square (pronounced *Lester*) was a model of formality and refinement when it was first laid out around 1630. By the 19th century the square was already bustling and disreputable, and although it's not a threatening place, you should still be on your guard, especially at night—any space so full of people is bound to attract pickpockets, and Leicester Square certainly does. Although a bit of residual glamour from the days of red-carpet film premieres remains, Londoners generally tend to avoid this windswept plaza, crowded as it is with suburban teenagers, wandering backpackers, and mimes. In the middle is a statue of a sulking Shakespeare, clearly wishing he were somewhere else and perhaps remembering the days when the cinemas were live theaters—burlesque houses, but live all the same. Here, too, are figures of Newton, Hogarth, Reynolds, and Charlie Chaplin. On the northeast corner, in Leicester Place, stands the church of **Notre Dame de France,** with a

wonderful mural by Jean Cocteau in one of its side chapels. For more in the way of atmosphere, head north and west from here, through Chinatown and the narrow streets of Soho. ⊠ *Covent Garden* Ⓜ *Leicester Sq.*

St. Paul's Church. If you want to commune with the spirits of Vivien Leigh, Noël Coward, Edith Evans, or Charlie Chaplin, this might be just the place. Memorials to them and many other theater greats are found in this 1633 work of the renowned Inigo Jones, who, as the King's Surveyor of Works, designed the whole of Covent Garden Piazza. St. Paul's Church has been known as "the actors' church" since the Restoration, thanks to the neighboring theater district and St. Paul's prominent parishioners. (Well-known actors often read the lessons at services, and the church still hosts concerts and small-scale productions.) Fittingly, the opening scene of Shaw's *Pygmalion* takes place under its Tuscan portico (you might know it better from the musical *My Fair Lady,* starring Audrey Hepburn). The western end of the Piazza is a prime pitch for street entertainers, but if they're not to your liking, you can repair to the serenity of the garden entered from King or Bedford streets. ⊠ *Bedford St., Covent Garden* Ⓜ *Covent Garden.*

Theatre Royal, Drury Lane. This is London's best-known auditorium and almost its largest. Since World War II, the Drury Lane's forte has been musicals (past ones have included *The King and I, My Fair Lady, South Pacific, Hello, Dolly!,* and *A Chorus Line*)—though David Garrick, who managed the theater from 1747 to 1776, made its name by reviving the works of the by-then-obscure William Shakespeare. The Drury Lane enjoys all the romantic accessories of a London theater—a history of fires (it burned down three times), riots (in 1737, when a posse of footmen demanded free admission), attempted regicides (George II in 1716 and his grandson George III in 1800), and even sightings of the most famous phantom of theaterland, the Man in Grey (in the Circle during matinees). ⊠ *Catherine St., Covent Garden* ☎ *020/7494–5000* Ⓜ *Covent Garden.*

Bloomsbury
and Holborn

WORD OF MOUTH

"We began to walk to the British Library in a leisurely manner.
[Then] we spent over an hour oohing and aahing (quietly!). Aus-
ten, Shakespeare, Carroll, Bronte, Milton, Wordsworth, Beowulf,
Gutenberg, Beatles, Handel. Beyond cool."

—texasbookworm

GETTING ORIENTED

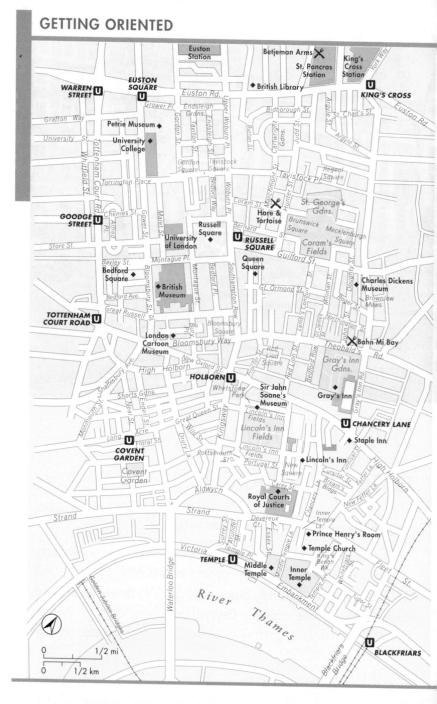

TOP REASONS TO GO

Take a tour of "Mankind's Attic": From the Rosetta Stone to the Elgin Marbles, the British Museum is the golden hoard of booty amassed by centuries of the British Empire.

The Inns of Court: Stroll through the quiet courts, leafy gardens, and magnificent halls that comprise the heart of Holborn—the closest thing to the spirit of Oxford London has to offer.

Time travel at Sir John Soane's Museum: Quirky and fascinating, the former home of the celebrated 19th-century architect is a treasure trove of antiquities and oddities.

Treasures at the British Library: In keeping with Bloomsbury's literary traditions, this great repository shows off the Magna Carta, a Gutenberg Bible, Shakespeare's First Folio, and other masterpieces of the written word.

Charles Dickens Museum: Pay your respects to the beloved author of *Oliver Twist* at his former residence.

FEELING PECKISH?

The Betjeman Arms. The Betjeman Arms, inside St. Pancras International's wonderfully Victorian station (shining star of the Harry Potter films), is the perfect place to stop for a pint and grab some traditional pub fare. Perched above the tracks of the Eurostar Terminal, the view of the trains will keep you entertained for hours. ⊠ *Unit 53, St. Pancras International Station* ☎ *020/7923–5440.*

The Hare and Tortoise Dumpling & Noodle Bar. This bright café serves scrumptious Asian fast food. A favorite with students, thanks to huge portions, reasonable bills, and all-natural ingredients. ⊠ *15–17 Brunswick Shopping Centre, opposite the Renoir Cinema, Brunswick Square, Bloomsbury* ☎ *020/7278–9799.*

GETTING THERE

The Russell Square Tube stop on the Piccadilly line leaves you right at the corner of Russell Square.

The best Tube stops for the Inns of Court are Holborn on the Central and Piccadilly lines or Chancery Lane on the Central line.

Tottenham Court Road on the Northern and Central lines is best for the British Museum.

Once you're in Bloomsbury, you can easily get around on foot.

5

MAKING THE MOST OF YOUR TIME

Bloomsbury can be seen in a day, or in half a day, depending on your interests and your time constraints.

If you plan to visit the Inns of Court as well as the British Museum, and you'd also like to get a feel for the neighborhood, then you may wish to devote an entire day to this literary and legal enclave.

An alternative scenario is to set aside a separate day for a visit the British Museum, which can easily consume as many hours as you have to spare.

It's a pleasure to wander through the quiet, leafy squares at your leisure, examining historic Blue Plaques or relaxing at a street-side café. The many students in the neighborhood add bit of street life.

Sightseeing ★★★ Nightlife ★★ Dining ★★ Lodging ★★★★ Shopping ★★	London can be a bit schizophrenic: Bloomsbury is only a mere couple of hundred yards from fun-loving, hedonistic Soho. Best known for the famous flowering of literary-arty bohemia in the early 20th century as personified by the Bloomsbury Group, the area encompasses the British Museum, the British Library, and the University of London. But don't let all this highbrow talk put you off: filled with beautiful historic buildings, Bloomsbury is simply a delightful part of the city in which to walk and explore.

Updated by
James O'Neill

Fundamental to the region's spirit of open expression and scholarly debate is the legacy of the Bloomsbury Group, an elite corps of artists and writers who lived in this neighborhood during the first part of the 20th century. **Gordon Square** was at one point home to Virginia Woolf, John Maynard Keynes (both at No. 46), and Lytton Strachey (at No. 51). But perhaps the best-known square in Bloomsbury is the large, centrally located **Russell Square,** with its handsome gardens. Scattered around the **University of London** campus are Woburn Square, Torrington Square, and Tavistock Square. The **British Library,** with its vast treasures, is a few blocks north, across busy Euston Road.

The area from Somerset House on the Strand, all the way up Kingsway to the Euston Road, is known as London's **Museum Mile** for the myriad historic houses and museums that dot the area. **Charles Dickens Museum,** where the author wrote *Oliver Twist,* pays homage to the master, and artists' studios and design shops share space with tenants near the bright and modern **British Museum.** And guaranteed to raise a smile from the most blasé and footsore tourist is **Sir John Soane's Museum,** where the colorful collection is a testimony to the namesake founder.

Bloomsbury also happens to be where London's legal profession was born. In fact, the buildings associated with Holborn were some of the few structures spared during the Great Fire of 1666, and so the serpentine alleys, cobbled courts, and historic halls frequented by the city's still-bewigged barristers ooze centuries of history. The massive Gothic-style **Royal Courts of Justice** ramble all the way to the Strand, and the **Inns of Court—Gray's Inn, Lincoln's Inn, Middle Temple,** and **Inner Temple**—are where most British trial lawyers have offices to this day.

TOP ATTRACTIONS

British Library. This collection of around 18 million volumes, formerly in the British Museum, now has a home in state-of-the-art surroundings. The library's greatest treasures are on view to the general public: the Magna Carta, a Gutenberg Bible, Jane Austen's writings, Shakespeare's First Folio, and musical manuscripts by G.F. Handel as well as Sir Paul McCartney are on display in the Sir John Ritblat Gallery. Also in the gallery are headphones with which you can listen to pieces in the **National Sound Archive** (it's the world's largest collection), such as the voice of Florence Nightingale and an extract from the Beatles' last tour interview. Marvel at the six-story glass tower that holds the 65,000-volume collection of George III, plus a permanent exhibition of rare stamps. On weekends and during school vacations there are hands-on demonstrations of how a book comes together, and the library frequently mounts special exhibitions. If all this wordiness is just too much, you can relax in the library's piazza or restaurant, or take in one of the occasional free concerts in the amphitheater outside. ✉ *96 Euston Rd., Bloomsbury* ☎ *0870/7412–7332* ⊕ *www.bl.uk* ✆ *Free, donations appreciated, charge for special exhibitions* ⊙ *Mon. and Wed.–Fri. 9:30–6, Tues. 9:30–8, Sat. 9:30–5, Sun. and bank holiday Mon. 11–5* Ⓜ *Euston, Euston Sq., King's Cross.*

Fodor's Choice **British Museum.**

★ *See the highlighted listing in this chapter.*

Fodor's Choice **Charles Dickens Museum.** This is the only one of the many London houses Charles Dickens (1812–70) inhabited that is still standing, and it would have had a real claim to his fame in any case because he wrote *Oliver Twist* and *Nicholas Nickleby* and finished *Pickwick Papers* here between 1837 and 1839. The house looks exactly as it would have in Dickens's day, complete with first editions, letters, and a tall clerk's desk (where the master wrote standing up, often while chatting with visiting friends and relatives). Down in the basement is a replica of the Dingley Dell kitchen from *Pickwick Papers*. A program of changing special exhibitions gives insight into the Dickens family and the author's works, with sessions where, for instance, you can try your own hand with a quill pen. Visitors have reported a "presence" upstairs in the Mary Hogarth bedroom, where Dickens's sister-in-law died—see for yourself! Christmas is a memorable time to visit, as the rooms are decorated in traditional style: better than any televised costume drama, this is the real thing. The museum also houses a shop and café. ✉ *48 Doughty St., Bloomsbury* ☎ *020/7405–2127* ⊕ *www.dickensmuseum.com* ✆ *£7* ⊙ *Daily 10–5; last admission 4:30* Ⓜ *Chancery La., Russell Sq.*

Continued on page 104

THE BRITISH MUSEUM

Anybody writing about the British Museum had better have a large stack of superlatives close at hand: most, biggest, earliest, finest. This is the golden hoard of nearly three centuries of the Empire, the booty brought from Britain's far-flung colonies.

The first major pieces, among them the Rosetta Stone and the Parthenon Sculptures (Elgin Marbles), were "acquired" from the French, who "found" them in Egypt and Greece. The museum has since collected countless goodies of worldwide historical significance: the Black Obelisk, some of the Dead Sea Scrolls, the Lindow Man. And that only begins the list.

The British Museum is a vast space split into 94 galleries, generally divided by continent or period of history, with some areas spanning more than one level. There are marvels wherever you go, and—while we don't like to be pessimistic—it is, yes, impossible to fully appreciate everything in a day. So make the most of the tours, activity trails, and visitors guides that are available.

The following is a highly edited overview of the museum's greatest hits, organized by area. Pick one or two that whet your appetite, then branch out from there, or spend two straight hours indulging in the company of a single favorite sculpture. There's no wrong way to experience the British Museum, just make sure you do!

⊠ Great Russell St., Bloomsbury WC1

☎ 020/7323–8000

⊕ www.britishmuseum.org

▧ Free; donations encouraged. Tickets for special exhibits vary in price.

⊙ Galleries (and Reading Room exhibition space): Sat.–Thurs. 10–5:30, Fri. 10–8:30. Great Court: Sat.–Thurs. 9–6, Fri. 9–8:30.

Ⓤ Russell Square, Holborn, Tottenham Court Rd.

(left) The Great Court
(top) *Cradle to Grave* by Pharmacopoeia

MUSEUM HIGHLIGHTS

Ancient Civilizations

The Rosetta Stone. Found in 1799 and carved in 196 BC by decree of Ptolemy V in Egyptian hieroglyphics, demotic, and Greek, it was this multilingual inscription that provided French Egyptologist Jean-François Champollion with the key to deciphering hieroglyphics. *Room 4.*

Colossal statue of Ramesses II. A member of the 19th dynasty (ca. 1270 BC), Ramesses II commissioned innumerable statues of himself—more than any other preceding or succeeding king. This one, a 7-ton likeness of his perfectly posed upper half, comes from his mortuary temple, the Ramesseum, in western Thebes. *Room 4.*

(top) Portland vase
(bottom) Colossal statue of Ramesses II

The Parthenon Sculptures. Perhaps these marvelous treasures of Greece shouldn't be here—but while the debate rages on, you can steal your own moment with the Elgin Marbles. Carved in about 440 BC, these graceful decorations are displayed along with an in-depth, high-tech exhibit of the Acropolis; the **handless, footless Dionysus** who used to recline along its east pediment is especially well known. *Room 18.*

Mausoleum of Halikarnassos. All that remains of this, one of the Seven Wonders of the Ancient World, is a fragmented form of the original "mausoleum," the 4th-century tomb of Maussollos, King of Karia. The highlight of this gallery is the marble forepart of the **colossal chariot horse from the** *quadriga. Room 21.*

The Egyptian mummies. Another short flight of stairs takes you to the museum's most popular galleries, especially beloved by children: the Roxie Walker Galleries of Egyptian Funerary Archaeology have a fascinating collection of relics from the Egyptian realm of the dead. In addition to real corpses, wrapped mummies, and mummy cases, there's a menagerie of animal companions and curious items that were buried alongside them. *Rooms 62–63.*

Portland Vase. Made in Italy from cameo glass at the turn of the first century, it is named after the Dukes of Portland, who owned it from 1785 to 1945. It is considered a technical masterpiece—opaque white mythological figures cut by a gem-cutter are set on cobalt-blue background. *Room 70.*

The **Enlightenment Gallery** should be visited purely for the fact that its antiquarian cases hold the contents of the British Museum's first collections—Sir Hans Sloane's natural-history loot, as well as that of Sir Joseph Banks, who acquired specimens of everything from giant shells to fossils to rare plants to exotic beasts during his voyage to the Pacific aboard Captain Cook's *Endeavour*. *Room 1.*

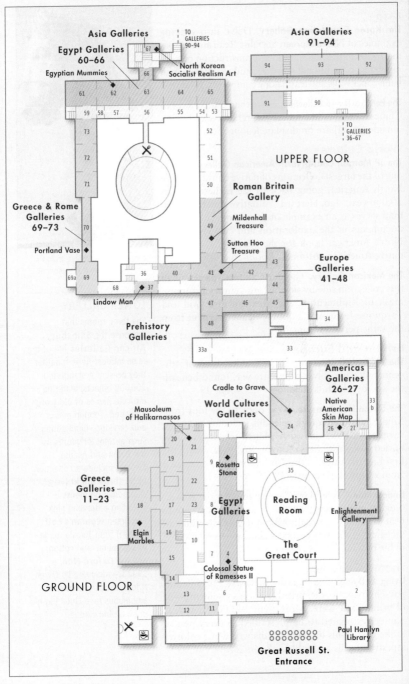

Asia

The Korea Foundation Gallery. Delve into striking examples of **North Korean Socialist Realism art** from the 1950s to the present and a reconstruction of a **sarangbang**, a traditional scholar's study, complete with hanji paper walls and tea-making equipment. *Room 67.*

The Percival David Collection. More than 1400 pieces of Chinese ceramics (the most comprehensive collection outside China) are on display. *Room 95.*

World Cultures

The JP Morgan Chase North American Gallery. This is one of the largest collections of native culture outside North America, going back to the earliest hunters 10,000 years ago. Here a 1775 **native American skin map** serves as an example of the importance of such documents in the exploration and cartography of North America. Look for the beautifully displayed **native American costumes.** *Room 26.*

The Mexican Gallery. The most alluring pieces sit in this collection side by side: a 15th-century **turquoise mask of Xiuhtecuhtli**, the Mexican Fire God and Turquoise Lord, and a **double-headed serpent** from the same period. *Room 27.*

Britain and Europe

The Mildenhall Treasure. This glittering haul of 4th-century Roman silver tableware was found beneath the sod of a Suffolk field in 1942. *Room 49.*

The Sutton Hoo Treasure. Next door to the loot from Mildenhall—and equally splendid, including brooches, swords, and jewel-encrusted helmets—the treasure was buried at sea with (it is thought) Redwald, one of the first English kings, in the 7th century, and excavated from a Suffolk field in 1938–39. *Room 41.*

Lindow Man. "Pete Marsh"—so named by the archaeologists who unearthed the body from a Cheshire peat marsh—was ritually slain, probably as a human sacrifice, in the 1st century and lay perfectly pickled in his bog until 1984. *Room 50.*

Theme Galleries

Living & Dying. The "Cradle to Grave" installation pays homage to the British nation's wellbeing—or ill-being, as it were. More than 14,000 drugs (the number estimated to be prescribed to every person in the U.K. in his lifetime) are displayed in a colorful tapestry of pills and tablets. *Room 24.*

Colossal chariot horse from the *quadriga* of the Mausoleum at Halikarnassos

LOWER GALLERY

The three rooms that comprise the **Sainsbury African Galleries** are of the main interest here: together they present a staggering 200,000 objects, featuring intricate pieces of old ivory, gold, and wooden masks and carvings—highlighting such ancient kingdoms as the Benin and Asante. The displays include a collection of **55 throwing knives**; ceremonial garments including a dazzling pink and green **woman's coif** (*qufiya*) from Tunisia made of silk, metal, and cotton; and the *Oxford Man, a* 1992 woodcarving by Owen Ndou, depicting a man of ambiguous race clutching his Book of Knowledge.

DID YOU KNOW?

Galleries help divide this sprawling space into manageable sizes for visitors. The Sainsbury African Galleries are just some of the 94 galleries; the British Museum's collection totals more than 7 million objects.

THE NATION'S ATTIC: A HISTORY OF THE MUSEUM

The collection began when Sir Hans Sloane, physician to Queen Anne and George II, bequeathed his personal collection of curiosities and antiquities to the nation. The collection quickly grew, thanks to enthusiastic kleptomaniacs after the Napoleonic Wars—most notoriously the seventh Earl of Elgin, who obtained the marbles from the Parthenon and Erechtheion on the Acropolis in Athens during his term as British ambassador in Constantinople.

Soon thereafter, it seemed everyone had something to donate—George II gave the old Royal Library, Sir William Hamilton gave antique vases, Charles Townley gave sculptures, the Bank of England gave coins. When the first exhibition galleries opened to visitors in 1759, the trustees agreed to admit only small groups guided by curators. The British Museum quickly became one of the most fashionable places to be seen in the capital, and tickets, which had to be booked in advance, were treated like gold dust.

The museum's holdings quickly outgrew their original space in Montague House. After the addition of such major pieces as the Rosetta Stone and other Egyptian antiquities (spoils of the Napoleonic War) and the Parthenon sculptures, Robert Smirke was commissioned to build an appropriately large and monumental building on the same site. It's still a hot ticket: the British Museum now receives more than 5 million visitors every year.

THE GREAT COURT & THE READING ROOM

The museum's classical Greek-style facade features figures representing the progress of civilization, and the focal point is the awesome Great Court, a massive glass-roofed space. Here is the museum's inner courtyard (now the largest covered square in Europe) that, for more than 150 years, had been used for storage.

The 19th-century Reading Room, an impressive 106-foot-high blue-and-gold-domed library, forms the centerpiece of the Great Court. The 104,000 ancient tomes are at the British Library until 2012. H.G. Wells, Thomas Hardy, Lord Tennyson, Oscar Wilde, George Orwell, T.S. Elliot, and Beatrix Potter are just a few writers who have used this space as a literary and academic sanctuary over the past 150 years or so. Temporary exhibitions here now include China's Terracotta Army, Hadrian, and Shah 'Abbas.

(above) Reading Room

PLANNING YOUR VISIT

Tours

The **50 minute eyeOpener tour (free)** by Museum Guides does just what it says; ask for details at the information desk. After this tour, you can then dip back into the collections that most captured your imagination at your leisure.

The popular interactive **Multimedia Guide (£5)** is a less-animated but perhaps more relaxed way to navigate the galleries. Other audio tours focus on the Enlightenment and Parthenon sculptures; another is designed for families.

Alternatively, the **Visitor's Guide (£3.50)** gives a brief but informative overview of the museum's history and is divided into self-guided themed tours.

Before you go, take a look at the online **COMPASS tour** using the museum's navigation tool (www.thebritishmuseum.org/compass), which allows users to browse past and present exhibits as well as search for specific objects. A children's version can also be found here. Computer stations in the Reading Room offer onsite access to COMPASS.

■**TIP→** The closest underground station to the British Museum is Russell Square on the Piccadilly line. However, since you will be entering via the back entrance on Montague Place, you will not experience the full impact of the museum's grand facade. To do so, alight at Holborn on the Central and Piccadilly lines or Tottenham Court Road on the Central and Northern lines. The walk from these stations is about 10 minutes.

WITH KIDS

■ Take a look at the "Objects to see with Children" page online. All the items are also on the family audio tour.

■ The Paul Hamlyn Library has trails for kids ages 3 to 5 and 6 to 11. The Ford Centre for Young Visitors has free activity backpacks.

■ Art materials are available for free from information points, where you can also find out about workshops, performances, storytelling sessions, and other free events.

■ Around the museum, there are Hands On desks open daily 11–4, which let visitors handle objects from the collections.

WHERE TO REFUEL

The British Museum's self-service **Gallery Café** gets very crowded but serves an acceptable menu beneath a plaster cast of a part of the Parthenon frieze that Lord Elgin didn't remove. It's open daily, but isn't particularly family friendly.

The **café in the Great Court** keeps longer hours and is a great place to people-watch and admire the spectacular glass roof while you eat your salad and sandwich.

If the weather is nice, exit the museum via the back entrance on Montague Place and amble over to **Russell Square**, which has grassy lawns, water fountains, and a glass-fronted café for post-sandwich coffee and ice cream.

5

IN FOCUS THE BRITISH MUSEUM

Fodor's Choice ★ **Sir John Soane's Museum.** Guaranteed to raise a smile from the most blasé and footsore tourist, this museum hardly deserves the burden of its dry name. Sir John (1753–1837), architect of the Bank of England, bequeathed his house to the nation on condition that nothing be changed. We owe him our thanks because he obviously had enormous fun with his home: in the Picture Room, for instance, two of Hogarth's *Rake's Progress* series are among the paintings on panels that swing away to reveal secret gallery pockets with even more paintings. Everywhere mirrors and colors play tricks with light and space, and split-level floors worthy of a fairground fun house disorient you. In

WORD OF MOUTH

"[For a nice stroll] head for Temple Tube station and walk east into inner/middle temple. Here you will find an oasis of calm, with just the sound of quill pens being wielded by all the barristers in their chambers. At lunchtime, the gardens of inner temple are open and make a nice spot for a picnic. Then cross over the strand, and wander around the Royal Courts of Justice—if you are interested, they hold the big libel trials and criminal appeals there—just ask at the enquiry desk at the entrance."
—annhig

a basement chamber sits the vast 1300 BC sarcophagus of Seti I, lighted by a domed skylight two stories above. (When Sir John acquired this priceless object for £2,000, after it was rejected by the British Museum, he celebrated with a three-day party.) The elegant, tranquil courtyard gardens with statuary and plants are open to the public, and a below-street-level passage joins two of the courtyards to the museum. Because of the small size of the museum, limited numbers are allowed entry at any one time, so you may have a short wait outside. On the first Tuesday of the month, the museum opens for a special candlelit evening from 6 to 9 pm, but expect to wait in a queue for this unique experience. ⊠ *13 Lincoln's Inn Fields, Bloomsbury* ☏ *020/7405–2107* ⊕ *www.soane.org* ✉ *Free, Sat. tour £5* ⊙ *Tues.–Sat. 10–5; also 6–9 on 1st Tues. of month* Ⓜ *Holborn.*

WORTH NOTING

Gray's Inn. Although the least architecturally interesting of the four Inns of Court and the one most damaged by German bombs in the 1940s, Gray's still has romantic associations. In 1594 Shakespeare's *Comedy of Errors* was performed for the first time in the hall—which was restored after World War II and has a fine Elizabethan screen of carved oak. You must make advance arrangements to view the hall, but the secluded and spacious gardens, first planted by Francis Bacon in 1606, are open to the public. ⊠ *Gray's Inn Rd., Holborn* ☏ *020/7458–7800* ⊕ *www. graysinn.org.uk* ✉ *Free* ⊙ *Weekdays noon–2:30* Ⓜ *Holborn, Temple.*

★ **Lincoln's Inn.** There's plenty to see at one of the oldest, best preserved, and most attractive of the Inns of Court—from the Chancery Lane Tudor brick gatehouse to the wide-open, tree-lined, atmospheric Lincoln's Inn Fields and the 15th-century chapel remodeled by Inigo Jones in 1620. Visitors are welcome to attend Sunday services in the chapel; otherwise, you must make prior arrangements to enter the buildings. ✉ *Chancery La., Bloomsbury* 🕿 *020/7405-1393* ⊕ *www.lincolnsinn.org.uk* 💷 *Free* ⊙ *Gardens weekdays 7–7, chapel weekdays noon–2:30; public may also attend Sun. service in chapel at 11:30 during legal terms* Ⓜ *Chancery La.*

Royal Courts of Justice. Here is the vast Victorian Gothic pile of 35 million bricks containing the nation's principal law courts, with 1,000-odd rooms running off 3½ miles of corridors. This is where the most important civil law cases—that's everything from divorce to fraud, with libel in between—are heard. You can sit in the viewing gallery to watch any trial you like, for a live version of Court TV. The more dramatic criminal cases are heard

KING'S CROSS STATION

Now looking decidedly the poorer relation to the sumptuously renovated St. Pancras station next-door, Kings Cross still has something that no other rail terminus in the world can boast: it's where Harry Potter and his fellow aspiring wizards took the *Hogwarts Express* to school from the imaginary platform 9¾. Not bad for an otherwise humdrum station built in 1851–52 as the London terminus for the Great Northern Railway. By the way, the station has put up a sign for platform 9¾ if you want to take a picture there—just don't try to run through the wall.

at the Old Bailey. Other sights are the 238-foot-long main hall and the compact exhibition of judges' robes. ✉ *The Strand, Bloomsbury* 🕿 *020/7947–6000* ⊕ *www.hmcourts-service.gov.uk* 💷 *Free* ⊙ *Weekdays 9–4:30* Ⓜ *Temple.*

Temple Church. Featuring "the Round"—a rare, circular nave—this church was built by the Knights Templar in the 12th century. The Red Knights (so called after the red crosses they wore—you can see them in effigy around the nave) held their secret initiation rites in the crypt here. Having started poor, holy, and dedicated to the protection of pilgrims, they grew rich from showers of royal gifts, until in the 14th century they were charged with heresy, blasphemy, and sodomy, thrown into the Tower, and stripped of their wealth. You might suppose the church to be thickly atmospheric, but Victorian and postwar restorers have tamed the air of antique mystery. Nevertheless, this is a fine Gothic-Romanesque church. ✉ *King's Bench Walk, The Temple, Bloomsbury* 🕿 *020/7353–8559* ⊕ *www.templechurch.com* 💷 *£3* ⊙ *Check website for details* Ⓜ *Temple.*

University College London. The college was founded in 1826 and set in a classical edifice designed by the architect of the National Gallery, William Wilkins. In 1907 it became part of the University of London, providing higher education without religious exclusion. The college has within its portals the **Slade School of Fine Art,** which did for many of Britain's artists what the nearby Royal Academy of Dramatic Art (on Gower Street) did for actors. The South Cloisters contain one of London's weirder treasures: the skeleton of one of the university's founders, Jeremy Bentham, who bequeathed himself to the college. Legend has it that students from a rival college, King's College London, once stole Bentham's head and played football with it. Whether or not the story is apocryphal, Bentham's clothed skeleton, stuffed with straw and topped with a wax head, now sits (literally) in the UCL collection. Be sure to take a look at the stunning Gotham-esque Senate House on Malet Street.

Petrie Museum. If you didn't get your fill of Egyptian artifacts at the British Museum, you can see more in the neighboring Petrie Museum, accessed from the DMS Watson building. The museum houses an outstanding, huge collection of fascinating objects of Egyptian archaeology—jewelry, toys, papyri, and some of the world's oldest garments. ☎ *020/7679–2884* ⊕ *www.petrie.ucl.ac.uk* ▣ *Free, donations appreciated* ☾ *Tues.–Sat. 1–5; closed over Christmas and Easter holidays* ✉ *Malet Pl., Bloomsbury* Ⓜ *Euston Sq., Goodge St.*

The City

WORD OF MOUTH

"Do you know about the Ceremony of the Keys at the Tower of London? Tickets are free, and attendees are limited to a small group. [Check out www.hrp.org.uk in advance.] It is a cool, and very authentic, ceremony they do every evening at sunset, to lock up the tower. They explain it as they go, and we thought it was neat to be there as the sun goes down." —PeaceOut

GETTING ORIENTED

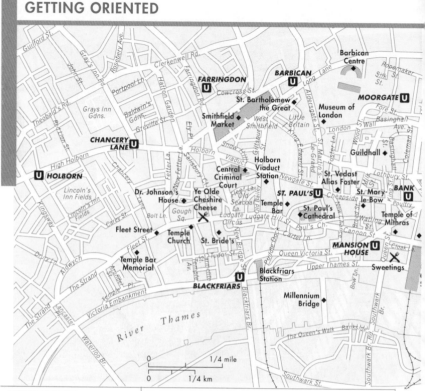

GETTING THERE

The City area is well served by a concentrated selection of Underground stops in London. St. Paul's and Bank are on the Central line, and Mansion House, Cannon Street, and Monument are on the District and Circle lines. Liverpool Street and Aldgate border The City's eastern edge, whereas Chancery Lane and Farringdon lie to the west. Barbican and Moorgate provide easy access to the theaters and galleries of the Barbican, and Blackfriars, to the south, leads to Ludgate Circus and Fleet Street.

TOP REASONS TO GO

St. Paul's Cathedral, the "Symbolic Heart of London": Now nudged by skyscrapers, St. Paul's still dominates the skyline—and once inside, you'll see the genius of Sir Christopher Wren's 17th-century masterpiece.

Linger on the Millennium Bridge: Hurtle the centuries with this promenade between the Tate Modern and St. Paul's—and get a great river view, too.

Treachery and Treasures at the Tower: This minicity of melodramatic towers is stuffed to bursting with heraldry, pageantry, and the stunning Crown Jewels (bring sunglasses).

Channel history at the Museum of London: From Oliver Cromwell's death mask to Queen Victoria's crinoline gowns; from Selfridges' art deco elevators to a diorama of the Great Fire (sound effects! flickering flames!), this gem of a museum's got it all.

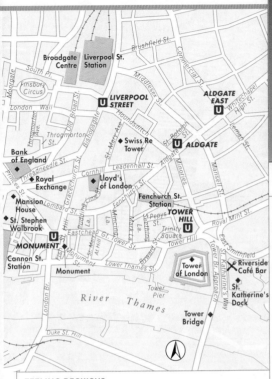

MAKING THE MOST OF YOUR TIME

The "Square Mile" is as compact as the nickname suggests, with little distance between points of interest, making an afternoon stroll a rewarding experience. For full immersion in the Tower of London, however, set aside half a day, especially if seeing the Crown Jewels is a priority. Allow an hour minimum each for the Museum of London, St. Paul's Cathedral, and the Tower Bridge. On weekends, without the scurrying suits, The City is nearly deserted, making it hard to find lunch—and yet this is when the major attractions are at their busiest.

A GOOD WALK

Crossing the Millennium Bridge from the Tate Modern to St. Paul's is one of the finest walks in London—with the river to either side and Christopher Wren's iconic dome towering at one end. Dubbed the "blade of light," the shiny aluminum-and-steel span was the result of a collaboration between architect Norman Foster and sculptor Anthony Caro.

FEELING PECKISH?

Riverside Café Bar. The friendly Riverside Café Bar is one of the few places you're sure to find a good cup of hot chocolate and hot and cold meals, with waterside views of the luxurious yachts and gin palaces moored at the docks. Closed in the evenings. ⊠ *St. Katherine's Dock, St. Katherine's Way* ☎ *020/7481–1464.*

Sweetings. Sweetings has been here since 1889. It's not cheap, takes no reservations, and closes at 3 pm, but it serves one of the best fish lunches in London. Refuel here on Dover sole and Black Velvet, the local brew, and observe the pinstripes at play in their natural habitat. ⊠ *39 Queen Victoria St.* ☎ *020/7248–3062.*

Ye Olde Cheshire Cheese. When you're finished exploring Fleet Street, head to the famed Ye Olde Cheshire Cheese for a pint of ale and a snack. Parts of the building date from 1667 and the pub is rightly admired for its roaring fires and dingy interior, barely changed since Dr. Johnson came here. Closed Sundays. ⊠ *145 Fleet St.* ☎ *020/7353–6170.*

6

Sightseeing
★★★★★
Nightlife
★
Dining
★★★
Lodging
★
Shopping
★★★

The City is the capital's fast-beating financial heart, with a powerful architectural triumvirate at its epicenter: the Bank of England, the Royal Exchange, and Mansion House, where the lord mayor of The City of London (not to be confused with the mayor of London) lives and entertains. The "Square Mile" also has currency as the place where London began, its historic heart. St. Paul's Cathedral has looked after Londoners' souls since the 7th century, and the Tower of London—that moat-surrounded royal fortress, prison, and jewel house—has occasionally taken care of their heads.

Updated by
James O'Neill

The City is a dizzying juxtaposition of the old and the new. You'll find yourself immersed in historic London if you begin your explorations on **Fleet Street,** the site of England's first printing press and the undisputed seat of British journalism until the 1980s. Nestled behind Fleet Street is **Dr. Johnson's House,** former home of the man who claimed that to be bored of London was to be bored of life and author of *Dictionary of the English Language.* The nearby church of **St. Bride's,** recognizable by its tiered wedding-cake steeple, is a Sir Christopher Wren gem and still the church for journalists, while eastward rises the iconic **St. Paul's Cathedral,** also designed by Wren and the architect's masterpiece. You'll encounter more of traditional London at the **Central Criminal Court** (nicknamed **Old Bailey,** and home to London's most sensational criminal trials) and the 800-year-old **Smithfield Market,** whose Victorian halls are the site of a daily early-morning meat market. Nearby are the ancient church of **St. Bartholomew the Great** and St. Bartholomew Hospital, both begun in 1123, as well as the **Guildhall,** the site of the only Roman amphitheater in London, the church of **St. Mary-le-Bow,** and the charmingly old-fashioned narrow maze of streets around **Bow Lane.**

You can put all this history into context at the **Museum of London,** where archaeological displays include a portion of the original **Roman Wall** that ringed The City.

A BRIEF HISTORY

First came the Romans, establishing the settlement of Londinium in AD 47 at the north bank of the Thames, an outpost of the Empire that soon became a sizable trading center. A thousand years later came the Normans and William the Conqueror, who began building the palace that was to become the Tower of London. The Tower would go from being Henry III's defensive shelter in the 13th century to, by Tudor times, the world's most forbidding and grisly prison, where two of Henry VIII's six wives were executed. During the Middle Ages, powerful guilds that nurtured commerce took root in the capital, followed by the foundation of great trading companies, such as the Honourable East India Company, which started up in 1600.

The City's history has been punctuated by periods of chaos that have threatened to destroy it. The Great Fire of 1666 spared only a few of the cramped, labyrinthine streets, where the Great Plague of the previous year had already wiped out a huge portion of the population. Yet the gutted wastelands enabled a new start, driving out the plague-carrying rodents that had menaced London since the Middle Ages and forcing an architectural renaissance, led by Sir Christopher Wren. Further punishment would come during the Blitz of World War II, when German bombers destroyed many buildings—but London's story has always been one of rebirth and regeneration; its eclectic skyline reflects that to this very day.

Just beyond rises the modern **Barbican Centre,** a concrete complex of arts venues and apartments that incites many observers to worry about the architectural direction of modern London. The sight of some other new structures rising above The City—especially the **Lloyd's of London Building** and the **Swiss Re Tower,** popularly known as "the Gherkin"—may or may not be more reassuring.

The **Monument,** near the banks of the Thames, was built to commemorate the Great Fire of London of 1666. From here, the river leads to one of London's most absorbing and bloody attractions, the **Tower of London. Tower Bridge** is a suitably giddying finale to an exploration of this fascinating part of London.

TOP ATTRACTIONS

Monument. Commemorating the "dreadful visitation" of the Great Fire of 1666, this is the world's tallest isolated stone column. It is the work of Sir Christopher Wren and Dr. Robert Hooke, who were asked to erect it "on or as neere unto the place where the said Fire soe unhappily began as conveniently may be." And so here it is—at 202 feet, exactly as tall as the distance it stands from Farriner's baking house in Pudding Lane, where the fire started (note the gilded urn of fire at the column's pinnacle). If climbing the 311 steps is enough to put you off your lunch, cheat a little and watch the live views that are relayed from the top. ✉ *Monument St., The City* ☎ *020/7626–2717* ⊕ *www.themonument. info* 🎟 *£3; combined ticket with Tower Bridge exhibition £9* ☾ *Daily 9:30–5:30; last admission 5* Ⓜ *Monument.*

⟳ ★ **Museum of London.** If there's one place to absorb the history of London, from 450,000 BC to the present day, it's here: Oliver Cromwell's death mask, Queen Victoria's crinoline gowns, Selfridges' art deco elevators, the London's Burning exhibition, fans, guns and jewelry, an original Newgate Prison Door, and the incredible late-18th-century Blackett Dolls House—7,000 objects to wonder at in all. The museum appropriately shelters a section of the 2nd- to 4th-century London wall, which you can view through a window, and permanent displays include "London Before London," "Roman London," "Medieval London," and "Tudor London." The Galleries of Modern London are enthralling: Experience the "Expanding City," "People's City," and "World City," each gallery dealing with a section of London's history from 1666 until the 21st century. Innovative interactive displays abound, and you can even wander around a 19th-century London street with impressively detailed shop fronts and interiors, including a pawnbrokers, a pub, a barber, even a bank manager's office, in case you're running short on holiday money. ⊠ *London Wall, The City* ☎ *020/7001–9844* ⊕ *www.museumoflondon.org.uk* ⧉ *Free* ⊙ *Mon.–Sun. 10–6; last admission 5:30* Ⓜ *Barbican, St. Paul's.*

| A VIEW TO REMEMBER |

At the top of the Monument's 311-step spiral staircase (think of it as the trip to the gym you didn't make that day) is a gallery providing fantastic views from the heart of The City that is helpfully caged to prevent suicidal jumps, which were a trend for a while in the 19th century.

Fodor's Choice ★ **St. Paul's Cathedral.**

See the highlighted listing in this chapter.

⟳ **Fodor's Choice** ★ **Tower Bridge.** Despite its medieval, fairy-tale appearance, this is a Victorian youngster. Constructed of steel, then clothed in Portland stone, the Horace Jones masterpiece was deliberately styled in the Gothic persuasion to complement the Tower next door, and it's famous for its enormous bascules—the 1,200-ton "arms" that open to allow large ships to glide beneath. This still happens occasionally, but when river traffic was dense, the bascules were raised about five times a day.

The **Tower Bridge Exhibition** is a child-friendly tour where you can discover how one of the world's most famous bridges actually works before heading out onto the walkways for the wonderful city views. First, take in the romance of the panoramas from the east and west walkways between those grand turrets. On the east are the modern superstructures of the Docklands, and on the west is the Tower of London, St. Paul's, the Monument, and the steel-and-glass "futuristic mushroom" that is Greater London Assembly's City Hall. Then it's back down to explore the Victorian engine rooms and discover the inner workings, which you learn about through hands-on displays and films. ⊠ *Tower Bridge Rd., The City* ☎ *020/7403–3761* ⊕ *www.towerbridge. org.uk* ⧉ *£8* ⊙ *Apr.–Sept., daily 10–6:30; Oct.–Mar., daily 9:30–6; last admission 30 mins before closing* Ⓜ *Tower Hill.*

Fodor's Choice ★ **Tower of London.**

See the highlighted listing in this chapter.

Continued on page 120

ST. PAUL'S CATHEDRAL

Sir Christopher Wren's maxim "I build for eternity" proves no empty boast.

Sublime, awesome, majestic, and inspirational are just some of the words to describe Wren's masterpiece, St. Paul's Cathedral—even more so now that the restoration for the 300th anniversary is expected to finish in 2010.

This is the spiritual heart of the nation, where people and events are celebrated, mourned, and honored. As you approach the cathedral your eyes are inevitably drawn skyward to the great dome, one of the largest in the world and an amazing piece of engineering. Visit in the late afternoon for evensong, and let the choir's voices transport you to a world of absolute peace in a place of perfect beauty, as pristine as the day it was completed.

TOURING ST. PAUL'S

Enter the cathedral via the main west entrance, and walk straight down the length of the nave to the central Dome Altar. Nobody can resist making a beeline for the dome, so start your tour beneath it, standing dead center on the beautiful sunburst floor, Wren's focal mirror of the magnificent design above. A simple quotation marks the floor "Lector si momentum requiris, circumspice" (Reader if you seek his monument, look around). The dome crowns the center of the cathedral and rises to 364 feet—but save your strength for the "great climb" to get some fantastic views.

THE CATHEDRAL FLOOR

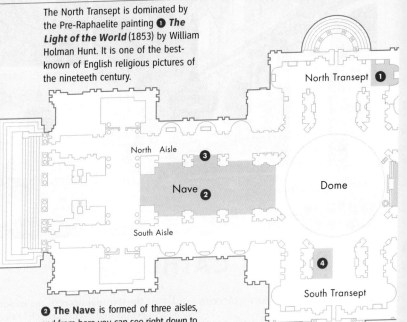

The North Transept is dominated by the Pre-Raphaelite painting ❶ *The Light of the World* (1853) by William Holman Hunt. It is one of the best-known of English religious pictures of the nineteeth century.

North Transept ❶

North Aisle ❸

Nave ❷

South Aisle

Dome

❹

South Transept

❷ **The Nave** is formed of three aisles, and from here you can see right down to the High Altar at the far end of the Choir, more than 100 yards away. Take time to admire the mastery of space and light.

In the north aisle of the Nave is Flaxman's grandiose ❸ **monument to the Duke of Wellington,** who sits astride his faithful charger, Copenhagen, the horse that carried him through the Battle of Waterloo.

The South Transept displays a ❹ **monument to Admiral Lord Nelson,** Britain's favorite naval hero, with an anchor. Other memorials commemorate the explorer Captain Robert Scott and the darling of British landscape painting J.M.W. Turner.

CELEBRITY STATUS

St. Paul's has witnessed many momentous processions along its checkered nave. The somber state funerals of heroes Admiral Lord Nelson and the Duke of Wellington, and of Sir Winston Churchill, drew huge crowds. It was here, also, that the fairy-tale wedding of Prince Charles and Lady Diana Spencer took place, and the jubilees of Queen Victoria, George V, and the present Queen were celebrated.

6

IN FOCUS ST. PAUL'S CATHEDRAL

The North Choir Aisle features the beautiful ❺ **gilded gates** by Jean Tijou, perhaps the most accomplished artist in wrought iron of all time, as well as Henry Moore's sculpture ❻ *Mother and Child,* its simple lines complementing the ornate surroundings.

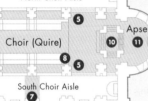

North Choir Aisle

Choir (Quire)

Apse

South Choir Aisle

The South Choir Aisle contains a ❼ **marble effigy of poet John Donne,** who was Dean of old St. Paul's for his final 10 years (he died in 1631). This is the only statue to have survived the Great Fire of London intact. You can see the scorch marks at the base of the statue.

The Choir contains the ❽ **Bishop's Throne** or cathedra, hence the name cathedral. Look aloft to the fabulous mosaics. Don't miss the exquisite, delicate carvings by Grinling Gibbons, in particular on the case of the ❾ **grand organ,** one of the Cathedral's greatest artifacts. It was designed by Wren and played by such illustrious figures as Handel and Mendelssohn.

❿ **The High Altar,** with its glorious canopy, is a profusion of marble and carved and gilded oak.

The Apse is home to the ⓫ **American Memorial Chapel,** which honors the more than 28,000 U.S. soldiers who died while stationed in the U.K. during World War II. The lime-wood paneling incorporates a rocket as a tribute to the United States' achievements in space.

MUSICAL FRICTION

The organ, with its cherubs and angels, was not installed without controversy. The mighty instrument proved a tight fit, and the maker, known as Father Schmidt, and Wren nearly came to blows. Wren was reputed to have said he would not adapt his cathedral for a mere "box of whistles."

THE DOME

The dome is the crowning glory of the cathedral, a must for visitors.

At 99 feet, the ❶ **Whispering Gallery** is reached by 259 spiral steps. This is the part of the cathedral with which you bribe children—they will be fascinated by the acoustic phenomenon: whisper something to the wall on one side, and a second later it transmits clearly to the other side, 107 feet away. The only problem is identifying your whisper from the cacophony of everyone else's. Look down onto the nave from here and up to the monochrome frescoes of St. Paul by Sir James Thornhill.

More stamina is required to reach the ❷ **Stone Gallery**, at 173 feet and 378 steps from ground level. It is on the exterior of the cathedral and offers a vista of the city and the River Thames.

For the best views of all—at 280 feet and 530 steps from ground level—make the trek to the small ❸ **Golden Gallery**, the highest point

of the outer dome. A hole in the floor gives a vertiginous view down. You can see the lantern above through a circular opening called the oculus. If you have a head for heights you can walk outside for a spectacular panorama of London.

The top of the dome is crowned with a ❹ **ball and cross.** At 23 feet high and weighing approximately 7 tons, it is the pinnacle of St. Paul's.

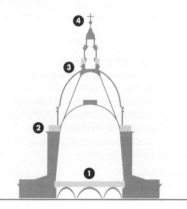

A BRIEF HISTORY

The cathedral is the masterpiece of Sir Christopher Wren (1632–1723), completed in 1710 after 35 years of building and much argument with the Royal Commission. Wren had originally been commissioned to restore Old St. Paul's, the Norman cathedral that had replaced, in its turn, three earlier versions, but the Great Fire left so little of it standing that a new cathedral was deemed necessary.

Wren's first plan, known as the New Model, did not make it past the drawing board; the second, known as the Great Model, got as far as the 20-foot oak rendering you can see here today before it, too, was rejected, whereupon Wren is said to have burst into tears. The third, however, known as the Warrant Design (because it received the royal warrant), was accepted, with the fortunate coda that the architect

be allowed to make changes as he saw fit. Without that, there would be no dome, because the approved design had featured a steeple. Parliament felt that building was proceeding too slowly (in fact, 35 years is lightning speed, as cathedrals go) and withheld half of Wren's pay for the last 13 years of work. He was pushing 80 when Queen Anne finally coughed up the arrears.

■ TIP→ To see Wren's Great Model, you must join a Triforium Tour (Mon. and Tues. at 11:30 and 2, Fri. at 2). These one-hour tours include a visit to the library and a glimpse of the famous Geometric staircase. The visit ends in the Trophy Room, where Wren's Great Model is on display. The tour costs £19.50 per person and includes entry to the cathedral and access to the crypt and galleries. It's best to book in advance by calling 020/7246–8357 or sending an e-mail to visits@stpaulscathedral.org.uk.

THE CRYPT

A visit to the vast crypt is a time for reflection and contemplation, with some 200 memorials to see. If it all becomes too somber, take solace in the café or shop near the crypt entrance.

Here lies ❶ **Admiral Nelson,** killed at the Battle of Trafalgar in 1805. His body was preserved in alcohol for the journey home, and his pickled remains were buried here beneath Cardinal Wolsey's unused 16th-century sarcophagus.

The ❷ **tomb of the Duke of Wellington** comprises a simple casket made from Cornish granite. He is remembered as a hero of battle, but his name lives on in the form of boots, cigars, beef Wellington, and the capital of New Zealand.

Surrounded by his family and close to a plethora of iconic artists, musicians, and scientists, the ❸ **tomb of Sir Christopher Wren** is a modest simple slab.

The beautiful ❹ **O.B.E. Chapel** (dedicated 1960) is a symbol of the Order of the British Empire, an order of chivalry established in 1917 by George V. The theme of sovereign and Commonwealth is represented in the glass panels.

The vast ❺ **treasury** houses the cathedral's plate, although a good deal has been lost or stolen over the centuries—in particular in a daring robbery of 1810—and much of the display comes from other London churches.

6

IN FOCUS ST. PAUL'S CATHEDRAL

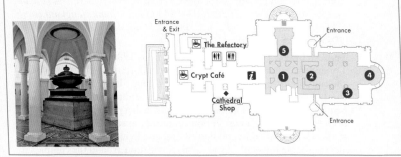

PLANNING YOUR DAY

WHAT'S NEARBY: Stroll over the Millennium Bridge (look back for a great view of St. Paul's) and have lunch at Tate Modern. The restaurant at the top of the gallery has spectacular views of London. ■ TIP➔ To avoid lines visit early in the morning. For a different experience return for Evensong at 5 pm.

CONTACT INFO: ✉ *St. Paul's Churchyard, Ludgate Hill EC4 8AD* ☎ *020/7236–4128* 🌐 *www.stpauls.co.uk* Ⓤ *St. Paul's.*

ADMISSION: Adults: cathedral, crypt, ambulatory, and gallery £15 (includes multimedia guides and guided tours). **Family ticket** (2

adults, 2 children): £34.50. **Children:** £5.50.

TOURS: A guided tour of the cathedral and crypt lasts 90 minutes. Tours start at 10:45, 11:15, 1:30, and 2. Reserve a place at the guiding desk when you arrive at the cathedral (it's not possible to make reservations in advance).

HOURS: The cathedral is a house of worship. Services may cause changes to the visiting hours on any given day, so be sure to call ahead.

Cathedral: Mon.–Sat. 8:30–4.
Shop: Mon.–Sat. 9–5, Sun. 10–5.
Crypt café: Mon.–Sat. 9–5, Sun. noon–4.

WORTH NOTING

Bank of England. The country's top vault has been central to the British economy since 1694. Known for the past couple of centuries as "the Old Lady of Threadneedle Street," after the name appeared in a caption to a political cartoon (which can be seen in the museum), the bank manages the national debt and the foreign exchange reserves, issues banknotes, sets interest rates, looks after England's gold, and regulates the country's banking system. Sir John Soane designed the neoclassical hulk in 1788, wrapping it in windowless walls, which are all that survives of his original building. The bank's history is traced in the Bank of England Museum (entrance is around the corner on Bartholomew Lane), where interactive exhibits chart the bank's more recent history and offer the chance to try your hand at controlling inflation. But most visitors still make a beeline for the solid-gold bar that can be stroked and held in the central trading hall (but before you get any ideas, there's security everywhere). ⊠ *Threadneedle St., The City* ☎ *020/7601–5545* ⊕ *www.bankofengland.co.uk* ✉ *Free* ☉ *Weekdays and Lord Mayor's Show day (2nd Sat. in Nov.) 10–5* Ⓜ *Bank, Monument.*

SUMMER FESTIVAL

Every year, for three weeks in June and July, the City of London Festival (⊕ *www.colf.org*) has numerous walks, dances, street arts, and concerts taking place in buildings that are usually closed to the public.

★ **Barbican Centre.** The Barbican is an enormous 1980s concrete maze that Londoners either love or hate—but the importance of the complex to the cultural life of the capital is beyond dispute. It houses two theaters; the London Symphony Orchestra and its auditorium; the Guildhall School of Music and Drama; a major art gallery for changing exhibitions; two cinemas; a convention center; an upscale restaurant, cafés, terraces with fountains, and bookshops; and living space in some of the most desirable tower blocks in town. Navigation around the complex is via the yellow lines running, Wizard-of-Oz-like, along the floors, with signs on the walls, although it's still easy to get lost. Actors and audiences alike rate the theater for its excellent acoustics and sight lines. The dance, music, and theater programs have been transformed into a yearlong fest named BITE, which stands for Barbican International Theatre Events, and encompasses dance, puppetry, and music. Emphasis is on presenting tomorrow's names today, although there are performances by established companies and artists as well. ⊠ *Silk St., The City* ☎ *020/7638–8891 box office* ⊕ *www.barbican.org.uk* ✉ *Barbican Centre free, art gallery £6–£8, films £7.50–£11.50, concerts £6.50–£45, theater £7–£50* ☉ *Barbican Centre Mon.–Sat. 9 am–11 pm, Sun. and holidays noon–11; gallery Thurs. 11–10, Mon. and Fri.–Sun. 11–8, Tues. and Wed. 11–6* Ⓜ *Moorgate, Barbican.*

★ **Dr. Johnson's House.** This is where Samuel Johnson lived between 1748 and 1759. Built in 1700, the elegant Georgian residence, with its paneled rooms and period furniture, is where the Great Bear (as he was known) compiled his *Dictionary of the English Language* in the attic

Interior of the "Inside-Out" Lloyd's of London building, designed by Richard Rogers Partnership

as his health deteriorated. Two early editions are on view, among other mementos of Johnson and his friend, diarist, and later, his biographer, James Boswell. After soaking up the atmosphere, repair around the corner in Wine Office Court to the famed **Ye Olde Cheshire Cheese** pub, once Johnson and Boswell's favorite watering hole. ✉ *17 Gough Sq., The City* ☎ *020/7353–3745* ⊕ *www.drjohnsonshouse.org* ✉ *£4.50* ⊙ *May–Sept., Mon.–Sat. 11–5:30; Oct.–Apr., Mon.–Sat. 11–5; closed bank holidays* Ⓜ *Holborn, Chancery Lane, Temple.*

Guildhall. The Corporation of London, which oversees The City, has ceremonially elected and installed its Lord Mayor here for the last 800 years. The Guildhall was built in 1411, and though it failed to avoid either the 1666 or 1940 flames, its core survived. The Great Hall is a psychedelic patchwork of coats of arms and banners of the City Livery Companies, which inherited the mantle of the medieval trade guilds. Tradesmen couldn't even run a shop without kowtowing to these pro-totypical unions, and their grand banqueting halls, the plushest private dining venues in The City, are testimony to the wealth they amassed. Inside the hall, Gog and Magog, the pair of mythical giants who founded ancient Albion and the city of New Troy, upon which London was said to be built, glower down from their west-gallery grandstand in 9-foot-high painted lime wood. The hall was also the site of famous trials, including that of Lady Jane Grey in 1553, before her execution at the Tower of London. To the right of Guildhall Yard is the **Guild-hall Art Gallery,** which includes portraits of the great and the good, cityscapes, famous battles, and a slightly cloying pre-Raphaelite section. The construction of the gallery in the 1980s led to the exciting discovery of London's only **Roman amphitheater,** which had lain underneath Guildhall Yard undisturbed for more than 1,800 years. It was excavated, and now visitors can walk among the remains, although most of the relics can be seen at the Museum of London. ⊠ *Aldermanbury, The City* ☎ *020/7606–3030, 020/7332–3700 gallery* ⊕ *www.cityoflondon. gov.uk* 🎟 *Free (fee for some gallery exhibitions)* ⊘ *Mon.–Sat. 9:30–5; gallery Mon.–Sat. 10–5, Sun. noon–4; last admission 4:30 or 3:30* Ⓜ *St. Paul's, Moorgate, Bank, Mansion House.*

Old Bailey. This is the place to watch the real-life drama of justice in action in one of the 16 courtrooms that are open to the public. Previous trials have included those of Crippen and Christie, two of England's most notorious wife murderers, as well as the controversial trials of Oscar Wilde and the notorious East End gangsters, the Kray twins. The day's hearings are posted on the sign outside, but your best bet is to consult the previous day's tabloid newspapers for an idea of the trials that are making waves. There are security restrictions, and children under 14 are not allowed in; call the information line first. The present-day **Central Criminal Court** is where Newgate Prison stood from the 12th century until the beginning of the 20th century. Called by the novelist Henry Fielding the "prototype of hell," few survived for long in the version pulled down in 1770. The Central Criminal Court replaced Newgate in 1907, and the most famous feature of the solid Edwardian building is the 12-foot gilded statue of Justice perched on top; she was intended to mirror the dome of St. Paul's. ⊠ *Newgate St., The City* ☎ *020/7248–3277 information* ⊕ *www.cityoflondon.gov. uk* ⊘ *Public Gallery weekdays 9:45–12:45 and 1:45–4 (approx.); line forms at Newgate St. entrance or in Warwick St. Passage; closed bank holidays and day after* Ⓜ *St. Paul's.*

St. Bartholomew the Great. Reached via a perfect half-timber gatehouse atop a 13th-century stone archway, this is one of London's oldest churches. Construction on the church and the hospital nearby was begun in 1123 by Henry I's favorite courtier, Rahere, who caught malaria and, surviving, vowed to dedicate his life to serving the saint who had visited him in his fevered dreams. With the dissolution of the monasteries, Henry VIII had most of the place torn down; the Romanesque choir loft is all that survives from the 12th century. The ancient church has appeared in *The Other Boleyn Girl, Four Weddings and a Funeral,* and *Shakespeare in Love.* ⊠ *Cloth Fair, West Smithfield, The City* ☎ *020/7606–5171* ⊕ *www.greatstbarts.com* 🎟 *Church £4, museum free* ⊘ *Church weekdays 9–5, Sat. 10:30–4, Sun 8:30–8. Museum Tues.–Fri. 10–4* Ⓜ *Barbican, Farringdon.*

St. Bride's. According to legend, the distinctively tiered steeple of this Christopher Wren–designed church gave rise to the shape of the traditional wedding cake. One early couple inspired to marry here were the parents of Virginia Dare, the first European child born in colonial America in 1587. As St. Paul's (in Covent Garden) is the actors' church, so St. Bride's belongs to journalists, many of whom have been buried or memorialized here. By 1664 the crypts were so crowded that diarist Samuel Pepys, who was baptized here, had to bribe the gravedigger to "justle together" some bodies to make room for his deceased brother.

Continued on page 130

THE TOWER OF LONDON

The Tower is a microcosm of the city itself—a sprawling, organic hodgepodge of buildings that inspires reverence and terror in equal measure. See the block on which Anne Boleyn was beheaded, marvel at the Crown Jewels, and pay homage to the ravens who keep the monarchy safe.

An architectural patchwork of time, the oldest building of the complex is the fairytale White Tower, conceived by William the Conqueror in 1078 as both a royal residence and a show of power to the troublesome Anglo-Saxons he had subdued at the Battle of Hastings. Today's Tower has seen everything, as a palace, barracks, a mint for producing coins, an armoury, and the Royal menagerie (home of the country's first elephant). The big draw is the stunning opulence of the Crown Jewels, kept on-site in the heavily fortified Jewel House. Most of all, though, the Tower is known for death: it's been a place of imprisonment, torture, and execution for the realm's most notorious traitors as well as its martyrs. These days, unless you count the killer admission fees, there are far less morbid activities taking place in the Tower, but it still breathes London's history and pageantry from its every brick and offers hours of exploration.

TOURING THE TOWER

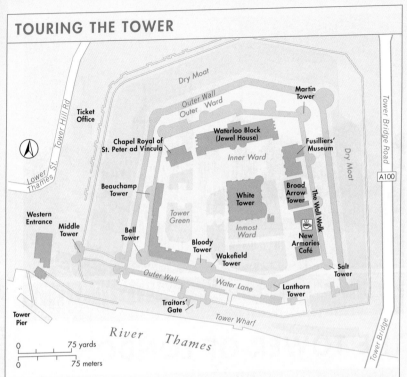

Entry to the Tower is via the **Western Entrance** and the **Middle Tower,** which feed into the outermost ring of the Tower's defenses.

Water Lane leads past the dread-inducing **Traitors' Gate,** the final point of entry for many Tower prisoners.

Toward the end of Water Lane, the **Lanthorn Tower** houses by night the ravens rumored to keep the kingdom safe, and by day a timely high-tech reconstruction of the Catholic Guy Fawkes's plot to blow up the Houses of Parliament in 1605.

The **Bloody Tower** earned its name as the apocryphal site

of the murder of two young princes, Edward and Richard, who disappeared from the Tower after being put there in 1483 by their uncle, Richard III. Two little skeletons (now in Westminster Abbey) were found buried close to the White Tower in 1674 and are thought to be theirs.

The **Beauchamp Tower** housed upper-class miscreants: Latin graffiti about Lady Jane Grey can be glimpsed today on its walls.

Like a prize gem set at the head of a royal crown, the **White Tower** is the centerpiece of the complex. Its four towers dominate the Inner

GOLD DIGGER?

Keep your eyes peeled as you tour the Tower: according to one story, Sir John Barkstead, goldsmith and Lieutenant of the Tower under Cromwell, hid £20,000 in gold coins here before his arrest and execution at the Restoration of Charles II.

Ward, a fitting and forbidding reminder of Norman strength at the time of the conquest of England.

Once inside the White Tower, head upstairs for the **Armouries,** where the biggest attraction, quite literally,

Jewel House, Waterloo Barracks

ROYAL BLING

The Crown of Queen Elizabeth, the Queen Mother, from 1937, contains the exotic 105-carat Koh-i-Noor (mountain of light) diamond.

TIME KILLERS

Some prisoners managed to keep themselves plenty amused: Sir Walter Raleigh grew tobacco on Tower Green, and in 1561 suspected sorcerer Hugh Draper carved an intricate astronomical clock on the walls of his Salt Tower cell.

is the suit of armor worn by a well-endowed Henry VIII. There is a matching outfit for his horse.

Other fascinating exhibits include the set of Samurai armor presented to James I in 1613 by the emperor of Japan, and the tiny set of armor worn by Henry VIII's young son Edward.

The **Jewel House** in Waterloo Block is the Tower's biggest draw, perfect for playing pick-your-favorite-crown from the wrong side of bul-

letproof glass. Not only are these crowns, staffs, and orbs encrusted with heavy-duty gems, they are invested with the authority of monarchical power in England, dating back to the 1300s.

Outside, pause at **Tower Green,** permanent departure point for those of noble birth. The hoi polloi were dispatched at nearby Tower Hill. The Tower's most famous female victims—Anne Boleyn, Margaret Countess of Salisbury, Catherine Howard, and Lady Jane Grey—all went this "priviledged" way.

Behind a well-kept square of grass stands the **Chapel Royal of St. Peter ad Vincula,** a delightful Tudor church and final resting place of six beheaded Tudor bodies. ■TIP→ **Visitors are welcome for services and can also enter after 4:30 pm daily.**

The **Salt Tower,** reputedly the most haunted corner of the complex, marks the start of the **Wall Walk,** a bracing promenade along the stone spiral steps and battlements of the Tower that looks down on the trucks, taxis, and shimmering high-rises of modern London.

The Wall Walk ends at the **Martin Tower,** former home of the Crown Jewels and now host to the crowns and diamonds exhibition that explains the art of fashioning royal headwear and tells the story of some of the most famous stones.

On leaving the Tower, browse the gift shop, and wander the wharf that overlooks the Thames, leading to a picture-postcard view of Tower Bridge.

WHO ARE THE BEEFEATERS?

First of all, they're Yeoman Warders, but probably got the nickname "beefeater" from their position as Royal Bodyguards which entitled them to eat as much beef as they liked. Part of the "Yeoman of the Guard," started in the reign of Edmund IV, the warders have formed the Royal Bodyguard as far back as 1509 when Henry VIII left a dozen of the Yeoman of the Guard at the Tower to protect it.

Originally, the Yeoman Warders also served as jailers of the Tower, doubling as torturers when necessary. (So it would have been a Beefeater tightening the thumb screws, or ratchetting the rack another notch on some unfortunate prisoner. Smile nicely.) Today 36 Yeoman Warders (men and women since 2007), along with the Chief Yeoman Warder and the Yeoman Gaoler, live within the walls of the Tower with their families, in accommodations in the Outer Ward. They stand guard over the Tower, conduct tours, and lock up at 9:53 pm every night with the Ceremony of the Keys.

■ TIP➡ Free tickets to the Ceremony of the Keys are available by writing several months in advance; check the Tower Web site for details.

HARK THE RAVENS!

Legend has it that should the hulking black ravens ever leave, the White Tower will crumble and the kingdom fall. Charles II, no doubt jumpy after his father's execution and the monarchy's short-term fall from grace, made a royal decree in 1662 that there should be at least six of the carrion-eating nasties present at all times. There have been some close calls. During World War II, numbers dropped to one, echoing the precarious fate of the war-wracked country. In 2005, two (of eight) died over Christmas when Thor—the most intelligent but also the largest bully of the bunch—killed new recruit Gundolf, named after the Tower's 1070 designer. Pneumonia put an end to Bran, leaving lifelong partner Branwen without her mate.

■ DID YOU KNOW? In 1981 a raven named Grog, perhaps seduced by his alcoholic moniker, escaped after 21 years at the Tower. Others have been banished for "conduct unbecoming."

The six that remain, each one identified by a colored band around a claw, are much loved for their fidelity (they mate for life) and their cheek (capable of 440 noises, they are witty and scolding mimics). It's not only the diet

of blood-soaked biscuits, rabbit, and scraps from the mess kitchen that keeps them coming back. Their lifting feathers on one wing are trimmed, meaning they can manage the equivalent of a lop-sided air-bound hobble but not much more. For the first half of 2006 the ravens were moved indoors full-time as a preventive measure against avian flu but have since been allowed out and about again. In situ they are a territorial lot, sticking to Tower Green and the White Tower, and lodging nightly by Wakefield Tower. They've had free front-row seats at all the most grisly moments in Tower history—Anne Boleyn's execution included.

■ TIP➡ Don't get too close to the ravens: they are prone to pecking and not particularly fond of humans, unless you are the Tower's Raven Master.

And *WHAT* are they wearing?

A **pike** (or halberd), also known as a partisan, is the Yeoman Warder's weapon of choice. The Chief Warder carries a staff topped with a miniature silver model of the White Tower.

Anyone who refers to this as a costume will be lucky to leave the Tower with head still attached to body: this is the ceremonial uniform of the Yeoman Warders, and it comes at a cool £13,000 a throw.

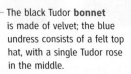

The black Tudor **bonnet** is made of velvet; the blue undress consists of a felt top hat, with a single Tudor rose in the middle.

This **Tudor-style ruff** helps date the ceremonial uniform, which was first worn in 1552.

Insignia on a Yeoman Warder's upper right arm denote the rank he carried in the military.

The **medals** on a Yeoman Warder's chest are more than mere show: all of the men and women have served for at least 22 years in the armed forces.

This version of the **royal livery** bears the insignia of the current Queen ("E" for Elizabeth) but originally dates from Tudor times. The first letter changes according to the reigning monarch's Christian name; the second letter is always an "R" for *rex* (king) or *regina* (queen).

Slits in the **tunic** date from the times when Beefeaters were expected to ride a horse.

Red socks and **black patent shoes** are worn on special occasions. Visitors are more likely to see the regular blue undress, introduced in 1858 as the regular working dress of the Yeoman Warders.

The **red lines down the trousers** are a sign of the blood from the swords of the Yeoman Warders in their defense of the realm.

6

IN FOCUS THE TOWER OF LONDON

(IN)FAMOUS PRISONERS OF THE TOWER

Anne Boleyn   Lady Jane Grey   Sir Walter Raleigh

Sir Thomas More. A Catholic and Henry VIII's friend and chancellor, Sir Thomas refused to attend the coronation of Anne Boleyn (Henry VIII's second wife) or to recognize the multi-marrying king as head of the Church. Sent to the Tower for treason, in 1535 More was beheaded.

Anne Boleyn. The first of Henry VIII's wives to be beheaded, Anne, who failed to provide the king with a son, was accused of sleeping with five men, including her own brother. All six got the chop in 1536. Her severed head was held up to the crowd, and her lips were said to be mouthing prayer.

Margaret, Countess of Salisbury. Not the best-known prisoner in her lifetime, she has a reputation today for haunting the Tower. And no wonder: the elderly 70-year-old was condemned by Henry VIII in 1541 for a potentially treacherous bloodline (she was the last Plantagenet princess) and hacked to death by the executioner after she refused to put her head on the block like a common traitor and attempted to run away.

Queen Catherine Howard. Henry VIII's fifth wife was locked up for high treason and infidelity and beheaded in 1542 at age 20. Ever eager to please, she spent her final night practicing how to lay her head on the block.

Lady Jane Grey. The nine-days-queen lost her head in 1554 at age 16. Her death was the result of sibling rivalry gone seriously wrong, when Protestant Edward VI slighted his Catholic sister Mary in favor of Lady Jane as heir, and Mary decided to have none of it.

Guy Fawkes. The Roman Catholic soldier who tried to blow up the Houses of Parliament and kill the king in the 1605 Gunpowder plot was first incarcerated in the chambers of the Tower, where King James I requested he be tortured in ever-worsening ways. Perhaps unsurprisingly, he confessed. He met his seriously grisly end in the Old Palace Yard at Westminster, where he was hung, drawn, and quartered in 1607.

Sir Walter Raleigh. Once a favorite of Elizabeth I, he offended her by secretly marrying her Maid of Honor and was chucked in the Tower. Later, as a conspirator against James I, he paid with his life. A frequent visitor to the Tower (he spent 13 years there in three stints), he managed to get the Bloody Tower enlarged on account of his wife and growing family. He was finally executed in 1618 in Old Palace Yard, Westminster.

Josef Jakobs. The last man to be executed in the Tower was caught as a spy when parachuting in from Germany and executed by firing squad in 1941. The chair he sat in when he was shot is preserved in the Royal Armouries' artifacts store.

FOR FURTHER EVIDENCE . . .

A trio of buildings in the Inner Ward, the **Bloody Tower, Beauchamp Tower,** and **Queen's House,** all with excellent views of the execution scaffold in Tower Green, are the heart of the Tower's prison accommodations and home to a permanent exhibition about notable inmates.

TACKLING THE TOWER (without losing your head)

✉ H.M. Tower of London, Tower Hill
☏ 0844/482-7777/7799 ⊕ www.hrp.org.
uk ✇ Adult: £19, children under 16: £10.45,
Family tickets (2 adults plus up to 6 children):
£55, children under 5, free. ◷ Mar.–Oct.,
Tues.–Sat. 9–5:30, Sun. and Mon. 10–5:30; last
admission at 5. Nov.–Feb., Tues.–Sat. 9–4:30,
Sun. and Mon. 10–4:30; last admission at 4
Ⓤ Tower Hill

■TIP→ You can buy tickets from automatic kiosks on arrival, or up to seven days
in advance at any Tube station. Avoid lines
completely by booking by telephone (0844
482 7777/7799 weekdays 9–5), or online.

MAKING THE MOST OF YOUR TIME:
Without doubt, the Tower is worth two to
three hours. A full hour of that would be well
spent by joining one of the Yeoman Warders' tours (included in admission). It's hard to
better their insight, vitality, and humor—they
are knights of the realm living their very own
fairytale castle existence.

The Crown Jewels are worth the wait, the
White Tower is essential, and the Medieval
Palace and Bloody Tower should at least be
breezed through.

■TIP→ It's best to visit on weekdays,
when the crowds are smaller.

WITH KIDS: The Tower's centuries-old
cobblestones are not exactly stroller-friendly,
but strollers are permitted inside most of the
buildings. If you do bring one, be prepared
to leave it temporarily unsupervised (the
stroller, that is—not your child) outside the
White Tower, which has no access. There are
baby-changing facilities in the Brick Tower
restrooms behind the Jewel House. Look for
regular free children's events such as the
Knight's school where children can have a go
at jousting, sword-fighting, and archery.

■TIP→ Tell your child to find one of the
Yeoman Warders if he or she should get
lost; they will in turn lead him or her to the
Byward Tower, which is where you should
meet.

IN A HURRY? If you have less than an hour,
head down Wall Walk, through a succession
of towers, which eventually spit you out at
the Martin Tower. The view over modern London is quite a contrast.

TOURS: Tours given by a Yeoman Warder
leave from the main entrance near Middle
Tower every half-hour from 10–4, and last
about an hour. Beefeaters give occasional
30-minute talks in the Lanthorn Tower about
their daily lives. Both tours are free. Check
website for talks and workshops

6

IN FOCUS THE TOWER OF LONDON

Now the crypts house a museum of the church's rich history, and a bit of Roman sidewalk. ✉ *Fleet St., The City* ☎ *020/7427–0133* ⊕ *www. stbrides.com* 🎫 *Free* ⊙ *Weekdays 8–6, Sat. call to confirm, Sun. for services only 10–6:30* Ⓜ *St. Paul's, Blackfriars.*

St. Mary-le-Bow. Various versions of this church have stood on the site since the 11th century. In 1284 a local goldsmith took refuge here after committing a murder, only to be killed inside the church by enraged relatives of his victim. The church was abandoned for a time afterward, but started up again, and was rebuilt in its current form after the Great Fire. Wren's 1673 incarnation has a tall steeple (in The City, only St. Bride's is taller) and one of the most famous sets of bells around—a Londoner must be born within the sound of the "Bow Bells" to be a true Cockney. The origin of that idea may have been the curfew rung on the bells during the 14th century, even though "Cockney" only came to mean "Londoner" centuries later, and then it was an insult. The Bow takes its name from the bow-shaped arches in the Norman crypt. The garden contains a statue of local boy Captain John Smith, who founded Virginia in 1606 and was later captured by Native Americans. ✉ *Cheapside, The City* ☎ *020/7248–5139* ⊕ *www.stmarylebow.co.uk* ⊙ *Mon.–Wed. 7–6, Thurs. 7–6:30, Fri. 7–4; closed weekends* Ⓜ *Mansion House, St. Paul's.*

QUICK
BITES

Café Below. The Café Below, in St. Mary-le-Bow's Norman crypt, is packed with City workers weekdays from 7:30 am until 9 pm for a menu covering breakfasts, scrumptious light lunches, and delicious dinners. ☎ *020/7329–0789* ⊕ *www.cafebelow.co.uk.*

The East End

WORD OF MOUTH

"I would guess that at least 30% on any of the Jack the Ripper tours through the East End think that JtR is fictional. They also expect it to be some kind of Dickens-type romp. They certainly don't expect the very vivid descriptions of what he did. To give you an idea, and expect this to be explained in close detail: 'That's the flesh from her thigh on the side table,' for instance." —Cholmondley_Warner

GETTING ORIENTED

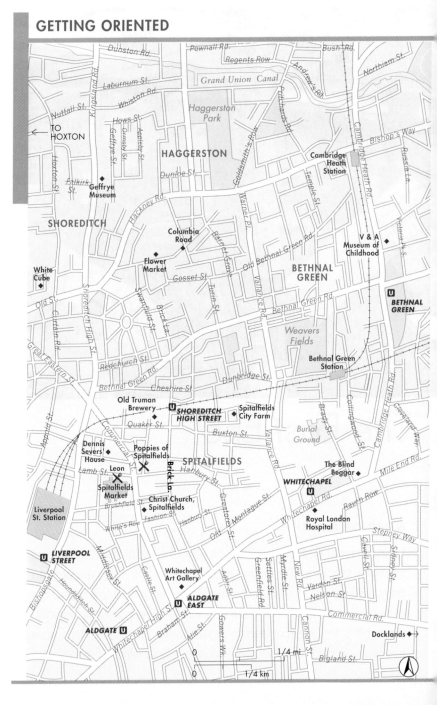

TOP REASONS TO GO

Take a candlelight tour of **Dennis Severs' House**: This handsome Georgian town house is stage-set to suggest that its 18th- and 19th-century occupants have just stepped out.

Go clubbing: For London's most hedonistic bar- or club-crawl, head to Hoxton and Shoreditch.

Check out London's coolest, hottest art scene: The East End isn't picturesque, but the art scene is vibrant, and small galleries are interspersed with larger collections.

Walk in the footsteps of **Jack the Ripper:** Track the very footsteps of the world's most infamous serial killer through the Victorian slum streets of the East End.

Peek into the lives of Londoners at the Geffrye Museum: The magical collection of this museum showcases an array of period rooms rich in antiques, brocades, and crystal.

FEELING PECKISH?

Leon. Inside Spitalfields Market is this branch of the small London chain; top bets are seasonable and yummy fast food including sandwiches, wraps, curries, and salads. ☎ 0207/247–4369.

Poppies of Spitalfields. Poppies of Spitalfields strikes a balance between trendy and traditional with retro-diner decor and efficient service. The specialty is fish-and-chips, but if fresh fish (from Billingsgate Market) isn't your thing, grilled chicken is also available. ✉ 6-8 Hanbury St., Spitalfields/East End ☎ 0207/247–0892 ⊕ www.poppiesfishandchips.co.uk.

SAFETY

Around the central hubs of Hoxton, Shoreditch, Spitalfields, and Brick Lane, most streets are safe during daylight hours; even after dark these areas are relatively safe. Be on your guard at all times, however, if venturing into the mean streets of Whitechapel, Bethnal Green, and Mile End.

GETTING THERE

The Tube is the easiest way to reach the East End from central London, and the best Tube stops to start from are Whitechapel or Aldgate East on the District–Hammersmith and City lines, and Aldgate on the Metropolitan and Circle lines.

MAKING THE MOST OF YOUR TIME

To experience the East End at its most lively, make sure you visit on the weekend, when it's possible to shop, eat, drink, and party your way through a whole 72 hours. Spitalfields Market bustles all weekend, while Brick Lane is at its best on a Sunday morning—also the time to visit Columbia Road for its glorious flower market. If you're planning to explore the East End art scene, pick up a free art map at the Whitechapel Art Gallery. As far as booming nightlife scene here, there's no time limit.

GUIDED TOURS

There are some thrilling walks that take you to the haunts of Jack the Ripper and other East End murderers: researcher and actor Declan McHugh leads the **Blood and Tears Walk: London's Horrible Past** (☎ 020/7625–5155), which departs daily from Barbican Tube station and is particularly recommended. There are also nifty Ripper walks sponsored by several companies.

7

Sightseeing
★★★
Nightlife
★★★★★
Dining
★★★★
Lodging
★
Shopping
★★★★

Made famous by Dickens and infamous by Jack the Ripper, the East End is one of London's most enduringly evocative neighborhoods. It may have fewer conventional tourist attractions but it is rich in folk history, architectural gems, feisty burgeoning culture, and one of the hottest gallery scenes in the world. Once home to French Huguenots, then Ashkenazi Jews, and now a large Bangladeshi community, the area has also attracted—since the early 1990s—hip artists and designers attracted by affordable Georgian buildings and converted industrial lofts.

Updated by
Ellin Stein

Nowadays the East End is one of London's most exciting neighborhoods, bohemian in places, culturally diverse, and though hit hard during the Blitz of World War II, historically charming here and there, with a surprising number of fine early Georgian houses. Your explorations, accordingly, will reward you with a rich variety experiences.

Two hot districts are Spitalfields and Shoreditch, together with Hoxton, which are filling up fast with stylish boutiques (especially on Cheshire Street) and cafés, artists' studios, and galleries in once-derelict industrial spaces that were bought up cheaply and have been imaginatively remodeled. **Brick Lane,** the heart of the Bangladeshi East End, is lined with innumerable curry houses and glittering sari shops, and is also home to the **Old Truman Brewery,** a remnant of the old East End and now converted to studios and gallery space.

Markets bring shoppers to the East End from all over London. The Sunday morning junk market on Brick Lane complements the neighborhood's many vintage-clothing shops, while Columbia Road is enlivened with a fun and fab flower market; Spitafields Market, with its crafts and designers booths, is open daily, but weekends are the liveliest. Some of London's most distinctive attractions are tucked away in the East End. The **Geffrye Museum,** a collection of domestic interiors, occupies a row of early-18th-century alms-houses, and Whitechapel Art Gallery and the East End branch of the **White Cube** gallery are bastions of contemporary art. Pockets of notable historic buildings remain. **Christ Church, Spitalfields,** Nicholas Hawkmoor's masterpiece, soars above Fournier Street. **Dennis Severs's House,** in a Georgian terrace, has been transformed into a "living house museum" that authentically re-creates several periods. The **Spitalfields City Farm** offers rare open space in this built-up area and is a favorite with kids, as is the quirky **V&A Museum of Childhood** in Bethnal Green.

WORD OF MOUTH

"The Geffrye Museum is off the beaten tourist path. It's well worth checking out [the museum's] special events. I attended a ceramics fair there in the fall, which featured many wonderful contemporary artists. Around the holidays, various rooms are decorated in period style. My daughter and I have enjoyed that on a couple of occasions." —obxgirl

TOP ATTRACTIONS

Fodor's Choice ★ **Dennis Severs' House.** Dennis Severs (1948–99), a performer-designer-scholar from Escondido, California, dedicated his life to restoring this Georgian terraced house. More than that, he created "still life dramas" using sight, sound, and smell to evoke the world of a fictitious family of Huguenot silk weavers, the Jervises, who might have inhabited the house between 1728 and 1914. Each of the 10 rooms has a distinctive, compelling atmosphere that encourages visitors to become lost in another time through the use of details like rose-laden Victorian wallpaper in the Victorian Chamber, Georgian wing chairs in the drawing room, and drab, late-17th-century "Protestant" colors upstairs. ■ TIP➔ The "Silent Night" candlelight tours, each Monday and Wednesday evening, are the most theatrical and memorable way to "feel" the house; this is a magical experience relished by both Londoners and out-of-towners. ⊠ 18 Folgate St., Spitalfields/East End ☎ 020/7247–4013 ⊕ www.dennissevershouse.co.uk ☎ £10 Sun., £7 Mon., £14 Mon. and Wed. evenings ⊗ Sun. noon–4 (last admission 3:15); 1st and 3rd Mon. noon–2 (last admission 1:15); Mon. and Wed. 6–8 (reservations essential) Ⓜ Liverpool St.

Fodor's Choice ★ **Geffrye Museum.** Here's where you can explore the life of London' middle class over the years (in contrast to the lifestyle evoked by the West End's grand aristocratic town houses). Originally a row of almshouses built in 1714 by Sir Robert Geffrye, a former Lord Mayor of London, this charming museum contains a series of 11 rooms that re-create everyday domestic interiors from the Elizabethan period through the 1950s to the present day. The almshouses were transformed into a museum after the pensioners who lived here were relocated to a healthier part of town in 1914, and one almshouse was restored to its original condition (to visit the almshouse you must go as part of a tour, which is offered at specific times each month). Outside, four period gardens chart the evolution of the town garden over the past 400 years, and next to them is a walled herb garden. The museum's extension wing houses the 20th-century galleries, a lovely café overlooking the gardens, and a bookshop. ⊠ *136 Kingsland Rd., Hoxton* ☎ *020/7739–9893* ⊕ *www. geffrye-museum.org.uk* ✉ *Free (charge for special exhibitions); almshouse £2.50* ⊙ *Tues.–Sat. 10–5, Sun. and bank holiday Mon. noon–5; gardens: Apr. 1–Oct. 31* Ⓜ *Hoxton (London Overground); Old St., then Bus 243; Liverpool St., then Bus 149 or 242.*

Spitalfields Market. A gorgeous piece of architecture in itself, this large restored Victorian market hall (covered by a glass canopy) is one part bazaar and one part food court. There's a notable antiques markets on Thursday and a fashion market on Friday (plus, on every first and third Friday, a record fair), as well as markets on other days selling goods ranging from vintage clothes to toys, hats, and jewelry. While some of the quality is pedestrian, you can also find interesting clothes, accessories, and leather goods by new designers. The adjoining brick market building houses upscale shops. ■TIP→ **The nearer the weekend, the busier it all gets.** *For more on Spitalfields, see* ⇨ *Chapter 18, Shopping.* ⊠ *65 Brushfield St., Spitalfields/East End* ☎ *020/7247–8556* ⊕ *www.visitspitalfields.com* ✉ *Free* ⊙ *Shops daily 10–7; market stalls Tues.–Fri. 10–4, Sun. 9–5* Ⓜ *Liverpool St.*

Ⓒ ★ **V&A Museum of Childhood.** This is a children-of-all-ages alert! The East End outpost of the Victoria & Albert Museum—in an iron, glass, and brown-brick building transported here from South Kensington in 1868—houses one of the world's biggest toy collections. One highlight (among many) is the large Dolls' Houses collection—a bit like the ⇨ *Geffrye Museum* zapped into miniature, with houses from 1673 up to the present—but other favorites range from board games to teddy bears and train sets. The collection is organized into galleries: Moving Toys, which includes everything from rocking horses to Xboxes; Creativity, which encompasses dolls, puppets, chemistry sets, play kitchens, construction toys, and musical instruments; and Childhood, with areas devoted to baby paraphernalia and baby dolls, an exhibit of children's clothes from the mid-1600s to the present, and toys inspired by adult pursuits, such as toy soldiers, toy guns, and toy hospitals. Don't miss the magnificent 18th-century *commedia dell'arte* puppet theater thought to have been made in Venice. ⊠ *Cambridge Heath Rd., East End* ☎ *020/8983–5200* ⊕ *www.vam.ac.uk/moc* ✉ *Free* ⊙ *Daily 10–5:45* Ⓜ *Bethnal Green.*

★ **Whitechapel Art Gallery.** Founded in 1901, this gallery has expanded into fabulous new spaces and presents internationally renowned shows that are often on the cutting edge of contemporary art. The American painter Jackson Pollock exhibited here in the 1950s, as did pop artist Robert Rauschenberg in the 1960s; David Hockney had his first solo show here in the 1970s. The gallery also hosts talks, film screenings, concerts, poetry readings, and other events. Pick up a free East End art map to

EAST END STREET SMARTS

Brick Lane and the narrow streets running off it offer a paradigm of the East End's development. Its population has moved in waves: communities seeking refuge, others moving out in an upwardly mobile direction.

Brick Lane has seen the manufacture of bricks (during the 16th century), beer, and bagels, but nowadays it's becoming the hub of artistic bohemia, especially at the Old Truman Brewery with its calendar of diverse cultural activities. It's also the heart of Banglatown—Bangladeshis make up one-third of the population in this London borough, and you'll see that the names of the surrounding streets are written in Bengali—where you find many kebab and curry houses along with shops selling videos, colorful saris, and stacks of sticky sweets. On Sunday morning the entire street becomes pedestrianized. Shops and cafés are open, and several stalls are set up, creating a companion market to the one on nearby **Petticoat Lane.**

Fournier Street contains fine examples of the neighborhood's characteristic Georgian terraced houses, many of them built by the richest of the early-18th-century Huguenot silk weavers (note the enlarged windows on the upper floors). Most of those along the north side of Fournier Street have been restored, but some still contain textile sweatshops—only now the workers are Bengali.

Wilkes Street, with more 1720s Huguenot houses, is north of the Christ Church, Spitalfields, and neighboring **Princelet Street** was once important to the East End's Jewish community. Where No. 6 stands now, the first of several thriving Yiddish theaters opened in 1886, playing to packed houses until the following year, when a false fire alarm, rung during a January performance, ended with 17 people being crushed to death. The tragedy so demoralized the theater's founder, Jacob Adler, that he moved his troupe to New York, where he played a major role in founding that city's great Yiddish theater tradition—which, in turn, had a significant effect on Hollywood.

Elder Street, just off Folgate, is another gem of original 18th-century houses. On the south and east side of Spitalfields Market are yet more time-warp streets that are worth a wander, such as **Gun Street,** where artist Mark Gertler (1891–1939) lived at No. 32.

help you with the rest of your gallery hopping. ⊠ 77–82 *Whitechapel High St., East End* ☎ *020/7522-7888* ⊕ *www.whitechapelgallery.org* ⊠ *Free, charge for some special exhibits* ☉ *Tues.–Wed., Fri.–Sun. 11–6; Thurs. 11–9* Ⓜ *Aldgate East.*

WORTH NOTING

The Blind Beggar. Salvation Army founder William Booth preached his first sermon in 1865 outside the Blind Beggar, a dark den of iniquity during Victorian times but now a rather unremarkable neighborhood pub. The event is commemorated by an inscribed stone on the south side of the street and a statue of Booth near the pub. The Blind Beggar's main claim to fame, however, is considerably less high-minded: its saloon

Blimey, Gov'nor, It's Jack the Ripper!

Gigantic shadows, fires blazing on the corner, leering looks by the homeless, and the spirit of "Jack" himself: all may show up on one of London's most unforgettable experiences, the "Jack the Ripper Walk" that tracks the very footsteps of the world's most infamous serial killer. You'll see the deserted squares ("Did you know that you're standing on the very spot where his second victim was found?"), warehouse alleys, and the ground-floor flat—today occupied by an Indian restaurant—where he literally butchered one of his poor victims.

At No. 90 Whitechapel High Street once stood George Yard Buildings, where Jack the Ripper's first victim, Martha Turner, was discovered in August 1888. A second murder occurred some weeks later, and Hanbury Street, behind a seedy lodging house at No. 29, is where Jack the Ripper left his third mutilated victim, "Dark" Annie Chapman. A double murder followed, and then, after a

month's lull, came the death on this street of Marie Kelly, the Ripper's last victim and his most revolting murder of all. He had been able to work indoors this time, and Kelly, a young widow, was found strewn all over the room, charred remains of her clothing in the fire grate. Jack the Ripper's identity never has been discovered, although theories abound, including, among others, the cover-up of a prominent member of the British aristocracy, the artist Walter Sickert, and Francis Tumblety, an American quack doctor.

Today, many outfitters offer walking tours of the Victorian slum streets that once Jack called his own: the most popular is run by Original London Walks (⊕ www.walks.com) and led by Donald Rumbelow, "the leading authority on Jack the Ripper"; it leaves every night from Tower Hill at 7:30 pm (Don only shows up a few nights a week).

bar is notorious as the scene where Ronnie Kray—one of the gangster Kray twins, former kings of the East End's underworld—shot dead rival gang member George Cornell in March 1966. As well, beer lovers will appreciate that the first modern brown ale was created at the adjoining Albion Brewery, built by the pub's landlord in 1808. During World War II, the brewery's stables suffered a direct hit, killing many of the beloved shire horses who pulled the delivery wagons. The brewery was closed in 1979 and is now a supermarket. ⊠ *337 Whitechapel Rd., East End* ☎ *0207/247–6195* ⊕ *www.theblindbeggar.com* Ⓜ *Whitechapel.*

Christ Church, Spitalfields. This is the 1729 masterpiece of Sir Christopher Wren's associate Nicholas Hawksmoor, one of his six London churches. It was commissioned as part of Parliament's 1711 "Fifty New Churches Act," passed in response to the influx of immigrants with the idea of providing for the religious needs of the "godless thousands"—actually, to ensure they joined the Church of England as opposed to such nonconformist denominations as the Protestant Huguenots. (It must have worked; you can still see gravestones with epitaphs in French in the churchyard.) As the local silk industry declined, the church fell into disrepair, and by 1958 the structure was crumbling, with the looming

On Sunday, additional clothing and crafts stalls surround Spitalfields covered market.

prospect of demolition. But after 25 years—longer than it took to build the church—and a huge local fund-raising effort, the structure was completely restored and is a joy to behold, from the colonnaded Doric portico and tall spire to its soaring, heavily-ornamented English Baroque plaster ceiling. As a concert venue it truly comes into its own. Tours that take you "backstage" to the many hidden rooms and passages, from the tower to the vaults, are offered on Tuesday and Sunday, other times by appointment. ■ TIP→ Don't miss the chance to attend one of the classical concerts held year- round in this atmospheric ecclesiastical venue. ✉ Commercial St., Spitalfields/East End ☎ 020/7377–2440 ✇ Free, tours £3 ◷ Tues. 10–4, Sun. 1–4. Ⓜ Aldgate East.

OFF THE BEATEN PATH

Estorick Collection. West of Hoxton, towards the eastern end of Islington, is this small, restored Georgian mansion with an extraordinary collection of early-20th-century Italian art. The works were acquired by Eric Estorick, an American collector and sociologist, who was particularly keen on Italian Futurists; there are works by Balla, Boccioni, and Severini, among others. The downstairs Estorick Caffè is a good place to grab a bite, especially in summer when you can sit outdoors. ✉ 39A Canonbury Sq., off Canonbury Rd., Islington ☎ 020/7704–9522 ⊕ www.estorickcollection.com ✇ £5 ◷ Wed., Fri., Sat. 11–6; Thurs. 11–8; Sun. noon–5 Ⓜ Highbury & Islington.

Old Truman Brewery. The last East End brewery still standing—a handsome example of Georgian and 19th-century industrial architecture, and in late Victorian times the largest brewery in the world—has been transformed into a cavernous hipster mall housing galleries, independent shops, fashion-forward boutiques, bars, clubs, and restaurants.

The East End Art Scene

It was only inevitable that the once arty Islington area (the N1 postal district, which rubs streets with the less elegant end of the Regent's Canal toward The City, EC1) would become too expensive and gentrified for the artists themselves. Hoxton, on a corner of Islington just off the City Road, with its cheap industrial units and more artisan Georgian–Victorian terraced streets, was the logical next stop.

The seal of boho approval came when Damien Hirst's agent and the most important modern art dealer in town, Jay Jopling, set up the White Cube gallery at 48 Hoxton Square. Impoverished artists, however, are not newcomers to the area—in the 1960s, Bridget Riley set up an outfit here to find affordable studio space for British artists—but the latest wave this side of the millennium has changed the face of this formerly down-at-the-heels neighborhood. It's now undeniably hip to be in Hoxton.

From the Barbican in The City to Whitechapel in the East End, as many as 25 art galleries have opened, showing the latest works of the YBAs (Young British Artists). A spread of trendy real estate has taken a firm grip across the City Road into E1, principally Shoreditch, Spitalfields, and "Banglatown"—the nickname for the neighborhood around Brick Lane where Bengali shops and homes have created a slice of south Asia. Where less-than-glam buildings for the poor (such as the Jewish Soup Kitchen off Commercial Street, Spitalfields) once stood are now loft-style luxury apartments. Boutiques, bars, clubs, and restaurants have followed in their wake, and the Eastside—as the neighborhood has been coined—is unapologetically brimming with energy.

The retailers are at street level with offices and studios on the upper floors. Events include fashion shows for both new and established designers, excellent sample sales, art installations, and, on weekends, a food hall and a vintage clothes fair. The Vibe Bar is a hot spot to chill out behind a traditional Georgian facade—it also has a great outdoor space. ⊠ *91 Brick La., Spitalfields/East End* ⊕ *www.trumanbrewery. com* Ⓜ *Aldgate East.*

Royal London Hospital Museum. Founded in 1740, the Royal London was in its early days as nasty as its former neighborhood near the Tower of London. Waste was carried out and dumped in the street, bedbugs and alcoholic nurses were rife, and, according to hsopital records, patients didn't die—they were "relieved." In 1757 the hospital moved to its present site and was soon one of the most up-to-date hospitals in London. Care was enhanced further by the addition of a small medical school in 1785 and again by an entire state-of-the-art medical college in 1855. The Royal London grew to become the largest general hospital in the United Kingdom—and it still is. A new hospital has opened alongside the existing one, which is undergoing a complete overhaul. To get an idea of the huge medical leaps made over the past centuries, you could walk through the new building to the Royal London Hospital museum in the crypt of St. Augustine located within the Victorian St. Philip's Church. But it is best to enter the church directly from Newark Street.

Located in the crypt of Victorian church, the Royal London Hospital Museum uses exhibits of historic medical equipment, surgical instruments, and archives to document the history of this East London institution from its foundation in 1740 to the present day. Highlights include a forensic medicine section with original material on the Jack the Ripper murders and the RLH surgeon who helped investigate them, artifacts and documents relating to Joseph Merrick—better known as "The Elephant Man"—who spent his final years in the hospital, and a set of dentures worn by George Washington. Opening hours are subject to change on short notice, so call before you go. ⊠ *Newark St., East End* ⊕ *www.bartsandthelondon.nhs.uk/museums* ☉ *Tues.–Fri. 10–4:30* Ⓜ *Whitechapel.*

☺ **Spitalfields City Farm.** An oasis of rural calm in an urban landscape, this little community farm raises a variety of animals, including some rare breeds, to help educate city kids about life in the country. A tiny farm shop sells freshly laid eggs, along with organic seasonal produce. ⊠ *Buxton St., East End* ☎ *020/7247–8762* ⊕ *www.spitalfieldscityfarm. org* ⊠ *Free* ☉ *Tues.–Sun. 10–4:30* Ⓜ *Aldgate East, Whitechapel, Liverpool Street.*

White Cube. The original White Cube once had cramped quarters in genteel St. James's but set up this outpost to take advantage of the massive open spaces of the East End's former industrial buildings. Damien Hirst—a moving force behind the Britart phenomenon best known for his large vitrines containing animals preserved in formaldehyde and the high prices his work commands—Tracey Emin, Gilbert and George, Sam Taylor-Wood, and other trailblazers have shown here and gone on to become internationally renowned (or, in some cases, notorious). The building looks, appropriately enough, like a white cube. For directions to the many other galleries that followed White Cube to the East End, pick up a map from the Whitechapel Art Gallery. ⊠ *48 Hoxton Sq., Hoxton* ☎ *020/7930–5373* ⊕ *www.whitecube.com* ⊠ *Free* ☉ *Tues.–Sat. 10–6* Ⓜ *Old St.; Hoxton (London Overground).*

The South Bank

WORD OF MOUTH

"To me the London Eye is an absolute must—one of the very first things to do—thrilling ride perched above the Thames and great way to orient yourself to the relief map of London stretched out below—all the famous landmarks clearly visible. Take a London map with you to pinpoint Hyde Park, Greenwich, Canary Wharf, etc. . ."

—PalenQ

GETTING ORIENTED

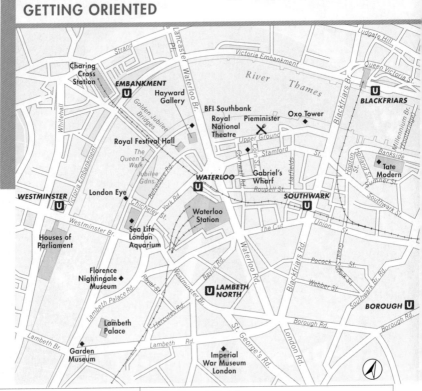

GETTING THERE	TOP REASONS TO GO

GETTING THERE

For the South Bank, use Embankment on the District, Circle, Northern, and Bakerloo lines, from where you can walk across the Golden Jubilee Bridges; or Waterloo on the Northern, and Bakerloo lines, from where it's a 10-minute walk to the Royal Festival Hall (slightly longer from the Jubilee line station).

London Bridge on the Northern and Jubilee lines is a five-minute stroll from Borough Market and Southwark Cathedral.

TOP REASONS TO GO

Join the "groundlings" at Shakespeare's Globe: Get caught up in the Bard's great words from the Elizabethan-style standing-room pit of this celebrated theater.

Marvel at the Tate Modern: One of the world's great shrines of contemporary and modern art, this branch of the Tate is noted for a spectacularly renovated electric turbine hall.

Be a ghoul at the London Dungeon: Did you ever wonder what a disembowelment looks like? That's just one of the torture tableaux on view in this old-fashioned "chamber of horrors." You'll be amazed how many children adore this place.

Channel Vivien Leigh on Waterloo Bridge: Take in one of London's most romantic views with St. Paul's to the east and the Houses of Parliament to the west, then head east along a fairy-light embankment toward the Oxo Tower.

MAKING THE MOST OF YOUR TIME

Don't attempt the South Bank all in one go. Not only will you exhaust yourself, but you will miss out on the varied delights that it has to offer.

The Tate Modern alone deserves a whole morning or afternoon, especially if you want to do justice to both the temporary exhibitions and the permanent collection.

The Globe requires about two hours for the exhibition theater tour and two to three hours for a performance. Finish with drinks at the Oxo Tower with its spectacular view or dinner at one of the many restaurants in the Southbank Centre.

You can return across the river to central London via Southwark on the Jubilee line from Tate Modern, although it's a good 15-minute walk from the station.

Crossing the elegant Millennium Bridge for St. Paul's on the Central line or the Golden Jubilee Bridges to Embankment offer longer but more-scenic alternatives.

FEELING PECKISH?

Pieminister. At the Gabriel's Wharf branch of Pieminister, which began life as a Borough Market stall, have a hot meat pie in pastry made with locally sourced and ethically farmed ingredients, such as chicken, bacon and tarragon, or stilton and beef (there are also vegetarian options). Take away or eat at the outside tables. ⊠ *56 Upper Ground, Gabriel's Wharf, South Bank* ☎ *020/7928–5755.*

Konditor & Cook. Known for its exquisite handmade cakes, cookies, and pastries, most baked on-site, this small chain of bijou patisseries also offers daily specials such as chicken paella or vegetarian moussaka. ⊠ *Borough Market 10 Stoney St., Southwark* ☎ *020/0844-854-9363.*

SAFETY

At night, it's best to stick to where the action is at the Butler's Wharf and Gabriel's Wharf restaurants, the Southbank Centre, and the Cut near the Old Vic. Stray farther away from these areas and the streets quickly begin to feel deserted.

8

For decades, tourists rarely ventured south of the river, except to go to Waterloo station. Now a host of attractions draws visitors from all over London: The reconstruction of Shakespeare's Globe, the world-class Tate Modern museum, the Southbank Centre, and, dominating the skyline, the London Eye—a giant Ferris wheel—are all huge draws. No longer off the beaten track, South London has become one of London's most popular places to be.

Updated by
Ellin Stein

That old, snide North London dig about needing a passport to cross the Thames has not been heard for the past decade. Before, natives rarely ventured beyond the watery curtain that divides the city in half; tourists, too, rarely troubled the area unless they were departing from Waterloo station. But now that the South Bank encompasses high-caliber art, music, film, and theater venues as well as an aquarium, a historic warship, and two popular food markets, South Londoners now sometimes look down on their northern cousins.

A borough of the City of London since 1327, Southwark first became well known for its inns (the pilgrims in Chaucer's *A Canterbury Tale* set off from one), theaters, prisons, and brothels, as well as entertainments such as bear-baiting. For four centuries, this was where Londoners went to let their hair down and behave badly.

Today, the **Thames Path** that skirts the South Bank is alive with skateboarders, secondhand booksellers, and street entertainers. At one end the **London Eye**, a millennium project that's a favorite with both Londoners and out-of-towners, rises next to the **London Aquarium and** the **Southbank Centre**, home to the recently renovated **Royal Festival Hall**, the **Hayward Gallery**, the **BFI Southbank** and the **National Theatre**. Farther east you'll come to a reconstruction of Sir Francis Drake's ship the **Golden Hinde; Butlers Wharf**, where some notable restaurants occupy what were once shadowy Dickensian docklands; and, next to **Tower Bridge**, the massive headlight-shape **City Hall**. Nearby Bermondsey (or "Beormund's

Eye" as it was known in Saxon times), with its bright yellow Fashion Museum, trendy boutiques, and cafés, is rapidly becoming one of the city's hippest enclaves. Meanwhile, younger visitors will enjoy the **London Dungeon** and the HMS *Belfast,* a decommissioned Royal Navy cruiser, while food lovers will head for London's oldest food market **Borough Market,** now reinvented as a gourmet mecca where independent stallholders provide farm-fresh produce, artisanal bread and cheese, and specialty fish and meat.

TOP ATTRACTIONS

The Globe Theatre.

Fodor's Choice ★ *See the highlighted listing in this chapter.*

Golden Hinde. Famed Elizabethan explorer Sir Francis Drake circumnavigated the globe in a little galleon just like this one. Launched in 1973, this exact replica made two round-the-world voyages and called in at ports—many along the Pacific and Atlantic coasts of the United States—to do duty as a maritime museum. Now berthed at the St. Mary Overie Dock, the ship continues its educational purpose, complete with "crew" in period costumes and five decks of artifacts. Call for information on guided tours. ⊠ *St. Mary Overie Dock, Cathedral St., Southwark* ☎ *020/7403–0123* ⊕ *www.goldenhinde.com* ⬚ *£6* ☉ *Daily 10–5:30* Ⓜ *London Bridge, Mansion House.*

QUICK BITES

Gabriel's Wharf. This cluster of specialty shops (jewelry, art, clothing, and ceramics) is nicely interspersed with informal restaurants (the place was renovated by the same group that converted the nearby **Oxo Tower Wharf,** an art deco warehouse topped by the famed Oxo Tower Restaurant, with levels of designer shop-studios).

You can rent bicycles at Gabriel's Wharf from the **London Bicycle Tour Company.** ⊠ *56 Upper Ground, South Bank* ☎ *020/7021–1686* ⊕ *www. coinstreet.org* ⬚ *Free* ☉ *Shops and studios Tues.–Sun. 11–6* Ⓜ *Blackfriars, Waterloo.*

Southbank Centre. The public has never really warmed to the Southbank Centre's hulking concrete buildings, products of the Brutalist style popular when the Centre was built in the 1950s and '60s, but they flock to its concerts, recitals, and exhibitions. The Royal Festival Hall is truly a People's Palace, with seats for 2,900, and a schedule that ranges from major symphony orchestras to pop stars (catch the new summer Meltdown Festival, where Lou Reed, Patti Smith, and Elvis Costello have put together way-cool calendars of concerts); the smaller Queen Elizabeth Hall is more strictly classically oriented. For art, head to the Hayward Gallery, home to shows on top contemporary artists such as Tracey Emin and George Condo (the terrace here is home to some exciting restaurants). Not officially part of the Southbank Centre but moments away on the east side of Waterloo Bridge, the National Theatre is home to some of the best productions in London (several, such as War Horse

8

and The History Boys, have become films) at prices well below the West End. Meanwhile, film buffs will appreciate the BFI Southbank (formerly the National Film Theatre), which has a schedule that true connoisseurs of the cinema will relish. ☒ *Southbank Centre, Belvedere Rd., South Bank* ☎ *020/7960–4200* ⊕ *www.southbankcentre.co.uk* ✉ *Varies; check website* ☼ *Varies according to venue; check website* Ⓜ *Waterloo, Embankment.*

London Eye. To mark the start of the new millennium, architects David Marks and Julia Barfield conceived a beautiful and celebratory structure that would allow people to see this great city from a completely new perspective. They came up with a giant Ferris wheel, which, as well as representing the turn of the century, would also be a symbol of regeneration. The London Eye is the largest cantilevered observation wheel ever built and among the tallest structures in London. The 25-minute slow-motion ride inside one of the enclosed passenger capsules is so smooth you'd hardly know you were suspended over the Thames. On a clear day you can see for up to 25 miles, with a bird's-eye view over London's most famous landmarks as you circle through 360 degrees. If you're looking for a special place to celebrate, champagne and canapés can be arranged ahead of time. ∎**TIP**➔ Buy your ticket online to avoid the long lines and get a 10% discount. For an extra £10, you can save even more time with a Fast Track flight for which you check in 15 minutes before your "departure." You can buy a combination ticket for the Eye and other London attractions—check online for details—or board the London Eye River Cruise here for a 40-minute sightseeing voyage on the Thames. ☒ *Riverside Bldg., County Hall, Westminster Bridge Rd., South Bank* ☎ *0870/990–8883* ⊕ *www.londoneye.com* ✉ *£18.60; cruise £12* ☼ *June and Sept., daily 10–9; July and Aug., daily 10–9:30; Oct.–Mar., daily 10–8:30* Ⓜ *Waterloo.*

Fashion and Textile Museum. The bright yellow and pink museum (it's hard to miss) designed by Mexican architect Ricardo Legorreta features changing exhibitions devoted to fashion design, textiles, and jewelry, with a strong emphasis on the 1960s and 1970s. Founded by designer Zandra Rhodes—an icon of Swinging London—and now owned by Newham College, the FTM is a favorite with fashionistas and offers weekday lectures on aspects of fashion history, along with an excellent gift shop selling books on fashion and one-of-a-kind pieces by local designers. After your visit, check out the many trendy spots that have bloomed in Southwark, in particular the restaurants, cafés, and boutiques on Bermondsey Street, as well as the latest—and largest—branch of the famed White Cube gallery. ☒ *83 Bermondsey St., Southwark* ☎ *020/7407–8664* ⊕ *www.ftmlondon.org* ✉ *£7* ☼ *Tues.–Sat. 11–6* Ⓜ *London Bridge.*

Tate Modern.

Fodor's Choice
★   *See the highlighted listing in this chapter.*

Continued on page 154

"Within this wooden O..."

—William Shakespeare, Henry V

SHAKESPEARE AND THE GLOBE THEATRE

At Shakespeare's Globe Theatre, they say the Bard does not belong to the British; he belongs to the world. Not a day has gone by since the Restoration when one of his plays isn't being performed or reinterpreted somewhere. But here, at the site of the original Globe, in a painstaking reconstruction of Shakespeare's own open-air theater, is where seeing one of his plays can take on an ethereal quality.

If you are exceedingly well read and a lover of the Bard, then chances are a pilgrimage to his Globe Theatre is already on your list. But if Shakespeare's works leave you wondering why exactly the play is the thing, then a trip to the Globe—to learn more about his life or to see his words come alive—is a must.

The Globe Theatre in Shakespeare's Day

In the 16th and 17th centuries, a handful of theaters—the Rose, the Swan, the Globe, and others whose names are lost—rose above the higgledy-piggledy jumble of rooftops in London's rowdy Southwark neighborhood. They were round or octagonal open-air playhouses, with galleries for the "quality" members of society, and large, open pits for the raucous mobs. People from all social classes, from royalty down to the hoi polloi, shared the communal experience of drama in these places. Shakespeare's Globe was one.

A fire in 1613 destroyed the first Globe, which was quickly rebuilt; however, Oliver Cromwell and waves of other reformers put an end to all the Southwark

playhouses in the 1640s. By the time American actor and director Sam Wanamaker visited in 1949, the only indication that the world's greatest dramatist created popular entertainment here was a plaque on a brewery wall. Wanamaker was shocked to find that all evidence of the playwright's legendary playhouse had vanished into air.

And thereby hangs a tale.

Wanamaker's Dream

Over the next several decades, Wanamaker devoted himself to the Bard. He was director of the New Shakespeare Theatre in Liverpool and, in 1959, joined the Shakespeare Memorial Theatre Company (now the Royal Shakespeare Company) at Stratford-upon-Avon. Finally, in the 1970s he began the project

SHAKESPEARE'S ALL-TIME TOP 10

1. *Romeo and Juliet.* Young love, teenage rebellion, and tragedy are the ingredients of the greatest tearjerker of all time.

2. *Hamlet* (right). The very model of a modern antihero and origin of the most quoted line of any play: "To be or not to be…"

3. *A Midsummer Night's Dream.* Spells and potions abound as the gods use humans for playthings; lovers' tiffs are followed by happy endings for all.

4. *Othello.* Jealousy poisons love and destroys a proud man.

5. *The Taming of the Shrew.* The eternal battle of the sexes.

6. *Macbeth.* Ambition, murder, and revenge. Evil gets its just reward.

7. *The Merry Wives of Windsor.* A two-timing rascal gets his comeuppance from a pack of hysterically funny gossips.

8. *Richard III.* One of literature's juiciest villains. The whole audience wants to hiss.

9. *The Tempest.* On a desert island, the concerns of men amaze and amuse the innocent Miranda: "Oh brave new world, that has such people in't."

10. *King Lear.* A tragedy of old age, filial love, and grasping, ungrateful children.

that would dominate the rest of his life: reconstructing Shakespeare's theater, as close to the original site as possible.

Today's Globe was re-created using authentic Elizabethan materials and craft techniques—green oak timbers joined only with wooden pegs and mortise-and-tenon joints; plaster made of lime, sand, and goat's hair; and the first thatched roof in London since the Great Fire of 1666. The complex, 200 yards from the site of the original Globe, includes an exhibition center, cafés, and restaurants. (The shell of a 17th-century-style theater, built adjacent to the Globe to a design by Inigo Jones, awaits further funds for completion.)

FUN FACT: Plays are presented in the open air (and sometimes the rain) to an audience of 1,000 on wooden benches in the bays, and 500 "groundlings," who stand on a carpet of hazelnut shells and cinder, just as they did nearly four centuries ago.

The eventual realization of Wanamaker's dream, a full-scale, accurate replica of the Globe, was the keystone that supported the revitalization of the entire district. The new Globe celebrates Shakespeare, his work, and his times, and as an educational trust it is dedicated to making the Bard continually fresh and accessible for new audiences. Sadly, Wanamaker died before construction was completed, in 1997. In Southwark Cathedral, a few hundred yards west of the Globe, a memorial to him stands beside the statue memorializing Shakespeare himself.

8

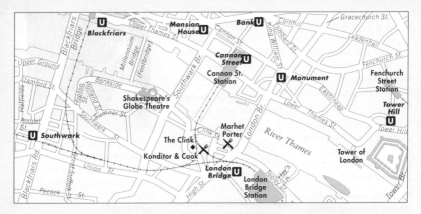

The season of plays is limited to the warmer months, from Shakespeare's Birthday (April 23) to the first week in October, with the schedule announced in late January on the theater's website. Tickets go on sale in mid-February. The box office takes phone and mail orders as well as in-person sales, but the most convenient way to buy tickets is online. Book as early as possible.

FUN FACT: "Groundlings"—those with £5 standing-only tickets—are not allowed to sit during the performance. Reserve an actual seat, though, on any one of the theater's three levels, and you can join the "Elizabethan" crowd.

If you do have a seat, you can rent cushions for £1 (or bring your own) to soften the backless wooden benches. A limited number of backrests are also available for rent for £4. The show must go on, rain or shine, warm or chilly—so come prepared for whatever the weather throws at you. Umbrellas are banned, but you can bring a raincoat or buy a cheap Globe rain poncho, which doubles as a great souvenir.

MAKING THE MOST OF YOUR TIME
Give yourself plenty of time: there are several cafés and restaurants, as well as fascinating interactive exhibitions, and theater tours with occasional live demonstrations. Performances can last up to three hours.

SPECIAL EVENT

The Frost Fair, held annually the weekend before Christmas, commemorates several extraordinary winters in the 17th century when the Thames froze over and fairs took place on the ice. It includes street theater, Morris Dancing, sword fighting, and food and crafts stalls. Admission is free, and there is special reduced admission to the Theatre and Exhibition during the fair.

Year-Round at Shakespeare's Globe

Shakespeare's Globe Exhibition is a comprehensive display built under the theater (the entry is adjacent) that provides background material about the Elizabethan theater and about the surrounding neighborhood, Southwark. The exhibition describes the process of building the modern Globe and the serious research that went into it.

FUN FACT: In Shakespeare's day, this was a rough part of town. The Bear Gardens, around the corner from the Globe, was where bear baiting, a cruel animal sport, took place. Farther along, the Clink (now a museum) was the local *gaol* (jail).

Daily live demonstrations include Elizabethan dressing, stage fighting, and swordplay, performed by drama students and stage-fighting instructors from the Royal Academy of Dramatic Art (RADA) and the London Academy of Music and Dramatic Art (LAMDA).

FUN FACT: Many performances are done in Elizabethan dress. Costumes are handmade from period materials—wool, silk, cotton, animal skins, and natural dyes.

Admission also includes a tour of the theater. On matinee days, the tour visits the archaeological site of the nearby (and older) Rose Theatre.

FUN FACT: Shakespeare's casts were all male, with young men and boys playing the female roles. A live demonstration in the costume exhibit shows how this was done—and how convincing it can be.

Visiting the Globe

✉ 21 New Globe Walk, Bankside, South Bank SE1 9DT

☎ 020/7902–1400 box office, 7401–9919 New Shakespeare's Globe Exhibition

🌐 www.shakespeares-globe.org

💲 Exhibition & tour £13.50, family ticket (2 adults, 3 children) £35; ticket prices for plays vary (£5–£35)

🕐 Exhibition Apr. 23–Early Oct., daily 10–5; Mid-Oct.–Apr. 22, daily 9–12:30 and 1–5; plays Apr. 23–early Oct., call for performance schedule.

Ⓤ Southwark, then walk to Blackfriars Bridge and descend the steps; Mansion House, then cross Southwark Bridge; Blackfriars, then walk across Blackfriars Bridge; St. Paul's, then cross Millennium Bridge or London Bridge.

TATE MODERN

✉ *Bankside, South Bank*
☎ *020/7887–8888* ⊕ *www. tate.org.uk/modern* 💷 *Free, charge for special exhibitions* 🕑 *Sun.–Thurs. 10–6, Fri. and Sat. 10–10 (last admission to exhibitions 45 mins before close)* Ⓜ *Southwark, Mansion House, St. Paul's.*

TIPS

■ Join one of the free, 45-minute guided tours. Each one covers a different gallery: Poetry and Dream at 11, Collection Highlights at noon, States of Flux at 2, and Energy and Process at 3. No need to book; just show up in the appropriate room.

■ Level 4 is devoted to temporary exhibitions, for which there's usually a charge of around £15. Bypass it if you're just here to see the main collection, which is free.

■ Make it a two-for-one art day by taking advantage of the Tate Boat, which takes visitors back and forth between Tate Britain and Tate Modern every 40 minutes.

■ Private "Tate Tours for Two" can be booked online from £100 to £120, with an afternoon tea for an additional £20 or a champagne dinner for an additional £90.

This spectacular renovation of a mid-20th-century power station is the most-visited museum of modern art in the world. Its great permanent collection, which starts in 1900 and ranges from Modern masters like Matisse to the most cutting-edge contemporary artists, is arranged thematically—Landscape, Still Life, and the Nude. Its blockbuster temporary exhibitions showcase the work of individual artists like Gaugin, Warhol, and Gerhard Richter.

HIGHLIGHTS

The vast **Turbine Hall** is a dramatic entrance point used to showcase big, audacious installations that tend to generate a lot of publicity. Past highlights include Olafur Eliasson's massive glowing sun and Carsten Holler's huge metal slides.

The **Material Gestures** galleries on Level 3 feature an impressive offering of post–World War II painting and sculpture. Room 7 contains a breathtaking collection of Rothkos and Monets; there are also paintings by Matisse, Pollock, and Picasso, and newer works from the likes of the sculptor Anish Kapoor.

Head to the Restaurant on Level 7 or the Espresso Bar on Level 4 for stunning vistas of the Thames. The view of St. Paul's from the Espresso Bar's balcony is one of the best in London.

An extension to the front of the building is not ony ambitious but also controversial—you won't be alone if you don't care for it.

Borough Market brings hungry shoppers to the London Bridge area every Friday and Saturday.

WORTH NOTING

Fodor's Choice ★

Dulwich Picture Gallery. Famed for its regal old-master painting collection, the Dulwich Picture Gallery (pronounced "Dull-ich") was Britain's first purpose-built art museum when it opened in 1811. The permanent collection includes landmark works by Rembrandt, Van Dyck, Rubens, Poussin, and Gainsborough, and it also hosts three major international exhibitions each year. As one British art critic puts it, "we would all travel bravely for a day in Tuscany or Umbria in order to see much less." The gallery also has a lovely café serving meals and drinks. Most of the land around here belongs to Dulwich College, a local boys' school, which keeps strict control over development. Consequently, Dulwich Village feels a bit like a time capsule, with old-fashioned street signs and handsome 18th-century houses strung out along its main street. Take a short wander and you'll find a handful of cute clothing and crafts stores and the well-manicured Dulwich Park, with lakeside walks and a fine display of rhododendrons in late May. ✉ *Gallery Rd., Dulwich* ☎ *020/8693–5254* 🌐 *www.dulwichpicturegallery.org.uk* 🎫 *£5–£9. Free guided tours weekends at 3* ⏲ *Tues.–Sun. and bank holiday Mon. 10–5* Ⓜ *National Rail: West Dulwich from Victoria or North Dulwich from London Bridge.*

Florence Nightingale Museum. Compact, highly visual, and engaging, this museum is dedicated to Florence Nightingale, who founded the first school of nursing and played a major role in establishing modern standards of health care. Exhibit are divided into three areas: one focuses on Nightingale's Victorian childhood, while the other two cover her work tending soldiers during the Crimean War (1854–56)

The Royal Festival Hall, the heart of the Southbank Centre, is home to many world-class musical performances.

and her subsequent health-care reforms. The museum is creative and accessible, incorporating photographs and personal items (including Nightingale's own books, bed, and famous lamp), as well as interactive displays of medical instruments and medicinal herbs. ⊠ *2 Lambeth Palace Rd., Lambeth* ☎ *020/7620–0374* ⊕ *www.florence-nightingale. co.uk* ⊠ *£5.80* ☉ *Mon.–Sun. 10–5; last admission 4* Ⓜ *Waterloo, Westminster, Lambeth North.*

★ **The Garden Museum.** This rather unassuming museum was created in the mid-1970s after two gardening enthusiasts came upon a medieval church which, they were horrified to discover, was about to be bulldozed. The churchyard contained the tomb of John Tradescant, an adventurous 17th-century plant collector who introduced many new species to England. Inspired to action, they rescued the church and opened this museum. With the support of a dedicated team of volunteers, it has subsequently acquired one of the largest collections of historic garden tools, artifacts, and curiosities in the world, in addition to creating beautiful walled gardens that are maintained year-round with seasonal plants. One section contains a perfect replica of a 17th-century knot garden, built around Tradescant's tomb; another is devoted entirely to wildflowers. It's also worth visiting the church itself, which contains the tombs of William Bligh, captain of the *Bounty*, and several members of the Boleyn family. As well, there's a green-thumb gift shop and the **Garden Café** serving vegetarian lunches and home-baked cakes—the toffee-apple variety is a must! ⊠ *5 Lambeth Palace Rd., Lambeth* ☎ *020/7401–8865* ⊕ *www.gardenmuseum.org.uk* ⊠ *£6 (includes garden and all exhibitions)* ☉ *Sun.–Fri. 10:30–5; Sat. 10:30–4;*

closed 1st Mon. of month M *Lambeth North, Vauxhall.*

HMS Belfast. At 613.5 feet, this is one of the last remaining big-gun armored warships from World War II, in which it played an important role in protecting the Arctic convoys and supporting the D-Day landings off Normandy. ⊠ *Morgan's La., Tooley St., Southwark* ☎ *020/7940–6300* ⊕ *hmsbelfast.iwm. org.uk* ⊠ *£14, children under 16 free* ⊗ *Mar.–Oct., daily 10–6; Nov.– Feb., daily 10–5; last admission 1 hr before closing* M *London Bridge.*

London Dungeon. Here's the goriest, grisliest, most gruesome attraction in town, where unfortunate prisoners (or at least realistic waxworks) are subjected in graphic detail to all the historical horrors that the Tower of London merely describes. Perhaps most shocking are the crowds of children roaring to get in—kids absolutely adore this place, although those with more a sensitive disposition may find it too frightening (that goes for adults as well). Replete with campy mannequins, penny-dreadful stage sets, and lurid colored spotlights, a series of tableaux depicts famously bloody moments alongside the torture, murder, and ritual slaughter of lesser-known victims, all to a sound track of screaming, wailing, and agonized moaning. There are displays on the Great Plague, the Great Fire of London, and Jack the Ripper, and, to add to the fear and fun, costumed characters leap out of the gloom to bring the exhibits to life. If you ever imagined what a disembowelment looked like, here's your chance. Be sure to get the souvenir booklet to impress all your friends back home. ■**TIP**➜ Expect long lines on weekends and during school holidays. Savings are available for online booking. ⊠ *28–34 Tooley St., Southwark* ☎ *020/7403–7221* ⊕ *www.thedungeons.com* ⊠ *From £18.52* ⊗ *Sept.–Feb., daily 10–5; Mar.–July, daily 9:30–6; Aug., daily 9:30–7; phone or check website to confirm times* M *London Bridge.*

Fodor's Choice ★

8

Oxo Tower. Long a London landmark to the insider, the art deco–era Oxo building has graduated from its former incarnations as a power-generating station and warehouse into a vibrant community of artists' and designers' workshops, a pair of restaurants, and five floors of community homes. There's an observation deck for a super river vista (St. Paul's to the east and Somerset House to the west), and a performance area on the first floor, which comes alive all summer long—as does the entire surrounding neighborhood. All the artisans expect you to disturb them whenever they're open, whether buying, commissioning, or just browsing. The biggest draw remains the Oxo Tower Restaurant for a meal or a martini. ⊠ *Bargehouse St., South Bank* ☎ *020/7021–1686* ⊕ *www.oxotower.co.uk* ⊠ *Free* ⊗ *Studios and shops Tues.–Sun. 11–6* U *Blackfriars, Waterloo.*

Sea Life London Aquarium. The curved, colonnaded, neoclassic former County Hall that once housed London's local government administration is now home to a superb three-level aquarium full of sharks and stingrays, along with many other aquatic species, both common and rare. There are also feeding and hands-on displays, including a tank full of shellfish that you can touch. It's not the biggest aquarium you've ever seen, but it will delight marine lovers. ☒ *County Hall, Westminster Bridge Rd., South Bank* ☎ *0871/663–1678* ⊕ *www.sealife.co.uk* ▤ *£19.02* ☉ *Mon.–Thurs. 10–6, last admission 5; Fri.–Sun. 10–7, last admission 6* Ⓜ *Westminster, Waterloo.*

Southwark Cathedral. Pronounced "Suth-uck," this is the second-oldest Gothic church in London, after Westminster Abbey, with parts dating back to the 12th century. Although it houses some remarkable memorials, not to mention a program of lunchtime concerts, it's seldom visited. It was promoted to cathedral status only in 1905; before that it was the priory church of St. Mary Overie (as in "over the water"—on the South Bank). Look for the gaudily renovated 1408 tomb of the poet John Gower, friend of Chaucer, and for the Harvard Chapel. Another notable buried here is Edmund Shakespeare, brother of William. ■TIP→ The Refectory serves full English breakfasts, light lunches, and tea daily 10–6. ☒ *London Bridge, South Bank* ☎ *020/7367–6700* ⊕ *www.southwark. anglican.org* ▤ *Free, suggested donation £4* ☉ *Daily 8–6* Ⓤ *London Bridge.*

Kensington, Chelsea, and Knightsbridge

WORD OF MOUTH

"The new V&A galleries are absolutely splendid. In a lesser city (i.e., anywhere else on earth) they'd be regarded as a major new museum in their own right."

—flanneruk

GETTING ORIENTED

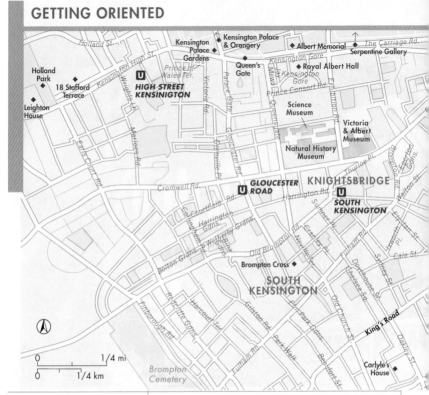

GETTING THERE

There are several useful Tube stations for this area: Sloane Square and High Street Kensington on the District and Circle lines; Knightsbridge and Hyde Park Corner on the Piccadilly line; Earl's Court, South Kensington, and Gloucester Road on the District, Circle, and Piccadilly lines; Holland Park on the Central line; and Victoria on the District, Circle, and Victoria lines.

SAFETY

This entire, posh region is quite safe but beware of pickpockets in shopping areas.

TOP REASONS TO GO

Treasure-hunt the V&A Museum: The Victoria & Albert Museum is the greatest museum of decorative arts in the world—even Edwardians got "interactive" by sketching in the Sculpture Court (stools are still provided today).

Encounter a dinosaur at the Natural History Museum: Watch children catch on that the museum's animatronic T. rex has noticed *them*—and is licking its dinosaur chops. Then see some of those fearsome teeth for real in the dinosaur room.

Get a glimpse of royal lifestyles at Kensington Palace: Home to royal personages including Queen Victoria, Princess Diana, and current residents the Duke and Duchess of Cambridge (William and Kate). Selections from the massive Royal Dress Collection are always on display.

Go Wilde at 18 Stafford Terrace: Filled with Victorian and Edwardian antiques and art, the charming Linley Sambourne House could be the perfect setting for *The Importance of Being Earnest.*

MAKING THE MOST OF YOUR TIME

You could fill three or four days in this borough: A shopping stroll along the length of the King's Road is easily half a day. Add lunch and some time weaving back and forth between the King's Road and the river and you can fill a day. Give yourself a half day, at least, for the Victoria & Albert Museum and a half day for either the Science or Natural History Museum.

9

FEELING PECKISH?

The Café at the V&A. The Café at the V&A serves breakfast, light snacks, tea, and full meals throughout the day, all in a grand room at modest prices (stop by just to see the original Arts and Crafts decor, one of William Morris's earliest commissions, with stained-glass by Edward Burne-Jones). Eat in the courtyard if the weather's good, or have a buffet supper on Friday late nights. ✉ *Victoria & Albert Museum, Cromwell Rd., South Kensington* ☎ *020/7942–2000.*

NEAREST PUBLIC RESTROOMS

Most old-style public restrooms have been replaced by futuristic "autoloos"—podlike booths on street corners that usually cost £1 to use. If you're not brave enough to trust the push-button locks, try the free and clean restrooms at department stores Peter Jones or Harvey Nichols. Or ask for the "loo" in a pub but be prepared for "sorry" if you're not a paying customer.

A GRAZER'S PARADISE

West London's answer to Borough Market, the Duke of York Square Food Market (☎ 020/7823–5577), an open-air market at 80 Duke of York Square, a chic shopping precinct, hosts 40 stalls every Saturday, from 10 to 4. Purveying artisanal and locally produced meat, game, fish, breads, cakes, cupcakes, honey, pasta, cheese, and chocolate from more than 150 small specialty food producers, this is a true grazer's paradise, with everything from around the world, ranging from paellas to pirogi to pad Thai to empanadas.

Sightseeing
★★★★
Nightlife
★★
Dining
★★★★
Lodging
★★★★
Shopping
★★★★★

In the Royal Borough of Kensington & Chelsea (or "K&C" as the locals call it) you'll find London at its richest, and not just in the moneyed sense. Once-bohemian Chelsea is where James McNeill Whistler and the Pre-Raphaelites painted and Mick Jagger partied. In South Kensington you'll come upon a concentration of great museums near Cromwell Road, including the Victoria & Albert, the Natural History Museum, and, within Hyde Park, historic Kensington Palace. Knightsbridge has become a playground for the international wealthy, with shopping to match their tastes. It is all summed up in adjacent Belgravia: comprised of block after block of cream-beige and white-porticoed mansions, this eminently walkable enclave of imposing residences and splendid embassies is like a stage set designed by Cecil Beaton.

KENSINGTON AND CHELSEA

Updated by
Ellin Stein

Chelsea was settled before the Domesday Book and was already fashionable when two of Henry VIII's wives lived there. On the banks of the Thames are the vast grounds of the **Royal Hospital,** designed by Christopher Wren. A walk along the riverside embankment will take you to **Cheyne Walk,** a lovely street dating back to the 18th century. Several of its more notable residents—who range from J.M.W. Turner and Henry James to Laurence Olivier and Keith Richards—are commemorated by blue plaques on their former houses.

The **Albert Bridge,** a candy-color Victorian confection of a suspension bridge, provides one of London's great romantic views, especially at night. Nearby is one of London's most exciting shopping streets, the **King's Road** (Charles II's private way from St. James's to Fulham). Leave time to explore the tiny Georgian lanes of pastel-color houses that veer off the King's Road to the north—especially **Jubilee Place** and **Burnsall Street**, leading to the hidden "village square" of **Chelsea Green**. On Saturday there's an excellent farmers' market up from the Saatchi Gallery selling artisanal cheese and chocolates, local oysters, and organic meats, plus stalls serving international food.

Kensington laid its first royal stake when King William III, fed up with the vapors of the Thames, bought a country place there in 1689 and converted it into **Kensington Palace.** Queen Victoria's consort, Prince Albert, added the jewel in the borough's crown when he turned the profits of the Great Exhibition of 1851 into South Kensington's metropolis of museums: **Victoria & Albert Museum (V&A),** the **Science Museum,** and the **Natural History Museum.** His namesakes in the area include **Royal Albert Hall,** with its bas-reliefs that make it resemble a giant, redbrick Wedgwood pot, and the lavish **Albert Memorial.**

Turn into Derry Street or Young Street and enter **Kensington Square,** one of the most complete 17th-century residential squares in London. Holland Park is about ¾ mile farther west; both **Leighton House** and **18 Stafford Terrace**—two of London's most gorgeously decorated Victorian-era houses (the lavish use of Islamic tiles, inlaid mosaics, gilded ceilings, and marble columns make the former into an Arabian Nights fantasy)—are nearby as well.

EXPLORING

Albert Memorial. This gleaming, neo-Gothic shrine to Prince Albert created by Sir Gilbert Scott epitomizes the Victorian era. After Albert's early death from typhoid in 1861, his grieving widow, Queen Victoria, had this elaborate confection erected to the west of where the Great Exhibition had been held a decade before. A 14-foot bronze gilt statue of the prince—depicted thumbing through a catalogue for his Great Exhibition—rests on a 15-foot-high pedestal, along with other statues representing his passions and interests. ⊠ *Kensington Gardens, Hyde Park, Kensington* Ⓜ *South Kensington, High Street Kensington.*

Fodor's Choice
★

18 Stafford Terrace. The home of *Punch* cartoonist Edward Linley Sambourne in the 1870s is filled with delightful Victorian and Edwardian antiques, fabrics, and paintings (as well as several samples of Linley Sambourne's work for *Punch*) and is one of the most charming 19th-century London houses extant—small wonder that it was used in Merchant Ivory's *A Room with a View.* The Italianate house was the scene for society parties when Anne Messel was in residence in the 1940s. This being Kensington, there's inevitably a royal connection: Messel's son, Antony Armstrong-Jones, was married to the late Princess Margaret, and their son has preserved the connection by taking the title Viscount Linley. Admission is by guided tour only. Apart from the 11:15 tour on weekends and all Wednesday tours, these are given by costumed actors. ⊠ *18 Stafford Terr., Kensington* ☏ *0207/602–3316* ⊕ *www.rbkc.gov.uk/subsites/ museums.aspx* ⊒£6 ۞ *Guided tours Wed. 11:15, 2:15, weekends 11:15, 1, 2:15, 3:30. Closed mid-June–mid-Sept.* Ⓜ *High Street Kensington.*

Holland Park. Formerly the grounds of an aristocrat's house and open to the public only since 1952, Holland Park is an often-overlooked gem and possibly London's most romantic park. The notrhern "Wilderness" end offers woodland walks among native and exotic trees first planted in the early 18th century. Foxes, rabbits, and hedgehogs are among the residents The central part of the park is given over to the manicured lawns—still stalked by raucous peacocks—one would expect at a stately home, although Holland House itself, originally built by James I's chancellor and later the site of a 19th-century salon frequented by Byron, Dickens, and Disraeli, was largely destroyed by incendiary bombs in 1940. The east wing was reconstructed and has been incorporated into a youth hostel, while the remains of the front terrace provide an atmospheric backdrop for the open-air performances of the April–September **Holland Park Opera Festival** (☎ *0207/361–3570 box office* ⊕ *www.operahollandpark.com*). The glass-walled Garden Ballroom (every home should have one) is now the **Orangery,** which hosts art exhibitions and other public events, as does the **Ice House,** while an adjoining former granary has become the upmarket Belvedere restaurant. In spring and summer the air is fragrant with aromas from a rose garden, great banks of rhododendrons, and an azalea walk. Garden enthusiasts will also not want to miss the tranquil, traditional **Kyoto Garden,** a legacy of London's 1991 Japan Festival. The southern part of the park is given over to sport: cricket and football pitches, a golf practice area, and tennis courts, and a well-supervised children's Adventure Playground. And don't miss a new addition, the giant outdoor chess set. ⊠ *Holland Park, Holland Park* ☉ *Daily 7:30–30 mins before dusk* Ⓜ *Holland Park, High Street Kensington.*

★ **Kensington Palace.**
See the highlighted listing in this chapter.

Natural History Museum.
Fodor's Choice
★   *See the highlighted listing in this chapter.*

Royal Albert Hall. Its terra-cotta exterior surmounted by a mosaic frieze depicting figures engaged in artistic, scientific, and cultural pursuits, this famously domed, circular 5,223-seat auditorium was made possible by the Victorian public, who donated the money to build it. After funds were diverted toward the Albert Memorial (opposite), more money was raised by selling 999-year leases for 1,276 "Members'" seats at £100 apiece—today a box with five Members' Seats goes for half a million pounds. The notoriously poor acoustics were fixed after a 2004

KENSINGTON PALACE

✉ *The Broad Walk, Kensington Gardens, Kensington* ☎ *0844/482–7799 advance booking, 0844/482-7777 information, 0203/166–6000 from outside U.K.* ⊕ *www.hrp.org.uk* 🎫 *£14.50* ⏰ *Mar.–Sept., daily 10–6; Oct.–Feb., daily 10–5; last admission 1 hr before closing* Ⓜ *Queensway, High Street Kensington.*

TIPS

■ If you also plan to visit the Tower of London, Hampton Court Palace, Banqueting House, or Kew Palace, become a member of Historic Royal Palaces. It costs £43 per person, or £83 for a family, and gives you free entry to all five sites for a year.

■ Picnicking is allowed on the benches in the palace grounds. (You can also picnic anywhere in the adjoining Kensington Gardens.)

■ There's a delightful café in the Orangery, near the Sunken Garden. Built for Queen Anne, it's a great place for formal afternoon tea, although it gets busy during peak hours.

Neither as imposing as Buckingham Palace nor as charming as Hampton Court, Kensington Palace is something of a Royal Family commune, with various close relatives of the Queen occupying large apartments in the private part of the palace. Bought in 1689 by Queen Mary and King William III, it was converted into a palace by Sir Christopher Wren and Nicholas Hawksmoor, and Royals have been in residence ever since. Its most famous resident, Princess Diana, lived here with her sons after her divorce, and this is where Prince William now lives with his wife, Catherine.

On March 2012, the palace unveiled a £12 million refurbishment, with four new "visitor routes," showcasing four famous phases of the palace's history: Queen Victoria (with the theme "love, duty, and loss"); the splendid King's State Apartments, with a peek into the age of George II ("the curious world of the court"); the regal Queen's State Apartments (the private life of Queen Anne); plus a special exhibition of Princess Diana's dresses ("it's not easy being a princess"). There's also a new café, restored garden, and underground visitors' center.

HIGHLIGHTS

In addition, the palace is home to the **Royal Ceremonial Dress Collection,** a collection of 10,000 items that include royal raiments ranging from the elaborate (an 18th-century mantua—a dazzling court dress with a 6-foot-wide skirt) to the downright odd (King George III's socks). Also of special note are the King's Staircase, with its panoramic trompe l'oeil painting, and the King's Gallery, with royal artworks in a jewel-box setting of rich red damask walls, intricate gilding, and a beautiful painted ceiling.

9

Ice-skaters outside the Natural History Museum in South Kensington

renovation and the sight lines are excellent. The RAH hosts everything from pop and classical headliners to Cirque du Soleil, ballet on ice, awards ceremonies, and Sumo wrestling championships, but is best known as the venue for the annual July–September BBC Promenade Concerts—the "Proms"—with bargain-price standing (or promenading, or sitting-on-the-floor) tickets sold on the night of the concert. ⊠ *Kensington Gore, Kensington* ☎ *0845/401–5045 from U.K., 0207/589–8212 from outside U.K.* ⊕ *www.royalalberthall.com* ✉ *Prices vary with event* Ⓜ *South Kensington, High Street Kensington.*

Royal Hospital Chelsea. Charles II founded this hospice for elderly and infirm soldiers in 1682 to reward the troops who had fought for him in the civil wars of 1642–46 and 1648. Charles wisely appointed the great architect Sir Christopher Wren to design this small village of brick and Portland stone set in manicured gardens (which you can visit) surrounding the Figure Court—the figure being a 1682 bronze statue of Charles II dressed as a Roman general—the Great Hall (dining room), and a chapel. The chapel is enhanced by choir stalls created by the great Grinling Gibbons (who made the statue of Charles as well), the Great Hall by Antonio Verrio's vast oil of Charles on horseback, and both are open to the public at certain times during the day. The real attraction, along with the building, is the pensioners themselves. Recognizable by their traditional scarlet frock coats with gold buttons, medals, and tricorne hats, they are all actual veterans, who wear the uniform, and the history it conveys, with a great deal of pride.

Chelsea Flower Show. Also in May (usually the third week), the Chelsea Flower Show (☎ *0844/338–7505 in U.K., 121/767–4063*

NATURAL HISTORY MUSEUM

✉ *Cromwell Rd., South Kensington* ☎ *0207/942–5000* ⊕ *www.nhm.ac.uk* 🎫 *Free (some fees for special exhibitions)* ⊙ *Daily 10–5:50, last admission at 5:30* Ⓜ *South Kensington.*

TIPS

■ "Nature Live" is a program of free, informal talks given by scientists, covering a wildly eclectic range of subjects, usually at 2:30 (and on some days at 12:30) in the David Attenborough Studio in the Darwin Centre.

■ The museum has an outdoor ice-skating rink from November to January, and a popular Christmas fair.

■ Free, daily behind-the-scenes Spirit collection tours of the museum can be booked on the day—although space is limited, so come early. Recommended for children over eight years old.

■ Got kids under seven with you? Check out the museum's free "Explorer Backpacks." They contain a range of activity materials to keep the little ones amused, including a pair of binoculars and an explorer's hat.

The delightfully ornate terra-cotta facade of this enormous Victorian museum is strewn with relief panels depicting living creatures to the left of the entrance and extinct ones to the right (although some species have subsequently changed categories). It's an appropriate design, for within these walls lie more than 70 million different specimens.

Only a small percentage is on public display, but you could still spend a day here and not come close to seeing everything. The museum is full of cutting-edge exhibits, with all the wow-power and interactives necessary to secure interest from younger visitors.

HIGHLIGHTS

A giant diplodocus skeleton dominates the vaulted, cathedral-like entrance hall, affording you perhaps the most irresistible photo opportunity in the building. It's just a cast, but the **Dinosaur Gallery** (Gallery 21) contains plenty of real-life dino bones, fossils—and some extremely long teeth.

You'll also come face to face with a giant animatronic Tyrannosaurus rex—who is programmed to sense when human prey is near and "respond" in character. When he does, you can hear the shrieks of fear and delight all the way across the room.

A dizzyingly tall escalator takes you into a giant globe in the **Earth Galleries,** where there's a choice of levels—and Earth surfaces—to explore. Don't leave without checking out the earthquake simulation in Gallery 61.

The centerpiece of a major expansion is the **Darwin Centre,** which houses some of the (literally) millions of items they don't have room to display, including "Archie," a 28.3-foot giant squid.

9

Historic Plaque Hunt

CLOSE UP

As you wander around London, you'll see lots of small blue, circular plaques on the sides and facades of buildings, describing which famous, infamous, or obscure but brilliant person once lived there. The first was placed outside Lord Byron's birthplace (now no more) by the Royal Society of Arts. There are about 700 blue plaques, erected by different bodies—you may even find some green ones that originated from Westminster City Council—but English Heritage now maintains the responsibility, and if you want to find out the latest, check the website ⊕ *www. english-heritage.org.uk. Below are some of the highlights:*

James Barrie (✉ 100 Bayswater Rd., Bayswater); **Frederic Chopin** (✉ 4 St. James's Pl., St. James's); **Sir Winston Churchill** (✉ 28 Hyde Park Gate, Kensington Gore); **Captain James Cook** (✉ 88 Mile End Rd., Tower Hamlets); **T.S. Eliot** (✉ 3 Kensington Court Gardens, Kensington); **Benjamin Franklin** (✉ 36 Craven St., Westminster); **Mahatma Gandhi** (✉ *20 Baron's Court Rd., West Kensington*); **George Frederic Handel** and **Jimi Hendrix** (✉ 23 Brook St., Mayfair); **Alfred Hitchcock** (✉ *153 Cromwell Rd., Earl's Court*); **Karl Marx** (✉ 28 Dean St., Soho); **Wolfgang Amadeus Mozart** (✉ 180 Ebury St., Pimlico); **Horatio Nelson** (✉ 103 New Bond St., Mayfair); **Sir Isaac Newton** (✉ 87 Jermyn St., St. James's); **Florence Nightingale** (✉ 10 South St., Mayfair); **George Bernard Shaw** (✉ 29 Fitzroy Sq., Fitzrovia); **Percy Bysshe Shelley** (✉ 15 Poland St., Soho); **Mark Twain** (✉ 23 Tedworth Sq., Chelsea); **H.G. Wells** (✉ 13 Hanover Terr., Regent's Park); **Oscar Wilde** (✉ 34 Tite St., Chelsea); **William Butler Yeats** (✉ 23 Fitzroy Rd., Primrose Hill).

from outside U.K.) ⊕ www.rhs.org.uk), the year's highlight for thousands of garden-obsessed Brits, is held here. Run by the Royal Horticultural Society, this mammoth event takes up vast acreage, and the surrounding streets throng with visitors. ✉ *Royal Hospital Rd., Chelsea* ☎ *020/7881–5298* ⊕ *www.chelsea-pensioners.org.uk* ✒ *Free* ☉ *Museum open weekdays 10–noon and 2–4, Sun. 2–4. Closed weekends, also closed holidays and for special events. Grounds, Chapel, Courts, and Great Hall open Mon.–Sat. 10–noon and 2–4.* Ⓜ *Sloane Sq.*

Saatchi Gallery. Charles Saatchi made his fortune building an advertising empire that successfully "rebranded" Margaret Thatcher's Conservative Party but then went on to find worldwide fame as Britain's most highly regarded collector of contemporary (and often scandalous) art. The result is this museum—its third in 10 years—located at the very imposing Duke of York's HQ, just off Chelsea's King's Road. Built in 1803, its suitably grand period exterior belies its imaginatively restored modern interior, which was transformed into 14 gallery exhibition spaces of varying size and shape. Unlike Tate Modern, there is no permanent collection; instead the galleries are given over to a single exhibition that normally runs for about three months—they are cutting-edge and excellent. There's also a nifty café (open late). ✉ *Duke of York's HQ Bldg., King's Rd., Chelsea* ☎ *020/7811–3085* ⊕ *www.saatchigallery. com* ✒ *Free* ☉ *Daily 10–6* Ⓜ *Sloane Sq.*

★ **Science Museum.** One of the three great South Kensington museums, this stands next to the Natural History Museum in a far plainer building. It has loads of hands-on painlessly educational exhibits, with entire schools of children apparently decanted inside to interact with them. Highlights include the *Puffing Billy,* the oldest steam locomotive in the world and the actual *Apollo 10* capsule, plus six floors devoted many subjects, from the history of flight to steam power. Also here are a 450-seat IMAX cinema and the Legend of Apollo, an advanced motion simulator that combines seat vibration with other technical gizmos to simulate the experience of a moon landing. ■TIP→ If you're a family of at least five, you might be able to get a place on one of the popular new Science Night sleepovers by booking well in advance. Aimed at kids 8–11 years old, these nighttime science workshops offer the chance to camp out in one of the galleries, and include a free IMAX show the next morning. Check the website for details. ⊠ *Exhibition Rd., South Kensington* ☎ *0870/870–4868* ⊕ *www.sciencemuseum.org.uk* ⊠ *Free, charge for cinema shows and special exhibitions* ⊙ *Daily 10–6, 10–7 during school holidays (check website)* Ⓜ *South Kensington.*

> **ARTISTIC CHELSEA**
>
> Artists and writers flocked to the area in the 19th century, establishing a creative colony in Cheyne Walk; at one time Turner, Whistler, John Singer Sargent, Dante Gabriel Rossetti, and Oscar Wilde were residents. In the 1960s it was the turn of the Rolling Stones and the Beatles; in the 1970s Bob Marley wrote "I Shot the Sheriff" in a flat off Cheyne Walk. It's now one of London's most expensive streets, completely unaffordable for latter-day Bob Marleys.

Serpentine Gallery. Overlooking the large Serpentine stream that winds its way through Hyde Park, this small brick building set in Kensington Gardens—once a favorite cause of Princess Diana—is one of London's foremost showcases for contemporary art, and has featured exhibitions by lumiaries such as Damien Hirst, Louise Bourgeois, John Currin, and Gerhard Richter. From May through September, check out the annually redesigned Serpentine pavilion (Frank Gehry, Daniel Liebeskind, and Jean Nouvel have been among the designers). ⊠ *Kensington Gardens, Kensington* ☎ *0207/402–6075* ⊕ *www.serpentinegallery.org* ⊠ *Free* ⊙ *Daily 10–6* Ⓜ *Lancaster Gate, Knightsbridge, South Kensington.*

☺ **Victoria & Albert Museum.**

Fodor's Choice
★ *See the highlighted listing in this chapter.*

KNIGHTSBRIDGE

There's no getting away from it. London's wealthiest enclave (not many other neighborhoods are plagued with street racers in Maseratis) is shop-'til-you-drop territory of the highest order. With two world-famous department stores, **Harrods** and **Harvey Nichols,** a few hundred yards apart, and every bit of space between and around taken up with designer boutiques, chain stores, and jewelers, it's hard to imagine why anyone who doesn't like shopping would even think of coming here.

VICTORIA & ALBERT MUSEUM

✉ Cromwell Rd., South Kensington ☎ 020/7942–2000
⊕ www.vam.ac.uk ☞ Free
⊙ Sat.–Tues. 10–5:45, Fri. 10–10 Ⓜ South Kensington.

TIPS

■ The V&A is a tricky building to navigate, so be sure to use the free map.

■ You could take a free one-hour tour at 10:30, 11:30, 12:30, 1:30, 2:30, or 3:30. There are also tours devoted just to the British Galleries at 12:30 and 2:30. Occasional public lectures during the week are delivered by visiting bigwigs from the art and fashion worlds (prices vary.) There are free lectures throughout the week given by museum staff.

■ Whatever time you visit, the spectacular sculpture hall will be filled with artists, both amateur and professional, sketching the myriad artworks on display there. Don't be shy; bring a pad and join in.

■ Although the permanent collection is free, the V&A also hosts high-profile special exhibitions that run for up to three months (from £5).

Always referred to as the V&A, this huge museum is devoted to the applied arts of all disciplines, all periods, and all nationalities. Full of innovation, it's a wonderful, generous place in which to to get lost. First opened as the South Kensington Museum in 1857, it was renamed in 1899 in honor of Queen Victoria's late husband and has since grown to become one of the country's best-loved cultural institutions.

Many collections at the V&A are presented not by period but by category—textiles, sculpture, jewelry, and so on. Nowhere is the benefit of this more apparent than in the **Fashion Gallery** (Room 40), where formal 18th-century court dresses are displayed alongside the haute couture styles of contemporary designers, creating an arresting sense of visual continuity.

The **British Galleries** (rooms 52–58), devoted to British art and design from 1500 to 1760, are full of beautiful diversions—among them the Great Bed of Ware (immortalized in Shakespeare's *Twelfth Night*). Here, a series of actual rooms have been painstakingly reconstructed piece by piece after being rescued from historic buildings. These include an ornate music room and the Henrietta St. Room, a breathtakingly serene parlor dating from 1722.

The **Asian Galleries** (rooms 44–47) are full of treasures, but among the most striking items on display is a remarkable collection of ornate samurai armor in the **Japanese Gallery** (Room 44). There are also galleries devoted to China, Korea, and the Islamic Middle East. Several new galleries opened in 2009: a Buddhist Sculpture gallery, a new Ceramics gallery, and a Medieval and Renaissance gallery, which has the largest collection of works from the period outside of Italy.

World-famous Harrods has been attracting shoppers since 1834.

If the department stores seem overwhelming, **Beauchamp Place** (pronounced "Beecham") is a good tonic. It's lined with equally chic and expensive boutiques, but they tend to be smaller, more personal, and less hectic. Nearby Sloane Street is lined with top-end designer boutiques such as Prada, Dior, and Tods.

Another place to find peace and quiet is a divinely peaceful stroll in fashionable Belgravia, one of the most gorgeous set-pieces of urban 19th-century planning. Street after street is lined with grand white terraces of aristocratic town houses, still part of the Grosvenor estate, and owned by the Dukes of Westminster. Many are leased to embassies, but a remarkable number around **Lowndes Square, Belgrave Square,** and **Eaton Square** remain homes of the discreet, private wealthy and outright super-rich. Some people call the area near **Elizabeth Street** Belgravia, others Pimlico–Victoria. Either way, now that you've had a break, it's time to shop again, and this street is the place to be.

EXPLORING

Belgrave Square. This is the heart of Belgravia, once the epicenter of posh London though now mostly occupied by organizations, embassies, and the international rich. The square and the streets leading off it share a remarkably consistent stately yet elegant architectural style thanks to all being part of a Regency redevelopment scheme commissioned by the Duke of Westminster and designed by Thomas Cubitt with George Basevi. The grand, porticoed mansions were snapped up by aristocrats and politicians due to their proximity to Buckingham Palace just around the corner, and still command record prices on the rare occasion when they come onto the market. The private garden in the center is open to the public once a year (see *www.opensquares.org*). Walk down Belgrave Place toward Eaton Place and you pass two of Belgravia's most beautiful mews: Eaton Mews North and Eccleston Mews, both fronted by grand rusticated entrances right out of a 19th-century engraving. ■ TIP➔ Traffic can really whip around Belgrave Square, so be careful. ✉ *Belgrave Sq., Belgravia* Ⓜ *Hyde Park Corner.*

Harrods. Just in case you don't notice its 4.5-acre bulk, this legendary shopping destination frames its domed terra-cotta exterior in thousands of small white lights each night. The store's motto is *Omnia, omnibus, ubique* (Everything, for everybody, everywhere), and, if the days when it provided an alligator as a Christmas gift for Noel Coward or embalming services to the body of Sigmund Freud are long gone, you can still find pretty much every luxury brand under the sun here, along with esoteric services like a custom-made Madame Tussaud's waxwork, should you be in the market for one. Don't miss the extravagant Food Hall, with its stunning Edwardian Rococo ceilings, art deco marble pillars and art nouveau mouldings and ceramic tiles. Repair to the excellent fifth-floor Urban Retreat spa if it all gets to be too much. *For more on Harrods, see* ⇨ *Shopping, Chapter 18.* ✉ *87–135 Brompton Rd., Knightsbridge* ☎ *020/7730–1234* ⊕ *www.harrods.com* ☉ *Mon.–Sat. 10–8, Sun. 11:30–6* Ⓜ *Knightsbridge.*

Harvey Nichols. Tourists flock to Harrods, but Harvey Nicks (as it's familiarly known to its well-heeled fashionista aficionados) is where in-the-know locals shop. The Fifth Floor Restaurant, Café, and Champagne Bar offer outstanding views and stylish refreshments that attract an equally stylish clientele. *For more on Harvey Nichols, see* ⇨ *Shopping, Chapter 18.* ✉ *109–125 Knightsbridge, Knightsbridge* ☎ *020/7235–5000* ⊕ *www.harveynichols.com* ☉ *Mon.–Sat. 10–8, Sun. 11:30–6* Ⓜ *Knightsbridge.*

Leighton House Museum. Leading Victorian artist Frederic, Lord Leighton lived and worked in this building on the edge of Holland Park, spending 30 years (and quite a bit of money) transforming it into an opulent "private palace of art" infused with an orientalist aesthetic sensibility. The interior is a sumptuous Arabian Nights fantasy, with walls lined in peacock blue tiles designed by Leighton's friend, the ceramic artist William de Morgan, and beautiful mosaic wall panels and floors, marble pillars, and gilded ceilings. The centerpiece is the Arab Hall, its marble walls adorned with even more intricate murals made from 16th- and 17th-century ceramic tiles imported from Syria, Turkey, and Iran, surmounted by a domed ceiling covered in gold leaf with a gold mosaic frieze running underneath. You can also visit Leighton's studio, with its huge north window and dome, and the house is filled with several of his paintings along with works by other Pre-Raphaelites. There are free tours of the house on Wednesday at 3. ✉ *12 Holland Park Rd., Holland Park* ☎ *020/7332–3316* ⊕ *www.rbkc.gov.uk* ☉ *Wed.–Mon. 10–5:30* Ⓜ *Holland Park.*

Notting Hill and Bayswater

WORD OF MOUTH

"Early in the AM on Saturday is great for the Portobello Road Market—by mid-morning it is a zoo." —janisj

"But if you're not that interested in the market, the area of Westbourne Grove/Ledbury Road has some very nice shops and restaurants. Not busy, even on a Saturday." —tulips

GETTING ORIENTED

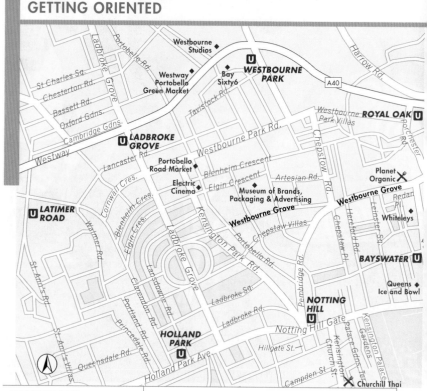

GETTING THERE

For Portobello Market and environs, the best Tube stops are Ladbroke Grove and Westbourne Park (Hammersmith and City lines); ask for directions when you emerge. The Notting Hill stop on the District, Circle, and Central lines enables you to walk the length of Portobello Road on a downhill gradient.

A GOOD WALK

To gape at Notting Hill's grandest houses, stroll over to Lansdowne Road, Lansdowne Crescent, and Lansdowne Square—two blocks west of Kensington Park Row.

TOP REASONS TO GO

Find a bargain on Portobello Road: Seek and ye shall find; go early-morning antiques hunting at London's best and most famous market on Saturday, or come during the week for a leisurely browse.

Shop for vintage clothing: In addition to the Portobello market, you can search for vintage designer pieces at Notting Hill's numerous secondhand and retro clothing stores.

See and be seen on Westbourne Grove: Watch the locals stroll the streets as if they were one big catwalk, then drop in for lunch at one of the Grove's colorful ethnic restaurants.

Catch a film at the Electric Cinema: Recline on a two-seater leather sofa, beer and bar snacks in hand, at this restored early-20th-century theater—then splurge for dinner at its fantastic Electric Brasserie.

Become a member of café society: There are few better places to study the passing parade than from a sidewalk café seat here.

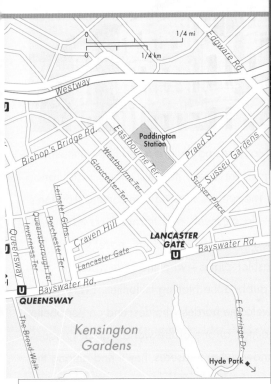

MAKING THE MOST OF YOUR TIME

Saturday is Notting Hill and Portobello Road's most fun and frenetic day. You could easily spend the whole day shopping, eating, and drinking here.

The market can get crowded by noon in warm weather so come early if you are serious about shopping.

You may prefer to start at the end of Portobello Road and work backward, using the parks for relaxation after your shopping exertions. Do the same on Friday if you're a flea-market fan.

Sunday, the Hyde Park and Kensington Gardens railings all along Bayswater Road are lined with artists peddling their (often dubious) work, which may slow your progress.

This is also the day when the well-heeled locals are out in force, filling the pubs at lunchtime or hitting the parks with their kids if it's sunny.

FEELING PECKISH?

Churchill Thai Kitchen. The triumphant image of Winston Churchill on the sign outside speaks to the eccentric, cult appeal of **Churchill Thai Kitchen**, attached to a traditional pub swamped in Churchill memorabilia. It's so popular that diners are usually given an hour in which to finish their meal, but the food is delicious—and at around £7 per dish, a real bargain for this part of town. ⊠ *119 Kensington Church St., Notting Hill* ☎ *020/7792–1246.*

Planet Organic. A haven for the health conscious, **Planet Organic** serves upscale vegetarian meals at nongourmet prices, with a wide selection of specials to take out. ⊠ *42 Westbourne Grove, Bayswater* ☎ *020/7727–2227.*

SAFETY

At night, be wary of straying too far off the main streets, as it gets "edgier" toward Ladbroke Grove's high-rise estates and surrounding areas. The Notting Hill Carnival is colorful but attracts massive crowds—and crime.

10

Sightseeing
★★
Nightlife
★★★
Dining
★★★
Lodging
★★★
Shopping
★★★★

Notting Hill is a trendsetting square mile full of multiethnicity, music, magnificent street markets, bars, restaurants, and chic shops. The area is studded with some of London's most handsome old crescents and terraces, now home to those well-dressed residents—musicians, novelists, film-biz workers, and fashion-plates—who the style-watching London media has dubbed the Notting Hillbillies. Every weekend, the locals welcome hordes who descend on Portobello Road to go "flea-ing" at one of the world's great antiques markets. Who knows what treasures they'll find among the acres of bric-a-brac and curios?

Updated by
Jack Jewers

Notting Hill, as we know it, was born in the 1840s when the wealthy Ladbroke family laid out a small suburb to the west of London. Before then the terrain had been known as "the Potteries and the Piggeries," in honor of its two industries: ceramics and pig farming.

During the 1980s, Notting Hill was quickly transforming from poverty-stricken backwater to super-trendy enclave. By the early 2000s the neighborhood was clearly established as chic—helped massively by the Julia Roberts hit movie that bore its name. For the Notting Hill of the silver screen, head straight for **Westbourne Grove,** replete with quirky boutiques and charity shops laden with the castoffs from wealthy residents. (Don't forget to check out the Travel Bookshop on Blenheim Crescent—Hugh Grant is the proprietor in the movie). This is also where you'll find a smattering of boutique art galleries, such as **England and Co.,** which welcome browsers as much as serious collectors.

The whole area has mushroomed around the **Portobello Road,** with the beautifully restored early-20th-century **Electric Cinema** at No. 191. The famous Saturday antiques market and shops are at the southern end; **Westway Portobello Green Market,** under the Westway overpass, is occupied by bric-a-brac, secondhand threads, and clothes and accessories by young, up-and-coming designers.

In Bayswater, the main thoroughfare of **Queensway** is a rather peculiar, cosmopolitan street of late-night cafés and restaurants, multiethnic food shops, and the **Whiteleys** shopping-and-movie mall. Nearby **Paddington station**, one of London's most handsome railway terminuses, is the namesake for the world's most famous marmalade fan: Paddington Bear.

NOTTING HILL CARNIVAL

Loud, colorful, and very crowded, the annual Carnival (⊕ *www. nottinghillcarnival.biz*) was started by Afro-Caribbean immigrants in the 1960s. Held the last weekend in August, it attracts hundreds of thousands of visitors, mostly young and raucous. Very high crime rates make this a no-no for families—even on "family day." Be careful.

EXPLORING

England & Co. This small gallery specializes in new and up-and-coming contemporary artists, presenting their work alongside that of more established names in the modern art world, from Britain and overseas. Exhibitions change regularly, but there's always a good selection of new and interesting work on display, from artists such as Grayson Perry, Peter Blake, and Gillian Ayres. The gallery is also a major dealer in contemporary art, so you might even go home with one of the exhibits—if you're feeling flush. ⊠ *215 Westbourne Grove, Bayswater* ☎ *020 7221–0417* ⊕ *www.englandgallery.com* Ⓜ *Notting Hill Gate.*

☾ **Hyde Park and Kensington Gardens.**

★ *See the highlighted listing in this chapter.*

☾ **Museum of Brands, Packaging and Advertising.** This extraordinary little museum does exactly what it says on the package. The massive collection of toys, fashion, food wrappers, advertising, and the assorted detritus of everyday life is from all corners of the globe and presents a fascinating and eccentric chronicle of how consumer culture has developed since the Victorian age. ⊠ *2 Colville Mews, Lonsdale Rd., Notting Hill* ☎ *020/7908–0880* ⊕ *www.museumofbrands.com* ☒ *£6.50* ☾ *Tues.–Sat. 10–6, Sun. 11–5; last entry 45 mins before closing. Closed during Notting Hill Carnival* Ⓜ *Notting Hill.*

★ **Portobello Road.** Tempted by tassels, looking for a 19th-century snuff spoon, on the hunt for a Georgian objet d'art? Fancy an original sixties minidress, or a dashingly deco party frock? Then head to Portobello Road, world famous for its Saturday antiques market. Arrive at about 9 am to find the real treasures-in-the-trash; after 10, the crowds pack in wall-to-wall. Actually, the Portobello Market is three markets: Antiques, "fruit and veg," and a flea market. Portobello Road begins at Notting Hill Gate, though the antiques stalls start a couple of blocks north, around Chepstow Villas. Lining the sloping street are also dozens of antiques shops and indoor markets, open most days—in fact,

10

Continued on page 184

HYDE PARK AND KENSINGTON GARDENS

Every year millions of visitors descend on the royal parks of Hyde Park and Kensington Gardens, which sit side by side and roll out over 625 acres of grassy expanses that provide much-craved-for respite from London's frenetic pace. The two parks incorporate formal gardens, fountains, sports fields, great picnic spots, shady clusters of ancient trees, and even an outdoor swimming pool.

10

Although it's probably been centuries since any major royal had a casual stroll here—you're more likely to bump into Chris Martin and Gwyneth Paltrow than Her Royal Highness these days—the parks remain the property of the Crown, which saved them from being devoured by the city's late-18th-century growth spurt.

Today the luxury of such wide open spaces continues to be appreciated by the Londoners who steal into the parks before work for a session of tai chi, say, or on weekends when the sun is shining. Simply sitting back in a hired deck chair or strolling through the varied terrain is one of the most enjoyable ways to spend time here.

KENSINGTON GARDENS

At the end of the 17th century, William III moved his court to the impeccably kept green space that is now **Kensington Gardens**. He was attracted to the location for its clean air and tranquillity and subsequently commissioned Sir Christopher Wren to overhaul the original redbrick building, resulting in the splendid **Kensington Palace**.

To the north of the palace complex is the early-20th-century **Sunken Garden**, complete with a living tunnel of lime trees (i.e., linden trees) and golden laburnum.

On western side of the **Long Water** is George Frampton's 1912 *Peter Pan*, a bronze of the boy who lived on an island in the Serpentine and never grew up and whose creator, J.M. Barrie, lived at 100 Bayswater Road, not 500 yards from here.

Back toward Kensington Palace, at the intersection of several paths, is George Frederick Watts's 1904 bronze of a muscle-bound horse and rider, entitled **Physical Energy**. The **Round Pond** is a magnet for model-boat enthusiasts and duck feeders.

Near the Broad Walk, toward Black Lion Gate, is the **Diana Princess of Wales**

Afternoon tea taken at the Orangery, a short walk from the Sunken Garden on the palace grounds, is a quintessentially English experience.

Memorial Playground, an enclosed space with specially designed structures and areas on the theme of Barrie's Neverland. Hook's ship, crocodiles, "jungles" of foliage, and islands of sand provide a fantasy land for kids—more than 70,000 visit every year. Just outside its bounds is Ivor Innes's *Elfin Oak*, the remains of a tree carved with scores of tiny woodland creatures.

One of the park's most striking monuments is the **Albert Memorial**. This Victorian high-Gothic celebration of Prince Albert is

adorned with marble statues representing his interests and amusements.

Diminutive as it may be, the **Serpentine Gallery** has not been afraid of courting controversy with its temporary exhibitions of challenging contemporary works.

Hyde Park was once the hunting ground of King Henry VIII. This stout, bawdy royal more or less stole Hyde Park, along with the smaller St. James's and Green parks, from the monks of Westminster in 1536. The public wasn't to be granted access

HYDE PARK

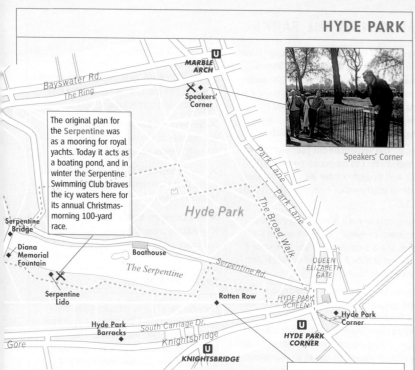

Speakers' Corner

The original plan for the **Serpentine** was as a mooring for royal yachts. Today it acts as a boating pond, and in winter the Serpentine Swimming Club braves the icy waters here for its annual Christmas-morning 100-yard race.

Rotten Row was the first artificially lit highway in Britain. In the late 17th century, William III was concerned that his walk to from Kensington Palace to St. James's Park was too dangerous, so he ordered 300 lamps to be placed along the route.

to Hyde Park's delights until James I came to the throne and opened up limited parts to "respectably dressed" plebeians.

It was Charles I, in the 1700s, however, who was to shape the Hyde Park that visitors see today. Once he had created **the Ring** (North Carriage Drive), which forms a curve north of the **Serpentine** and boathouses, Charles allowed the general public to roam free. During the Great Plague of 1665, East Enders and City dwellers fled to the park, seeking refuge from the black bilious disease.

The **Serpentine Bridge**, built in 1826 by George Rennie, marks the boundary between Hyde Park and Kensington Gardens. **Rotten Row**, a corruption of the French *route de roi* (king's road), runs along the southeastern edge of Hyde Park and is still used by the Household Cavalry, who live at the **Hyde Park Barracks**—a high-rise and a long, low, red block—to the left. This is where the brigade that mounts the guard at Buckingham Palace resides; you can see them at about 10:30 am, as they leave to perform their duty in full regalia, or await the return of the guard about noon.

On the south side of the 1930s **Serpentine Lido** (open to swimmers from June to September) is the £3.6 million oval **Diana Memorial Fountain**.

Ever since the 1827 legislation of public assembly, **Speakers' Corner** near Marble Arch has provided an outlet for political debate: on Sundays, it's a spectacle of vehement, sometimes comical, and always entertaining orators.

10

ENJOYING THE PARKS

Ride. **Hyde Park Riding Stables** keeps horses for hacking the sand tracks. Group lessons (usually just a few people) are £64 per person per hour. Private lessons are £89 Tuesday–Friday, £99 on weekends. ⊠ 63 Bathurst Mews, Bayswater W2 ☎ 020/7723–2813 ⊕ www.hydeparkstables.com Ⓤ Lancaster Gate.

Row. **The Serpentine** has paddleboats and rowboats for £10 per person per hour, kids £5, April through October from 10 am to dusk, later in good weather in summer. ☎ 020/7262–1330.

Run. You can run a **4-mi route** around the perimeter of Hyde Park and Kensington Gardens or a **2½-mi route** in Hyde Park alone if you start at Hyde Park Corner or Marble Arch and encircle the Serpentine.

Skate. On Friday, skaters of intermediate ability and upward meet at 8 pm at the Duke of Wellington Arch, Hyde Park Corner, for the **Friday Night Skate,** an enthusiastic two-hour mass skating session, complete with music and whistles. If you're a bit unsure on your wheels, arrive at 6:30 pm for the free lesson on how to break and turn. The **Sunday Rollerstroll,** a more laid-back version of the same thing, runs on Sunday afternoons; meet at 2 pm on the east side of Serpentine Road ⊕ www.thefns.com Ⓤ Hyde Park Corner.

Swim. **Serpentine Lido** is technically a beach on a lake, but a hot day in Hyde Park is surreally reminiscent of the seaside. There are changing facilities, and the swimming section is chlorinated. There is also a paddling pool, sandpit, and kids' entertainer in the afternoons. It's open daily from June through September, 10–6; admission £4, ☎ 020/7706–3422 ⊕ www.royalparks.org.uk Ⓤ Knightsbridge.

WHERE TO REFUEL

✗ The **Lido Café,** near the Diana Memorial Fountain, has plenty of seating with views across the Serpentine Lake.

✗ **Serpentine Bar and Kitchen** on the eastern side of the lake, is a good pit stop for tasty snacks, salads, and sandwiches.

✗ The **Broadwalk Café & Playcafe** next to the Diana Memorial Playground has a children's menu.

✗ The **Orangery** beside Kensington Palace is a distinctly more grown-up affair for tea and cakes.

SPEAKERS' CORNER

Once the site of public executions and the Tyburn hanging trees, the corner of Hyde Park at Cumberland Gate and Park Lane now harbors one of London's most public spectacles: Speakers' Corner. This has been a place of assembly and vitriolic outpourings and debates since the mid-19th century. The pageant of free speech takes place every Sunday afternoon.

Anyone is welcome to mount a soapbox and declaim upon any topic, which makes for an irresistible showcase of eccentricity—one such being the (now-deceased) Protein Man. Wearing his publicity board, the Protein Man proclaimed that the eating of meat, cheese, and peanuts led to uncontrollable acts of passion that would destroy Western civilization. The pamphlets he sold for four decades are now collector's items. Other more strait-laced campaigns have been launched here by the Chartists, the Reform League, the May Day demonstrators, and the Suffragettes.

PRACTICAL INFO

ADMISSION: Free for both parks

HOURS: Kensington Gardens 6 am–dusk; Hyde Park 5 am–midnight

CONTACT INFO: ☎ 030/0061–2000, ⊕ www.royalparks.gov.uk

GETTING HERE: Ⓤ Kensington Gardens: Kensington High Street, Queensway, Lancaster Gate, South Kensington. **Hyde Park:** Hyde Park Corner, Knightsbridge, Lancaster Gate, Marble Arch

EVENTS: Major events, such as rock concerts and festivals, road races, and talks, are regular features of the parks' calendar; check online for what's on during your visit.

Each summer, a different modern architect designs an outdoor pavilion for the contemporary Serpentine Gallery, the venue for outdoor film screenings, readings, and other such cultural soirees.

Every June or July, Hyde Park hosts The Wireless, one of the U.K.'s biggest music festivals. It's held over a weekend, on several stages, and attracts some of the biggest global names in pop, indie, and rock.

(left) Horseback riding, Hyde Park

(top) The Fountains, Kensington Gardens

(bottom) Both parks are lovely year-round, but spring blooms are spectacular.

TOURS: There are **themed guided walks** about once a month, usually on Thursday or Friday afternoons. They are free but must be booked in advance. Check online or call the park offices for dates and details.

A 45-minute tour (£6) of the **Albert Memorial** is available. It's held at 2 and 3 pm on the first Sunday of the month from March to December. For information call ☎ 020/7495–0916.

Kensington Palace reopened March 2012 after a vast refurbishment, with new "visitor routes" touting the palace's famous residents, from Queen Anne to Princess Diana. Hours are March to September, daily, from 10 to 6 and October to February from 10 to 5. For tickets £15 and information call ☎ 0844/482–7777 or visit ⊕ www.hrp.org.uk.

serious collectors will want to do Portobello on a weekday, when they can explore the 90-some antiques and art stores in relative peace. Where the road levels off, around Elgin Crescent, youth culture and a vibrant neighborhood life kicks in, with all manner of interesting small stores and restaurants interspersed with the fruit-and-vegetable market. This continues to the Westway overpass ("flyover" in British), where on Friday and Saturday you'll find London's best flea market—a ragtag of high-class, vintage, antique, and secondhand clothing, together with jewelry and assorted junk. There's a strong West Indian flavor to Notting Hill, with a Trinidad-style Carnival centered along Portobello Road on the August bank-holiday weekend. *For more on Portobello Road, see ⇨ Shopping, Chapter 18.* ⊕ *www.portobelloroad.co.uk* Ⓜ *Notting Hill Gate, Ladbroke Grove.*

Regent's Park and Hampstead

WORD OF MOUTH

"Abbey Road? An unforgettable day out. Taking a detour to just see a building and a zebra crossing is no way worth it. However, to see history and what it stands for: definitely worth it!" —AR

"Oh, go for it! We did it and took the requisite photos. It was a lotta fun, and we had great photos to send out with our Christmas cards that year." —Canterbury

GETTING ORIENTED

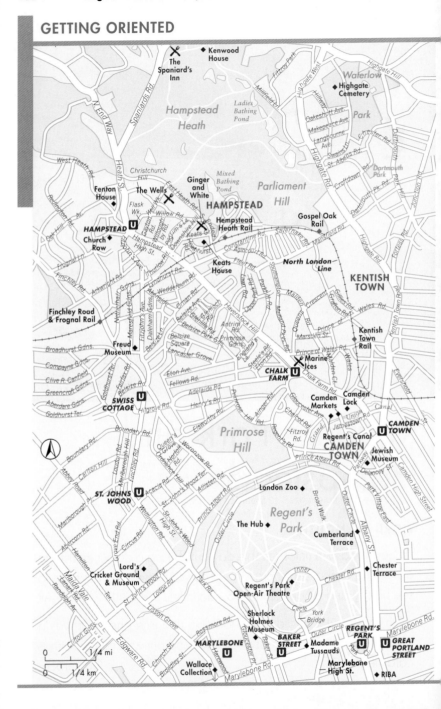

TOP REASONS TO GO

Enjoy the gilt at the Wallace Collection: Home to fabulous Fragonards and gilded French furniture, this 18th-century mansion is a homage to prerevolutionary France.

Ramble across Hampstead Heath: Londoners adore the Heath for its wild, unkempt beauty—and the unparalleled views across the city.

Listen to your muse at Keats House: Stroll through the very garden where the great Romantic strolled while writing "Ode to a Nightingale."

Marvel at London's grandest Regency terraces: With their Wedgwood-blue pediments, snow-white statuary, and porticos of Ionic columns, Nash's 18th-century mansions make a splendid backdrop for Regent's Park.

Strawberry Beatles Forever!: For countless Beatlemaniacs and baby boomers, a visit to No. 3 Abbey Road is an unforgettable experience.

FEELING PECKISH?

Ginger and White. Family-friendly and thoroughly modern, Ginger and White is a delightful fusion of continental-style café and traditional British coffee shop—all bound up with a sophisticated Hampstead vibe. ⊠ *9 South End Rd., Hampstead* ☎ *020/7431–9098* ⊕ *www.gingerandwhite.com.*

Marine Ices. Marine Ices, near the Camden Lock market, has some of London's best ice cream, while the indoor Italian restaurant section lures diners. ⊠ *8 Haverstock Hill, Camden Town* ☎ *020/7482–9003* ⊕ *www.marineices.co.uk.*

SAFETY

It's best to stay out of Hampstead Heath and Regent's Park proper at night unless there's an event taking place; both are perfectly safe during the day. Also to be avoided after dark: the Heath, Camden High Street, and the Canal towpath.

GETTING THERE

Reaching Hampstead by Tube is as easy as it looks: Simply take the Edgware branch of the Northern line to Hampstead station, or the overground North London line to Hampstead Heath. The south side of Hampstead Heath can also be reached by the Gospel Oak station on the North London line. To get to Regent's Park, take the Bakerloo line to Regent's Park Tube station or, for Primrose Hill, the Chalk Farm stop on the Northern line.

MAKING THE MOST OF YOUR TIME

Depending on your pace and inclination, Marylebone, Regent's Park, and Hampstead can realistically be covered in a day. It might be best to spend the morning in Hampstead, with at least a brief foray onto the Heath, then head south toward Regent's Park and Marylebone in the afternoon so that you're closer to central London come nightfall, if that is where your hotel is located. If you have time, you may want to return to Hampstead another day for a longer walk across the Heath.

A GOOD WALK

These are two of the most walkable districts in London. Everything from Hampstead "village" to Regent's Park (and its outlying terraced streets) are best explored on foot—even Hampstead Heath has marked footpaths.

Sightseeing
★★★★
Nightlife
★★★
Dining
★★
Lodging
★★
Shopping
★★★

As civilized as a Gainsborough landscape, Regent's Park and Hampstead contain some of the prettiest and most aristocratic architecture that London has to offer. The city becomes noticeably calmer and greener as you head north from Oxford Street, past the newly chic shopping streets of Marylebone and immensely regal mansions that encircle Regent's Park, up to the well-tended lawns of Primrose Hill (no wonder Madonna and Gwyneth Paltrow chose to live here) and the handsome Georgian streets of Hampstead. All in all, this area will provide a taste of how laid-back (moneyed) Londoners can be.

Updated by
Jack Jewers

Rather like the Left Bank in Paris or Greenwich Village in New York, the residential areas north of Regent's Park have long been associated with artists and writers—even though it's been a long time since most of them could afford to live here. John Keats (1795–1821) lived in **Hampstead** as a virtual pauper; you'll find **Keats House**, where the poet wrote his most famous work, among the homes of artistic types who these days are more likely to be millionaire film stars or musicians. However the neighborhood still retains a gorgeously bohemian vibe, which all but shimmers through the moneyed haze of swank boutiques and artisan food stores. Perhaps it's something to do with the high concentration of wonderful, atmospheric pubs.

Also hidden among Hampstead's winding streets are **Fenton House,** a Georgian town house with a lovely walled garden, and **Kenwood House,** with its remarkable art collection. Overlooking it all is **Hampstead Heath** (known locally as just "The Heath"), a huge, wild urban park with great views across London—although **Primrose Hill** has perhaps the most spectacular view you can find without getting onto the London Eye.

A BRIEF HISTORY

The well-worn, but entirely accurate cliché about the enclaves north of Regent's Park (Primrose Hill, Belsize Park, and Hampstead) is that several of the residents claim to be artists—and yet the cost of a coffee at a café along Regent's Park Road will run you as much as, if not more than, one in central London. In the last decade, real estate prices have skyrocketed, and the elephants of the London Zoo now count some of the best-dressed folks in town as their neighbors.

In the early 18th century, the commercial development of the mineral springs in Hampstead led to its success as a spa; people traveled from miles around to drink the pure waters from Hampstead Wells, and small cottages were hastily built to accommodate the influx. Though the spa phenomenon was short-lived, Hampstead remained a favorite place for many artistic figures whose legacies still mark the landscape as much as they permeate the culture.

A livelier, cooler vibe prevails at **Camden Market,** a magnet for dedicated followers of fashion, while kids will adore **London Zoo** at the northern end of **Regent's Park.**

This, the youngest of London's great parks, was laid out in 1812 by John Nash, working, as ever, for his patron, the Prince Regent (hence the name), who was crowned George IV in 1820. The idea was to re-create the feel of a grand country residence close to the center of town, with all those magnificent white-stucco terraces facing in on the park. As you walk "the Outer Circle," you'll see how successfully Nash's plans were carried out. The most famous and impressive of Nash's terraces would have been in the prince's line of vision from the planned palace, so was extra-ornamental. Cumberland Terrace has a central block of Ionic columns surmounted by a triangular Wedgewood-blue pediment and giant statuary personifying Britannia and her empire further single it out from the pack. There are those who find nearby Chester Terrace to be even more regal.

The southeastern exit of the park is just around the corner from two of London's most traditional tourist destinations, the **Sherlock Holmes Museum** and **Madame Tussauds.**

Before you plunge back into the frenetic activity of central London, you can wander down the stylish **Marylebone High Street** and, just north of Oxford Street, check out the patrician **Wallace Collection,** an extraordinary collection of old-master paintings and palace furniture housed in an 18th-century mansion.

TOP ATTRACTIONS

Fodor'sChoice
★

Hampstead Heath. For an escape from the ordered prettiness of Hampstead, head to the Heath—a unique remnant of London's original countryside, with habitats ranging from wide grasslands to ancient woodlands and spread over some 791 acres. **Parliament Hill,** one of the highest points in London, offers a stunning panorama over the city. There are signposted paths, but these can be confusing. Maps are available from ⇨ *Kenwood House*, or the Education Centre near the Lido off Gordon House Road, where you can also get details about the history of the Heath and the flora and fauna growing there. An excellent café near the Athletics Field offers light refreshment under the trees. ⊠ *Hampstead* ☎ *020/7482–7073 Heath Education Centre* ⊕ *www. cityoflondon.gov.uk/hampstead* ☒ *Free* Ⓜ *To reach the south of the Heath, tube it to the Highbury & Islington Underground station,* then switch to the North London Overground platforms at the same station and go to Gospel Oak or Hampstead Heath stations; for the eastern part of the Heath, take the tube to Hampstead station, then walk through Flask Walk or Well Walk; for the north and west of the Heath, take the tube to Golders Green Underground station, then Bus 210, 268 to Whitestone Pond.

WORD OF MOUTH

"I am at a loss to describe their treasures of 18th century French paintings, porcelain, furniture, bibelots, medieval and Renaissance works, and "the finest collections of princely arms and armour in Britain." Their website—wallacecollection.org—gives an excellent overview of the mansion and its holdings."

—latedaytraveler

★ **Highgate Cemetery.** Highgate is not the oldest cemetery in London, but it is probably the best known. After the cemetery was consecrated in 1839, Victorians came from miles around to appreciate the ornate headstones, the impressive tombs, and the view. Such was its popularity that 19 acres on the other side of the road were acquired in 1850, and this additional East Cemetery contains what may be the most visited grave, of Karl Marx, and those of other famous names including George Eliot and Malcolm McLaren. At the summit is the **Circle of Lebanon**, a ring of vaults built around an ancient cypress tree—a legacy of 17th-century gardens that occupied the site previously. Leading from the circle is the **Egyptian Avenue**, a subterranean stone tunnel lined with catacombs, itself approached by a dramatic colonnade that screens the main cemetery from the road. If you wish to tour Highgate, contact the Friends of Highgate Cemetery; space on tours is limited to 15, so call to book. Please dress respectfully, whether you come here on your own or on a tour. ⊠ *Swains La., Highgate* ☎ *020/8340–1834* ⊕ *www. highgate-cemetery.org* ☒ *East Cemetery £3, tours £7; West Cemetery tours £7. No credit cards.* ☉ *Daily; usually Apr.–Oct. 10–5, Nov.–Mar. 10–4, but call ahead as hrs vary according to whether a funeral service is scheduled. East Cemetery tours, Sat. 2. West Cemetery tours, Mar.–Nov., weekdays 1:45, weekends hourly 11–3* Ⓜ *Archway, then Bus 210, 271, or 143 to Highgate Village.*

Keats House. It was in February 1820 that John Keats (1795–1821) coughed blood up into his handkerchief and exclaimed, "That drop of blood is my death warrant. I must die." He duly left his beloved home in Hampstead and moved to Rome, where he died of consumption, at just 25. Here you can see the plum tree under which the young Romantic poet composed "Ode to a Nightingale"; many of his original manuscripts; his library; and other possessions he managed to acquire in his short life. There are frequent guided tours and special events, such as poetry readings. The house has been restored to its original Regency style of decoration, and the design of the gardens is inspired by elements of Keats's poetry, such as "autumn" and "nightingale." The ticket gives you entry for a full year, so you can come back as often as you like. ■TIP➔ Picnics can be taken into the grounds during the summer. ✉ *Wentworth Pl., Keats Grove, Hampstead* ☎ *020/7332–3868* ⊕ *www.keatshouse.cityoflondon.gov.uk* ✉ *£5* ⊘ *Apr.–Oct., Tues.–Sun. 1–5; Nov.–Mar., Fri.–Sun. 1–5; closed Good Friday and Christmas wk* Ⓜ *Hampstead; then exit to walk down Hampstead High St., with a left on Downshire Hill, then a right onto Keats Grove..*

Ⓒ ★ **Kenwood House.** This gracious Georgian villa was first built in 1616 and remodeled by Robert Adam between 1764 and 1779. Adam refaced most of the exterior and added the splendid library, which, with its curved painted ceiling and gilded detail, is the highlight of the house for lovers of the decorative arts and interior design. Kenwood is also home to the **Iveagh Bequest,** an extraordinary collection of paintings that the Earl of Iveagh gave the nation in 1927, including a wonderful self-portrait by Rembrandt and works by Reynolds, Van Dyck, Hals, Gainsborough, and Turner. Most iconic among them is Vermeer's *Guitar Player,* considered by many to be among the most beautiful paintings in the world. In front of the house, a graceful lawn slopes down to a little lake crossed by a trompe-l'oeil bridge—all in perfect 18th-century upper-class taste. The grounds are skirted by Hampstead Heath. ■TIP➔ In summer the grounds host a series of popular and classical concerts, culminating in fireworks on the last night. A popular café, the Brew House, is part of the old coach house, with outdoor tables in the courtyard and terraced garden. ✉ *Hampstead La., Hampstead* ☎ *020/8348–1286* ⊕ *www.english-heritage.org.uk* ✉ *Free* ⊘ *House daily except Dec. 24–26 and Jan. 1, 11:30–4. Gardens daily dawn–dusk* Ⓜ *Golders Green, then Bus 210.*

Ⓒ **Fodor's Choice** ★ **London Zoo.** The zoo, owned by the Zoological Society of London (a charity), opened in 1828. A recent modernization program has seen several big attractions open, with a focus on wildlife conservation, education, and the breeding of endangered species. The zoo's Reptile House is a special draw for Harry Potter fans—it's where Harry first talks to snakes, to alarming effect on his horrible cousin, Dudley. Other major attractions include the huge **BUGS** pavilion (Biodiversity Underpinning Global Survival), a self-sustaining, contained ecosystem with 140 species of exotic plants, animals, and creepy-crawlies; **Gorilla Kingdom,** where you can watch the four residents—Effie, Kesho, Jookie, and Zaire—at close range; **Rainforest Life,** a recreated nighttime rain-forest environment, home to tiny marmosets and other rain-forest-dwelling creatures, including bats; and state-of-the-art **Penguin Beach,** the most popular place in the zoo at 11:30, when the penguins receive their main feed. ■TIP➔ Check the website or the information board out front for free events, including creature close encounters and ask the keeper' sessions. ✉ *Regent's Park* ☎ *020/7722–3333* ⊕ *www.zsl.org* ✉ *£16.60–£18.60, depending on season* ⊘ *2nd wk in Nov.–Feb., daily 10–4; Mar.–1st*

There are more than 30,000 rosebushes of 100 separate varieties in Queen Mary's Gardens, within the Inner Circle of Regent's Park.

wk in Sept., daily 10–6; 2nd wk in Sept.–Oct., daily 10–5:30; 1st wk in Nov., daily 10–4:30; last admission 1 hr before closing Ⓜ *Camden Town, then Bus 274.*

★ **Marylebone High Street.** A favorite of newspaper style sections everywhere, this street forms the heart of Marylebone (pronounced "Marr-le-bone") Village, a vibrant, upscale neighborhood that encompasses the squares and streets around the High Street and nearby Marylebone Lane. It's hard to believe that you're just a few blocks north of Oxford Street as you wander in and out of Marylebone's small shops and boutiques, the best of which include La Fromagerie (2–6 Moxon Street), an excellent cheese shop; Daunt Books (Nos. 83–84), a travel bookshop; "Cabbages and Frocks" market on the grounds of the St. Marylebone Parish Church, held Saturday 11–5, which purveys specialty foods and vintage clothing; and on Sunday 10–2, a large farmers' and artisan food market in a parking lot on Cramer Street, just behind the High Street. ✉ *Marylebone* Ⓜ *Bond St.*

Ⓒ **Regent's Park.**
★ *See the highlighted listing in this chapter.*

Ⓒ **Wallace Collection.** Assembled by four generations of Marquesses of
Fodor's Choice Hertford and given to the nation by the widow of Sir Richard Wal-
★ lace (1818–90), bastard son of the fourth, this fabled collection of art and antiques is important, exciting, undervisited—and free. The salons of Hertford House, an 18th-century mansion, began to be filled by Wallace's father, the 4th Marquess of Hartford, a particularly shrewd connoisseur and dealer. After the French Revolution he took a house

in Paris, where he went about snapping up paintings by what were then dangerously unpopular artists—Boucher, Fragonard, Watteau, Lancret—for a song. Frans Hals's *Laughing Cavalier* is probably the most famous painting here, or perhaps Jean-Honoré Fragonard's *The Swing*, which perfectly encapsulates the frilly decadence of the Rococo style and the playful eroticism of prerevolutionary French art. Everyone else is here, from Rubens and Rembrandt to Van Dyck and Velázquez. English works include paintings by Gainsborough and Turner, plus a dozen by Joshua Reynolds. Some American artists are also on view, including Thomas Sully's pretty portrait of Queen Victoria, which is fittingly housed in a rouge-pink salon (just to the right of the main entrance). Almost more famous than the paintings are the examples of French 18th-century palace furniture, including legendary examples by Riesener, Oeben, and B.V.R.B., many created for the Bourbon kings to use at Versailles. The museum restaurant is elegantly sited in a glass-roofed courtyard. ⊠ *Hertford House, Manchester Sq., Marylebone* ☎ *020/7563–9500* ⊕ *www.wallacecollection.org* ⊠ *Free* ☉ *Daily 10–5* Ⓜ *Bond St.*

Wallace Restaurant. Bringing the outside in, this lovely restaurant is located in the glass-roofed courtyard of the Wallace Collection and is open for breakfast, lunch, and afternoon tea, and for dinner on weekends. The menu highlights French brasserie food, from pâtés and cheeses to oysters, lobster, and succulent steaks, or you can just linger over coffee or afternoon tea. It's open Sunday–Thursday 10–5, Friday and Saturday 10 am–11 pm. ⊠ *Wallace Collection, Manchester Sq., Marylebone* ☎ *020/7563–9505.*

WORTH NOTING

Burgh House. One of Hampstead's oldest buildings, Burgh House was built in 1704 to take advantage of the natural spa waters of the then-fashionable Hampstead Wells. A private house until World War II, Burgh was saved from near-dereliction in the 1970s by local residents, who have been restoring and maintaining it ever since. The building is a fine example of the gentle elegance common to the Queen Anne period, with its redbrick box frontage, oak panelled rooms, and terraced garden (originally designed by Gertrude Jekyll). Today the house contains a small but diverting museum on the history of the area, and also hosts regular talks, concerts, and recitals. The secluded garden courtyard of the café is a lovely spot for lunch, tea, or glass of wine on a summer's afternoon. Call ahead if you're visiting on a weekend, however, as the house is often hired out as a wedding venue on Saturdays. ⊠ *New End Square, Hampstead* ☎ *020/7431–0144* ⊕ *www.burghhouse.org.uk* ⊠ *Free* ☉ *Wed.–Fri. 11–5:30; weekends 9:30–5:30.*

Camden Market. What started as a small group of clothing stalls in the 1970s has since grown into one of London's biggest (and most crowded) tourist attractions. Centered on the Grand Union Canal, this isn't actually a single market, but a vast honeycomb of them that sell crafts,

REGENT'S PARK

✉ *Marylebone Rd., Regent's Park* ☎ *0300/061–2000* ⊕ *www.royalparks.gov.uk* ☑ *Free* ◷ *5 am–dusk* Ⓜ *Baker St., Regent's Park, Great Portland St.—it's at the very edge of the park on the northeastern side.*

TIPS

■ Soccer, rugby, tennis, hockey, and softball are played on the park's many sports grounds. Head up to the area around the Hub (0300/061–2324)—a state-of-the-art sports pavilion—to watch some action. You'll have to book in advance if you want to join in, but you're just as likely to find an informal soccer match in progress anywhere in the park, especially on a warm Sunday afternoon.

■ At the Garden Café (Inner Circle, Regent's Park; 020/7935–5729), enjoy breakfast, lunch, or supper on a patio next to the rose gardens, or take away some smoked-salmon bagels and champagne (or cappuccinos) for an elegant picnic.

■ Check the Regent's Park Open-Air Theatre schedule—they have been mounting summer Shakespeare productions here since 1932 (0844/826–4242; www.openairtheatre.org).

Cultivated and formal, compared with the relative wildness of Hampstead Heath, Regent's Park was laid out in 1812 by John Nash in honor of the Prince Regent, who was later crowned George IV. The idea was to re-create the feel of a grand country residence close to the center of town. Most of Nash's plans were carried out successfully, although the focus of it all—a palace for the prince—was never built. Now the park is a favorite destination for sporty types and dog owners. Not for nothing did Dodie Smith set her novel *A Hundred and One Dalmatians* in an Outer Circle house. (Nearby along East Heath Road is the Gothic manse that inspired Cruella DeVil's Hell Hall.)

HIGHLIGHTS

The most famous and impressive of Nash's white-stuco terraces facing the park, **Cumberland Terrace** has a central block of Ionic columns surmounted by a triangular Wedgwood-blue pediment that looks like a giant cameo. The noted architectural historian Sir John Summerson described it as "easily the most breathtaking architectural panorama in London."

The **Broad Walk** is a good vantage point from which to glimpse the minaret and the golden dome of the **London Central Mosque** on the far west side of the park. As in all London parks, planting here is planned with the aim of having something in bloom in all seasons, but if you hit the park in summer, head first to the Inner Circle. Your nostrils should lead you to **Queen Mary's Gardens**, a fragrant 17-acre circle that riots with 400 different varieties of roses in summer. Spend a vigorous afternoon rowing about **Regent's Park Boating Lake**, where rowboats hold up to five adults and cost £6.50 per hour per person. Times vary with seasons and weather. ☎ *020/7724–4069*

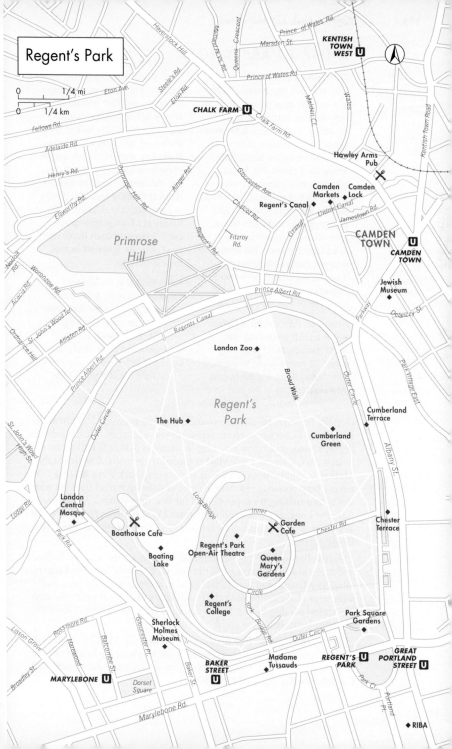

A TRIP TO ABBEY ROAD

For countless Beatlemaniacs and baby boomers, No. 3 Abbey Road is one of the most beloved spots in London. Here, outside the legendary Abbey Road Studios, is the most famous zebra crossing in the world, immortalized on the Beatles' 1969 *Abbey Road* album. This footpath became a mod monument when, on August 8 of that year, John, Paul, George, and Ringo posed for photographer Iain Macmillan's famous cover shot. The recording facility's Studio 2 is where the Beatles recorded their entire output, from "Love Me Do" onward, including *Sgt. Pepper's Lonely Hearts Club Band* (early 1967).

Meanwhile, there's never any shortage of tourists re-creating "the photo" outside. ■TIP→ Be very careful if you're going to attempt this. Abbey Road is a dangerous intersection. One of the best—and

safer—ways Beatle lovers can enjoy the history of the group is to take one of the excellent walking tours offered by the **Original London Walks** (☎ 020/7624–3978 ⊕ *www.walks.com*), including **The Beatles In-My-Life Walk** (11:20 am outside Marylebone Underground on Saturday and Tuesday) and **The Beatles Magical Mystery Tour** (Wednesday at 2 pm, Thursday at 11 am, and Sunday at 11 am at Underground Exit 3, Tottenham Court Road), which cover nostalgic landmark Beatles spots in the city.

Abbey Road is in the elegant neighborhood of St. John's Wood, a 10-minute ride on the Tube from central London. Take the Jubilee line to the St. John's Wood Tube stop, head southwest three blocks down Grove End Road, and be prepared for a view right out of Memory Lane.

clothing (vintage, ethnic, and young designer), antiques, and just about everything in between. Here, especially on weekends, the crowds are dense, young, and relentless, with as many as 100,000 visitors on the busiest days. **Camden Lock Market** specializes in crafts; **Camden Stables Market** is popular with Goth kids and aspiring rock stars. ■TIP→ Print out the (appropriately psychedelic) map of Camden Market from the website before coming; it's super-helpful for first-time visitors. *For more on Camden Lock, see* ⇨ *Shopping, Chapter 18.* ⊠ *Camden High St., Camden Town* ⊕ *www.camdenmarkets.org* ⊙ *Daily 10–6* Ⓜ *Camden Town, Chalk Farm.*

Electric Ballroom. A nightclub that doubles as a retro/designer fashion and music market on weekends, the Electric Ballroom has been a scuzzy, dilapidated, wild, and wonderful Camden institution for decades. Sadly, long-term plans to demolish the building are afoot, but so far the club has staved off developers. ⊠ *184 Camden High St.* ☎ *020/7485–9006* ⊕ *www.electricballroom.co.uk*

Hawley Arms Pub. Just around the corner, the Hawley Arms Pub gained fame as a hangout for celebrities such as Kate Moss and the late Amy Winehouse. It's a good spot for an inexpensive pub lunch. ⊠ *2 Castlehaven Rd.* ☎ *020/7428–5979*

The fabled cover of the Beatles *Abbey Road* album, with Hampstead's most famous traffic crossing.

QUICK BITES

You will not go hungry in Camden Town, with its countless cafés, bars, and pubs, plus appealing restaurants at all price points on Parkway. Within the market at Camden Lock there are various stalls selling the usual hot dogs and burgers, but you can also find good value at the stalls selling ethnic food if you don't mind standing as you eat outdoors, or perching on a canal-side bench.

Fenton House. Hampstead's oldest surviving house, a National Trust property, shows off a fine collections of porcelain and Georgian furniture and has a superb walled garden, complete with an apple orchard that dates back to the 17th century. Baroque music enthusiasts can join a tour of the important collection of keyboard instruments, and there's a summer series of concerts on these very same instruments on Thursday evenings. Check the website for details. ⊠ *Hampstead Grove, Hampstead* ☎ *020/7435–3471* ⊕ *www.nationaltrust.org.uk* 🎟 *£6.50, garden only £2* ⊙ *Late Mar.–Oct., Wed.–Sun. 11–5; last admission 30 mins before closing. Closed some Thurs. mornings, June and July; call to confirm.* Ⓜ *Hampstead.*

Freud Museum. The father of psychoanalysis lived here for a year, between his escape from Nazi persecution in his native Vienna in 1938 and his death in 1939. Many of his possessions emigrated with him and were set up by his daughter, Anna (herself a pioneer of child psychoanalysis), as a shrine to her father's life and work. Shortly after Anna's death in 1982 the house was opened as a museum. It replicates Freud's famous consulting rooms, particularly through the presence of *the* couch. You'll

PUBS WITH A PAST

Hampstead has some of the most storied pubs in London—although a few have distinctly shady pasts.

Holly Bush. Tucked away down the lolloping hills and leafy side roads of old Hampstead is this gorgeously unspoiled old pub, built in 1807. The dim, cozy interior has an open fireplace and wooden booths. The classic British food is excellent; take it in the bar with a pint, or in the rather swankier dining room. ⊠ *22 Holly Mount, Hampstead* ☎ *020/7435–2892.*

Magdala. Meanwhile, a much sadder tale is associated with the Magdala, the site of a notorious murder in 1955 for which Ruth Ellis was the last woman in Britain to be hanged. It's a sedate place these days, but the famous bullet holes near the door have been left untouched. ⊠ *2A South Hill Park* ☎ *020/7435–2503.*

Spaniard's Inn. The legendary highwayman Dick Turpin is said to have been born at the Spaniard's Inn, which was once frequented by the likes of Dickens, Shelley, and Stoker. The owners will happily tell you how the latter borrowed one of their many resident ghost stories to furnish the plot of *Dracula.* After a few hours in this atmospheric spot, you might even believe it. ⊠ *Spaniards Rd.* ☎ *020/8731–8406.*

Wells. A plaque outside this Georgian pub delicately informs visitors that it was originally built to provide "facilities for the celebration of unpremeditated and clandestine marriages." These days the spot is far better known as one of the finest gastropubs in the area. ⊠ *30 Well Walk* ☎ *020/7794–3785.*

find Freud-related books, lectures, and study groups here, too. ⊠ *20 Maresfield Gardens, Hampstead* ☎ *020/7435–2002* ⊕ *www.freud.org. uk* ⊠ *£6* ⊙ *Wed.–Sun. noon–5* Ⓜ *Swiss Cottage, Finchley Rd.*

Jewish Museum. The focus is on the history of the Jewish people in Britain from medieval times to the present day, although most of the exhibits date from the 17th century—when Cromwell repealed the laws against Jewish settlement—and later. "History: A British Story" provides a general overview of the Jewish people in Britain over the centuries, through a mix of rare artifacts and interactive displays, including a re-creation of a Victorian street from what was then the legendary Jewish quarter of East London. The Holocaust Gallery focuses on the incredible story of Leon Greenman (1910–2008), a British Jew who survived six concentration camps. Here, too, is one of the world's largest collections of Jewish art. ⊠ *Raymond Burton House, 129–131 Albert St., Camden Town* ☎ *020/7284–7384* ⊕ *www.jewishmuseum.org.uk* ⊠ *£7.50* ⊙ *Sat.–Thurs. 10–5, Fri. 10–2; last admission 30 mins before closing. Closed on major Jewish festivals* Ⓜ *Camden Town.*

OFF THE
BEATEN
PATH

London Canal Museum. Near the St. Pancras International train station, in this former ice-storage house, you can learn about the rise and fall of London's once extensive canal network. Children enjoy the activity zone and learning about Henrietta, the museum's horse. Outside, on the Battlebridge Basin, float the painted narrow boats of modern canal

221B Baker Street and "Holmes" himself

dwellers—a few steps and a world away from King's Cross, which was once one of London's least salubrious neighborhoods. The quirky little museum is a half-hour walk along the towpath from Camden Lock— you can download a free audio tour to accompany the route, or join one of the several guided walking tours (£6 per person). ⊠ *12–13 New Wharf Rd., King's Cross* ☎ *020/7713–0836* ⊕ *www.canalmuseum.org. uk* ⊠ *£4* ⊗ *Tues.–Sun. and holiday Mon. 10–4:30; last admission 30 mins before closing. First Thurs. open until 7:30. Closed Dec. 24–Jan. 1* Ⓜ *King's Cross.*

Lord's Cricket Ground & Museum. If you can't manage to lay your hands on tickets for a cricket match, the next best thing is to take a tour of the spiritual home of this most English of games. Founded by Thomas Lord, the headquarters of the MCC (Marylebone Cricket Club) opens its "behind the scenes" areas to visitors. You can see the Long Room with cricketing art on display; the players' dressing rooms; and the world's oldest sporting museum, where the progress from gentlemanly village-green game to worldwide sport over 400 years is charted. Don't miss the prize exhibit: the urn containing the sport's most iconic trophy, the Ashes (the remains of a cricket ball presented to the English captain in 1883, a jokey allusion to a newspaper's premature obituary for the death of English cricket published after the home team's defeat by Australia). The two nations still play for possession of the Ashes every two years. ⊠ *St. John's Wood Rd., St. John's Wood* ☎ *020/7616–8595* ⊕ *www.lords.org* ⊠ *£15. Museum only, £7.50 match days* ⊗ *Museum Apr.–Oct., daily 10–5, except during major matches; Nov.–Mar., daily 11:30–5 (closes at 4 Fri.). Tours Apr.–Oct., daily 10, noon, 2, and 3;*

Nov.–Mar, weekdays 11, noon, and 2; weekends 10, 11, and noon. Ⓜ *St. John's Wood.*

Ⓒ **Madame Tussauds.** One of London's busiest tourist attractions, this is nothing less—but also nothing more—than the world's most famous exhibition of lifelike waxwork models of celebrities. Madame T. learned her craft while making death masks of French Revolution victims, and in 1835 she set up her first show of the famous ones near this spot. Top billing still goes to the murderers in the Chamber of Horrors, who stare glassy-eyed at visitors—one from an electric chair, one sitting next to the tin bath where he dissolved several wives in quicklime. What, aside from ghoulish prurience, makes people stand in line to invest in one of London's most expensive museum tickets? It must be the thrill of all those photo opportunities with royalty, Hollywood stars, and world leaders—all in a single day. ■ **TIP→** Beat the crowds by calling in advance for timed entry tickets, or booking online—where you can also buy non-timed, "priority access" tickets at a premium. ✉ *Marylebone Rd., Regent's Park* ☎ *0870/400–3000 for timed entry tickets* ⊕ *www.madame-tussauds. com* ✆ *£15–£32 according to time; call or check website. Combination ticket with London Eye, London Dungeons, and London Aquarium from £60.50* ☺ *Weekdays 9–5:30 (last admission); weekends 9:30–6 (last admission)* Ⓜ *Baker St.*

Regent's Park Open-Air Theatre. The theater has mounted productions of Shakespeare productions every summer since 1932; everyone from Vivien Leigh to Jeremy Irons has performed here. Today it also hosts musicals, concerts, and comedy shows. However, *A Midsummer Night's Dream* is the one to catch—never is that enchanted Greek wood more lifelike than it is here, enhanced by genuine birdsong and a rising moon. You can buy light suppers or choose from a (somewhat limited) barbecue selection in the evening, or prebook a picnic lunch for matinees. The park can get chilly, so bring a blanket; only very heavy rain stops the plays, in which case you can exchange your ticket (umbrellas aren't allowed during performances). ✉ *Open-Air Theatre, Inner Circle, Regent's Park* ☎ *0844/826–4242* ⊕ *www.openairtheatre.org* ✆ *£15–£45* ☺ *June–mid-Sept., evening performances at 8, matinees at 2:30* Ⓜ *Baker St., Regent's Park.*

Sherlock Holmes Museum. Outside Baker Street station, by the Marylebone Road exit, is a 9-foot-high bronze statue of the celebrated detective. Nearby is number 221B Baker Street—the address of Arthur Conan Doyle's fictional detective. Inside, Mrs. Hudson, "Holmes's housekeeper," conducts you into a series of Victorian rooms full of Sherlock-abilia. There's more than enough photo ops, and it's all carried off with such genuine enthusiasm that you almost believe that the fictional "great detective" really lived here. ✉ *221B Baker St., Regent's Park* ☎ *020/7224–3688* ⊕ *www.sherlock-holmes.co.uk* ✆ *£6* ☺ *Daily 9:30–6* Ⓜ *Baker St.*

Greenwich

WORD OF MOUTH

"We took a Thames river cruise starting just above the Westminister Bridge and got off at Greenwich and walked to the observatory. That way we were able to see the Tower Bridge, etc. along the way."

— 120aks

GETTING ORIENTED

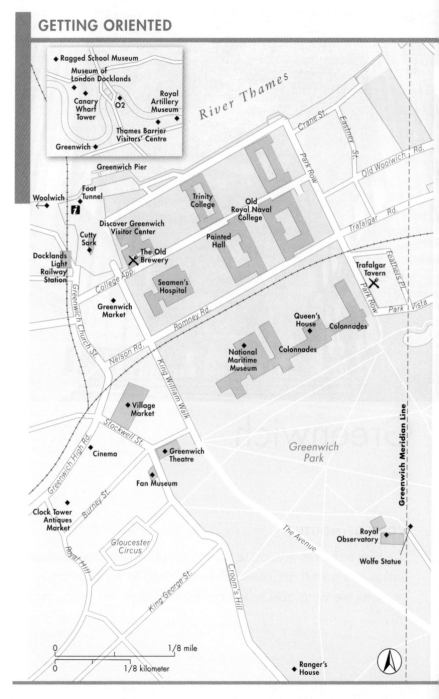

Ragged School Museum

Museum of London Docklands

Canary Wharf Tower

O2

Royal Artillery Museum

Thames Barrier Visitors' Centre

Greenwich

River Thames

Crane St.

Eastney St.

Old Woolwich Rd.

Greenwich Pier

Foot Tunnel

Woolwich

Trinity College

Old Royal Naval College

Trafalgar Rd.

Park Row

Discover Greenwich Visitor Center

Painted Hall

Cutty Sark

The Old Brewery

Trafalgar Tavern

Feathers Pl.

Docklands Light Railway Station

College App.

Seamen's Hospital

Park Row

Park Vista

Greenwich Church St.

Greenwich Market

Romney Rd.

Queen's House

Colonnades

Nelson Rd.

Colonnades

National Maritime Museum

King William Walk

Village Market

Stockwell St.

Greenwich Park

Cinema

Greenwich High Rd.

Greenwich Theatre

Burney St.

Fan Museum

Clock Tower Antiques Market

Gloucester Circus

Royal Hill

Greenwich Meridian Line

Royal Observatory

Wolfe Statue

King George St.

Croom's Hill

The Avenue

0   1/8 mile

0   1/8 kilometer

Ranger's House

12

TOP REASONS TO GO

Stand astride the Greenwich Meridian Line: At the Royal Observatory—where the world's time is set—you can be in the eastern and western hemispheres simultaneously.

Pay a call to Sir Inigo Jones's Queen's House: This 17th-century building was massively influential in its day, being the first in England to embrace the styles of the Italian Renaissance. See what all the fuss was about.

Step into the Old Royal Naval College: Come to the chapel at lunchtime to catch a free concert by one of Britain's most prestigious music schools.

Discover Britain's seafaring past at the **National Maritime Museum:** See how Britannia ruled the seas and helped shape the modern world.

Step aboard the *Cutty Sark:* Take a stroll along the deck of the last surviving 19th-century tea clipper, newly shipshape after years of renovation.

FEELING PECKISH?

Old Brewery. Right next to Discover Greenwich, the Old Brewery is a relaxed café by day and a sophisticated restaurant at night. The artful, high-ceiling dining room merits a visit but the modern British cuisine is also among the best in this part of London—and reasonably priced, too. The bar serves 200 different types of ale. ⊠ *Pepys Bldg., Royal Naval College, Greenwich* ☎ *020/3327–1280* ⊕ *www. oldbrewerygreenwich.com.*

Trafalgar Tavern. With its excellent vista of the Thames, there is no more handsomely situated pub in Greenwich than the Trafalgar Tavern. Featured in Charles Dickens's *Our Mutual Friend*, it's still as grand a place to have a pint and some (upscale) pub grub as it ever was. ⊠ *Park Row* ☎ *020/8858– 2909* ⊕ *www.trafalgartavern.co.uk.*

GETTING THERE

Docklands Light Railway (DLR) is a zippy way to get to Cutty Sark station, from Canary Wharf and Bank Tube stations in The City. Or take the DLR to Island Gardens and walk the old Victorian Foot Tunnel under the river. (Sitting at the front of a train can be disconcerting, as you watch the controls in the fully automated driver's cab move about, as if a ghost were at the helm.) The best way to arrive, however—time and weather permitting—is like a sea captain of old: by water (though this way takes an hour from central London; *for more on cruising the Thames, see Chapter 13).*

MAKING THE MOST OF YOUR TIME

Set apart from the rest of London, Greenwich is worth a day to itself—those who love maritime history will want to spend at least two—to make the most of walks in the rolling parklands and to immerse yourself in the richness of Greenwich's history, science, and architecture. The boat trip takes about an hour from Westminster Pier (next to Big Ben), or 25 minutes from the Tower of London, so factor in enough time for the round-trip.

NEAREST PUBLIC RESTROOMS

Duck into the tourist information center (near the Old Royal Naval College), where loos are free.

Sightseeing
★★★★
Nightlife
★
Dining
★★
Lodging
★
Shopping
★★★

About 8 miles downstream—which means seaward, to the east—from central London lies a destination you'd think had been conceived to provide the perfect day out. The small borough of Greenwich is only small in size: it actually looms large in the imagination for it is not only home to the Old Royal Observatory, which measures time for our entire planet, and the Greenwich Meridian, which divides the world into two (you can stand astride it with one foot in either hemisphere) but this town also bears witness to Britain's incredible maritime history, thanks to the National Maritime Museum and the *Cutty Sark*. Add in Christopher Wren's Royal Naval College and Inigo Jones's Queen's House—two of the grandest buildings in English architectural history—and the pretty streets of Greenwich Village itself, and you have one of London's most splendid excursions.

Updated by
Jack Jewers

Bear in mind that the journey to Greenwich is an event in itself, especially if you approach by Old Father Thames, arriving at the best possible vista of the Royal Naval College, with the Queen's House behind. On the way, the boat glides past famous sights on the London skyline (there's a guaranteed spine chill on passing the Tower) and ever-changing docklands, and there's always a cockney navigator enhancing the views with his salty commentary. Of course, you can also arrive using the modern Docklands Light Railway (DLR). Either by train or by boat, Greenwich will wind up thrilling nearly everyone, from seafaring types to landlubbers, who will enjoy strolling the green acres of parkland that surround the venerable buildings, the quaint 19th-century houses, and the weekend crafts and antiques markets.

A visit to Greenwich feels like a trip to a rather elegant seaside town—albeit one with more than its fair share of historic sites. The grandiose **Old Royal Naval Hospital,** designed by Christopher Wren, was originally a home for veteran sailors. Today it's a popular visitor attraction, with a more glamorous second life as one of the most widely used movie locations in Britain.

FUN FACT

Hang out beneath the lightning-cracked Elizabeth Oak in Greenwich Park and you'll be following in illustrious footsteps—it's so called because Elizabeth I is supposed to have played in its branches as a girl.

12

Greenwich was originally home to one of England's finest Tudor palaces, and the birthplace of Henry VIII, Elizabeth I, and Mary I. Inigo Jones built what is considered the first "classical" building in England in 1616—the **Queen's House,** which now houses a collection of fine art. Right next door, the excellent **National Maritime Museum** details the history of the glorious seafaring past of Britain, this island kingdom. Its prize exhibits include the coat worn by Admiral Lord Nelson (1758–1805) in his final battle—bullet hole and all.

Greenwich Park, London's oldest royal park, is still home to fallow red deer, just as it has been since they were first introduced here for hunting by Henry VIII. The **Ranger's House** now houses a private art collection, next door to a beautifully manicured rose garden. Above it all is the **Royal Observatory,** where you can be in two hemispheres at once by standing along the **Greenwich Meridian Line,** before seeing a high-tech planetarium show.

In town, opposite the Greenwich Theatre, the **Fan Museum** is home to 4,000 fans dating as far back as the 11th century. The **Clock Tower Antiques Market** and the lively **Greenwich Market** keep bargain-hunters busy on weekends.

Toward north Greenwich, the hopelessly ambitious Millennium Dome has been successfully reborn as the O2 and now hosts major concerts and stand-up comedy gigs. In the opposite direction, downstream in Woolwich, lies the modern engineering marvel of the **Thames Flood Barrier.**

TOP ATTRACTIONS

Clock Tower Antiques Market. The weekend Clock Tower Antiques Market on Greenwich High Road draws crowds for its vintage shopping. Browsing among the "small collectibles" makes for a good half-hour diversion even if you are not buying. ⊠ *166 Greenwich High Rd., Greenwich* ⊕ *www.clocktowermarket.co.uk* ☉ *Weekends 10–5.* Ⓜ *DLR: Greenwich.*

Discover Greenwich. Intended as a kind of anchor point for Greenwich's big three attractions—the Old Royal Naval College, *Cutty Sark,* and National Maritime Museum—this excellent, state-of-the-art visitor center includes interactive exhibitions on the history of Greenwich, plus an assortment of local treasures and artifacts. Most intriguing among them is a 17th-century "witch bottle," once used to ward off evil spirits. Modern X-rays have revealed it to contain a mixture of human

ROYAL OBSERVATORY

✉ *Romney Rd., Greenwich*
☎ *020/8858–4422* ⊕ *www.*
rog.nmm.ac.uk ✉ *Astronomy*
Galleries free; Flamstead
house and Meridian Line
courtyard £7; planetarium
shows £6.50 ⊗ *Daily 10–5*
(May–Aug., Meridian courtyard
until 6); last entry 30 mins
before closing; last planetar-
ium show 4 Ⓜ *DLR: Greenwich.*

TIPS

■ A brass line laid among
the cobblestones here marks
the meridian, one side being
the eastern, one the western
hemisphere. As darkness falls,
a funky green laser shoots
out across London for several
miles, following exactly the
path of the meridian line.

■ The Time Ball atop Flamsteed House is one of the
world's earliest time signals.
Each day at 12:55, it rises
halfway up its mast. At 12:58
it rises all the way to the top,
and at 1 exactly, the ball falls.

■ The steep hill that is home
to the observatory gives
fantastic views across London,
topped off with £1-a-slot
telescopes to scour the skyline. Time a walk to catch the
golden glow of late-afternoon
sun on Canary Wharf Tower
and head back into Greenwich
via the rose garden behind
Ranger's House. Youngsters
under five are not usually
allowed into the auditorium.
Tickets can be purchased
ahead online.

Greenwich is on the prime meridian at 0° longitude, and
the ultimate standard for time around the world has
been set here since 1884, when Britain was the world's
largest and most important maritime power.

HIGHLIGHTS

The observatory is actually split into two sites, a short
walk apart—one devoted to astronomy, the other to the
study of time. The enchanting **Peter Harrison Planetarium** is London's only planetarium, its bronze-clad turret
poking out of the ground like a crashed UFO. Shows
on black holes and how to interpret the night sky are
enthralling and enlightening. Even better for kids are
the high-technology rooms of the **Astronomy Galleries,**
where cutting-edge touch screens and interactive programs give young explorers the chance to run their own
space missions to Ganymede, one of Jupiter's moons.

Across the way is **Flamsteed House,** designed by Christopher Wren in 1675 for John Flamsteed, the first Royal
Astronomer. A climb to the top of the house reveals the
28-inch telescope, built in 1893 and now housed inside
an onion-shape fiberglass dome. It doesn't compare
with the range of modern optical telescopes, but it's
still the largest in the United Kingdom. Regular viewing
evenings reveal startlingly detailed views of the lunar
surface. In the **Time Galleries,** linger over the superb
workmanship of John Harrison (1693–1776), whose
famous **Maritime Clocks** won him the Longitude Prize
for solving the problem of accurate timekeeping at sea
and greatly improved navigation.

DID YOU KNOW?

Once sailors could determine their distance from the Greenwich meridian (longitude), maritime navigation was greatly improved. Look for the brass line marking the two hemispheres throughout the cobblestone streets.

hair, fingernails, and urine. ✉ *Pepys Bldg., King William Walk, Greenwich* ☎ *020/8269–4799* ⊕ *www.oldroyalnavalcollege.org* 🎫 *Free* ⊙ *Daily 10–5* Ⓜ *DLR: Greenwich.*

Greenwich Market. Established as a fruit-and-vegetable market in 1700, and granted a royal charter in 1849, the covered market now offers mixed stalls of art and crafts on Wednesday, Saturday, and Sunday; antiques, and collectibles on Tuesday, Thursday, and Friday. You can get food-to-go on each market day, although the offerings are usually best on weekends. Shopping for handicrafts is a pleasure here, as in most cases you're buying directly from the artist. ✉ *College Approach, Greenwich* ☎ *020/8269–5093* ⊕ *www.shopgreenwich.co.uk* ⊙ *Tues.–Sun. 10–5:30* Ⓜ *DLR: Cutty Sark.*

National Maritime Museum. From the time of Henry VIII until the 1940s Britain was the world's preeminent naval power, and the collections here trace half a millennia of that seafaring history. The story is as much about trade as it is warfare; the "Atlantic Worlds" gallery explores how trade in goods—and people—helped shape the New World, while "Voyagers: Britons and the Sea" focuses on stories of the ordinary people who took to the waves over the centuries. One gallery is devoted to Admiral Lord Nelson, Britain's most famous naval commander, and among the exhibits are the uniform he was wearing, complete with bloodstains, when he died in 1805. Temporary exhibitions here are usually fascinating; those in recent years have included the Arctic convoys of World War II and the history of piracy. ■TIP➔ The museum has a good café with views over Greenwich Park. The adjacent **Queen's House** is home to the museum's art collection, the largest collection of maritime art in the world, including works by William Hogarth, Canaletto, and Joshua Reynolds. Construction was granted by Queen Anne only on condition that the river vista from the house be preserved, and there are few more majestic views in London than Inigo Jones's awe-inspiring symmetry. Completed around 1638, the Tulip Stair, named for the fleur-de-lis–style pattern on the balustrade, is especially fine, spiraling up without a central support to the Great Hall. The Great Hall itself is a perfect cube, exactly 40 feet in all three dimensions, decorated with paintings of the Muses and the Virtues. ✉ *Romney Rd., Greenwich* ☎ *020/8858–4422* ⊕ *www.nmm.ac.uk* 🎫 *Free* ⊙ *Daily 10–5; last admission 30 mins before closing* Ⓜ *DLR: Greenwich.*

Old Royal Naval College. Begun by Christopher Wren in 1694 as a rest home for ancient mariners, the college became instead a school for

Without a central support, the Tulip Stair spirals up to the Great Hall of Queen's House.

young ones in 1873. Today the University of Greenwich and Trinity College of Music have classes here. Architecturally, you'll notice how the structures part to reveal the **Queen's House** across the central lawns. Behind the college are two more buildings you can visit: the **Painted Hall,** the college's dining hall, derives its name from the baroque murals of William and Mary (reigned 1689–95; William alone 1695–1702) and assorted allegorical figures. James Thornhill's frescoes, depicting scenes of naval grandeur with a suitably pro-British note of propaganda, were painstakingly done over installments in 1708–12 and 1718–26, and were good enough to earn him a knighthood. In the opposite building stands the **College Chapel,** which was rebuilt after a fire in 1779 in an altogether more restrained, neo-Grecian style. ■TIP➔ Check the website for special events. Trinity College of Music holds free classical music concerts in the chapel every Tuesday lunchtime during the school year. ⊠ *Old Royal Naval College, King William Walk, Greenwich* ☎ *020/8269–4747* ⊕ *www.oldroyalnavalcollege.org* 🖾 *Free, guided tours £6* ☉ *Painted Hall and chapel daily 10–5 (Sun. chapel from 12:30); grounds 8–6* Ⓜ *DLR: Greenwich.*

Royal Observatory.

See the highlighted listing in this chapter.

WORTH NOTING

Cutty Sark. This sleek, romantic clipper was built in 1869, one among fleets and fleets of tall-masted wooden ships that plied the oceanic highways of the 19th century, trading in exotic commodities—in this case,

THE DOCKLANDS RENAISSANCE

For centuries the Thames was a fevered hub of activity. Great palaces were built along the river, most long gone (such as Whitehall, which dwarfed even Versailles in splendor). Dock warehouses sprang up to the east of London in the 18th century to cater to the burgeoning trade in luxury goods, from tea, coffee, and spices to silks and exotic pets. By the 1950s, however, this trade had all but disappeared—partly due to the devastation of World War II, but also because trading vessels had simply gotten too big to fit along the river. The area all but died until a massive regeneration scheme known as Docklands was completed in the 1980s. It brought renewal in the form of cutting-edge architecture, galleries, restaurants, and bars. Many of the old warehouses were restored and are now used as museums or shopping malls, such as Hay's and Butler's Wharves. The best way to explore is on the **Docklands Light Railway (DLR)**, whose elevated track appears to skim over the water past the swanky glass buildings. If you explore on foot, the Thames Path has helpful plaques along the way, with nuggets of historical information.

Museum of London Docklands. The wonderful old warehouse building, on a quaint cobbled quayside, beside the tower of Canary Wharf, is alone worth a visit. With uneven wood floors, beams, and pillars, the museum used to be a storehouse for coffee, tea, sugar, and rum from the West Indies—hence the name West India Quay.

The fascinating story of the old port and the river is told using films, together with interactive displays

and reconstructions, and a permanent exhibition, London, Sugar and Slavery, highlights the capital's involvement in the slave trade. The museum runs a highlights tour (free) on Wednesday and Sunday at 3 pm. ■TIP→ On the second Friday of every month the museum hosts the Docklands Cinema Club, which shows rare and classic films, together with talks, inside the old warehouse. ⊠ *No. 1 Warehouse, West India Quay, Hertsmere Rd., East End* ☎ *020/7001–9844* ⊕ *www.museumindocklands.org.uk* 🎟 *Free* ⊙ *Daily 10–6; last admission 5:40* Ⓜ *Canary Wharf; DLR: West India Quay.*

🖢 **Ragged School Museum.** In its time, the Ragged School Museum was the largest school in London and a place where impoverished children could get free education and a good meal. The museum recreates a classroom dating from the 1880s. It's an eye-opener for adults, and fun for kids, who get the chance to work just like Victorian children did in one of the many organized workshops.

■TIP→ If you really want to get into the spirit, visitors of all ages can attend a Victorian-style lesson (complete with fully costumed schoolmistress) from 2:15 to 3:30 on the first Sunday of every month. ⊠ *46–50 Copperfield Rd., East End* ☎ *020/8980–6405* ⊕ *www.raggedschoolmuseum.org.uk* 🎟 *Free; £2 donation requested for Victorian lessons* ⊙ *Wed. and Thurs. 10–5, 1st Sun. of month 2–5* Ⓜ *Mile End; DLR: Limehouse.*

tea. *Cutty Sark* (named after an old Scottish term for women's undergarments) was the fastest, sailing the China–London route in 1871 in only 107 days. The clipper has been preserved in dry docks as a museum ship since the 1950s, but was severely damaged in a devastating fire in 2007. As luck would have it, however, roughly half the ship had been dismantled for cleaning at the time, so a near-full restoration was possible and the boat reopened as one of Greenwich's most famous attractions in Spring 2012. Check the website for opening hours and other details before you go. ⊠ *King William Walk, Greenwich* ☎ *020/8858–2698* ⊕ *www.cuttysark.org.uk* Ⓜ *DLR: Cutty Sark.*

Fan Museum. An arcane but frequently alluring marriage between art and function, the simple fan is more than a mere fashion accessory; historically, fans can tell as much about fashion and social mores as they can about craftsmanship. There are 2,000 of them here, dating from the 17th century onward, often exquisitely crafted from ivory, mother-of-pearl, and tortoiseshell. It was the personal vision—and collection—of Helene Alexander that brought this enchanting museum into being, and the workshop and conservation–study center that she has also set up ensure that this art form continues to have a future. If your interest is really piqued, you can attend fan-making workshops (on the first Saturday of every month only—£20 for the afternoon; call ahead or visit the website for booking details). ■TIP➔ Afternoon tea is served in the café on Tuesday and Sunday at 3 pm. ⊠ *12 Croom's Hill, Greenwich* ☎ *020/8305–1441* ⊕ *www.fan-museum.org* 🖰 *£4* ☉ *Tues.–Sat. 11–5, Sun. noon–5* Ⓜ *DLR: Greenwich.*

Ranger's House. This handsome, early-18th-century villa, which was the Greenwich Park ranger's official residence during the 19th century, is hung with Stuart and Jacobean portraits. But the most interesting diversion is the Wernher Collection, more than 700 works of art amassed by diamond millionaire Julius Wernher (1850–1912). The collection ranges from Old and Dutch Master paintings to Renaissance jewelry and assorted pieces of decorative art and curios from the medieval period onwards. Wernher's American wife, Birdie, was a strong influence and personality during the belle époque, which is easy to imagine from her striking portrait by Sargent. ⊠ *Chesterfield Walk, Greenwich Park, Greenwich* ☎ *020/8853–0035* ⊕ *www.english-heritage.org.uk* 🖰 *£6.30* ☉ *Apr.–Sept., Mon.–Wed. guided tours only, 11:30 and 2:30; Sun. 11–5; call ahead to confirm* Ⓜ *DLR: Greenwich; no direct bus access, only to Vanbrugh Hill (from east) and Blackheath Hill (from west).*

OFF THE BEATEN PATH

Thames Barrier Visitors' Centre. Learn what comes between London and its famous river—a futuristic-looking metal barrier that has been described as the eighth wonder of the world. Multimedia presentations, a film on the Thames's history, working models, and views of the barrier itself put the importance of the relationship between London and its river in perspective. ⊠ *Unity Way, Eastmoor St., Woolwich* ☎ *020/8305–4188* ⊕ *www.environment-agency.gov.uk* 🖰 *£3.50* ☉ *Apr.–Sept., Thurs.–Sun. 10:30–5; last entry 4:30* Ⓜ *National Rail: Charlton (from London Bridge), then Bus 177 or 180; North Greenwich (Jubilee line), then Bus 161 or 472.*

The Thames Upstream

WORD OF MOUTH

"You can take a boat down the Thames to Hampton Court or back, and it is a fascinating journey, and a lovely way to beat the heat if the weather is warm . . . the Thames is of such historic importance to London, traveling to or from Hampton Court on the river can really enrich your understanding."

—zeppole

GETTING ORIENTED

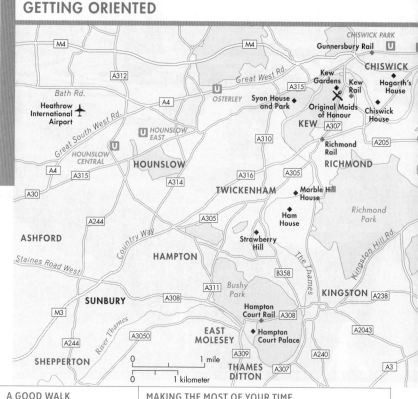

A GOOD WALK

From Chiswick House, follow Burlington Lane and take a left onto Hogarth Lane—which is anything but a lane, in reality—to reach Hogarth's House. Chiswick's Church Street (reached by an underpass from Hogarth's House) is the nearest thing to a sleepy country village street you're likely to find in London. Follow it down to the Thames and turn left at the bottom to reach the 18th-century riverfront houses of Chiswick Mall, referred to by locals as "Millionaire's Row." There are several pretty riverside pubs near Hammersmith Bridge.

MAKING THE MOST OF YOUR TIME

Hampton Court Palace requires at least half a day to experience its magic fully, although you could make do with a couple of hours for any of the other attractions. Because of the distance between the sights, too much traveling eats into your day. Best to concentrate on one principal sight, add in a stately home or village stroll, then a riverside promenade before a pint at a pub.

FEELING PECKISH?

The Original Maids of Honour. Most traditional of Old English tearooms, this is named for a type of jam tart invented here and still baked by hand on the premises. Legend has it that Henry VIII loved them so much he had the recipe kept under guard. Tea is served daily 2:30–6, lunch in two sittings at 12:30 and 1:30. ✉ *288 Kew Rd., Kew* ☏ *020/8940-2752* ⊕ *www.theoriginalmaidsofhonour.co.uk.*

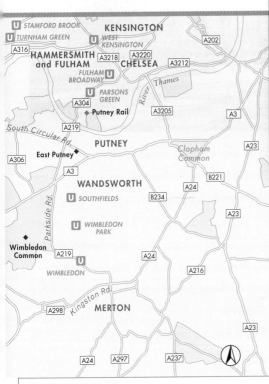

13

GETTING THERE

The District line is the best of the Tube options, stopping at Turnham Green (in the heart of Chiswick but a fair walk from the houses), Gunnersbury (for Syon Park), Kew Gardens, and Richmond. For Hampton Court, overland train is your quickest option: South West trains run from Waterloo twice an hour, with most requiring a change at Surbiton. There are also regular, direct trains from Waterloo to Chiswick station (best for Chiswick House), Kew Bridge, Richmond (for Ham House), and St. Margaret's (best for Marble Hill House). London overground trains also stop at Gunnersbury, Kew Gardens, and Richmond.

A pleasant, if slow, way to go is by river. Boats depart upriver from Westminster Pier, by Big Ben, for Kew (1½ hours), Richmond (2 hours), and Hampton Court (3 hours) several times a day in summer, less frequently from October through March. The boat trip is worth taking only if you make it an integral part of your day out, and be aware that it can get very breezy on the water.

TOP REASONS TO GO

Explore Hampton Court Palace: Go ghost hunting or just admire the beautiful Tudor architecture at Henry VIII's beloved home, then lose yourself in the maze as dusk begins to fall.

Go "Goth" at Strawberry Hill: The 19th-century birthplace of connoisseur Horace Walpole's "Gothick" style, this mock-castle is a joyous riot of color and invention.

Escape to magical Kew Gardens: See the earth from above by visiting Kew's treetop walkway at the famous Royal Botanic Gardens.

Pay your respects to Father Thames: Enjoy a pint from the creaking balcony of a centuries-old riverside pub as you watch the boats row by on the loveliest stretch of England's greatest river.

NEAREST PUBLIC RESTROOMS

Richmond Park, Kew Gardens, and all the stately homes have public restrooms available.

The upper stretch of the Thames unites a string of fashionable districts—Chiswick, Kew, Richmond, and Putney—taking in winding old streets, horticultural delights, cozy pubs nestling at water's edge, and Henry VIII's fiendish outdoor labyrinth at Hampton Court Palace. The neighborhoods dotted along the way are as proud of their village-y feel as of their stately history, witnessed by such handsome and historic estates as Strawberry Hill and Syon House. After the sensory overload of the West End, it's easy to forget you're in a capital city at all.

CHISWICK AND KEW

Updated by
Jack Jewers

On the banks of the Thames just west of central London, far enough out to escape the crush and crowds you've probably just started to get used to, Chiswick is a low-key, upmarket district, content with its run of restaurants, stylish shops, and film-star residents. No doubt its most famous son wouldn't approve of all the conspicuous wealth, though; Chiswick was home to one of Britain's best-loved painters, William Hogarth, who tore the fabric of the 18th-century nation to shreds with his slew of satirical engravings. **Hogarth's House** has been restored to its former glory. Incongruously stranded among Chiswick's terraced houses are a number of fine 18th-century buildings, which are now some of the most desirable suburban houses in London. By far the grandest of all is **Chiswick House,** a unique Palladian-style mansion borne from the 3rd Earl of Burlington's love of classical and Renaissance architecture—a radical style at the time. A mile or so beyond Chiswick is Kew, a leafy suburb with little to see other than its two big attractions: the lovely **Kew Palace** and the **Royal Botanic Gardens**—anchored in the landscape for several miles around by a towering, mock-Chinese pagoda.

EXPLORING

★ **Chiswick House.** Completed in 1729 by the 3rd Earl of Burlington (of Burlington House—home of the Royal Academy—and Burlington Arcade fame), this extraordinary Palladian mansion was envisaged as a kind of temple to the arts. Burlington was fascinated by the architecture he saw in Italy while on the Grand Tour as a young man. When his country home was destroyed by fire in 1725, he seized the chance to rebuild it in homage to those classical and Renaissance styles. The building is loosely modeled on the Villa Capra near Vicenza, while the colonnaded frontage is a partial replica of the Pantheon in Rome (which also inspired the domed roof). The sumptuous interiors were the work of the top decorator of 18th-century England, William Kent (1685–1748). His extraordinary salons, like the Blue Velvet Room, with its gilded decoration and intricate painted ceiling, along with the layout of Chiswick House, sparked a great deal of interest—such ideas were radical in England at the time—and you'll see its influence reflected in numerous later buildings. The rambling gardens are one of the hidden gems of West London. Italianate in style (of course), they are filled with classical temples, statues, and obelisks. ⊠ *Burlington La., Chiswick* ☎ *020/8995–0508* ⊕ *www.chgt.org.uk* ⊠ *£5.50* ☉ *Grounds daily 7–dusk; house Mar.–Oct., daily 10–4* Ⓜ *Turnham Green, Chiswick.*

Hogarth's House. Besieged by a roaring highway that somewhat spoils the atmosphere, and now fully restored after a major fire, the home of the satirist and painter William Hogarth (1697–1764) is worth a visit by fans of his amusing, moralistic engravings (such as "The Rake's Progress" and "Marriage à la Mode"). The artist's tomb is in the cemetery of St. Nicholas's church on nearby Chiswick Mall. ⊠ *Hogarth La., Great West Rd., Chiswick* ☎ *020/8994–6757* ⊕ *www.hounslow.info/arts/hogarthshouse* ⊠ *Free* ☉ *Tues.–Sun. noon–5* Ⓜ *Turnham Green.*

HOGARTH HEAVEN

Fosters Bookshop. A great place to buy Hogarth prints is at Fosters Bookshop, the oldest shop in Chiswick. The shop has its original Georgian frontage, creaking floorboards, and a glorious number of original Victorian novels and essays. It also offers handwritten gift vouchers from £10 to £50,000. ⊠ *183 Chiswick High Rd.* ☎ *020/8995–2768* ⊕ *www.fostersbookshop.co.uk.*

13

QUICK BITES

Some of the loveliest pubs in London sit beside the Thames at Chiswick, stretching along the northern bank of the river as far as Hammersmith Mall—the last remaining fragment of what was once a pretty old village, now all but replaced by urban sprawl.

Blue Anchor. Briefly famous in the late 1990s, thanks to the movie *Sliding Doors*, the Blue Anchor is a cozy 18th-century watering hole with rowing memorabilia lining the walls. ⊠ *13 Lower Mall, Hammersmith* ☎ *020/8748–5774* ⊕ *www.blueanchorlondon.com.*

City Barge. Opposite a tiny island in the middle of the Thames, the City Barge has a lovely riverside terrace and honest pub grub. ⊠ *27 Strand-on-the-Green, Chiswick* ☎ *020/8994–2148.*

Dove Inn. This spot retains the charm of its 300-plus-year heritage, and the tiny terrace is a tranquil place to watch the river flow by. The food is good here, too (especially Sunday lunch). ⊠ *19 Upper Mall, Hammersmith* ☎ *020/8748–9474* ⊕ *www.fullers.co.uk.*

🕘 **Kew Gardens.**

★ *See the highlighted listing in this chapter.*

★ **Kew Palace and Queen Charlotte's Cottage.** The elegant redbrick exterior of Kew, the smallest of Britain's royal palaces, seems almost humble when compared with the grandeur of, say, Buckingham or Kensington Palaces. Yet inside is a fascinating glimpse into life at the uppermost end of society from the 17th to the 19th century. This was one of the havens to which George III retired when insanity forced him to withdraw from public life. Queen Charlotte had an orné—a rustic-style cottage retreat—added in the late 18th century. In a marvelously regal flight of fancy, she kept kangaroos in the paddock outside. The main house and gardens are maintained in the 18th- century style. There are extended tours of the palace on a few Sunday evenings each summer that cover areas not usually on show, such as the Tudor undercroft. Check the website for details. ⊠ *Kew Gardens, Kew* ☎ *0844/482 7777* ⊕ *www.hrp.org.uk* ⊠ *£5.30, in addition to ticket for Kew Gardens* ☉ *Apr.–Sept., Tues.–Sun. 10–5, Mon. 11–5* Ⓜ *Kew Gardens.*

RICHMOND

Named after the (long-vanished) palace Henry VII started here in 1500, Richmond is still a welcoming suburb with a small-town feel, marred only by choking levels of traffic. Duck away from the main streets to find many handsome Georgian and Victorian houses, antiques shops, a Victorian theater, a grand stately home—and, best of all, the largest of London's royal parks.

EXPLORING

★ **Ham House.** To the west of Richmond Park, overlooking the Thames and nearly opposite the memorably named Eel Pie Island, Ham House was built in 1610 and remodelled 50 years later. It's one of the most complete examples in Europe of a lavish 17th-century house, together with a restored formal garden that has become an influential source for other European palaces and grand villas. The original decorations in the Great Hall, Round Gallery, and Great Staircase have been replicated, and all the furniture and fittings are on permanent loan from the Victoria & Albert Museum. A tranquil and scenic way to reach the house is on foot, which takes about 30 minutes, along the eastern riverbank south from Richmond Bridge. ⊠ *Ham St., Richmond* ☎ *020/8940–1950* ⊕ *www. nationaltrust.org.uk* ⊠ *House, gardens, and outbuildings £10.90; gardens only £3.65* ☉ *House mid-Feb.–Mar., Sat.–Mon. 11:30–3:30; Apr.–Sept., Sat.–Wed. noon–4; Oct. and Nov., Sat.–Tues. 11:30–3. Gardens Nov.–early Feb., daily 11–4; mid-Feb.–Oct., daily 11–5* Ⓜ *Richmond, then Bus 65 or 371.*

KEW GARDENS

✉ *Royal Botanic Gardens, Kew, Richmond, Surrey (main entrance is between Richmond Circus and traffic circle at Mortlake Rd.)* ☏ *020/8332–5655* 🌐 *www.kew.org* 🎟 *£13.90* ⊙ *Mid-Feb.–mid Mar., daily 9:30–5:30; late Mar.–Aug., weekdays 9:30–6:30, weekends 9:30–7:30; Sept. and Oct., 9:30–6; Nov.–early Feb. 9:30–4:15. Glasshouses and galleries close 5:30 (3:45 Nov.–early Feb., 5 mid-Feb.–late Mar.)* Ⓜ *Kew Gardens.*

TIPS

■ Free guided tours by garden volunteers leave daily from the Guides' desk inside Victoria Plaza at 11 and 1:30, and a seasonally themed tour leaves at noon. Come early as tours are limited to 15 people.

■ The Kew Explorer bus runs on a 40-minute, hop-on, hop-off route around the gardens every hour from 11 am. Tickets cost £2.

■ Discovery Tours are specially adapted for disabled visitors. Options include walking tours designed for deaf or blind visitors, or bus tours for those with mobility problems. Walking tours are £5 per group, bus tours £30 per group.

■ Fresh air and natural beauty made you peckish? Treat your taste buds to a light tea at the Victoria Terrace Café or a meal at the elegant Orangery, or dine outside at White Peaks.

■ Download the official Kew Gardens guide as an app for your mobile phone, free on the website.

Enter Kew Gardens and you are enveloped by blazes of color, extraordinary blooms, hidden trails, and lovely old follies. Beautiful though it all is, Kew's charms are secondary to its true purpose as a major center for serious research. Academics are hard at work on more than 300 scientific projects across as many acres, analyzing everything from the cacti of eastern Brazil to the yams of Madagascar. First opened to the public in 1840, Kew has been supported by royalty and nurtured by landscapers, botanists, and architects since the 1720s, and with more than 30,000 species of plants, there is interest and beauty in spades.

Although the plant houses make Kew worth visiting even in the depths of winter (there's also a seasonal garden), the flower beds are, of course, best enjoyed in the fullness of spring and summer.

HIGHLIGHTS

Two great 19th-century greenhouses—the **Palm House** and the **Temperate House**—are filled with exotic blooms, and many of the plants have been there since the final glass panel was fixed into place. The Temperate House, once the biggest greenhouse in the world, today contains the largest greenhouse plant in the world, a Chilean wine palm rooted in 1846. You can climb the spiral staircase to the roof and look down on it. Architect Sir William Chambers built a series of temples and follies, of which the crazy 10-story **Pagoda**, visible for miles around, is the star turn. The Princess of Wales conservatory houses 10 climate zones, and the Rhizotron and Xstrata Treetop Walkway takes you 59 feet up into the air.

Fodor's Choice **Hampton Court Palace.**
★ *See the highlighted listing in this chapter.*

Marble Hill House. Set in 66 acres of parkland on the northern bank of the Thames, this handsome Palladian mansion is located almost opposite Ham House. Marble Hill House was built in the 1720s by George II for his mistress, the "exceedingly respectable and respected" Henrietta Howard. Later the house was occupied by Mrs. Fitzherbert, who was secretly married to the Prince Regent (later George IV) in 1785. Restored in 1901 it now looks like it did in Georgian times, with extravagant gilded rooms in which Ms. Howard entertained such literary superstars as Pope, Gay, and Swift. A ferry service from Ham House operates during the summer; access on foot is a half-hour walk south along the west bank of the Thames from Richmond Bridge. Entry is by guided tours, which start at 10:30 and noon at weekends, with additional tours at 2:15 and 3:30 on Sunday. ⊠ *Richmond Rd., Twickenham, Richmond* ☎ *020/8892–5115* ⊕ *www.english-heritage.org.uk* ☛ *£5.30 (guided tour only)* ☉ *Apr.–Oct., Sat. 10–2, Sun. and bank holidays 10–5; Nov.–Mar., prebooked tours only* Ⓜ *Richmond.*

☼ **Richmond Park.** Like practically all other London parks, this enormous park was enclosed in 1637 for use as a royal hunting ground. Unlike the others, however, Richmond Park still has wild red and fallow deer roaming its 2,360 acres (that's three times the size of New York's Central Park). Of special note is the Isabella Plantation (near the Ham Gate entrance), an enchanting and colorful woodland garden, first laid out in 1831. ■TIP➔ There's a splendid, protected view of St. Paul's Cathedral from King Henry VIII's Mound, the highest point in the park. Find it and you have a piece of magic in your sights. The park is also home to White Lodge, a 1727 hunting lodge that now houses the Royal Ballet School. ⊠ *Richmond* ☎ *020/8948–3209* ⊕ *www.royalparks.org.uk* ☉ *Mar.–late Dec., daily 7–dusk; late Dec.–Feb., daily 7:30–dusk* Ⓜ *Richmond, then Bus 371 or 65.*

White Lodge Museum. Though the school isn't open to the public, it does contain the small White Lodge Museum dedicated to the history of the school and ballet in general. Entry is on Tuesday and Thursday afternoons during the school year only and prebooking is essential. ☎ *020/8392–8440* ⊕ *www.royal-ballet-school.org.uk* ☛ *Free* ☉ *School term, Tues. and Thurs. 1:30–3:30; occasional days in school holidays (call to check)* Ⓜ *Mortlake rail*

QUICK BITES

White Cross. Overlooking the Thames so closely that the waters almost lap at the door in high tide, the White Cross is a popular spot that serves traditional pub grub. ⊠ *Water La., Richmond* ☎ *020/8940–6844* ⊕ *www.youngs.co.uk.*

HAMPTON COURT PALACE

✉ *Hampton Court Palace, East Molesley, Surrey* ☎ *0844/482–7799 tickets, 0844/482–7777 information (24 hrs)* ⊕ *www.hrp.org.uk/hamptoncourtpalace* 💷 *Palace, maze, and gardens £16; maze only £3.85; gardens only £5.30.* ⊙ *Late Mar.–Oct., daily 10–6 (last ticket sold at 5; last entry to maze at 5:15); Nov.–late Mar., daily 10–4:30 (last ticket sold at 3:30; last entry to maze at 3:45); check website before visiting* Ⓜ *Richmond, then Bus R68; National Rail, South West: Hampton Court station, 35 mins from Waterloo (most trains require change at Surbiton).*

TIPS

■ Avoid the queue and save by buying your tickets online. Family tickets can mean big savings, with £43.50 covering two adults and up to six children.

■ Choose which parts of the palace to explore based on a number of self-guided audio walking tours. Come Christmas time, there's ice-skating on a rink before the West Front of the palace.

■ Special programs, such as cooking demonstrations in the cavernous Tudor kitchens, bring the past to life. In summer months, arrive in style by riverboat (see "A Tour of the Thames" special section).

The beloved seat of Henry VIII's court, sprawled elegantly beside the languid waters of the Thames, this beautiful palace really gives you two for the price of one: the magnificent Tudor redbrick mansion, begun in 1514 by Cardinal Wolsey to curry favor with the young Henry, and the larger 17th-century baroque building, which was partly designed by Christopher Wren (of St. Paul's fame). The earliest buildings on this site belonged to a religious order founded in the 11th century and were expanded over the years by its many subsequent residents, until George II moved the royal household closer to London in the early 18th century.

HIGHLIGHTS

Wander through the **State Apartments,** decorated in the Tudor style, complete with priceless paintings, and on to the wood-beamed magnificence of **Henry's Great Hall,** before taking in the strikingly azure ceiling of the **Chapel Royal.** Topping it all is the **Great House of Easement,** a lavatory that could sit 28 people at a time.

Feel a chill in the air? Watch out for the ghost of Henry VIII's doomed fifth wife, Catherine Howard, who literally lost her head yet is said to scream her way along the **Haunted Gallery.** Weirdly, the ambient temperature really is prone to drop noticeably and nobody knows why. Latter-day masters of the palace, the joint rulers William and Mary (reigned 1689–1702), were responsible for the beautiful **King's and Queen's Apartments, Georgian Rooms,** and a fine collection of porcelain.

Don't miss the world's most famous **maze,** its ½ mile of pathways among clipped hedgerows still fiendish to negotiate. There's a trick, but we won't give it away here: It's much more fun to go and lose yourself. Also on the grounds, the **Lower Orangery Exotic Garden** shows off thousands of exotic species that William and Mary, avid plant collectors, gathered from around the globe.

★ **Strawberry Hill.** From the outside, this Rococo mishmash of towers, crenulations, and dazzling white stucco is almost fairy-tale-ish in its faux-medieval splendor. Its architect, Sir Horace Walpole (1717–97), knew a thing or two about imaginative flights of fancy—the flamboyant son of the first British prime minister, Robert Walpole, he all but single-handedly invented the Gothic Revival style with his novel *The Castle of Otranto* (1764). Once inside, the forbidding exterior gives way to a veritable explosion of color and light, for Walpole boldly decided to take elements from the exteriors of Gothic cathedrals and move them inside for interior accents. The detail is extraordinary, from the cavernous entrance hall with its vast Gothic trompe l'oeil, to the Great Parlour with its Renaissance stained glass, to the Gallery, whose extraordinary fan vaulting is a replica of the vaults found in Henry VIII's chapel at Westminster Abbey. Neglected for years, Strawberry Hill reopened in 2011 after a stunningly successful £9 million restoration. The gardens have also been meticulously returned to their original 18th-century design, right down to a white marble love seat sculpted into the shape of a shell. ⊠ *268 Waldegrave Rd., Twickenham* ☎ *020/8744–3124* ⊕ *www.strawberryhillhouse.org.uk* 🎟 *£8* ⊙ *Timed entry, every 20 mins; Apr.–early Nov., weekends noon–4:20, Mon.–Wed. 2–4:20* Ⓜ *Richmond, then Bus 33; National Rail: Strawberry Hill station.*

☺ **Syon House and Park.** The residence of the Duke and Duchess of Nor-
Fodor's Choice thumberland, this is one of England's most lavish stately homes—and, ★ even better, the only one reachable by Tube stop. Set in a 55-acre park landscaped by Capability Brown, the core of the house is Tudor—Henry VIII's fifth wife, Catherine Howard, and the extremely short-lived monarch, Lady Jane Grey ("Queen for thirteen days"), made pit stops here before they were sent to the Tower. However, it was spectacularly remodeled in the Georgian style in 1761 by famed decorator Robert Adam. He had just returned from studying the sights of classical antiquity in Italy and created two rooms sumptuous enough to wow any Grand Tourist: the entryway is an amazing study in black and white, pairing neoclassical marbles with antique bronzes, and the Ante-Room contains 12 enormous verd-antique columns surmounted by statues of gold—and this was just a waiting room for the duke's servants and retainers. The Red Drawing Room is covered with crimson Spitalfields silk, and the Long Gallery is one of Adam's noblest creations. Also on view, for a peek through the keyhole, are the duke's and duchess's private (and very lavish) sitting rooms. On the grounds is a famous "Tropical Zoo," a wonderful rescue sanctuary for rare species. ⊠ *Syon Park* ☎ *020/8847–4730* ⊕ *www.tropicalzoo.org* 🎟 *£7.50* ⊙ *Daily 10–5:30* Ⓜ *Gunnersbury, then Bus 237 or 267 to Brentlea stop* ⊠ *Syon Park, Brentford* ☎ *020/8560–0882* ⊕ *www.syonpark.co.uk* 🎟 *£10 for house, gardens, conservatory, and rose garden; £5 for gardens and conservatory* ⊙ *House mid-Mar.–Oct., Wed., Thurs., Sun., and bank holidays 11–5; gardens mid-Mar.–Oct., daily 10:30–5; Nov.–mid-Mar., weekends 10:30–4; Tropical Zoo daily 10–5:30. Last admission 1 hr before closing* Ⓜ *Gunnersbury, then Bus 237 or 267 to Brentlea stop.*

Tower Bridge

A TOUR OF THE THAMES

"I have seen the Mississippi. That is muddy water.
I have seen the St. Lawrence. That is crystal water.
But the Thames is liquid history."
—John Burns

The twists and turns of the Thames River through the heart of the capital make it London's best thoroughfare and most compelling viewing point. Once famous for sludge, silt, and sewage, the Thames is now the cleanest city river in the world. Whether you take a river cruise or a leisurely stroll along its banks and bridges, traveling on or alongside the river is an unforgettable way to soak up views of the city.

MILLENNIUM BRIDGE TO THAMES FLOOD BARRIER

Tower Bridge

The **Millennium Bridge** is the newest span across the river: St. **Paul's Cathedral** and **Tate Modern** eye each other magnificently from either side of the once worryingly wobbly strip of a bridge. Farther east, the reconstructed **Shakespeare's Globe Theatre** is resplendent in whitewash and brown timber on the South Bank.

Between Southwark and London bridges, look for the southside *Golden Hinde*, an exact scale reconstruction of Sir Francis Drake's galleon that sailed around the world.

Moored outside the Victorian shopping mall **Hay's Galleria** is HMS *Belfast*, Europe's last existing armored warship that saw action in World War II, now a floating naval museum on nine decks.

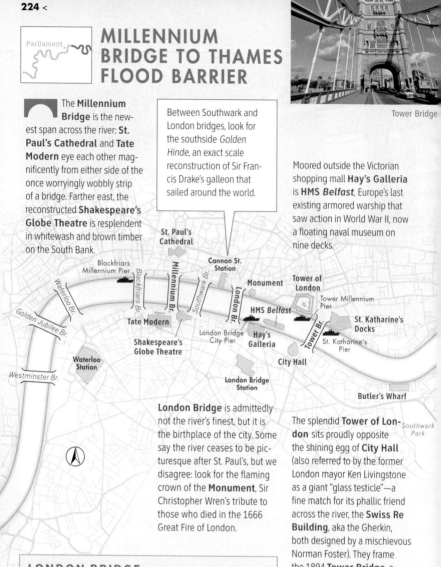

London Bridge is admittedly not the river's finest, but it is the birthplace of the city. Some say the river ceases to be picturesque after St. Paul's, but we disagree: look for the flaming crown of the **Monument**, Sir Christopher Wren's tribute to those who died in the 1666 Great Fire of London.

The splendid **Tower of London** sits proudly opposite the shining egg of **City Hall** (also referred to by the former London mayor Ken Livingstone as a giant "glass testicle"—a fine match for its phallic friend across the river, the **Swiss Re Building**, aka the Gherkin, both designed by a mischievous Norman Foster). They frame the 1894 **Tower Bridge**, a magnificent feat of engineering and style, which leads past the elegant confines of **St. Katharine's Docks**, the trendy restaurants of **Butler's Wharf**, and the **Design Museum**.

LONDON BRIDGE

Viking invaders destroyed London Bridge in 1014, hence the nursery rhyme "London Bridge is falling down." By 1962, London Bridge really was falling down again, its 1831 incarnation unable to take the strain of traffic. It was saved by American tycoon Robert McCulloch, who—possibly confusing the bridge with its much more splendid neighbor, Tower Bridge—bought it in 1968 for $2.46 million and had it shipped, stone by stone, to Lake Havasu in Arizona.

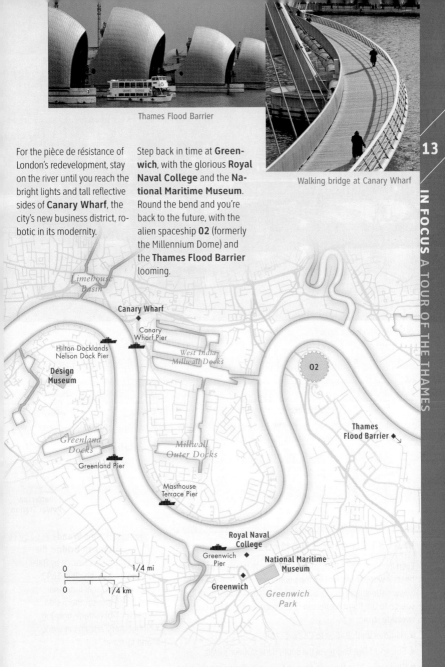

Thames Flood Barrier

Walking bridge at Canary Wharf

For the pièce de résistance of London's redevelopment, stay on the river until you reach the bright lights and tall reflective sides of **Canary Wharf**, the city's new business district, robotic in its modernity.

Step back in time at **Greenwich**, with the glorious **Royal Naval College** and the **National Maritime Museum**. Round the bend and you're back to the future, with the alien spaceship **O2** (formerly the Millennium Dome) and the **Thames Flood Barrier** looming.

Limehouse Basin

Canary Wharf

Canary Wharf Pier

Hilton Docklands Nelson Dock Pier

Design Museum

West India Millwall Docks

O2

Thames Flood Barrier

Greenland Docks

Greenland Pier

Millwall Outer Docks

Masthouse Terrace Pier

Royal Naval College

Greenwich Pier

National Maritime Museum

Greenwich

Greenwich Park

0   1/4 mi
0   1/4 km

WANDSWORTH TO BLACKFRIARS

Parliament

Blackfriars Bridge at night.

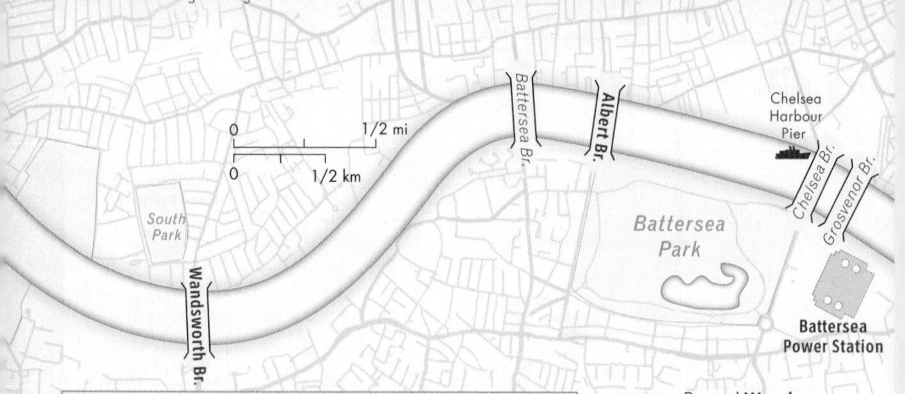

Battersea Br.

Albert Br.

Chelsea Harbour Pier

Chelsea Br.

Grosvenor Br.

South Park

Battersea Park

0   1/2 mi

0   1/2 km

Wandsworth Br.

Battersea Power Station

WALKING THE THAMES

Even if you lack sea legs, you can still enjoy the river: not much beats a wander beside London's waterway. The Thames Path (www.nationaltrail.co.uk) follows the river 184 miles, from its source to the flood barriers in Greenwich. Some of the best riverside strolls:

- Hammersmith Bridge to Chiswick Mall
- Golden Jubilee Bridges to the South Bank's Queen's Walk
- Cleopatra's Needle to Parliament along Victoria Embankment
- Tate Modern to St. Paul's over Millennium Bridge

Beyond **Wandsworth Bridge**, the early part of this stretch by Battersea Bridge, rebuilt in 1890, was London's real industrial heartland, the southern side chock full of cottage housing for laborers, artisans at work, and factories.

The real treat of this stretch is the view of the **Houses of Parliament** and, beyond that, **Westminster Abbey**. **Victoria Embankment**, stretching all the way from Westminster to Blackfriars, was once all grim mudflats. In 1878 it became the country's first electrically illuminated street, and today its fine architecture, trees, and gardens are perfect strolling territory.

View from London Eye (left); House's of Parliament (right)

You can't miss the **London Eye**, whose parts were brought down the Thames one by one before being assembled on-location. Look out too for the London Aquarium and the Dalí museum, housed in the baroque-style County Hall.

Cleopatra's Needle, overlooking the Thames by Embankment, dates back to Heliopolis in 1450 BC. Look for World War I shrapnel holes and gouges at the base.

St. James Park

Charing Cross Station

Cleopatra's Needle

Victoria Embankment

Waterloo Br.

Golden Jubilee Brs.

Oxo Tower

Blackfriars Br.

Blackfriars Pier

Westminster Millennium Pier

Victoria Station

Westminster Abbey

Westminster Br.

Queen's Walk

Houses of Parliament

London Eye

South Bank

The Victoria Tower Gardens

Lambeth Palace

Tate Britain

Lambeth Br.

Vauxhall Br.

Vauxhall Park

Further on is the **Oxo Tower**, whose red-glass letters were designed in 1928 to spell out the brand name while circumventing tight laws on exterior advertising.

By **Blackfriars Bridge**, named after the monks who wore black robes and lived on the north bank during the Middle Ages, the river used to run red by the riverside tanneries and slaughterhouses.

After **Albert Bridge**—glorious at night, with lights like luminescent pearls sweeping down on strings—the Thames is a metropolitan glory of a river, charging through fashionable **Chelsea** and past the now derelict **Battersea Power Station**, under Chelsea, Vauxhall and Lambeth Bridges, with **Lambeth Palace** to the south.

The **Golden Jubilee Bridges** by **Embankment**, two beautifully lit steel-cabled pedestrian walkways, are perfect for reaching the **South Bank**.

Look out for the golden eagle, a monument to World War I RAF fighters, and **Cleopatra's Needle**. For the ultimate double-decker bus-viewing moment, look at **Waterloo Bridge**, once known as Ladies Bridge because it was built by female labor during World War II. The bridge has great views of the South Bank.

Blackfriars Bridge

Parliament

HAMPTON COURT PALACE TO PUTNEY

The Great Conservatory at Syon Park

Hampton Court Palace is a suitably lavish start or end to any trip on the Thames. The river skirts the grounds, giving magnificent views over the Tudor palace that Henry VIII and his daughter Elizabeth I made home, and continues north to **Kingston Bridge**, starting point for the river voyage of Jerome K. Jerome's *Three Men in a Boat* and home to hectic summer regattas. At **Teddington**, where the poet Alexander Pope and writer Horace Walpole entertained their female admirers in the 18th century, the river turns tidal but remains quiet and unspoiled all the way to **Kew**, passing herons and fine stately homes standing proud on the banks. From **Twickenham Bridge** you round the old deer park (to the south) and **Syon Park** (north), which has belonged to the Duke of

Waterlily House at Kew Gardens

Northumberland's family for centuries. Beyond that is an even greater treat—the UNESCO World Heritage Site of **Kew Botanical Gardens**. All manner of rowboats set up for one, two, four, or eight people pull hard under **Chiswick Bridge** and **Barnes (railway) Bridge**, past the expensive riverside frontage of Chiswick Mall and under **Hammersmith Bridge**, to **Putney** and **Fulham**—smart urban villages facing each other across the banks.

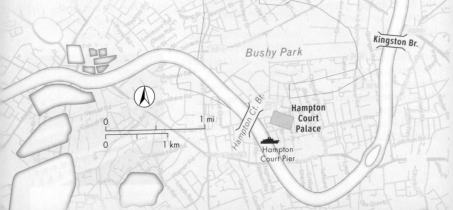

Syon Park

Kew Botanical Gardens

Twickenham Br.

Richmond Landing Stage

Richmond Br.

Marble Hill Park

Eel Pie Island

Teddington

Kingston Br.

Bushy Park

Hampton Ct. Br.

Hampton Court Palace

Hampton Court Pier

0   1 mi

0   1 km

The stretch between Kew and Hammersmith is real rowing and riverside-pub territory, with a picturesque parade past Strand-on-the-Green by Kew Bridge.

ROWERS' ROW Every spring Britain's oldest universities, Oxford and Cambridge, compete not with their brains but with their brawn, in the **Boat Race**, which began in 1829. The race is 4¼ miles upstream from Putney Bridge to Chiswick Bridge: expect clashing oars, clenched teeth, and the occasional sinking (there have been six). The best views are from Hammersmith at the Surrey bend, which is also where most of the pubs are clustered. ⊕ www.theboatrace.org

A BRIEF HISTORY

An engraving by Claes Van Visscher showing Old London Bridge in 1616, with Southwark Cathedral in the foreground

The Thames has come a long way—and not just from its 344-km (214-mi) journey from a remote Gloucestershire meadow to the sea. In the mid-19th century, the river was dying, poisoned by sewers that flushed into the river. The "Big Stink" was so awful that cholera and typhoid killed more than 10,000 in 1853, and Parliament abandoned sitting in 1858. "The odour is hardly that of frankincense," said one contemporary of the 1884 drought that forced down water levels, leaving elegant Victorian nostrils exposed to slimy ooze on the banks.

Joseph Bazalgette, star civil engineer of his time, was commissioned to design a new sewage system, and by the 1900s nearly all was forgiven. (His efforts did not go unappreciated: Bazalgette was later knighted.) Today 7.2 million people get their drinking water from the Thames River.

PLANNING A THAMES BOAT TOUR

"On the smallest pretext of holiday or fine weather the mighty population takes to the boats," wrote Henry James in 1877. You can follow in the footsteps of James, who took a boat trip from Westminster to Greenwich, or make up your own itinerary.

■ Frequent daily tourist-boat services are at their height between April and October.

■ In most cases you can turn up at a pier, and the next departure won't be far away. However, it never hurts to book ahead if you can.

■ Westminster and Tower piers are the busiest starting points, usually with boats heading east.

■TIP➔ For a rundown of all the options, along with prices and timetables, contact **London River Services** (☎ 020/7222–1234 ⊕ www.tfl.gov.uk/river), which gives details of all the operators sailing various sections of the river.

■ The trip between Westminster Pier and the Tower of London takes about 30 minutes, as does the trip between the Tower and Greenwich.

■ A full round-trip can take several hours. Ask about flexible fares and hop on/off options at the various piers.

THE BEST WAYS TO EXPERIENCE THE THAMES WHILE...

GOING OFF THE BEATEN PATH (LITERALLY)	020/7928–3132	www.londonducktours.co.uk	£21
	London Ducktours offers sightseeing with a twist—amphibious patrol vehicles used in World War II have been painted like rubber duckies and traverse land and sea.	Departs from the London Eye (on land): Daily, according to demand, 9:30 am–dusk. Approximately 1½ hrs.	
SAVING TIME AND MONEY	020/7887–8888	www.tate.org.uk/tatetotate	£5.50 one-way
	The playfully polka-dotted *Tate Boat* sails across the river from the Tate Britain to the Tate Modern with a London Eye stop in between.	Departs from the pier at either museum: Daily every 40 mins. Approximately 13 mins. one-way.	
IMPRESSING A DATE OR CLIENT	0870/429–2451	www.bateauxlondon.com	£29.50–£41.50 (lunch), £76–£125 (dinner)
	For ultimate glamour (and expense), look into lunch and dinner cruises with **Bateaux London**, often formal affairs with surprisingly good two- to five-course meals. Variations include jazz brunch cruises on Sundays.	Departs from Embankment Pier for lunch at 12. For dinner, Weds.–Sun. 8 pm (boarding begins 45 mins before departure; some extra sailings in summer). About 3 hours.	
ENJOYING ON-BOARD ENTERTAINMENT	020/7740–0400	www.citycruises.com	£75
	The *London Showboat* lives up to its name, with four-course meals, snazzy cabaret acts from West End musicals, and after-dinner dancing.	Departs from Westminster Pier 7:30 pm (boarding 7:15) April and Oct., Thurs.–Sat.; May–Sept., Wed.–Sun.; Nov., Thurs.–Sun., Dec., Tues.–Sat.; Jan.–Feb., Fri.–Sat. Approximately 3½ hours.	

Where to Eat

WORD OF MOUTH

"Rules [pictured above], on Maiden Lane near Covent Garden, is incredible! Possibly the oldest restaurant in London and the menu is wonderful, especially if you like game."

—mnapoli

THE SCENE

Updated by Alex Wijeratna

As anyone knows who reads the Sunday paper's travel section, London has had a restaurant boom, or rather, a restaurant atomic bomb explosion.

More than ever, Londoners love their restaurants—all 6,700 of them—from its be-here-right-now, wow-factor West End gastro-emporiums, to its tiny neighborhood joints, from stripped-back gastropubs where young-gun foodniks find their feet to swank boîtes where well-traveled, soon-to-be celebrity chefs launch their madcap ego flights. You, too, will be smitten, because you'll be spending, on average, 25% of your travel budget on eating out.

Today, nearly everything on the culinary front has dramatically changed from the days of steamed puddings and overboiled brussels sprouts. Everyone seems to be passionate about food, while a never-ending wall of City money has souped-up standards unimaginably. Celebrity chefs abound. One week it's Heston Blumenthal at the Mandarin Oriental that's flavor of the month, the next it's Jason Atherton at the Pollen Street Social in Mayfair. Thankfully, pride in the best of authentic British food—local, regional, wild, foraged, and seasonal—has made a resurgence and appears on more menus by the day. The new wave of waste-not, want-not "nose-to-tail" eating—where every scrap of meat is deemed fair game for the plate—made its first spectacular comeback at St. John's in Clerkenwell, and fits perfectly with the new age of austerity.

Needless to say, it's the top of the food chain that makes all the news. Throughout London you'll find an ambitious bunch of haute cuisine heroes kickin' butt to world-class standards. Clare Smyth sets the highest bar as head chef at Restaurant Gordon Ramsay in Chelsea; Heston Blumenthal protégé Ashley Palmer Watts single-handedly revives olde-English gastronomy with ultramodern methods at Dinner by Heston Blumenthal; Aussie Brett Graham is cooking on gas at the Ledbury; Portuguese Nuno Mendes creates a modernist escapade at Viajante in Bethnal Green; and French whizzo Hélène Darroze does it sublimely for the girls at the regal Connaught.

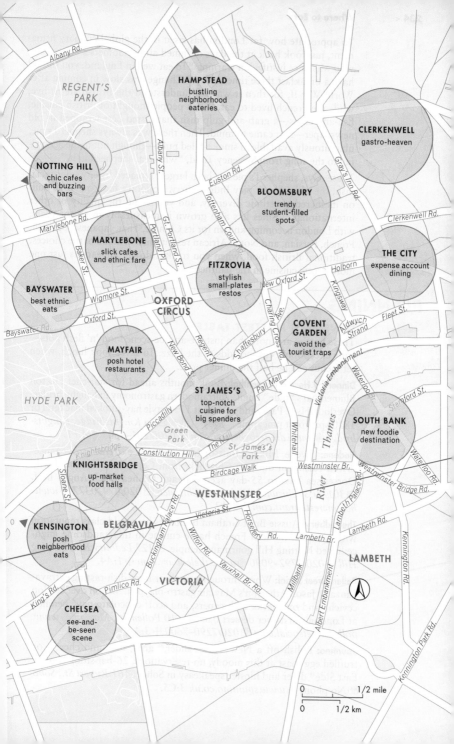

To appreciate how far London has risen in the global culinary firmament, just look back at the days of famed author Somerset Maugham, who was once justified in warning "To eat well in England, you should have a breakfast three times a day." Change was slow in coming after World War II, for then it was still understood the British ate to live, while the French lived to eat. When people thought of British cuisine, fish-and-chips—a grab-and-gulp dish that tasted best wrapped in old newspaper—first came to mind. Then there was always shepherd's pie, ubiquitously available in smoke-filled pubs—though not made according to the song from Sweeney Todd, "with real shepherd in it."

These days, shepherd's pie has been largely replaced by city's unofficial dish, the ubiquitous spicy Indian curry. London's food quake is built on its incredible ethnic diversity, and you'll find the quality of other international cuisines has also grown immeasurably in recent years, with London becoming known for its Chinese, Thai, Japanese, Spanish, French, Persian, and North African restaurants. With all of the choices, traditional British food, when you track it down, appears as just one more exotic cuisine in the pantheon.

PLANNING

LONDON'S HOTTEST TABLES

These hotties are more than just see-and-be-scene food 'n' flesh pots—truly exceptional cuisine adds to the buzz. To save, book lunch, when set menus can be half the dinner price.

Dinner by Heston Blumenthal: Book months ahead for star-chef Heston Blumenthal's "olde" English ultramodern gastronomy in Knightsbridge. Overlook Hyde Park, and marvel at 1730-style hay-smoked mackerel or 1810 spit-roast pineapple "Tipsy" cake. ⊠ *66 Knightsbridge, Knightsbridge* ⊕ *www.dinnerbyheston.com* ☎ *020/7201–3833* ✛ *4:F1.*

Hedone: Swede Mikael Jonsson debuts with extreme provenance-driven cuisine in outlying Chiswick, from Cévennes onions and wild Dorset sea bass to 55-day aged Darragh O'Shea Black Angus beef. ⊠ *301–303 Chiswick High Rd., Chiswick* ☎ *020/874–0377* ⊕ *www.hedonerestaurant.com* ✛ *1:A2.*

The Ledbury: Aussie Brett Graham burnishes his world-class reputation with complex modern French haute cuisine in this handsome, high-ceilinged Notting Hill gourmand temple. ⊠ *127 Ledbury Rd., Notting Hill* ☎ *020/7792–9090* ⊕ *www.theledbury.com* ✛ *1:A4.*

Pollen Street Social: Whizz through a small-or-large dish-tasting extravaganza at Jason Atherton's Mayfair gastro-playpen. Swoon over scallop ceviche and ox cheeks with capers, and scoff chocolate pavé perched at London's first-ever dessert bar. ⊠ *8–10 Pollen St., Mayfair* ⊕ *www.pollenstreetsocial.com* ☎ *020/7290–7600* ✛ *3:A5.*

Spuntino: Polish off a New York "slider," grits, mac and cheese, or truffled egg toast at this moody, no-reservations, 26-bar-stool "Lower East Side" diner and hipster speakeasy in Soho. ⊠ *61 Rupert St., Soho* ☎ No phone ⊕ *www.spuntino.co.uk 3:C5.*

Viajante: El Bulli–trained Portuguese star Nuno Mendes bedazzles with urban foraged and art-on-a-plate contemporary cuisine in far-off but happening Bethnal Green. ⊠ *Patriot Sq., Bethnal Green* ☎ *020/7871–0461* ⊕ *www.viajante.co.uk* ✛ *4:G1.*

EATING OUT STRATEGY

Where should you eat? With thousands of London eateries competing for your attention, it may seem like a daunting question. But fret not—our expert writers and editors have done most of the legwork. The selections here represent the best this city has to offer—from hot pudding to haute cuisine. *Search "Best Bets" for top recommendations by price, cuisine, and experience. Sample local flavor in the neighborhood features. Or find a review quickly in the neighborhood listings. Whichever way you look at it, you're sure to get a taste of London.*

14

RESERVATIONS

Plan ahead if you're determined to snag a sought-after reservation. Some renowned restaurants are booked weeks or even months in advance. In the reviews, we mention reservations only when they're essential or not accepted, though it's always a good idea to book as far ahead as you can and reconfirm when you arrive in London. Note that some top restaurants also now take credit-card details and charge a penalty fee if you're a no-show.

WHAT TO WEAR

When in England's style capital, do as the natives do: Dress up to eat out. Whatever your style, dial it up a notch. Have some fun while you're at it. Pull out the clothes you've been saving for a special occasion and get a little glamorous. As unfair as it seems, the way you look can influence how you're treated—and where you're seated. Generally speaking, jeans and a button-down shirt will suffice at most table-service restaurants in the $ to $$ range. Moving up from there, many pricier restaurants require jackets, and some insist on ties. Shorts, sweatpants, and sports jerseys are rarely appropriate. Note that in reviews we mention dress only when men are required to wear a jacket, or a jacket and tie.

TIPPING AND TAXES

Do not tip bar staff in pubs and bars—though you can always offer to buy them a drink. In restaurants, tip 12.5% of the check for full meals if service is not already included; tip a small token if you're just having coffee or tea. If paying by credit card, double-check that a tip has not already been included in the bill.

CHILDREN

Unless your children behave impeccably, it's best to avoid the high-class establishments; you're unlikely to find a children's menu there, anyway. London's many Italian restaurants and pizzerias are popular with kids. Other family-friendly establishments include chains like Byron, Pizza Express, Wagamama, Giraffe, and Carluccio's.

HOURS

In London you can find breakfast all day, but it's generally served between 7 am and 11 am. Lunch is between noon and 3 pm, and brunch between 11 am to 2 pm. Tea, often a meal in itself, is taken between

Continued on page 250

BEST BETS FOR LONDON DINING

With thousands of restaurants to choose from, how will you decide where to eat? Fodor's writers and editors have selected their favorite restaurants by price, cuisine, and experience in the Best Bets lists below. In the first column, Fodor's Choice properties represent the "best of the best" in every price category. You can also search by neighborhood for excellent eats—just peruse the following pages. Or find specific details about a restaurant in the full reviews, listed later in the chapter by neighborhood.

Fodor's Choice ★

Chez Bruce, p. 266
Clos Maggiore, p. 260
Dean Street Town-house, p. 258
Dinner by Heston Blumenthal, p. 271
Giaconda Dining Room, p. 258
Great Queen Street, p. 261
Harwood Arms, p. 268
Hedone, p. 276
Hélène Darroze at the Connaught, p. 253
Hibiscus, p. 253
Hix, p. 259
The Ledbury, p. 274
Les Deux Salons, p. 262
The Orange, p. 269
Pollen Street Social, p. 254
Rules, p. 262
Scott's, p. 255

Seven Park Place, p. 251
Spuntino, p. 259
St. John, p. 265
Viajante, p. 265
Wiltons, p. 251

Best by Price

$

Baozi Inn, p. 256
Busaba Eathai, p. 258
Côte, p. 258
Golden Hind, p. 255
Koya, p. 241

$$

Giaconda Dining Room, p. 258
Great Queen Street, p. 261
Harwood Arms, p. 268
The Orange, p. 269
Viajante, p. 265

$$$

Dean Street Town-house, p. 258
Hix, p. 259
St. John, p. 265

$$$$

Dinner by Heston Blumenthal, p. 271
Hélène Darroze at the Connaught, p. 253
L'Atelier de Joël Robuchon, p. 261
The Ledbury, p. 274
Marcus Wareing at the Berkeley, p. 272
Restaurant Gordon Ramsay, p. 269
Scott's, p. 255
Tom Aikens, p. 268

Best by Cuisine

BRITISH

Great Queen Street, p. 261
Harwood Arms, p. 268
Hereford Road, p. 274
Hix, p. 259
The Orange, p. 269
St. John, p. 265

CHINESE

Baozi Inn, p. 256
Yauatcha, p. 260

FRENCH

Hélène Darroze at the Connaught, p. 253
Koffmann's, p. 272
La Petite Maison, p. 253
The Ledbury, p. 274
Restaurant Gordon Ramsay, p. 269
Seven Park Place, p. 251

ITALIAN

Bocca di Lupo, p. 257
Cecconi's, p. 251
L'Anima, p. 264

JAPANESE

Aqua Kyoto, p. 256
Koya, p. 241

SEAFOOD

Golden Hind, p. 255
J Sheekey, p. 261
Scott's, p. 255
Sweetings, p. 264

Best by Experience

BRASSERIE

Cecconi's, p. 251
Côte, p. 258
Dean Street Town-house, p. 258
Les Deux Salons, p. 262
Racine, p. 269
The Riding House Café, p. 254
The Wolseley, p. 251

BRUNCH

Cecconi's, p. 251
Dean Street Town-house, p. 258
Hélène Darroze at the Connaught, p. 253
The Modern Pantry, p. 245
PJ's Bar & Grill, p. 267

BUSINESS DINING

Bistrot Bruno Loubet, p. 265
Corrigan's Mayfair, p. 252
Dinner by Heston Blumenthal, p. 271
The Greenhouse, p. 253
The Ledbury, p. 274
Scott's, p. 255

CELEB SPOTTING

Hix, p. 259
J Sheekey, p. 261
Le Caprice, p. 250

Nobu Berkeley Street, p. 254
Scott's, p. 255
The Wolseley, p. 251

GASTROPUBS

The Cow, p. 272
Great Queen Street, p. 261
Harwood Arms, p. 268
The Orange, p. 269
Riding House Cafe, p. 254

GOOD FOR GROUPS

Boundary, p. 263
Lemonia, p. 276
The Orange, p. 269

HISTORIC

Maison Bertaux, p. 259
Rules, p. 262
Simpson's Tavern, p. 264
Sweetings, p. 264
Wiltons, p. 251

HOTEL DINING

Bar Boulud at the Marndarin Oriental, p. 271
Bistro Bruno Loubet at The Zetter, p. 265
Dinner by Heston Blumenthal at the Mandarin Oriental, p. 271
Hélène Darroze at the Connaught, p. 253
Koffmann's at the Berkeley, p. 272

Marcus Wareing at the Berkeley, p. 272

HOT SPOTS

Dinner by Heston Blumenthal, p. 271
Pollen Street Social, p. 254
The Ledbury, p. 274
Scott's, p. 255
Spuntino, p. 259

LATE-NIGHT DINING

Café Boheme, p. 241
Dean Street Town-house, p. 258
J Sheekey, p. 261
The Wolseley, p. 251

LOCAL FAVORITES

Alounak, p. 249
Chez Bruce, p. 266
Hedone, p. 276
The Henry Root Lemonia, p. 276

LUNCH PRIX-FIXE

Galvin Bistrot de Luxe, p. 255
Hereford Road, p. 274
Koffmann's, p. 272
Luxe, p. TK
Le Gavroche, p. 254
Racine, p. 269

PRETHEATER

Côte, p. 258
Dean Street Town-house, p. 258
Savoy Grill, p. 263
Wild Honey, p. 255

QUIET MEAL

Hibiscus, p. 253
The Greenhouse, p. 253
L'Oranger, p. 250
Seven Park Place, p. 251

14

ROMANTIC

Andrew Edmunds, p. 256
Hélène Darroze at the Connaught, p. 253
J Sheekey, p. 261
Le Gavroche, p. 254
Scott's, p. 255

SPECIAL OCCASION

Dinner by Heston Blumental, p. 271
Hélène Darroze at the Connaught, p. 253
Koffmann's, p. 272
The Ledbury, p. 274
Restaurant Gordon Ramsay, p. 269

WINE LISTS

The Greenhouse, p. 253
The Ledbury, p. 274
Marcus Wareing at the Berkeley, p. 272
Restaurant Gordon Ramsay, p. 269

EXPERIMENTAL

Hedone, p. 276
Hibiscus, p. 253
Tom Aikens, p. 268
Viajante, p. 265

ST. JAMES'S, MAYFAIR, AND MARYLEBONE

Mayfair and St. James's—home to Buckingham Palace and Clarence House, where Prince Charles and Camilla live—have a decidedly old-world, royal feel. Appropriately, most of the restaurants here are fit for a future king or queen.

This is where you'll find London's top restaurants, including Pollen Street Social, Hélène Darroze at the Connaught, Scott's, Bibiscus, and ageless Le Gavroche—dining experiences that are geared toward a well-heeled, deep-pocketed clientele. Mere mortals should make reservations well in advance to dine at any of these restaurants for dinner (and reserve for the earlier shank of the evening, when demand is less). Keep in mind that no-shows mean last-minute tables often crop up, and lunching here can be a great money-saving strategy.

If you're looking for something more wallet-friendly, head north to Marylebone, formerly dowdy but now prized for its chic "village"-like feel. Here are an array of low-key little cafés, boîtes, and tapas bars, offering everything from Moroccan and Spanish to Thai and Japanese.

"POP-UPS" AND . . .

An underground food revolution of here-today-gone-tomorrow "pop-up" restaurants, chef-led supper clubs, and home-based supper nights is sweeping the London foodie scene. Start your hunt for supper clubs and "anti-restaurants" at ⊕ supperclubfangroup.ning.com. A top pop-up is the Rambling Restaurant (⊕ www.ramblingrestaurant.com). Originally founded by star chef Nuno Mendes, "supper club" meals cooked by leading guest chefs are featured at the Loft Project (⊕ www.theloftproject.co.uk), with tasting-menu extravaganzas for 16 people around a communal table in a trendy loft in east-side Dalston (£120).

BRITISH TO A "T": TOP LONDON TEAS

It was a peckish Anna, 7th Duchess of Bedford, who began the tradition of British afternoon tea in the 1840s, and taking tea is now once more the height of fashion. Here's the best around. (Sorry: longtime favorite Fortnum & Mason has one of the worst!)

Tea at the Palm Court at the **Ritz** (⊠ The Ritz, 150 Piccadilly, St. James's ☎ 020/7493–2687 ⊕ www.theritzlondon.com) would moisten the eye of Marie Antoinette and is still an ultimate afternoon tea experience, with a rococo star-burst of gilt work, crystal chandeliers, and vast floral displays. Expect egg and cress and cucumber sandwiches on three-tiered silver cake stands, plus scones, cakes, and dainty pastries (£54–£64).

A Hungarian quartet play at suave and swank **Claridge's** (⊠ Brook St., Mayfair ⊕ www.claridges.co.uk ☎ 020/7629–8860), where the green-and-white-striped porcelain tea service is straight out of the Mad Hatter's Tea Party. You'll find 30 loose-leaf teas to choose from, including rare Darjeeling First Flush tea (prices from £38, or £62 for a Rosé Champagne tea).

Not far away off Mount Street in Mayfair, fashionistas splurge on flourless caramel sponge cake at the soigné **Connaught** (⊠ Carlos Pl., Mayfair ⊕ www.the-connaught.co.uk ☎ 020/3147–7100). Loyalists dig the open fires, Laurent-Perrier bubbles, smoked salmon and wasabi finger sandwiches, Christine Ferber jams, and loose-leaf Ceylon tea.

If you can't afford to stay at London's best hotel, why not take tea for an hour or two and indulge in the fantasy of Noel Coward's favorite city spot for a fraction of the cost. Just a few blocks over from Mayfair in Soho, the **Savoy** (⊠ Strand, Soho ⊕ www.claridges.co.uk ☎ 020/7836–4343) offers the prettiest settings in London. In the heavenly Upper Thames Foyer—all pink orchids and a black-and-white chinoiserie fabric—be sure to check out the hotel's own Savoy Tea boutique, with great bespoke tea accessories. In adjacent Thames Foyer savor the Savoy's High Tea.

HOTEL DINING

14

Some of London's finest restaurants are found inside its top-end hotels. **Dinner by Heston Blumenthal** (⊠ Mandarin Oriental, 66 Knightsbridge, Knightsbridge ☎ 20/7201–3833) wows at the Mandarin Oriental with modern takes on olde-English dishes like "Meat fruit" mandarin-shape chicken liver parfait (circa 1500) and "Spiced pigeon" with ale and artichokes (circa 1780).

French dynamo **Hélène Darroze** shows off virtuoso skills at her self-named wood-paneled Edwardian dining room (⊠ The Connaught, 6 Carlos Pl., Mayfair ☎ 020/3147–7200). Catch veteran Pierre Koffmann while you can at **Koffmann's** (⊠ The Berkeley, Wilton Place, Knightsbridge) where you simply must try his pig's trotters with morels and pistachio soufflé before he retires.

Star chef Daniel Boulud pulls in a crowd for his posh French charcuterie and Yankee hamburgers at **Bar Boulud** (⊠ Mandarin Oriental, see above).

COVENT GARDEN

Soho and Covent Garden are the city's playground, an all-day, all-night jostling neon wonderland of glitz, glamour, and greasepaint. This area is London's cultural heart, with old and new media companies, late-night dive bars, West End musicals, and highbrow theater, ballet, and opera houses.

In the last decade, high rents have forced out many of Soho's seedier businesses and ushered in top-notch restaurants, including French brasserie deluxe **Les Deux Salons** (⊠ *40–42 William IV St., Covent Garden* ☎ *020/7734–0623* ✛ *3:E6*), speakeasy diner **Spuntino** (⊠ *61 Rupert St., Soho* ✛ *3:C5*), Italian upstairs hideaway **Polpetto** (⊠ *Upstairs at the French House, 49 Dean St., Soho* ☎ *020/7734–1969* ✛ *3:D5*) and high-quality Spanish tapas bar **Barrafina** (⊠ *54 Frith St., Soho* ☎ *020/7813–8016* ✛ *3:D4*), a magnet for modern Iberian food. Because of its popularity with visitors, Soho prices can be absurdly expensive: £12 cocktails and £30 main courses are not unheard of. For a quick bite without breaking the bank, head to Chinatown's festooned and cobbled streets.

STREET EATS

Head to **Mooli's** on Frith St. (⊠ *50 Frith St., Soho* ☎ *020/7494–9075* ⊕ *www.moolis.com* ✛ *3:D4*), where you can find fine Indian street food. Try the unleavened flatbread roti wraps crammed with Punjabi goat and cumin potato. Other good-to-go rotis, which cost under £5.50, are stuffed with Goan pork and pomegranate seeds or the Keralan beef with coconut. Just around the corner, there's a friendly welcome, comfy booths, and a longer street-based Thai menu at **Rosa's** (⊠ *48 Dean St., Soho* ☎ *020/7494–1638* ⊕ *www.rosaslondon.com* ✛ *3:D5*), where it would be a crime to miss the deep-fried Thai calamari or soft shell crabs.

MEAL DEALS AND STEALS

PRE- AND POST-THEATER DINING

Opening night West End and Hollywood stars celebrate at **J Sheekey** (✉ *28–32 St. Martin's Ct., Covent Garden* ☎ *020/7240-2565* ⊕ *www.j-sheekey.co.uk* ✛ *3:E6*) for late-night seafood dishes in a low-lighted chic mahogany salon and raised-counter oyster bar.

For a highly romantic £19.50 set French meal in a cute con-servatory, head to candle-lighted **Clos Maggiore** (✉ *33 King St., Covent Garden* ☎ *020/7379-9696* ⊕ *www.closmaggiore. com* ✛ *3:F5*), just off Covent Garden piazza. Meander through duck rillettes, French charcuterie, and natural terroirs-based wines at **Terroirs** (✉ *5 William IV St., Covent Garden* ☎ *020/7036-0660* ⊕ *www.terroirswinebar.com* ✛ *3:E6*). Savor watercress soup and cod with sea purslane in a classy French brasserie deluxe at **Les Deux Salons** (✉ *40–42 William IV St., Covent Garden* ☎ *020/7420-2050* ⊕ *www.lesdeuxsalons.com* ✛ *3:E6*), where three-course theater deals are only £15.95. **Polpetto** (✉ *Upstairs at the French House, 49 Dean St., Soho* ☎ *020/7734-1969* ⊕ *www.polpetto.co.uk* ✛ *3:C5*) above the historic French House pub is a moody, tin-tile-ceiling, 28-seat hidden gem, which whips up winning Italian small plates like hare papardelle, char-grilled octopus, or pork in milk.

BUDGET EATS

European: Regular Twitter feeds from **Fernandez & Wells** (✉ *43 Lexington St., Soho* ☎ *020/7734-1546* ⊕ *www. fernandezandwells.com* ✛ *3:B5*) about their latest European stews, soups, cheese, and cured meat baguettes help pull in the punters.

Pan-Asian: Try the great Japanese udon noodles with mack-erel and green leaves for £10.50 at no-reservations **Koya** in Soho (✉ *49 Frith St., Soho* ☎ *020/7434-4463* ⊕ *www.koya. co.uk* ✛ *3:D5*), or hit **Busaba Eathai** (✉ *106–110 Wardour St., Soho* ☎ *020/7255-8686* ⊕ *www.busaba.com* ✛ *3:C4*), a wildly popular Thai canteen with low lighting and shared tables.

BARS AND PUBS

One of the top spots for a truly romantic date is the elegant champagne bar at **Brasserie Max** inside the stylish Covent Garden Hotel (✉ *10 Monmouth St., Covent Garden* ☎ *020/7806-1007* ✛ *3:E4*).

Café Bohème (✉ *13 Old Compton St., Soho* ☎ *020/7734-0623* ✛ *3:D5*) opposite the Prince Edward Theatre has an atmospheric zinc bar, low-risk brasserie fare, curbside tables, and is popular with the fashion crowd (open until 3 am Monday–Sat-urday). The snazzy base-ment hangout **Mark's Bar** (✉ *66–70 Brewer St., Soho* ☎ *020/7292-3518* ⊕ *www.hixsoho.co.uk* ✛ *3:C5*) has old-fashioned bar billiards and English heritage cocktails (think Picador's, Hanky Panky's, milk punches, and lovage gin). Or mind the bouncer and battered front door at the **Experimental Cock-tail Club** in Chinatown (✉ *13A Gerrard St., China-town* ☎ *020/7434-3559* ✛ *3:D5*) where it's all fanatical cocktail bar staff and antiques-shop chic.

14

BLOOMSBURY, FITROVIA, MARYLEBONE, AND HAMPSTEAD

From money-is-no-object expense-account dining in Fitzrovia to the bluestocking haunts of Bloomsbury and the bracing fresh-air and leafy tranquillity of Hampstead, you couldn't imagine three more strikingly different dining zones.

Show off with the Gucci Gucci crowd at sceney sushi sanctum and robata bar **Roka** (⊠ *37 Charlotte St., Fitzrovia* ☎ *020/7580–6464* ⊕ *www.rokarestaurant.com* ✚ *3:C2*) on restaurant-central Charlotte Street, where there's lush scallop skewers and sea bass sashimi. Or hang with the asymmetric fringed, design-school hipsters that koo over the squirrel taxidermy at New York–style **Riding House Café** (⊠ *43–51 Great Titchfield St., Bloomsbury* ☎ *020/7927–0840* ⊕ *www.ridinghousecafe.co.uk* ✚ *3:A2*) where gourmet burgers are a snip at £9.60. Or experience classic English flavor at one of the homey Georgian gastropubs of Hampstead (more millionaires in Britain than anywhere else): the **Wells** (⊠ *30 Well Walk* ☎ *020/7794–3785* ⊕ *www.thewellshampstead.co.uk* ✚ *1:E1*), just off the Heath, serves traditional roast beef and Yorkshire pudding (£16).

THE SERVICE SITUATION

What London's restaurant boom of seismic proportions means to you, the visitor, is, naturally, a great many more choices, though the hot competition among the hundreds of new restaurants for the handful of good staff means there's been no improvement in the standard of service—in fact, quite the opposite. If you don't expect your waiter to introduce him or herself, smile, notice your frantic semaphoring, know anything about the dishes, or apologize for whatever goes amiss, you'll be quite happy. Sir Terrance Conran tried to remedy this situation with a restaurant school but, alas, that shut its doors some time ago.

DINING TWO WAYS

	SAVE	SPLURGE
French	**Le Relais de Venise L'Entrecôte** (⊠ 120 Marylebone La., Marylebone ☎ 020/7486–0878 ✛ 1:H3) is a cult no-reservations, no-choice, steak, frites, and salad Parisian-style brasserie.	**Galvin Bistrot de Luxe** (⊠ 66 Baker St., Fitzrovia ☎ 020/7935–4007 ✛ 1:G3) conjures exemplary upmarket French bistro food in a handsome and grown-up brasserie deluxe on Baker Street.
Indian	**Trishna** (⊠ 15–17 Blandford St, Marylebone ☎ 020/7935–5624 ✛ 1:G3) has delicate £18 set three-course South Indian seafood-based aromatic modern curries.	**Rasa Samudra** (⊠ 5 Charlotte St., Fitzrovia ☎ 020/7637–0222 ✛ 3:C2) impresses with spicy Keralian seafood specialties, ranging from tilapia to kingfish.
Japanese	**Sushi of Shiori** (⊠ 144 Drummond St., Euston ☎ 020/7388–9962 ✛ 2:B3) offers mind-blowing sushi canapés or omakase chef's selection sushi and sashimi at this tidy eight-seater in Euston.	**Roka's** (⊠ 37 Charlotte St., Fitzrovia ☎ 020/7580–6464 ✛ 3:C2) robata grill attracts a glamourpuss crowd for its black cod, king crab, scallops, and skewered chicken dishes.

GLOBAL TAPAS

The small-plates trend marches on in London, especially in Bloomsbury and Fitzrovia. Here's where to go: **Barrica** (⊠ 62 Goodge St., Fitzrovia ☎ 020/7436–9448 ✛ 3:B2) serves notable Spanish tapas in a long Madrid-style tapas room. Plough through meatballs, pork, and oxtail or squid or veal cheeks. At **Salt Yard** (⊠ 54 Goodge St., Fitzrovia ☎ 020/7637–0657 ✛ 3:B2) the tapas have a seamless Spanish–Italian twist. And **Siam Central** (⊠ 14 Charlotte St., Fitzrovia ☎ 020/7436–7460 ✛ 3:C2) is a popular corner spot on buzzy Charlotte Street that offers 30 Thai tapas, such as tamarind duck, battered mussels, and drunken noodles with beef and Thai basil.

14

CUPCAKE CENTRAL

London's turned into cupcake central, and Bea's of Bloomsbury (⊠ 44 Theobald's Rd., Bloomsbury ☎ 020/7242–8330 ⊕ www.beasofbloomsbury.com ✛ 3:H1) is one of the best cupcake and tea shops in town.

With its on-site bakery, Bea's churns out freshly baked sugary delights like blackberry cupcake with vanilla sponge, butter cream, and a fresh blackberry on top, or heavenly chocolate fudge cupcake with fudge icing.

Don't miss the brightly colored peanut butter, praline, or carrot cake cupcakes. And try not to drool over the cornucopia of three-layered chocolate truffle cakes, New York cheese cakes, lemon drizzle Bundts, fruit cakes, and pecan pies.

Afternoon tea (noon–7 pm weekdays and Saturday, and 2–7 pm on Sunday) with cupcakes, scones, minimeringues, flavored marshmallows, and Valrhona brownies is £22.

THE CITY, CLERKENWELL, AND SOUTH BANK

Historic and just-beyond-The-City-limits, Clerkenwell is one of the most cutting-edge, radical, and trendy quarters for London gastro-dining, which sets it in marked contrast to the adjacent City, which caters overwhelmingly to business-focused conservative dining. Across the Thames, the South Bank anchors itself to its foodie mecca, the Borough Food Market.

For The City, join the bailed-out City bankers trooping over to **Hawksmoor** (✉ *157 Commercial St., The City* ☎ *020/7247–7392* ⊕ *www.thehawksmoor.com* ✛ *2:G1*) for dictionary-thick, 35-day-aged, char-grilled British Longhorn steaks. Farther over toward Clerkenwell, there's a more relaxed, trendy vibe at **Morito** (✉ *32 Exmouth Market, Clerkenwell* ☎ *020/7608–1550* ✛ *2:E3*), where a bright orange Formica counter often displays high-quality Spanish tapas at fair prices.

THE BOROUGH MARKET FOR UNDER £10

Follow the Tumblr online photo feed at the amazing brick-walled **Elliot's Café** (✉ 12 Stoney St., Borough ☎ 020/7403–7436 ⊕ www.elliotscafe.com ✛ 5:H1) bang opposite Borough Market for incredible curios like cage-caught gray squirrel rillettes on toast for £7.50. Or for slightly more traditional "olde" English fare, sit at wooden oyster barrels and treat yourself to four Cumbrae rock oysters for under £10 at **Wright Brothers Oyster & Porter House** (✉ 11 Stoney St., Borough ☎ 020/7403–9554 ⊕ www.wrightbros.eu.com ✛ 5:H1).

OFF THE TOURIST TRACK

CHEF-CENTRIC CLERKENWELL

The area where the buttoned-up starchiness of The City fades into the relaxed artiness of Clerkenwell is a fertile ground for avant-garde chefs and restaurants. Within walking distance of Farringdon Tube and the Smithfield Meat Market, **Bistrot Bruno Loubet** (⊠ *86–88 Clerkenwell Rd., Clerkenwell* ☎ *020/7324–4455* ⊕ *www.bistrotbrunoloubet.com* ✛ *2:F3*) at the Zetter hotel pulls no punches with highly expressive southwestern French cuisine like hare royale or daube of beef. Facing Loubet's on St. John's Square, New Zealander Anna Hansen's **Modern Pantry** (⊠ *47–48 St. John's Sq., Clerkenwell* ☎ *020/7553–9210* ⊕ *www.themodernpantry.co.uk* ✛ *2:F3*) is doing something extremely rare and special with modern fusion food at this all-day two-floor pantry and deli. Her sugar-cured New Caledonian prawn omelet with Sri Lankan chili "sambol" is famed. At nearby stark-white fronted **St. John** (⊠ *26 St. John St., Smithfield* ☎ *020/7251–0848* ⊕ *www.stjohnrestaurant.com* ✛ *2:F4*) pioneering Fergus Henderson prepares British nose-to-tail carnivorous cuisine, famed for its no-nonsense approach to offal and all fiddly bits in between.

BUSTLING BOROUGH MARKET

First mentioned in 1276 and believed to have existed in Roman times, Borough Market on the South Bank is a firm favorite with tourists, chefs, and foodies alike. From Thursday to Saturday, the unassuming location under Victorian wrought-iron railway arches at London Bridge is packed with food trekkers eager to pick up the finest and freshest fruit, veg, and grub in the capital. There are more than 140 stalls, plus a bunch of pubs, bars, and restaurants and specialist shops like **Neal's Yard Dairy** (⊠ *6 Park St., Borough* ☎ *020/7367–0799* ⊕ *www.nealsyarddairy.co.uk* ✛ *5:H1*), where you'll be bowled over by the great truckles of pungent blue Stilton cheese stacked floor to ceiling.

MONDO VINO

It's all about the wine at **28°–50° Wine Workshop & Kitchen** (⊠ *140 Fetter La., The City* ☎ *020/7242–8877* ⊕ *www.2850.co.uk* ✛ *2:E5*) at this oenophiles' honeypot and French restaurant.

Here, sommelier and co-owner Xavier Rousset has assembled a cracking wine list of 40-odd wines available by the glass, carafe, or bottle.

Plus he offers an awesome collectors' list with rare vintages seldom seen in London restaurants—all sold at bargain prices. With bottles sourced directly from private collectors, look out for gems like Château Cheval Blanc Grand Cru 1976 from Bordeaux for £399.

Another top selection was a highly prized Château Rieussec 2003 Sauternes sweet dessert wine for a knockdown £59.

Authentic French breads, charcuterie, duck rillettes, and cheese selections provide a tasty foil for the outstanding wines on offer.

14

KENSINGTON, CHELSEA, AND KNIGHTSBRIDGE

If you *think* you're fabulous, famous, wealthy, or all three, chances are you'll be living—and dining—in one of these neighborhoods among its world-class museums, parks, shops, hotels, monuments, fashion stores, and top restaurants (do super-chef Heston Blumenthal and Harvey Nichols ring a bell?).

Chelsea, made famous in the swinging 60s, is where today's Prada velour–clad yummy mummies bomb around in Range Rovers 4x4s, which locals have dubbed "Chelsea tractors." Known for its shopping, Chelsea's restaurants range from bijou boîtes to exclusive little places ideal for a girly gossip and a bite on the go. Over in upscale Knightsbridge, you'll find Harrods and the high-end fashion boutiques of Sloane Street, plus a heap of world-class hotel-based restaurants. Come here for an amazing dining experience, but don't expect bargains (except at lunch). Nearby, Kensington is a residential neighborhood with a wider range of restaurants, from French bistros to funky Vietnamese hideaways.

CULTURAL EATS

The food's almost as good as the art and artifacts at some chic London locales. Marvel at portraits of pop stars and queens before bagging a seat with an amazing view of Trafalgar Square at the rooftop **Portrait Restaurant** (✉ *National Portrait Gallery, St. Martin's Pl., St. James's* ☎ *020/7312–2490* ⊕ *www.npg.org.uk* ✛ *3:E6*), which offers fairly decent British fare. At the world-famous auction house, the **Café at Sotheby's** (✉ *34–35 New Bond St., Mayfair* ☎ *020/7293–5077* ⊕ *www.sothebys.com/cafe*) attracts a classy in-the-know crowd for bargain afternoon tea services (£7 to £12).

PIT STOPS FOR SHOPPERS

Whether you're looking for a quick bite or a more relaxing meal, there are plenty of options for every shopper.

Londoners still adore **Wagamama** (✉ 26 Kensington High St. ☎ 020/7376–1717 ⊕ www.wagamama.com ✛ 4:B1) for its healthful, cheap, and cheerful Asian noodles, ramen, and rice dishes.

This branch overlooks Kensington High Street and is clogged with mummies, toddlers, and buggies.

Slip in for a lemon sole or a Botanist salad—with squash, Jerusalem artichoke, and spinach—at the **Botanist** (✉ 7 Sloane Sq., Chelsea ☎ 020/7730–0077 ⊕ www. thebotanistonsloanesquare.com ✛ 4:G2), the ultimate posh hangout on Sloane Square.

Or dispatch a cheeseburger topped with Monterey Jack and courgette fries at **Byron** (✉ 93–95 Old Brompton Rd., Chelsea ☎ 020/7590–9040 ⊕ www.byronhamburgers.com ✛ 4:D3).

It's bright, breezy, and perfect for young families, with two courses for kids for £6.25.

RISING STAR: MIKAEL JONSSON

Swedish food blogger, former lawyer, and extreme-provenance fiend Mikael Jonsson shakes up the London dining scene with his ultrasourced produce-driven set menus at **Hedone** (✉ 301–303 Chiswick High Rd., Chiswick ☎ 020/7747–0377 ⊕ www.hedonerestaurant.com ✛ 1:A2) in leafy Chiswick.

His hand-dived Devon scallops are the most scallopy scallops that you'll have tasted, his Cévennes onion the most indescribably oniony.

Eschewing grains and carbs, Jonsson lets rip with fully marbled 55-day aged Darragh O'Shea Black Angus beef, wild sea bass with wild chives, and his steamed John Dory with a stuffed courgette flower tastes like no other.

MUSICAL FOOD

It's hard to hear yourself speak, and the food's a bit pricey, but everyone enjoys the 1950s bohemian scene, folksy live music, and poetry readings at the **Troubadour** (✉ 263–267 Old Brompton Rd., Chelsea ☎ 020/7370–1434 ⊕ www.troubadour.co.uk ✛ 4:B3), a restaurant, coffee shop, and music venue. The site of Bob Dylan's first London gig and host to Led Zep, Joni Mitchell, Jimmy Hendrix, and Nick Drake, this place is where latter-day bohemians lounge around and dine on breakfasts, burgers, pastas, omelets, and strong coffee. Nearby off the King's Road, there's more live music at the **606 Club** (✉ 90 Lots Rd., Chelsea ☎ 020/7352–5953 ⊕ www.606club.co.uk ✛ 4:C6).

Enjoy the sounds as you dine on grilled sea bass with fennel, or Welsh lamb and rosemary gravy while enjoying up-close-and-personal live jazz in a low-ceiling basement setting.

NOTTING HILL AND BAYSWATER

World-renowned Notting Hill's trendy atmosphere, designer shops, and oh-so-hip residents, and nearby Bayswater's ethnic eateries, entice Londoners and travelers in droves.

Notting Hill has a reputation as one of London's most fashionable neighborhoods, with numerous boutiques, chic cafés, pâtisseries and restaurants, buzzing bars, and the famous Portobello Road market's collection of antiques shops, bric-a-brac, vintage-clothing stands, and delicious food stalls. The gentrification of Notting Hill has led to hordes of bankers and high flyers moving into the area, and hence prices are stratospheric. If you are in London at the end of August, be sure to check out the fanfare of the multiethnic Notting Hill Carnival street parade—a celebration of Caribbean and West Indian culture.

Bayswater is seedier, more transient, and known for its diversity. This neighborhood's main artery, Queensway, boasts some of the best cheap ethnic restaurants in London. Here, the Greek, Indian, Chinese and Persian restaurants are all cheek by jowl. Visitors love the affordable hotels and shops here.

SNACKING SPOT

Portobello Road market is one of London's most popular outdoor street markets. Get there early on Saturday morning (the market is open 8 am–6 pm) to beat the crowds. Peruse the antiques and vintage clothes and when you want to snack head to the north end of the market. Get ready for fresh fruit and veggie stands, bakeries, Spanish olive and French cheese purveyors, and numerous hot-food stalls peddling savory crêpes, hamburgers, German chicken, wraps, paella, kebabs, and Malaysian noodles.

How to get there: Take the Tube to Ladbroke Grove or Notting Hill Gate station and follow the signs (and crowds).

GASTROPUB TOUR

These upscale pubs specialize in high-quality, innovative fare in a low-key bar setting. The **Cow** (✉ *89 Westbourne Park Rd., Notting Hill* ☎ *020/7221–0021* ⊕ *www.thecowlondon. co.uk* ✛ *1:B3*) is one of the best-known gastropubs in London. Eat oysters or prawns and down a pint of Guinness at the stylish '50s bar or head upstairs to the slightly more formal dining room. Over the road, the **Westbourne** (✉ *101 Westbourne Park Villas, Notting Hill* ☎ *020/7221–1332* ⊕ *www. thewestbourne.com* ✛ *1:A3*) attracts a good-looking boho-chic set and serves hearty regional food and rustic dishes, with specials like cuttlefish with capers, and sea bream with olive tapenade (£14). Lauded Italian eatery **Assaggi** (✉ *2nd fl., 39 Chepstow Rd., Notting Hill* ☎ *020/792–5501* ✛ *1:B4*) sits above the Chepstow pub and excels with regional dishes like stuffed squid and grilled sea bass. The **Mall Tavern** (✉ *71–73 Palace Gardens Terr., Notting Hill* ☎ *020/7229–3374* ✛ *1:B5*) specializes in nostalgic British favorites like pork scratchings, chicken Kiev, Cow pie, and Arctic Roll ice creams.

CHEAP EATS

If you're looking for a filling meal that's not too pricey, head to Bayswater and Queensway. **Alounak** (✉ *44 Westbourne Grove, Bayswater* ☎ *020/7229–4158* ✛ *1:B4*) is a local favorite featuring lively Persian cuisine served in a cramped dining room. Set piece lobster noodle platters, king oysters, and fried baby squid are three super-popular Chinese dishes at the **Mandarin Kitchen** (✉ *14–16 Queensway, Queensway* ☎ *020/7727–9012* ✛ *1:C5*). **Hereford Road** (✉ *3 Hereford Rd., Bayswater* ☎ *020/7727–1144* ⊕ *www.herefordroad.org*; *see review* ✛ *1:B4*) champions pared-back British seasonal fare like roast guinea fowl, game chips, and the rice pudding with baked fig. Or there's always a big fat Greek party going on at **Aphrodite Taverna** (✉ *15 Hereford Rd., Queensway* ☎ *020/7229–2206* ⊕ *www. aphroditerestaurant.co.uk* ✛ *1:B4*), festooned with Greek drachmas, bouzouki mandolins, and a big bottle of Metaxa brandy.

AROUND THE PARK

A Sunday afternoon stroll around Holland Park can lead you in many culinary directions.

After a glimpse of its flower gardens and resident peacocks, you may be inclined to stop for a scoop or two of luscious Italian ice cream at **Gelato Mio** (✉ *138 Holland Park Ave., Notting Hill* ☎ *020/7727–4117* ⊕ *www.gelatomio.co.uk* ✛ *1:B1*), an ice-cream parlor on nearby Holland Park Avenue.

Try their fantastic Sicilian pistachio, Piedmont hazelnut, black cherry, or their *biscotto* (cookies and cream).

If you're not in the mood for ice cream, head down Portland Road and sit outside at pavement tables at **Julie's Restaurant & Bar** (✉ *135 Portland Rd., Notting Hill* ☎ *020/7727–7985* ⊕ *www.juliesrestaurant. com* ✛ *1:B1*) at quaint Clarendon Cross.

Here you can enjoy a Kir Royale or dry martini, along with a bowl of vegetable tempura with French beans, courgette, and sage leaves (£14.25).

14

3 pm and 6 pm, and dinner or supper is typically eaten between 7 pm and 11 pm, though it can be taken earlier. Many ethnic restaurants, especially Indian, serve food until midnight. Sunday is proper lunch day, and some restaurants are open for lunch only. Over the Christmas period, London virtually shuts down and it seems only hotels are prepared to feed travelers

PRICES

London is a very expensive city by global standards. A modest meal for two can easily cost £45, and the £120-a-head meal is not unknown. Damage-control strategies include making lunch your main meal—the top places have bargain midday menus—going for early- or late-evening deals, or sharing an à la carte entrée and ordering a second appetizer instead. Seek out fixed-price menus, and watch for hidden extras on the check, that is, bread or vegetables charged separately.

RESTAURANT REVIEWS

Listed alphabetically within neighborhoods. Use the coordinate (✛ 1:B2) at the end of each listing to locate a property on the Where to Eat and Stay in London atlas at the end of this chapter. Prices in the reviews are the average cost of a main course at dinner or, if dinner is not served, at lunch.

ST. JAMES'S AND MAYFAIR

ST. JAMES'S

$$$
MODERN
EUROPEAN
★

✕ **Le Caprice.** Celeb-ville old-timer Le Caprice commands the deepest loyalty of any restaurant in London. *Why?* Because it gets practically everything right. It's the quarter-century celebrity history—think Liz Taylor and Lady Di—the David Bailey black-and-white photos, designer Martin Brudnizki's updated decor, Jesus Adorno the veteran maitre'd, the perfect service, and the appealing menu that sits somewhere between Euro peasant and trendy fashion plate. Sit at the raised counter and enjoy calves' liver with crispy bacon, roast pheasant with caramelized quince, and signature Scandinavian iced berries with white chocolate sauce—all served with an ample dollop of "*Shush!* -don't-look-now-dear" star spotting. ⑤ *Average main: £23* ⊠ *Arlington House, Arlington St., St. James's* ☎ *020/7629–2239* ⊕ *www.caprice-holdings.co.uk* ☖ *Reservations essential* Ⓜ *Green Park* ✛ *5:A1.*

$$$$
FRENCH
★

✕ **L'Oranger.** Very discrete, very plush, very intimate, L'Oranger's French haute cuisine reaches gobsmacking heights at this swanky spot in St. James's. Whether you opt for scallops and white truffles, sea bass with girolles, or the fillet beef Rossini, the perfection of the kitchen is nicely on show. Don't look for fireworks in the decor, but the charming dining room—beige walls, brown chairs, bright art and flowers—and a hidden conservatory are both hushed and reassuringly attractive. Service is straight-backed and formal, just the way the well-bred courtiers (from nearby royal residence Clarence House) and business barons who revel here like it. ⑤ *Average main: £32* ⊠ *5 St. James's St., St. James's*

☎ 020/7839–3774 ⊕ *www.loranger.co.uk* ⚐ *Reservations essential* *Jacket required* ⊙ *Closed Sun. No lunch Sat.* Ⓜ *Green Park* ✛ *5:A1.*

$$$$ ✕ **Seven Park Place.** Is this London's best-kept gourmand's *secret?* The

MODERN FRENCH incredible clarity of modest chef William Drabble's wonderful neo-

Fodor's Choice French haute cuisine is turning foodie blogger heads at the St. James's

★ Hotel and Club (near Clarence House and Buckingham Palace). Serious foodie-trekkers squeeze into a diminutive and Diana Vreeland–esque opulent wonderland of black-and-gilt patterned wallpaper and strik-ing ladies' portraits for Drabble's three- to six-course set-meal extrava-ganzas, which might include sublime slithers of scallops ceviche with Jerusalem artichokes or pink and unbeatable Lune Valley lamb with rosemary and garlic purée. ⑤ *Average main: £30* ✉ *7–8 Park Pl., St. James's* ☎ *020/7316–1600* ⚐ *Reservations essential* Ⓜ *Green Park* ✛ *5:A1.*

$$$$ ✕ **Wiltons.** Double-barreled blue bloods, aristocrats, and the *extremely*

BRITISH well-to-do blow the family bank at this old-fashioned bastion of English

Fodor's Choice fine dining on pedigreed Jermyn Street (the place first opened on the

★ Haymarket as a shellfish stall in 1742). Invariably fresh from a snooze in their nearby St. James's gentlemen's clubs, male diners are required to wear jackets for luncheon and dinner at this clubby time capsule and *frightfully* snooty ode to all things English. Signet ring-sporting posh patrons take half a dozen finest Colchester oysters, followed by grilled Dover sole on the bone, or fabulous native game in season, such as grouse, woodcock, partridge, or teal. There are long-forgotten savo-ries like anchovies and mushrooms on toast, plus nursery desserts like sherry trifle and bread-and-butter pudding. Service, naturally, would put Jeeves to shame. ⑤ *Average main: £30* ✉ *55 Jermyn St., St. James's* ☎ *020/7629–9955* ⊕ *www.wiltons.co.uk* ⚐ *Reservations essential. Jacket required* ⊙ *Closed weekends* Ⓜ *Green Park* ✛ *5:A1.*

$$ ✕ **The Wolseley.** The whole of beau London comes for the always-on-

AUSTRIAN show spectacle and soaring elegance at this double-height Viennese-style

★ *Mitteleuropa* grand café on Piccadilly. Framed with black laquerware, silver service, and a few doors down from the Ritz, this all-day brasserie begins its long decadent days with breakfast at 7 am and serves until midnight. Don't be shy to pop in on spec (they hold seats back precisely for this) to enjoy such highlights as Hungarian goulash, Matjes herrings with pumpernickel, chicken soup, chopped liver, kedgeree, steak tartare, or the breaded Wiener schnitzel. Don't forget to book a return table to savor the Viennoiserie pastries at one of their classy afternoon teas. ⑤ *Average main: £18* ✉ *160 Piccadilly, St. James's* ☎ *020/7499–6996* ⊕ *www.thewolseley.com* Ⓜ *Green Park* ✛ *5:A1.*

MAYFAIR

$$$ ✕ **Cecconi's.** Enjoy all-day buzz and spot the odd celebrity at this ever-

ITALIAN fashionable Italian brasserie wedged handily between Old Bond Street, Cork Street, and Savile Row, and over the road from the Royal Acad-emy of Arts. The Miu Miu and private jet set spill out onto the street for breakfast, brunch, and *cicchetti* (Italian tapas) and return with friends later in the day for something more substantial. À-la-mode designer Ilse Crawford's green-and-brown interior is a stylish backdrop for classics like veal Milanese, Venetian calves' liver, crab ravioli, lobster spaghetti

14

A juicy burger and fries served at meat specialist Goodman

and a decent pick-me-up tiramisu. This is just the spot for a pit stop during a blow-out West End shopping spree. ⑤ *Average main: £23* ✉ *5A Burlington Gardens, Mayfair* ☎ *020/7434–1500* ⊕ *www.cecconis.co.uk* Ⓜ *Green Park, Piccadilly Circus* ✛ *3:A6.*

$$$
BRITISH

✕ **Corrigan's Mayfair.** The surrounding Mayfair streets may be eerily quiet, but there's a warm welcome and a lively scene at burly Irish chef Richard Corrigan's flagship British haute cuisine haven off Park Lane. Self-assured and on top of its game, the dark blue banquettes, crisp Irish linen, and huntin', shootin' and fishin' motifs provide a handsome setting for a high-powered clientele who return repeatedly for dishes like partridge salad, steamed pollack with clams, wild duck with prunes, and heartier plates like haunch of venison, saddle of rabbit, or pork with pear and dandelion. ⑤ *Average main: £27* ✉ *28 Upper Grosvenor St., Mayfair* ☎ *020/7499–9943* ⊕ *www.corrigansmayfair.com* ✍ *Reservations essential* ⊘ *No lunch Sat.* Ⓜ *Marble Arch* ✛ *1:G5.*

$$$
STEAKHOUSE
★

✕ **Goodman.** This Russian-owned, Manhattan-themed, Mayfair-based steakhouse, named after Chicago jazz and swing legend Benny Goodman, has everyone in agreement—here you'll find the best steaks in town. USDA-certified, corn-fed and dry-aged Nebraska Red and Black Angus T-bones, Rib eye, Porterhouse and New York sirloin steaks compete for taste and tenderness with heavily marbled grass-fed prime cut fillets from Scotland and Ireland. There's token Russian sweet herring, lobster bisque and seafood risotto, but everyone here has only got one thing on their mind: the juicy 250g-400g charcoal oven grilled steaks, which come with fries, creamed spinach and either lush Béarnaise, pepper, or Stilton sauce. ⑤ *Average main: £27* ✉ *26 Maddox St., Mayfair*

☎ *020/7499–3776* ⊕ *www.goodmanrestaurants.com* ⚱ *Reservations essential* ☉ *Closed Sun* Ⓜ *Oxford Circus* ✛ *1:H4.*

$$$$ ✕ **The Greenhouse.** Discretely tucked away amid imposing Mayfair
FRENCH mansions and approached via a spotlighted garden, this ultra-elegant ground-floor dining salon quietly screams "Stealth wealth!" and attracts aficionados of top-class French haute cuisine at any price. Feast on snail risotto, wild turbot with lemon-caper sauce, grouse with cep mushrooms, or the signature pink Anjou pigeon breast with turnip purée. The mainly private equity/hedge fund/dark-pool business clientele come for the achingly smooth service, the glassed-off private dining room, and the awesome 90-page wine list. ⑤ *Average main: £31* ⊠ *27A Hay's Mews, Mayfair* ☎ *020/7499–3331* ⊕ *www.greenhouserestaurant.co.uk* ⚱ *Reservations essential* ☉ *Closed Sun. No lunch Sat.* Ⓜ *Green Park* ✛ *1:H5.*

$$$$ ✕ **Hélène Darroze at the Connaught.** La crème de la crème flock here
FRENCH for dazzling regional French haute cuisine, served in a Edwardian
Fodor's Choice wood-paneled hotel dining salon sumpuiously kitted out by Pari-
★ sian It-designer India Mahdavi. Taking inspiration from Les Landes in southwest France, Darroze sallies forth with a procession of magical dishes. Caviar d'Acquitaine wows with oyster tartare in a sleek martini glass, topped with black caviar jelly and white haricot bean velouté. Spit-roasted and flambéed pigeon is served wonderfully pink, with duck foie gras and mini–Brussels sprouts. To finish, choose pear jelly or rose petal panna cotta with almond sponge. It's perfect for celebrations or special occasions, but note the high prices: £35 for lunch, £55 for Sat. brunch, and £85 or £115 for dinner. ⑤ *Average main: £85* ⊠ *The Connaught, Carlos Pl., Mayfair* ☎ *020/7107–8880* ⊕ *www.the-connaught.co.uk* ⚱ *Reservations essential. Jacket required* ☉ *Closed Sun. and Mon.* Ⓜ *Green Park* ✛ *1:H5.*

$$$$ ✕ **Hibiscus.** Is Claude Bosi the *new* Heston Blumenthal? Such are the
MODERN FRENCH global accolades showered on this burly French chef that—*whisper*
Fodor's Choice *it!*—Bosi's now talked about in the same breath as Blumenthal, Brit-
★ ain's current supernova TV chef. Chef Bosi naturally bosses the scene at his disarmingly neutral Mayfair spot with peerless, take-no-prisoners nouvelle dishes like carpaccio of hand-dived Isle of Skye scallops with blobs of truffle and pickled radish, or Cornish John Dory with autumnal girolle mushrooms and specks of Morteau sausage. His desserts are as original as his mains, with an unlikely mushroom-flavored cep tart standing out. Celebration, business folk, and top-end international gastro-tourists are well served by a wine list studded with unique choices. ⑤ *Average main: £80* ⊠ *29 Maddox St., Mayfair* ☎ *020/7629–2999* ⊕ *www.hibiscusrestaurant.co.uk* ☉ *Closed Sun. and Mon.* Ⓜ *Oxford Circus, Piccadilly* ✛ *3:A5.*

$$$ ✕ **La Petite Maison.** Star and food blogger Gwyneth Paltrow rates seen-
FRENCH and-be-seen La Petite Maison, off New Bond Street, as her all-time favorite London restaurant, and no wonder—there's nothing on the impeccably well-sourced carbo-lite French Mediterranean and Provençale menu that fails to delight. Try figure-friendly broad bean and Pecorino salad, the soft Burrata cheese with Camone tomato spread, or the wonderfully aromatic baked turbot with artichokes, chorizo,

14

spices, and white wine sauce. Based on the style of the original La Petite Maison in Nice in France, dishes come to the table as and when they're ready, and the *jolie* and informal waitstaff make for a convivial Gucci Gucci Eurotrash vibe. *Rosé*, anyone? $ *Average main: £23* ⊠ *53–54 Brook's Mews, Mayfair* 🕾 *020/7495–4774* ⊕ *www.lpmlondon.co.uk* Ⓜ *Bond St.* ✛ *1:H4.*

$$$$ ✕ **Le Gavroche.** "Master Chef" judge Michel Roux Jr. thrives and works
FRENCH the floor at this clubby basement national institution in Mayfair—established by his father and uncle in 1967—and which many still rate to this day as the best formal dining in London. With silver domes and old-fashioned unpriced ladies' menus, Roux's mastery of classical French cuisine hypnotizes all comers with signature dishes like foie gras with cinnamon-scented crispy duck pancake, langoustine with snails and Hollandaise, pig's trotters, or saddle of rabbit with Parmesan cheese. Desserts like Roux's famous chocolate omelet soufflé or upside-down apple tart are equally accomplished. Weekday three-course set lunches (at £51) are the sanest way to experience such unashamed overwrought flummery—with a half bottle of wine, water, coffee, and petit fours thrown in. Sadly, the decor will win no prizes. $ *Average main: £38* ⊠ *43 Upper Brook St., Mayfair* 🕾 *020/7408–0881* ⊕ *www.le-gavroche. co.uk* ⌕ *Reservations essential. Jacket required* ☉ *Closed Sun. and 10 days at Christmas* Ⓜ *Marble Arch* ✛ *1:G5.*

$$$$ ✕ **Nobu Berkeley Street.** Supermodels, soccer stars, F1 drivers, groupies,
JAPANESE and the global fashion crowd pay silly money for new-style sashimi with a Peruvian flair at this so-hip-it-hurts Nobu spin-off near Piccadilly. Louder, more thumping, and more fashion-forward than nearby flagship Nobu on Park Lane, this sibling version seems to triple up successfully with a combined ground-floor scene cocktail bar, a first-floor restaurant, and a wraparound '90s West End nightclub vibe. Once past security and firmly seated, the oh-so-beautiful people go bonkers for miso black cod, California sushi rolls, tuna teriyaki, yellowtail sashimi, Bento boxes, grilled peppers, and extortionate Wagyu beef. Prices are downtown-Tokyo extreme, but the piping-hot people-watching is just *sooo* good. $ *Average main: £30* ⊠ *15 Berkeley St., Mayfair* 🕾 *020/7290–9222* ⊕ *www.noburestaurants.com* Ⓜ *Green Park* ✛ *1:H5.*

$$$ ✕ **Pollen Street Social.** El Bulli–trained and unstoppable star Jason Ather-
MODERN ton knocks the London dining scene for a loop at his smash-hit Pollen
EUROPEAN Street Social set in a side alleyway off Regent Street. Fans mix-and-max
Fodor's Choice on edgy but refined small-or-larger dishes ranging from a "full English"
★ starter—a miniature of eggs, bacon, morels, and croutons—to sublime Dingley Dell pork belly or the Atlantic hake with cod cheeks and seaweed. Glam punters perch at London's first dessert bar, and strike up and watch staff prepare immaculate creamy goats' milk rice pudding with hay ice-cream or sensational pressed watermelon with basil sorbet. $ *Average main: £26* ⊠ *8–10 Pollen St., Mayfair* 🕾 *020/7290–7600* ⊕ *www.pollenstreetsocial.com* ⌕ *Reservations essential* Ⓜ *Oxford Circus, Piccadilly Circus* ✛ *3:A5.*

$$ ✕ **The Riding House Cafe.** Stuffed-squirrel lamp holders peer down on
BURGER trendy diners at this groovy New York–style small-plates-and-deluxe-burgers all-dayer just north of Oxford Circus. Everything's reclaimed,

salvaged, or bespoke, so you'll find stuffed birds and taxidermy dotted around, reclaimed blue theater seats at the counter bar, bright orange leather banquettes, or old snooker table legs holding up your dining table. Opt for a £5 small plate of sea bass ceviche with lime and chili, and head straight for the poached-egg chorizo hash browns or a mighty decadent foie gras hamburger, with gherkin and chips—a bargain at £13.90. ⑤ *Average main: £14* ✉ *43 Great Titchfield St., Noho* ☎ *020/7927–0840* ⊕ *www.ridinghousecafe.co.uk* ✎ *Reservations essential* Ⓜ *Oxford Circus* ✛ *3:A2.*

$$$$
SEAFOOD
Fodor's Choice
★

✕ **Scott's.** Liveried doormen greet the triple-A list with a nod at this glamorlicious seafood haven and crustacean bar on fashion central Mount Street in Mayfair. Orginally founded in 1851, and a former haunt of James Bond author Ian Fleming (he loved the potted shrimps), you'll now likely see loaded former Brit-pack artists Tracy Emin or Damien Hirst playing up at a banquette in a corner. Scott's draws London's real movers-and-shakers and the beautiful ones, who enjoy Whitstable oysters, shrimp burgers, cod cheeks, roast halibut, and Stargazy pie (Cornish pie with fish heads gazing out of a pastry crust). Standouts like red mullet with scallops and saffron broth or lobster thermador with garlic butter are to die for. Prices are heart-murmur-inducing high, but fear not: this really is *the* hottest joint in town. ⑤ *Average main: £32* ✉ *20 Mount St., Mayfair* ☎ *020/7495–7309* ⊕ *www.scotts-restaurant. com* ✎ *Reservations essential* Ⓜ *Bond St.* ✛ *1:G5.*

14

$$
MODERN
EUROPEAN

✕ **Wild Honey.** Just follow the stream of savvy art dealers to a side road behind Christie's salesrooms (in New Bond Street) and you'll discover this hidden gem, wildly popular thanks to its set lunches (£16.95) or pre- and post-theater evening deals (£19.95). Set in a long oak-paneled former gentlemen's club, but nicely spruced up with attractive modern abstracts, Wild Honey has a kitchen that showcases hearty, unpretentious, but artfully presented, food: best bets include the shoulder of venison with creamy polenta, the Cornish plaice with squash and wild mushrooms, or the Norfolk hare with celery and chestnuts. ⑤ *Average main: £18* ✉ *12 St. George St., Mayfair* ☎ *020/7758–9160* ⊕ *www. wildhoneyrestaurant.co.uk* ✎ *Reservations essential* Ⓜ *Oxford Circus* ✛ *3:A5.*

MARYLEBONE

$$
BISTRO

✕ **Galvin Bistrot de Luxe.** The publicity-shy Chris and Jeff Galvin brothers blaze a trail for the French "bistrot deluxe" concept on a fast-moving stretch of Baker Street in Marylebone. Seasoned fans and an older crowd go for the impeccable food and service in a handsome mahogany-paneled and slate-floored Parisian-style salon. There's no finer Dorset crab lasagna around, and main courses punch above their weight: Corsican bream, calves liver with Alsace bacon, stuffed pig's trotter, and veal kidneys with girolles are all gastronomic triumphs. The £17.50 three-course set lunches or £19.50 early evening dinners (6–7 pm) are unbeatable value. ⑤ *Average main: £18* ✉ *66 Baker St., Marylebone* ☎ *020/7935–4007* ⊕ *www.galvinrestaurants.com* ✎ *Reservations essential* Ⓜ *Baker St.* ✛ *1:G3.*

$
SEAFOOD

✕ **The Golden Hind.** You'll land some of the best fish-and-chips in London at the Golden Hind, a great British "chippy" (or traditional fish-and-chip shop), run by a Greek family in a retro 1914 art deco café, off Marylebone High Street. Gaggles of tourists and hungry Marylebone village locals alike hunker down for the homemade cod fishcakes, skate wings, feta fritters, and breaded scampi tails, but it's the perfectly prepared and nongreasy deep-fried or steamed battered cod, plaice, and haddock from Grimsby (£4–£6.20); the classic hand-cut Maris Piper chips; and the mushy peas that are the big draws. It's BYO and take away, but note it's only open noon–3 pm weekdays, and 6–10 pm Monday to Saturday. $ *Average main: £6* ⊠ *73 Marylebone La., Marylebone* ☎ *020/7486–3644* ⏌⏉ *BYOB* ☺ *Closed Sun. No lunch Sat.* Ⓜ *Bond St.* ✛ *1:H3.*

SOHO AND COVENT GARDEN

SOHO

$$ ✕ **Andrew Edmunds.** Candle-lighted, well-worn, and with an overwhelming Dickensian vibe to it, Andrew Edmunds is a permanently packed, deeply romantic Soho institution—though it could be larger, less creaky, and the church-pew wooden bench seats more forgiving. Tucked away behind Carnaby Street, it's a favorite with the insider Soho media mafia that come for daily changing, photo-copied, fixed-price lunch menus and the overall quirky/historic vibe. Satisfyingly rustic and keenly priced starters and mains draw on the tastes of Ireland, the Mediterranean, and the Middle East. Harissa-spiced mackerel, woodcock on toast, goose rillettes, seafood paella, and pork belly with apple purée are all hale and hearty. $ *Average main: £15* ⊠ *46 Lexington St., Soho* ☎ *020/7437–5708* ⏉ *Reservations essential* Ⓜ *Oxford Circus, Piccadilly Circus* ✛ *3:C5.*

MEDITERRANEAN

$$$ ✕ **Aqua Kyoto.** Japanese spectacular Aqua Kyoto is a high-concept import from Hong Kong that looks like a set from a moody James Bond film, with a sunken central sushi counter that's straight out of the *Starship Enterprise.* Set on the fifth floor of the former Dickens & Jones building off Regent Street, there's enough culinary theater and high-end sushi, sashimi, tempura, and grilled tepanyaki dishes to keep the rich kids, glamour gals, and after-work suits coming back for more. Try beef teriyaki with chili ponzu sauce, green tea noodles with Wagyu sashimi, or miso black cod. There's a wonderful, open-air terrace in summer overlooking Liberty department store. $ *Average main: £17* ⊠ *240 Regents St.(entrance on Argyll St.), 5th fl., Soho* ☎ *020/7478–0540* ⊕ *www.aqua-london.com* ⏉ *Reservations essential* Ⓜ *Piccadilly Circus, Oxford Circus* ✛ *3:A4.*

JAPANESE

$ ✕ **Baozi Inn.** Vintage Chairman Mao posters and Communist Party paraphernalia decorate the walls of this handy hole-in-the-wall Szechuan café on a busy side street in Chinatown. Baozi steamed buns—pork and onion, or shrimp and radish—are house specials, and there's dragon wonton broth, Dan Dan noodles with mustard greens and sesame paste, or Chengdu pork dumplings with chili oil. Top choices include the ginger juice spinach and the Peace and Happiness noodle soup, topped with duck and Chinese toon tree shoots. Tables are cramped, prices are low, turnover is fast, and customer service is *bang! bang! bang!* $ *Average*

CHINESE

Busaba Eathai's tasty fried calamari

main: £6 ⊠ *25 Newport Ct., Soho* ☎ *020/7287–6877* ✍ *Reservations not accepted* Ⓜ *Leicester Sq.* ✛ *3:E5.*

$ **CAFÉ** ✕ **Bar Italia.** This legendary 1949 landmark stand-up-or-sit-down Italian coffee bar is a 24-hour Soho institution. Football crazy, and a honey-pot for a weird and wonderful assortment of roués and Soho-ites, most regulars grab a frothy cappuccino, espresso, or sobering *macchiato* and wolf down a cheap slice of pizza, panettone, or rich chocolate cake at one of the mirrored counters (or at pavement seats out *da* front). The walls are plastered with Italian flags and fading old pictures of lusty Italian singers, boxing champs, and movie legends, and it's the *primo numero uno* spot in London to watch Italy play in—or get dumped out of—the football World Cup. Ⓢ *Average main: £6* ⊠ *22 Frith St., Soho* ☎ *020/7437–4520* ⊕ *www.baritaliasoho.co.uk* ▭ *No credit cards* Ⓜ *Leicester Sq.* ✛ *3:D5.*

$$ **SPANISH** ✕ **Barrafina.** Soho's favorite tapas bar on Frith Street is modeled on Cal Pep, the famed tapas joint in Barcelona, and similarly has only a few—23 in total—raised counter seats. It's no-reservations but you can strike up with fellow queuers, and the tapas is supreme. Nosh on small plates of shrimp, chorizo, quail, salt cod fritters, sardines, and octopus, or classics like cured Jabugo ham and Spanish tortilla. There's a decent selection of reds, whites, and sparkling Cava, and leave room for desserts like the crema Catalana or almond-based Santiago tart. Ⓢ *Average main: £9* ⊠ *54 Frith St., Soho* ☎ *020/7813–8016* ⊕ *www.barrafina. co.uk* ✍ *Reservations not accepted* Ⓜ *Tottenham Court Rd.* ✛ *3:D4.*

$$$ **ITALIAN** ✕ **Bocca di Lupo.** The place is packed, the tables are too close together, and the acoustics can be shattering, but everyone comes for the *craic* (lively talk) and the lush regional Italian cuisine. Redbrick fronted and set in an unlikely street off Soho's seedy red-light district, this place offers a succession of small plates and peasant-based dishes from Bologna to Veneto, Lombaria to Campania. Try goodies like buffalo mozzarella, fried squid, or Wigeon duck, or go for mussels with basil and celery, or *baccala* home-salted pollack. You won't be able to hear yourselves speak properly, but at least the milk-free espresso ice cream will make up for the loss. ⑤ *Average main: £14* ⊠ *12 Archer St., Soho* ☎ *020/7734–2223* ⊕ *www.boccadilupo.com* ⌂ *Reservations essential* ⊙ *Closed Sun.* Ⓜ *Piccadilly Circus* ✛ *3:C5.*

$ ✕**Busaba Eathai.** It's top Thai nosh for little moolah at this sleek and
THAI sultry canteen in the heart of Soho. Fitted with dark-wood bench seats
★ and hardwood tables, this flagship restaurant has communal dining, rapid service, low lighting, and often fast-moving queues out the front. Pour yourself a lemongrass tea, then try ginger beef with Thai pepper, classic green papaya salad, chicken with shiitake, monkfish curry, vermicelli with prawns, squid, and scallops, or other winners here. All in all, this makes for a fine pit stop during a West End shopping safari. ⑤ *Average main: £10* ⊠ *106–110 Wardour St., Soho* ☎ *020/7255–8686* ⊕ *www.busaba.com* ⌂ *Reservations not accepted* Ⓜ *Tottenham Court Rd.* ✛ *3:C4.*

$ ✕**Côte.** Where else can you get a surprisingly good three-course French
FRENCH meal for £13.65? The Côte brasserie—softly lighted and smoothly decked out with nifty gray-and-white striped awning, banquettes, and Parisian-style round tables—does just the trick, and offers these meal deals weekdays from noon until 7 pm, and weekends from noon 'til 6 pm. With four choices per course, you'll find all your firm favorites: tuna Nicoise salad, beef bourguignonne, Breton chicken, *moules marinières* (mussels with white wine), steak haché, and crème caramel for afters. If you're attending the nearby Royal Opera House, this is a handy standby for pre-theater. ⑤ *Average main: £10* ⊠ *17-21 Tavistock St., Covent Garden* ☎ *020/7379–9991* ⊕ *www.cote-restaurants.co.uk* Ⓜ *Covent Garden.* ✛ *3:G5.*

$$$ ✕**Dean Street Townhouse.** Everyone feels at least 10 times more glamorous
BRITISH once they step into this buzzy Soho spot, attached to the stylish 39-room
Fodor's Choice Georgian hotel of the same name. Soft lighting, dark-wood floors, red
★ leather banquettes, raised bar seats, and walls crammed with Brit-artist pics creates a hip hangout for London's good-looking and self-obsessed media darlings. No-frills, no-fuss retro-British favorites include pea-and-ham soup, Scottish haggis, fish fingers, chicken and leek pie, or toad-in-the-hole, plus yumptious sherry trifle, Trinity burnt cream, or steamed sponge pudding. You'll find buttered crumpets for afternoon tea, Welsh rarebit for "high tea," and a good smattering of celebs fiddling around on their new iPhones. ⑤ *Average main: £20* ⊠ *69–71 Dean St., Soho* ☎ *020/7434–1775* ⊕ *www.deanstreettownhouse.com* ⌂ *Reservations essential* Ⓜ *Tottenham Court Rd.* ✛ *3:D5.*

$$ ✕**The Giaconda Dining Room.** A bite-size gastro-landmark with an indie
MODERN spirit on Denmark Street's Tin Pan Alley (think Bowie, Marley, and The
EUROPEAN Clash), this super-friendly Australian-run dining room may only seat
Fodor's Choice 35, but the eclectic menu is genius and inspired. Chef Paul Merrony
★ sends out mighty starters—creamed shallots with horseradish, crispy

pig's trotters, or chicken livers with juniper mousse—and a full range of luscious main entrées at extremely low prices. Try the ox tongue, rack of lamb with gnocchi, crab spaghetti, or heartier dishes like veal kidneys, black pudding with potatoes, or ham-hock hash with a fried egg on top. Puddings, like peach melba or Eton Mess, are a snip at £6 a pop. ⑤ *Average main: £13* ⊠ *9 Denmark St., Soho* ☎ *020/7240–3334* ⊕ *www.giacondadining.com* ⊙ *Closed Sun. and Mon. No lunch Sat.* Ⓜ *Tottenham Court Rd.* ✛ *3:D4.*

$$$ ✗ **Hix.** Restauranteur and *bon viveur* Mark Hix's spunky Soho spot
BRITISH oozes class and panache, and remains a magnet for launch-night and
Fodor's Choice post-performance A-list celebrations. It serves simple but brilliant Brit-
★ ish fare: think hanger steak with a chunk of bone marrow, red-leg par-
tridge with curly kale, or Shetland coley with cockles and sea purslane.
You'll also find epic feasts for tables of eight: chop and oysters, goose, or suckling pig, and riffs on classic dishes, like rabbit and crayfish Stargazy pie. Check out the Brit artist Sarah Lucas and Damian Hirst mobiles, the bar billiards, and famed mixologist Nick Strangeway's heritage cocktails in the winning basement bar, known appropriately as . . . Mark's Bar. ⑤ *Average main: £22* ⊠ *66–70 Brewer St., Soho* ☎ *020/7292–3518* ⊕ *www.hixsoho.co.uk* ⌂ *Reservations essential* Ⓜ *Piccadilly Circus* ✛ *3:C5.*

$ ✗ **Maison Bertaux.** Romantics and Francophiles cherish this quirky, two-
CAFÉ story 1871 French pâtisserie, tea parlor, and occasional pop-up art space, where nothing seems to have changed since the 1940s. Framed with vintage blue-and-white awnings, the *choux* pastry, tarts, gateaux, and gooey cakes at this time-warp Soho institution are renowned and baked on-site. The chocolate or cream-and-fruit éclairs, Saint-Honoré, and Black Forest gâteaux, marzipan figs, apricot tarts, and almond croissants won't fail to delight. Run by glamorous Soho legend Michelle Wade, Bertaux also hosts a retro and cheery tea service, which comes with tasty savories, like broccoli quiche or a Dijon slice, with cheese, peppers, and Dijon mustard. ⑤ *Average main: £4* ⊠ *28 Greek St., Soho* ☎ *020/7437–6007* ⊕ *www.maisonbertaux.com* ▭ *No credit cards* Ⓜ *Leicester Sq.* ✛ *3:D5.*

$$ ✗ **Manchurian Legends.** Chinatown's bustin' out from Szechuan and Can-
CHINESE tonese cuisine, and now embraces this regional Dongbei flag bearer from Manchuria and the hardy northeast of China. Set off by vintage black-and-white photos and modern dark-wood tables, with service that is Chinatown industry standard—it's seriously hot and cold—this spot has a mazy 122-dish menu in which you can get lost among all the cold vegetable starters, dumplings, stews, and hotpots. Best to swerve the tripe, duck's tongue, and chicken gizzard, but opt for Dongbei faves like chili-ed Xinjiang-style fried lamb with cumin, pork belly with spin-ach and glass noodles, and Bang Bang king prawns. ⑤ *Average main: £11* ⊠ *12 Macclesfield St., Chinatown* ☎ *020/7437–8785* ⌂ *Reserva-tions essential* Ⓜ *Leicester Sq., Piccadilly Circus* ✛ *3:D5 .*

$$ ✗ **Spuntino.** Moody tin-tile ceilings, dangly low-wattage filament light
DINER bulbs, tattooed waitstaff, bluegrass tunes, and only 26 raised coun-
Fodor's Choice ter stools at this pewter-topped rectangular bar and Lower East Side/
★ Italian-inspired Soho diner makes this the absolute, undisputed, most

14

unimaginably *cool* gig in town. Naturally, there's no phone, no reservations, and minimal signage, but that only adds to the speakeasy vibe. Once seated, try truffle egg toast, grits, or Yankee sliders—like beef and bone marrow, or lamb and pickled cucumber—and there's also old-school mac and cheese (£8) or manly steak and eggs (£10). $ *Average main: £12* ⊠ *61 Rupert St., Soho* ☎ *No telephone* ⌖ *Reservations not accepted* Ⓜ *Piccadilly Circus* ✛ *3:C5.*

$$$ ✕ **St. John Hotel Restaurant.** Chef Fergus Henderson and the St. John crew
MODERN BRITISH   are the dons of British nose-to-tail dining, so make sure you're not too squeamish if you venture to their (late-night) hotel dining room, handily placed off Leicester Square in the dinky St. John Hotel. Whether it's deviled kidneys for breakfast, lambs' tongues for lunch, or pig skin followed by bread-and-butter pudding for dinner, everything's sure to be well sourced and austerely presented. The all-white dining room's as bare as a Puritan church, service comes in and out of focus, and luckily last orders for food are taken until midnight. $ *Average main: £21* ⊠ *St. John Hotel, 1 Leicester St., Chinatown* ☎ *020/3301–8020* ⊕ *www.stjohnhotellondon.com* ⌖ *Reservations essential* Ⓜ *Leicester Sq.* ✛ *3:D6.*

$$$ ✕ **Yauatcha.** Hurrah! for the all-day dim sum at this Cantonese Soho
CHINESE   classic. Slinkily designed by the chic Christian Liaigre—with black gran-
★   ite floors, purple-lighted aquarium, candles, exposed-brick light wall, and a starry ceiling—the theatrical setting is the perfect stage for the wicked dim sum—try king crab, cuttlefish, and zucchini, or prawn and Chinese chives—plus the crispy duck rolls, hot-and-sour soup, *congee* rice porridge, venison puffs, and sea bass and lotus root. You'll also find fancy cocktails, plus exquisite Oriental loose-leaf teas and delicate cakes and fancies in the first-floor tearoom. Be sure to request a table in the more happening and romantic basement at night. $ *Average main: £16* ⊠ *15 Broadwick St., Soho* ☎ *020/7494–8888* ⊕ *www.yauatcha.com* ⌖ *Reservations essential* Ⓜ *Oxford Circus* ✛ *3:C4.*

COVENT GARDEN

$$$ ✕ **Clos Maggiore.** Bag a seat in the low-lighted conservatory at this seri-
FRENCH   ously romantic Provençal country inn–style refuge in the heart of Cov-
Fodor's Choice   ent Garden. A bouquet's throw away from the Royal Opera House,
★   and a favorite with amorous Prince Harry, service is formal and the warren of candle-lighted, wood-panel rooms, open fires, oil paintings, and convex mirrors never fails to enchant. Meal deals and theater specials (£19.50–£22.50) are a cute way in, where you'll be wooed by refined French cuisine, such as Loire valley rabbit ballotine, Weymouth sea bass, or Charolais beef cheeks with fine French beans. $ *Average main: £24* ⊠ *33 King St., Covent Garden* ☎ *020/7379–9696* ⊕ *www.closmaggiore.com* ⌖ *Reservations essential* Ⓜ *Covent Garden* ✛ *3:F5.*

$ ✕ **Food for Thought.** This hippy-vibey '70s-style subterranean BYO veg-
VEGETARIAN   etarian café has a cult veggie following, so be prepared to wait with the best of them. You'll find wooden communal tables and a daily changing menu of wholesome soups, salads, stews, quiches, stir-fries, bakes, and casseroles. Wheat-free, gluten-free, GM–free, vegan, Fair Trade, and organic options are available throughout, and there's puddings like their famous oat-based strawberry-and-banana "Scrunch." Take-away,

but no credit cards, and note that it's only open until 8:30 pm Monday through Saturday and until 5:30 on Sunday. $ *Average main: £7* ⊠ *31 Neal St., Covent Garden* ☎ *020/7836–9072* ⌕ *Reservations not accepted* ▭ *No credit cards* ⌷ *BYOB* Ⓜ *Covent Garden* ✛ *3:F4.*

$$ ✕ **Great Queen Street.** Expect a noisy foodie-loving crowd at Covent
MODERN BRITISH Garden's top gastropub that showcases the kind of classic retro-English
Fodor's Choice dishes that Londoners can't get enough of. Not far from the Royal
★ Opera House, the eatery is done up in a burgundy walls and bare oak-floor-and-table setting. Rowdy diners dive into old-fashioned offerings like pressed tongue, potato soup, chicken, ham and asparagus pie, Old Spot pork, or mackerel with rhubarb. Dishes from a bygone era, like brown crab on toast, venison pie, and roasts for the whole table—such as the seven-hour shoulder of lamb with dauphinoise potatoes—are highly convivial. $ *Average main: £19* ⊠ *32 Great Queen St., Covent Garden* ☎ *020/7242–0622* ⌕ *Reservations essential* ⊘ *No dinner Sun.* Ⓜ *Covent Garden, Holborn* ✛ *3:G4.*

$$$ ✕ **The Ivy.** The triple-A list tend to spurn the Ivy for its upstairs private
BRITISH members' club and other luxe spots like Scott's, Hix, and J Sheekey, but nonetheless this landmark still takes a thousand calls a day! An intriguing mix of daytime-and-satellite TV stars, gawkers, and out-of-towners dine on salt-beef hash, squash risotto, Thai-baked sea bass, salmon fish cakes, eggs Benedict, and English classics like Shepherd's pie or *kedgeree* (curried rice with haddock, egg and parsley) in a handsome mullioned stained-glass and oak-paneled dining salon. Service is exemplary, and for low-to-mid wattage West End star-spotting this is a prime spot. Tip: If you can't snag a reservation by phone, try walking in for a table on spec—it's been known to work. $ *Average main: £23* ⊠ *1–5 West St., Covent Garden* ☎ *020/7836–4751* ⊕ *www.the-ivy.co.uk* ⌕ *Reservations essential* Ⓜ *Covent Garden* ✛ *3:E5.*

$$$ ✕ **J Sheekey.** West End and Hollywood superdooperstars slip into this
SEAFOOD classy 1896 seafood classic as an alternative to Scott's, C London, or
★ Hix in Soho. Linked with nearby Theaterland, J Sheekey is one of Londoners' all-time favorite West End haunts. Smoothly orchestrated by incorrigibly amusing maitre'd John Andrews, Sheekey charms with warm wood paneling, showbiz monochromes, a warren of alcove tables, and lava-rock bar tops. Opt for snappingly fresh Atlantic prawns, Arctic herring, crab bisque, Cornish sardines, or famous Sheekey fish pie. Better still, have Gaston Chiquet champagne and six Maldon Rock oysters at the old mirrored raised-counter oyster bar for the ultimate in true romance, or take advantage of the £26.50 weekend set lunch deals. $ *Average main: £22* ⊠ *28–32 St. Martin's Ct., Covent Garden* ☎ *020/7240–2565* ⊕ *www.j-sheekey.co.uk* Ⓜ *Leicester Sq.* ✛ *3:E6.*

$$$$ ✕ **L'Atelier de Joël Robuchon.** A few doors down from the Ivy and arguably
FRENCH one of London's least publicized best restaurants, L'Atelier attracts both
★ *glitterati* and food cognoscenti to sit side-by-side at the open-kitchen and graze tapas-style at this hyper-seductive staging post for French superchef Joël Robuchon. Framed with a green-leafy wall, moody lighting, and signature red glasses and raised counter seats, this space is custom-tailored for those who want to pig out on an orgy of exquisite French tapas—from frogs' legs and egg cocotte to scallops, pig's trotters,

14

foie gras, and quail with buttery truffle mash. The £125 eight-course tasting menu is a wanton way to blow the inheritance, but the £25 and £29 lunch and pre-theater deals are an altogether saner way to go. There's a more formal restaurant, La Cuisine, on the first floor, and a cozy open-fired top-floor snug bar, too. Ⓢ *Average main: £27* ⊠ *13–15 West St., Covent Garden* ☎ *020/7010–8600* ⊕ *www.joel-robuchon.net* Ⓜ *Leicester Sq.* ✛ *3:E5.*

$$$
BRASSERIE
Fodor'sChoice
★

╳**Les Deux Salons.** You're bound to spot a late-night theaterland celeb like Sienna Miller in one of those dark green leather bays at this classic 1930s-style French brasserie off St. Martin's Lane. The two-floor mezzanine dining salons are an elegant profusion of brass rails, mosaic floors, white linen, and flattering globe lights, where you'll find masterful classics, from Marseille bouillabaisse fish soup to Bavette steak. Some mains are truly outstanding—grilled sea bass with seashore vegetables, perhaps, or roast cod with peas and bacon—but it's the great people-watching that makes it sparkle. Tip: try the excellent pre- and post-theater meals for £15.95. Ⓢ *Average main: £18* ⊠ *42–44 William IV St., Covent Garden* ☎ *020/7420–2050* ⊕ *www.lesdeuxsalons.co.uk* ⌂ *Reservations essential* Ⓜ *Leicester Sq.* ✛ *3:E6.*

$$
TAPAS

╳**Opera Tavern.** Mouthwatering Iberico pig's head terrine and char-grilled salt marsh lamb with broad beans and mini pork-and–foie gras burgers are just a few of the smashing Spanish/Italian tapas presented at the handily situated Opera Tavern, not far from Covent Garden piazza. Clamber in at the overcrowded ground-floor tapas bar (avoiding the acoustically challenged second-floor salon if you can) and, after enjoying the amuse-bouche of crispy pig's ears, gun for the swooningly rich empanadas of venison, the Italian Scotch eggs, or Venetian-style sardines. Authentic? The menu warns that all game here may have "shot" in it. Ⓢ *Average main: £14* ⊠ *23 Catherine St., Covent Garden* ☎ *020/7836–3680* ⊕ *www.operatavern.co.uk* ⌂ *Reservations essential* Ⓜ *Leicester Sq.* ✛ *3:G5.*

$$$$
BRITISH
Fodor'sChoice
★

╳**Rules.** Come, escape the 21st century. Opened by Thomas Rule in 1798, London's oldest restaurant is, according to some, still London's most beautiful. This is to London what Maxim's is to Paris, although in this case the art nouveau decor is High Regency. Plush red banquettes, lacquered yellow walls, and spectacular etched-glass skylights make up the frame, then every nook and cranny is filled in vintage needlepoints, Victorian oil paintings, antique clocks, stuffed pheasants, antlers, bronze figurines, and hundreds of framed engravings. No wonder this stage has been pranced across by everyone from Charles Dickens to Laurence Olivier. For your shining day—be sure to ask for a table in one of the "glass house" skylight rooms, the bar area, or the cute Maggie Thatcher corner—dig in to the menu's pricey and historic British dishes, such as steak-and-kidney pie, jugged hare, or roast beef and Yorkshire pudding. True: movie stars no longer come and some diners appear in shirtsleeves at lunch, but no other place in London can give you such a grand old vibe as this beloved landmark. Ⓢ *Average main: £27* ⊠ *35 Maiden La., Covent Garden* ☎ *020/7836–5314* ⊕ *www.rules.co.uk* ⌂ *Reservations essential. Jacket required* Ⓜ *Covent Garden* ✛ *3:F6.*

$$$$
BRITISH

✕ **The Savoy Grill.** You can feel the history in this glamorous 1889 art deco power dining salon, which has hosted everyone from Oscar Wilde and Sir Winston Churchill to Audrey Hepburn and Marilyn Monroe. Nowadays, the place is masterminded by Gordon Ramsay for business buccaneers, high rollers, and top-end tourists who come to enjoy the Grill's famous table-side trolley, which might trundle up bearing gifts like rack of roast Dingley Dell pork, sumptuous roast leg of lamb, or traditional roast beef Wellington. Other classics, such as T-bone, rib-eye, and Porterhouse steaks, or Dover sole or braised halibut, have gotten the Ramsay makeover. For an infinitely more chic surround, repair, instead, to the Savoy's Thames Foyer, a "winter-garden" setting just off the main lobby: it offers a lighter menu and one of the most elegant teas in the city. $ *Average main: £28* ⊠ *The Savoy, 100 Strand, Covent Garden* ☎ *020/7592–1600* ⊕ *www.gordonramsay.com/thesavoygrill* ⌖ *Reservations essential* Ⓜ *Charing Cross, Covent Garden* ✛ *3:G5.*

14

$
MEXICAN
☾

✕ **Wahaca.** Brace for queues for the fab-value Mexican street food at chef Thomasina Mier's brightly colored Covent Garden favorite. Mud walls and bench seats make for buzzy basement surrounds, but it's the cheap-as-chips and sustainably sourced £3.95–£6.95 tacos, enchiladas, quesadillas, and burritos that pull in the cost-conscious student-type crowds. A £19.95 spread for two hungry honchos will produce a feast of broad bean quesadillas, pork tacos, slaw, chicken taquitas with green rice, tostadas, black beans, and guacamole, but note that it is often heaving by 6:30 pm. $ *Average main: £8* ⊠ *66 Chandos Pl., Covent Garden* ☎ *020/7240–1883* ⊕ *www.wahaca.co.uk* ⌖ *Reservations not accepted* Ⓜ *Covent Garden* ✛ *3:F6.*

THE CITY

$$$
BRASSERIE

✕ **Boundary.** Restaurateur and design-god Sir Terence Conran scores a golden bull's-eye at Boundary in east-side über-trendy Hoxton/ Shoreditch. A theatrically glass-fronted open kitchen and sparkling lighting, acoustics, and Technicolor seats, make this plush 100-seat chic French basement brasserie the glamorati's East End destination of choice. The menu's a wish list of crowd-pleasers designed to impress: shellfish bisque, escargots à la bourguignonne, cassoulet Toulousain (haricot beans with pork, lamb and garlic sausage), and *lapin à la moutarde* (rabbit with mustard). Keep an eye out for the £19.50 and £23.50 prix-fixes deals. $ *Average main: £20* ⊠ *2–4 Boundary St., entrance at 9 Redchurch St., The City* ☎ *020/7729–1051* ⊕ *www. theboundary.co.uk* ⌖ *Reservations essential* ◷ *No lunch Mon.* Ⓜ *Liverpool St.* ✛ *2:G1.*

$
CAFÉ

✕ **E Pellicci.** It's non-stop Cockney banter and all-day English breakfasts at this tiny 1900 Italian family-run listed landmark café near the great Brick Lane and Columbia Road street markets in Bethnal Green. With stained glass, art deco marquetry, and signed photos of *East Enders* TV soap stars, it's the hole-in-the-wall for the greasy fry-ups that Londoners love: eggs, bacon, toast, baked beans, tomatoes, mushrooms, black pudding and "bubble 'n' squeak" (cabbage and mash potatoes). Your arteries most certainly will clog up, but at least the wallet will breathe easily. Everything's less than £9, but remember this is the East

End and hence it's cash-only, mate! $ *Average main: £8* ✉ *332 Bethnal Green Rd., The City* ☎ *020/7739–4873* ▭ *No credit cards* ⊘ *Closed Sun.* Ⓜ *Bethnal Green* ✛ *2:H1.*

$$$ ✕ **L'Anima.** Brilliant southern Italian cuisine in a (love-it-or-loathe-it)
ITALIAN modern glass-sided shoe box of a restaurant characterizes the breezy business-based scene here in The City district. Chef Francesco Mazzei draws inspiration from Sicily, Puglia, Sardinia, and Calabria, and prowls the bar, floor, and clear-fronted kitchen like the proud owner he is. Simple, modern, and restrained dishes like wild mushroom and black truffle *tagliolini* and Sardinian fish stew are near perfection, as is the wood-roasted turbot with artichoke and Calabrian sausage—as succulent as you could wish. Desserts, like licorice zabayon wine custard, are *bellissimo,* and the wine list, naturally, is nearly all Italian. $ *Average main: £24* ✉ *1 Snowden St., The City* ☎ *020/7422–7000* ⊕ *www. lanima.co.uk* ⊘ *Closed Sun.* Ⓜ *Liverpool St.* ✛ *2:G1.*

$ ✕ **Simpson's Tavern.** This Old World Dickensian back-alley City chop-
BRITISH house and tavern was founded in 1757 and is probably as raucous now as the day it opened. It draws well-fed, ruddy-faced, pinstriped City folk, who revel in the boarding school atmosphere and guzzle down shed-loads of old-school grub: oxtail stew, steak-and-kidney pie, potted shrimps (preserved in butter), and "stewed cheese," the house special of cheese on toast with béchamel sauce. Puddings, of course, are public-schoolboy favorites, like spotted dick and custard. Shared oak bench stalls and magnificently grumpy service only seems to add to the charm. Note that it is only open weekdays for lunch from noon until 3. $ *Average main: £10* ✉ *38½ Cornhill, at Ball Ct., The City* ☎ *020/7626–9985* ⊕ *www.simpsonstavern.co.uk* ⊘ *Closed weekends. No dinner* Ⓜ *Bank* ✛ *2:G2.*

$ ✕ **Sông Quê Café.** An urban safari through Hoxton's east-side hip bou-
VIETNAMESE tiques, record shops, furniture stores, and art galleries is topped off at this cracking-value Vietnamese canteen and all-round urban hot spot. Block out the scuzzy Hackney Kingsland Road location, the bright lights, and the oh-so-gaudy green decor and focus on sampling a slew of Sông Quê's 180 wicked dishes, including green papaya salad, tamarind prawns, beef in betel leaves, Vietnamese pancakes, and steaming bowls of Vietnamese *pho,* or beef broth with steak and rice noodles. $ *Average main: £8* ✉ *134 Kingsland Rd., Hackney* ☎ *020/7613–3222* ⊕ *www. songque.co.uk* ⌚ *Reservations essential* Ⓜ *Old St.* ✛ *2:G1.*

$$$ ✕ **Sweetings.** A time-warp traditional City seafood institution, Sweetings
SEAFOOD was established in 1889 and it powers on serenely as if the sun never went down on the British Empire. There are some things Sweetings really *doesn't* do: dinner, reservations, coffee, or weekends. It does, mercifully, do seafood. Not far from St. Paul's Cathedral, it's patronized by self-assured and minted City gents who down tankards of Black Velvet (Guinness and champagne) and eat soused herrings, roe on toast, and succulent skate wings with black butter at linen-covered raised counters. The oysters are fresh, and desserts like spotted dick and baked jam roll are classic favorites. $ *Average main: £22* ✉ *39 Queen Victoria St., The City* ☎ *020/7248–3062* ⌚ *Reservations not accepted* ⊘ *Closed weekends. No dinner* Ⓜ *Mansion House* ✛ *2:H6.*

$ **✕ Tayyabs.** City bankers and heroic medics from the nearby Royal Lon-
don Hospital swamp this high-turnover Pakistani curry canteen in east-
side Whitechapel. Expect lines after dark, and bear in mind it's BYO,
jam-packed, noisy, and sometimes maddeningly chaotic. Nonetheless,
prices are keen and you can gorge handsomely for £16 on a mixed
char-grill extravaganza which includes chicken and fish tikka. Other
best bets include Karachi okra, slow-cooked "dry meat," minced meat
seekh kebabs, Karahi prawns, naan bread, and their famous char-grilled
spicy lamb chops. ⑤ *Average main: £11* ✉ *83 Fieldgate St., The City*
☎ *020/7247–9543* ⊕ *www.tayyabs.co.uk* ⌕ *Reservations not accepted*
🍷 *BYOB* Ⓜ *Aldgate East* ✛ *2:H2.*

PAKISTANI

CLERKENWELL

$$$ **✕ Bistrot Bruno Loubet.** Prodigal French chef Bruno Loubet rules the roost
at this distinctive hotel dining room and bistro at the Zetter hotel in
cutting-edge Clerkenwell. He creates so many must-try dishes it is genu-
inely hard to pick: deliciously pink quail comes with pistachio and soft
egg-yolk ravioli, while guinea fowl *boudin blanc* sausages sit perfectly
with leeks and chervil sauce, to name two winners. You'll find snails
and meatballs and hare royale, followed by crêpe suzette served in a
shiny copper pan. The ground-floor bistro is kitted out with retro lamps
and artifacts and overlooks St. John's Square. ⑤ *Average main: £18*
✉ *The Zetter, 86–88 Clerkenwell Rd, Clerkenwell* ☎ *020/7324–4455*
⊕ *www.bistrotbrunoloubet.com* ⌕ *Reservations essential* Ⓜ *Farringdon
St.* ✛ *2:F3.*

FRENCH

$$$ **✕ St. John.** Foodies travel the world for pioneering chef Fergus Hen-
derson's ultra-British nose-to-tail cooking at this no-frills stark-white
converted smokehouse in Clerkenwell. Henderson uses all parts of a
carcass, and his waste-not, want-not chutzpah is laudable: one appetizer
is pigskin, and others, like ox heart or pig's ear and calves' brain and
chicory, are marginally less extreme. Signatures like bone marrow and
parsley salad, or chitterlings with dandelion, appear stark on the plate,
but arrive with aplomb. Expect a cracking all-French wine list and finish with quince jelly, Eccles cakes, or half a dozen golden madeleines.
⑤ *Average main: £20* ✉ *26 St. John St., Clerkenwell* ☎ *020/7251–0848*
⊕ *www.stjohnrestaurant.com* ⌕ *Reservations essential* ⊘ *No dinner
Sun.* Ⓜ *Farringdon* ✛ *2:F4.*

BRITISH
Fodor's Choice
★

14

THE EAST END

$$$ **✕ Viajante.** It's a schlep from the West End to Viajante in Bethnal Green,
but Portuguese chef/patron Nuno Mendes's ultra-contemporary, avant-
garde cuisine is the hottest, most exciting in London—bar none. Armed
with tweezers in a fascinating open-kitchen, El Bulli–trained Mendes
doubles down with 3- to 12-course tasting extravaganzas (£28–£90)
in the modishly converted former Bethnal Green Town Hall. Unlikely
tastes, textures, and flavors abound—like skate with roasted yeast, crab
milk with beach herbs, or Thai basil panna cotta—but every dish excels,
and looks like high art. Expect rare micro-herbs and local urban-foraged
goodies on the plate, such as wood sorrel, sweet violets, and honey-
suckle, and don't be surprised to be served at your table by Mendes

MODERN
EUROPEAN
Fodor's Choice
★

Harwood Arms' modern take on the classic British dish, Scotch eggs

himself. Our advice is simple: *Go!!* $ *Average main: £25* ✉ *Town Hall Hotel, Patriot Sq., East End* ☎ *020/7871–0461* ⊕ *www.viajante.co.uk* ⌁ *Reservations essential* Ⓜ *Bethnal Green tube/rail* ✛ *2:H1.*

THE SOUTH BANK

$$
MODERN BRITISH

✕ **Anchor & Hope.** Great meaty dishes at friendly prices emerge from the open kitchen at this permanently packed leading gastropub on The Cut in Waterloo: pot roast duck, Herefordshire beef, Orkney kippers, and cuttlefish with snails and bacon stand out. It's a few doors down from the fabulous Young Vic contemporary theater and bear in mind that it's noisy, cramped, overflowing, and informal. That said, it's highly original, and there are great dishes for groups—like slow-roasted leg of lamb. Eager diners wait for a table over a pint in the pub's convivial saloon bar and be prepared to share a dining table with others once seated, too. $ *Average main: £17* ✉ *36 The Cut, South Bank* ☎ *020/7928–9898* ⌁ *Reservations not accepted* ⊗ *No dinner Sun. No lunch Mon.* Ⓜ *Waterloo, Southwark* ✛ *5:F2.*

$$$
MODERN FRENCH
Fodor's Choice
★

✕ **Chez Bruce.** Bullsy French cuisine, faultless service, a winning wine list, and a glossy and upbeat local neighborhood vibe make for one of London's all-time favorite celebration restaurants. Take a cab or overland train south of the river to chef Bruce Poole's cozy haunt overlooking Wandsworth Common and expect wonders ranging from delicious offal to lighter, simply grilled fish dishes. Pot roast pig's cheek with polenta, pollack with wild mushrooms, and bream with orange vinaigrette are all immaculately presented. The desserts and wines are great, the sommelier's superb, and, pound-for-pound, Bruce is nigh impossible to beat.

$ *Average main: £25* ✉ *2 Bellevue Rd., Wandsworth* ☎ *020/8672–0114* ⊕ *www.chezbruce.co.uk* ⌕ *Reservations essential* Ⓜ *Tube: Wandsworth Common rail* ✛ *4:E6.*

$$
TAPAS
✕**Jose.** Rising Spanish chef Jose Pizarro packs 'em in like so many slices of *jamon jamon* at this tapas-and-sherry treasure trove in Bermondsey, south of the river near London Bridge. With only 30 seats and no reservations, you'll be hard-pressed to find a spot at the tapas bar or a perch at an upturned barrel after 6 pm, but stick with it *hombre*—the tapas is astounding. Quaff a glass of Amontillado sherry, and keep those small white plates comin': green padron peppers . . . pisto and crispy duck eggs . . . hake and aioli . . . razor clams with chorizo . . . paprika-specked Iberico pork fillets. You'll either love or hate the crush. $ *Average main: £8* ✉ *104 Bermondsey St., South Bank* ☎ *020/7403–4902* ⊕ *joserestaurant.co.uk* ⌕ *Reservations not accepted* Ⓜ *London Bridge* ✛ *5:H2.*

$$$
MODERN BRITISH
✕**Magdalen.** South of the river between London and Tower bridges, Magdalen is a self-assured beacon of class in a markedly up-and-coming part of town. It specializes in inventive but unpretentious modern British cuisine at keen prices; poached hake with fennel (£9), calves' sweetbreads with salsify (£18), wild turbot and clams (£19), and treacle tart for £6 will hardly break the bank. With dark-wood and bent-wood chairs, chandeliers, tea candles, the pleasing ox-blood-color surrounds invite you to sit back with the clever wine list and ponder whether to have a feast of whole hare or the stuffed suckling pig instead. $ *Average main: £18* ✉ *152 Tooley St., South Bank* ☎ *020/7403–1342* ⊕ *www.magdalenrestaurant.co.uk* ⌕ *Reservations essential* ⊗ *Closed Sun. No lunch Sat.* Ⓜ *London Bridge* ✛ *5:H2.*

14

KENSINGTON, CHELSEA, AND KNIGHTSBRIDGE

KENSINGTON

$$$$
MODERN BRITISH
✕**Bibendum.** Magnificent stained-glass windows of a bulging Michelin Man reminds diners in Latin that *Nunc est Bibendum* —""Now is the time to drink"—at this landmark special-occasion showpiece in the extraordinary art deco Michelin Building in south Kensington. Today, seasoned chef Matthew Harris cooks with classical French brasserie flair, consistently churning out quality favorites like pigeon salad, grilled squid with aioli, steak au poivre, ox cheeks with pearl barley, and *escargots de Bourgogne* (snails). Desserts like quince and almond clafoutis tart are just as impressive, and the weekend £30–£32 lunches are super-popular. $ *Average main: £27* ✉ *Michelin House, 81 Fulham Rd., Kensington* ☎ *020/7581–5817* ⊕ *www.bibendum.co.uk* ⌕ *Reservations essential* Ⓜ *South Kensington* ✛ *4:E3.*

$$
AMERICAN
✕**PJ's Bar & Grill.** Enter PJ's and assume the Polo Joe lifestyle: wooden floors and stained glass, a slowly revolving propeller from a World War I 1911 Vickers Vimy flying bomber, and vintage polo gear and mementos galore. A notorious magnet for the well-tanned, upmarket, foot-loose-and-fancy-free Chelsea jet set, the place is packed yet relaxed, and the menu, which includes all-American staples like 28-day steaks, club sandwiches, Caesar salads, and brownies pleases

all except vegetarians. $ *Average main: £17* ⊠ *52 Fulham Rd., Kensington* ☎ *020/7581–0025* ⊕ *www.pjsbarandgrill.co.uk* ⌂ *Reservations essential* Ⓜ *South Kensington* ✛ *4:E3.*

$$$$
FRENCH

✕ **Tom Aikens.** Is flame-haired so-called wonderchef Tom Aikens the real thing? The former bad boy is always in the gossip columns for having bust-ups, winning awards, hob-knobbing with the gentry, or for flirting with bankruptcy. Nonetheless, it's all splashes and dashes on the plate at his strikingly revamped gastro-lair in residential Chelsea, and many are mighty impressed. You'll totally swoon over his foie gras with Sauternes jelly, sea bass with pickled fennel, partridge with truffle mash, and his honeycomb-and-poppy-seed ice cream. The £49 set lunch is practically a romantic gesture. $ *Average main: £32* ⊠ *43 Elystan St., Kensington* ☎ *020/7584–2003* ⊕ *www.tomaikens.co.uk* ⌂ *Reservations essential* Ⓜ *South Kensington* ✛ *4:E3.*

CHELSEA

$$$
MODERN BRITISH

✕ **The Botanist.** Tally-ho with the horse-and-hound set at this Sloane-ranger mustering point on the corner of Sloane Square in South Kensington. An ultrablonde, Alice band–wearing, good-looking Sloaney crew jack up the decibels at this cream, green, and serene restaurant, hangout, and after-works drinks hub. Framed with intriguing Sir Hans Sloane botany prints, the figure-conscious restaurant menu takes itself seriously, so you'll find well-executed Isle of Man king scallops, Atlantic cod, salmon fishcakes, or pot-roast poussin all carried off with panache and aplomb. $ *Average main: £24* ⊠ *7 Sloane Sq., Chelsea* ☎ *020/7730–0077* ⊕ *www.thebotanistonsloanesquare.com* ⌂ *Reservations essential* Ⓜ *Sloane Sq.* ✛ *4:G2*

$$
MODERN BRITISH
Fodor's Choice
★

✕ **Harwood Arms.** Modern British game doesn't get any better—or more inventive—than at this game-lovers' paradise gastropub off Fulham Broadway. Enthusiast and co-owner Mike Robinson shoots and bags all the wild venison on the menu here in season, and you'll find a catalog of awesome game-based dishes like Berkshire roe deer with junipers or North Yorkshire grouse with Earl Grey–soaked prunes. Tuck into game pie with Somerset cider jelly or wood pigeon with pickled apricots in a relaxed sofas-and-newspapers Sloaney-pub type setting. Some dishes are served on a slab of wood, and there are popular carve-your-own roast beef, lamb, or pork joints for the table. $ *Average main: £17* ⊠ *27 Walham Grove, Chelsea* ☎ *020/7386–1847* ⊕ *www.harwoodarms.com* ⌂ *Reservations essential* ☉ *No lunch Mon* Ⓜ *Fulham Broadway* ✛ *4:A5.*

$$
WINE BAR

✕ **The Henry Root.** Named after the hilarious upper-class serial spoof letter writer, Henry Root, you'll find there's nothing fake about this winsome neighborhood joint-cum-wine-bar that serves up a quirky menu in a friendly nonstop party salon. Wealthy local Chelsea denizens think nothing about using their fingers to pick their way through a whole globe artichoke with Dijon vinaigrette, and they rave about the hearty jellied ham hock or cured meat and Piccadilly charcuterie platters. Besides small plates and salad bowls, there's satisfying mains like lemon chicken or the smoked haddock in champagne sauce. $ *Average main: £15* ⊠ *9 Park Walk, Chelsea* ☎ *020/7352–7040* ⊕ *www.*

thehenryroot.com ⌦ *Reservations essential* Ⓜ *Fulham Broaₐ₁*
Kensington ✛ *4:D4.*

$$$ ✕ **Medlar.** What's there *not* to like about Medlar? Sensationally assu.
MODERN modern European cuisine, effortless service, and elegant oak-wooᵤ
EUROPEAN floors, mirrored walls, and a luxe gray/lime-green stenciled color scheme
make for a complete neighborhood package at the quieter World's End
stretch of the King's Road. Set lunch is a steal at £25, where you'll find
such winners as crab ravioli with fondant leeks and samphire, rabbit
with red onion marmalade, or fillet steak with snails and triple-cooked
chips. Desserts—like pear-and-frangipane tart and clotted cream—
couldn't be more delicious. Ⓢ *Average main: £22* ⌧ *438 King's Rd.,*
Chelsea ☎ *020/7349–1900* ⊕ *www.medlarrestaurant.co.uk* ⌦ *Reserva-*
tions essential Ⓜ *Fulham Broadway, Sloane Sq.* ✛ *4:D4*

$$ ✕ **The Orange.** Four-square and handsome, this Pimplico gastropub gets
MODERN BRITISH everything right, which is why it's packed with well-shod braying locals
Fodor's Choice most nights and all weekend. The stage is set—light and airy, with
★ stripped wood, a tony ocher color scheme, and mini-potted orange
trees—for service that is noticeably smiley, polite, and well-mannered.
You can't go wrong with the chicken liver parfait, Trealy Farm–cured
meat platters, and the wood-fired pizzas, or enjoy a leisurely Sunday
roast like Castle of Mey rib beef, Kilravock pork rack, or chicken with
sage-and-bacon stuffing, all served with duck-fat roast potatoes and
Yorkshire pudding goodies. Ⓢ *Average main: £15* ⌧ *37 Pimlico Rd.,*
Chelsea ☎ *020/7881–9844* ⊕ *www.theorange.co.uk* ⌦ *Reservations*
essential Ⓜ *Sloane Sq.* ✛ *4:G3.*

$$ ✕ **Racine.** There's always an upscale buzz at this star of the Brompton
BRASSERIE Road dining scene, not far from the V&A, Harrods, and the packed-to-
the-rafters upmarket Holy Trinity Brompton Church. This smooth-run-
ning chic-and-cheerful classic French brasserie excels in doing the simple
things well—and not costing the earth. Chef Henry Harris's signatures
like roast partridge, foie gras with Calvados, soft roe on toast, rack of
lamb, or the adventurous *tete de veau*—poached calf's head—all hit
the high notes. Many of the happy-looking patrons are stealth-wealth
local regulars, but even they are tempted by the £15.50–£17.75 prix-fixe
lunch or dinners (6–8 pm). Ⓢ *Average main: £18* ⌧ *239 Brompton Rd.,*
Chelsea ☎ *020/7584–4477* ⊕ *www.racine-restaurant.com* ⌦ *Reserva-*
tions essential Ⓜ *South Kensington* ✛ *4:E2.*

$$$$ ✕ **Restaurant Gordon Ramsay.** Modest Gordon Ramsay protégée and head
FRENCH chef Clare Smyth wins three stars and the highest Michelin award in
London at this special-occasion showstopper near Chelsea Embank-
ment. It's mighty hard to book a table at anything like short notice, so
if you do bag a seat you'd be slightly mad not to splurge on the £120
seven-course tasting menu, where you'll experience divine dishes like
lobster ravioli with chervil sauce, Bresse pigeon with date and polenta,
and Cornish turbot with girolles, followed perhaps by a dessert of Agen
prune crème brûlée. There's an incoming battalion of *amuse bouche* at
every meal, service is neat and tidy, and the wine list goes on forever.
Ⓢ *Average main: £35* ⌧ *68 Royal Hospital Rd., Chelsea* ☎ *020/7352–*
4441 ⊕ *www.gordonramsay.com/royalhospitalroad* ⌦ *Reservations*
essential. Jacket required ☉ *Closed weekends* Ⓜ *Sloane Sq.* ✛ *4:F4.*

14

DON'S BEST CURRIES

...oom. Curry is England's sur-
... national dish and in Lon-
...you'll find some of the best.
...oom near Leicester Square is
...deled on the Persian-run all-day
...ii cafés of Victorian Bombay and
it skillfully churns out marvelous
street food, from hot naan bread
and *roomali* roti wraps, to masala
Bombay chipolata sausages, Mulli-
gatawny soup, and sweet yogurt-
and-milk-based *lassi* drinks. Average
price of dinner for two: £20. ⊠ *12
Upper St. Martin's La., Covent Garden*
☎ *020/7420–9320* ⊕ *www.dishoom.
com* Ⓜ *Leicester Sq.* ✛ *3:E5.*

Hot Stuff. Hot Stuff in Vauxhall
offers some of the best-loved and
best-priced curries in London. Run by
Raj Dawood, it's a cult BYO café with
its own Facebook appreciation society. Home-cooked specials include
king prawn *biryani*, thick lamb bhuna
curry, and cubed chili paneer white
cheese. There's also wonderful pilau
rice, onion bhaji snacks, Peshwari
naan bread, and earthy *dhal* (curried
lentils). Average price of dinner for
two: £26. ⊠ *19–23 Wilcox Rd., South
Bank* ☎ *020/7720–1480* ⊕ *www.
welovehotstuff.com* ⓘ *BYOB* Ⓜ *Vauxhall* ✛ *5:C6.*

Indian Zing. Indian Zing's chef/
owner Manoj Vasaikar woos the west
London curry mafia with updated
eclectic regional Indian cuisine on
King's Street emergent '"Curry Mile."
Start with tamarind-spiced Rasam
mussels and move onto Khyber Pass
shank of lamb or Barbary duck with
Chettinad spices. Average price of
dinner for two: £68. ⊠ *236 King St.,
Hammersmith* ☎ *020/8748–5959*
⊕ *www.indianzing.co.uk* ⌕ *Reservations essential* Ⓜ *Hammersmith*
✛ *1:A2.*

Rasoi. Rasoi's Indian chef/owner
Vineet Bhatia concocts Michelin-
star modern Indian cuisine at this
tony special-occasion Chelsea town
house off the King's Road, where
fans with chubby wallets swoon over
spiced foie gras, skewered scallops,
tandoori lobster, South Indian crab
cakes, and Keralean lamb lasagna.
"Average" price of dinner for two:
£180. ⊠ *10 Lincoln St., Knightsbridge*
☎ *020/7225–1881* ⊕ *www.rasoi-uk.
com* Ⓜ *Sloane Sq.* ✛ *4:F3.*

Tayyabs. Half-hour-long lines sometimes form here at this throbbing
east-side Whitechapel mecca and
all-round Karahi curry madhouse.
Best bets include the fiery Pakistani
curries, char-grilled meats, and spicy
seekh and *shami* kebabs. Average
price of dinner for two: £36. ⊠ *83-89
Fieldgate St., The City* ☎ *020/7247–
9543* ⊕ *www.tayyabs.co.uk* ⌕ *Reservations essential* ⓘ *BYOB* Ⓜ *Aldgate
East* ✛ *2:H2.*

Trishna's. Trishna's £20 four-course
(early evening) tasting menus are
a smart way to savor this Mumbai-
inspired seafood ace in Marylebone
village. Tiger prawn seafood salad
with Goan sausages, crispy squid,
fish tikka, and spiced brown crab all
come with basmati rice, Hydrabadi
dhal, naan bread, and a choice of
Indian desserts. Average price for
dinner for two: £80. ⊠ *15–17 Bland-
ford St., Marylebone* ☎ *020/79351–
5624* ⊕ *www.trishnalondon.com*
⌕ *Reservations essential* Ⓜ *Bond
St.* ✛ *1:G3.*

Prosciutto-topped wood-fired pizza served at the Orange.

KNIGHTSBRIDGE

$$$
FRENCH

✗ **Bar Boulud.** U.S.-based star French chef Daniel Boulud combines the best of French high-end brasserie fare with a dash of superior Yankee gourmet burgers and fries at this popular street-level hang out in the luxe Mandarin Oriental hotel in Knightsbridge. Lilliputian-size platters of the most delicate Gilles Verot charcuterie, or chunky Beaujolaise sausages with Lyonnaise mashed potatoes are followed by palm-size Yankee, Frenchie, or Piggie burgers and fries in sesame-seed buns. The knock-out grazing menu has something for everyone, and pro but informal waitstaff make for a convivial vibe in this handy spot opposite Harvey Nichols department store. $ *Average main: £20* ⊠ *Mandarin Oriental Hyde Park, 66 Knightsbridge, Knightsbridge* ☏ *020/7201–3899* ⊕ *www.danielnyc.com/barbouludlondon.html* ⚎ *Reservations essential* Ⓜ *Knightsbridge* ✛ *4:F1.*

$$$$
BRITISH
Fodor's Choice
★

✗ **Dinner by Heston Blumenthal.** Genius "olde" English-inspired dishes executed with modern precision in an open-kitchen is the schtick at Heston Blumenthal's incredible award-winner at the Mandarin Oriental hotel. As you take in the view overlooking Hyde Park, you can slice into a "Meat Fruit" starter (c.1500) shaped like a orange mandarin, but encasing the smoothest, most creamy chicken liver parfait imaginable. "Rice and flesh" (c.1390) is a picture of yellow saffron rice with calf's tails and red wine, and fans will recognize his snail-and-girolle "Savoury porridge" (c.1660). There's juicy Beef Royale (c.1720) cooked *sous-vide* at 56°C for 72 hours, plus Salamagundy salad with calf's hearts, walnuts, and horseradish. Head off with the spit-roast pineapple "Tipsy cake" (c.1810)—an homage to English spit-roasting from yesteryear. $ *Average main: £32* ⊠ *Mandarin Oriental Hyde*

Park, 66 Knightsbridge, Knightsbridge ☎ *020/7201–3833* ⊕ *www. dinnerbyheston.com* ⌕ *Reservations essential* Ⓜ *Knightsbridge* ✚ *4:F1.*

$$$
FRENCH

✗ **Koffmann's.** Perfectly seared scallops with black squid ink and famed pig's trotters with sweetbreads and morels are two all-time signature French classics at Pierre Koffmann's eponymous last-hurrah! at the Berkeley in Knightsbridge. In his mid-sixties, and the antithesis of a celebrity chef, Koffmann showcases 35-odd years of experience and the best of regional Gascony cuisine in a *jolie* and well-appointed informal basement setting. Alongside celebs and minor royalty, sample snails with garlic and parsley, wild duck à l'orange, and Gascon apple tart or the signature pistachio soufflé with ice cream—before it is too late. ⑤ *Average main: £23* ⊠ *The Berkeley, Wilton Place, Knightsbridge* ☎ *020/7235–1010* ⌕ *Reservations essential* Ⓜ *Knightsbridge* ✚ *4:G1.*

$$$$
MODERN
EUROPEAN

✗ **Marcus Wareing at the Berkeley.** *Will-he-Won't-he?* master chef Marcus Wareing would do anything for a coveted third Michelin star, but will he ever jump from two to three and reach the top? Hedge funders, Russian "supermodels," and the petro-dollar elite settle into the David Collins–designed plush salon—all clarets, deep carpet, velvet, and burgundy leather seats—where Wareing pulls out all the haute cuisine stops with a succession of world-class British-sourced seasonal dishes. Standouts include Galloway beef with Jerusalem artichokes, Scottish halibut with charred leeks, Anjou pigeon, oozing chocolate *moëlleux* with Cointreau, or killer custard tarts with chestnuts and pear jelly. The wine list is *stuffed* with prestige cuvées. ⑤ *Average main: £30* ⊠ *The Berkeley, Wilton Pl., Knightsbridge* ☎ *020/7235–1200* ⊕ *www.the-berkeley.co.uk* ⌕ *Reservations essential* ⊘ *Closed Sun. No lunch Sat.* Ⓜ *Knightsbridge* ✚ *4:G1.*

$$$$
INDIAN

✗ **Rasoi.** Star Indian chef Vineet Bhatia showcases the finest new-wave Indian cuisine in London at this tony Victorian town house off the King's Road. Ring the doorbell on arrival at this romantic celebration venue, which is decked out with colorful Indian silks, prints, masks, brass bells, and ornaments. Bhatia pushes the boundaries with signatures like wild mushroom rice with tomato ice cream, spiced lamb with coconut and morel Korma sauce, or grilled lobster with cocoa powder. Prices are pretty extreme, but don't leave without sampling mango and saffron panna cotta or the famous warm chocolate samosas, dubbed "Chocamosas." ⑤ *Average main: £30* ⊠ *10 Lincoln St., Knightsbridge* ☎ *020/7225–1881* ⊕ *www.rasoirestaurant.co.uk* ⌕ *Reservations essential* Ⓜ *Sloane Sq.* ✚ *4:F3.*

NOTTING HILL AND BAYSWATER

NOTTING HILL

$$
MODERN BRITISH

✗ **The Cow.** Supermodel Kate Moss and her rocker hubby Jamie Hince often crash this popular archetypal boho-chic Notting Hill gastropub, which packs 'em in cheek-by-jowl in a faux-Dublin '50s backroom saloon bar that serves Fines de Claires oysters, bowls of whelks and winkles, and whole Dorset crab with aioli. Upstairs the chef whips up Brit specialties like deviled kidneys on toast, Stilton cheese and hazelnut salad, or smoked eel with horseradish. Post–double dip recession

British Food Decoder

In London, local could mean any global flavor, but for pure Britishness, roast beef and Yorkshire pudding top the list. If you want the best-value traditional Sunday lunch, go to a traditional pub. Updated gastropubs, where Sunday roasts are generally made on-site with top-quality ingredients, are an excellent bet, too. The meat is usually served with duck-fat crisp roast potatoes and carrots, and with Yorkshire pudding, a savory batter baked in the oven until crisp. A rich, dark, meaty gravy is poured on top.

Other tummy liners include shepherd's pie, made with stewed minced lamb and a mashed-potato topping and baked until lightly browned on top; cottage pie is a similar dish, but made with minced beef instead of lamb. Steak-and-kidney pie is a delight when done properly: with chunks of lean beef and ox kidneys, braised with onions and mushrooms in a thick meaty gravy, and topped with a light puff-pastry crust.

Fish-and-chips, usually battered deep-fried cod, haddock, or plaice, comes with thick chips, or french fries, as we call them in the States. A ploughman's lunch in a pub is crusty bread, a strong-flavored English cheese with bite (Cheddar, blue Stilton, crumbly white Cheshire, or smooth red Leicester), and tangy pickles with a side-salad garnish. For a hot, comforting dessert, seek out a sweet bread-and-butter pudding, made from layers of bread and dried currants baked in cream until crisp. And one can't forgo English cream tea, which consists of fruit scones served with jam and clotted cream, and sandwiches made with wafer-thin slices of cucumber—served as an accompaniment to properly brewed tea.

14

ex-mill'aire Notting Hill locals seem to be addicted to the house special in the bar: draft Guinness with a pint of prawns and mayonnaise (£9.95). ⑤ *Average main: £18* ⊠ *89 Westbourne Park Rd., Notting Hill* ☎ *020/7221–0021* ⊕ *www.thecowlondon.co.uk* ⌲ *Reservations essential* Ⓜ *Westbourne Park* ⊹ *1:B3.*

$$$ ✕ **E&O.** Madonna, Gywneth, and Stella, and a million fashionistas and
ASIAN the private jet set give a well-manicured thumbs-up to this Asian tapas supremo off Portobello Road street market. E&O's figure-friendly mix of Chinese, Japanese, Vietnamese, and Thai favorite dishes includes a slew of low-carb veggie options. Don't skip lychee martinis in the seen-and-be-scene bar, before moseying over for miso black cod, chili tofu, papaya salad, Thai rare beef, or green fried rice; the sea bass sashimi is achingly fresh. There are pavement tables and curbside bench seats to watch the world go by on Portobello, and it is cool for a girly girls' night get-together. ⑤ *Average main: £18* ⊠ *14 Blenheim Crescent, Notting Hill* ☎ *020/7229–5454* ⊕ *www.rickerrestaurants.com/eando* ⌲ *Reservations essential* Ⓜ *Ladbroke Grove* ⊹ *1:B1.*

$$$ ✕ **Julie's.** Does Julie's really have a draped-off dining area known affec-
BRITISH tionately as "the G-spot"? The warren of peekaboo alcoves and opulent Victoriana dining rooms at this cute 1969 throwback ooze sensuality and *allegedly* have witnessed all manner of naughtiness over the years. Royalty and rockers—from Mick Jagger to Lady Di—have all

famously cavorted here (note: now it's their kids that turn up). Situated at quaint Clarenden Cross, off Holland Park Avenue, the food is fun in an unashamedly unreconstructed kinda-way. Poached lobster with Russian salad, swordfish carpaccio, pork and Calvados, quail with Swiss *rösti* potatoes, and crab spaghetti are all popular faves, but overall its more about the vibe than the food. $ *Average main: £23* ⊠ *135 Portland Rd., Notting Hill* ☎ *020/7229–8331* ⊕ *www.juliesrestaurant.com* ⩲ *Reservations essential* M *Holland Park* ✛ *1:B1.*

$$$$

MODERN FRENCH

Fodor's Choice

★

✕ **The Ledbury.** Aussie chef Brett Graham wins hearts and minds—and global accolades—at this high-ceilinged destination fine-dining landmark on the crumbier edges of Notting Hill. In a handsome room full of drapes, mirrored walls, and leather seats, you won't find a more amazing veg dish than his ash-baked celeriac, and it's hard to better his frog's legs *beignets* or Cornish turbot with fennel and elderflower. Graham's famous for inventive desserts, so why not finish with his banana *galette* with passion fruit, salted caramel, and peanut oil? Seamless service and a sunny sommelier round out this winning proposition—one of London's finest. $ *Average main: £30* ⊠ *127 Ledbury Rd., Notting Hill* ☎ *0207/7792–9090* ⊕ *www.theledbury.com* ⩲ *Reservations essential* M *Westbourne Park* ✛ *1:A4.*

$$

BRITISH

✕ **The Mall Tavern.** It's all things British at this exemplary Notting Hill gastropub, which overflows with discerning local natives. Check out all the Coronation mugs and various royal wedding and Prince Charles and Lady Di crockery and memorabilia after sampling great British bar snacks like pork scratchings, brawn (head cheese), or lop-eared sausage rolls. Move through to dine on cow pie with bone marrow poking through the crust, or wallow in nostalgia with oozing chicken Kiev or fish fingers and mushy peas. There's old-school "Arctic Roll" ice cream, and Hello to the Queen! glacé bananas with hot chocolate sauce. $ *Average main: £12* ⊠ *71 Palace Gardens Terr., Notting Hill* ☎ *020/7229–3374* ⊕ *www.themalltavern.com* ⩲ *Reservations essential* M *Notting Hill Gate* ✛ *1:B5.*

BAYSWATER

$$$

FRENCH

✕ **Angelus.** Owner, sommelier, and former pro-rugby union player Thierry Tomasin scores with this distinctive French brasserie in Lancaster Gate. Styled with art nouveau mirrors and button-back banquettes in a 200-year-old converted former pub, Angelus has a reputation for unrivaled Paris-style *brasserie de luxe* cuisine. The foie gras crème brûlée, egg cocotte, frog's legs and snails, partridge ballotine, or chocolate soufflé are as good as they get. Light bites, like steak sandwich, are served at the bar, service is notoriously *Gallic,* and Tomasin is sure to select an interesting bottle from the offbeat wine list. $ *Average main: £26* ⊠ *4 Bathurst St., Bayswater* ☎ *020/402–0083* ⊕ *www.angelusrestaurant.co.uk* ⩲ *Reservations essential* M *Lancaster Gate* ✛ *1:D4.*

$$

MODERN BRITISH

✕ **Hereford Road.** Bespeckled chef/co-owner Tom Pemberton mans the front-of-house grill and prep station at this must-visit Bayswater favorite for pared-down and pomp-free British fare. With an accent on well-sourced honest-to-goodness regional and seasonal British ingredients, many dishes are as unfussy as you'll find. Work your way though uncluttered razor clams and lovage, lemon sole with sea dulse, pigeon

LOCAL CHAINS WORTH A TASTE

When you're on the go or don't have time for a leisurely meal, you might want to try a local chain restaurant or sandwich bar. *The ones listed below are well priced and are the best in their category.*

Busaba Eathai: It's always jam-packed at these seven Thai canteen supremos where you'll find Thai noodles, rice dishes, and spicy all-in-one meals in a bowl in sultry dark-wood surrounds. ⊕ *www.busaba.com.*

Byron: Bright and child-friendly, this 18-strong line of superior hamburger joints storms the market with its delicious Scotch beef hamburgers, onion rings, Cobb salads, and fries. ⊕ *www.byronhamburgers.com.*

Café Rouge: A classic 35-strong French bistro chain that's been around for eons and does great £6.50–£10.50 prix-fixe deals—so uncool that it's now almost fashionable. ⊕ *www.caferouge.co.uk.*

Carluccio's Caffè: The Carluccio's chain of 16 all-day Italian café/bar/food shops are freshly sourced, family-friendly, and make for brilliant pasta and salad stops on a shopping spree. ⊕ *www.carluccios.com.*

Ed's Easy Diner: Overdose on milk shakes, ice-cream floats, chili dogs, and made-to-order hamburgers at this four-strong chain of shiny, retro 1950s-theme American diners. ⊕ *www.edseasydiner.com.*

Le Pain Quotidien: Try tartine open sandwiches, soups, salads, and cakes at the communal wooden tables. There are 14 branches, including at the stunning St. Pancras station and Eurostar terminus. ⊕ *www.lepainquotidien.co.uk.*

Pizza Express: Serving classic thin-crust pizzas, old-favorite Pizza Express is everywhere (there are nearly 100 in London). The Soho branch has a famed live jazz program. ⊕ *www.pizzaexpress.com.*

Pret à Manger: London's high-street take-out supremo isn't just for store-made sandwiches: there are wraps, toasties, noodles, sushi, salads, fruit, porridge, and tea cakes, too. ⊕ *www.pret.com.*

Ranoush Juice: Chewy shawarma lamb kebabs are the draw at these four-strong mirrored late-night kebab and juice bars (open 8 am to 3 am daily). They also serve falafel, meze, and tabbouleh. ⊕ *www.maroush.com.*

Strada: Stop at this 30-strong chain for authentic hand-stretched pizzas baked over a wood fire, plus classic pastas, steaks, and risottos. It's cheap, stylish, and generally packed. ⊕ *www.strada.co.uk.*

Wagamama: Londoners drain endless bowls of Asian ramen and noodle soups at this high-tech, child-friendly chain of canteens. ⊕ *www.wagamama.com.*

14

and pickled walnut salad, and damson sorbet. Expect to bump into the entire well-heeled Tory party leadership and Notting Hill set on the way in and out. Ⓢ *Average main: £16* ✉ *3 Hereford Rd., Bayswater* ☎ *020/7727–1144* ⊕ *www.herefordroad.org* ⚱ *Reservations essential* Ⓜ *Bayswater, Queensway* ✛ *1:B4.*

REGENT'S PARK AND HAMPSTEAD

REGENT'S PARK

$$
GREEK
✗**Lemonia.** Hollywood-*ville* Primrose Hill's favorite Greek Cypriot restaurant, vine-decked and '80s taverna-style Lemonia is large and light, and always packed with hordes of hungry locals. Besides an endless supply of small-dish *mezédes* dips and starters, there are rustic mains like slow-baked *kleftiko* lamb in lemon, aubergine and potato *moussaka*, and beef stewed in red wine. Expect generous Greek hospitality, tons of noise, and the odd fly-by from the ritzy boho-chic Primrose Hill/super-megastar set. Top-value weekday luncheons are a bargain £11.50. ⑤ *Average main: £12* ⌧ *89 Regent's Park Rd., Regent's Park* ☎ *020/7586–7454* ⌲ *Reservations essential* ⊘ *No lunch Sat. No dinner Sun.* Ⓜ *Chalk Farm* ✛ *1:F1.*

THE THAMES UPSTREAM

$$$
MODERN
EUROPEAN
Fodor's Choice
★
✗**Hedone.** Only a loony or genius would serve an appetizer of half a white Cevennes onion with a few pear shavings, but, luckily, maverick Swedish chef Mikael Jonsson falls in the latter camp at his spectacular debut in Chiswick. A food blogger and former lawyer, Jonsson's extremist approach to the provenance of his ingredients—often wild or foraged—means his dishes are some of the most intense around. Watch him in an open kitchen prepare wonders like wild Dorset sea bass with pickled black radishes and hyssop oil, the Devon scallops with a vividly stuffed courgette flower, or the gloriously marbled 55-day-aged Darragh O'Shea Black Angus beef. Such is Hedone's acclaim that reservations are often needed weeks in advance. ⑤ *Average main: £25* ⌧ *301–303 Chiswick High Rd., Chiswick* ☎ *020/8747–0377* ⊕ *www.hedonerestaurant.com* ⌲ *Reservations essential* ⊘ *Closed Sun. and Mon.* Ⓜ *Chiswick Park* ✛ *1:A2.*

London Dining
and Lodging
Atlas

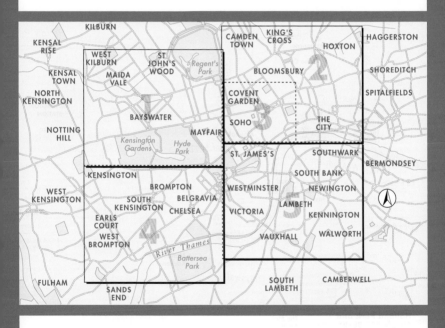

KILBURN

KENSAL
RISE

WEST
KILBURN

ST
JOHN'S
WOOD

Regent's
Park

CAMDEN
TOWN

KING'S
CROSS

HOXTON

HAGGERSTON

KENSAL
TOWN

MAIDA
VALE

BLOOMSBURY

2

SHOREDITCH

NORTH
KENSINGTON

1

COVENT
GARDEN

SPITALFIELDS

BAYSWATER

SOHO

3

THE
CITY

NOTTING
HILL

MAYFAIR

Kensington
Gardens

Hyde
Park

ST. JAMES'S

SOUTHWARK

BERMONDSEY

KENSINGTON

SOUTH BANK

WEST
KENSINGTON

BROMPTON

WESTMINSTER

NEWINGTON

SOUTH
KENSINGTON

BELGRAVIA

LAMBETH

5

CHELSEA

VICTORIA

KENNINGTON

EARLS
COURT

4

WEST
BROMPTON

River Thames

VAUXHALL

WALWORTH

Battersea
Park

FULHAM

SANDS
END

SOUTH
LAMBETH

CAMBERWELL

KEY	
☐	Hotels
■	Restaurants
■	Restaurant in Hotel
U **WESTMINSTER**	
	Station
London Underground	
⇌	National Rail Connection

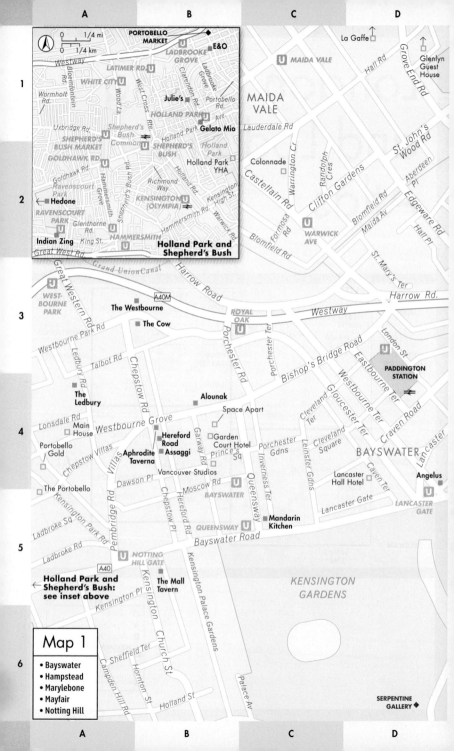

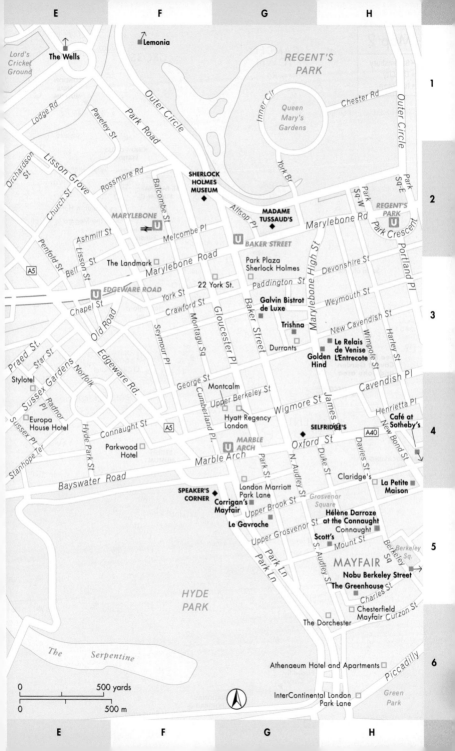

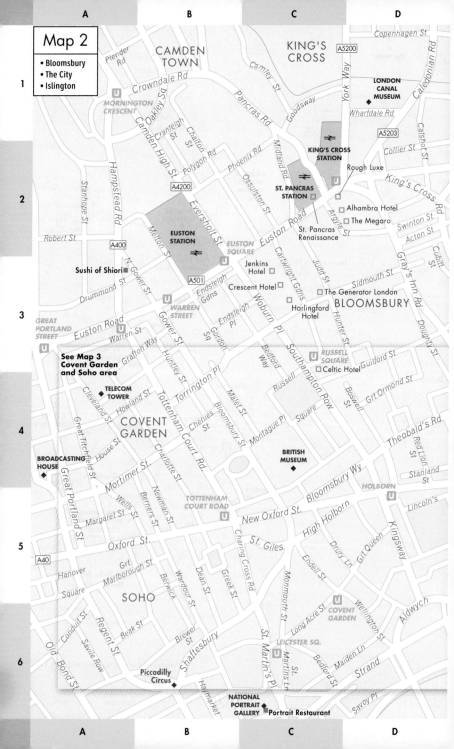

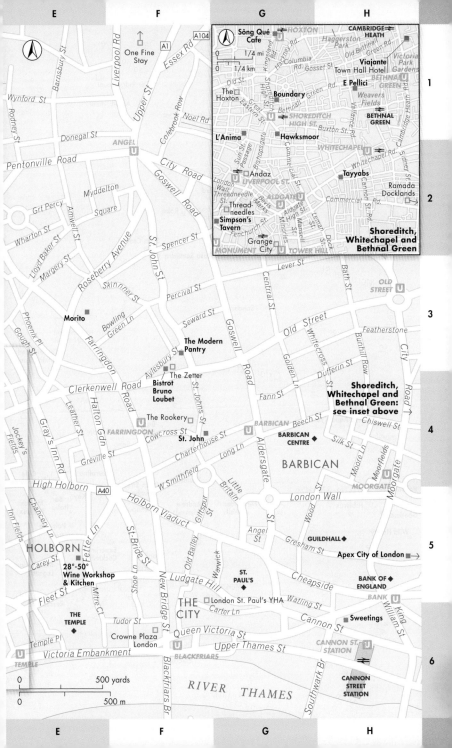

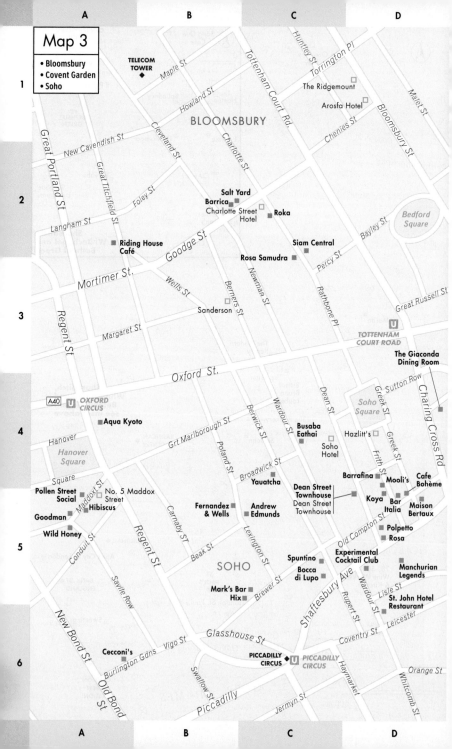

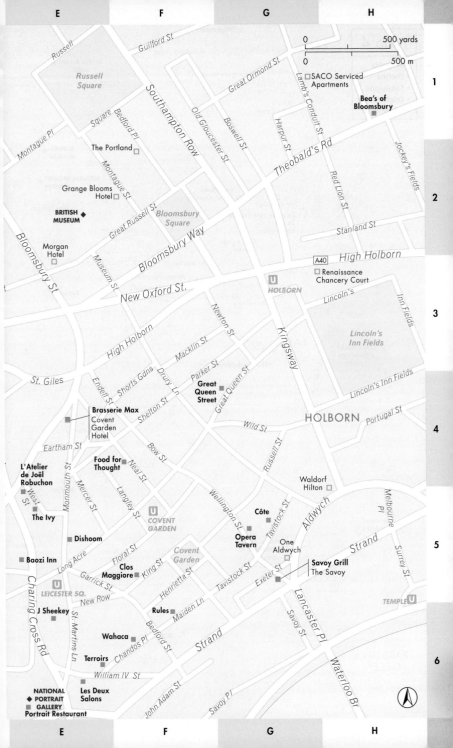

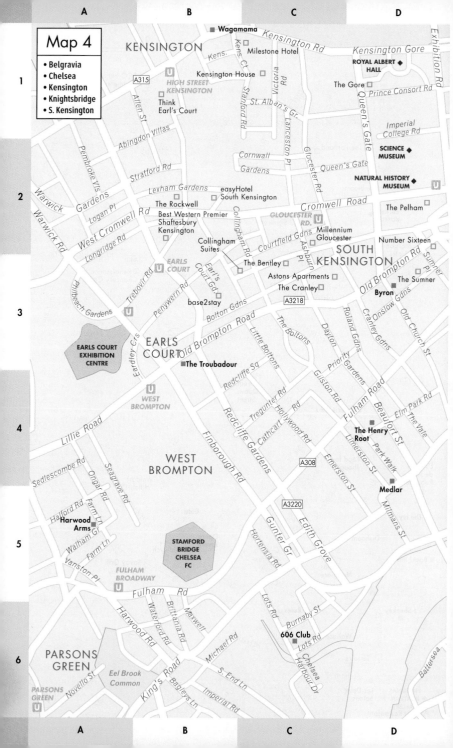

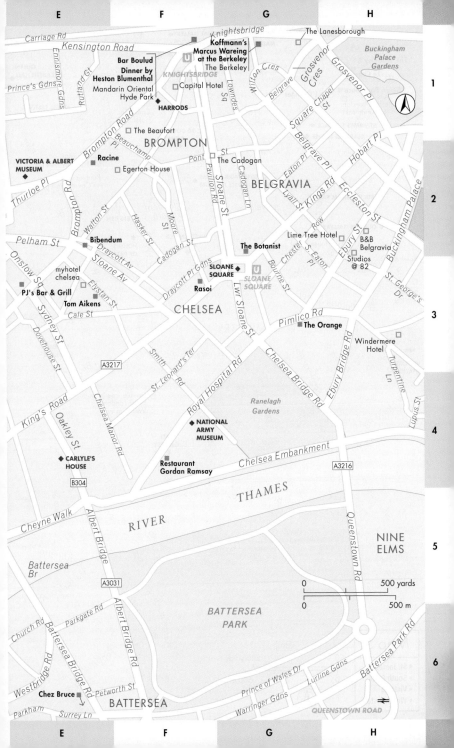

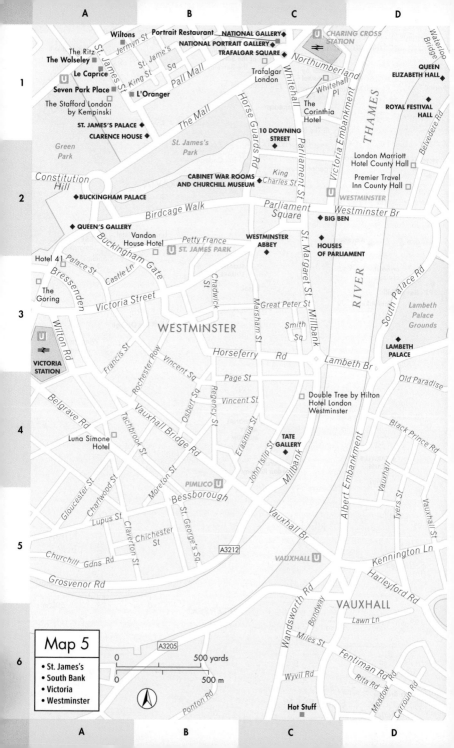

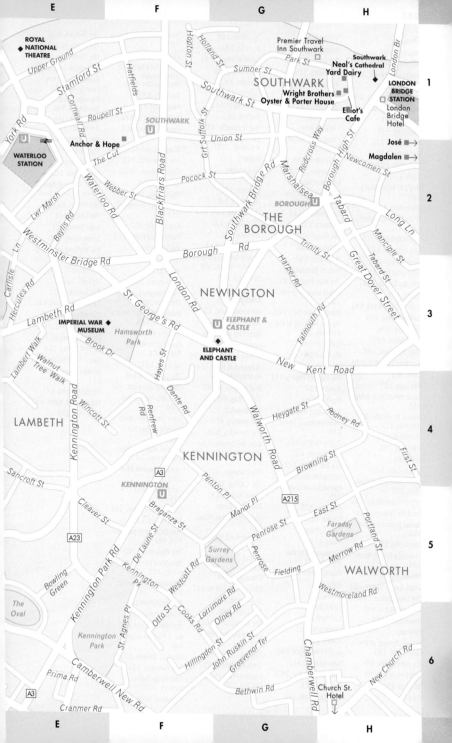

Where to Stay

WORD OF MOUTH

"Don't forget the Goring, close to Buckingham Palace. It was the first hotel in London to have a bathroom with every bedroom and has a nicely old-fashioned feel to it. BTW, that's where Kate Middleton stayed the night before the royal wedding."

—Underhill

THE SCENE

Updated by
Jack Jewers

Queen Elizabeth hasn't invited you this time? No matter. Staying at one of London's grand dame hotels is the next best thing—some say better—to being a guest at the palace. Royally resplendent decor abounds and armies of extra-solicitous staff are stuck in the pampering mode—the Windsors should have it so good at such fabled landmarks as Claridge's, the Goring, and the Dorchester. Happily, however, there is no dearth of options where friendliness outdistances luxe—London, thank goodness, has plenty of atmospheric places that won't cost a king's ransom.

During the past year, however, a vast new array of spectacular hotels has opened. Head to the Corinthia and you'd never know the recession has struck. But almost as if to launch a broad counterattack, the city's mid-range hotel scene has at long last gotten its act together, and there is now a choice range of reasonably priced, high-quality hotels that regularly offer good deals and bargain rates.

Leaders in this field are places like the Hoxton—which even makes a handful of rooms available for £1 per night, if you're lucky enough to snatch one. Several mid-range hotels have dropped their average prices in response to the choppy waters of the global economy, which has pulled some fantastic places, such as Hazlitt's and Town Hall, back into the affordable category. And there's a clutch of new, stylish and super-cheap hotels that are a real step forward for the city, with places like Stylotel making heads turn with its small-is-beautiful approach. The downside is that these places tend to be a little out of the way, but that's often a price worth paying. Another newly attractive alternative are hotels in the Premier and Millennium chains, which offer sleek, modern rooms, lots of modern conveniences, and sales that frequently bring room prices well below £100 a night.

At the budget level, small and interesting bed-and-breakfasts such as the Parkwood and the Church Street Hotel stand out in a sea of battered and old-fashioned B&Bs. An alternative is the easyHotel chain, with its tiny, bright orange "pod" rooms. There's also the more sophisticated (and more expensive) base2stay, which falls somewhere between budget and moderate. And if you're willing to fend for yourself, the city has some great rental options, including the innovative One Fine Stay—a new service that lets you borrow gorgeous apartments from real Londoners, with an on-call concierge service to turn to should you need it.

But if you are interested in Luxury, London is just the place. Although the image we love to harbor about Olde London Towne may be fast fading in the light of today's glittering city, when it comes time to rest your head, the old-fashioned clichés remain enticing. Who wouldn't want their cream tea served by a frock-coated retainer while lounging in an overstuffed brocade armchair? Or to breakfast on coffee, toast, and croissants in a handmade bed in your powder-blue-and-white Syrie Maughamesque boudoir, as the Thames flows lazily past your French windows? Choose one of London's heritage-rich hotels—Brown's or Claridge's supply perfect parlors; the Savoy has that river view—and these fantasies can, and always will, be fulfilled.

15

PLANNING

LODGING STRATEGY

Where should you stay? With hundreds of London hotels, it may seem like a daunting question. But it doesn't have to be. The 130-plus selections here represent the best this city has to offer—from the most-for-your-money budget B&Bs to the sleekest designer hotels. Scan "Best Bets" on the following pages for top recommendations by price and experience. Or look through the reviews. To find one quickly, search by neighborhood, then alphabetically. Happy hunting!

NEED A RESERVATION?

Yes. Hotel reservations are an absolute necessity when planning your trip to London, so book your room as far in advance as possible. The further in advance you can book, the better the deal you're likely to get. Just watch out if you change your mind—cancellation fees can be hefty. On the other hand, it is possible to find some amazing last-minute deals at mid- to high-range places, but this is a real gamble as you could just as easily end up paying full rate. Fierce competition means properties undergo frequent improvements, so when booking inquire about any ongoing renovations that may interrupt your stay.

CHECKING IN

Typical check-in and checkout times are 2 pm and noon, respectively. Many flights from North America arrive early in the morning, but having to wait six hours for a room after arriving jet-lagged at 8 am isn't the ideal way to start a vacation. Alert the hotel of your early arrival; large hotels can often make special early check-in arrangements, but almost all will look after your luggage in the meantime. Be prepared to drop your bags and strike out for a few hours. On the plus side, this can effectively give you a whole extra day for sightseeing.

HOTEL QUALITY

Note that rooms can vary considerably in a single hotel. If you don't like the room you're given, ask to see another. Be prepared for the fact that, while smoking is now banned in public, this doesn't apply to hotel rooms—so be firm and ask to change if you're given a smoking room and didn't request one. Hotels often renovate room by room—you might find yourself allocated a dark, unrenovated room, whereas a bright, newly decorated room awaits just down the hall.

BREAKFAST

Some hotels include breakfast in the price of the room. It ranges from a gourmet spread to what is known as the "full English" (one fried egg, two sausage links, two thick slices of bacon, a grilled tomato, sautéed mushrooms, and toast). In most budget hotels and B&Bs, this is the only hot breakfast available. Most expensive hotels (and the most imaginative small ones) may also offer pancakes, French toast, waffles, and omelets. Luckily, virtually all accommodations also offer packaged cereals, muffins, yogurt, and fresh fruit, so when the sausage-and-bacon brigade begins to get you down, go continental.

FACILITIES

Keep in mind that some facilities come with the room rate while others cost extra. So, when pricing accommodations, always ask what's included. Modern hotels usually have air-conditioning, but B&Bs and hotels in older buildings often do not, and it is generally not the norm in London. Wi-Fi is much more common than it was even a year or two ago, but don't assume it's free (large hotels in particular can charge outrageous fees). If you want a double room, specify whether you want a double bed or a twin (two single beds next to each other). All hotels listed here have private baths unless otherwise noted.

PRICES

If you're planning to visit in the fall, winter, or early spring, start monitoring bargain online prices a few months before your trip and book whenever you see a good rate. Chains such as Hilton, Premier, and Millennium are known for their low-season sales in which prices can be as little as half the normal rate.

The exchange rate between the pound and the dollar is also unpredictable, so if it's looking good when you book, an advance payment deal could end up saving you a decent amount of money. ■TIP→ The Visit London Accommodation Booking Service (☎ 020/7932-2020 ⊕ www.visitlondon.com) offers a best-price guarantee.

Prices in the reviews are the lowest cost of a standard double room in high season, including 20% V.A.T.

WHERE SHOULD I STAY?

	Neighborhood Vibe	Pros	Cons
Westminster and Royal London	This historic section, aka "Royal London," is home to major tourist attractions like Buckingham Palace.	Central area near tourist sites; easy Tube access; considered a safe area to stay.	Mostly expensive lodging options; few good restaurants and entertainment venues nearby.
St. James's and Mayfair	Traditional, old money; a mixture of the business and financial set with fashionable shops.	In the heart of the action; some of London's best hotels are found here.	Pricey part of town; the city-that-never-sleeps buzz makes peace and quiet hard to come by.
Soho and Covent Garden	A tourist hub with endless entertainment on the streets and in theaters and clubs—this is party central for young adults.	Buzzing area with plenty to see and do; late-night entertainment abounds; wonderful shopping district.	Perhaps London's busiest (and noisiest) district after dark; few budget hotels; keep your wits about you at night, and watch out for pickpockets.
Bloomsbury, Holborn, and Islington	Diverse area that is part bustling business center and part tranquil respite with tree-lined streets and parks.	Easy access to Tube, and 15 minutes to city center; major sights, like British Museum in Bloomsbury; great nightlife in Islington.	Holborn has busy streets filled with honking trucks and roving students; the area around King's Cross can be sketchy—particularly at night.
The City and South Bank	London's financial district, where most of the city's banks and businesses are headquartered.	Central location with easy transportation access; great hotel deals; cultural center of South Bank.	It can be as quiet as a tomb after 8 pm; many nearby restaurants and shops close over the weekend.
East End	Increasingly trendy area east of the city center, with a great arts scene.	Great for art lovers, shoppers, and business execs with meetings in Canary Wharf.	Still a transitional area, parts of Hoxton can be a bit dodgy at night; 20-minute Tube ride from central London.
Kensington, Chelsea, and Knightsbridge	These are some of London's most upscale neighborhoods and a hub of London's tourist universe. A glittering galaxy of posh department stores, boutiques, and fabulous hotels.	Diverse hotel selection; great area for meandering urban walks; London's capital of high-end shopping with Harrods and many boutiques.	Depending on where you are, the nearest Tube might be a hike; residential area might be too quiet for some. Few budget hotel or restaurant options; beware of pickpockets.
Notting Hill and Bayswater	This is an upscale, trendy area favored by locals, with plenty of good hotels.	Hotel deals abound if you know where to look; gorgeous greenery in Hyde Park; great shopping districts.	Choose the wrong place and you may end up in a fleapit; residential areas may be too quiet at night for some.
Regent's Park and Hampstead	A mix of arty, fashionable districts with a villagelike feel in other places.	Good access to central London; easy to fall in love with this part of town.	Some distance from center; lack of hotel/dining options.

15

HOTELS REVIEWS

Listed alphabetically by neighborhood. Use the coordinate (✛ 1:B2) at the end of each listing to locate a site on the corresponding map. To locate the property on a map, turn to the London Dining and Lodging Atlas at the end of the Where to Eat chapter. The first number after the ✛ symbol indicates the map number. Following that is the property's coordinate on the map grid.

For expanded hotel reviews, visit Fodors.com.

WESTMINSTER AND ROYAL LONDON

WESTMINSTER

$$$$
HOTEL
Fodor'sChoice
★

The Corinthia. No one can deny that this is the most spectacular of the new crop of hotels that opened in London in 2011, the only argument is which is the most photogenic spot in the place: the eye-popping Moderne lobby, or the Northall restaurant—an amazing symphony of soaring while columns, apricot-hued seats, Edwardian woodwork, and futuristic chandeliers—or the Massimo restaurant (a ravishing David Collins masterpiece, whose candy-striped columns make a nod to medieval Siena) or even the drop-dead chic shop; no matter, wherever you are in this hotel it is design heaven-on-earth and will make anyone feel like a VIP. **Pros:** so much luxury and elegance you'll feel like royalty; the staggeringly beautiful Edwardian building (a wow illuminated at night). **Cons:** prices jump to the stratosphere once the cheapest rooms sell out. **TripAdvisor:** "perfect luxury," "excellent high tea," "best hotel shower ever." ⑤ *Rooms from: £329* ✉ *Whitehall Pl., Westminster* ☎ *020/7930–8181* ⊕ *www.corinthia.com* ⌨ *294 rooms* Ⓜ *Charing Cross* ✛ *5:C1.*

$$$
HOTEL
☾

DoubleTree by Hilton Hotel London Westminster. Spectacular views of the river, Big Ben, and the London Eye fill the floor-to-ceiling windows in this rather stark, steel-and-glass building steps from the Tate Britain, and techy perks include Skype-enabled phones (allowing for free calls) and Macs in every room; cots, baby baths, Nickelodeon, special menus, and baby food are on tap for kids. **Pros:** amazing views; flat screens and other high-tech gadgetry. **Cons:** small bedrooms; tiny bathrooms; TV has to be operated through a computer (confusing if you're not used to it). **TripAdvisor:** "great location for Tate Britain," "friendly staff," "very nice modern hotel." ⑤ *Rooms from: £210* ✉ *30 John Islip St., Westminster* ☎ *020/7630–1000* ⊕ *www.minthotel.com* ⌨ *444 rooms, 16 suites* Ⓜ *Pimlico* ✛ *5:C4.*

$
HOTEL

Vandon House Hotel. Accommodations are the very definition of cheap and cheerful at this simply decorated hotel close to Westminster Abbey and Buckingham Palace, where bathrooms are either shared or have showers only. **Pros:** excellent location; comfortable beds; very friendly. **Cons:** simple decor; few extras; some rooms share bathrooms. **TripAdvisor:** "good for one night," "great location," "comfortable and clean." ⑤ *Rooms from: £75* ✉ *1 Vandon St., Westminster* ☎ *020/7799–6780* ⊕ *www.vandonhouse.com* ⌨ *32 rooms; 1 apartment* ⊠ *Breakfast* Ⓜ *St. James's Park* ✛ *5:B2.*

BEST BETS FOR LONDON LODGING

Fodor's offers a selective listing of high-quality lodging experiences at every price range, from the city's best budget motel to its most sophisticated luxury hotel. Here, we've compiled our top recommendations by price and experience. The very best properties—in other words, those that provide a particularly remarkable experience in their price range—are designated in the listings with the Fodor's Choice logo.

15

Fodor's Choice ★

The Berkeley, p. 318

Chancery Court Hotel, p. 304

Church Street Hotel, p. 312

Claridge's, p. 297

The Connaught, p. 298

The Corinthia, p. 294

Covent Garden Hotel, p. 303

Dean Street Town-house, p. 302

The Dorchester, p. 298

Egerton Hotel, p. 319

Hotel 41, p. 296

The Hoxton Hotel, p. 311

Hyatt Regency London—The Churchill, p. 300

The Lanesborough, p. 319

The Main House, p. 322

Mandarin Oriental Hyde Park, p. 319

Number Sixteen, p. 317

The Pelham Hotel, p. 317

The Rookery, p. 310

The Savoy, p. 303

The Stafford London by Kempinski, p. 297

The Zetter, p. 311

Best by Price

$

easyHotel, p. 315

The Glenlyn, p. 324

Parkwood Hotel, p. 323

Stylotel, p. 324

$$

Church Street Hotel, p. 312

Harlingford Hotel, p. 306

The Hoxton Hotel, p. 311

The Luna Simone Hotel, p. 296

Morgan Hotel, p. 307

The Rockwell, p. 317

$$$

Athenaeum Hotel and Apartments, p. 298

The Cadogan, p. 318

Chancery Court Hotel, p. 304

Number Sixteen, p. 317

The Rookery, p. 310

$$$$

Claridge's, p. 297

The Connaught, p. 298

The Corinthia, p. 294

The Dorchester, p. 298

Mandarin Oriental Hyde Park, p. 319

The Savoy, p. 303

Best by Experience

BEST SPAS

The Bentley, p. 315

Chancery Court Hotel, p. 304

Claridge's, p. 297

One Aldwych, p. 303

HISTORIC HOTELS

The Cadogan, p. 318

Claridge's, p. 297

The Dorchester, p. 298

The Rookery, p. 310

BEST BREAKFAST

Church Street Hotel, p. 312

The Dorchester, p. 298

Milestone Hotel, p. 316

BUSINESS TRAVELERS

Crowne Plaza London—The City, p. 308

Grange City, p. 308

Threadneedles, p. 310

The Zetter, p. 311

BEST CONCIERGE

The Connaught, p. 298

The Dorchester, p. 298

The Lanesborough, p. 319

Mandarin Oriental Hyde Park, p. 319

MOST KID-FRIENDLY

Mint Hotel Westminster, p. 294

No. 5 Maddox Street, p. 301

Premier Travel Inn County Hall, p. 313

MOST ROMANTIC

Number Sixteen, p. 317

The Pelham, p. 317

The Rookery, p. 310

The Stafford London by Kempinski, p. 297

VICTORIA

$$
B&B/INN
🛏 **B&B Belgravia.** At this modern guesthouse near Victoria station, a clean, chic white color scheme, simple modern furniture, and a lounge where a fire crackles away in the winter are all geared to stylish comfort. **Pros:** nice extras like free use of a laptop in the hotel lounge; coffee and tea always available. **Cons:** bathrooms and rooms are small; unimaginative breakfasts; can be noisy, especially on lower floors. **TripAdvisor:** "very good value," "heart of the city," "modern and clean." $ *Rooms from: £135* ✉ *64–66 Ebury St., Victoria* ☎ *020/7259–8570* ⊕ *www. bb-belgravia.com* ⇆ *17 rooms* ⦿ *Breakfast* Ⓜ *Knightsbridge* ✛ *4:H2.*

$$$$
HOTEL
🛏 **The Goring.** Buckingham Palace is just around the corner, so this hotel, built in 1910 and now run by third-generation Gorings, has always been a favorite among discreet VIPs—it was picked by Kate Middleton's family to be their London "home" the night before her royal wedding at Westminster Abbey—who love its Edwardian style: striped wallpapers, floral curtains, patterned carpets, and brass fittings make it luxurious and welcoming at the same time. **Pros:** comfortable beds; spacious rooms. **Cons:** price is too high for what you get; decor is a bit fussy. **TripAdvisor:** "first class experience," "finest hotel in the UK," "perfect evening cocktails." $ *Rooms from: £455* ✉ *15 Beeston Pl., Grosvenor Gardens, Victoria* ☎ *020/7396–9000* ⊕ *www.thegoring. com* ⇆ *68 rooms, 6 suites* Ⓜ *Victoria* ✛ *5:A3.*

$$$$
HOTEL
Fodor's Choice
★
🛏 **Hotel 41.** Designer credentials are everywhere in these impeccably coordinated black-and-white rooms, some of them split-level and all gorgeously furnished with extraordinary pieces drawn from every corner of the globe and equipped with a plethora of high-tech gadgets, exquisite bed linens, feather duvets, and luxurious marble baths. **Pros:** unique place opposite Buckingham Palace; great service. **Cons:** the unusual design is not for everyone. **TripAdvisor:** "professional and friendly staff," "simply the best," "eclectic boutique hideaway." $ *Rooms from: £299* ✉ *41 Buckingham Palace Rd., Victoria* ☎ *020/7300–0041* ⊕ *www.41hotel. com* ⇆ *26 rooms, 4 suites, 2 apartments* ⦿ *Breakfast* Ⓜ *Victoria* ✛ *5:A3.*

$$
HOTEL
🛏 **Lime Tree Hotel.** In a central neighborhood where hotels veer from grimy bolt-holes at one extreme to wildly overpriced at the other, the homey Lime Tree stands out for its gracious proprietors, the Davies family, who offer comfortable, contemporary rooms and hearty cooked breakfasts that set you up nicely for the day. **Pros:** lovely and helpful hosts; great location; rooms are decent size (though the cheaper rooms are small). **Cons:** some rooms are up several flights of stairs, and there's no elevator; family rooms don't allow kids under five. **TripAdvisor:** "a true gem," "great service and location," "fun hotel." $ *Rooms from: £150* ✉ *135–137 Ebury St., Victoria* ☎ *020/7730–8191* ⊕ *www. limetreehotel.co.uk* ⇆ *25 rooms* ⦿ *Breakfast* Ⓜ *Victoria* ✛ *4:H2.*

$$
HOTEL
🛏 **The Luna Simone Hotel.** This delightful and elegant little hotel, a short stroll from Buckingham Palace, is a real find for the price in central London, and though rooms are on the small side, they are clean and comfortable, with queen-size beds and power showers; a few have balconies that look out over the bustling Georgian street. The home-cooked English breakfasts—included in the price—are delicious. ■TIP➔ Bus no. 24, which stops opposite the hotel, goes past several major sights, including

Westminster Abbey, the Houses of Parliament, and Trafalgar Square. Pros: friendly and comfortable; family rooms are outstanding value; superb location. Cons: no lift or air-conditioning. **TripAdvisor:** "great location for exploring London," "awesome service," "friendly and efficient." ⑤ *Rooms from: £120* ✉ *47–49 Belgrave Rd.Belgravia* ☎ *020/7834 5897* ⊕ *www.lunasimonehotel.com* ✎ *36 rooms* ✚ *5:A4.*

$
RENTAL
🛏 **Studios @ 82.** A new side operation from ⇨ *B&B Belgravia*, these self-catering apartments represent fantastic value for money; they're pleasant, contemporary spaces that have everything you need, plus a few useful extras such as free Wi-Fi. **Pros:** great price; lovely location; all the independence of self-catering. **Cons:** lots of stairs and no elevator. ⑤ *Rooms from: £99* ✉ *64–66 Ebury St., Victoria* ☎ *020/7259–8570* ⊕ *www.bb-belgravia.com* ✎ *9 apartments* ⑩ *Breakfast* Ⓜ *Knightsbridge* ✚ *4:H2.*

$$
HOTEL
🛏 **Windermere Hotel.** This sweet old hotel occupies the former premises of London's first B&B, which opened here in 1881, and is a cheery little place, with comfortable (if small) bedrooms draped in floral fabrics of the kind your grandmother would love, thoroughly modern bathrooms, and a restaurant serving good British and European cuisine. **Pros:** good location; free Wi-Fi. **Cons:** price is a bit high for what you get; rooms and bathrooms are tiny; no elevator. **TripAdvisor:** "nice quiet hotel," "friendly and relaxing," "home away from home." ⑤ *Rooms from: £155* ✉ *142–144 Warwick Way, Victoria* ☎ *020/7834–5163* ⊕ *www.windermere-hotel.co.uk* ✎ *22 rooms* Ⓜ *Victoria* ✚ *4:H3.*

ST. JAMES'S AND MAYFAIR

ST. JAMES'S

$$$$
HOTEL
Fodor's Choice
★
☾
🛏 **Claridge's.** Perhaps Spencer Tracy said it best when he remarked that, when he died, he wanted to go not to heaven, but to Claridge's, and he was just one of the famed names to sign the guestbook here—little wonder they chose this place as their London home-away-from-home, since all guests are tended to by a friendly staff that is not in the least condescending and accommodated in quarters that are never less than luxurious (with soothing, modern decor in tones of taupe and cream and spacious bathrooms with enormous showerheads). **Pros:** serious luxury everywhere—this is an old-money hotel; kids won't be bored, with comics, books, and DVDs to help keep them amused. **Cons:** better pack your designer wardrobe—the guests in the hotel bar can be almost cartoonishly snobbish. **TripAdvisor:** "the home of Kings and Queens," "fabulous service," "first class as expected." ⑤ *Rooms from: £300* ✉ *Brook St., St. James's* ☎ *020/7629–8860, 866/599–6991 in U.S.* ⊕ *www.claridges.co.uk* ✎ *203 rooms* Ⓜ *Bond St.* ✚ *1:H4.*

$$$$
HOTEL
Fodor's Choice
★
🛏 **The Stafford London by Kempinski.** Many praise this as a rare find: a posh hotel that is equal parts elegance and friendliness, and while all the accommodations are luxurious and chic, it boasts 13 especially pleasant rooms installed in an 18th-century stable block, with cobbled mews entrances, gas-fueled fireplaces, and exposed beams. **Pros:** great staff; big, luxurious rooms; quiet location. **Cons:** traditional decor is not to all tastes; men must wear jackets in the bar. **TripAdvisor:** "quiet haven in busy London," "no reason to stay anywhere else,"

15

"outstanding all around." ⑤ *Rooms from: £300* ☒ *St. James's Pl., St. James's* ☎ *020/7493–0111* ⊕ *www.kempinski.com/london* ⤳ *81 rooms* Ⓜ *Green Park* ✛ *5:A1.*

MAYFAIR

$$$ 　🎫 **Athenaeum Hotel and Apartments.** This grand hotel overlooking Green
HOTEL　 Park offers plenty for the money: rooms are both comfortable and lavishly decorated, with deeply comfortable Hypnos beds, plasma-screen TVs, luxurious fabrics, and original contemporary artworks, and breakfasts are luxurious and varied, with endless continental and cooked options. **Pros:** peaceful park views; handy for Buckingham Palace and Piccadilly; great value for elegant setting. **Cons:** bathrooms are almost all small. **TripAdvisor:** "very nice hotel," "lovely location," "for business or pleasure." ⑤ *Rooms from: £276* ☒ *116 Piccadilly, Mayfair* ☎ *020/7640–3557* ⊕ *www.athenaeumhotel.com* ⤳ *111 rooms, 46 suites and apartments* ⏁Ⓞ⏁ *Breakfast* Ⓜ *Green Park* ✛ *1:H6.*

$$$　 🎫 **Chesterfield Mayfair Hotel.** Set deep in the heart of Mayfair, the former
HOTEL　 town house of the Earl of Chesterfield welcomes guests in wood-and-leather public rooms that match the dark-wood furnishings in the small bedrooms, which are done in burgundy, fawn, gray, or forest green. **Pros:** laid-back atmosphere; attentive service. **Cons:** prices rise sharply if you don't get the cheapest rooms; some rooms are tiny; restaurant is old-fashioned and very expensive; free Wi-Fi in lounges and restaurants, but broadband access only in rooms. **TripAdvisor:** "hidden gem," "good old-fashioned service," "comfort in the ideal location." ⑤ *Rooms from: £200* ☒ *35 Charles St., Mayfair* ☎ *020/7491–2622, 877/955–1515 in U.S.* ⊕ *www.chesterfieldmayfair.com* ⤳ *94 rooms, 13 suites* Ⓜ *Green Park* ✛ *1:H5.*

$$$$　 🎫 **The Connaught.** This huge favorite of the monied set since its opening
HOTEL　 in 1917 has many dazzlingly modern compliments to its historic fea-
Fodor's Choice　 tures, including up-to-date rooms done in smooth taupes and creams
　★　 and, the ultimate sign of devil-may-care swagger, a swanky bar with platinum-plated walls. **Pros:** legendary hotel; great for star-spotting. **Cons:** history comes at a price; bathrooms are small. **TripAdvisor:** "London with no attitude," "post-refurbished excellence," "perfection." ⑤ *Rooms from: £400* ☒ *Carlos Pl., Mayfair* ☎ *020/7499–7070 in U.S., 866/599–6991* ⊕ *www.the-connaught.co.uk* ⤳ *92 rooms* Ⓜ *Bond St.* ✛ *1:H5.*

$$$$　 🎫 **The Dorchester.** The glamour level is off the scale here with gold leaf
HOTEL　 and marble public rooms and guest quarters awash in English coun-
Fodor's Choice　 try-house-style furnishings, with more than a hint of art deco—along
　★　 with Irish linen sheets on canopied beds, acres of brocades and velvets, and Italian marble and etched-glass bathrooms with exclusive toiletries created by Floris. **Pros:** historic luxury in 1930s building; lovely views of Hyde Park; top-notch star-spotting; lots of modern technology, including Web TVs. **Cons:** traditional look is not to all tastes; prices are high; some rooms are rather small. **TripAdvisor:** "truly amazing," "never miss afternoon tea," "traditional English comfort." ⑤ *Rooms from: £365* ☒ *Park La., Mayfair* ☎ *020/7629–8888* ⊕ *www. thedorchester.com* ⤳ *195 rooms, 55 suites* Ⓜ *Marble Arch, Hyde Park Corner* ✛ *1:H6.*

Claridge's

The Connaught

The Dorchester

The Stafford London by Kempinski

$$$ 🔲 **Durrants Hotel.** Wonderfully old-fashioned Durrants sits on a quiet
HOTEL   corner not far from the Wallace Collection and, occupying premises
that have served as a hotel since the late 18th century, is awash in old-
English good taste—with wood paneling, leather armchairs, patterned
carpets, and genteel guest quarters. **Pros:** comfortable; relaxed base
for exploring; Oxford Street and the smaller, posher shops of Maryle-
bone High Street are just outside the door. **Cons:** not all rooms are air-
conditioned; some rooms are small; breakfast is expensive. **TripAdvisor:**
"excellent service in a lovely area," "compact but clean and pleas-
ant," "great place for tea." ⑤ *Rooms from: £210* ✉ *26–32 George St.,
Mayfair* ☎ *020/7935–8131* ⊕ *www.durrantshotel.co.uk* ⟿ *87 rooms,
5 suites* Ⓜ *Bond St.* ✛ *1:G3.*

$$$$ 🔲 **Hyatt Regency London – The Churchill.** You don't need to be a genius to
HOTEL   figure out why this hotel (one of London's largest) is usually packed
Fodor's Choice   with customers smiling at the purring perfection they find here: a lobby
★   that shimmers in Robert Adamesque 19th-century style; the warmly
personalized service; the exceptional Locanda Locatelli restaurant; the
calmly alluring guest rooms; and the chic art-world connections with
the Frieze Art Fair—let other hotels take you for "silly money" and
über-hip decor, but the Churchill (the hotel's name when it was opened
by NYC's Tisch family as a homage to Sir Winston) does not. **Pros:**
decent prices; our-home-is-your-home vibe; a style that pleases every-
one. **Cons:** world-is-ending noise when kitchen disposes of glass bottles
every morning. **TripAdvisor:** "excellent location and customer experi-
ence," "friendly sophistication," "great traditional hotel." ⑤ *Rooms
from: £350* ✉ *30 Portman Sq., Marylebone* ☎ *020/7486–5800* ⟿ *434
rooms* Ⓜ *Marble Arch, Bond. St.* ✛ *1:G4.*

$$$ 🔲 **InterContinental London Park Lane.** Overlooking busy Hyde Park Corner
HOTEL   and the Queen's back garden (much to her chagrin, allegedly), these
luxurious rooms aimed at high-end business travelers are comfortable
and slightly masculine, incorporating dark woods, with rich curtains
and bedspreads. **Pros:** central location; business facilities. **Cons:** no
park views with standard rooms; only half the rooms are non-smoking;
£15 a day charge for Internet access is a bit rich given the room rates.
TripAdvisor: "fab hotel with all you need," "friendly luxury," "great
location." ⑤ *Rooms from: £260* ✉ *1 Hamilton Pl., Park La., Mayfair* ☎ *020/7409–3131 or 871/423–4901* ⊕ *www.intercontinental.com*
⟿ *447 rooms, 60 suites* Ⓜ *Hyde Park Corner* ✛ *1:H6.*

$$$ 🔲 **London Marriott Park Lane.** The ornate facade and beautiful public
HOTEL   rooms of this swanky hotel date to 1919, though the sizable bedrooms
are standard Marriott fare, with neutral decor, comfortable mattresses,
and lots of business accoutrements. **Pros:** great location; big bedrooms.
Cons: a bit nondescript; very busy streets outside. **TripAdvisor:** "great
hotel in best location," "fantastic service," "perfect base for a family hol-
iday." ⑤ *Rooms from: £280* ✉ *140 Park La., Mayfair* ☎ *020/7493–7000*
⊕ *www.marriott.co.uk* ⟿ *148 rooms, 9 suites* Ⓜ *Marble Arch* ✛ *1:G4.*

$$$ 🔲 **The Montcalm.** This grand hotel at the edge of Park Lane might have
HOTEL   a modern look—along with contemporary rooms decorated in tones of
toffee and cream and furnished with comfortable king-size beds—but the
attitude toward providing solid comfort and luxury seems old fashioned.

Pros: great location off Park Lane; dedication to luxury and comfort. **Cons:** service can be patchy; old-fashioned approach might seem stuffy to some; marble bathrooms are not large, but they do have soothing rain showers. **TripAdvisor:** "pure luxury," "geared towards foreign tourists," "very central to everything." ⑤ *Rooms from: £280* ⊠ *34–40 Great Cumberland Pl., Mayfair* ☎ *0207/402–4288, 877/898–1587 in U.S.* ⊕ *www.montcalm.co.uk* ⇨ *170 rooms* ◎| *Breakfast* Ⓜ *Marble Arch* ✛ *1:G4.*

$$$ 🖼 **No. 5 Maddox Street.** It doesn't get more boutique than this: 12 luxury
RENTAL   suites, some with balconies and working fireplaces, are decorated with
ℭ   subtle, Asian-inspired touches like bamboo and delicate art and filled with everything you could ever need. **Pros:** handy kitchens stocked with everything from cookies to herbal tea; extremely attentive room service; a great option for those who tire of traditional travel. **Cons:** you can feel isolated, as there's no communal lobby. **TripAdvisor:** "lovely secret hideaway," "Alice in Wonderland feeling," "great location and value." ⑤ *Rooms from: £270* ⊠ *5 Maddox St., Mayfair* ☎ *020/7647–0200* ⊕ *www.living-rooms.co.uk* ⇨ *12 suites* Ⓜ *Oxford Circus* ✛ *3:A5.*

MARYLEBONE

$$$$ 🖼 **The Landmark London Hotel.** A glass-covered, eight-story atrium sets
HOTEL   the scene at one of the truly grand London hotels, where the huge bedrooms are done in rich fabrics and have white marble bathrooms (odd-numbered rooms overlook the Winter Garden that flourishes beneath the glass roof). **Pros:** amazing levels of luxury; spacious rooms; one of the few really posh London hotels that doesn't make you dress up; grandeur comes at a hefty price, but there are good discounts available. **Cons:** two-night minimum stay at certain times. **TripAdvisor:** "like going home," "excellent service," "amazing Sunday brunch." ⑤ *Rooms from: £310* ⊠ *222 Marylebone Rd., Marylebone* ☎ *020/7631–8000* ⊕ *www.landmarklondon.co.uk* ⇨ *299 rooms, 47 suites* Ⓜ *Marylebone* ✛ *1:F3.*

$$ 🖼 **Park Plaza Sherlock Holmes Hotel.** In honor of the fictional detective who
HOTEL   had his home on Baker Street, rooms here have a masculine edge with lots of earth tones and pinstripe sheets (along with hyper-modern bathrooms stocked with fluffy bathrobes) and the bar has a relaxing, clubby feel, with wood floors and leather furniture. **Pros:** nicely decorated; near Marylebone High Street; international electrical outlets, including those that work with American equipment. **Cons:** have to walk through the bar to get to reception; not well soundproofed from the noisy street. **TripAdvisor:** "style and service," "close to all you need," "excellent food." ⑤ *Rooms from: £190* ⊠ *108 Baker St., Marylebone* ☎ *020/7486–6161* ⊕ *www.sherlockholmeshotel.com* ⇨ *119 rooms* Ⓜ *Baker St.* ✛ *1:G3.*

$$ 🖼 **22 York Street.** This Georgian town house has a cozy, family feel, with
B&B/INN   polished pine floors and plenty of quilts and French antiques in the homey, individually furnished bedrooms, but pride of place goes to the communal dining table where guests share a varied continental breakfast. **Pros:** handy guesthouse in a great location for shoppers; friendly hosts. **Cons:** some rooms could do with a refurb; location aside, you're still paying a lot for a B&B. **TripAdvisor:** "great location," "a quiet friendly corner," "wonderful B and B." ⑤ *Rooms from: £130* ⊠ *22 York St., Mayfair* ☎ *020/7224–2990* ⊕ *www.22yorkstreet.co.uk* ⇨ *10 rooms* ◎| *Breakfast* Ⓜ *Baker St.* ✛ *1:G3.*

15

BED-AND-BREAKFASTS

You can stay in small, homey B&Bs for an up-close-and-personal brush with city life (Parkwood Hotel; The Arosfa), or find yourself in what is really a modern guesthouse, where you never meet the owners (B&B Belgravia; The Main House). The main benefit of staying in a B&B is that the price is usually cheaper than a hotel room of comparable quality, and you receive more personal service. However, the limitations may be off-putting for some: although you can sometimes arrange for daily maid service, there's usually no restaurant or bar, and no concierge should you have a question. Prices start at around £70 a night, and in that bracket the grimmer places are legion, so make your choice carefully. Prices usually (though not always) go up for more central neighborhoods and larger and more luxurious

homes. It's a nice option, both for seasoned travelers who want a more authentic taste of London, and for those trying to travel well without busting their budgets.

Host & Guest Service. Host & Guest Service can find you a room in London as well as in the rest of the United Kingdom. $ Rooms from: £32 ⊠ 103 Dawes Rd., Fulham ☎ 0870/220–2640 ⊕ www.host-guest.co.uk ☞ Full payment in advance.

London B&B. The long-established family-run agency London B&B has some truly spectacular—and some more modest—homes in central London. $ Rooms from: £130 ⊠ 437 J St., Suite 210, San Diego, California, U.S. ☎ 800/872–2632 in U.S. ⊕ www.londonbandb.com ☞ 30% deposit required.

SOHO AND COVENT GARDEN

SOHO

$$
HOTEL
Fodor'sChoice
★
🛏 **Dean Street Townhouse.** At this discreet, unpretentious, but oh-so-stylish place to stay in the heart of Soho, walls are papered in tones of subtle cream, gray, or pale green; comfy sofas and heavy upholstered chairs jostle for space; and many beds are four-poster—minus the canopy, which somehow just adds to the bohemian vibe. **Pros:** über-cool; rooms resemble a kind of upper-class pied–à–terre. **Cons:** at full rate you're paying more for the address than what you get; some rooms are quite small; rooms at the front can be noisy, especially on weekends; occasional two-night minimum stay. **TripAdvisor:** "great location," "very helpful and attentive staff," "cool but cozy." $ *Rooms from: £170 ⊠ 69–71 Dean St., Soho* ☎ *020/7434–1775* ⊕ *www.deanstreettownhouse.com* ⤴ *39 rooms* Ⓜ *Leicester Sq., Tottenham Court Rd.* ✥ *3:D5.*

$$
HOTEL
🛏 **Hazlitt's.** Three connected early-18th-century houses, one of which was the last home of essayist William Hazlitt (1778–1830), make up this disarmingly friendly place, full of personality, robust antiques, and claw-foot tubs but devoid of certain modern amenities (as the owners say, "In 1718 there were no elevators, and there still aren't"). **Pros:** great for art and antiques lovers; historic atmosphere with lots of small sitting rooms and wooden staircases; truly beautiful and relaxed. **Cons:** no in-house restaurant; breakfast is extra; no elevators. **TripAdvisor:** "beautiful and relaxing," "classic London," "country house comforts."

$ *Rooms from: £180* ✉ *6 Frith St., Soho* ☎ *020/7434–1771* ⊕ *www. hazlittshotel.com* ⤴ *20 rooms, 3 suites* Ⓜ *Tottenham Court Rd.* ✛ *3:D4.*

$$$$ Ⓣ **The Soho Hotel.** At this redbrick, loftlike getaway, public rooms are
HOTEL boldly designed with bright colors and big artworks, while the large
bedrooms are calmer, most with neutral, beige-and-cream tones, or
subtle, sophisticated pinstripes, all offset by modern furniture. **Pros:**
small and sophisticated; comfortable beds, great in-house restaurant.
Cons: bar can be crowded and noisy on weeknights. **TripAdvisor:**
"hip comfortable room," "beautiful in every respect," "warm and
trendy." $ *Rooms from: £354* ✉ *4 Richmond Mews, off Dean St., Soho*
☎ *020/7559–3000* ⊕ *www.sohohotel.com* ⤴ *91 rooms, 4 apartments*
Ⓜ *Tottenham Court Rd.* ✛ *3:C4.*

COVENT GARDEN

$$$$ Ⓣ **Covent Garden Hotel.** It's little wonder the Covent Garden is now the
HOTEL London home-away-from-home for off-duty celebrities, actors, and
Fodor's Choice style mavens: with painted silks, style-anglais ottomans, and 19th-
★ century Romantic oils, the public salons are perfect places to decom-
press over a glass of wine, while guest rooms are *World of Interiors*
stylish, each showcasing mix-and-match couture fabrics to stunning
effect. **Pros:** great for star-spotting, super-trendy. **Cons:** you can feel you
don't matter if you're not famous; setting in Covent Garden can be a bit
boisterous. **TripAdvisor:** "wonderful location," "home sweet home,"
"excellent service." $ *Rooms from: £300* ✉ *10 Monmouth St., Covent
Garden* ☎ *020/7806–1000, 800/553–6674 in U.S.* ⊕ *www.firmdale.
com* ⤴ *55 rooms, 3 suites* Ⓜ *Covent Garden* ✛ *3:E4.*

$$$$ Ⓣ **One Aldwych.** An Edwardian building is an understated blend of
HOTEL contemporary and classic, resulting in pure, modern luxury, with an
artsy lobby and guest rooms equipped with feather duvets, Italian linen
sheets, and ample elegance. **Pros:** understated luxury; ultracool atmosphere. **Cons:** all this luxury doesn't come cheap; fashionable ambience
is not always relaxing; design sometimes verges on form over function.
TripAdvisor: "very trendy," "personal touch," "superbly comfortable."
$ *Rooms from: £342* ✉ *1 Aldwych, Covent Garden* ☎ *020/7300–1000*
⊕ *www.onealdwych.co.uk* ⤴ *93 rooms, 12 suites* Ⓜ *Charing Cross,
Covent Garden* ✛ *3:G5.*

$$$$ Ⓣ **The Savoy.** One of London's most famous hotels has recently emerged
HOTEL from a £220 million renovation, and the old girl is looking like a super-
Fodor's Choice star again; guest rooms are individually designed, and are as cosseting
★ as they were (thanks to chandeliers, silk wall coverings, and Edwardian-
or art deco–style furnishings, with huge marble bathrooms) when they
welcomed Elizabeth Taylor on her first honeymoon; even better, there is
still no grander stage-set in London than the main stately-house lobby—
replete with velvet armchairs, carved wood friezes, and blazing fire-
places—or a more glamorous setting than the adjacent Thames Foyer, a
dreamy salon done up in black-and-white chinoiserie and pink orchids:
no wonder most of Hollywood stays here. **Pros:** the best hotel in London, period; Thames-side location; less snooty than many others of its
pedigree. **Cons:** everything comes with a price tag (even Wi-Fi), but if
you're going to really splurge anywhere in town, this should be near the
top of your short list; bedrooms can be surprisingly noisy, particularly

15

on lower floors; right off super-busy Strand Avenue. **TripAdvisor:** "fabulous old world elegance," "big hotel with a bigger heart," "fantastic location and atmosphere." ⑤ *Rooms from: £350* ✉ *Strand, Covent Garden* ☎ *020/7836–4343, 800/257–7544 in U.S.* ⊕ *www.the-savoy. com* ⇄ *268* Ⓜ *Covent Garden, Charing Cross* ✛ *3:G5.*

$$$ ⊡ **The Trafalgar London.** The guest rooms here, in either sky-blue or beige
HOTEL color schemes, keep many of the 19th-century office building's original features, and some have floor-to-ceiling windows with extraordinary views of Trafalgar Square and The City; 21 are split-level, with upstairs space for chilling out and sleeping space below. **Pros:** amazing location and views; spacious rooms; a fresh, contemporary hotel that defies the Hilton norm; good reductions on weekends. **Cons:** decor is somewhat austere; service is patchy. **TripAdvisor:** "perfect location and great service," "lovely accommodation," "boutique ambience." ⑤ *Rooms from: £222* ✉ *2 Spring Gardens, Covent Garden* ☎ *020/7870–2900* ⊕ *www. hilton.co.uk* ⇄ *127 rooms, 2 suites* Ⓜ *Charing Cross* ✛ *5:C1.*

$$$ ⊡ **Waldorf Hilton.** Understated bedrooms, with white-marble baths and
HOTEL plenty of amenities (such as plasma-screen TVs and laptop chargers) nicely meet the demands of modern travelers. **Pros:** tradition meets modern life comfortably here. **Cons:** prices are quite high for a Hilton; few discounts or deals. **TripAdvisor:** "beautiful character," "pure luxury," "fabulous afternoon tea." ⑤ *Rooms from: £180* ✉ *Aldwych, Covent Garden* ☎ *020/7836–2400* ⊕ *www.hilton.co.uk* ⇄ *303 rooms* Ⓜ *Charing Cross* ✛ *3:H5.*

HOLBORN

$$$ ⊡ **Chancery Court Hotel.** This landmark structure, built by the Pearl
HOTEL Assurance Company in 1914 and so striking it was featured in the film
Fodor's Choice *Howards End,* houses a beautiful hotel, with spacious bedrooms that
★ are popular with business travelers and have a masculine edge—lots of leather and dark-red fabrics, with luxurious mattresses—and a day spa in the basement that is a peaceful cocoon. **Pros:** gorgeous space; great spa; your every need catered to. **Cons:** area is deserted at night and on weekends. **TripAdvisor:** "luxury in heart of London," "charm and tradition," "beautiful grand hotel." ⑤ *Rooms from: £215* ✉ *252 High Holborn, Holborn* ☎ *020/7829–9888* ⊕ *www.marriott.com* ⇄ *342 rooms, 14 suites* Ⓜ *Holborn* ✛ *3:G3.*

$$$ ⊡ **SACO Serviced Apartments, Holborn.** Down a quiet backstreet, a
RENTAL 10-minute walk from the British Museum, these apartments are spacious, modern, and extremely well equipped—each has its own kitchen (with dishwasher and washing machine) and those on the top floor have large terraces, ideal for a morning coffee or alfresco dining. **Pros:** more independence than hotels; pleasant and spacious accommodations. **Cons:** exterior is dated; you must provide own bedding for baby cots. ⑤ *Rooms from: £214* ✉ *82 Lamb's Conduit St., Holborn* ☎ *020/7269– 9930* ⊕ *www.sacoapartments.co.uk* ⇄ *30 apartments (mixture of studios, 1, 2, and 3 bed)* Ⓜ *Russell Sq.* ✛ *3:G1.*

BLOOMSBURY AND HOLBORN

$ 🏨 **Alhambra Hotel.** One of the best bargains in Bloomsbury is a stone's
HOTEL throw from King's Cross and the Eurostar terminal, and though rooms
are very small and the neighborhood is still "edgy," few places are this
cheery and clean for the price. **Pros:** low price, with breakfast included;
friendly service; central location. **Cons:** zero frills; stairs to climb; some
rooms have shared bathrooms. **TripAdvisor:** "great value and location," "great base in London," "clean and well situated." ⑤ *Rooms
from: £75* ✉ *17–19 Argyle St., Bloomsbury* ☎ *020/7837–9575* ⊕ *www.
alhambrahotel.com* 🛏 *52 rooms* ⎮⊙⎮ *Breakfast* Ⓜ *King's Cross* ✛ *2:C2.*

$$ 🏨 **Arosfa Hotel.** Friendly owners; simple, quirky charm (from the
B&B/INN 1940s-style phone on the painted sign out front); and the clean and
contemporary look of the public areas all set this B&B—in what was
once the home of pre-Raphaelite painter Sir John Everett Millais—apart
from the Gower Street hotel pack. **Pros:** friendly staff; check-in from
7 am; good location for museums and theaters; free Wi-Fi. **Cons:** some
rooms are very small; few services. **TripAdvisor:** "yummy breakfast and
clean rooms," "great location and superb service," "warm and friendly
atmosphere." ⑤ *Rooms from: £107* ✉ *83 Gower St., Bloomsbury*
☎ *020/7636–2115* ⊕ *www.arosfalondon.com* 🛏 *15 rooms* ⎮⊙⎮ *Break-
fast* Ⓜ *Goodge St.* ✛ *3:D1.*

$ 🏨 **Celtic Hotel.** At this clean and comfortable budget accommodation
HOTEL with basic amenities, bedrooms aren't fussy and the cheaper rooms have
shared bathrooms, but the staff is friendly and helpful and the British
Museum and London's West End are nearby. **Pros:** good prices; friendly
staff recommends restaurants and pubs; handy location at the edge of
Bloomsbury. **Cons:** no-frills approach means few extras; cheaper rooms
don't have private bathrooms. **TripAdvisor:** "wonderful people," "great
location," "clean and quirky." ⑤ *Rooms from: £98* ✉ *61–63 Guilford
St., Bloomsbury* ☎ *020/7837–6737* 🛏 *35 rooms* ⎮⊙⎮ *Breakfast* Ⓜ *Rus-
sell Sq.* ✛ *2:C3.*

$$$ 🏨 **Charlotte Street Hotel.** Modern flair and the traditional are fused with
HOTEL real style in public spaces and bedrooms beautifully decorated with
unique printed fabrics from designer Kit Kemp; bathrooms are truly
impressive, lined with gleaming granite and oak—with walk-in showers
and flat-screen TVs, so you can catch up on the news while you soak in
the deep baths. **Pros:** elegant, luxurious; great attention to detail. **Cons:**
the popular bar can be noisy; reservations are necessary for the restaurant. **TripAdvisor:** "fab hotel with excellent service," "lovely Valentine's
treat," "a true boutique gem." ⑤ *Rooms from: £288* ✉ *15 Charlotte
St., Bloomsbury* ☎ *020/7806–2000, 800/553–6674 in U.S.* ⊕ *www.
charlottestreethotel.com* 🛏 *46 rooms, 6 suites* Ⓜ *Goodge St.* ✛ *3:C2.*

$$ 🏨 **Crescent Hotel London.** At this friendly, attractive B&B on one of
B&B/INN Bloomsbury's grand old squares, rooms are small and simply decorated
in cheery colors and breakfasts are big and hearty—but although the
overall effect is somewhat utilitarian, but the basics are well covered.
Pros: lovely, convenient location; friendly staff. **Cons:** price too high
for what you get; decor needs a face-lift; no elevator; bathrooms are
tiny and some have only a bath, so if you want a shower, ask when you

15

book. TripAdvisor: "quiet," "clean and nice," "great character and location." ⑤ *Rooms from: £110* ✉ *49–50 Cartright Gardens, Bloomsbury* ☎ *020/7387–1515* ⊕ *www.crescenthoteloflondon.com* ⇆ *27 rooms, 10 with bath* ❶⊙❘ *Breakfast* Ⓜ *Russell Sq.* ✛ *2:C3.*

$ ⊞ **The Generator, London.** This former police barracks, with decor that
B&B/INN makes the most of the nightclub-with-bunk-beds vibe, is where the young, enthusiastic traveler comes to find fellow partyers and provides singles, twins, and dormitory rooms, each with a washbasin, locker, and free bed linens. **Pros:** youthful attitude; funky design; good security; great location. **Cons:** bar is crowded and noisy; nonstop party atmosphere not for everyone; it's still a hostel, so will always be a bit hit-or-miss. **TripAdvisor:** "great way to meet backpackers," "friendly and safe," "not the best but you'll survive." ⑤ *Rooms from: £32* ✉ *MacNaghten House, Compton Pl. off 37 Tavistock Pl., Bloomsbury* ☎ *020/7388–7666* ⊕ *www.generatorhostels.com/london* ⇆ *214 beds* ❶⊙❘ *Breakfast* Ⓜ *Russell Sq.* ✛ *2:C3.*

$$ ⊞ **Grange Blooms Hotel.** At this white Georgian town-house hotel just
HOTEL around the corner from the British Museum, rooms are not too tiny by London standards—and those in the back of the hotel look out onto a leafy green garden—and service is excellent, with a concierge and porter always on hand to help. **Pros:** great location; overall good value; good prices if you book early through the website. **Cons:** bathrooms could use an upgrade; guests can be bumped to sister hotel if fully booked; no air-conditioning; street noise in some rooms. **TripAdvisor:** "calm oasis," "elegant and comfortable," "lovely overnight stay." ⑤ *Rooms from: £114* ✉ *7 Montague St., Bloomsbury* ☎ *020/7323–1717 or 800/2247–2643* ⊕ *www.grangehotels.com* ⇆ *26 rooms, 1 suite* Ⓜ *Russell Sq.* ✛ *3:F2.*

$$ ⊞ **Harlingford Hotel.** The most contemporary of the Cartwright Gar-
HOTEL dens hotels offers sleek, quiet, and comfortable bedrooms and perfectly appointed public rooms. **Pros:** good location; friendly staff; wider breakfast choice than many small London hotels. **Cons:** rooms are quite small; no elevator. **TripAdvisor:** "great little find in central London," "good breakfast," "comfortable and well-appointed rooms." ⑤ *Rooms from: £115* ✉ *61–63 Cartwright Gardens, Bloomsbury* ☎ *020/7387–1551* ⊕ *www.harlingfordhotel.com* ⇆ *43 rooms* ❶⊙❘ *Breakfast* Ⓜ *Russell Sq.* ✛ *2:C3.*

$ ⊞ **Jenkins Hotel.** A classic Georgian exterior belies the simply designed,
B&B/INN homey interior, where bedrooms are decorated in traditional color schemes—creams and blues with walnut furniture and heavy floral curtains—and bathrooms are miniscule. **Pros:** good location for theaters and restaurants. **Cons:** thin mattresses; very small bathrooms; cheaper rooms have shared bathrooms; lots of stairs but no elevator. **TripAdvisor:** "location is tops," "quiet and comfortable," "great breakfast." ⑤ *Rooms from: £98* ✉ *45 Cartwright Gardens, Bloomsbury* ☎ *020/7387–2067* ⊕ *www.jenkinshotel.demon.co.uk* ⇆ *14 rooms* ❶⊙❘ *Breakfast* Ⓜ *Russell Sq., King's Cross, Euston* ✛ *2:C3.*

$$ ⊞ **The Megaro.** These snazzy, well-designed, modern bedrooms just
HOTEL across the street from St. Pancras International station surround guests with startlingly contemporary decor and amenities that include

powerful showers and espresso machines. **Pros:** unbeatable location for Eurostar; short hop on Tube to city center. **Cons:** neighborhood isn't great; standard rooms are small; decor may be a bit stark for some. **TripAdvisor:** "a haven of peace," "big modern room," "tranquil atmosphere." Ⓢ *Rooms from: £160* ⊠ *Belgrove St., King's Cross* ☎ *020/7843–2222* ⊕ *www.hotelmegaro.co.uk* ⚲ *49 rooms* ✛ *2:D2.*

$$
B&B/INN

🛏 **Morgan Hotel.** This Georgian house is a handy option for those traveling on a budget: don't expect many bells or whistles, but the basic rooms are sunny and attractive—some are quite spacious, some have floor-to-ceiling windows, and some overlook the British Museum. **Pros:** friendly staff; double and triple rooms are large by London standards; right by the museum and near West End theaters. **Cons:** mattresses are quite thin, as are walls; no elevator. **TripAdvisor:** "charming and cheapish," "pleasant staff," "great location and service." Ⓢ *Rooms from: £125* ⊠ *24 Bloomsbury St., Bloomsbury* ☎ *020/7636–3735* ⊕ *www. morganhotel.co.uk* ⚲ *15 rooms, 5 apartments* ⓘ⃝*Breakfast* Ⓜ *Tottenham Court Rd., Russell Sq.* ✛ *3:E2.*

$$
HOTEL

🛏 **The Portland Hotel.** Just around the corner from leafy Russell Square, the Portland is good value-for-money in a swank neighborhood, offering bedrooms that are spacious and comfortable, with large bathrooms and seating areas, and all with their own kitchenettes. **Pros:** great location an easy walk from the British Museum and Covent Garden; large rooms; kitchenettes offer alternative to restaurants; staff is friendly. **Cons:** restaurant is in neighboring hotel, requiring a walk down the street to breakfast. **TripAdvisor:** "really pleasant," "good for shopping," "nice room." Ⓢ *Rooms from: £102* ⊠ *31–32 Bedford Pl., Bloomsbury* ☎ *020/7580–7088* ⊕ *www.grangehotels.com* ⚲ *18 rooms* Ⓜ *Holborn Rd.* ✛ *3:F2.*

$
B&B/INN

🛏 **The Ridgemount Hotel.** Mere blocks away from the British Museum and London's West End theaters, this handsomely fronted guesthouse has clean, neat, and plainly decorated rooms at a bargain, and the welcoming public areas, especially the family-style breakfast room, resemble sweetly cluttered Victorian-style parlors. **Pros:** good location for theaters and museum; helpful staff; family rooms accommodate up to five. **Cons:** decor is basic; no elevator; cheapest rooms have shared bathrooms. **TripAdvisor:** "great value," "try to get renovated room," "very clean." Ⓢ *Rooms from: £74* ⊠ *65 Gower St., Bloomsbury* ☎ *020/7636–1141* ⊕ *www.ridgemounthotel.co.uk* ⚲ *32 rooms, 15 with bath* ⓘ⃝*Breakfast* Ⓜ *Goodge St.* ✛ *3:D1.*

$$$
B&B/INN

🛏 **Rough Luxe.** Bloomsbury's quirkiest hotel, a strange combination of shabby chic and swanky luxury, occupies a 19th-century building that has been renovated to keep bits of old battered walls and flooring in place—elegant beds, designer lighting, and original artwork are cast in stark relief and antique claw-foot tubs and designer sinks are set alongside remnants of the old, torn wallpaper. **Pros:** art and design lovers will be dazzled; it's all very avant-garde. **Cons:** not to everyone's taste; no restaurant or bar; near King's Cross train station in a neighborhood locals would describe as "dodgy"; some rooms share baths. **TripAdvisor:** "fantastic service," "cute but small," "charming oasis." Ⓢ *Rooms from: £180* ⊠ *1 Birkenhead St., Bloomsbury*

15

☎ *020/7837–5338* ⊕ *www.roughluxe.co.uk* ➲ *10 rooms, 4 with shared bath* Ⓜ *Kings Cross* ✚ *2:C2.*

$$$ 🛏 **Sanderson Hotel.** At this fashionable and surreal "urban spa" housed
HOTEL in a converted 1950s textile factory, the lobby looks like a design museum, bedrooms have sleigh beds and a mix of over-the-top Louis XV and postmodern furnishings, and amenities include holistic bath house, indoor-outdoor fitness classes, and a gorgeous courtyard. **Pros:** popular with design mavens; your every whim gratified. **Cons:** "designer cool" can be self-consciously hip; bar and restaurant are so exclusive it's hard to get in. **TripAdvisor:** "hip and happening," "excellent staff," "charming and professional." Ⓢ *Rooms from: £270* ✉ *50 Berners St., Bloomsbury* ☎ *020/7300–1400* ⊕ *www.sandersonlondon.com* ➲ *150 rooms* Ⓜ *Oxford Circus, Tottenham Court Rd.* ✚ *3:B3.*

THE CITY

$$ 🛏 **Apex City of London.** At this sleek, modern branch of the small Apex
HOTEL chain near the Tower of London, bedrooms are reasonably spacious, with contemporary color schemes and little sofas and desks that make life easier for the traveler. **Pros:** great location; helpful staff; full of modern comforts. **Cons:** geared more to business than leisure travelers; price can rise sharply during busy times. **TripAdvisor:** "welcoming staff," "great decor," "like a luxury cruise suite." Ⓢ *Rooms from: £119* ✉ *1 Seething La., The City* ☎ *020/7702–2020* ⊕ *www.apexhotels.co.uk* ➲ *179 rooms* Ⓜ *Tower Hill* ✚ *2:H5.*

$$$ 🛏 **Crowne Plaza London—The City.** The shell of an old stationery ware-
HOTEL house, on the former site of Henry VIII's Bridewell Palace, has found its most recent reincarnation as a polished hotel with small, minimalist rooms done in cool shades of gray and cream and a Michelin-starred restaurant, Refettorio, serving high-quality rustic Italian cuisine by acclaimed chef Giorgio Locatelli. **Pros:** good prices available with advance booking; kids stay free; lots of amenities. **Cons:** neighborhood is super-busy during the day and graveyard-quiet at night—you'll have to go elsewhere for a party scene. **TripAdvisor:** "excellent staff," "chic hotel with lovely rooms," "great city getaway." Ⓢ *Rooms from: £189* ✉ *19 New Bridge St., The City* ☎ *0871/423–4828* ⊕ *www.crowneplaza. com* ➲ *203 rooms, 3 suites* Ⓜ *Blackfriars* ✚ *2:F6.*

$$$ 🛏 **Grange City Hotel.** With an eye on business, this sleek hotel in London's
HOTEL City has everything the workaholic needs to feel right at home—chic bedrooms subtly decorated in creams and chocolates, modern furnishings, plenty of space (by London standards), and more. **Pros:** good-size rooms; women-only rooms are great for female travelers. **Cons:** location is a bit off the tourist track; some rooms overlook train platform; online discounts tend to not allow changes or cancellation. **TripAdvisor:** "perfect position," "excellent service," "very comfortable." Ⓢ *Rooms from: £144* ✉ *8–14 Cooper's Row, The City* ☎ *020/7863–3700* ⊕ *www. grangehotels.com* ➲ *307 rooms, 11 suites* Ⓜ *Tower Hill, Aldgate, Monument* ✚ *2:G2.*

$ 🛏 **London St. Pauls YHA.** Once a choir school, this hostel has an oak-
B&B/INN panel chapel that's now a meeting room and, the best feature of all, is on the doorstep of St. Paul's Cathedral and the Millennium Bridge (the

Renaissance Chancery Court

One Aldwych

The Generator, London

LONDON CHAIN HOTEL PRIMER

England has a number of hotel chains—worth considering—some are moderately priced, others are luxurious. Here's a quick run-down of our favorites:

easyhotel: One of the first chains to bring so-called "pod hotels" to London, the easyhotel chain specializes in very cheap (less than £50 a night for a double) rooms that are clean, secure and offer all the basics, but are teeny-tiny, and have no extras at all. ⊕ www.easyhotel.com.

Grange Hotels: This chain includes a good mix of large and small hotels, with reliable (if somewhat dull) neutral decor, good service, and plenty of gadgets for business travelers. Prices vary, although most are moderately priced. ⊕ www.grangehotels.com.

Malmaison: With lavish, elegant small hotels around the country, this upscale chain offers luxurious designer style, good restaurants, and trendy bars. ⊕ www.malmaison.com.

Millennium: Similar in style to Premier Inns, Millennium (and its other brand, Copthorne) hotels are targeted at both business and leisure travelers. They offer well-designed rooms with plenty of gadgets and have frequent sales. ⊕ www.millenniumhotels.co.uk.

myhotel: A small chain of pricey boutique hotels, with a designer decor, trendy bars, and a modern approach, myhotels offer reliable comfort and service, if you don't mind the price tag. ⊕ www.myhotels.com.

Premier Inns: This widespread chain features medium-size, moderately priced hotels. They're known for their attractive if bland look, and for frequent sales, which keep prices cheap. ⊕ www.premierinn.com.

pathway to the Tate Modern). **Pros:** outstanding location; friendly and safe; family rooms available. **Cons:** lively and often noisy; piped music in some public areas; geared to the young. **TripAdvisor:** "comfy and cheap," "convenient and friendly," "wonderful location." ⑤ *Rooms from: £46* ⊠ *36 Carter La., The City* ☎ *0845/371–9012* ⊕ *www.yha.org.uk* ⥅ *210 beds* ⑩ *Breakfast* Ⓜ *St. Paul's* ✛ *2:F5.*

$$$
HOTEL
Fodor's Choice
★

🏨 **The Rookery.** An absolutely unique and beautiful 1725 town house, surrounded by office buildings, the Rookery is the kind of place where you want to allow some proper time to enjoy and soak up the hotel atmosphere—in the elegant, Regency-style drawing room, which has a well-stocked honesty bar, and in the huge, wood-paneled bedrooms, with heavy raw silk drapes, antique furniture, antiquarian books artfully scattered here and there, and white marble bathrooms with deep claw-foot tubs big enough for two. **Pros:** beautiful; helpful staff; good deals to be had in the off-season. **Cons:** breakfast costs extra; short Tube ride to tourist sites. **TripAdvisor:** "very pleasant," "great service and luxury," "independent hotel with character." ⑤ *Rooms from: £198* ⊠ *12 Peter's La., at Cowcross St., The City* ☎ *020/7336–0931* ⊕ *www.rookeryhotel.com* ⥅ *30 rooms, 3 suites* Ⓜ *Farringdon* ✛ *2:F4.*

$$$$
HOTEL

🏨 **Threadneedles Hotel.** The elaborate building housing this grand hotel is a former bank, and the vast old banking hall has been beautifully adapted as the lobby, with luxurious marble and mahogany panels, while the stylish guest rooms are spacious, with modern bathrooms, big comfortable beds, and neutral coffee and cream colors, with dashes of deep burgundy. **Pros:** lap of luxury; excellent service. **Cons:** a bit stuffy for some tastes; neighborhood is quiet at night. **TripAdvisor:** "consistently excellent," "a little gem," "stunning." ⑤ *Rooms from: £294* ⊠ *5 Threadneedle St., The City* ☎ *020/7657–8080* ⊕ *www. theetoncollection.com* ⤳ *63 rooms, 6 suites* Ⓜ *Bank* ✛ *2:G2.*

$$$ **⌂ The Zetter.** The dizzying five-story atrium, art deco staircase, and slick
HOTEL European restaurant are your first indications of what to expect at
Fodor's Choice this converted warehouse: a breath of fresh air and rooms smoothly
★ done up in soft dove gray and vanilla fabrics, with wonderful views of The City from the higher floors. **Pros:** big rooms; lots of gadgets; free Wi-Fi; gorgeous "rain-forest" showers. **Cons:** rooms with good views cost more. **TripAdvisor:** "clean and quiet," "quirky but nice," "great service in a stylish setting." ⑤ *Rooms from: £222* ⊠ *86–88 Clerkenwell Rd., Holborn* ☎ *020/7324–4444* ⊕ *www.thezetter.com* ⤳ *59 rooms* Ⓜ *Farringdon* ✛ *2:F3.*

15

THE EAST END

$$$$ **⌂ Andaz.** This swanky, upscale hotel sports a modern, masculine design,
HOTEL and rooms are sparsely decorated with designer furniture, intensely comfortable beds, and white walls, charcoal floors, and ruby-red touches. **Pros:** nice attention to detail; guests can borrow an iPod from the front desk; no standing in line to check in; "healthy minibars" are stocked with nuts, fruit, and yogurt. **Cons:** sparse decor is not for all. **TripAdvisor:** "great service," "style and tradition," "perfect hip hotel." ⑤ *Rooms from: £276* ⊠ *40 Liverpool St., East End* ☎ *020/7961–1234, 800/492–8804 in U.S.* ⊕ *london.liverpoolstreet.andaz.hyatt.com* ⤳ *267 rooms* Ⓜ *Liverpool St.* ✛ *2:G2.*

$$ **⌂ The Hoxton Hotel.** The design throughout this trendy East London
HOTEL lodging is contemporary—but not so modern as to be absurd, and in
Fodor's Choice keeping with a claim to combine a country-lodge lifestyle with true
★ urban living, a fire crackles in the lobby, the chic but casual restaurant is packed with friendly youth, and the comfortable guest rooms have Frette linen sheets and down comforters. **Pros:** cool vibe and neighborhood known for funky galleries and small boutiques; huge weekend discounts; way-cool restaurant; price includes one hour of free international calls. **Cons:** price shoots up during the week; area is away from tourist sights; competition for £1 rooms is so intense that you're unlikely to get one (they sell out months ahead). **TripAdvisor:** "hipster central," "great atmosphere," "lovely people." ⑤ *Rooms from: £80* ⊠ *81 Great Eastern St., East End* ☎ *020/7550–1000* ⊕ *www. hoxtonhotels.com* ⤳ *208 rooms* ⧖ *Breakfast* Ⓜ *Old St.* ✛ *2:G1.*

$$ **⌂ Ramada Hotel and Suites Docklands.** Many of the sleek and modern
HOTEL rooms at this hotel dramatically set at the edge of the river in the rejuvenated Docklands area of East London have water views, and others have views of the city. **Pros:** waterfront views. **Cons:** lacks character; area is tumbleweed quiet on weekends; about a 20-minute Tube ride to central London. **TripAdvisor:** "good hotel at a fair price," "convenient

and friendly," "very uncomfortable beds." $ Rooms from: £109 ✉ Ex-Cel, 2 Festoon Way, Royal Victoria Dock, East End ☎ 020/7540–4820 ⊕ www.ramadadocklands.co.uk ➶ 224 rooms ❍ Breakfast Ⓜ Old St. ✛ 2:H2.

$$ ⬚ **Town Hall Hotel and Apartments.** What used to be one of London's
HOTEL living ghosts—an art deco town hall that was abandoned in the early 1980s and turned into a chic hotel in 2010—is now lively and stylish, with the best of the building's elegant original features intact and bright and airy rooms done in masculine color schemes of cream, brown, and metallic gray. **Pros:** beautifully designed; lovely staff; big discounts for weekend stays. **Cons:** not a good part of town; a 15-minute Tube ride away from central London. **TripAdvisor:** "amazing renovation," "for the design conscious," "excellent service and great location." $ Rooms from: £163 ✉ Patriot Square, Bethnal Green, East End ☎ 020/7657–8080 ⊕ www.townhallhotel.com Ⓜ Bethnal Green ✛ 2:H1.

THE SOUTH BANK

$$ ⬚ **Church Street Hotel.** Like rays of sunshine in gritty south London, these
HOTEL rooms above a popular tapas restaurant are individually decorated in
Fodor's Choice rich, bold tones and authentic Central American touches, from elabo-
★ rately painted crucifixes to tiles that were handmade in Guadalajara to homemade iron bed frames. **Pros:** unique and arty; great breakfasts; lovely staff; closer to central London than it might appear. **Cons:** not a great part of town; would suit adventurous young things more than families; a mile from a Tube station (though bus connections are handier); some rooms have shared bathrooms. **TripAdvisor:** "welcome oasis," "a piece of Mexico in London," "unique rooms and relaxed atmosphere." $ Rooms from: £95 ✉ 29–33 Camberwell Church St., South East ☎ 020/7961–1234 ⊕ www.churchstreethotel.com ➶ 267 rooms, 22 with shared bath Ⓜ Oval St. ✛ 5:H6.

$$$ ⬚ **London Bridge Hotel.** Steps away from the London Bridge rail and Tube
HOTEL stations, this thoroughly modern, stylish hotel is popular with business travelers, but leisure travelers find it just as handy and the diminutive but sleek rooms, with their understated, contemporary decor, just as calming. **Pros:** good location to visit South Bank attractions; good deals available online in the off-season. **Cons:** small rooms; bathrooms underwhelming for the price. **TripAdvisor:** "comfortable and relaxed," "friendly hotel in a good location," "cozy hotel." $ Rooms from: £200 ✉ 8–18 London Bridge St., South Bank ☎ 020/7855–2200 ⊕ www.london-bridge-hotel.co.uk ➶ 138 rooms, 3 apartments Ⓜ London Bridge ✛ 5:H1.

$$$ ⬚ **London Marriott Hotel County Hall.** Housed in part of what was, until
HOTEL the 1980s, the seat of London's government, many of the warmly deco-rated, modern rooms in this grand hotel on the Thames enjoy perhaps the most iconic view of any in the city: right next door is the London Eye, and directly across the River Thames are Big Ben and the Houses of Parliament. **Pros:** handy location for South Bank arts scene, London Eye and Westminster; great gym; good weekend discounts. **Cons:** decor is overdone; breakfasts are pricey; rooms facing the river inevitably cost extra. **TripAdvisor:** "wonderful swimming pool," "excellent location,"

"fantastic building." $ *Rooms from: £225* ⊠ *County Hall, Westminster Bridge Rd., South Bank* ☎ *020/7928–5200, 888/236–2427 in U.S.* ⊕ *www.marriott.com* ⤴ *200 rooms* Ⓜ *Westminster* ✛ *5:D2.*

$$
HOTEL
Ⓒ
 🛏 **Premier Travel Inn County Hall.** Though the small but nicely decorated rooms at this budget choice share the County Hall complex with the London Marriott Hotel County Hall, they have none of the spectacular river views; that said, they have the same convenient location, and they are decidedly cheaper, too. **Pros:** good location for the South Bank; bargains to be had if you book in advance, including very cheap breakfast and dinner rates; kids stay free. **Cons:** no river views; limited services. **TripAdvisor:** "very friendly," "nice breakfast," "lovely location." $ *Rooms from: £132* ⊠ *Belvedere Rd., South Bank* ☎ *0871/527–8648* ⊕ *www.premiertravelinn.com* ⤴ *313 rooms* Ⓜ *Westminster* ✛ *5:D2.*

$$
HOTEL
 🛏 **Premier Travel Inn Southwark.** This excellent branch of the Premier Travel Inn chain is a bit out of the way on the South Bank, but it sits on a quiet cobbled lane and offers the chain's simply decorated rooms with 6-foot-wide beds (really two 3-foot-wide beds zipped together). **Pros:** ideally located for visiting the Tate Modern or the Globe Theatre. **Cons:** small rooms; uninspiring building; limited extras or services; rooms near elevators can be a little noisy (ask for one farther down the hall). **TripAdvisor:** "fantastically placed," "top service," "quiet night." $ *Rooms from: £117* ⊠ *34 Park St., South Bank* ☎ *0871/527–8676* ⊕ *www.premiertravelinn.com* ⤴ *56 rooms* Ⓜ *London Bridge* ✛ *5:H1.*

15

KENSINGTON, CHELSEA, AND KNIGHTSBRIDGE

KENSINGTON

$$
RENTAL
 🛏 **Astons Apartments.** Three redbrick Victorian town houses on a quiet residential street are the setting for Astons's comfortable studios and apartments; all are simple and small but well designed with tiny kitchenettes, and larger units have marble bathrooms and other extra touches as well. **Pros:** decent alternative to full-service hotel rooms; kitchenettes help save money on long stays. **Cons:** modern (if rather functional) blond-wood furnishings advertised as "designer" but look a bit cheap; few customer services; weekly discounts are hardly generous. **TripAdvisor:** "good London base," "fantastic staff and service," "clean but very small." $ *Rooms from: £100* ⊠ *31 Rosary Gardens, South Kensington* ☎ *020/7590–6000, 800/525–2810 in U.S.* ⊕ *www.astons-apartments.com* ⤴ *43 rooms, 12 suites* Ⓜ *Gloucester Rd.* ✛ *4:D3.*

$$
RENTAL
 🛏 **base2stay Kensington.** This near-budget option in a creamy white Georgian town house offers comfortable double rooms that have a stylish, modern look with white walls and bedding and dark throws and pillows; all have tiny kitchenettes and some even have bunk beds for traveling friends or children. **Pros:** great value alternative to hotel; attractive rooms; handy mini-kitchens. **Cons:** bathrooms are small but well designed; 15-minute Tube ride to central London. **TripAdvisor:** "a great family-oriented place," "green and contemporary," "small room but comfortable and practical." $ *Rooms from: £113* ⊠ *25 Courtfield Gardens, South Kensington* ☎ *020/7244–2255, 800/511–9821 in U.S.* ⊕ *www.base2stay.com* ⤴ *67 rooms* Ⓜ *Earls Court Station* ✛ *4:B3.*

Fodor's Choice ★

Mandarin Oriental Hyde Park

Church Street Hotel

The Hoxton

Number Sixteen

The Zetter

The Rookery

$$$$
HOTEL
The Bentley London. This opulent hotel, owned by Hilton, is an elegant escape—housed in a creamy-white Victorian building, its lobby is a gorgeous explosion of marble, with high ceilings and chandeliers, and bedrooms are almost palatial in size, with silk wallpaper, golden furnishings, and fine marble bathrooms with whirlpool baths—some even have steam rooms. **Pros:** luxurious rooms; gorgeous spa; great location. **Cons:** can be a bit stuffy; old-fashioned style won't please everyone. **TripAdvisor:** "lovely afternoon tea," "old-fashioned service," "opulence and sheer class." $ *Rooms from: £306* ✉ *27–33 Harrington Gardens, South Kensington* ☎ *020/7244–5555* ⊕ *www.thebentley-hotel. com* ⬦ *52 rooms, 12 suites* Ⓜ *Gloucester Rd.* ✛ *4:C3.*

$$
HOTEL
Best Western Premier Shaftesbury Kensington. These fresh and relaxing guest rooms, done in cool grays and earth tones and with firm queen-size beds, are just steps from Earl's Court Tube station and offer a lot for your money. **Pros:** good neighborhood; two-minute walk from the Tube; frequent online sales. **Cons:** small rooms; temperamental booking system, so make sure you bring your confirmation details; at the far edge of Kensington, farther from the museums than you might expect. **TripAdvisor:** "nice place for gentle people," "great stay in Kensington," "convenient location." $ *Rooms from: £137* ✉ *33–37 Hogarth Rd., Kensington* ☎ *020/7370–6831* ⊕ *www.bw-shaftesburykensingtonhotel. co.uk* ⬦ *133 rooms* ⑩ *Breakfast* Ⓜ *Earl's Court* ✛ *4:B2.*

$$
RENTAL
Collingham Suites. Most of the suites and small apartments in this attractive Georgian building have separate living rooms and kitchens and all rooms are tastefully decorated in contemporary style, with neutral carpets and a creamy pallet. **Pros:** more space than you usually get with a serviced apartment; no minimum length of stay. **Cons:** still a bit pricey for what you get; no in-house restaurant or bar. **TripAdvisor:** "very comfortable stay," "lovely apartment in central location," "great alternative to a regular hotel." $ *Rooms from: £180* ✉ *26–27 Collingham Gardens, Kensington* ☎ *020/7244–8677* ⊕ *www. collinghamapartments.com* ⬦ *26 rooms* Ⓜ *Gloucester Rd.* ✛ *4:C3.*

$$$
HOTEL
The Cranley Hotel. Old-fashioned British propriety is the overall feeling at this small, Victorian town-house hotel, where high ceilings, huge windows, and a pale, creamy color scheme make the bedrooms light and bright and antique desks and four-poster or half-tester beds give the place historic authenticity. **Pros:** good-size rooms; attractive decor; friendly staff; free evening nibbles are a nice touch. **Cons:** steep stairs into lobby; no restaurant. **TripAdvisor:** "good up market traditional hotel," "intimate boutique," "quiet neighborhood." $ *Rooms from: £230* ✉ *10–12 Bina Gardens, South Kensington* ☎ *020/7373–0123* ⊕ *www.thecranley.com* ⬦ *29 rooms, 5 suites, 4 apartments* Ⓜ *Gloucester Rd.* ✛ *4:C3.*

$
HOTEL
easyHotel South Kensington. London's first "pod hotel" has 34 tiny rooms, all with a double bed, private bathroom, and little else, each brightly decorated in the trademark orange and white of the easyGroup (which includes the budget airline easyJet). **Pros:** amazing price; safe and pleasant space. **Cons:** not for the claustrophobic; most rooms have no windows; six floors and no elevator; everything costs extra, from a TV in your room (£5 per day), to Wi-Fi (£3 per hour) and even fresh

15

towels (£1 each). **TripAdvisor:** "ideal for short stays," "tiny but it's fun," "clean and simple." Ⓢ *Rooms from: £35* ✉ *14 Lexham Gardens, Kensington* ☎ *020/7216–1717* ⊕ *www.easyhotel.com* ⤢ *34 rooms* Ⓜ *Gloucester Rd.* ✛ *4:B2.*

$$$
HOTEL

⛾ **The Gore Hotel.** Just down the road from the Albert Hall, this gorgeous, friendly hotel has a luxurious mixture of the comfortable and the extraordinary; the lobby evokes a wealthy estate from centuries past, and upstairs most rooms are spacious and beautifully decorated in calming neutral tones with rich fabrics. **Pros:** gorgeously designed and spacious rooms; staff lavishes attention on you. **Cons:** prices rather high; bar can be noisy. **TripAdvisor:** "exclusivity and elegance," "upscale Victorian charm," "traditional and modern." Ⓢ *Rooms from: £246* ✉ *189 Queen's Gate, Kensington* ☎ *020/7584–6601, 888/757–5587 in U.S* ⊕ *www.gorehotel.com* ⤢ *50 rooms* Ⓜ *Gloucester Rd.* ✛ *4:D1.*

$
B&B/INN

⛾ **Holland Park YHA.** Clean, bright, modern dorm rooms in the most celebrated (and certainly the most pastoral) of London's super-cheap places to stay occupy a historic Jacobean mansion and overlook the wooded park, where peacocks strut around the Kyoto Gardens. **Pros:** friendly and bright; beautiful setting. **Cons:** only a handful of rooms aren't dorms; youthful atmosphere can be boisterous. **TripAdvisor:** "beautiful building," "warm and welcoming," "great staff." Ⓢ *Rooms from: £21* ✉ *Holland Walk, Kensington* ☎ *0845/371–9122* ⊕ *www.yha.org. uk* ⤢ *200 beds* ⍾⃝ *Breakfast* Ⓜ *High Street Kensington* ✛ *1:B2.*

$$
HOTEL

⛾ **Kensington House Hotel.** Streamlined, contemporary rooms in this refurbished 19th-century town house off High Street Kensington have large windows and plenty of light, and comfortable beds with luxurious fabrics and soft comforters. **Pros:** attractive design; relaxing setting. **Cons:** rooms are small; bathrooms are minuscule; the elevator is Lilliputian. **TripAdvisor:** "great small hotel," "great location for the price," "friendly staff." Ⓢ *Rooms from: £115* ✉ *15–16 Prince of Wales Terr., Kensington* ☎ *020/7937–2345* ⊕ *www.kenhouse.com* ⤢ *39 rooms, 2 suites* ⍾⃝ *Breakfast* Ⓜ *High Street Kensington* ✛ *4:C1.*

$$$$
HOTEL

⛾ **Milestone Hotel.** This pair of intricately decorated Victorian town houses overlooking Kensington Palace and Gardens is an intimate, luxurious alternative to the city's more famous high-end hotels, offering thoughtful hospitality and sumptuous, distinctively decorated rooms full of antiques. **Pros:** beautiful and elegant space; big rooms, many with park views; excellent location. **Cons:** service can be a bit stuffy (it seems you're not expected to do anything for yourself). **TripAdvisor:** "best afternoon tea ever," "our luxurious home from home," "service the old London way." Ⓢ *Rooms from: £366* ✉ *1 Kensington Ct., Kensington* ☎ *020/7917–1000* ⊕ *www.milestonehotel.com* ⤢ *44 rooms, 12 suites, 6 apartments* Ⓜ *High Street Kensington* ✛ *4:C1.*

$$$
HOTEL

⛾ **Millennium Gloucester.** Although the sleek lobby, with polished wood columns, a warming fireplace, and glittering chandeliers, is quite opulent, guest rooms have a traditionally masculine look, done in neutral creams and earth tones and furnished with blond-wood desks and leather chairs. **Pros:** good deals available if you book in advance. **Cons:** lighting in some bedrooms is a bit too subtle; bathrooms are relatively small but have all you need; public areas and restaurant can get crowded. **TripAdvisor:** "very handy location," "excellent customer service," "stylish weekend break." Ⓢ *Rooms from: £145* ✉ *4–18 Harrington Gardens, Kensington* ☎ *020/7373–6030* ⊕ *www. millenniumhotels.co.uk/millenniumgloucester* ⤵ *143 rooms* ⦿| *Breakfast* Ⓜ *Gloucester Rd.* ✛ *4:C2.*

$$$ 🏨 **Number Sixteen.** Guest rooms at this lovely luxury guesthouse just
HOTEL around the corner from the Victoria & Albert Museum look like they
Fodor's Choice come from the pages of an interior design magazine—chic yet homey,
★ with beautiful furniture and heavy fabrics, offset by nice little touches like piles of antiquarian books and flat-screen TVs set into the wall; bathrooms are clad in dark marble and polished oak. **Pros:** just the right level of helpful service; decor is gorgeous. **Cons:** no restaurant; small elevator. **TripAdvisor:** "little known gem," "beautiful breakfast," "special place for a special occasion." Ⓢ *Rooms from: £210* ✉ *16 Sumner Pl., South Kensington* ☎ *020/7589–5232, 888/559–5508 in U.S.* ⊕ *www. firmdale.com* ⤵ *42 rooms* ⦿| *Breakfast* Ⓜ *South Kensington* ✛ *4:D3.*

$$$ 🏨 **The Pelham Hotel.** One of the first and most stylish of London's famed
HOTEL "boutique" hotels, this still-chic choice is but a short stroll away from
Fodor's Choice the Natural History, Science, and V&A museums; at the end of a day's
★ sightseeing you can settle down in front of the fireplace in the gorgeous, wood-paneled drawing room with its honor bar or retire to the stylish, contemporary guest rooms by the doyenne designer of boutique hotels, Kit Kemp. **Pros:** great location for museum-hopping; gorgeous marble bathrooms; soigné decor; lovely staff; good package deals for online booking. **Cons:** taller guests will find themselves cursing the top-floor rooms with sloping ceilings. **TripAdvisor:** "fantastic home away from home," "beautiful interior design," "impeccable service." Ⓢ *Rooms from: £252* ✉ *15 Cromwell Pl., South Kensington* ☎ *020/7589–8288, 888/757–5587 in U.S.* ⊕ *www.pelhamhotel.co.uk* ⤵ *47 rooms, 4 suites* Ⓜ *South Kensington* ✛ *4:D2.*

$$ 🏨 **The Rockwell.** Bedrooms, done in earthy, slightly retro tones, are com-
HOTEL fortable, well designed, and very spacious by London standards, and out back is a pleasant walled garden where you can relax with a drink or join a summertime barbecue. **Pros:** large bedoooms; stylish surroundings; helpful staff; windows have good soundproofing. **Cons:** on a busy, unattractive road; 15-minute Tube ride to central London. **TripAdvisor:** "large and good location," "nice interior," "unusually accommodating." Ⓢ *Rooms from: £162* ✉ *181 Cromwell Rd., South Kensington* ☎ *020/7244–2000* ⊕ *www.therockwell.com* ⤵ *40 rooms* ✛ *4:B2.*

$$$ 🏨 **The Sumner.** You can feel yourself relaxing the minute you enter this
HOTEL elegant Georgian town house, where the interior design has a modern flair and guest rooms are painted in neutral tones with splashes of rich color. **Pros:** excellent location for shopping; small enough that the staff knows your name; attractive conservatory and garden. **Cons:** services are limited but prices high. **TripAdvisor:** "classy," "spotless hotel in good location," "friendly and attractive." Ⓢ *Rooms from: £210* ✉ *5 Sumner Pl., South Kensington* ☎ *020/7723–2244* ⊕ *www.thesumner. com* ⤵ *20 rooms* ⦿| *Breakfast* Ⓜ *South Kensington* ✛ *4:D3.*

$$ 🏨 **Think Earl's Court.** These serviced apartments are a stone's throw from
RENTAL Kensington High Street and each has everything you need, including

15

a well-equipped kitchen with washing machine and dishwasher, plus cable TV and free Wi-Fi. **Pros:** brand-new building; self-catering offers greater independence. **Cons:** payment is made when you book; bland, officelike exterior. **TripAdvisor:** "strange but good place," "comfortable and clean," "great base of operations." Ⓢ *Rooms from: £100 ⊠ 26A Adam and Eve Mews, Kensington ☎ 020/3465–9100 ⊕ www.think-apartments.com ↝ 133 rooms* Ⓜ *High Street Kensington ✛ 4:B1.*

CHELSEA

$$$
HOTEL

📺 **The Cadogan Hotel.** Elegant creams and golds and postmodern guest-room decor now prevail at one of London's most historically naughty hotels, once the home of Lillie Langtry, a "scandalous" actress and King Edward's mistress in the 1890s, and where Oscar Wilde was staying in 1895 (in Room 118) when he was arrested for "indecency" with a young man. **Pros:** luxurious but not stuffy; friendly staff; great location for shopping; good advance discounts online. **Cons:** rooms are quite small. **TripAdvisor:** "great tasting menu," "best-in-class service," "best hotel and staff in London." Ⓢ *Rooms from: £285 ⊠ 75 Sloane St., Chelsea ☎ 020/7235–7141 ⊕ www.cadogan.com ↝ 65 rooms* Ⓜ *Sloane Sq. ✛ 4:F2.*

$$$
HOTEL

📺 **myhotel chelsea.** Rooms at this small, chic charmer tucked away down a side street are bijou tiny but sophisticated, with mauve satin throws atop crisp white down comforters, and the beauty is in the details—the fire-warmed bar serves light meals and tea; there's a relaxing spa; and the guest library lends DVDs and books and is a quiet place to relax. **Pros:** stylish rooms made for relaxation; upscale neighborhood. **Cons:** price a bit high for what you get; tiny rooms; no restaurant. **TripAdvisor:** "refreshingly different," "very personal," "a little gem in Chelsea." Ⓢ *Rooms from: £216 ⊠ 35 Ixworth Pl., Chelsea ☎ 020/7225–7500 ⊕ www.myhotels.com ↝ 45 rooms, 9 suites* Ⓜ *South Kensington ✛ 4:E3.*

KNIGHTSBRIDGE

$$$
HOTEL

📺 **The Beaufort.** The high-ceilinged, contemporary rooms at this gracious guesthouse have muted, sophisticated colors and a plethora of thoughtful extras—such as flowers, chocolates, free afternoon tea, and even free drinks in the evening; listen carefully and you can almost hear the cash registers ringing from nearby Harrods. **Pros:** gorgeous decor; friendly staff. **Cons:** two-night minimum on some dates; standard doubles are much smaller than the price might indicate. **TripAdvisor:** "the perfect London boutique hotel," "peaceful and comfortable," "quiet excellence." Ⓢ *Rooms from: £300 ⊠ 33 Beaufort Gardens, Knightsbridge ☎ 020/7584–5252 ⊕ www.thebeaufort.co.uk ↝ 20 rooms, 7 suites* ⦿ *Breakfast* Ⓜ *Knightsbridge ✛ 4:F1.*

$$$$
HOTEL
Fodor's Choice
★

📺 **The Berkeley.** Conveniently located for Knightsbridge shopping, the very elegant Berkeley is known for its talked-about restaurants and luxuries that culminate—literally—in a splendid penthouse swimming pool and include spacious bedrooms, decorated with William Morris prints and art deco flourishes, and lavish marble bathrooms. ■**TIP→** In winter the roof terrace becomes a deliciously festive open-air cinema showing Christmas movies, complete with blankets, hot water bottles and hot chocolate. It's open to nonresidents for £55. **ros:** lavish and elegant; attentive service; prices aren't quite so stratospheric as some other high-end places. **Cons:** even if you do decide to splurge, you'll still need your best designer clothes to fit in. **TripAdvisor:** "slick service and great beds," "a very fashionable afternoon tea," "impeccable service." ⑤ *Rooms from: £319* ⊠ *Wilton Pl., Knightsbridge* ☎ *020/7235–6000, 800/637–2869 in U.S.* ⊕ *www.the-berkeley.co.uk* ⌿ *103 rooms, 55 suites* Ⓜ *Knightsbridge* ✛ *4:G1.*

$$$$
HOTEL
🖫 **The Capital Hotel.** Nothing is ever too much at this elegant hotel that was formerly a private house—mattresses are handmade, sheets are 450-thread count, bathrooms are marble, and everything is done in impeccable taste: fine-grain woods, original prints, soothing, country-chic furnishings, and understated service. **Pros:** beautiful space; handy for shopping at Harrods. **Cons:** breakfast is expensive. **TripAdvisor:** "small but perfectly formed," "food was exceptional," "perfect location for a special occasion." ⑤ *Rooms from: £300* ⊠ *22–24 Basil St., Knightsbridge* ☎ *020/7589–5171, 800/628–8929 in U.S.* ⊕ *www. capitalhotel.co.uk* ⌿ *42 rooms, 8 suites* Ⓜ *Knightsbridge* ✛ *4:F1.*

$$$$
HOTEL
Fodor's Choice
★
🖫 **Egerton House.** Sensationally soigné, chicly decorated, and feeling like your own private London home, this option has some gorgeous pluses, including guest rooms lavishly decorated with luxurious fabrics in rich colors, a knockout white-on-gold dining room—and did we mention all the prints and posters by Matisse, Picasso, and Toulouse-Lautrec? **Pros:** lovely staff; great location; magnificent decor; striking art. **Cons:** some decor touches may be a little too frou-frou, but Toulouse-Lautrec would have approved. **TripAdvisor:** "ideally situated in Knightsbridge," "excellent boutique hotel," "service and comfort." ⑤ *Rooms from: £312* ⊠ *17–19 Egerton Terr., Knightsbridge* ☎ *020/7589–2412, 877/955–1515 in U.S.* ⊕ *www.egertonhousehotel.co.uk* ⌿ *22 rooms, 6 suites* Ⓜ *Knightsbridge, South Kensington* ✛ *4:F2.*

$$$$
HOTEL
Fodor's Choice
★
🖫 **The Lanesborough.** A gilded cocoon for the seriously wealthy, this hotel exudes a spectacular richness and, when built by a Texan heiress, was the talk of the town, thanks to the magnificent 19th-century antiques (even in the guest rooms), the personal butler service (for your every whim), and that 1770 cognac on the menu—like a weekend spent in Bath, this place recreates the splendor of Georgian England and whether you're a high-roller or a high-style connoisseur, you'll be absolutely delighted. **Pros:** lap of luxury; your wish is their command. **Cons:** prices are extraordinary; not everybody likes the constantly hovering service. **TripAdvisor:** "a London classic," "wonderful afternoon tea," "beautiful hotel." ⑤ *Rooms from: £555* ⊠ *Hyde Park Corner, Belgravia* ☎ *020/7259–5599, 800/999–1828 in U.S.* ⊕ *www.lanesborough.com* ⌿ *50 rooms, 43 suites* Ⓜ *Hyde Park Corner* ✛ *4:G1.*

$$$$
HOTEL
Fodor's Choice
★
🖫 **Mandarin Oriental Hyde Park.** Built in 1880, the Mandarin Oriental welcomes you with one of the most exuberantly Victorian facades in town, then fast-forwards you to high-trend modern London, thanks to strikingly decorated guest rooms (filled with hidden high-tech gadgets and luxuries like Frette linen duvets, fresh orchids, and gourmet chocolates) and the spectacular restaurant, Dinner by Heston Blumenthal, probably London's most talked-about eatery these days. ■ **TIP→** For the 99% of us who can't afford to stay here, a visit to the Mandarin Bar for cocktails is a glamorous (and surprisingly relaxed) peek into the world of London high society. **Pros:** the three greats of Knightsbridge—Hyde Park,

15

APARTMENT RENTALS & HOME EXCHANGES

APARTMENT RENTALS

For a home base that's roomy enough for a family and that comes with cooking facilities, consider renting furnished "flats" (the British word for apartments).

These can save you money, especially if you're traveling as a family or with a group. You also have the freedom to cook for yourselves if you want—surprisingly liberating after several days of restaurant food.

If you're interested in home exchange, but don't feel like sharing, some home-exchange directories list rentals as well.

If you want to deal directly with local agents, get a personal recommendation from someone who has used the company; there's no accredited rating system for apartment-rental standards like the one for hotels.

INTERNATIONAL AGENTS

Hideaways International. Hideaways International offers boutique hotels, tours, and cruises. $ *Rooms from: £195 ⊠ 767 Islington St., Portsmouth, New Hampshire, U.S. ☎ 603/430–4433 or 800/843–4433 ⊕ www.hideaways.com.*

Interhome. Interhome has dozens of flats all over London starting at about £400 per week per person. $ *Rooms from: £400 ⊠ c/o Resort-Quest, 2860 State Rd. 84, Suite 116/PMB 214, Fort Lauderdale, Florida, U.S. ☎ 800/882–6864 ⊕ www. interhome.us.*

LOCAL AGENTS

Acorn Apartments. Acorn Apartments offers attractive small flats in Clerkenwell and Bloomsbury starting at around £100. $ *Rooms from: £100 ⊠ Ground Fl., 19 Bedford Pl., Bloomsbury ☎ 020/7636–8325 ⊕ www.acorn-apartments.co.uk.*

The Apartment Service. The Apartment Service specializes in executive apartments for business travelers, so prices are high, but so is the level of quality. $ *Rooms from: £75 ⊠ 5 Francis Grove, Wimbledon ☎ 020/8944–1444 ⊕ www. apartmentservice.com.*

At Home in London. At Home in London offers rooms in private homes in Knightsbridge, Kensington, Mayfair, Chelsea, and West London. $ *Rooms from: £90 ⊠ 70 Black Lion La., Hammersmith ☎ 020/8748–1943 ⊕ www.athomeinlondon.co.uk.*

The Bed and Breakfast Club. The Bed and Breakfast Club offers delightful little London flats in Knightsbridge, Kensington, and Chelsea. $ *Rooms from: £50 ⊠ 405 Kings Rd., Suite 192, Chelsea ☎ 01243/370692 ⊕ www. thebedandbreakfastclub.co.uk* ☞ *There's a 2.5% fee for using a credit card; debit cards incur no fees; the full price of room must be paid in advance. Check cancellation policies carefully.*

Coach House London Vacation Rentals. Coach House London Vacation Rentals arranges stays in the properties of Londoners who are temporarily away. $ *Rooms from: £130 ⊠ 2 Tunley Rd., Balham ☎ 020/8133–8332 ⊕ www.rentals. chslondon.com* ☞ *Payment by credit card only; 10% deposit required.*

Landmark Trust. Landmark Trust has London apartments in unusual and historic buildings; prices start at around £100 a night, but many buildings require a minimum stay of seven days. ⑤ *Rooms from: £100* ✉ *Shottesbrooke, Maidenhead, Berkshire* ☎ *01628/825925* ⊕ *www. landmarktrust.org.uk.*

One Fine Stay. What sets One Fine Stay apart is the quality of the properties on offer and the outstanding support you get during your stay—fresh linen, toiletries, a kitchen full of basic supplies, iPhones helpfully loaded with maps, and, in a lovely touch, a package of tips about the area from the owners themselves. ⑤ *Rooms from: £90* ☎ *020/7097–8948* ⇨ *N/A* ⊹ *2:F1.*

Uptown Reservations. Uptown Reservations accepts only upscale addresses, and specializes in hosted homes or apartments for Americans, often business executives. ⑤ *Rooms from: £105* ✉ *8 Kelso Pl., Kensington* ☎ *020/7937–2001* ⊕ *www. uptownres.co.uk.*

In addition, travelers at Fodors.com recommend these rental services:

"I've used **London Guest Suites** (⊕ *www.londonguestsuites.com*) many times and like them. They have rentals of all lengths. I also just booked a flat at **A Place Like Home** (⊕ *www.aplacelikehome.co.uk*)." —carrybean

"We stayed in 1 Sloane Ave. and were extremely happy and pleased with the apartment and the company **The Apartments** (⊕ *www. theapartments.co.uk*)." —jrecm

"Try the biggest rental site in Europe: **Holiday-Rentals from Home Away** (⊕ *www.holiday-rentals.co.uk*)." —travel_tomato

"Check out **VRBO** (⊕ *www.vrbo.com*), lots of London listings, and **Farnum-Christ** (⊕ *www.farnum-christ.com*), which is a high-ish end agency with some wonderful flats." —janisj

"I've used **London Connections** (⊕ *www.londonconnections.com*) several times and I've been very pleased." —Tinathread

HOME EXCHANGES
If you would like to exchange your home for someone else's, join a home-exchange organization, which will send you its updated listings of available exchanges for a year and will include your own listing in at least one of them. It's up to you to make specific arrangements.

Exchange Clubs HomeLink International (✉ *2937 N.W. 9th Terr., Fort Lauderdale, Florida, U.S.* ☎ *954/566–2687 or 800/638–3841* ⊕ www. homelink.org); $119 yearly for a listing and online access.

Intervac U.S (✉ *Box 590504, San Francisco, California, U.S.94159* ☎ *800/756–4663* ⊕ *www.intervacus. com*); $99 yearly for a listing and online access.

15

Harrods, and Harvey Nichols—are at your doorstep; amazing views of Hyde Park; excellent service; gorgeous decor. **Cons:** nothing here comes cheap; you must dress for dinner (and lunch and breakfast). **TripAdvisor:** "unexpected excellence," "elegant and luxurious," "very elegant." ⑤ *Rooms from: £475* ⊠ *66 Knightsbridge, Knightsbridge* ☎ *020/7201–3773 or 800/2828–3838* ⊕ *www.mandarinoriental.com/london* ➲ *177 rooms, 23 suites* Ⓜ *Knightsbridge* ✛ *4:F1.*

NOTTING HILL AND BAYSWATER

NOTTING HILL

$ **Lancaster Hall Hotel.** This cheap and cheerful choice just north of Hyde
HOTEL Park offers clean, simple rooms at a decent price, along with a good buffet breakfast. **Pros:** decent, inexpensive, no-frills accommodation; excellent central location five-minute walk to Hyde Park; short Tube or bus ride away from many sights. **Cons:** just the basics; no nonsmoking rooms; beds could be better; all double rooms have twin beds. **TripAdvisor:** "basic accommodation in great location," "nice and clean," "wonderful staff." ⑤ *Rooms from: £87* ⊠ *35 Craven Terr.,Bayswater* ☎ *020/7723–9276* ⊕ *www.lancaster-hall-hotel.co.uk* ➲ *180 rooms* ⊟ *No credit cards* Ⓜ *Lancaster Gate* ✛ *1:D4* .

$$ **The Main House.** A stay in this Victorian building with four bedrooms
B&B/INN and clean white linens, polished wood floors, modern furniture, and
Fodor's Choice Asian art in the uncluttered and delightful spaces feels more like sleeping
★ over at a friend's house than in a B&B. **Pros:** unique and unusual place; charming and helpful owners. **Cons:** few services; two-night minimum stay. **TripAdvisor:** "style and class," "stylish flat in upscale Notting Hill," "for the independent traveler." ⑤ *Rooms from: £110* ⊠ *6 Colvile Rd., Notting Hill* ☎ *020/7221–9691* ⊕ *www.themainhouse.com* ➲ *4 rooms* ⊦⊙⊧ *Breakfast* Ⓜ *Notting Hill Gate* ✛ *1:A4.*

$ **Portobello Gold.** This no-frills B&B in the heart of the Portobello
B&B/INN Road antiques area is on the floor above the pub and restaurant of the same name and offers small but comfortable accommodations; in the tiny doubles, beds take up almost the entire room. **Pros:** great location; friendly, laid-back atmosphere; free Wi-Fi in guest rooms plus an internet café that charges £1 per half hour on the premises. **Cons:** "wet rooms" replace proper bathrooms (be prepared to shower by the sink); can be noisy; no elevator. **TripAdvisor:** "nice location," "relaxed atmosphere," "shabby chic." ⑤ *Rooms from: £80* ⊠ *95–97 Portobello Rd., Notting Hill* ☎ *020/7460–4910* ⊕ *www.portobellogold.com* ➲ *6 rooms, 1 apartment* ⊦⊙⊧ *Breakfast* Ⓜ *Notting Hill Gate* ✛ *1:A4.*

$$$ **The Portobello Hotel.** One of London's quirkiest hotels, the little Por-
HOTEL tobello (formed from two adjoining Victorian houses) is seriously hip, attracting scores of celebrities to its small but stylish rooms that are decorated with joyous abandon—you're likely to be surrounded with an assortment of antiques, luxurious fabrics, statues, and bizarre bric-a-brac, such as the extraordinary Victorian "bathing machine" (found in Room 16) that actor Johnny Depp is said to have once filled with champagne for Kate Moss, a former flame. **Pros:** stylish; celebrity vibe; guests have use of nearby gym and pool. **Cons:** most rooms are quite small; may be too eccentric for some. **TripAdvisor:** "charming," "lovely

friendly staff," "colonial decadence." Ⓢ *Rooms from: £234* ⊠ *22 Stanley Gardens, Notting Hill* ☎ *020/7727–2777* ⊕ *www.portobello-hotel. co.uk* ↻ *24 rooms* ☉ *Closed 10 days at Christmas* ⊺⊙⊦ *Breakfast* Ⓜ *Notting Hill Gate* ✛ *1:A5.*

BAYSWATER

$$
HOTEL

Colonnade. Each room is different in this lovely town house near a canal filled with colorful narrow boats in the Little Venice neighborhood—some are split-level or have balconies and all are filled with rich brocades, velvets, and antiques. **Pros:** beautifully decorated; unique and little-known part of London, five minutes from Paddington station; ongoing renovations are smoothing out some previously time-worn edges. **Cons:** you have to go through shoddier parts of town to get there; rooms are small. **TripAdvisor:** "a little quirky," "a lot of history," "quiet central location." Ⓢ *Rooms from: £138* ⊠ *2 Warrington Crescent, Bayswater* ☎ *020/7286–1052* ⊕ *www.theetoncollection.com* ↻ *15 rooms, 28 suites* Ⓜ *Warwick Ave.* ✛ *1:C2.*

$
B&B/INN

Europa House Hotel. Don't expect much more than the basics in this old-fashioned B&B near Hyde Park, but the small rooms are cozy and the owners who have been running the place since the 1970s are adept at directing visitors to the area's best pubs and restaurants. **Pros:** bargain price; close to two Tube stations. **Cons:** no extras; dated decor; tiny bathrooms; no elevator. **TripAdvisor:** "great location and great room," "cheap and cheerful," "good breakfasts." Ⓢ *Rooms from: £70* ⊠ *151 Sussex Gardens, Bayswater* ☎ *020/7723–7343* ⊕ *www. europahousehotel.org.uk* Ⓜ *Paddington, Lancaster Gate* ✛ *1:E4.*

$
B&B/INN

Garden Court Hotel. Each room in this small hotel formed from two 19th-century town houses in a quiet garden square has a character of its own—some, such as those with original Victorian fittings, are nicer than others, but all share the lush little garden, a lovely hideaway when the sun shines. **Pros:** lovely garden; lots of charm; new elevator makes the upper floors more pleasant. **Cons:** price jumps by nearly 50% if you want a private bathroom; some rooms much better than others. **TripAdvisor:** "simple and lovely," "great place for a weekend," "quiet and nice." Ⓢ *Rooms from: £80* ⊠ *30–31 Kensington Gardens Sq., Bayswater* ☎ *020/7229–2553* ⊕ *www.gardencourthotel.co.uk* ↻ *12 rooms, 10 with bath* ⊺⊙⊦ *Breakfast* Ⓜ *Bayswater, Queensway* ✛ *1:B4.*

$
B&B/INN

Parkwood Hotel. Located mere seconds from Hyde Park in one of London's swankiest enclaves, this sweet little guesthouse is an oasis of value-for-money, with warm and helpful hosts and bright bedrooms simply furnished with pastel color schemes and reproduction antique beds. **Pros:** lovely hosts; price guaranteed to match any other hotel of its class in the area. **Cons:** often booked up in advance; no elevator; front-facing rooms can be noisy. **TripAdvisor:** "fantastic service and great value," "good breakfast," "perfect location for a weekend stay." Ⓢ *Rooms from: £70* ⊠ *4 Stanhope Pl., Bayswater* ☎ *020/7402–2241* ⊕ *www.parkwoodhotel.com* ↻ *18 rooms* Ⓜ *Marble Arch* ✛ *1:F4 .*

$$
RENTAL

Space Apart Hotel. These 30 studio apartments near Hyde Park are done in soothing tones of white and gray, with polished wood floors and attractive modern kitchenettes equipped with all you need to make small meals. **Pros:** especially good value for the money; the larger suites

15

have space for four people; handy location. **Cons:** no in-house restaurant or bar; minimum two-night stay required. **TripAdvisor:** "spacious room," "good amenities and helpful staff," "quiet and pleasant stay." ⑤ *Rooms from: £140* ✉ *32–37 Kensington Gardens Sq., Bayswater* ☎ *020/7908–1340* ⊕ *www.aparthotel-london.co.uk* ↘ *30 rooms* Ⓜ *Bayswater* ✛ *1:B4.*

$ Ⓣ **Stylotel.** Just around the corner from Paddington station, this funkylooking little place has small, functional rooms done to death in contemporary style and even tinier bathrooms but is clean, cheerful, and perfectly comfortable. **Pros:** bargain price; helpful staff; unique style. **Cons:** style will be too unique for some; small bedrooms and bathrooms; serves breakfast only; website is frequently down, which can make booking online a challenge. **TripAdvisor:** "perfect for a short stay," "retro and futuristic," "decent area and friendly staff." ⑤ *Rooms from: £90* ✉ *160–162 Sussex Gardens Sq., Bayswater* ☎ *0207/223–1026* ⊕ *www. stylotel.com* ↘ *40 rooms* Ⓜ *Paddington, Edgware Rd* ✛ *1:E4.*
HOTEL

$$ Ⓣ **Vancouver Studios.** All guest rooms in this Victorian town house are similar to efficiency apartments, with mini-kitchens and microwaves, and you can even preorder groceries, which are stocked in your minirefrigerator on arrival. **Pros:** more space than a hotel room; unique little apartments. **Cons:** a bit out of the way; a bargain only if several people share the space. **TripAdvisor:** "nice and on the small side," "London gem," "very nice accommodation." ⑤ *Rooms from: £130* ✉ *30 Prince's Sq., Bayswater* ☎ *020/7243–1270* ⊕ *www.vancouverstudios. co.uk* ↘ *45 studios* Ⓜ *Bayswater, Queensway* ✛ *1:B4.*
RENTAL

REGENT'S PARK AND HAMPSTEAD

$ Ⓣ **Glenlyn Guest House.** A few miles north of Hampstead, this is an excellent option for travelers who don't mind being a long Tube ride away from the action; you'll enjoy collapsing in this converted Victorian town house which offers a high standard of accommodation, with spacious bedrooms, huge flat-screen TVs, and a conservatory breakfast room that opens onto a garden. **Pros:** comfortable and friendly; adjoining rooms can be converted to family suites; five-minute walk to Tube station. **Cons:** half-hour Tube ride to central London; no restaurant. **TripAdvisor:** "great room," "cheap and well located," "friendly and helpful staff." ⑤ *Rooms from: £80* ✉ *6 Woodside Park Rd., North Finchley* ☎ *020/8445–0440* ↘ *27 rooms* Ⓜ *Woodside Park* ✛ *1:D1.*
B&B/INN

$$ Ⓣ **La Gaffe.** The name of these early-18th-century row houses is an ironic French play on "Gaff," which is British slang for a small and simple residence—and that rather neatly sums up the bedrooms, which are tiny and with few amenities, although some have four-poster beds, and the honeymoon suite (a mere £30 more than a basic room) has its own Jacuzzi. **Pros:** pretty area of town; friendly staff; small but private bathrooms. **Cons:** few services; no elevator; outside city center. **TripAdvisor:** "professionally run," "homey Italian restaurant," "lovely hotel in a wonderful location." ⑤ *Rooms from: £100* ✉ *107–111 Heath St., Hampstead* ☎ *020/7435–8965* ⊕ *www.lagaffe.co.uk* ↘ *18 rooms, 3 suites* ⓘ| *Breakfast* Ⓜ *Hampstead* ✛ *1:D1.*
B&B/INN

Pubs and Nightlife

WORD OF MOUTH

"London has two types of pubs. One is the local where neighbors visit. The second is an open type hosting casual visitors. Inquire at your hotel about a local. Be prepared to buy a round. At the casual bar, ask for a recommendation of a beer or ale. Ask at your hotel for a nearby pub with the best pub grub."

—GSteed

Updated by
Julius Honnor

There isn't a London nightlife scene—there are lots of them. As long as there are crowds for obscure teenage rock bands, Dickensian-style pubs, comedy cabarets, and "bodysonic" dance nights, someone will create clubs and venues for them in London. The result? London has become a veritable utopia for excitement junkies, culture fiends, and those who—simply put—like to party. Nearly everyone who visits London these days will be mesmerized by the city's energy, which reveals itself in layers. Whether you prefer rhythm and blues with fine French food, the gritty guitar riff tunes and boutique beers of East London, a pint and gourmet pizza at a local gastropub, or swanky cocktails and sushi at London's sexiest lair, London is sure to feed your fancy.

PLANNING

GETTING AROUND

If you're out past 12:30 am, the best way to get home is by taxi (the Tube stops running around 12:30 am Monday–Saturday and midnight on Sunday), though the city's night buses have improved hugely in recent years. The best place to hail a taxi is at the front door of one of the major hotels; you can also have the staff at your last stop of the evening call one for you. Avoid unlicensed taxis that tout for business around closing time.

REGENT'S PARK

HAMPSTEAD
villagey pubs
for long Sunday
lunches

CLERKENWELL
urban
cutting edge

NOTTING HILL
arty but smart
and rich-hip
drinking holes

BLOOMSBURY
heritage,
learning,
bowling

HOXTON
arty and
on the pulse

FITZROVIA
secret chic

OXFORD CIRCUS

SOHO
lowlife and
highlife,
music and dance

COVENT GARDEN
a drink before
the show

MAYFAIR
wine and
spirits

HYDE PARK

ST JAMES'S
jacket
required

SOUTH BANK
real ale,
real food

KNIGHTSBRIDGE
hotel bar
martinis

Green
Park

St. James's
Park

WESTMINSTER

River Thames

HAMMERSMITH
relaxed and
upmarket,
evenings
by the river

BELGRAVIA
hidden mews
gems

LAMBETH

VICTORIA

CHELSEA
sophisticated
and moneyed

0   1/2 mile
0   1/2 km

LIQUOR AND SMOKING LAWS

Recent laws have allowed London drinking establishments to extend their opening hours beyond the traditional 11 pm closing and banned smoking. Most pubs and bars still close at 11 and some others at midnight or a few short hours later, and in general you'll find yourself drinking in environs that are healthier and certainly more pleasant.

CAN I TAKE MY KIDS TO THE PUB?

As pubs increasingly emphasize what's coming out of the kitchen rather than what's flowing from the tap, bringing the kids is more of an option. The law dictates that children 14 to 17 may enter a pub but are not permitted to purchase or drink alcohol, and children under 14 are not permitted in the bar area of a pub unless the pub has a "Children's Certificate" and they are accompanied by an adult. Some pubs have a section set aside for families, especially during the day.

WHAT TO WEAR

As a general rule, you won't see too many people in the upscale London nightspots wearing jeans and sneakers. British women are also prone to baring a bit of skin, so that sparkly, backless top you were saving for a Caribbean soiree might be just as suitable for a night out in London. In general, people are more likely to dress down than up for an evening in the pub.

FIND OUT WHAT'S PLAYING WHERE

Because today's cool spot is often tomorrow's forgotten or closed venue, you'll want to be sure to check out the weekly listings in the print editions (some with websites) of the *Evening Standard* (⊕ *www.thisislondon.co.uk*), *Time Out London* (⊕ *www.timeout.com/london*), *Where London*, and *In London*. Other websites to check out are ⊕ www.londontown.com, ⊕ www.allinlondon.co.uk, and ⊕ *www.viewlondon.co.uk*. *Tatler*, the monthly, super-stylish magazine about England's blue-blood set, is the insider's bible for the hottest places to go. Although many clubs are for under-thirties, many others are popular with patrons of all ages and types.

PUBS

Pubs are where Londoners go to hang out, to see and be seen, act out the drama of life, and, for some, occasionally drink themselves into varying degrees of oblivion. Even today, the traditional pub is still a vital part of British life. It also should be a part of the visitor's experience, as there are few better places to meet Londoners in their local habitat. There are somewhere around 4,000 pubs in London—some are dark and woody, others plain and functional, a few still have original Victorian etched glass, Edwardian panels, and art nouveau carvings. *The list below offers a few pubs selected for central location, historical interest, a pleasant garden, music, or good food, but you might just as happily adopt your own temporary "local."*

Pubs in the capital are changing as gastropub fever has swept through London. At many places, char-grills are installed in the kitchen and nouveau pub grub, such as Moroccan chicken, is on the menu. Even so, the English take their drink very seriously, and regardless of what you eat, you'll definitely want to order a pint.

The big decision is what to drink. The beers of choice among Britons are "bitters," lightly fermented with an amber color that get their bitterness from hops. They are usually served at cellar temperature (that is, cooler than room tempera-

ture but not actually chilled). Real ales, served from wooded kegs and made without chilling, filtering, or pasteurization, are flatter than regular bitters and enjoying a renaissance. Stouts, like Guinness, are a meal in themselves and something of an acquired taste—they have a burned flavor and look like thickened flat Coke with a frothy top. Lagers, most familiar to American drinkers, are light color and carbonated. ■TIP➜ Remember that what Americans call beer, the British call lager, and those on offer are often beers from continental Europe. Designer and American beers have been making their way to bars across London.

Note that many English pubs are affiliated with or owned by particular breweries and are beholden to sell only beers produced by that brewery. Some of these larger chain owners, sometimes identified on the pub's sign, include Bass, Chef and Brewer, Mitchells and Butlers, Courage, Punch Taverns, Samuel Smith, and Whitbread. In contrast, independently owned pubs, called "free houses," tend to offer a more extensive selection. Other potations now available also include ciders, ranging from sweet to dry, which are made from apples (Irish cider, served over ice, is now ubiquitously fashionable) and shandies, a mix of lager beer and lemonade. Friendly pubs will usually be happy to give you a taste of the brew of your choice before you order. After discussing your choice of drink with the barman, turn to your neighbor, raise the glass, and utter that most pleasant of toasts, "Cheers."

BLOOMSBURY AND HOLBORN

BLOOMSBURY

★ **The Lamb.** Charles Dickens and his contemporaries drank here, but today's enthusiastic clientele make sure this intimate and eternally popular pub avoids the pitfalls of feeling too old-fashioned. For private chats at the bar, you can close a delicate etched-glass "snob screen" to the bar staff, opening it only when you fancy another pint. ⊠ *94 Lamb's Conduit St., Bloomsbury* ☏ *020/7405–0713* Ⓜ *Russell Sq.*

★ **Museum Tavern.** Across the street from the British Museum, this friendly and classy Victorian pub makes an ideal resting place after the rigors of the culture trail. Karl Marx unwound here after a hard day in the library. He could have spent his *Kapital* on any of seven well-kept beers available on tap. ⊠ *49 Great Russell St., Bloomsbury* ☏ *020/7242–8987* Ⓜ *Tottenham Court Rd.*

Market Porter pub is directly across from foodie favorite Borough Market.

The Queen's Larder. The royal associated with this tiny pub is Queen Charlotte, who is said to have stored food here for her "mad" husband, George III, when he was being treated nearby. The interior preserves its antique feel, with dark wood and old posters, and in the evenings fills up quickly with office workers and students. In good weather, you might prefer to grab one of the seats outdoors. ✉ *1 Queen's Sq., Bloomsbury* ☎ *020/7837–5627* ⊕ *www.queenslarder.co.uk* Ⓜ *Russell Sq.*

HOLBORN

Princess Louise. This fine, popular pub is an exquisite museum piece of a Victorian interior, with glazed tiles and intricately engraved glass screens that divide the bar area into cozy little annexes. It's not all show, either: There's a good selection of excellent-value Yorkshire real ales. ✉ *208 High Holborn, Holborn* ☎ *020/7405–8816* Ⓜ *Holborn.*

THE CITY AND CLERKENWELL

THE CITY

Fodor'sChoice ★ **Black Friar.** A step from Blackfriars Tube stop, this spectacular pub has an Arts-and-Crafts interior that is entertainingly, satirically ecclesiastical, with inlaid mother-of-pearl, wood carvings, stained glass, and marble pillars all over the place. In spite of the finely lettered temperance tracts on view just below the reliefs of monks, fairies, and friars, there is a nice group of ales on tap from independent brewers. The 20th-century poet Sir John Betjeman once led a successful campaign to save the pub from demolition. ✉ *174 Queen Victoria St., The City* ☎ *020/7236–5474* ⊕ *www.nicholsonspubs.co.uk/theblackfriarblackfriarslondon* Ⓜ *Blackfriars.*

Viaduct Tavern. Queen Victoria opened the nearby Holborn Viaduct in 1869, and this eponymous pub honored the waterway by serving its first pint the same year. Much of the Victorian decoration is still extant, with gilded mirrors, carved wood, and engraved glass. The Viaduct Tavern's haunted reputation stems from its proximity to the former Newgate Gaol, which once stood on the site (in fact, ex-prison cells in the basement can be seen with a free tour before or after the lunchtime rush and before 5 pm). There are usually three or four ales on tap; lunch is also served. ⊠ *126 Newgate St., The City* ☎ *020/7600–1863* ⊘ *Closed weekends* Ⓜ *St. Paul's.*

Ye Olde Cheshire Cheese. Yes, this extremely historic pub (it dates from 1667, the year after the Great Fire of London) is full of tourists, but it deserves a visit for its sawdust-covered floors, low wood-beam ceilings, and the 14th-century crypt of Whitefriars' monastery under the cellar bar. This was the most regular of Dr. Johnson's and Dickens's *many* locals. ⊠ *145 Fleet St., The City* ☎ *020/7353–6170* ⊘ *Open noon–3 Sun.* Ⓜ *Blackfriars.*

Ye Olde Mitre. Hidden off the side of 8 Hatton Gardens, this cozy pub's roots go back to 1547, though it was rebuilt around 1772. Originally built for the staff of the Bishop of Ely, whose London residence was next door, it remained officially part of Cambridgeshire until the 20th century. It's a friendly little place, with a fireplace, well-kept ales, wooden beams, and traditional bar snacks. ⊠ *1 Ely Ct., The City* ☎ *020/7405–4751* ⊘ *Closed weekends* Ⓜ *Chancery La.*

Ye Olde Watling. This busy corner pub has been rebuilt at least three times since 1666. One of its incarnations was supposedly as a hostel for Christopher Wren's workmen while nearby St. Paul's was being built. The ground floor is a laid-back pub, while upstairs houses an atmospheric restaurant, complete with wooden beams and trestle tables, with a basic English pub menu. ⊠ *29 Watling St., The City* ☎ *020/7248–8935* Ⓜ *Mansion House.*

CLERKENWELL

Fodor's Choice
★ **Jerusalem Tavern.** Owned by the well-respected St. Peter's Brewery from Suffolk, the Jerusalem Tavern is one-of-a-kind, small, and endearingly eccentric. Ancient Delft-style tiles meld with wood and concrete in a converted watchmaker and jeweler's shop dating back to the 18th century. The beer, both bottled and on tap, is some of the best available anywhere in London. It's often busy, especially after work. ⊠ *55 Britton St., Clerkenwell* ☎ *020/7490–4281* Ⓜ *Farringdon.*

THE EAST END

Prospect of Whitby. Named after a ship, this is London's oldest riverside pub, dating from around 1520. Once upon a time it was called the Devil's Tavern because of the lowlife criminals—thieves and smugglers—who congregated here. Ornamented with pewter ware and nautical objects, this much-loved "boozer" is often pointed out from boat trips up the Thames. ⊠ *57 Wapping Wall, East End* ☎ *020/7481–1095* Ⓜ *Wapping.*

CHELSEA AND KNIGHTSBRIDGE

CHELSEA

Admiral Codrington. Named after a hero of the Napoleonic Wars, this smart pub is a popular meeting place for the upwardly mobile of Sloane Square (Lady Diana Spencer is said to have been a regular in her teaching days). The "Admiral Cod," as it's known, houses a modern restaurant where excellent English fare is served at lunch and dinnertime (treat yourself to a delicious raspberry soufflé to finish). Activity at the island bar centers on the wine list; well-off Chelsea residents pack the bare wood interior on weekend evenings. ⊠ *17 Mossop St., Chelsea* ☎ *020/7581–0005* ⊕ *www.theadmiralcodrington.co.uk* Ⓜ *South Kensington.*

KNIGHTSBRIDGE

★ **The Nag's Head.** The landlord of this classic little mews pub in Belgravia runs a tight ship, and no cell phones are allowed. If that sounds like misery, the lovingly collected Victorian artifacts (including antique penny arcade games), high-quality beer, and old-fashioned pub grub should make up for it. ⊠ *53 Kinnerton St., Belgravia* ☎ *020/7235–1135* Ⓜ *Hyde Park Corner.*

MAYFAIR

The Running Horse. Wood paneling lends an authentic feel to the ground floor of this smart Mayfair pub, a pleasant stopover during your jaunt around the elegant neighborhood. Upmarket pub grub is served in the restaurant upstairs. ⊠ *50 Davies St., Mayfair* ☎ *020/7493–1275* ⊕ *www.therunninghorselondon.co.uk* Ⓜ *Bond St.*

NOTTING HILL

The Cow. Crowds head to this chic mix of fun, haute food, and friendly, quaint decor for Guinness and oysters, either enjoying them in the unpretentious downstairs bar or the upstairs more formal restaurant. The food is excellent, if pricey for pub grub, with lots of seafood and steaks (and sometimes a mix, as in the smoked eel with mash and bacon). The atmosphere? Always warm, welcoming, and buzzing. ⊠ *89 Westbourne Park Rd., Notting Hill* ☎ *020/7221–0021* ⊕ *www. thecowlondon.co.uk* Ⓜ *Royal Oak, Westbourne Park.*

REGENT'S PARK AND HAMPSTEAD

REGENT'S PARK

Camden Arms. On the site of the last fatal duel in Britain, this funky-yet-chill place has plenty of interesting features—check out the ornate spiral staircase after a good pint of beer. House tunes spun by DJs pervade this pub–lounge every Friday night, and often on Saturday. Modern cocktails are served alongside Thai cuisine. ⊠ *1 Randolph St., Camden* ☎ *020/7267–9829* ⊕ *www.thecamdenarms.com* Ⓜ *Camden.*

HAMPSTEAD

The Holly Bush. A short walk up the hill from Hampstead Tube station, the friendly Holly Bush was a country pub before London spread this far north. It retains something of a rural feel, with stripped wooden floors and an open fire, and is an intimate place to enjoy great ales and organic and free-range pub food. Try the homemade pork scratchings and pickled eggs. ✉ *22 Holly Mount, Hampstead* ☎ *020/7435–2892* ⊕ *www.hollybushpub.com* Ⓜ *Hampstead.*

Spaniards Inn. Ideal as a refueling point when you're on a Hampstead Heath hike, this historic oak-beam pub has a gorgeous garden, scene of the tea party in Dickens's *Pickwick Papers.* Dick Turpin, the highwayman, frequented the inn before Dickens's time, and Shelley, Keats, and Byron hung out here as well. The place is extremely popular, especially on Sunday, when Londoners roll in. It's also very dog friendly—there's even a dog wash in the garden. ✉ *Spaniards Rd., Hampstead* ☎ *020/8731–8406* ⊕ *www.thespaniardshampstead.co.uk* Ⓜ *Hampstead.*

SOUTHBANK

16

Fodor's Choice **Anchor & Hope.** One of London's most popular gastropubs, the Anchor
★ & Hope doesn't take reservations (except for Sunday lunch). Would-be diners snake around the red-walled, wooden-floored pub, kept happy by some good real ales and a fine wine list as they wait for hours for a table. The food is old-fashioned English (think salt cod, tripe, and chips) with a few modern twists. ✉ *36 The Cut, South Bank* ☎ *020/7928–9898* Ⓜ *Southwark.*

★ **Market Porter.** Opposite Borough Market, this atmospheric pub opens at 6 am for the stallholders, and always seems busy. Remarkably, the place manages to remain relaxed, with helpful staff and happy customers spilling out onto the road right through the year. The wide selection of real ales is lovingly tended. ✉ *9 Stoney St., South Bank* ☎ *020/7407–2495* ⊕ *www.markettaverns.co.uk* Ⓜ *London Bridge.*

Mayflower. An atmospheric 17th-century riverside inn (rebuilt in the following century) with exposed beams and a terrace is near the onetime berth of the famous ship on which the Pilgrims sailed to what became the American colonies. The pub has a jetty where customers can sit or opt to enjoy the quaint wood-beamed interiors, although the interior can get quite packed with sightseers. ✉ *117 Rotherhithe St., South Bank* ☎ *020/7237–4088* Ⓜ *Rotherhithe.*

COVENT GARDEN AND SOHO

COVENT GARDEN

Harp. This is the sort of friendly little local you might find on some out-of-the-way backstreet, except that it's right in the middle of town, between Trafalgar Square and Covent Garden. As a result, the Harp can get crowded, especially since it was named British pub of the year by the Campaign for Real Ale, but the squeeze is worth it for the excellent real ales (there are usually eight traditional ales available, often featuring rare brands) and a no-frills menu of high-quality British sausages, cooked behind the bar. ⊠ *47 Chandos Pl., Covent Garden* ☎ *020/7836–0291* Ⓜ *Charing Cross.*

Lamb & Flag. This refreshingly un-gentrified 17th-century pub was once known as the Bucket of Blood because the upstairs room was used as a ring for bare-knuckle boxing. Now it's a friendly—and bloodless—place, serving food (lunch only) and real ale. It's on the edge of Covent Garden, up a hidden alley off Garrick Street. ⊠ *33 Rose St., Covent Garden* ☎ *020/7497–9504* Ⓜ *Covent Garden.*

★ **White Hart.** Claiming to be the oldest licensed pub in London, this elegant, family-owned place on Drury Lane had already been here for more than 500 years when it served highwayman Dick Turpin in 1739 just before he was hanged. Nowadays it is one of the best places to mix with cast and crew of the stage. A female-friendly environment, a cheery skylight above the lounge area, and above-average pub fare make the White Hart a particularly sociable spot for a drink. ⊠ *191 Drury La., Covent Garden* ☎ *020/7242–2317* Ⓜ *Holborn, Covent Garden, Tottenham Court Rd.*

SOHO

French House. In the pub where the French Resistance convened during World War II, Soho hipsters and eccentrics rub shoulders now with theater people and the literati—more than shoulders, actually, because this tiny, tricolor-waving, photograph-lined pub is almost always packed. Note that in French style, beer is served in half-pints only. If you're around on July 14, come and join in the rapturous Bastille Day celebrations. ⊠ *49 Dean St., Soho* ☎ *020/7437–2799* ⊕ *www.frenchhousesoho. com* Ⓜ *Tottenham Court Rd.*

THE THAMES UPSTREAM

HAMMERSMITH

Blue Anchor. This unaltered Georgian pub has been seen in the movie *Sliding Doors* and was the site where *The Planets* composer Gustav Holst wrote his *Hammersmith Suite.* Sit out by the river, or shelter inside with a good ale. ⊠ *13 Lower Mall, Hammersmith* ☎ *020/8748–5774* ⊕ *www.blueanchorlondon.com* Ⓜ *Hammersmith.*

Dove Inn. Read the list of famous ex-regulars, from Charles II and Nell Gwyn to Ernest Hemingway, as you wait for a beer at this smart, comely, and popular 16th-century riverside pub by Hammersmith Bridge. After a few pints you can practice your singing skills to the English patriotic song that was composed here, "Rule, Britannia!" If (as is often the case) the Dove is too full, stroll upstream along the bank to the Old Ship or the Blue Anchor. ⊠ *19 Upper Mall, Hammersmith* ☎ *020/8748–9474* Ⓜ *Hammersmith.*

RICHMOND

Roebuck. Perched on top of Richmond Hill, the Roebuck has perhaps the best view of any pub in London. The most sought-after seats are the benches found directly across the road, which look out over the Thames as it winds its way into the countryside below. Friendly and

Order a pint at the 17th-century Lamb & Flag pub in Covent Garden.

surprisingly unpretentious, given its lofty surrounds, it is well worth the long climb up the hill from the center of Richmond. ✉ *130 Richmond Hill, Richmond* ☎ *020/3582–664* Ⓜ *Richmond.*

NIGHTLIFE

As is true of nearly all cosmopolitan centers, the pace with which bars and clubs go in and out of fashion in London is mind-boggling. New trends, likewise, emerge all time. In one recent development, the dreaded velvet rope has been usurped by the doorbell-ringing mystique of members-only drinking clubs. Some of the city's most talked-about nightlife spots these days are those attached to some of the best restaurants and hotels—no wonder, when you consider the increased popularity of London cuisine in international circles. Moreover, the gay scene in London continues to flourish. One constant on the nightlife scene is variety. The understated glamour of North London's Primrose Hill, which makes movie stars feel so at ease, might be considered dull by the über-trendy club goers of London's East End. Likewise, the price of a pint in Chelsea would be dubbed blasphemous by the musicians and poets of racially diverse Brixton.

Whatever your pleasure, however your whim turns come evening, chances are you'll find what you're looking for in London's ever-changing arena of activity and invention.

BARS

Time was, bars in London were just stopovers in an evening full of fun—perhaps the pub first, then a bar, and off to boogie the night away at the nearest dance club. These days, however, bars are not just pit stops but all-night or all-day destinations in themselves. With the addition of dinner menus, DJs, and dance floors, at many of London's most fashionable bars patrons stay into the wee small hours of the morning. The scene is known for its bizarre blends, its pioneering panache, and its highly stylish regulars. From exotic spaces designed to look like African villages to classic art deco creations to cavernous structures housed in old railway stations, London's bar culture is as diverse as it is delicious.

COMEDY AND CABARET

From renowned comedians such as Eddie Izzard to amateurs who try their luck on stage, in London you'll find plenty of comedy and cabaret acts to keep you entertained all night long.

DANCE CLUBS

The city that practically invented raves is always on the verge of creating something new, and on any given night there's a club playing the latest in dance music. Because London is so ethnically diverse, the tunes that emanate from the DJ box are equally varied—an amalgamation of sounds infusing drum 'n' bass, hip-hop, deep house, Latin house, breakbeat, indie, and R&B.

The club scene here ranges from mammoth-size playgrounds like Fabric and Cargo to more intimate venues where you can actually hear your friends talk. Check the daily listings in *Time Out* for "club nights," which are theme nights that take place the same night every week, sometimes at the same clubs but often shifting locations. Another good way to learn about club nights is by picking up flyers in your favorite bar.

ECLECTIC MUSIC

The eclectic music scene in London is constantly becoming more of a mishmash—the electro scene has evolved into the "nu rave" scene, and the constant arrival of new bands adds to the capital's already diverse music scene.

JAZZ AND BLUES

Jazz in London is highly eclectic. You can expect anything from danceable, smooth tunes played at a supper club to groovy New Orleans–style blues to exotic world-beat rhythms, which can be heard at some of the less central venues throughout the capital. London hosts the **London Jazz Festival** (⊕ *www.londonjazzfestival.org.uk*) in November, which showcases top and emerging artists in experimental jazz. The **Ealing Jazz Festival** (⊕ *www.ealing.gov.uk*), at the end of July, claims to be the biggest free jazz event in Europe.

ROCK

Ever since the Beatles hit the world stage in the early 1960s, London has been at the epicenter of rock and roll. The city is a given stop on any burgeoning or established band's international tour. Fans here are both loyal and enthusiastic. It is, therefore, a good idea to buy show tickets ahead of time. The "Gigs and Tickets" section on ⊕ *www.nme.com* is a

THE GAY SCENE

The U.K. capital's gay and lesbian culture is as thriving as it is in New York or Los Angeles, with Soho serving as the hub of gay London.

Clubs in London cater to almost every desire, whether that be the suited-up Tommy Hilfiger–look-alike scene, cruisers taking on dingy dives, flamboyant drag shows, lesbian tea dances, or themed fetish nights.

There's also a cornucopia of queer theater and performance art that runs throughout the year. Whatever your tastes, you'll be able to satisfy them with a night on the town in London.

Choices are admittedly much better for males than females here; although many of the gay clubs are female-friendly, those catering strictly to lesbians are in the minority.

The British Film Institute puts on the BFI London Lesbian and Gay Film Festival in late March and early April (⊕ www.bfi.org.uk/llgff) every year.

Pride London in June (an annual event encompassing a parade, sports, art, comedy, theater, music, cabaret, and dance) welcomes anyone and everyone, and claimed a million participants in 2010.

This extravagant pageant spirals its way through London's streets, with major events taking place in Trafalgar Square and Leicester Square, then culminates in Victoria Embankment with ticketed parties continuing on afterward (⊕ www.pridelondon.org for details).

For up-to-date listings, consult *Time Out* (⊕ www.timeout.com/london/gay), *Boyz* (⊕ www.boyz.co.uk), *Gay Times* (⊕ www.gaytimes.co.uk), *Attitude* (⊕ www.attitude.co.uk), or the lesbian monthly *Diva* (⊕ www.divamag.co.uk).

Online resources include Rainbow Network (⊕ www.rainbownetwork.com).

BARS, CAFÉS, AND PUBS
Most bars in London are gay-friendly, though there are a number of cafés and pubs that are known as gay hangouts after hours. The latest serve drinks until 3 am (11 pm on Sunday).

CLUBS
Many of London's best gay dance clubs are in mixed clubs like Fabric on theme nights designated for gays.

Almost all dance clubs in London are gay-friendly, but if you want to cruise or mingle only with other gays, it's best to call ahead or check website listings.

16

comprehensive search engine where you can easily book tickets online; *Time Out* is another good source for upcoming shows.

BLOOMSBURY, FITZROVIA

BLOOMSBURY
BARS
All Star Lanes. One of London's most chic bars is an unlikely combination—it's in a sleek, underground, retro bowling alley in the heart of literary Bloomsbury. Here, surrounded by 1950s Americana, you can sit

on the red leather seats and choose from the largest selection of bourbons in London. DJs play on Friday and Saturday nights; there are also locations in Bayswater, Brick Lane, and Stratford. ⊠ *Victoria House, Bloomsbury Pl., Bloomsbury* ☎ *020/7025–2676* ⊕ *www.allstarlanes. co.uk* ⊗ *Mon.–Wed. 5 pm–11:30 pm, Thurs. 5–midnight, Fri. and Sat. noon–2 am, Sun. noon–11* Ⓜ *Holborn.*

Booking Office. Taking full advantage of the soaring Victorian redbrick vaults and arches of the newly restored St. Pancras hotel, Booking Office is closer in feel to a cathedral than a traditional station bar. Seasonal cocktails using traditional English ingredients are high on flavor and low on mixers and there's live music Thursday through Saturday evenings. ⊠ *St Pancras Renaissance London Hotel, Euston Rd.* ☎ *020/7841–3566* ⊕ *www.bookingofficerestaurant.com* Ⓜ *King's Cross.*

ROCK

Water Rats. This high-spirited pub hosted Bob Dylan on his 1963 tour, as well as the first Oasis gig. Alt-country, hip-hop, and indie guitar bands thrash it out most nights of the week. ⊠ *328 Gray's Inn Rd., Bloomsbury* ☎ *020/7837–7269* ⊕ *www.themonto.com* 🎫 *£6 and up* ⊗ *Mon.–Sat. noon–11:30* Ⓜ *King's Cross.*

SOHO

ECLECTIC MUSIC

12 Bar Club. This small and rough-and-ready acoustic club hosts notable singer-songwriters. Four different acts of new folk, contemporary country, blues, and even ska and punk perform each night in the intimate venue. There's a good selection of bottled beer and gastropub food here. ⊠ *22–23 Denmark Pl., Soho* ☎ *020/7240–2622* ⊕ *www.12barclub.com* 🎫 *£3–£10* ⊗ *Fri. and Sat. 7 pm–3 am, Sun. 6 pm–12:30 am. Café serves food 9–9* Ⓜ *Tottenham Court Rd.*

FITZROVIA

Fodor'sChoice ★ **Crazy Bear.** This sexy basement bar with cowhide stools and croc-skin tables feels like Casablanca in Fitzrovia. As you enter Crazy Bear, a spiral staircase leads to a mirrored parlor over which presides a 1947 Murano chandelier. But don't let the opulence fool you: Waitstaff here are warm and welcoming to an all-ages international crowd abuzz with chatter. The menu advertises high-quality Thai, Chinese, and Japanese food alongside the drinks. ⊠ *26–28 Whitfield St., Fitzrovia* ☎ *020/7631–0088* ⊕ *www.crazybeargroup.co.uk* ⊗ *Sun.–Wed. noon–midnight, Thurs.–Sat. noon–1 am* Ⓜ *Goodge St.*

Long Bar at Sanderson Hotel. The 80-foot-long shimmering white onyx bar in the Philippe Starck–designed Sanderson Hotel attracts a trendy crowd, while the large but welcoming outdoor area exudes a relaxing, Zen-like feel, with soothing running water mixed with dim lighting and decorative vegetation. The hotel's **Purple Bar** provides a more intimate and romantic setting and serves excellent chocolate martinis. ⊠ *50 Berners St., Fitzrovia* ☎ *020/7300–5588* ⊕ *www.sandersonlondon.com* ⊗ *Mon. 11 am–1 am, Tues. and Wed. 11 am–1:30 am, Thurs.–Sat. 11 am–3 am, Sun. noon–10:30 pm* Ⓜ *Oxford Circus.*

THE EAST END

HOXTON

DANCE CLUBS

Fabric. This sprawling subterranean club is now a firm fixture on the London scene. "Fabric Live" hosts drum 'n' bass, dubstep, and hip-hop crews and live acts on Friday; international big-name DJs play slow, sexy bass lines and cutting-edge music on Saturday. The devastating sound system and "bodysonic" dance floor ensure that bass riffs vibrate through your entire body. ■TIP➜ Get there early to avoid a lengthy queue, and don't wear a suit. ⊠ *77A Charterhouse St., East End* ☎ *020/7336–8898* ⊕ *www.fabriclondon.com* ▦ *£15–£20* ⊙ *Fri. 10 pm–6 am, Sat. 11 pm–8 am, Sun. 11 pm–6 am* Ⓜ *Farringdon.*

SHOREDITCH

BARS

Book Club. Light and friendly, the Book Club tops off a dose of Shoreditch's fashionable industrial chic with a dollop of culture. White tiles, bricks, and big black-and-white photos set the tone and there's a separate room for table-tennis. Breakfast is served morning weekdays, a full lunch menu is offered through the week, and a modern menu of cocktails accompanies music, book launches, and workshops in the evenings. ⊠ *100 Leonard St., Shoreditch* ☎ *020/7684–8618* ⊕ *www. wearetbc.com* ⊙ *Mon.–Wed. 8 am–midnight, Thurs.–Sat. 8 am–2 am, Sun. 10 am–midnight.* Ⓜ *Shoreditch High St.*

Mason and Taylor. This hip industrial Shoreditch bar specializes in ales, lagers, and stouts from boutique producers and offers them in unique third-of-a-pint glasses on tasting boards, thus maximizing your chances of working your way through the menu. There's a tapas-style food menu through the week and brunches and roasts at weekends. ⊠ *51-55 Bethnal Green Rd, Shoreditch* ☎ *020/7749–9670* ⊕ *www.masonandtaylor. co.uk* Ⓜ *Shoreditch High St..*

DANCE CLUBS

Cargo. Housed under a series of old railway arches, this vast brick-wall bar, restaurant, dance floor, and live-music venue pulls a young, international crowd with its hip vibe and diverse selection of music. Long tables bring people together, as does the food, which draws on global influences and is served tapas-style. Drinks, though, are expensive. ⊠ *83 Rivington St., Shoreditch* ☎ *020/7739–3440* ⊕ *www.cargo-london.com* ▦ *Free–£20* ⊙ *Mon.–Thurs. noon–1 am, Fri. noon–3 am, Sat. 6 pm– 3 am, Sun. 1 pm–midnight* Ⓜ *Old St.*

333. Fashionable bright young Shoreditch things dance to indie rave, dubstep, twisted disco, and underground dance genres. There are three floors, each with its own theme. You can chill on leather sofas at the relaxed Mother Bar upstairs, which is open from 8 pm daily and always has DJs. ⊠ *333 Old St., Shoreditch* ☎ *020/7739–5949* ⊕ *www.333mother.com* ▦ *Free–£10* ⊙ *Fri. and Sat. 10 pm–3 am, bar Mon.–Sun., 8 pm–3 am* Ⓜ *Old St.*

16

KENSINGTON, CHELSEA, AND KNIGHTSBRIDGE

CHELSEA

JAZZ AND BLUES

606 Club. This civilized Chelsea club showcases mainstream and contemporary jazz by well-known British-based musicians. ■TIP➔ You must eat a meal in order to consume alcohol, so allow for an extra £20. Reservations are advisable. Sunday lunchtime jazz takes place once or twice a month; call ahead. ⊠ *90 Lots Rd., Chelsea* ☎ *020/7352–5953* ⊕ *www.606club.co.uk* 🍽 *£8–£12 music charge added to bill* ⊗ *Mon. 7:30 pm–12:30 am, Tues.–Thurs. 7 pm–12:30 am, Fri. and Sat. 8 pm–1:30 am, Sun. 7 pm–midnight* Ⓜ *Earl's Court, Fulham Broadway.*

KNIGHTSBRIDGE

BARS

Fodor's Choice ★ **The Blue Bar at the Berkeley Hotel.** With low-slung gray-blue walls, this hotel bar is ever so slightly sexy. Immaculate service, an excellent cocktail list—try the Sex in the City—and a trendy David Collins design make this an ideal spot for a secretive tête-à-tête, complete with jazzy music in the background. ⊠ *Wilton Pl., Knightsbridge* ☎ *020/7235–6000* ⊕ *the-berkeley.co.uk* ⊗ *Mon. 4 pm–1 am, Tues.–Sat. 9 am–1 am, Sun. 4–11 pm* Ⓜ *Knightsbridge.*

NOTTING HILL

BARS

Beach Blanket Babylon. In a Georgian house in Notting Hill, close to Portobello Market, this always-packed bar is distinguishable by its eclectic indoor-outdoor spaces with Gaudí-esque curves and snuggly corners—like a fairy-tale grotto or a medieval dungeon. A sister restaurant-bar-gallery offers a slightly more modern take on similar themes in an ex-warehouse in Shoreditch (at 19 Bethnal Green Road). ⊠ *45 Ledbury Rd., Notting Hill* ☎ *020/7229–2907* ⊕ *www.beachblanket. co.uk* ⊗ *Tues.–Sun. noon–midnight, Mon. 5 pm–midnight* Ⓜ *Notting Hill Gate.*

DANCE CLUBS

★ **Notting Hill Arts Club.** Rock stars like Liam Gallagher and Courtney Love have been seen at this small basement club-bar. What the place lacks in looks it makes up for in mood, and an alternative crowd swills beer to eclectic music that spans Asian underground, hip-hop, Latin-inspired funk, deep house, and jazzy grooves. ⊠ *21 Notting Hill Gate, Notting Hill* ☎ *020/7460–4459* ⊕ *www.nottinghillartsclub.com* 🍽 *Free–£8* ⊗ *Weekdays 7 pm–2 am, Sat. 4 pm–2 am, Sun. 4 pm–1 am* Ⓜ *Notting Hill Gate.*

ST. JAMES'S AND MAYFAIR

MAYFAIR

BARS

Fodor's Choice ★ **Claridge's Bar.** This elegant Mayfair meeting place remains unpretentious even when it brims with beautiful people. The bar has an art deco heritage made hip by the sophisticated touch of designer David

Cargo dance club is a huge venue for live music of all types.

Collins. A library of rare champagnes and brandies as well as a delicious choice of traditional and exotic cocktails—try the Flapper or the Black Pearl—will occupy your taste buds. Request a glass of vintage Cristal in the Macanudo Fumoir. ⊠ *55 Brook St., Mayfair* ☎ *020/7629–8860* ⊕ *www.claridges.co.uk* ✆ *Mon.–Sat. noon–1 am, Sun. noon–midnight* Ⓜ *Bond St.*

JAZZ AND BLUES

Dover Street Restaurant & Jazz Bar. Put on your blue-suede shoes and prepare to dance the night away—that is, after you've feasted from the French Mediterranean menu. Fun for dates as well as groups, Dover Street Restaurant has three bars, a DJ, and a stage with the latest live bands performing everything from jazz to soul to R&B, all this encircling linen-covered tables with a friendly staff catering to your every whim. ⊠ *8–10 Dover St., Mayfair* ☎ *020/7491–7509* ⊕ *www.doverst. co.uk* ✆ *£7–£15* ✆ *Mon.–Thurs. 5:30 pm–3 am, Fri. and Sat. 7 pm–3 am* Ⓜ *Green Park.*

ST. JAMES'S

BARS

★ **American Bar.** Festooned with a chin-dropping array of club ties, signed celebrity photographs, sporting mementos, and baseball caps, this sensational hotel cocktail bar has superb martinis. ■ TIP➜ Jacket required. ⊠ *Stafford Hotel, 16–18 St. James's Pl., St. James's* ☎ *020/7493–0111* ⊕ *www.thestaffordhotel.co.uk* ✆ *Weekdays 11:30–11, weekends noon–11* Ⓜ *Green Park.*

The Thameside Bulls Head has live jazz every night.

THE SOUTH

BRIXTON
BARS

★ **Dogstar.** This popular South London hangout is frequented by local hipsters and counterculture types. It was the first DJ bar in the world and has since enjoyed a fabulous reputation. The vibe at this "surrealist boudoir" is unpretentious, with top-name DJs playing cutting-edge sounds every night (free Tuesday–Thursday) and pizza for sale until midnight. ✉ *389 Coldharbour La., Brixton* ☎ *020/7733–7515* ⊕ *www.antic-ltd. com/dogstar* 🖅 *Free–£8* ⊗ *Tues.–Thurs. 4 pm–2 am, Fri. 4 pm–4 am, Sat. noon–4 am, Sun. noon–10:30 pm* Ⓜ *Brixton.*

DANCE CLUBS

Mass. In what was previously St. Matthew's Church (whose crypt now houses the Babalou bar), Mass is an atmospheric club with Gothic overtones. Winding stone steps lead to the main room where an extended balcony hangs over the dance floor. An unpretentious and friendly crowd dances, on rotating club nights, to reggae, drum 'n' bass, and R&B. ✉ *Brixton Hill, St. Matthew's Church, Brixton* ☎ *020/7738–7875* ⊕ *www.mass-club.com* 🖅 *£5–£20* ⊗ *Wed. and Thurs. 10 pm–2 am, Fri. and Sat. 9 pm–6 am* Ⓜ *Brixton.*

ECLECTIC MUSIC

Fodor's Choice **O2 Academy Brixton.** This legendary Brixton venue has seen it all—mods
★ and rockers, hippies and punks—and it remains one of the city's top indie and rock venues. Despite a capacity for almost 5,000, this refurbished Victorian hall with original art deco fixtures retains a clublike charm; it has plenty of bars and upstairs seating. ✉ *211 Stockwell Rd.,*

Brixton ☎ *020/7771–3000* ⊕ *www.brixton-academy.co.uk* 🎫 *£10–£50* ⊙ *Opening hrs vary* Ⓜ *Brixton.*

SOUTH BANK

DANCE CLUBS

Ministry of Sound. It's more of an industry than a club, with its own record label, online radio station, and international DJs. The stripped-down warehouse-style club has a super sound system and pulls in the world's most legendary names in dance. There are chill-out rooms, two bars, and three dance floors. ⊠ *103 Gaunt St., South Bank* ☎ *020/740–8600* ⊕ *www.ministryofsound.com* 🎫 *£15–£23* ⊙ *Fri. 10:30 pm–6 am, Sat. 11 pm–7 am* Ⓜ *Elephant & Castle.*

SOHO AND COVENT GARDEN

LEICESTER SQUARE

BARS

Le Beaujolais. Around 60 lovingly selected French wines are available, and you can snack on olives, charcuterie, and homemade *croque monsieur* (grilled ham and cheese) sandwiches while snug and warm under the bottle-laden ceiling as a funky blues sound track plays. The romantically shabby-around-the-edges feel and authentically French insouciance may come as a surprise in the heart of tourist-centric London. ⊠ *25 Litchfield St., Leicester Square* ☎ *020/7836–2955* ⊙ *Weekdays noon–11, Sat. 5–11* Ⓜ *Leicester Sq.*

★ **Le Salon Bar.** Renowned chef Joël Robuchon's intimate, relaxed, and elegant bar with red undertones is in the same premises as his L'Atelier and La Cuisine restaurants. New cocktails await you, as the drink menu changes every six months, with new flavors and textures sure to entice your taste buds. ⊠ *13–15 West St., Leicester Square* ☎ *020/7010–8600* ⊕ *www.joel-robuchon.com* ⊙ *Mon.–Sat. 2:30 pm–2 am, Sun. 2:30 pm–10:30 pm* Ⓜ *Leicester Sq.*

COVENT GARDEN

BARS

Cafe des Amis. This relaxed basement wine bar near the Royal Opera House is the perfect pre- or post-theater spot, popular among musicians and performers alike. More than 30 wines are served by the glass, along with a good selection of cheeses and plates of charcuterie as well as more substantial dishes for those with more of an appetite (there's also a French restaurant with a Mediterranean twist on the ground floor serving everything from moules marinières to risotto). ⊠ *11–14 Hanover Pl., Covent Garden* ☎ *020/7379–3444* ⊕ *www.cafedesamis.co.uk* ⊙ *Mon.–Sat. noon–11:30 pm, Sun. noon–8 pm* Ⓜ *Covent Garden.*

Terroirs. Specializing in "natural wines" (organic and sustainably produced with minimal added ingredients), Terroirs has an unusually careful selection of 200 wines from artisan French and Italian winemakers. These are served, along with charcuterie, tapas, and more substantial French-inspired dishes, at a bar and tables in white-washed, wooden-floored environs. ⊠ *5 William St., Covent Garden* ☎ *020/7036–0660* ⊙ *Mon.–Sat. noon–11 pm* Ⓜ *Covent Garden.*

16

THE GAY SCENE

Fodor's Choice

★

Heaven. With the best light show on any London dance floor, Heaven is unpretentious, loud, and huge, with a labyrinth of rooms, bars, and live-music parlors. Friday and Saturday nights there's a gay comedy night (£10 in advance, 7–10 pm). If you go to just one gay club in London, Heaven should be it. ✉ *The Arches, Villiers St., Covent Garden* ☎ *020/7930–2020* ⊕ *www.heaven-london.com* ⊠ *£4–£12* ⊙ *Mon. 11 pm–6 am, Tues.–Thurs. 11 pm–5 am, Wed. 10:30 pm–4 am, Fri. 11 pm–5 am, Sat. 10:30 pm–5 am* Ⓜ *Charing Cross, Embankment.*

SOHO

BARS

★ **Nordic.** With shooters called "Husky Poo" and "Danish Bacon Surprise" and crayfish tails and meatballs on the smorgasbord menu, Nordic takes its Scandinavian feel the whole way. This secluded, shabby-chic bar serves many couples cozied up among travel brochures promoting the Viking lands. If you can't decide what to drink, the cocktail roulette wheel on the wall may help. ✉ *25 Newman St., Soho* ☎ *020/7631–3174* ⊕ *www.nordicbar.com* ⊙ *Mon.–Thurs. noon–11 pm, Fri. noon–midnight, Sat. 6 pm–midnight* Ⓜ *Tottenham Court Rd.*

Sketch. One seat never looks like the next at this collection of esoteric living-room bars. The exclusive Parlour Bar, a patisserie during the day, exudes plenty of rarefied charm; the intimate East Bar at the back is reminiscent of a sci-fi film set; and in the Glade it's permanently sunset. ✉ *9 Conduit St., Soho* ☎ *020/7659–4500* ⊕ *www.sketch.uk.com* ⊙ *Parlour Bar Mon.–Thurs. 6:30–10 pm, Fri. and Sat. 6:30–9 pm, members only after 9 pm; East Bar 7 pm–2 am; The Glade 6 pm–2 am* Ⓜ *Oxford Circus.*

COMEDY AND CABARET

Amused Moose. This Soho basement/retro nightclub is often considered the best place to see breaking talent as well as household names doing "secret" shows. Ricky Gervais, Eddie Izzard, and Russell Brand are among those who have graced the stage, and every summer a handful of the Edinburgh Fringe comedians preview here. The bar is open late (and serves food), and there's a DJ and dancing until 5 am after the show. Tickets are often discounted with a printout from their website, and shows are mainly on Saturday. ✉ *Moonlighting, 17 Greek St., Soho* ☎ *020/7287–3727* ⊕ *www.amusedmoose.com* ⊠ *£9 and up* ⊙ *Doors open at 7:30 pm* Ⓜ *Tottenham Court Rd.*

★ **Comedy Store.** Known as the birthplace of alternative comedy, this is where the United Kingdom's funniest stand-ups have cut their teeth before being launched onto prime-time TV. Comedy Store Players, a team with six comedians doing improvisation with audience suggestions, entertain on Wednesday and Sunday; the Cutting Edge steps in every Tuesday. Thursday, Friday, and Saturday with the best stand-up acts. There's also a bar with food. Note that children under 18 are not admitted to this venue. ✉ *1A Oxendon St., Soho* ☎ *0844/847–1728* ⊕ *www.thecomedystore.co.uk* ⊠ *£13–£18* ⊙ *Shows daily 8 pm, with extra shows Fri. and Sat. at midnight* Ⓜ *Piccadilly Circus, Leicester Sq.*

100 Club. Since this small club opened in 1942, many of the greats have played here, from Glenn Miller and Louis Armstrong to The Who and the Sex Pistols. Saved from closure in 2010 by a campaign led by Paul McCartney, the space now reverberates to jazz and northern soul. ✉ *100 Oxford St., Soho* ☎ *020/7636–0933* ⊕ *www.the100club.co.uk* 💷 *£7–£15* ⊙ *Mon. 7:30–midnight, Tues.–Thurs. 7:30–11, Fri. 7:30 pm–12:30 am, Sat. 7:30 pm–2 am, Sun. 7:30–11* Ⓜ *Oxford Circus, Tottenham Court Rd.*

Fodor'sChoice ★ **Soho Theatre.** This innovative theater's programs include comedy shows by established acts and up-and-coming comedians and new writers. The refurbished Soho Theatre Bar has a late license until 1am for members and ticket holders. Check local listings or the website for what's on, and book tickets in advance. ✉ *21 Dean St., Soho* ☎ *020/7478–0100* ⊕ *www.sohotheatre.com* 💷 *£10–£22.50* ⊙ *Mon.–Sat. usually 7–11 although show times vary* Ⓜ *Tottenham Court Rd.*

JAZZ AND BLUES

Ain't Nothin' but . . . The Blues Bar. The name sums up this bar that whips up a sweaty environment. Local musicians, as well as some notable names, squeeze onto the tiny stage. There's good bar food of the chili-and-gumbo variety. Most weekday nights there's no cover. ✉ *20 Kingly St., Soho* ☎ *020/7287–0514* ⊕ *www.aintnothinbut.co.uk* 💷 *Free–£5* ⊙ *Mon.–Thurs. 5 pm–1 am, Fri. 5 pm–2:30 am, Sat. 3 pm–2:30 am, Sun. 3 pm–midnight* Ⓜ *Oxford Circus.*

Fodor'sChoice ★ **Pizza Express Jazz Club Soho.** One of the capital's most ubiquitous pizza chains also runs a great Soho jazz venue. The dimly lighted restaurant hosts top-quality international jazz acts every night. The Italian-style thin-crust pizzas are good, too, though on the small side. ✉ *10 Dean St., Soho* ☎ *0845/602–7017* ⊕ *www.pizzaexpresslive.com* 💷 *£10–£25* ⊙ *Daily from 11:30 am for food; music 7:30 pm–11 pm* Ⓜ *Tottenham Court Rd.*

Ronnie Scott's. This legendary jazz club has attracted big names since the 1960s. It's usually crowded and hot, the food isn't great, and service is slow—but the mood can't be beat, even since the sad departure of the eponymous founder and saxophonist. Reservations are recommended. ✉ *47 Frith St., Soho* ☎ *020/7439–0747* ⊕ *www.ronniescotts.co.uk* 💷 *£20–£36 nonmembers, 20% off for members, annual membership £175* ⊙ *Mon.–Sat. 6 pm–3 am, Sun. 6:30 pm–11 pm* Ⓜ *Leicester Sq.*

THE GAY SCENE

Candy Bar. London's top girls' bar is intimate, chilled, and cruisey, with DJs mixing the latest sounds. Pole dancing and striptease are also featured on some nights. Men are welcome only as guests of female patrons. ✉ *4 Carlisle St., Soho* ☎ *020/7287–5041* ⊕ *www.candybarsoho.com* 💷 *Free–£5* ⊙ *Mon.–Sat. 1 pm–3 am, Sun. 1 pm–12:30 am* Ⓜ *Tottenham Court Rd.*

Fodor'sChoice ★ **Friendly Society.** This haute moderne hot spot hops with activity almost any night of the week; the basement feels a bit like something out of *Star Trek* with its white-leather pod seats. The place is known for being gay yet female-friendly. ✉ *79 Wardour St., Soho* ☎ *020/7434–3805* ⊙ *Weekdays 4–11, Sat. 2–11, Sun. 2–10:30* Ⓜ *Leicester Sq.*

16

Rupert Street. For smart boyz, this gay chic island among the sleaze has a lounge feel with brown-leather sofas and floor-to-ceiling windows. It's crowded and cruisey at night with preclubbers, bright, civilized and cafélike by day and a good spot for brunch. Traditional British food is served until 10 pm. ⊠ *50 Rupert St., Soho* ☎ *020/7494–3059* ⊗ *Mon.–Wed. noon–11, Thurs.–Sat. noon–11:30, Sun. noon–10:30* Ⓜ *Leicester Sq., Piccadilly Circus.*

★ **The Shadow Lounge.** This fabulous little lounge and dance club glitters with faux jewels and twinkling fiber-optic lights over its sunken dance floor, which comes complete with pole for those inclined to do their thing around it. It has a serious A-list celebrity factor, with the glamorous London glitterati camping out in the VIP booth. Members are given entrance priority when the place gets full, especially on weekends, so show up early, book onto the guest list online, or prepare to queue. Free entry on Monday. ⊠ *5 Brewer St., Soho* ☎ *020/7317–9270* ⊕ *www.theshadowlounge.co.uk* ☎ *£5–£10* ⊗ *Mon.–Sat. 10 pm–3 am; occasionally open Sun.* Ⓜ *Leicester Sq.*

REGENT'S PARK AND HAMPSTEAD

CAMDEN

DANCE CLUBS

★ **KOKO.** This Victorian theater, formerly known as Camden Palace, has seen acts from Charlie Chaplin to Madonna, and genres from punk to rave. Updated with lush reds not unlike a cockney Moulin Rouge, this is still one of London's most stunning venues. Sounds of live indie rock, cabaret, funky house, and club classics keep the big dance floor moving, even when it's not heaving. ⊠ *1A Camden High St., Camden Town* ☎ *0870/432–5527* ⊕ *www.koko.uk.com* ☎ *£3–£20* ⊗ *Opening hrs vary, depending on shows* Ⓜ *Mornington Crescent.*

JAZZ AND BLUES

★ **Jazz Café.** A palace of high-tech cool in bohemian Camden remains an essential hangout for fans of both the mainstream end of the jazz repertoire and hip-hop, funk, world music, and Latin fusion. It's also the unlikely venue for Saturday "I Love the 80s" nights. Book ahead if you want a prime table in the balcony restaurant overlooking the stage. ⊠ *5 Parkway, Camden Town* ☎ *020/7688–8899 restaurant reservations, 020/7485–6834 venue info, 0844/847–2514 tickets (Ticketmaster)* ⊕ *venues.meanfiddler.com/jazz-cafe/home* ☎ *£6–£35* ⊗ *Daily 7 pm–2 am* Ⓜ *Camden Town.*

ROCK

★ **Barfly Club.** At one of the finest small clubs in the capital, punk, indie guitar bands, and new metal rock attract a nonmainstream crowd. Weekend club nights upstairs host DJs (and live bands) who rock the decks. ⊠ *49 Chalk Farm Rd., Camden Town* ☎ *020/7424–0800 venue, 0844/847–2424 tickets* ⊕ *www.barflyclub.com* ☎ *£5–£11* ⊗ *Mon. and Tues. 7–midnight, Wed. and Thurs. 7 pm–2 am, Fri. and Sat. 7 pm–3 am* Ⓜ *Camden Town, Chalk Farm.*

ISLINGTON
ECLECTIC
 Union Chapel. The beauty of this sublime old chapel and its impressive multicultural programming make this spot one of London's best musical venues, especially for acoustic shows. Performers have included Björk, Beck, and Goldfrapp, though now you're more likely to hear lower-key alternative country, world music, and jazz, alongside poetry and literary events. ⊠ *Compton Terr., Islington* ☎ *020/7226–1686 venue (no box office; ticket sales numbers vary with each event)* ⊕ *www.unionchapel. org.uk* ☖ *Free–£25* ⊗ *Opening hrs vary* Ⓜ *Highbury & Islington.*

KENTISH TOWN
ROCK
The HMV Forum. The best medium-to-big-name rock performers consistently play at this 2,000-capacity club. It's a converted 1920 art deco cinema, with a balcony overlooking the grungy dance floor. ⊠ *9–17 Highgate Rd., Kentish Town* ☎ *020/7428–4099 venue, 0843/221–0100 tickets* ⊕ *www.meanfiddler.com* ☖ *£12–£25* ⊗ *Opening hrs vary, depending on concert schedule* Ⓜ *Kentish Town.*

LITTLE VENICE
COMEDY AND CABARET
Canal Café Theatre. Famous comics and cabaret stars perform every night of the week in this intimate, canal-side venue. The long-running News-Revue is a topical song-and-sketch show performed Thursday–Sunday evenings. ⊠ *Bridge House, Delamere Terr., Little Venice* ☎ *020/7289–6054* ⊕ *www.canalcafetheatre.com* ☖ *£5–£11* ⊗ *Mon.–Sat. 7:30–11, Sun. 7–10:30* Ⓜ *Warwick Ave., Royal Oak, Paddington.*

16

WESTMINSTER

CHARING CROSS
BARS
Bedford and Strand. The wine bar enjoyed something of a renaissance in the first decade of the 21st century in London, and this is one of the best of a new generation. It's sunk atmospherically down below the streets of Covent Garden, with dark wood and hanging shades; the wine list is short but well chosen, the service is faultless, and the bistro food is created with plenty of care. ⊠ *1A Bedford St., Charing Cross* ☎ *020/ 7836–3033* ⊕ *www.bedford-strand.com* ⊗ *Weekdays noon–midnight, Sat. 5 pm–midnight* Ⓜ *Charing Cross.*

HAYMARKET
BARS
The Mint Leaf Bar. The renowned long bar is stocked with more than 500 spirits and serves more than 1,000 well-prepared cocktails. Nibbles and light snacks with an Indian twist are available, and if you're up for some more substantial spicy food, treat yourself to a meal at the sophisticated restaurant. There is a sister bar and restaurant in Angel Court in The City. ⊠ *Suffolk Pl., Haymarket* ☎ *020/7930–9020* ⊕ *www. mintleafrestaurant.com* ⊗ *Mon.–Wed. noon–midnight, Thurs. and Fri. noon–1 am, Sat. 5 pm–1 am, Sun. 5 pm–midnight* Ⓜ *Piccadilly Circus.*

VICTORIA
DANCE CLUBS

Pacha. London's version of the Ibizan superclub is in a restored 1920s dance hall next to Victoria Coach station. The hedonistic surroundings include a (smoking) roof terrace for alfresco clubbing and a state-of-the-art VIP room. The stylish crowd is slightly older than average, but not necessarily as moneyed as you might expect. ⊠ *Terminus Pl., Victoria* 🕾 *0845/371–4489* ⊕ *www.pachalondon.com* 🗐 *£5–£20* ⊗ *Fri. and Sat. 10 pm–5 am* Ⓜ *Victoria.*

WESTMINSTER
BARS

Cinnamon Club. In the basement of what was once Old Westminster Library, the Club Bar of this contemporary Indian restaurant (treat yourself to a superb curry) has Bollywood scenes projected onto the glass back wall, Asian-theme cocktails (mango mojitos, Delhi mules), delicious bar snacks, and a clientele that includes fashionable young politicos. Upstairs, the Library Bar also serves cocktails through the day. ⊠ *The Old Westminster Library, Great Smith St., Westminster* 🕾 *020/7222–2555* ⊕ *www.cinnamonclub.com* ⊗ *Mon.–Sat. 6 pm–11:45 pm* Ⓜ *Westminster.*

Arts and Entertainment

WORD OF MOUTH

"We bought standing-room tickets to the Proms which go on sale a couple of hours before the concert. You don't really stand but sit on the floor in the top gallery. It's like a big picnic. It was fun!"

—Marija

Updated by
Julius Honnor

"All the world's a stage," said Shakespeare, immortal words heard for the first time right here in London. And whether you prefer your theater, music, and art classical or modern, or as contemporary twists on time-honored classics, you'll find that London's vibrant cultural scene holds its own on the world stage.

Divas sing original-language librettos at the Royal Opera House, Shakespeare's plays are brought to life at the reconstructed Globe Theatre, and challenging new writing is produced at the Royal Court. Whether you feel like basking in the lighthearted extravagance of a West End musical or taking in the next shark-in-formaldehyde at the White Cube, the choice is yours.

Shakespearean theater and contemporary musicals, enormous art installations and tiny Renaissance portraits, magnificent operas and cutting-edge physical theater—if you're into going out, London will suit your fancy. There are international theater festivals, innovative music festivals, and critically acclaimed seasons of postmodern dance. Short trip or long, you'll find the cultural scene in London is ever-changing, ever-expanding, and ever-exciting.

After starting out with the two main performing arts centers in London—the Barbican Centre and the Southbank Centre—this chapter is organized alphabetically by neighborhood. Within each neighborhood is a list of the main art or performing arts venue. In addition, "What's Happening Now" boxes highlight the current state of the arts in each of the main art groups, such as Dance, Theater, Opera, and Film. No matter where you head, you'll find that London's art and performing arts scenes have been setting global trends for decades—and when you include Shakespearean theater and Handel oratorios, for centuries. Fringe theater, classical ballet, participatory chorales, you name it, London probably did it first and often does it best.

PLANNING

TOP FIVE FOR THE ARTS

Stand with the "plebs" in Shakespeare's Globe Theatre. There are seats, but to really experience theater Shakespearean-style you should stand in the yard, with the stage at eye level (plus it's a bargain at £5).

Visit the latest grand art installation in the Turbine Hall at the Tate Modern. The enormity of the Tate's central space either intimidates or inspires artists challenged to fill it.

Catch a world-class performance at the Proms. There's a surprisingly down-to-earth atmosphere among the elated company at these great concerts.

Enjoy a night at the National Film Theatre. Mingle with the real aficionados at screenings of foreign, classic, and experimental films.

Watch a Hollywood star in a West End production. Film stars often come to London to boost their artistic credibility in small-scale theaters.

TOP THEATER TIPS

Behind the pillars. Many theaters and concert halls sell discounted seats with restricted views.

Matinees. Afternoon performances are almost always a better value than evening ones.

Previews. Tickets to shows are usually less expensive in the first few weeks of their run, before the critics have had their say.

Monday. Most cinemas and some theaters, including the Royal Court, have a reduced-price ticketing policy on Monday.

Standing. The Globe Theatre and the Proms are the two most prominent occasions where remaining upright saves you money.

FIND OUT WHAT'S PLAYING WHERE

To find out what's showing now, the weekly magazine *Time Out* (£3.25, issued every Tuesday) is invaluable.

The free *Evening Standard* carries listings, many of which are also available online at ⊕ *www.thisislondon.co.uk*. *Metro*, London's other widely available free newspaper, is also worth checking out, as are many Sunday papers, and the Saturday *Independent, Guardian,* and *Times*.

You can pick up the free fortnightly *London Theatre Guide* from hotels and tourist-information centers.

There are hundreds of small private galleries all over London with interesting work by famous and not-yet-famous artists.

The bimonthly free pamphlet "new exhibitions of contemporary art" (⊕ *www.newexhibitions.com*), available at most galleries, lists and maps nearly 200 art spaces in London.

17

THE TWO MAIN PERFORMING ARTS CENTERS

🌣 **Barbican Centre.** Opened in 1982, the Brutalist-style Barbican is the largest performing arts center in Europe. The main concrete theater is most famous as the home of the London Symphony Orchestra. As well as the LSO (⊕ *www.lso.co.uk*), the Barbican is also the frequent host of

Random Dance Company performs at Sadler's Wells.

the English Chamber Orchestra and the BBC Symphony Orchestra, and has an excellent concert season of big-name virtuosos. Performances by British and international theater companies make up part of its year-round **B.I.T.E.** (Barbican International Theatre Events), which also features groundbreaking performance, dance, drama, and musical theater. Innovative exhibitions of 20th-century and current art and design are shown in the Barbican Gallery and the Curve (usually free). In addition to Hollywood films, obscure classics and film festivals with Screen Talks are programmed in the three cinemas here. Saturday Family Film Club has adventure and animation to please all ages. You could catch "The Directorspective" on the films of Andrei Konchalovsky, see a fashion performance inspired by Japan, check out some Senegalese music, and peruse an exhibition on efficiency and elegance in building design, all in one evening. ⊠ *Silk St., The City* ☎ *020/7638–8891 box office* ⊕ *www.barbican.org.uk* ⊗ *Mon–Sat 9 am–11 pm, Sun noon–11 pm* Ⓜ *Barbican.*

★ **Southbank Centre.** The Royal Festival Hall is one of London's best spaces for large-scale choral and orchestral works and is home to the Philharmonia and London Philharmonic orchestras. Other venues in the Southbank Centre host smaller-scale music performances: The Queen Elizabeth Hall is a popular venue for chamber orchestras and top-tier soloists, and the intimate Purcell Room is known for chamber music and solo recitals. Southbank also hosts everything from the London International Mime festival to large-scale dance performances, including a diverse and exciting season of international and British-based contemporary dance companies. Also part of the complex is the **Hayward**

THE ARTS FOR FREE

CLASSICAL MUSIC AND JAZZ

The Barbican, the Royal National Theatre, and the Royal Opera House often have free music in their foyers or in dedicated spaces, usually of high standard. On the South Bank, free festivals and special performances often take place alongside the river.

Many of London's world-class music colleges give free concerts several times a week. The Royal Academy of Music and the Royal College of Music often have free recitals. St. Martin-in-the-Fields has free lunchtime concerts, as does Christchurch Spitalfields. Other churches, including Westminster Abbey, St. James's Piccadilly, and St. Paul's in Covent Garden, also have frequent free music. For the Proms, which run from July to September at the Royal Albert Hall, good seats are expensive, but hundreds of standing tickets are available at £5: not quite free, but a good value.

CONTEMPORARY MUSIC

Brixton's Dogstar pub has a great selection of DJs playing for free on weekday evenings. Ain't Nothing But the Blues Bar in Soho has live music most nights, often without a cover charge, and pubs such as the Monarch and the Hawley Arms near Camden Market offer the chance to see tomorrow's indie stars today. The largest of the music superstores, such as HMV Oxford Street, have occasional live performances of pop and rock bands, often to accompany album or single launches.

DRAMA AND PERFORMANCE ARTS

Look out for occasional festivals where innovative performances take place on the South Bank. Check the newspapers and *Time Out* for upcoming performances.

MUSEUMS AND GALLERIES

Few if any other cities in the world equal the number of free art venues offered in London. Most of the city's museums and galleries do not charge entrance fees. The monthly *Galleries* magazine, available from galleries themselves or online at ⊕ www.galleries.co.uk, has listings for all private galleries in the capital.

PARK LIFE

London's parks come to life in summer with a wide-ranging program of music, dance, and visual arts (⊕ *www.royalparks.gov.uk* for details or ☎ *020/7298–2000*). There are several summer festivals in London parks, some with lots of big-name pop stars, like the Wireless festival in Hyde Park and the somewhat more indie Lovebox in Victoria Park. Notable contemporary art fairs are October's Frieze in Regent's Park (⊕ *www. friezeartfair.com*) and the Affordable Art Fair in Battersea Park in spring (⊕ *www.affordableartfair.com*).

RADIO AND TELEVISION

With so much broadcast material made in London, much of it recorded in front of live audiences, there are often opportunities to watch a free quiz show, current-affairs debate, comedy, or even drama. Check the BBC website for forthcoming recordings (⊕ *www.bbc.co.uk/tickets*). **Hat Trick Productions** (☎ *020/184– 7777* ⊕ *www.hattrick.co.uk*) makes a number of good comedy programs, including the satirical current-affairs program *Have I Got News for You.*

17

For London's most glamorous night out, book seats for a performance at the Royal Opera House.

Gallery (Saturday–Wednesday 10–6, Thursday and Friday 10–8 during exhibitions), a landmark Brutalist-style 1960s building and one of London's major venues for contemporary art exhibitions. ⊠ *Belvedere Rd., South Bank* ☎ *020/7960–4200* ⊕ *www.southbankcentre.co.uk* Ⓜ *Waterloo.*

BLOOMSBURY, ISLINGTON, KILBURN, AND KING'S CROSS

BLOOMSBURY

DANCE

Peacock Theatre. Sadler's Wells's West End annex, this modernist theater near the London School of Economics (which uses it as a lecture hall during the day) focuses on younger companies and shows in popular dance genres like flamenco, tango, and hip-hop. ⊠ *Portugal St., Holborn* ☎ *020/7863–8065, 0844/412–4300 booking office* ⊕ *www.sadlerswells.com/page/peacock-theatre* Ⓜ *Holborn.*

The Place. The Robin Howard Dance Theatre is London's only theater dedicated to contemporary dance, and with tickets around £15 it's good value, too. "Resolution!" is the United Kingdom's biggest platform event for new choreographers. ⊠ *17 Duke's Rd., Bloomsbury* ☎ *020/7121–1100* ⊕ *www.theplace.org.uk* Ⓜ *Euston.*

ISLINGTON

ART GALLERY

Victoria Miro Gallery. This important commercial gallery has exhibited some of the biggest names on the British contemporary art scene—Chris Ofili, the Chapman brothers, and Peter Doig, to name a few. It also brings in exciting new talent from abroad. ⊠ *16 Wharf Rd., Islington* ☎ *020/7336–8109* ⊕ *www.victoria-miro.com* ⊠ *Free* ⊗ *Tues.–Sat. 10–6* Ⓜ *Old St., Angel.*

DANCE

Fodor'sChoice ★ **Sadler's Wells.** This gleaming building opened in 1998, the seventh on the site in its 300-year history, and is devoted to presenting leading classical and contemporary dance companies. The Random Dance Company is in residence, and the little Lilian Bayliss Theatre hosts avant-garde work. ⊠ *Rosebery Ave., Islington* ☎ *0844/412–4300 booking office, 020/7863-8198 general inquiries* ⊕ *www.sadlerswells.com* Ⓜ *Angel.*

THEATER

★ **Almeida Theatre.** This Off–West End venue premieres excellent new plays and exciting twists on the classics, often featuring high-profile actors. There's a good cafe and a licensed bar that serves "sharing dishes" as well as tasty main courses. ⊠ *Almeida St., Islington* ☎ *020/7359–4404* ⊕ *www.almeida.co.uk* Ⓜ *Angel, Highbury & Islington.*

KILBURN

FILM AND THEATER

Tricycle Theatre. The Tricycle is committed to representing the cultural diversity of its community and shows the best in black, Irish, Jewish, Asian, and South African drama, and also promotes new work. There is a gallery and cinema, too: Expect the best of new European and international cinema, including films from the United States, occasionally screened at film festivals the theater organizes. A year-round program of film-related activities is geared to children, and discounted cinema tickets are available on Monday. ⊠ *269 Kilburn High Rd., Kilburn* ☎ *020/7372–6611 information, 020/7328–1000 box office* ⊕ *www. tricycle.co.uk* Ⓜ *Kilburn.*

KING'S CROSS

CLASSICAL MUSIC

Kings Place. This airy concert venue opened in October 2008 near the Eurostar terminal in King's Cross, and is the permanent home of the London Sinfonietta and the Orchestra of the Age of Enlightenment. It offers weeklong programs by musicians in a range of genres, and the London Chamber Music Society performs Sunday concerts. There's also a hugely varied cultural calendar of jazz, comedy, folk, and political and literary lectures. ⊠ *90 York Way, King's Cross* ☎ *020/7520–1490 box office, 020/7520–1440 inquiries* ⊕ *www.kingsplace.co.uk* Ⓜ *King's Cross.*

17

DANCE: WHAT'S HAPPENING NOW

Dance fans in London can enjoy the classicism of the world-renowned Royal Ballet, as well as innovative works by several contemporary dance companies—including Rambert Dance Company, Matthew Bourne's New Adventures, and the Wheeldon Company—and scores of independent choreographers. The English National Ballet and visiting international companies perform at the Coliseum and at Sadler's Wells, which also hosts various other ballet companies and dance troupes. Encompassing the refurbished Royal Festival Hall, the Southbank Centre has a seriously good contemporary dance program that hosts top international companies and important

U.K. choreographers, as well as multicultural offerings ranging from Japanese Butoh and Indian Kathak to hip-hop. The Place and the Lilian Bayliss Theatre at Sadler's Wells are where you'll find the most daring, cutting-edge performances.

The following theaters are the key dance venues. Also check ⊕ *www. londondance.com* for current performances and fringe venues.

Dance Umbrella. The biggest annual event is Dance Umbrella, a four-week season in October that hosts international and British-based artists at various venues across the city. ☎ *020/7407–1200* ⊕ *www. danceumbrella.co.uk.*

THE CITY AND SOUTH BANK

THE CITY

See the Barbican Centre in the Two Main Performing Arts Centers, at the top of this chapter.

SOUTH BANK

Also see the Southbank Centre in the Two Main Performing Arts Centers, at the top of this chapter.

ART GALLERY

Fodor's Choice
★

Tate Modern. This converted power station is one of the largest modern-art galleries in the world, so give yourself ample time to take it all in. The permanent collection includes work by all the major 20th-century artists, though only a fraction is shown at any one time. There are also blockbuster touring shows and solo exhibitions of international artists. ■TIP→ The bar on the top floor has gorgeous views overlooking the Thames and St. Paul's Cathedral. ⊠ *Bankside, South Bank* ☎ *020/7887–8888* ⊕ *www.tate.org.uk* ⊡ *Free–£12.70* ⊗ *Sun.–Thurs. 10–6, Fri. and Sat. 10–10* Ⓜ *Southwark, St. Paul's, London Bridge.*

FILM

BFI London IMAX Cinema. The British Film Institute's glazed drum-shaped IMAX theater has the largest screen in the United Kingdom (approximately 75 feet wide and the height of five double-decker buses), showing state-of-the-art 2-D and 3-D films. ⊠ *1 Charlie Chaplin Walk, South Bank* ☎ *0870/7199–6000* ⊕ *www.bfi.org.uk/imax* Ⓜ *Waterloo.*

☺ **BFI Southbank.** With the best repertory programming in London, the
★ three cinemas and studio at what was previously known as the National
Film Theatre are effectively a national film center run by the British
Film Institute. They show more than 1,000 titles each year, favoring
art-house, foreign, silent, overlooked, classic, noir, and short films over
Hollywood blockbusters. The center also has a gallery, bookshop, and
"mediatheque," where visitors can watch film and television from the
National Archive. This is one of the venues for the Times BFI London
Film Festival; throughout the year there are minifestivals, seminars,
and guest speakers. ■TIP→ Members (£40) get priority bookings (useful for special events) and £1.50 off each screening. ⊠ *Belvedere Rd.,
South Bank* ☎ *020/7928–3535 information, 020/7928–3232 box office*
⊕ *www.bfi.org.uk* Ⓜ *Waterloo.*

THEATER

★ **BAC.** Battersea Arts Centre has a reputation for producing innovative
new work. Check out Scratch events, low-tech cabaret theater by emerg-
ing artists where the audience provides feedback on works-in-progress.
Tuesday shows usually have pay-what-you-can entry. ⊠ *176 Lavender
Hill, Battersea* ☎ *020/7223–2223* ⊕ *www.bac.org.uk* Ⓜ *National Rail:
Clapham Junction.*

★ **National Theatre.** When this theater opened in 1976, designed by Sir
Denys Lasdun, Londoners weren't all so keen on the low-slung, multilayered Brutalist block. Prince Charles described the building as "a
clever way of building a nuclear power station in the middle of London
without anyone objecting." But whatever its merits or demerits as a
feature on the landscape, the Royal National Theatre's interior spaces
are definitely worth a tour. Interspersed with the three theaters, the
1,120-seat Olivier, the 890-seat Lyttelton, and the 300-seat Cottesloe,
is a multilayered foyer with exhibitions, bars, and restaurants, and
free entertainment. Musicals, classics, and new plays are performed
by a top-flight company. Some shows offer £12 ticket deals. ⊠ *Southbank Centre, Belvedere Rd., South Bank* ☎ *020/7452–3000 box office,
020/7452–3400 information* ⊕ *www.nationaltheatre.org.uk* ▨ *Tour
£8.50* ☼ *Foyer Mon.–Sat. 9:30 am–11 pm; 75-min tour backstage up
to 6 times daily weekdays, twice on Sat., often on Sun.* Ⓜ *Waterloo.*

The Old Vic. This grand old theater, former haunting grounds of such
stage legends as John Gielgud, Vivien Leigh, Peter O'Toole, Richard
Burton, and Judi Dench, is now masterminded by American actor Kevin
Spacey. The theater had suffered decades of financial duress before being
brought under the ownership of a dedicated trust headed by Spacey. His
production record so far has been mixed but the theater seems to be
on financially firmer ground. ⊠ *The Cut, Southwark* ☎ *0844/871–7628*
⊕ *www.oldvictheatre.com* Ⓜ *Waterloo.*

Fodor'sChoice **Shakespeare's Globe Theatre.** This faithful reconstruction of the open-air
★ playhouse where Shakespeare worked and wrote many of his greatest
plays marvelously re-creates the 16th-century theatergoing experience.
Standing room in the "pit" right in front of the stage costs £5. The
season runs June through October. ⇨ *For more on the Globe Theatre,
see our special photo-feature, "Shakespeare and the Globe Theater" in*

17

CLASSICAL MUSIC: LONDON TODAY

Whether it's a concert by cellist Yo-Yo Ma or a Mozart requiem by candlelight, it's possible to hear first-rate musicians in world-class venues almost every day of the year. The London Symphony Orchestra is in residence at the Barbican Centre, although other top orchestras—including the Philharmonia and the Royal Philharmonic—also perform here. The Barbican also hosts chamber-music concerts, with celebrated orchestras such as the City of London Sinfonia. Kings Place, the new kid on London's concert block, has a great, and greatly varied calendar of musical events. The Southbank Centre has an impressive international music season, held in the Queen Elizabeth Hall and the small Purcell Room as well as in the Royal Festival Hall, now completely refurbished. Full houses are rare, so even at the biggest concert halls you should be able to get a ticket for £12. If you can't book in advance, arrive at the hall an hour before the performance for a chance at returns.

■TIP→ Lunchtime concerts take place all over the city in smaller concert halls, the big arts-center foyers, and churches; they usually cost less than £5 or are free, and feature string quartets, singers, jazz ensembles, or gospel choirs. St. John's, Smith Square, and St. Martin-in-the-Fields are popular locations. Performances usually begin about 1 pm and last one hour.

Classical-music festivals range from the stimulating avant-garde **Meltdown** (⊕ meltdown.southbankcentre. co.uk), curated each year by a prominent musician—recently Patti Smith and Ray Davies—at the Southbank Centre in June, to church hall recitals including the **Spitalfields Festival** (⊕ www.spitalfieldsfestival.org.uk), a program of recitals held in beautiful, historic East End churches in June, December, and January, and the monthlong **City of London Festival** (⊕ www.colf.org) in the Square Mile in summer. A great British tradition since 1895, the **Henry Wood Promenade Concerts** (more commonly known as the "Proms" ⊕ www.bbc. co.uk/proms) run eight weeks, from July to September, at the Royal Albert Hall. Despite an extraordinary quantity of high-quality concerts, it's renowned for its (atypical) last night: a madly jingoistic display of singing "Land of Hope and Glory," Union Jack–waving, and general madness. For regular Proms, tickets run £5–£90, with hundreds of standing tickets for £5 available at the hall on the night of the concert. ■TIP→ The last night is broadcast in Hyde Park on a jumbo screen, but even here a seat on the grass requires a paid ticket that can set you back around £25.

Chapter 8. ⊠ *21 New Globe Walk, Bankside, South Bank* ☎ *020/7401–9919 box office, 020/7902–1400 inquiries* ⊕ *www.shakespearesglobe. com* Ⓜ *Southwark, then walk to Blackfriars Bridge and descend steps; Mansion House, then cross Southwark Bridge; Blackfriars, then walk across Blackfriars Bridge; St. Paul's, then cross Millenium Bridge.*

Young Vic. In a home near Waterloo, big names perform alongside young talent, often in daring, innovative productions of classic plays. ⊠ *66 The Cut, Waterloo, South Bank* ☎ *020/7922–2800* ⊕ *www.youngvic. org* Ⓜ *Waterloo.*

THE EAST END

HACKNEY

THEATER

★ **Hackney Empire.** The history of this treasure of a theater is drama in its own right. Charlie Chaplin is said to have appeared here during its days as a thriving variety theater and music hall in the early 1900s. It now hosts traditional family entertainment and variety shows, opera, musical theater, dance, and drama, often with a multicultural slant. ☒ *291 Mare St., Hackney* ☎ *020/8985–2424* ⊕ *www.hackneyempire.co.uk* Ⓜ *National Rail: Hackney Central.*

HOXTON

ART GALLERY

★ **White Cube.** The English role in the exploding contemporary art scene has been major, thanks in good portion to Jay Joplin's influential gallery. Housed in a 1920s light-industrial building on Hoxton Square, it is home base for an array of artists who have won the Turner Prize—Hirst, Emin, Hume, et al.—with many of these superstars now residing in the East End (which supposedly has the highest concentration of artists in Europe). Farther west, White Cube has a second gallery in a striking building in Mason's Yard, St. James's, reflecting its central status in London's art world. A third outpost, south of the river in Bermondsey, opened in 2011 and is Europe's largest commercial gallery. ☒ *48 Hoxton Sq., Hoxton* ☎ *020/7930–5373* ⊕ *www.whitecube.com* ☐ *Free* ☉ *Tues.–Sat. 10–6* Ⓜ *Old St.*

SHOREDITCH

ART GALLERY

★ **Whitechapel Art Gallery.** Established in 1897 and newly expanded, this large, independent East End gallery is one of London's most innovative and consistently interesting. Jeff Wall, Bill Viola, Gary Hume, and Mark Rothko have exhibited here and there is an interesting program of events as well as an excellent restaurant. ☒ *80–82 Whitechapel High St., Shoreditch* ☎ *020/7522–7888* ⊕ *www.whitechapel.org* ☐ *Free* ☉ *Tues., Wed., Fri.–Sun. 11 am–6 pm, Thurs. 11 am–9 pm* Ⓜ *Aldgate East.*

KENSINGTON, CHELSEA, AND KNIGHTSBRIDGE

CHELSEA

ART GALLERY

Saatchi Gallery. Charles Saatchi lit the fuse to the contemporary art explosion in Britain and though he and his art investments may not be quite as ubiquitous as they once were, he remains a key figure. After

17

FILM: WHAT'S HAPPENING NOW

There are many wonderful movie theaters in London and several that are committed to nonmainstream and repertory cinema, in particular the excellent Curzon cinemas and the National Film Theatre. Now more than 50 years old, the **Times BFI London Film Festival** (⊕ www.lff.org.uk) brings hundreds of films made by masters of world cinema to London for 16 days each October, accompanied by often-sold-out talks and other events. The smaller, avant-garde **Raindance Film Festival** (⊕ www.raindance.co.uk) highlights independent filmmaking, September into October.

West End movie theaters continue to do good business. Most of the major houses, such as the Odeon Leicester Square and the Empire, are in the Leicester Square–Piccadilly Circus area, where tickets average £15. Monday and matinees are often cheaper, at around £6–£10, and there are also smaller crowds.

Check out *Time Out*, one of the London papers, or ⊕ www.viewlondon.co.uk for listings.

migrating to several museums and being shown around the world, Saatchi's collection now resides in this modern gallery that sprawls through 70,000 square feet of the Duke of York's HQ building in Chelsea, complete with a bookshop and café-bar. ⊠ *Duke of York's HQ, Sloane Sq., Chelsea* ☎ *020/7823-2332* ⊕ *www.saatchi-gallery.co.uk* 🖾 *Free* ☉ *Daily 10 am–6 pm* Ⓜ *Sloane Sq.*

THEATER

★ **Royal Court Theatre.** Britain's undisputed epicenter of new theatrical works, the RCT is now 50 years old and continues to produce gritty British and international drama. ■**TIP→** Don't miss the best deal in town—10-pence standing tickets go on sale one hour before each performance, and £10 tickets are available on Monday. ⊠ *Sloane Sq., Chelsea* ☎ *020/7565-5000* ⊕ *www.royalcourttheatre.com* Ⓜ *Sloane Sq.*

KENSINGTON

ART GALLERY

Serpentine Gallery. Built in 1934 as a tea pavilion in Kensington Gardens, the Serpentine has an international reputation for exhibitions of modern and contemporary art. Man Ray, Henry Moore, Andy Warhol, Bridget Riley, Damien Hirst, and Rachel Whiteread are a few of the artists who have had exhibits here. The annual Summer Pavilion, a striking temporary structure designed by a different leading architect every year, is always worth catching. ⊠ *Kensington Gardens, South Kensington* ☎ *020/7402-6075* ⊕ *www.serpentinegallery.org* 🖾 *Free* ☉ *Daily 10–6* Ⓜ *South Kensington, Lancaster Gate.*

CLASSICAL MUSIC

Cadogan Hall. Formerly a church, Cadogan Hall has been turned into a spacious concert venue. It's home to the Royal Philharmonic Orchestra, and the English Chamber Orchestra performs here regularly. ⊠ *5*

OPERA: WHAT'S HAPPENING NOW

The two key players in London's opera scene are the Royal Opera House (which ranks with the Metropolitan Opera House in New York) and the more innovative English National Opera (ENO), which presents English-language productions at the London Coliseum. Only the Theatre Royal, Drury Lane, has a longer theatrical history than the Royal Opera House—the third theater to be built on the site since 1858.

Despite occasional performances by the likes of Björk, the Royal Opera House struggles to shrug off its reputation for elitism and ticket prices that can rise to £800. It is, however, more accessible than it used to be—the cheapest tickets are less than £10. Conditions of purchase vary; call for information. Prices for the ENO are generally lower, ranging from around £20 to £95.

In summer, the increasingly adventurous Opera Holland Park presents the usual chestnuts alongside some obscure works under a canopy in leafy Holland Park.

International touring companies often perform at Sadler's Wells, the Barbican, the Southbank Centre, and Wigmore Hall, so check the weekly listings for details.

Sloane Terr., Kensington ☎ *020/7730–4500* ⊕ *www.cadoganhall.com* Ⓜ *Sloane Sq.*

★ **Royal Albert Hall.** Built in 1871, this splendid iron-and-glass–dome auditorium hosts music programs in a wide range of genres, including top-flight pop artists, as well as being the home of Europe's most democratic music festival, the Proms. The hall is also open daily for daytime guided tours (£8) and occasional backstage tours (£12). ⊠ *Kensington Gore, Kensington* ☎ *020/7589–8212* ⊕ *www.royalalberthall.com* Ⓜ *South Kensington.*

OPERA

Opera Holland Park. In summer, well-loved operas and imaginative productions of relatively unknown works are presented under a spectacular new canopy against the remains of Holland House, one of the first great houses built in Kensington. Ticket prices range from £12 to £65, with 1,100 tickets offered free to young people ages 9–18 every season. Tickets go on sale in April. ⊠ *Holland Park, Kensington High St., Kensington* ☎ *0845/230–9769* ⊕ *www.operahollandpark.com* Ⓜ *High Street Kensington, Holland Park.*

GREATER LONDON

OPERA

★ **Glyndebourne.** Fifty-four miles south of London, Glyndebourne is one of the most famous opera houses in the world. During the glamorous summer festival, six operas are presented from mid-May to late August. The best route by car is the M23 to Brighton, then the A27 toward Lewes. There are regular trains from London (Victoria) to Lewes with coach

17

London's Royal Opera House is also home to the Royal Ballet and an in-house orchestra.

connections to and from Glyndebourne. Call the information office for recommended trains for each performance. ⊠ *Lewes* ☎ *01273/815000* ⊕ *www.glyndebourne.com.*

NOTTING HILL

FILM

☾ **The Electric Cinema.** This refurbished Portobello Road art house screens
★ mainstream and international movies. The emphasis is on comfort, with leather sofas, armchairs, footstools, and mini–coffee tables for your tapas-style food and wine. Saturday matinees for kids are popular. The Electric also has an even more sumptuous cinema in east London—the Aubin, on Redchurch Street, with sofas and wine coolers. ⊠ *191 Portobello Rd., Notting Hill* ☎ *020/7908–9696* ⊕ *www.electriccinema.co.uk* Ⓜ *Ladbroke Grove, Notting Hill Gate.*

REGENT'S PARK

THEATER

Fodor'sChoice **Open Air Theatre.** On a warm summer evening, classical theater in the
★ pastoral and royal Regent's Park is hard to beat for a magical adventure. Enjoy a supper before the performance, a bite during the intermission on the picnic lawn, or drinks in the spacious bar. ⊠ *Inner Circle, Regent's Park* ☎ *0844/826–4242* ⊕ *www.openairtheatre.org* Ⓜ *Baker St., Regent's Park.*

ST. JAMES'S, MAYFAIR, AND MARYLEBONE

MARYLEBONE

ART GALLERY

Lisson. Owner Nicholas Logsdail represents about 40 blue-chip artists, including minimalist Sol Lewitt and Dan Graham, at one of the most respected galleries in London. The gallery is most associated with New Object sculptors like Anish Kapoor and Richard Deacon, many of whom have won the Turner Prize. A branch down the road at 29 Bell Street features work by younger, up-and-coming artists, and the gallery has another branch in Mian. ⊠ *52–54 Bell St., Marylebone* ☎ *020/7724–2739* ⊕ *www.lissongallery.com* 🖼 *Free* ⊘ *Weekdays 10–6, Sat. 11–5* Ⓜ *Edgware Rd., Marylebone.*

CLASSICAL MUSIC

Fodor'sChoice ★ **Wigmore Hall.** Hear chamber music and song recitals in this charming hall with near-perfect acoustics. Don't miss the Sunday morning concerts (11:30 am). ⊠ *36 Wigmore St., Marylebone* ☎ *020/7935–2141* ⊕ *www.wigmore-hall.org.uk* Ⓜ *Bond St.*

MAYFAIR

ART GALLERY

Royal Academy of Arts. Housed in an aristocratic mansion and home to Britain's first art school (founded in 1768), the academy is best known for its blockbuster special exhibitions—like a controversial Sensation show drawn from the Saatchi collection and a record-breaking Monet show—though it also has a permanent collection that includes Michelangelo's marble Taddei Tondo. The annual Summer Exhibition has been a popular London tradition since 1769. ⊠ *Burlington House, Mayfair* ☎ *020/7300–8000* ⊕ *www.royalacademy.org.uk* 🖼 *From £9, prices vary with exhibition* ⊘ *tSat. –Thurs. 10–6, Fri. 10–10* Ⓜ *Piccadilly Circus.*

ST. JAMES'S

ART GALLERY

Institute of Contemporary Arts. Housed in an elegant John Nash–designed Regency terrace, the ICA's two galleries have changing exhibitions of contemporary visual art. The ICA also programs performances, underground and vintage movies, talks, and photography, and there's an arts bookstore, cafeteria, and bar. ⊠ *Nash House, The Mall, St. James's* ☎ *020/7930–3647* ⊕ *www.ica.org.uk* 🖼 *Free* ⊘ *Wed. noon–11, Thurs.– Sat. noon–1 am, Sun noon–9 pm* Ⓜ *Charing Cross.*

CLASSICAL MUSIC

St. James's Church. The organ was brought here in 1691 after fire destroyed its former home, the Palace of Whitehall. St. James's holds regular classical-music concerts and free lunchtime recitals Monday, Wednesday, and Friday at 1:10 pm (free but donation of £3.50 suggested). ⊠ *197 Piccadilly, St. James's* ☎ *020/7381–0441 concert program and tickets* ⊕ *www. st-james-piccadilly.org* Ⓜ *Piccadilly Circus, Green Park.*

17

SOHO AND COVENT GARDEN

COVENT GARDEN

CLASSICAL MUSIC

★ **St. Martin-in-the-Fields.** Popular lunchtime concerts (free but £3.50 donation suggested) are held in this lovely 1726 church, as are regular evening concerts. ■TIP→ Stop for a snack at the Café in the Crypt. ⊠ *Trafalgar Sq., Covent Garden* ☎ *020/7766–1100* ⊕ *www. stmartin-in-the-fields.org* Ⓜ *Charing Cross.*

WORD OF MOUTH

"For me one thing stands out above all the others: London Theatre, where the houses are generally small, you can nearly always get a seat to almost any show at half price, and nobody races out before the curtain calls."
—NeoPatrick

DANCE

The London Coliseum. Ballet troupes are often booked into the spectacular Coliseum during the summer and the Christmas season, and generally any time when the resident English National Opera is not holding down the fort here. The restored Edwardian baroque theater (1904) is known for its magnificent auditorium and a rooftop glass dome. The top dance company to perform here is the English National Ballet (⊕ *www.ballet.org.uk*). ⊠ *St. Martin's La., Covent Garden* ☎ *020/7632–8300* ⊕ *www.eno.org* Ⓜ *Leicester Sq.*

Fodor's Choice **Royal Opera House.** As well as the Royal Opera, the renowned Royal
★ Ballet performs classical and contemporary repertoire in this spectacular theater, where the decor may be Victorian but the stagecraft behind the red velvet curtain is state-of-the-art. Backstage tours are £10.50. ⊠ *Bow St., Covent Garden* ☎ *020/7304–4000* ⊕ *www.roh.org.uk* ☉ *Backstage tours (1 hr 15 mins) weekdays 10:30, 12:30, and 2:30; Sat. 10:30, 11:30, and 12:30* Ⓜ *Covent Garden.*

THEATER

Fodor's Choice **Donmar Warehouse.** Hollywood stars often perform here in diverse and
★ daring new works, bold interpretations of the classics, and small-scale musicals. Under current artistic director Michael Grandage, who succeeded Sam Mendes, Nicole Kidman, Gwyneth Paltrow, and Ewan McGregor have all been featured. ⊠ *41 Earlham St., Covent Garden* ☎ *0844/871–7624* ⊕ *www.donmarwarehouse.com* Ⓜ *Covent Garden.*

Novello Theatre. Dating back to 1905 and refurbished a century later, the Novello specializes in popular contemporary musicals. ⊠ *Aldwych, Covent Garden* ☎ *020/7812–7498* ⊕ *www.delfontmackintosh.co.uk* Ⓜ *Covent Garden, Temple.*

OPERA

The London Coliseum. A vertible architectural extravaganza of Edwardian exoticism, the restored baroque-style theater (1904) has a magnificent auditorium and a rooftop glass dome with a bar and great views. As one of the city's largest and most venerable theaters, the Coliseum functions mainly as the home of the English National Opera. Seemingly in better financial shape than it has been for some time, ENO continues

THEATER: WHAT'S HAPPENING NOW

In London the play really *is* the thing, ranging from a long-running popular musical like *Mamma Mia!*, a groundbreaking reworking of Pinter, imaginative physical theater from an experimental company like *Complicite*, a lavish Disney spectacle, or a small fringe production above a pub. West End glitz and glamour continue to pull in the audiences, and so do the more innovative productions. Only in London will a Tuesday matinee of the Royal Shakespeare Company's *Henry IV* sell out a 1,200-seat theater.

In London the words "radical" and "quality," or "classical" and "experimental" are not mutually exclusive. The Royal Shakespeare Company (⊕ *www.rsc.org.uk*) and the National Theatre (⊕ *www.nationaltheatre.org.uk*) often stage contemporary versions of the classics. The Almeida, Battersea Arts Centre (BAC), Donmar Warehouse, Royal Court Theatre, Soho Theatre, and Old Vic attract famous actors and have excellent reputations for new writing and innovative theatrical approaches. These are the venues where you'll see an original production before it becomes a hit in the West End or on Broadway (and for a fraction of the cost).

The London theater scene remains vibrant throughout the summer months. Open-air productions of Shakespeare are particularly well served, whether in the faithful reconstruction of the Elizabethan Globe Theatre or under the stars in Regent's Park's Open Air Theatre. Theater festivals such as **LIFT** (⊕ *www. Liftfestival.com*), the London International Festival of Theatre, and **bite** (Barbican International Theater Events ⊕ *www.barbican.org.uk*) provide the chance to see international and cutting-edge companies throughout the year.

Theatergoing isn't cheap. Tickets less than £10 are a rarity, although designated productions at the National Theatre have seats at this price. At the commercial theaters you should expect to pay from £15 for a seat in the upper balcony to at least £25 for a good one in the stalls (orchestra) or dress circle (mezzanine). However, last-minute returns available on the night may provide some good deals. Tickets may be booked through ticket agents, at individual theater box offices, or over the phone by credit card. Be sure to inquire about any extra fees—prices can vary enormously, but agents are legally obliged to reveal the face value of the ticket if you ask. All the larger hotels offer theater bookings, but they tack on a hefty service charge. ■TIP➔ Be very wary of ticket touts (scalpers) and unscrupulous ticket agents outside theaters and working the line at "tkts" (a half-price ticket booth, www.tkts.co.uk).

Ticketmaster (☎ 0844/277–4321 ⊕ *www.ticketmaster.co.uk*) sells tickets to a number of different theaters, although they charge a booking fee. For discount tickets, **Society of London Theatre** (☎ 020/7557–6700 ⊕ *www.tkts.co.uk*) operates "tkts," a half-price ticket booth on the southwest corner of Leicester Square, and sells the best available seats to performances at about 25 theaters. It's open Monday–Saturday 10–7, Sunday 10–4; there's a £3 service charge (included in the price). Major credit cards are accepted.

17

Dominique Gonzalez-Foerster's installation, TH.2058, in the Turbine Hall of the Tate Modern

to produce innovative opera, sung in English, for lower prices than the Royal Opera House. During opera's off-season, the house hosts a number of dance troupes, including the English National Ballet (⊕ *www. ballet.org.uk*). ✉ *St. Martin's La., Covent Garden* ☎ *0871/911–0200 box office, 020/7836–0111 inquiries* ⊕ *www.eno.org* Ⓜ *Leicester Sq.*

Fodor's Choice
★
Royal Opera House. Along with Milan's La Scala, New York's Metropolitan, and Paris's Palais Garnier, this is one of the world's greatest opera houses. The resident troupe has mounted famously spectacular productions in the past, though recent productions have tended towards starker, more contemporary operas. Whatever the style of the performance, the extravagant theater itself—also home to the famed Royal Ballet—delivers a full dose of opulence. Tickets range in price from £8 to £800. The box office opens at 10 am, but queues for popular productions can start as early as 7 am; unsold tickets are offered at half price four hours before a performance. If you wish to see the hall but are not able to procure a ticket, you can join one of the daily tours of the auditorium (£8) or backstage (£10.50). There are free lunchtime recitals most Mondays in the Crush Room (arrive early to get a ticket—between 11 am and noon; some tickets are available online from nine days before the event). ROH2, the Opera House's contemporary arm, stages more experimental dance and voice performances in locations including the Linbury Studio Theatre, a 400-seater space below the Opera House. ✉ *Bow St., Covent Garden* ☎ *020/7304–4000* ⊕ *www.royalopera.org* ⊙ *Auditorium tours daily, 4; backstage tours weekdays 10:30, 12:30, and 2:30; Sat. 10:30, 11:30, 12:30, and 1:30* Ⓜ *Covent Garden.*

CONTEMPORARY ART: LONDON TODAY

In the 21st century, the focus of the city's art scene has shifted from the past to the future. Helped by the prominence of the Tate Modern, London's contemporary art scene has never been so high profile. In publicly funded exhibition spaces like the Barbican Gallery, the Hayward Gallery, the Institute of Contemporary Arts, and the Serpentine Gallery, London now has a modern-art environment on a par with Bilbao and New York. Young British Artists (YBAs, though no longer as young as they once were) Damien Hirst, Tracey Emin, and others are firmly planted in the public imagination. The celebrity status of British artists is in part thanks to the annual Turner Prize, which always stirs up controversy in the media during a monthlong display of the work, usually at Tate Britain.

Depending on whom you talk to, the Saatchi Gallery is considered to be either the savior of contemporary art or the wardrobe of the emperor's new clothes. After a couple of recent moves it has now reopened in the former Duke of York's barracks off Chelsea's Kings Road.

The South Bank's Tate Modern (recently expanded) may house the giants of modern art, but East London is where the innovative action is. There are dozens of galleries in the fashionable spaces around Old Street, and the truly hip have already moved even farther east, to areas such as Bethnal Green. The Whitechapel Art Gallery and Jay Jopling's influential White Cube in Hoxton Square remain at the epicenter of the new art establishment and continue to show exciting work by emerging British artists.

On the first Thursday of every month, more than 100 museums and galleries of East London stay open 'til late (more information at ⊕ *www.firstthursdays.co.uk*).

17

SOHO

ART GALLERY

★ **Photographer's Gallery.** Britain's first photography gallery brought world-famous photographers like André Kertesz, Jacques-Henri Lartigue, and Irving Penn to the United Kingdom, and continues to program cutting-edge and provocative photography. A grand renovation of the building means that, as of the May 2012 reopening, this prestigious institution will offer even more exhibitions, classes, and outreach programs. The gallery also has an impressive print sales room, bookstore, and café. ⊠ *16–18 Ramillies St., off Oxford St.,Soho* ☎ *0845/262–1618* ⊕ *www.photonet.org.uk* 🎟 *Free* ☉ *Tues., Wed., and Sat. 11–6; Thurs. and Fri. 11–8; Sun. noon–6* Ⓜ *Oxford Circus.*

Riflemaker. In the oldest public building in the West End, and a former Georgian rifle maker's workshop, this gallery exhibits ambitious works by emerging artists, having housed debuts by Francesca Lowe, Chosil Kil, Jaime Gili, and Jamie Shovin. ⊠ *79 Beak St., Soho* ☎ *020/7439–0000* ⊕ *www.riflemaker.org* 🎟 *Free* ☉ *Weekdays 10 am–6 pm, Sat. noon–6 pm* Ⓜ *Piccadilly Circus, Oxford Circus.*

FILM

★ **Curzon Soho.** This comfortable cinema runs an artsy program of mixed repertoire and mainstream films with a good calendar of director talks and other events, too. There are also branches in Mayfair, Bloomsbury, Chelsea, and Richmond. ✉ *99 Shaftesbury Ave., Soho* ☎ *0330/500–1331* Ⓜ *Piccadilly Circus, Leicester Sq.* ✉ *38 Curzon St., Mayfair* ☎ *0330/500–1331* ⊕ *www.curzoncinemas.com* Ⓜ *Green Park*

☾ **Prince Charles Cinema.** This repertory cinema right off Leicester Square offers a chance to catch up with independent features, documentaries, and even blockbusters you may have missed, and tickets are only £6.50, or £4 if you purchase a £10 membership. A second screen upstairs shows newer movies at more usual West End prices. This is where the "sing-along" screening originated—you can come in character and warble along to *The Sound of Music* and *The Rocky Horror Picture Show.* ✉ *7 Leicester Pl., Soho* ☎ *0207/494–3654* ⊕ *www.princecharlescinema. com* Ⓜ *Leicester Sq., Piccadilly Circus.*

THEATER

Soho Theatre. This sleek theater in the heart of Soho is devoted to fostering new work and is a prolific presenter of plays by emerging writers, comedy performances, cabaret shows, and other entertainment. ✉ *21 Dean St., Soho* ☎ *020/7478–0100* ⊕ *www.sohotheatre.com* Ⓜ *Tottenham Court Rd.*

Shopping

WORD OF MOUTH

"The museums and galleries in London all have great shops with interesting things to buy. Some museums have more than one shop, too; for example at the VA they often have a shop specializing in things to do with the special exhibition then showing as well as the normal shop goods."

—KayF

Updated by
Ellin Stein

As befits one of the great trading capitals of the world, London's shops have been known to boast, "You name it, we sell it." Finding and buying "it" can be a delight (the private fitting rooms at couturier Vivienne Westwood) or a trial (mobbed Oxford Street sales on a Saturday morning). No matter where you end up, you'll find plenty to tempt you. You can shop like royalty at Her Majesty's lingerie supplier, track down a leather-bound copy of *Wuthering Heights* at a Charing Cross bookseller, or find flea-market goodies on Portobello Road. Whether you're out for fun—there's nothing like the size, variety, and sheer street theater of the markets to stimulate the acquisitive instinct—or for fashion, London can be the most rewarding of hunting grounds.

Although it's impossible to pin down one particular look that defines the city, London style tends to fall into two camps: one is the quirky, individualistic, somewhat romantic look that draws on the city's Punk, Mod, and Boho heritage, exemplified by homegrown designers like Vivienne Westwood, Matthew Williamson, Liberty, and Temperley. The other reflects Britain's celebrated tradition of highly tailored classics, with labels like Mulberry, Paul Smith, and Burberry giving them a modern twist. The real thing can be found in the menswear stores of Jermyn Street and Savile Row—there's no better place in the city to buy custom-made shirts and suits. If your budget can't stretch to Savile Row, no problem; the city's chain stores like Topshop, Warehouse, Reiss, and Zara are excellent places to pick up designs copied straight from the catwalk, at a fraction of the price.

For buzzy fashionistas, the trick to smart shopping is to sniff out the most fashion-forward, on-trend places. Amazingly, the very designers

Continued on page 378.

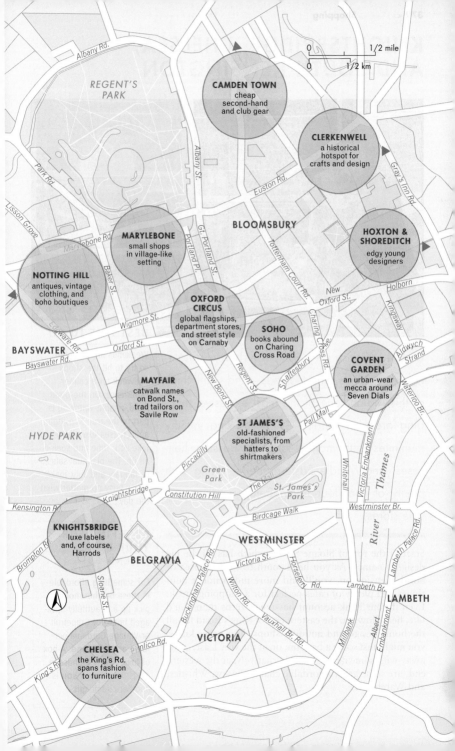

CAMDEN TOWN
cheap
second-hand
and club gear

CLERKENWELL
a historical
hotspot for
crafts and design

**HOXTON &
SHOREDITCH**
edgy young
designers

MARYLEBONE
small shops
in village-like
setting

NOTTING HILL
antiques, vintage
clothing, and
boho boutiques

**OXFORD
CIRCUS**
global flagships,
department stores,
and street style
on Carnaby

SOHO
books abound
on Charing
Cross Road

**COVENT
GARDEN**
an urban-wear
mecca around
Seven Dials

MAYFAIR
catwalk names
on Bond St.,
trad tailors on
Savile Row

ST JAMES'S
old-fashioned
specialists, from
hatters to
shirtmakers

KNIGHTSBRIDGE
luxe labels
and, of course,
Harrods

CHELSEA
the King's Rd.
spans fashion
to furniture

REGENT'S
PARK

BLOOMSBURY

BAYSWATER

HYDE PARK

GREEN
PARK

ST. JAMES'S
PARK

WESTMINSTER

BELGRAVIA

VICTORIA

LAMBETH

Thames

River

1/2 mile

1/2 km

KNIGHTSBRIDGE, CHELSEA, AND SOUTH KENSINGTON

Dream of British ultraluxury—Burberry, Pringle, Harvey Nichols, and Harrods—and you'll think of this region, one of the most exclusive shopping areas in London. Expect to find yummy mummies with money to burn, Russian heiresses, and Middle Eastern sheiks, along with plenty of chauffeur-driven Bentleys idling outside stores.

Start at the top of Sloane Street, which has all the big designer names. As you head south toward Chelsea or South Kensington, you'll find more independent boutiques and plenty of cafés perfect for a shopping break. Even if your bank account has fewer zeros than you'd like, head down to the eastern end of King's Road for all the home design and antiques shops. You never know, you might just score a bargain, or, at the very least, come away with some new ideas. Alternatively, at the western end, are some great affordable chains: Jigsaw, Whistles, and Warehouse.

BEST TIME TO GO

Weekends are crowded, so try to hit the shops midweek for a calmer experience. On the other hand, people-watching is part of the true Kensington and Chelsea experience, so take your time and soak it all up. The biannual sales, in January and July, make shops busy no matter what the day.

BEST FIND FOR YOUR BEST FRIEND

For something affordable in these neighborhoods, pick up a beautifully packaged bottle of Grapefruit or Vintage Gardenia perfume at **Jo Malone**. A box of luxury correspondence cards from **Smythson** is another classic gift.

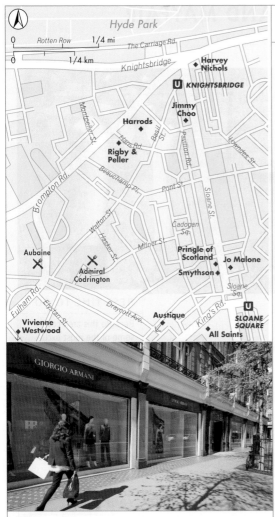

REFUELING

Chic ladies sip lattes and nibble on goat-cheese tarts or a salad Niçoise at **Aubaine**, a simple yet elegant French café and boulangerie. For something more substantial, tuck into a hearty meal at **Admiral Codrington**, a gastropub known as "The Cod" to the locals.

You can't go wrong with an order of crispy fish-and-chips served with chive butter, or salmon and crab cakes, all washed down with a pint of beer or a glass of wine.

WHAT YOU'LL WANT

TRUE BRIT

Harrods. Swanky, plush, and deep-carpeted as ever, it earns its motto— "Omnia, omnibus, ubique" ("everything, for everyone, everywhere")—thanks to its 230 departments.

Pringle of Scotland. There's nothing dowdy here. The traditional plaids still crop up, but the latest designs are edgy and cool.

A SENSUAL AFFAIR

Rigby and Peller. The Queen's corsetiere offers a selection of highest-quality lingerie and fitting expertise second to none.

Agent Provocateur. Want to get your wife to wear sexy and saucy lingerie? Take her here to stock up on their lushly alluring night wear.

TRENDSETTERS

All Saints. Limited stock and fresh-from-the-catwalk designs here mean original looks—you won't be walking around looking like everyone else.

Austique. For the über-feminine London shopper, look no further than this two-floor boutique on the King's Road, which offers chic dresses and accessories.

Harvey Nichols. The capital's chicest, most high-end department store is a must.

18

ST. JAMES'S AND MAYFAIR

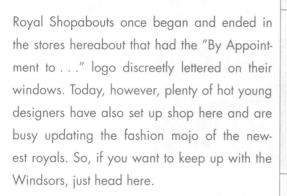

CLOTH SOLD BY THE METRE

Royal Shopabouts once began and ended in the stores hereabout that had the "By Appointment to . . ." logo discreetly lettered on their windows. Today, however, plenty of hot young designers have also set up shop here and are busy updating the fashion mojo of the newest royals. So, if you want to keep up with the Windsors, just head here.

Fabled addresses—like St. James's Jermyn Street—still retain their lost-in-time quality and give off a vibe that seems unchanged since Edwardian times. But even ageless Savile Row—synonymous with custom-made suits—now moves to a new beat: Prince Charles and rocker David Bowie have their clothing made there. In fact, the hottest names on the London catwalks have their headquarters here—Alexander McQueen's flagship store is at 4–5 Old Bond Street, Mayfair, and, nearby, Stella McCartney's collections are showcased in a townhouse at 30 Bruton Street.

BEST TIME TO GO

Because this area covers some of the most exclusive shopping streets in the capital, don't expect huge crowds. South Molton Street can get a bit busy, whereas the area surrounding Jermyn Street is relatively quiet. Many of the independent stores are closed on Sunday.

BEST FIND FOR YOUR DAD

Long-established shirt maker **Hilditch & Key** makes bespoke and ready-to-wear dress shirts. Alternatively, for something a bit less expensive, pick up a formal shirt from **Thomas Pink** or **Charles Tyrhwhitt.**

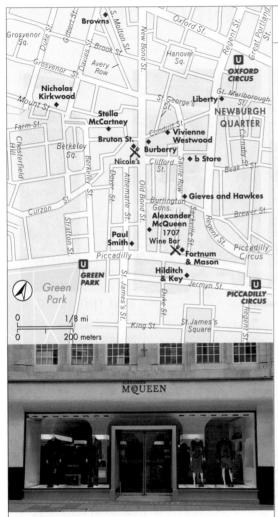

MQUEEN

REFUELING

Nicole's restaurant in the basement of the Nicole Farhi shop is ideal for a quick lunch between purchases. The two-story restaurant was designed by Ms. Farhi, as was the menu, which features modern British cuisine with a California twist. For the quickest service, head to the upper level; reservations are recommended for the more formal dining room. Or pop in for a glass of wine at the **1707 Wine Bar** inside Fortnum & Mason, one of four restaurants in what's known as the Queen's grocery store.

WHAT YOU'LL WANT

COOL BRITANNIA

Alexander McQueen. When Kate Middleton married Prince William, the future queen had to go to McQueen to find the best of British style, now headed by design genius Sarah Burton.

Vivienne Westwood. The queen of punk fashion reigns in a boutique stuffed with Punk-Pompadour gowns, Lady Hamilton vest coats, and other fabulously foppish get-ups.

Paul Smith. This furniture and curio shop has the same quirky aesthetic as the classics-with-a-twist clothing for which the designer is known.

Burberry. This once hidebound landmark label is now super-chic thanks to Christopher Bailey, the designer who transformed it into the British Gucci.

THE FRILL IS GONE

Stella McCartney. Sophisticated and sexy, these fashions are for women who like to frock-around-the-clock with cool lines and a cooler vibe.

Mackintosh. "Seams like old times" at this resurrected Victorian-era designer of the first rubberized raincoat but these astonishingly modern designs fit right into today.

18

SOHO AND COVENT GARDEN

If London has a buzzy, one-size-fits-all area that would make most fashionistas happy, it is Soho and Covent Garden: they both have a mix of achingly trendy boutiques and stylish chains such as Zara and H&M.

True, Soho may be better known for its restaurants than for its shops, but it is also home to many independent boutiques. Indeed, if you want to track down the next Alexander McQueen, just head to the Newburgh Quarter, set one block east of Carnaby Street (just off roaring Regent Street). This charming maze of pedestrian lanes is lined with an array of specialist boutiques, edgy stores, and young indy upstarts where the future of England's fashion is being incubated. A check of their ingredients reveals one part 60s London, one part Futuristic Fetishism, one part Dickensian charm, and one part British street swagger. Check out stores like Beyond the Valley, Peckham Rye, Sweaty Betty, and Lucy in Disguise to see what all the fuss is about. Other top spots: Covent Garden's Piazza, Neal's Yard courtyard, Seven Dials (Monmouth Street has lots of offbeat delights), nearby Floral Street (home to United Nude), and Neal Street.

BEST TIME TO GO

It's almost always crowded, so go with the flow—or get there early in the morning.

BEST FIND FOR YOUR ANGLOPHILE FRIEND

Couldn't make it to Scotland this trip? Leave room in your luggage for a bottle or two of single-malt whisky from **Milroy's of Soho**, on Greek Street, which stocks whiskies from every distillery in Scotland. Or stop by the **Tea House** on Neal Street, which sells more than 100 varieties of tea along with pots and mugs to make the perfect brew and the perfect gift.

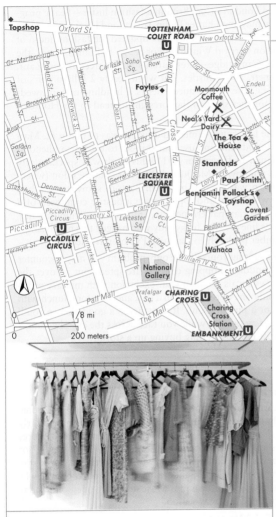

REFUELING

Wahaca serves delicious yet inexpensive dishes inspired by Mexican street food. The wait for a seat is worth it, and you'll have money left over to continue shopping your way through Covent Garden. If you're looking for a caffeine jolt, head to **Monmouth Coffee**, which roasts all its own beans and boasts some of the best coffee around, or pick up some delectable cheese to nibble on from the nearby **Neal's Yard Dairy**.

WHAT YOU'LL WANT

BOOKS AND PRINTS

Foyles. This bibliophile's wonderland has everything from art history to opera scores.

Stanfords. With the British long known as fabled explorers, it is little wonder London boasts the world's best travel bookshop.

QUIRKY COOL

Peckham Rye. Imagine *Brideshead Revisted* "legacy" looks given a mod spin and the results are on view here, a top stop in the cutting-edge Newburgh Quarter.

b store. Models flock here for the ever-changing stock of clothing and accessories by emerging talent.

United Nude. Innovative, surprisingly comfortable shoes incorporate up-to-the minute materials.

TOYS R THEM

Benjamin Pollock's Toyshop. Billionaires buy the antique toy theaters on sale in this legendary and historic emporium, while the rest of us adore the new paper reproductions, complete with dollhouse sets for *The Mikado*.

Hamleys. The city's biggest toy store is heaven to most children, although adults may be less enchanted with the highly commercial emphasis.

18

that have revived London's Cool Britannia fashion luster—Beatle progeny Stella McCartney, mad hatter Philip Treacy, and local genius Alexander McQueen—are the ones that have updated the fashion mojo of the new generation of royal Windsors. For her go-to brands, Kate—the new Duchess of Cambridge—likes various High Street stores: Zara, Reiss, L.K. Bennett, and Whistles. But when nearly 2 billion pairs of eyes are watching, the future queen needs a headline-making wedding gown and for that she had the foresight to head to the House of McQueen.

The genius of the late, much-lamented designer was to take a St. Martin's art school foundation and use that skill-set to become a phenomenal dress designer. In December 2011, this truth was spectacularly dramatized in a window of McQueen's Mayfair couture salon (where Kate's bridal gown was created by Sarah Burton) showcasing a ball gown made of white tulle and topped with a bustier composed of a mosaic of real Victorian-pattern pottery, cracked into a hundred tiny pieces. Fashion as fine art. The lucky lady who bagged this paralyzingly high priced number probably exclaimed "I've been framed!"

Apart from bankrupting yourself, the only problem you may encounter is exhaustion. London's shopping districts are spread out all over the city, so do as savvy locals do: plan your excursion with military precision, taking in only one or two areas in a day, and stop for a lunch with a glass of wine or a pint at a pub. If not, there's a good chance you'll wind up losing a few pounds while you race across the city shedding a goodly number of pounds sterling buying up a storm.

PLANNING

OPENING HOURS

Most shops are open from about 9:30 or 10 am to 6 or 6:30 pm. Some may open at 11 and stay open until 7. Because shop hours, particularly for the smaller shops, are varied, it's a good idea to phone ahead. Stores that have late shopping—and not all do—are usually open until 7 or 8 pm on Wednesday or Thursday only. Most department stores stay open late during the week. On Sunday, many shops open between 11 am and noon and close at 5 or 6 pm. Most stores are open on Sunday in December for the Christmas season.

WATCH YOUR LANGUAGE

Locals like to say that Brits and Americans are separated by a common language. Here are a few confusing terms to watch for when out and about in the shops:

Pants means underwear. Every other type of long-legged bottoms (except jeans) are called **trousers.**

Knickers are ladies' underwear. If you want pantyhose, ask for **tights.**

Jumper means sweater—unless it's a cardigan, in which case it's often shortened to **cardie.** If you ask for a **sweater,** you may be offered a sweatshirt.

Men use **braces** to hold up their trousers; in England **suspenders** is another word for garters.

If you want some Adidas- or Nike-type athletic shoes, ask for **trainers**, not sneakers.

Don't ask for a **pocketbook** or a **purse** if you mean a handbag—the former will be incomprehensible, and the latter will produce a coin purse.

Nightgowns are usually abbreviated to **nighties** and bathrobes may be **dressing gowns.**

A WORD ABOUT SERVICE

American standards of customer service are rare in London—you may find attentive customer service at old-school, traditional names and some independent stores, but salespeople elsewhere can seem abrupt or indifferent.

SPECIALTY STORES

ANTIQUES

Investment-quality items or lovable junk—London has loads. For the best range of merchandise, and plenty of character, try the markets first. Some argue that Portobello Road in Notting Hill has become a bit of a tourist trap, but if you acknowledge that it's a circus and get into the spirit, it's a lot of fun. Kensington Church Street and the shops along the King's Road have some of the best antiques in the city, but the prices are high, unless you're willing to wake up early and try your luck at the Lots Road Auction, near the swanky Chelsea Design Centre. Also stop by Alfie's Antique Market in Marylebone. The nearby small shops lining Church Street sell everything from large-scale 19th-century English and European furniture to art deco ceramics and vintage shop fittings.
■ TIP➜ Opening times vary: many places that are open on the weekend are closed Monday or Tuesday.

18

BEAUTY

Skin-care junkies and perfume fans will be hard-pressed to walk away empty-handed from London's beauty emporiums. Visitors should try to visit at least one of London's most venerable perfumeries—the old-school favorites Floris or Penhaligon, as well as relative newcomers like Miller Harris or Jo Malone. Space NK stocks upscale, hard-to-find cosmetic and skin-care brands while fans of natural beauty products flock to London's organic pioneer, Neal's Yard Remedies.

BOOKS AND PRINTS

Books—actual, physical books— are still popular in London and most decent London neighborhoods have a Waterstone's or local independent, some complete with coffee shops and, in some cases, even cocktail bars.

CLOSE UP

Know Your Shopping Personality

"Where is the best place to shop in London?" There are thousands of shops in the city, and dozens of neighborhoods worth shopping in. Start by identifying your shopping personality to narrow your choices for a successful outing.

Easygoing. If you want to pop in and out of a variety of shops, as well as avoid the crowds around Oxford Street, head to the King's Road in Chelsea. You'll find department store Peter Jones, plus Marks & Spencer and plenty of chains and trendy boutiques. Another safe bet is High Street Kensington for the usual big chains, in addition to some smaller ones less oriented toward disposable fashion, such as Cos, Karen Millen, and Oliver Bonas.

Eclectic. If you don't want to be pinned down and prefer beautiful workmanship and originality, start at Liberty on Regent Street, then head to either the Holland Park/Notting Hill, Marylebone, or Covent Garden neighborhoods. All provide enough idiosyncratic lifestyle shops for hours of browsing.

Fashionista. When only the top designers will do, start at Harvey Nichols in Knightsbridge, then take in the designer boutiques along Sloane Street before hopping on the Tube for Green Park. From there you can cover Bond Street (both Old and New), and finish at Fenwick, or veer off onto Conduit Street, designer-heavy Bruton Street, or, at the northwest end of Berkeley Square, ultrachic Mount Street. If you still have time and energy, check out South Molton Street opposite Bond Street Tube or St. Christopher's Place across Oxford Street.

Funky and Avant-Garde. For cutting-edge fashion and homewares, head east to the city's coolest neighborhoods, chiefly Hoxton and Shoreditch. Start at Columbia Road for the flower market and lovely shops on the street, then have a wander around Spitalfields and Brick Lane for their excellent street markets. Work your way north to Hoxton and Shoreditch, chock-full of out-of-the-mainstream stores. Right in the center of town, also check out the Newburgh Quarter, right off Carnaby Street (off Regent): this warren of cobblestoned streets is lined with the hippest shops in town.

Whirlwind. If you're after a one-stop shopping experience, head to one of London's biggest department stores. Selfridges and Liberty are near the Bond Street and Oxford Circus Tube stations, while Harvey Nichols and Harrods share the Knightsbridge Tube station.

The English gentleman's library, with its glass-front cabinets full of rare leather-bound books, may be a cliché from films and books, but there's no denying that London is also one of the world's great centers for rare-book collectors. Bloomsbury, around London University and the British Museum, is noted for its used and specialist bookstores, as is Charing Cross Road and its offshoot pedestrian alley Cecil Court (see ⊕ *www.cecilcourt.co.uk* for a full list of the shops in this unique enclave). Other well-respected specialists reside in Mayfair, while more humble used books can be found on the tables outside the British Film Institute in Southbank.

CLOTHING

Like Paris and New York, London is one of the world's fashion capitals, and every designer you've ever heard of is available. But it's the city's eccentric street style that gives fashion here its special edge. Instead of the put-together chic that appeals to many French and Italian women, many British women aim for experimentation and individuality, and many of the trends that show up on European catwalks really begin in London. What makes London clothes shopping so much fun—for both men and women—is that you can buy high-quality traditional British clothing, bespoke tailoring, leading contemporary fashion labels, exquisite vintage clothing, and outrageous directional street style without traveling farther than a couple of Tube stops.

WORD OF MOUTH

"If you're more interested in hip new stuff, and enjoy wandering through a warren of endless little shops, take the tube to Camden Town and spend a day lost in Camden Lock, a short walk from the Camden Town station. The area is also the site of street vendors, flea-style markets, and regular storefronts." —imaginaryjazz

London has shops to dress women in style whether their taste is trendy or traditional, and their budget rummage or royal. Chains like Miss Selfridge, Topshop, New Look, and Warehouse take aim at the young, adventurous, and slim; Hobbs, Whistles, L.K. Bennett, Joseph, Reiss, and Jaeger provide updated classics for the more sophisticated; and fashion-oriented department stores—Harvey Nichols, Harrods, Selfridges, Liberty, Fenwick—cater to women of all ages and tastes. The hottest names on the London catwalks have their headquarters here—Alexander McQueen's flagship store is at 4–5 Old Bond Street, Mayfair, and, nearby, Stella McCartney's collections are showcased in a town house at 30 Bruton Street. The Newburgh Quarter is home to the next generation's McQueens and McCartneys.

When it comes to stylish accessories, whether a sturdy umbrella, a traditional hat, or a bag that will last a lifetime, London's specialists are known for their high level of craftsmanship—and today's designers like Philip Treacy, Bill Amberg, and Anya Hindmarch draw on centuries of expertise.

London's menswear is considered even more trendsetting than its womenswear. The department stores have good menswear departments, but Selfridges and Liberty deserve special mention for interesting designer offerings. London's Savile Row tailors are still the spot where a man orders a bespoke suit once he has really "arrived," but British style has loosened up considerably in recent years. Ozwald Boateng, with his sharp tailoring and colorful suit linings, is typical of the new wave of bespoke tailors along with Richard James. Those with more flash than cash should seek out the trendsetting fashion chains: Topman, Reiss, and Zara.

Finally, several popular chains, including H&M, Next, Monsoon, and Zara, have cheap and cheerful children's lines. In select Jigsaw branches, Jigsaw Junior has classics with a twist for girls. London parents swear

LONDON SHOPPING STEALS AND DEALS

Even at the best of times London has never been known as a budget-shopping destination, and when the pound is strong prices can seem stratospheric. However, whatever the exchange rate, there are still bargains to be had as long as you know where, and when, to look. To get the maximum mileage out of your cash, visit during the widespread biannual sales, which kick off in late June and just after Christmas, and last about a month.

Fashion insiders attend the many sales held throughout the year, from big warehouse clearances, such as the Designer Warehouse Sales (⊕ www.designerwarehousesales. com) and Designer Sales UK (⊕ www. designersales.co.uk), to individual designers' sample sales—check out ⊕ www.fashionconfidential.co. uk, ⊕ www.dailycandy.com/London or *Time Out* (www.timeout.com) for information, and to register for updates. London outlets, such as Browns Labels for Less, Paul Smith Sale Shop, and the Joseph Sale Shop on King's Road, offer year-round designer bargains. If time permits, travel outside London to Bicester Village (⊕ www.bicestervillage.com), a luxury outlet mall in Oxfordshire.

It's completely worth the nearly one-hour train journey, if only for the opportunity to score an item from such highly coveted British brands as Alexander McQueen, Temperley, Mulberry, Burberry and Aquascutum, as well as top international labels.

If you're not fussy about labels, there are even more choices.

Pokit. Contemporary tailors Pokit offer sharp but comfortable made-to-measure suits for men and women from just £800 (jackets £500), plus a wide range of leather goods. ⊠ *132 Wardour St., Soho* ☎ *020/7434–2875* ⊕ *www.pokit.co.uk* ⊗ *Closed Sun.* Ⓜ *Tottenham Court Rd., Oxford Circus.*

Primark. Primark is fantastic for low-cost, trendy clothing. At the huge, two-story Oxford Street flagship (there are other branches in Hammersmith and Kilburn), keep in mind you get what you pay for; some of the fabrics and finishes reflect the store's budget prices. This is the home of fast, youthful, disposable fashion, so don't expect attentive service or classic styling and you won't be disappointed. ⊠ *499 Oxford St., Soho* ☎ *020/7495–0420* ⊕ *www. primark.co.uk* Ⓜ *Marble Arch.*

by no-nonsense department store John Lewis, on Oxford Street, for fair prices and high-quality goods. But if you're looking for something more than run of the mill, expect to pay for it.

DEPARTMENT STORES

London's department stores range from Harrods—which every visitor is obliged to visit— through many serviceable middle-range stores, with a something-for-everyone range. The best are Liberty, John Lewis, Selfridges, Harrods, and Harvey Nichols.

FOOD AND DRINK

London excels at posh nosh, and the selection has gotten even bigger with European integration—but be prepared to pay quite a lot for gourmet goods. The Food Halls at Harrods are internationally famous, almost as much for the beautiful displays and ceramic-tile ceilings as for the packaged teas, chocolates, biscuits, fresh produce, fish, and game. Selfridges is less daunting but more international in its selection, and the grande dame of London food halls is Fortnum & Mason. Marks & Spencer, almost as well known for its high-quality ready-made meals as its underwear, has M&S Simply Food stores around town.

BESPOKE LONDON

Having anything made to order used to be restricted to the upper class. One had one's tailor, one's milliner, one's dressmaker, and so forth. Things are more democratic these days, but whether you want a custom-made Savile Row suit or handmade leather shoes, the price is steep.

HOME DECOR

London's main department stores have just about everything you might need; John Lewis, on Oxford Street is especially good for practical items, such as kitchen equipment. For something more unusual, head to Cheshire Street in the East End. Independent home-design shops have sprouted up here over the past few years, including the wonderfully British Labour & Wait, which sells stylish yet practical goods. Some are open only on weekends, when the Brick Lane and Spitalfields markets bring customers to the area.

18

JEWELRY

If you are suddenly overcome with the need to invest in serious rocks, London won't let you down. All the major international players are here: Cartier, Tiffany, Bulgari, Fred, Boucheron, De Beers, Van Cleef and Arpels, Graff, David Morris, and Britain's own Mappin & Webb among them. Bond Street, in particular, is good hunting grounds for megawatt stocking fillers. ■TIP→ **Bargain hunters who know their gems head for Hatton Garden, London's traditional diamond center. It's lined with small, independent dealers.** For a selection of unusual designer jewelry under one roof, try Liberty, Selfridges, or Fenwick. Links of London, a widespread chain, is a good bet for classic sterling silver and gold pieces, especially charm bracelets and cuff links, and Melissa McArthur Jewellery is a fantastic little shop in Chelsea for purchasing beautifully handmade earrings or a necklace—all for prices that won't leave you gasping.

MUSIC

Although their supremacy is increasingly challenged by Internet downloads, global megastore HMV is still busy. There are also specialty stores galore for cutting-edge music mixed by club DJs, and for stocking

VINTAGE LONDON

The British, with their love of theatrical style, have embraced the trend for vintage clothing with particular gusto. Even mainstream places, like Liberty, Selfridges, and Topshop, all have vintage sections. And don't forget the retro finds to be found at Camden Market, Portobello Road, Brick Lane/Spitalfields, and the following top shops.

Absolute Vintage. Absolute Vintage is a warehouse of handpicked items from the 1930s through the 1980s, but the specialty here is shoes (more than 1,000 pairs) and bags. Best of all, prices are reasonable. There's a branch on Berwick Street in Soho. ⊠ 15 Hanbury St., Spitalfields/East End ☎ 020/7247–3883 ⊕ www.absolutevintage.co.uk Ⓜ Aldgate East, Liverpool St.

Beyond Retro. Beyond Retro stocks more than 10,000 vintage items for men and women. From bowling shirts to prom dresses, they've got the United Kingdom's largest collection of American retro. There's another outpost in Soho. ⊠ 110–112 Cheshire St., Spitalfields/East End ☎ 020/7729–9001 ⊕ www.beyondretro.com Ⓜ Shoreditch High St., Whitechapel.

Blitz. "Seams" like old times? It certain does at the world's first (self-proclaimed) "vintage department store." This vast former furniture factory now has separate floors devoted to antiques and vintage clothing. Look for racks filled with Marlboro Man leather jackets, sequined Indian silk tops, Sgt Pepper band uniforms, and Liberty shirts. ⊠ 98 55 Hanbury St., East End ☎ 020/377–0730 Ⓜ Bethnal Green.

Orsini. Eveningwear with Hollywood-style glamour is the trademark at this tiny but choice boutique, with clothes from the 1920s to the 1970s. Victoria Beckham is a fan. ⊠ 76 Earl's Court Rd., Kensington ☎ 020/7937–2903 Ⓜ Earl's Court.

Palette London. Every piece of clothing at Palette London is in immaculate condition. Owner Mark Ellis sells vintage Ossie Clark, Missoni, Pucci, as well as Chanel from the 1940s up to the '90s and new European designers. His selection of '80s Betsey Johnson is particularly strong. ⊠ 21 Canonbury La., Islington ☎ 020/7288–7428 ⊕ www.palette-london.com Ⓜ Highbury & Islington.

Rellik. Today favored by the likes of Kate Moss, Rellik began as a stall in the Portobello Market. Vintage hunters looking to splurge can find a selection of YSL, Alaia, and Dior. Prices range from £30 to £1,000. ⊠ 8 Golborne Rd., Notting Hill ☎ 020/8962–0089 ⊕ www.relliklondon.co.uk Ⓜ Westbourne Park.

Rokit. Rokit consists of two shops along Brick Lane that stock everything from handbags and ball gowns to jeans, military garb, and Western wear, from the 1920s to the 1990s. Magazine and rock stylists love it. Branches are in Camden and Covent Garden. ⊠ 101 and 107 Brick La., Spitalfields/East End ☎ 020/7375–3864 ⊕ www.rokit.co.uk Ⓜ Shoreditch High St.

Virginia. Virginia Bates's collection of vintage clothing may be the best in London. Dresses, hats, and accessories from the late Victorian era (circa 1880) to the early 1930s are available. ⊠ 98 Portland Rd., Holland Park ☎ 020/7727–9908 ⊙ Closed Sun.; open Sat. by appointment only Ⓜ Holland Park, Ladbroke Grove.

up your own collection of good old-fashioned vinyl. ■TIP➔ Consider that CDs cost anywhere from 10% to as much as 50% more in the United Kingdom than they do in North America. So look for the kind of music you really can't find at home. Soho's long-standing independent record-shop enclave Berwick Street has seen some recent closures, but survivors include the wide-ranging Sister Ray (Nos. 34–35), and Revival

Records (No. 30), while Rough Trade Records has outlets in Notting Hill and the East End's Old Truman Brewery. Camden Market is also good for a browse through secondhand and independent music stores.

SHOES

It's no accident that Manolo Blahnik, the luxury shoe designer, made his name in London and still lives here. Audrey Hepburn, Kate Moss, and even the *Sex and the City* girls have all worn Manolos. Blahnik still trades from his original shop in Chelsea, just off the King's Road, hidden away on Old Church Street. Jimmy Choo is another "native son" who began his career quietly in London's East End before Tamara Mellon (who's now left the company) turned his name into a global luxury brand. The British capital is still a hotbed of shoemaking talent: Nicholas Kirkwood, Beatrix Ong, and Rupert Sanderson are some of the most exciting names of the moment. Stop in at one of the King's Road or South Moulton street branches of Office, Kurt Geiger, Dune, or the more avant-garde United Nude for British-designed shoes at slightly more affordable prices. And don't miss the shoe department at Selfridges, the largest in the world where the shoes are presented like art.

TOYS AND MODELS

If you're traveling with kids in tow, there are plenty of shops that cater to children. Forget about taking them to check out the latest game system; London is the place to shop for traditional toys like soldiers, puppets, teddy bears, and those divinely wonderful toy theaters from Pollock's that have been delighting children ever since the days of Queen Victoria.

BLOOMSBURY, HOLBORN, AND ISLINGTON

BLOOMSBURY

ACCESSORIES

James Smith & Sons Ltd. This has to be the world's ultimate umbrella shop, and a must for anyone interested in real Victorian London. The family-owned shop has been in this location on a corner of New Oxford

18

BRING A BIT OF ENGLAND HOME

To avoid panic-buying a bulk pack of Cadbury chocolate at Heathrow, it's wise to plan your gift purchasing with care.

For everything under one roof, unique department store Liberty is hard to beat—here you'll find everything from exquisite Miller Harris fragrances by British perfumer Lyn Harris to small leather goods embossed with the famous Liberty prints.

Fortnum & Mason is even more sensational on its floors packed with carefully curated and sweetly stylish offerings, such as leather-covered hip flasks and model boats with Union Jack sails. Of course, it is world famous for its beautifully packaged biscuits, teas, and unusual condiments.

For the men back home, consider some traditional shaving cream from Geo. F. Trumper.

The museum shops are also bursting with original gift ideas, from Brit Art books and posters at Tate Modern to double-decker bus models and Tube-map mouse pads at the London Transport Museum in Covent Garden. *The shops below will inspire.*

A. Gold. All the traditional, old-school foodstuffs sold in this Dickensian-looking shop, occupying an old milliner's premises near Spitalfields Market, are from the United Kingdom. A bottle of mead, a jar of London-produced honey, or hand-made fudge are all great Brit gifts. Stylish gift baskets and old-fashioned picnic hampers are available. ✉ *42 Brushfield St., East End* ☎ *020/7247-2487* ⊕ *www.agoldshop.com* Ⓜ *Liverpool St.*

Geo. F. Trumper. If you don't have time for an old-fashioned hot towel shave, pick up some accessories to take home for yourself or as a gift. The Extract of West Indian Lime is a popular, zingy aftershave, and the Coconut Oil Hard Shaving Soap, which comes in a hand-turned wooden bowl, is a classic. There is also a store at 9 Curzon Street in Mayfair. ✉ *1 Duke of York St., St. James's* ☎ *020/7734-1370* ⊕ *www.trumpers.com* ⊘ *Closed Sun.* Ⓜ *Piccadilly Circus.*

Labour & Wait. Although such household items as colanders and clothespins may not sound like ideal souvenirs, this shop may make you reconsider. The owners are on a mission to revive functional, old-fashioned British goods, such as enamel kitchenware, "Brown Betty" glazed teapots, Guernsey sweaters, and vintage Welsh blankets. ✉ *85 Redchurch St., East End* ☎ *020/7729-6253* ⊘ *Closed Mon.* Ⓜ *Shoreditch High St.*

Street since 1857, and sells every kind of umbrella, cane, and walking stick imaginable. The decor is unchanged since the 19th century; you will feel as if you have stepped back in time. If the umbrellas are out of your price range, James Smith also sells smaller accessories and handmade wooden bowls. ✉ *Hazelwood House, 53 New Oxford St., Bloomsbury* ☎ *020/7836-4731* ⊕ *www.james-smith.co.uk* ⊘ *Closed Sun.* Ⓜ *Tottenham Court Rd., Holborn.*

Continued on page 393

TO MARKET, TO MARKET

Londoners love a good market. With their cluttered stalls and crowds of people, they are a visible reminder that, in this world of global chain stores and supermarkets, London is still, in many respects, an Old World European city.

Every neighborhood has its cluster of fruit, vegetable, and flower stalls, or its weekend car-boot sales—gigantic garage sales where ordinary people pay a fiver for the privilege of selling their castoffs. Some, like Broadway Market in London Fields, run for miles. Others, like Brixton Market, Europe's biggest Caribbean-food market, featuring more than 300 stalls, specialize in ethnic ingredients and products. Still others crop up in the most unexpected places: on Berwick Street in the heart of Soho, for example, media moguls, designers, ad execs, actors,

dancers, and ladies of the night mingle over the punnets of strawberries, wedges of cheddar, and slabs of wet fish.

The big specialty markets, traditionally open on weekends, are not only great for the occasional bargain but also for people-watching, photo ops, and all around great days out. And though the markets are popular with visitors, they aren't tourist traps. In fact, browsing the London markets is one of the few activities in London where natives and tourists mix and enjoy themselves as equals.

PORTOBELLO ROAD MARKET

🕘 Sat. 8 am–6:30 pm

✉ Portobello Rd., Notting Hill W11

Ⓤ Ladbroke Grove (Hammersmith & City Line), Notting Hill (District, Circle, or Central Line)

🛍 Antiques, fruits and vegetables, vintage and designer clothing, household goods

★ **Fodor's**Choice **London's most famous market** still wins the prize (according to some) for the all-around best. It sits in a lively multicultural part of town; the 1,500-odd antiques dealers don't rip you off (although you should haggle where you can); and it stretches over a mile, changing character completely as it goes.

The southern end, starting at Chepstow Villas, is lined with shops and stalls selling antiques and bric-a-brac; the middle, above Elgin Crescent, is where locals buy fruits and vegetables. This middle area was the setting for the lovely sequence in the movie *Notting Hill* where Hugh Grant walks along the market and through the changing seasons. The section near the elevated highway (called the Westway) has the best flea market in town, with vintage-clothing stores along the edges. Here, young designers sell their wares in and around the Portobello Green arcade. After that, the market trails off into a giant rummage sale of the kinds of cheap household goods the British call tat.

Some say Portobello Road has become a bit of a tourist trap, but if you acknowledge that it's a circus and get into the spirit, it's a lot of fun. Perhaps you won't find many bargains, but this is such a cool part of town that just hanging out is a good enough excuse to come. There are some food and flower stalls throughout the week, but to see the market in full swing, Saturday is the only day to come, although fashion designers prefer Friday mornings.

A PORTOBELLO DAY

In good weather the market gets very crowded by midday.

For a Londoner's day at Portobello, come as early as you can (7 am) and enjoy the market when the traders have time for a chat and you can actually get near the stalls.

By 10:30 you'll have seen plenty of the market and can stop for a late breakfast or brunch at the **Electric Brasserie** (✉ 191 Portobello Rd. ☎ 020/7908–9696), next to the area's famous Electric Cinema.

If you still have the will to shop, move on to the less crowded boutiques along Westbourne Grove, Blenheim Crescent, or Ledbury Road.

BOROUGH MARKET

🕙 **Thurs. 8–5, Fri. noon–4:30, Sat. 9–4**

✉ E Borough High St., Borough SE1 1TL

Ⓤ London Bridge (Jubilee or Northern Line),

☞ Cheese, olives, coffee, baked goods, meats, fish, fruits, vegetables

★ **There's been a market** in Borough since Roman times. This one, spread under the arches and railway tracks leading to London Bridge Station, is the descendant of a medieval market once held on London Bridge.

Post-millennium, it has been transformed from a noisy collection of local stalls to a trendy foodie center.

With a reputation as the best food market in London, the Farmers Market held on Thursdays, Fridays and Saturdays has attracted some of London's best merchants of comestibles.

Fresh coffees, gorgeous cheeses, olives, and baked goods complement the organically farmed meats, fresh fish, fruit, and veggies.

Don't make any other lunch plans for the day; celebrity chef Jamie Oliver's scallop man cooks them up fresh from the Dorset coast at Shell Seekers; wild boar sausages sizzle on a grill, and there is much more that's tempting to gobble on the spot.

There are chocolates, preserves, and Burnt Sugar's fudge, but the best souvenirs are the memories.

If you'd rather eat sitting down, pop into the sleek reataurant Roast, which specializes in local seasonal food—much of it purchased at the market.

A BARGAIN DAY ON THE SOUTH BANK

Combine a visit to the Tate Modern (free) and a walk across the Millennium Bridge from the Tate to St. Paul's with a Thames-side picnic of goodies foraged at Borough Market. There are gourmet breads and farmhouse cheeses from France and Italy.

Or how about a wedge of Stinking Bishop cheese (Wallace and Gromit's favorite) from Neal's Yard Dairy? Fishmonger Applebee's serves up freshly sautéed garlic prawns in a wrap with chili and crème fraîche.

A PUB RIGHT OUT OF DICKENS

On the way back to Borough Tube station, stop for a pint at the **George Inn** (✉ 77 Borough High St., Southwark SE1 ☎ 020/7407–2056 Ⓤ London Bridge), mentioned by Dickens in *Little Dorrit*. This 17th-century coaching inn was a famous terminus in its day, and is the last galleried inn in London. Now owned by the National Trust, it is leased to a private company and still operates as a pub.

18

THE EAST END MARKETS

Brick Lane. The noisy center of the Bengali community is a hubbub of buying and selling. Sunday stalls have food, hardware, household goods, electrical goods, books, bikes, shoes, clothes, spices, and saris. The CDs and DVDs may not be entirely legitimate, and the bargain iron may not have a plug—so be careful. But people come more to enjoy the ethnic buzz, eat curries and Bengali sweets, or indulge in salt beef on a bagel at Beigel Bake, London's 24-hour bagel bakery, a survivor of the neighborhood's Jewish past. Brick Lane's activity spills over into nearby Petticoat Lane Market with similar goods but with less atmosphere.

From Brick Lane it's a stone's throw to the **Columbia Road Flower Market.** It's only 52 stalls, but markets don't get much more photogenic than this. Flowers, shrubs, bulbs, and trees are sold at competitive prices, while 30 shops offer complementary accesories like garden tools and pots. The local cafés are superb.

Stop to smell the roses and have Sunday brunch on Columbia Road before plunging into **Spitalfields.** This restored Victorian market hall (once London's wholesale fruit and vegetable market) is at the center of this area's gentrified revival. The original building is now largely occupied by boutiques, with traders' stalls relegated to the courtyard and an adjoining, glass-canopied modern shopping precinct. Wares include crafts, retro clothing, handmade rugs, soap, cakes. And, from Spanish tapas to Thai satays, it's possible to eat your way around the world.

BRICK LANE
🕙 Sun. 9 am–5 pm

✉ Brick La., Shoreditch E1 6SE

Ⓤ Liverpool Street (Metropolitan, Hammersmith & City, Circle or Central Line), Shoreditch High Street (London Overground)

☞ Food, hardware, household goods, electric goods, books, bikes, shoes, clothes, spices, saris

COLUMBIA ROAD FLOWER MARKET
🕙 Sun. 8–4

✉ Columbia Rd., Shoreditch E2 7RG

Ⓤ Old Street (Northern Line), Hoxton (London Overground)

☞ Flowers, shrubs, bulbs, trees, garden tools, accessories

SPITALFIELDS
🕙 Stalls Tues.–Fri. 10–4, Sun. 9–5. Restaurants Mon.–Fri. 8 am–11 pm, Sun. 9–11. Retail shops daily 10–7.

✉ Brushfield St., East End

Ⓤ Liverpool St. (Hammersmith & City, Circle, Metropolitan, or Central Line),Shoreditch High Street (London Overground)

☞ Crafts, foods, retro and modern clothing, rugs, vintage vinyl

BERMONDSEY ANTIQUES MARKET

🕐 Fri. 4 am–about 1 pm

✉ Long La. and Bermondsey Sq., Bermondsey SE1 4QB

Ⓤ London Bridge (Jubilee or Northern Line), Borough (Nothern Line)

☞ Antiques (silverware, paintings, furniture)

Come before dawn and bring a flashlight to bag a bargain antique at this famous market. Dealers arrive as early as 4 AM to snap up the best bric-a-brac and silverware, paintings, objets d'art, fine arts, and furniture. The early start grew out of a wrinkle in the law under which thieves could sell stolen goods with impunity in the hours of darkness when provenance could not be ascertained. That law was changed, and the market has been shrinking ever since.

What should be one of London's most important antiques markets is in decline and in desperate need of a significant rebrand to survive. The recent establishment of the Saturday morning Bermondsey Farmer's Market, as well as the 2009 redevelopment of Bermondsey Square (⊕ www.bermondseysquare. co.uk) should attract more customers to the Antiques Market. The square now includes a hotel, an arthouse cinema, shops, and restaurants.

THE CAMDEN MARKETS

CAMDEN MARKET
🕐 Daily 10 am–6 pm

CAMDEN LOCK MARKET, STABLES MARKET, AND CANAL MARKET
🕐 Daily 10–6

ELECTRIC MARKET
🕐 Sun. 9–5:30

✉ Camden Town, Camden NW1

Ⓤ Camden Town, Chalk Farm (Northern Line)

☞ Vintage clothing, antiques, jewelry, textiles, shoes, ceramics, mirrors, toys

18

This area's actually several markets gathered around a pair of locks in the Regent's Canal. Camden Lock Market proper began in 1973 on the site of a former timber yard. The lock studios attracted artists with reasonable rents and gave customers the chance to see goods being made. Today, the market includes some of London's most creative types, with products designed on site and market stalls offering a spectacular array of merchandise: vintage and new clothes, antiques and junk, jewelry and scarves, candlesticks, ceramics, mirrors, shoes, and toys.

The markets on Camden High Street (both outdoors and within the Electric Ballroom) mainly sell cheap T-shirts, secondhand clothes, and tacky pop-culture paraphernalia; it's best to head to Camden Lock and Stable Markets. Though much of the merchandise is youth oriented, the markets have a lively appeal to aging hippies, fashion designers, and anyone with a taste for the bohemian who doesn't mind crowds and a bit of a madhouse scene. Don't miss the Horse Hospital (weekends only) for quirky antiques dealers.

THE GREENWICH MARKET

The center of Greenwich is given over to a series of markets—crafts, fresh produce and food-to-go on Wed.; antiques, vintage fashion, collectables and food-to-go on Thurs. and Fri.; and arts, crafts, curiosities, fresh produce, and food-to-go on Sat. and Sun. Less crowded than Camden, less touristy than Covent Garden, this part-indoor, part-outdoor market is surrounded by interesting shops and close to historic sites. If you make a day of it, you can see the Greenwich Observatory and stand on Longitude 0 (marked in brass and stone in front of the observatory), visit the tall ship Cutty Sark, and shop till you drop. Take the DLR to the Cutty Sark, right in the thick of it, or for more fun, ride the DLR through Canary Wharf, get off at Island Gardens, and walk through the ancient foot tunnel under the Thames. Alternatively, take a river taxi to Greenwich Pier.

🕐 Tues.–Sun. 10 am–5:30 pm

✉ Greenwich Market (off Greenwich Church St.), Greenwich SE10 9HZ

Ⓤ DLR: Cutty Sark for Maritime Greenwich

☞ Antiques, arts, crafts, food, jewelry, clothing, leather goods, books, toys paraphernalia

Know-How

■ **TWO MARKET TIPS TO REMEMBER →** In the end, if you like something and you can afford it, it's worth buying; you're the best judge of that. But it's annoying to buy an "English antique" only to find the Made in China label when you get home. To avoid disappointment:

Look for hallmarks. A lot of what passes for English silver is plate or outright fake. English gold and silver must, by law, be marked with hallmarks that indicate their material and the year in which they were made. Books of hallmarks are inexpensive to buy in London bookshops.

Buy crafts items directly from the makers. Ceramicists, jewelers, needleworkers and other artisans often sell their own work at markets. Besides buying the item, you may have a conversation worth remembering.

■ **MARKET ETIQUETTE →** You've probably heard that you're expected to bargain with the market traders to get the best price. That's true to a degree, but London markets

are not Middle Eastern souks, and most bargaining is modest. Unless you are an expert in the item you want to buy and really know how low you can go, don't offer a ridiculously low price. Instead ask the dealer, "Is that the best you can do?" If the dealer is willing to bargain, he or she will suggest a slightly lower price, maybe 10% less. You might try to get another 10% off and end up meeting in the middle.

BOOKS

Gay's the Word. Open since 1979, this is London's leading gay and lesbian bookshop. Thousands of titles, from literature and thoughtful nonfiction, erotica to pro-diversity children's books, fill the shelves. The shop is a well-loved fixture on the scene, and often hosts discussion groups, readings, and other events. ✉ *66 Marchmont St., Bloomsbury* ☎ *020/7278–7654* ⊕ *www.gaystheword.co.uk* ✿ *Closed Sun. morning* Ⓜ *Russell Sq.*

Persephone Books. A must for all lovers of feminist fiction and nonfiction, Persephone is a gem of a bookshop specializing in reprints of mostly neglected 20th-century works from predominately female writers. Exquisitely decorated endpapers make these books perfect gifts for your bibliophile friends. ✉ *59 Lamb's Conduit St., Bloomsbury* ☎ *020/ 7242–9292* ⊕ *www.persephonebooks.co.uk* ✿ *Closed Sun.* Ⓜ *Russell Sq., Holborn.*

STATIONERY

Paperchase. The stationery superstore of the United Kingdom sells writing paper in every conceivable shade and in a dozen mediums. There are lovely cards, artists' materials, notebooks, and loose stationery. The three-floor flagship store has a café. Other London branches can be found on Chelsea's King's Road and Covent Garden's Piazza. ✉ *213– 215 Tottenham Court Rd., Bloomsbury* ☎ *020/7467–6200* ⊕ *www. paperchase.co.uk* Ⓜ *Goodge St.*

HOLBORN

ANTIQUES

★ **London Silver Vaults.** Housed in a basement vault, this extraordinary space holds stalls from more than 30 silver dealers. Products range from the spectacularly over-the-top costing thousands to smaller items—like teaspoons, candlesticks, or a set of Victorian cake forks—starting at £25. ■TIP→ Most of the silver merchants actually trade out of room-size, underground vaults, which were originally rented out to London's upper crust to store their valuables. ✉ *53–64 Chancery La., Holborn* ☎ *020/7242–3844* ⊕ *www.thesilvervaults.com* ✿ *Closed Sat. after 1 and Sun.* Ⓜ *Chancery La.*

ISLINGTON

HOUSEHOLD

TwentyTwentyOne. TwentyTwentyOne showcases the best in modern and vintage furniture. There are design classics like a chaise longue from Le Corbusier, as well as curvy daybeds from designer Jacob Pringiers. The kids' range is particularly cool, with items like the classic elephant sculpture/toy from husband-and-wife design team Charles and Ray Eames. Small accessories like tote bags and cushions will easily fit into your luggage. ✉ *274–275 Upper St., Islington* ☎ *020/7288–1996* ⊕ *www. twentytwentyone.com* Ⓜ *Highbury & Islington.*

18

THE CITY AND SOUTH BANK

THE CITY

ART GALLERY

★ **Lesley Craze Gallery.** This serene gallery displays jewelry by some 100 young designers from around the world (with a strong British bias), who use precious and semiprecious stones. A sculpture and textiles room showcases colorful handmade scarves. Prices start at £45. ✉ *33–35A Clerkenwell Green, Clerkenwell* ☎ *020/7608–0393* ⊕ *www.lesleycrazegallery.co.uk* ⊘ *Closed Sun.; open Mon. in Nov. and Dec. only* Ⓜ *Farringdon.*

THE SOUTH BANK

ART

Oxo Tower Wharf. The artisans creating fashion, jewelry, home accessories, textiles, prints and photographs, furniture, and other design items have to pass rigorous selection procedures to set up in these prime riverside workshops where they make, display, and sell their work. The workshops are glass-walled, and you're welcome to explore, even if you're just browsing. There are around 30 studios, spread over three floors. The Oxo Tower Restaurant & Brasserie on the top floor is expensive, but with its fantastic view of London, it's worth popping up for a drink. There's also a public terrace where you can take in the view. ✉ *Oxo Tower Wharf, Bargehouse St., South Bank* ☎ *020/7021–1686* ⊘ *Closed Mon.* Ⓜ *Southwark, Waterloo.*

THE EAST END

SPITALFIELDS

ACCESSORIES: HATS

★ **Bernstock Speirs.** Paul Bernstock and Thelma Speirs turn traditional hats on their head with street-smart trilbies and knitted hats that feature unusual colors and quirky details. ✉ *234 Brick La., Spitalfields* ☎ *020/7739–7385* ⊕ *www.bernstockspiers.com* Ⓜ *Liverpool St., Bethnal Green.*

CLOTHING

★ **Junky Styling.** This brand was launched by designers Annika Sanders and Kerry Seager, who used to "deconstruct" old clothing when they wanted something unique to wear clubbing. They recycled traditional suits and shirts into wild outfits, and the business grew from there. Each piece is unique, and the highly original (and eco-friendly) garments, for both men and women, are funky but retain the sophistication of their tailored origins. ✉ *12 Dray Walk, The Old Truman Brewery, 91 Brick La., Spitalfields* ☎ *020/7247–1883* ⊕ *www.junkystyling.co.uk* Ⓜ *Liverpool St., Aldgate East.*

★ **The Laden Showroom.** Sienna Miller, Victoria Beckham, and Noel Gallagher are among the celebs who regularly check out emerging talent at this East End showroom for young designers. The store retails the work of more than 70 new designers, some selling one-off items—so the look you find is likely to be original. ⊠ *103 Brick La., Spitalfields* ☎ *020/7247–2431* ⊕ *www.laden.co.uk* Ⓜ *Shoreditch High St.*

Start London. Start London offers an ever-changing roster of cutting-edge designers like Rick Owens, Richard Nicoll, and Markus Lupfer and, for men (down the street at No. 59), everything from Comme des Garcons to Nudie Jeans. Although the emphasis is on chic directional fashion, co-owner and American expat Brix Smith-Start is more mother hen than formidable fashionista and is happy to gently guide customers into trying something new. ⊠ *42-44 Rivington St., Shoreditch* ☎ *020/7033–3951* ⊕ *www.start-london.com* Ⓜ *Old St., Shoreditch High St.*

MUSIC

★ **Rough Trade East.** While many London record stores are struggling, this veteran indie-music specialist seems to have gotten the formula right. The spacious surroundings are as much a hangout as a shop, complete with a stage for live gigs, a café, and Internet access. ⊠ *Dray Walk, Old Truman Brewery, 91 Brick La., Spitalfields* ☎ *020/7392–7788* Ⓜ *Liverpool St., Shoreditch High St.*

KENSINGTON, CHELSEA, KNIGHTSBRIDGE, AND BELGRAVIA

18

BELGRAVIA

ACCESSORIES

★ **Lulu Guinness.** Famous for her flamboyantly themed bags (think the satin "bucket" topped with roses or the elaborately beaded red snakeskin "lips" clutch). Guinness also showcases vintage-inspired luggage and beauty accessories in this frilly little shop, which is just as whimsical as her designs. ⊠ *3 Ellis St., Belgravia* ☎ *020/7823–4828* ⊕ *www.luluguinness.com* ⊘ *Closed Sun.* Ⓜ *Sloane Sq.*

Fodor'sChoice **Philip Treacy.** Treacy's magnificent hats are annual showstoppers on
★ Ladies Day at the Royal Ascot races and regularly grace the glossy magazines' society pages. Part Mad Hatter, part Cecil Beaton, Treacy's creations always guarantee a grand entrance (remember the eye-popping chapeaux that adorned many famous heads at the Westminster Abbey wedding of Prince William and his queen-to-be Kate?). In addition to the extravagant, haute couture hats handmade in the atelier, ready-to-wear hats and bags are also for sale. ⊠ *69 Elizabeth St., Belgravia* ☎ *020/7730–3992* ⊕ *www.philiptreacy.co.uk* ⊘ *Closed Sun.* Ⓜ *Sloane Sq.*

CHELSEA

ACCESSORIES

The Shop at Bluebird. The brainchild of the couple behind popular wom-enswear brand Jigsaw, this 10,000-square-foot space in the old Bluebird garage brings together fashion, furniture, books, and music—all cho-sen for style and originality. It's worth visiting for the displays alone, which change regularly, although the funky ceiling-light installation of more than 1,000 bulbs seems to be a constant feature. After browsing, unwind with a treatment at the on-site spa or join the ladies who lunch at the restaurant in the same complex. ■TIP➔ It's a good 20-minute walk from the nearest Tube station at Sloane Square, so catch a No. 11 or No. 22 bus along the King's Road. ⊠ *350 King's Rd., Chelsea* ☎ *020/7351–3873* ⊕ *www.theshopatbluebird.com* Ⓜ *Sloane Sq.*

ANTIQUES

Fodor's Choice ★ **Rupert Cavendish.** This most elevated of Chelsea dealers had the Bieder-meier market cornered so has now expanded to Empire and art deco antiques. The shop is a museum experience. ⊠ *610 King's Rd., Chelsea* ☎ *020/7731–7041* ⊕ *www.rupertcavendish.co.uk* Ⓜ *Sloane Sq.*

BOOKS

Green & Stone. This fabulous cave of artists' materials, papers, art books, easels, and mannequins is one of the longest-established shops on the King's Road, with a distinguished arts pedigree. It began life in 1927 as part of the Chenil Gallery, run by a distinguished group that included Augustus John and George Bernard Shaw. At the current location since 1934, the shop also has a framing service, antique paint boxes, and artists' tools. ⊠ *259 King's Rd., Chelsea* ☎ *020/7352–0837* ⊕ *www. greenandstone.com* Ⓜ *Sloane Sq.*

CLOTHING

Austique. For fans of such feminine brands as Shoshanna, Alice + Olivia, or Mara Hoffman, look no further than Austique. Situated along the trendy King's Road, this sophisticated boutique, created by sisters Linda Lopes and Katie Canvin, is home to a gorgeous array of dresses, lin-gerie, jewelry, and accessories for the ultimate fashionista. It's almost impossible to leave empty-handed. There's another branch in Maryle-bone. ⊠ *330 King's Rd., Chelsea* ☎ *020/7376–4555* ⊕ *www.austique. co.uk* Ⓜ *Sloane Sq.*

☾ **Brora.** The knitwear is cozy, but the style is cool in this contempo-rary Scottish cashmere emporium for men, women, and kids. There are dressed-up camisoles, sweaters and cardigans, and adorable baby ensembles, as well as noncashmere items such as picnic blankets and scarves. Other branches can be found in Notting Hill, Marylebone, Islington, Wimbledon, Richmond, Covent Garden, and Sloane Square. ⊠ *344 King's Rd., Chelsea* ☎ *020/7352–3697* ⊕ *www.brora.co.uk* Ⓜ *Sloane Sq.*

Fodor's Choice ★ **Jack Wills.** Wowie-zowie! The British preppie's answer to Abercrombie & Fitch, Jack Wills specializes in heritage and country sports-inspired styles for men and women but gives them a youthful, sexy edge. This means disco-like stores crammed with slim-line Fair Isle sweaters, fitted plaid shirts, and short floral sundresses for the girls, plus sweatshirts, blazers, skinny cords, hoodies, and rugby shirts for the boys. Add in a delightful array of shocking pink gypsy pillows, Union Jack carry-ons, bobble hats galore, knitted jackets for hot-water bottles, and other kitschy items and the result are crowds of plugged-in buyers. Branches are in Notting Hill, Covent Garden, Islington, and Soho (on Long Acre). ⊠ *72 Kings Rd., Chelsea* ☎ *020/7581–0347* ⊕ *www.jackwills. com* Ⓜ *Sloane Sq.*

CLOTHING: WOMEN'S

Rigby & Peller. Lovers of luxury lingerie shop here for brands like Prima Donna and Aubade, as well as R&P's own line. If the right fit eludes you and you fancy being fitted by the Queen's *corsetiére*, the Knightsbridge branch offers a made-to-measure service starting around £300. Many of London's most affluent women shop here, not only because of the royal appointment but also because the quality is excellent and the service is impeccably knowledgeable, while being much friendlier than you might expect. There are a number of branches around town, all of which are open on Sunday, except the Conduit Street location. ⊠ *13 Kings Rd., Chelsea* ☎ *0845/076–5545* ⊕ *www.rigbyandpeller.com* Ⓜ *Sloane Sq.*

FOOD

L'Artisan du Chocolat. Praised by top chefs Gordon Ramsay and Heston Blumenthal, L'Artisan raises chocolate to an art form. "Couture" chocolates are infused with fruits, nuts, and spices (including such exotic flavorings as Szechuan pepper and tobacco). This is one of the few chocolate shops in the world that makes liquid salted caramels. Leave the kiddies at home, though; this shop is total wish fulfillment for grown-up chocolate lovers. There's also a branch in Notting Hill. ⊠ *89 Lower Sloane St., Chelsea* ☎ *020/7824–8365* Ⓜ *Sloane Sq.*

HOUSEHOLD

★ **The Conran Shop.** This is the brainchild of Sir Terence Conran, who has been informing British taste since he opened Habitat in the 1960s. Although he is no longer associated with Habitat, his eponymous stores are still bastions of similarly clean, unfussy modernist design. Home enhancers from furniture to stemware and textiles—both handmade and mass-produced, by famous names and emerging designers—are displayed in a suitably gorgeous building that is a modernist design landmark in its own right. Both the flagship store and the branch on Marylebone High Street are bursting with great gift ideas. ⊠ *Michelin House, 81 Fulham Rd., South Kensington* ☎ *020/7589–7401* ⊕ *www. conranshop.co.uk* Ⓜ *South Kensington.*

Designers Guild. Tricia Guild's exuberantly colored modern fabrics, wallpapers, paints, furniture, and bed linens have inspired several decades' worth of home owners and apartment dwellers, and her soft-furnishings book has taught many a budget-conscious do-it-yourselfer how to reupholster a sofa or make lined draperies. The shop also stocks contemporary furniture, wallpapers, and home accessories by other designers. ⊠ *267-277 King's Rd., Chelsea* ☎ *020/351–5775* ⊕ *www. designersguild.com* ⊘ *Closed Sun.* Ⓜ *Sloane Sq.*

18

JEWELRY

★ **Butler & Wilson.** Long before anybody ever heard the word "bling," this shop was marketing the look—in diamanté, colored rhinestones, and crystal—to movie stars and secretaries alike. Specialists in bold costume jewelry, they've added semiprecious stones to the collections and the look is anything but subtle, so it may not suit all tastes unless you're in the market for a rhinestone Union Jack pin. Even if you're not a fan, the shop is worth a visit for its vintage (and vintage-influenced) clothes, once used only to display the jewelry. There's also another shop at 20 South Molton Street. ⊠ *189 Fulham Rd., South Kensington* ☎ *020/7352–3045* ⊕ *www.butlerandwilson.co.uk* Ⓜ *South Kensington.*

Melissa McArthur Jewellry. Tucked between Vivienne Westwood's shop and the Bluebird in Chelsea, this small but mighty jewelry store is a must-see on the King's Road. With everything handmade in-house using precious and semiprecious gems (don't forget the freshwater pearls), stocking up on gifts for female loved ones is easy here. The price points are also very reasonable for such eternally wearable and gorgeous items. ⊠ *378 King's Rd., Chelsea* ☎ *020/7351–1551* ⊕ *www.mmjlondon.com* Ⓜ *Sloane Sq., South Kensington.*

SHOES

★ **Manolo Blahnik.** Blink and you'll miss the discreet sign that marks fashionista footwear central. Blahnik, the man who single-handedly managed to revive the sexy stiletto and make it classier than ever, has been trading out of this small shop on a Chelsea side street since 1973. It's a must for shoe lovers with a generous budget. If you decide to wear your new Manolos, hop on the No. 11 or No. 22 bus or grab a cab—the nearest Tube is about a 20-minute totter away. ⊠ *49–51 Old Church St., Chelsea* ☎ *020/7352–3863* ⊕ *www.manoloblahnik.com* ⊙ *Closed Sun.* Ⓜ *Sloane Sq., South Kensington.*

KENSINGTON

HOUSEHOLD

Fodor's Choice
★ **Mint.** Owner Lina Kanafani has scoured the globe to stock an eclectic mix of furniture, art, ceramics, and home accessories. Mint also showcases works by up-and-coming designers and sells plenty of limited edition and one-off pieces. If you don't want to ship a couch home, consider a miniature flower vase or a handmade ceramic pitcher. ⊠ *2 North Terr., South Kensington* ☎ *020/7225–2228* ⊕ *www.mintshop. co.uk* Ⓜ *South Kensington.*

WOMEN'S WEAR

★ **Jigsaw.** Jigsaw specializes in clothes that are classic yet trendy, ladylike without being dull. The style is epitomized by the former Kate Middleton, who was a buyer for the company before her marriage. The quality of fabrics and detailing belie the reasonable prices and cuts are kind to the womanly figure. Although there are numerous branches across London, no two stores are the same. The pre-teen set have their own line, Jigsaw Junior. ⊠ *The Chapel, Duke of York Sq., King's Rd., Chelsea* ☎ *020/730–4404* ⊕ *www.jigsawonline.com* Ⓜ *Sloane Sq.*

KNIGHTSBRIDGE

ACCESSORIES

★ **Anya Hindmarch.** Exquisite leather bags and personalized, printed canvas totes are what made Hindmarch famous, along with her "I'm Not A Plastic Bag" eco-creation. Her designs are sold at Harrods and Harvey Nichols, but in her stores you can see her complete collection of bags and shoes and have your photograph immortalized on a "Be A Bag" that comes in a variety of sizes and styles. There are also branches around the corner on Bond Street in Mayfair and on Ledbury Road in Notting Hill. ⊠ *157–158 Sloane St., Knightsbridge* ☏ *020/7730–0961* ⊕ *www.anyahindmarch.com* Ⓜ *Sloane Sq., Knightsbridge.*

CLOTHING

Egg. Tucked away in a residential mews a short walk from Harvey Nichols, this shop is the brainchild of Maureen Doherty, once Issey Miyake's right-hand person. More than half the minimalist, unstructured styles for men and women in natural fabrics such as silk, cashmere, and antique cotton are handmade. The shop is a former Victorian dairy, and garments are casually hung on hooks or folded on wooden tables in the simple, white space. The price tags, however, are anything but humble. Unusual ceramics and jewelry are also on display. ⊠ *36 Kinnerton St., Knightsbridge* ☏ *020/7235–9315* ☉ *Closed Sun.* Ⓜ *Knightsbridge.*

CLOTHING: CHILDREN

☺ **Rachel Riley.** Looking for traditional English style for the younger ones? Riley's expensive, vintage-inspired collection includes classics like duffle coats, cashmere booties, and floral dresses for girls and teens. Mothers who love the Riley look can pick even up coordinating outfits for themselves at the Knightsbridge or Marylebone High Street locations. ⊠ *14 Pont St., Knightsbridge* ☏ *020/7259–5969* ⊕ *www.rachelriley. com* Ⓜ *Knightsbridge.*

CLOTHING: MENSWEAR

Hackett. If J. Crew isn't preppy enough for you, try Hackett. Originally a posh thrift shop recycling cricket flannels, hunting pinks, Oxford brogues, and other staples of the British gentleman's wardrobe, Hackett now creates its own line and has become a genuine—and very good— men's outfitter. The look is traditional and classic, with best buys including polo shirts, corduroys, and striped scarves. There's also a boys' line for the junior man-about-town. ⊠ *137/138 Sloane St., Chelsea* ☏ *020/7730–3331* ⊕ *www.hackett.com* Ⓜ *Sloane Sq.*

CLOTHING: WOMEN'S WEAR

★ **Agent Provocateur.** Created by Vivienne Westwood's son, this line of sexy, saucy lingerie in gorgeous fabrics and lace tends toward the kind of underwear that men buy for women, more provocative than practical. The original boudoir-like shop is in what was Soho's red-light district, but the brand has gone thoroughly mainstream and now sells bathing suits, bed linen, and luggage (along with paddles and pasties) in Knightsbridge, Notting Hill, and the City of London, as well as in Harrods, Harvey Nichols, and Selfridges. ⊠ *16 Pont St., Knightsbridge* ☏ *020/7235–0229* ⊕ *www.agentprovocateur.com* ☉ *Closed Sun.* Ⓜ *Knightsbridge.*

18

DEPARTMENT STORES

★ **Harrods.** With an encyclopedic assortment of luxury brands, this Knightsbridge institution has more than 300 departments and 20 restaurants, all spread over 1 million square feet on a 5-acre site. If you approach Harrods as a tourist attraction rather than as a fashion hunting ground, you won't be disappointed. Focus on the spectacular food halls, the huge ground-floor perfumery, the marble-lined accessory rooms, the excellent Urban Retreat spa, and the Vegas–like Egyptian Room. At the bottom of the nearby Egyptian escalator, there's a bronze statue depicting the late Princess Diana and Dodi Fayed, son of the former owner, dancing beneath the wings of an albatross. Nevertheless, standards of taste are enforced with a customer dress code (no shorts, ripped jeans, or flip-flops). ■TIP➔ Be prepared to brave the crowds (avoid visiting on a Saturday if you can), and be prepared to pay if you want to use the bathroom on some floors(!). ✉ *87–135 Brompton Rd., Knightsbridge* ☎ *020/7730–1234* ⊕ *www.harrods.com* Ⓜ *Knightsbridge.*

Fodor's Choice **Harvey Nichols.** While visiting tourists flock to Harrods, true London
★ fashionistas shop at Harvey Nichols, aka "Harvey Nicks." The womenswear and accessories departments are outstanding, featuring of-the-moment designers like Roland Mouret, Peter Pilotto, and 3.1 Phillip Lim. The furniture and housewares are equally gorgeous (and pricey), though they become somewhat more affordable during the twice-annual sales in January and July. The Fifth Floor restaurant is the place to see and be seen, but if you're just after a quick bite, there's also a more informal café on the same floor or sushi-to-go from Yo! Sushi. ✉ *109–125 Knightsbridge, Knightsbridge* ☎ *020/7235–5000* ⊕ *www. harveynichols.com* Ⓜ *Knightsbridge.*

SHOES

Jimmy Choo. Even though both designer Choo (who now runs a Connaught Street atelier selling couture handmade shoes) and Tamara Mellon, who built the brand, have now departed, Jimmy Choo designs remain a red carpet must-have for supermodels, fashionistas, and celebrities. The elegant yet sexy creations combine luxurious materials and details with classic shapes (pointy toes and slim high heels are signatures) to create timeless style—essential given the prices. The handbags are also firm favorites with the loyal clientele. ✉ *32 Sloane St., Knightsbridge* ☎ *020/7823–1051* ⊕ *www.jimmychoo.com* Ⓜ *Knightsbridge.*

NOTTING HILL

BOOKS

Books for Cooks. It may seem odd to describe a bookshop as delicious-smelling, but the aromas wafting out of Books for Cooks' test kitchen will whet your appetite even before you've opened one of the 8,000 cookbooks. Just about every world cuisine is represented along with a complete lineup of books by celebrity chefs. A tiny café at the back offers lunch dishes drawn from recipes on the shelves, as well as desserts and coffee. Menus change daily. ■TIP➔ Before you come to London, visit the shop's website, www.booksforcooks.com, to sign up for a cooking class.

✉ *4 Blenheim Crescent, Notting Hill* ☎ *020/7221–1992* ⊙ *Closed Sun. and Mon.* Ⓜ *Notting Hill Gate, Ladbroke Grove.*

CLOTHING

Aimé. French-Cambodian sisters Val and Vanda Heng-Vong launched this shop to showcase the best of French clothing and designer housewares. Expect to find fashion by Isabel Marant, Forte Forte, and A.P.C. You can also pick up A.P.C. candles, Rice homewares, and a well-edited collection of ceramics. Just next door at 34 Ledbury Road, Petit Aimé sells children's clothing. ✉ *32 Ledbury Rd., Notting Hill* ☎ *020/7221–7070* ⊕ *www.aimelondon.com* Ⓜ *Notting Hill Gate.*

☺ **Caramel Baby & Child.** Here you'll find adorable yet unfussy clothes for children six months and up: handcrafted Peruvian alpaca cardigans in sherbet colors, twill skirts, and floral cotton blouses and dresses for girls; check shirts and earth-tone tees for boys; comfortable pants in twill, corduroy, and cotton for both; and Merino/cashmere sweaters for extremely fashionable toddlers and babies. Caramel also sells a small selection of decorative/functional items like mobiles, child-friendly chairs and stools, teddy bears, and sheep-shape pillows. There are also branches in South Kensington and Chelsea. ✉ *77 Ledbury Rd., Notting Hill* ☎ *020/7727–0906* ⊕ *www.caramel-shop.co.uk* Ⓜ *Westbourne Park, Notting Hill Gate.*

MUSIC

Music & Video Exchange. This store—actually a rambling conglomeration of several shops on Notting Hill Gate—is a music collector's treasure trove, with a constantly changing stock refreshed by customers selling and exchanging as well as buying. The main store focuses on rock and pop, both mainstream and obscure, in a variety of formats ranging from vinyl to CD, cassette, and even mini-disk. Don't miss the discounts in the basement and the rarities upstairs. Soul and dance is found at No. 42, classical music at No. 36, video and computer games at No. 40, and movies at No. 34. There are also branches in Soho, Greenwich, and Camden. ✉ *38 Notting Hill Gate, Notting Hill* ☎ *020/7243–8574* Ⓜ *Notting Hill Gate.*

SHOES

Emma Hope. Emma Hope's signature look is elegant and ladylike, with pointed toes and kitten heels, often ornamented with bows, lace, crystal, or exquisite embroidery. Ballet flats and sneakers in velvet or animal prints provide glamour without sacrificing comfort. Both branches (Notting Hill and Sloane Square) also stock small-but-perfectly-formed handbags, as well as shoes and accessories for men. ✉ *207 Westbourne Grove, Notting Hill* ☎ *020/7313–7490* ⊕ *www.emmahope.com* Ⓜ *Notting Hill Gate.*

SPECIALTY STORES

Fodor's Choice ★ **The Village Bicycle.** With a style that might best be described as punk *luxe*, this "lifestyle concept store" offers witty, *haute* Goth homewares like a phone disguised as Damien Hirst's notorious artwork *For The Love of God* (a diamond-encrusted skull, except in this case the diamonds are glass) and an iPad stand in the form of an old-school arcade game. There are also toys, coffee-table books, trinkets, shoes, hi-tops, and art, as well as clothes—most involving leather, black, or fur from ultra-hip labels like House of Holland, Mark Fast, and Chloe Sevigny that are designed for girls with small frames and big credit limits. ⊠ *79-81 Ledbury Rd., Notting Hill* ☎ *020/7792–8601* Ⓜ *Notting Hill Gate, Westbourne Park.*

ST. JAMES'S, MAYFAIR, AND MARYLEBONE

MARYLEBONE

ANTIQUES

★ **Alfie's Antique Market.** This four-story, bohemian-chic labyrinth is London's largest indoor antiques market, housing dealers specializing in art, lighting, glassware, textiles, jewelry, furniture, and collectibles, with a particular strength in vintage clothing and 20th-century design. Here's where you come to pick up fabulous cocktail dresses and kitsch bar accessories at The Girl Can't Help It, an Alvar Aalto chair at Brent Plys, or a spectacular mid-20th-century Italian lighting fixture at Vincenzo Caffarrella. There's also a rooftop restaurant if you need a coffee break. In addition to the market, this end of Church Street is lined with excellent antiques shops. ⊠ *13–25 Church St., Marylebone* ☎ *020/7723–6066* ⊕ *www.alfiesantiques.com* ⊗ *Closed Sun. and Mon.* Ⓜ *Marylebone.*

BOOKS

Daunt Books. An independent bookstore chain (there are additional branches in Belsize Park, Chelsea, Hampstead, Holland Park, and Cheapside), Daunt favors a thoughtful selection of contemporary and classic fiction and nonfiction over self-help books and ghost-written celebrity "autobiographies." It is especially noted for its travel selection, which includes not only guidebooks but also relevant poetry and literature organized by country, and children's books. The striking Marylebone branch is an original Edwardian bookstore where a dramatic room lined with oak galleries under lofty skylights houses the travel section. Meanwhile, biographies and fiction are piled on tables at the entrance for eclectic browsing. ⊠ *83 Marylebone High St., Marylebone* ☎ *020/7224–2295* ⊕ *www.dauntbooks.co.uk* Ⓜ *Baker St.*

CERAMICS

Emma Bridgewater. Here's where you'll find fun and funky casual plates, mugs, jugs, and breakfast tableware embellished with polka dots, hens, hearts and flowers, amusing mottoes, or matter-of-fact labels (sugar or coffee). There's another branch in Fulham. ⊠ *81a Marylebone High St., Marylebone* ☎ *020/7486–6897* Ⓜ *Baker St., Bond St.*

CLOTHING

Margaret Howell. These quintessentially English clothes are understated yet manage to look utterly contemporary. Howell mixes impeccable British tailoring and traditional fabrics (linen, cashmere, and tweed) with relaxed modern cuts. A fan of 20th-century household design, the designer also showcases vintage Ercol furniture in her Wigmore

Street boutique. There's another branch on the Fulham Road. ✉ *34 Wigmore St., Marylebone* ☎ *020/7009–9006* ⊕ *www.margarethowell. co.uk* Ⓜ *Bond St.*

Matches. The rising British designers featured in these shops that pop up throughout London include Christopher Kane, Jonathan Saunders, Issa, and Goat, as well as more-established figures like McCartney and McQueen. International labels, including J Brand, Acne, Vanessa Bruno, Lanvin, Chloe, and Celine, are also represented. There's also an equally stylish menswear department, plus jewelry, lingerie, and accessories. ✉ *87 Marylebone High St., Marylebone* ☎ *020/7487–5400* ⊕ *www.matchesfashion.com* Ⓜ *Baker St., Regent's Park.*

DEPARTMENT STORES

Marks & Spencer. You'd be hard-pressed to find a Brit who doesn't have something in the closet from Marks & Spencer (or "M&S," as it's affectionately known). This major chain whips up classic, dependable clothing for men, women, and children and occasionally scores a fashion hit with its Per Una and Autograph lines. But the best buys here are the classics, such as cashmere and wool sweaters, socks and underwear, and believe it or not, machine-washable suits. The food department at M&S is consistently superb, especially for frozen food, and a great place to pick up a sandwich or premade salad on the go (look for M&S Simply Food stores all over town.) The flagship branch at Marble Arch and the Pantheon location at 173 Oxford Street have extensive fashion departments. ✉ *458 Oxford St., Marylebone* ☎ *020/7935–7954* ⊕ *www.marksandspencer.com* Ⓜ *Marble Arch.*

Fodor's Choice ★ **Selfridges.** This giant, bustling store (the second-largest in the United Kingdom after Harrods) gives Harvey Nichols a run for its money as London's leading fashion department store. Packed to the rafters with clothes ranging from mid-price lines to the latest catwalk names, the store continues to break ground with its striking modern design, especially the high-fashion Superbrands sections and the ground-floor Wonder Room showcasing extravagant jewelry and luxury gifts. There are so many zones that merge into one another—from youth-oriented Miss Selfridge to sports gear to audio equipment to the large, comprehensive cosmetics department—that you practically need a map. Don't miss the Shoe Galleries, the world's largest shoe department filled with more than 5,000 pairs from 120 brands, displayed like works of art under spotlights, plus comfy fuscia-pink seating. ■ TIP➔ Take a break with a glass of wine from the Wonder Bar, or pick up some rare tea in the Food Hall as a gift. ✉ *400 Oxford St., Marylebone* ☎ *0800/123400* ⊕ *www. selfridges.com* Ⓜ *Bond St.*

JEWELRY

★ **Kabiri.** A dazzling array of exciting contemporary jewelry by emerging and established designers from around the world is packed into this small shop. There is something to suit most budgets and tastes, from flamboyant statement pieces to subtle, delicate adornment. Look out for British talent Johanne Mills, among many others. ✉ *37 Marylebone High St., Marylebone* ☎ *020/7224–1808* ⊕ *www.kabiri.co.uk* Ⓜ *Baker St.*

18

MAYFAIR

ACCESSORIES

Fodor's Choice ★ **Mulberry.** Staying true to its roots in rural Somerset, this luxury goods company epitomizes *le style Anglais*, a sophisticated take on the earth tones and practicality of English country style. Best known for highly desirable luxury handbags such as the Alexa and the Bayswater, the company also produces gorgeous leather accessories, from wallets to luggage, as well as shoes and clothing. Aside from the New Bond Street flagship, there are branches in Knightsbridge and Covent Garden, and Mulberry is sold in the major department stores. The small store on St. Christopher's Place in Marylebone stocks accessories only. ⊠ *50 New Bond St., Mayfair* ☎ *020/7491–3900* ⊕ *www.mulberry.com* Ⓜ *Bond St.*

William & Son. William Aprey, scion of the jewelry dynasty, has decided to set up on his own and open a store that takes a more friendly, less formal approach to selling carefully chosen, British-made luxury goods. Here's where you'll find all sorts of items you didn't know you needed, like silver-tipped retractable pencils, lizard-skin passport holders, crocodile backgammon sets, or a silver piggy bank. The jewelry is tasteful rather than knock-your-eyes-out and the store encourages requests for custom-made pieces. ⊠ *10 Mount St., Mayfair* ☎ *020/7493–8385* ⊕ *www.williamandson.com* ✆ *Closed weekends* Ⓜ *Bond St.*

ANTIQUES

Grays Antique Market. Open daily except Sunday from 10 to 6 (not all stalls are open on Saturdays), Grays boasts approximately 200 dealers specializing in everything from Bakelite homewares to Mughal art. The majority focus on jewelry, ranging from contemporary to antique. Bargains are not out of the question, and proper pedigrees are guaranteed. Also try Grays in the Mews around the corner—stalls there sell less expensive merchandise, including antique dolls at Glenda's and excellent vintage clothing at Vintage Modes. ⊠ *58 Davies St., Mayfair* ☎ *020/7629–7034* ⊕ *www.graysantiques.com* ✆ *Closed Sun.* Ⓜ *Bond St.*

BOOKS AND STATIONERY

Maggs Brothers Ltd. How could any book lover resist a shop with such a deliciously Dickensian name? Located in a Georgian town house in one of Mayfair's most elegant squares, Maggs, established 1853, is one of the world's oldest and largest rare-book dealers. Shop staff is expert enough to advise important collectors, but is nonetheless friendly and helpful to all interested visitors. ⊠ *50 Berkeley Sq., Mayfair* ☎ *020/7493–7160* ⊕ *www.maggs.com* ✆ *Closed weekends* Ⓜ *Green Park.*

★ **Smythson of Bond Street.** Hands down, this is the most elegant stationer in Britain. No hostess of any standing would consider having a leatherbound guest book made by anyone else, and the shop's distinctive pale-blue–page diaries and social stationery are thoroughly British. Diaries, stationery, and small leather goods can be personalized. Smythson also produces a small range of leather handbags and purses. There are branches within Harvey Nichols, Harrods, and Selfridges. ⊠ *40 New Bond St., Mayfair* ☎ *020/7629–8558* Ⓜ *Bond St., Green Park.*

Waterstone's. At this mega-bookshop (Europe's largest) located in a former art deco department store near Piccadilly Circus, browse through your latest purchase or admire the view while sipping a glass of bubbly or getting a bite to eat at the sixth-floor Champagne and Seafood Bar, which is open until 9. Waterstone's is the country's leading book chain, and they've pulled out all the stops to make their flagship as comfortable and welcoming as a bookstore can be. There are several smaller branches located throughout the city. ⊠ *203–206 Piccadilly, Mayfair* ☎ *0843/290–8549* ⊕ *www.waterstones.com* Ⓜ *Piccadilly Circus.*

CLOTHING

Burberry. Burberry, known for its ubiquitous plaids, has cultivated an edgy, high-fashion image in recent years, with designs like fetish-y boots and sexy leather jackets perfect for any catwalk. The raincoats are still a classic buy, along with plaid scarves in every color imaginable. If you're up for a trek, there's a huge factory outlet in Hackney on Chatham Place that has clothes and accessories for men, women, and children at half price or less. There are also branches on Brompton Road in Knightsbridge and Regent Street in Soho. ⊠ *21–23 New Bond St., Mayfair* ☎ *020/3367–3000* ⊕ *www.burberry.com* Ⓜ *Piccadilly Circus.*

Fodor'sChoice
★ **Dover Street Market.** Visiting this six-floor emporium isn't just about buying; with its creative displays and eclectic, well-chosen mix of merchandise, it's as much art installation as store. The creation of Comme des Garçons' Rei Kawakubo, it showcases all of the label's collections for men and women alongside a changing roster of other designers including Erdem, Alaïa, and Givenchy—all of whom have their own customized mini-boutiques—plus avant-garde art books, vintage couture, and curiosities such as antique plaster anatomy models. You never know what you will find, which is half the fun. ■ TIP➔ **An outpost of the Rose Bakery on the top floor makes for a yummy break.** ⊠ *17–18 Dover St., Mayfair* ☎ *020/7518–0680* ⊕ *www.doverstreetmarket.com* ☉ *Closed Sun.* Ⓜ *Green Park.*

Mackintosh. Think of Victorian and you think of corsets, bodices, and frock coats—but did you know that the era also created the modern rubberized raincoat? Back in 1823, a Glasgow chemist named Mackintosh successfully came up with the way to interweave rubber with cloth and, in so doing, finally designed rainproof clothes (then used for horse riding). Now, just in time for the hot new "Steampunk" fashion—old Victorian meets mod engineering—this once-famous label has been reborn thanks to Japanese backers, who have also invested in a hip boutique. Far from a museum, it showcases the line's quasi-militaristic yet casual designs. Everything old is, indeed, new again. ⊠ *104 Mount St., Mayfair W1K 2TL* ☎ *020/7493–4678* ☉ *Closed Sun.* Ⓜ *Bond St.*

CLOTHING: MENSWEAR

Gieves and Hawkes. One of the grand mens' tailoring houses of Savile Row, this company made its name outfitting British Royals who served as officers in the armed forces and still supplies custom-made military uniforms, as well as beautifully tailored civilian wear. Prices for a

18

bespoke suit start around £3,800 but there are also off-the-peg designs starting at around £600. ✉ *1 Savile Row, Mayfair* ☎ *020/7434–2001* ⊕ *www.gievesandhawkes.com* Ⓜ *Piccadilly Circus.*

★ **Ozwald Boateng.** Ozwald Boateng's (pronounced Bwa-teng) dapper menswear combines contemporary funky style with traditional Savile Row quality. His made-to-measure suits have been worn by trendsetters such as Jamie Foxx, Mick Jagger, and Laurence Fishburne, who appreciate the sharp cuts, luxurious fabrics, and occasionally vibrant colors (even the more conservative choices sport jacket linings in bright silk). ✉ *30 Savile Row, Mayfair* ☎ *020/7437–2030* ⊕ *www.ozwaldboateng. co.uk* ⊘ *Closed Sun.* Ⓜ *Piccadilly Circus.*

CLOTHING: WOMEN'S WEAR

Fodor's Choice
★

Alexander McQueen. Today, the chorus of fashionistas intent on crowning a "new" McQueen are delighted that she was spotted right at the master's feet: since McQueen's death in 2010, his right-hand woman Sarah Burton has been at the helm, and has been receiving raves for continuing his tradition of theatrical, darkly romantic, and beautifully cut clothes incorporating corsetry, lace, embroidery, and hourglass silhouettes, all of which were exemplified in Burton's celebrated wedding dress for Kate Middleton. Ms. Burton is still the star of the moment, as her 2013 show in Paris won rave reviews for its spectacular feather-and-chiffon gowns and the fact that she remained true to the forms first forged by Lee McQueen's in the late 90s (such as the low-slung "bumster" trousers). Can't afford a gala gown? Go home with a skull-printed scarf. ✉ *4–5 Old Bond St., Mayfair* ☎ *020/7355–0088* ⊕ *www.alexandermcqueen. com* ⊘ *Closed Sun.* Ⓜ *Bond St.*

Fodor's Choice
★

Browns. This shop—actually a collection of small shops—was a pioneer designer boutique in the 1970s and continues to talent-spot the newest and best around. You may find the windows showcasing the work of top graduates from this year's student shows or displaying well-established designers such as Marni, Chloé, Alexander McQueen, Dries Van Noten, or Temperley. The men's store at No. 23 has a similar designer selection, while Browns Focus, across the street at Nos. 38–39, showcases youthful, hip designs and denim. There is a bargain outlet at No. 50 and a smaller boutique at 6C Sloane Street. If you're about to go down the aisle, check out the two bridal boutiques; one at 11–12 Hinde Street, which stocks various designers, and another at 59 Brook Street, off New Bond Street, devoted to Vera Wang gowns exclusive to Browns in the United Kingdom. ✉ *24–27 S. Molton St., Mayfair* ☎ *020/7514–0000* ⊕ *www.brownsfashion.com* ⊘ *Closed Sun.* Ⓜ *Bond St.*

Fodor's Choice
★

b Store. Some people regard b Store as the best small clothing boutique in London. Head here for cutting-edge pieces from avant-garde designers such as Sophie Hume, plus the store's quirky own-label shoes, men and women's clothing, and accessories. ✉ *21 Kingly St., Soho* ☎ *020/7734–6846* ⊕ *www.bstorelondon.com* ⊘ *Closed Sun.* Ⓜ *Piccadilly Circus, Oxford Circus.*

Fenwick. A manageably sized department store, Fenwick is a welcome haven of affordability in a shopping area where stratospheric prices are the norm. The store is particularly strong on accessories (notably lingerie, wraps, and hats), cosmetics, perfumes and chic, wearable fashion by both established and emerging designers such as Issa and Richard Nicholl. There are also three small spas (Chantecaille, Clarins, and Pure Massage), a nail bar, a brow bar, and a restaurant, plus a men's department in the basement. ✉ *163 New Bond St., Mayfair* ☎ *020/7629–9161* ⊕ *www.fenwick.co.uk* Ⓜ *Bond St.*

Matthew Williamson. Sinuous, feminine, and floaty, Williamson's designs—often incorporating bright prints and embellishment—are the epitome of rich-hippie chic, and are favorites with such well-heeled free spirits as Kate Moss and Sienna Miller. Even if you can't manage to get to a beach party on Ibiza, a Williamson dress will put you in the spirit. ✉ *28 Bruton St., Mayfair* ☎ *020/7629–6200* ⊕ *www.matthewwilliamson.com* Ⓜ *Bond St.*

Nicole Farhi. Busy working women who value unfussy quality invest in Farhi's softly tailored yet functional dresses and separates, and her contemporary yet timeless styles are wardrobe staples. There are several locations throughout the city, with the flagship New Bond Street store selling clothes for both men and women (as well as boasting a restaurant, Nicole's, that is more than just somewhere to resuscitate between purchases). A branch devoted to homewares is around the corner on Clifford Street, while the full men's collection is available at the Floral Street branch. ✉ *158 New Bond St., Mayfair* ☎ *020/7499–8368* ⊕ *www.nicolefarhi.com* Ⓜ *Bond St.*

★ **Stella McCartney.** It's not easy emerging from the shadow of a Beatle father, but Stella McCartney has become a major force in fashion in her own right. Her signature tuxedo pantsuits embody her design philosophy, combining minimalist tailoring with femininity and sophistication with ease of wear. Her love of functionality and clean lines has led to her branching off into sportswear, designing a line for Adidas and dressing Team GB for the London Olympics. Being a vegetarian like her mother Linda, her refusal to use fur or leather has made her a favorite with ethical fashionistas. There's another boutique on the Brompton Road. ✉ *30 Bruton St., Mayfair* ☎ *020/751–8310* ⊕ *www.stellamccartney.com.uk* ☯ *Closed Sun.* Ⓜ *Bond St.*

Fodor's Choice ★ **Vivienne Westwood.** From beginnings as the most shocking and outré designer around, Westwood has become a standard bearer for high-style British couture. The boutique under the backwards-spinning clock in Chelsea is where it all started: the lavish corseted ball gowns, the dandy-fied nipped-waist jackets, and the tartan with a punk edge that formed the core of her signature look. Here you can still buy ready-to-wear, mainly the more casual Anglomania diffusion line and the exclusive Worlds End label based on the archives. The small Davies Street boutique sells only the more exclusive, expensive Gold Label and Couture collections (plus bridal), while the flagship Conduit Street store carries all of the above. ✉ *44 Conduit St., Mayfair* ☎ *020/7439–1109* ☯ *Closed Sun.* Ⓜ *Oxford Circus* ✉ *Original boutique, 430 King's Rd., Chelsea* ☎ *020/7352–6551* ☯ *Closed Sun.* Ⓜ *Sloane Sq.*

18

DEPARTMENT STORES

Fodor'sChoice ★ **Liberty.** Liberty's wonderful black-and-white mock-Tudor facade created from the timbers of two Royal Navy ships reflects the store's origins in the late-19th-century's Arts and Crafts movement. Leading designers were recruited from this and the aesthetic movement to create the classic art nouveau Liberty prints that are still a centerpiece of the brand, gracing everything from cushions and silk kimonos to embossed leather bags and photo albums. Inside, Liberty's is a labyrinth of nooks and crannies stuffed with thoughtfully chosen merchandise. The carpet and furniture departments are worth a look even if you're not buying. Clothes for both men and women focus on high quality and high fashion. The store regularly commissions new prints from contemporary designers, and sells both these and its archival patterns by the yard. If you're not so handy with a needle, an interior design service will create soft furnishings for you. ⊠ *Regent St., Soho* ☎ *020/7734–1234* ⊕ *www. liberty.co.uk* Ⓜ *Oxford Circus.*

Thomas Goode. This spacious luxury homewares shop has been at the same smart Mayfair address since 1845. The china, silver, crystal, and linens are either of the store's own design and manufacture or are simply the best that money can buy, a legacy of its original customer base of international royals and heads of state. The store still holds two royal warrants, but anyone who can afford it can commission their own bespoke set of china. ■ TIP➔ If such luxury is beyond you, visit anyway for the shop's small museum of plates, either antique or designed for royalty, including some created for Princess Diana's wedding. ⊠ *19 S. Audley St., Mayfair* ☎ *020/7499–2823* ⊕ *www.thomasgoode.co.uk* Ⓜ *Green Park.*

FOOD

Charbonnel et Walker. Britain's master chocolatier since 1875, this Mayfair shop specializes in traditional handmade chocolates (violet and rose-petal creams, for example) and has been creating these beautifully packaged, high-quality sweets from long before most of today's fashionable brands appeared. ■ TIP➔ Their drinking chocolate—coarsely grated fine chocolate in a tin—is worth carrying home in a suitcase. *28 Old Bond St., Mayfair* ☎ *020/7491–0939* ⊕ *www.charbonnel.co.uk* ☾ *Closed Sun.* Ⓜ *Green Park.*

JEWELRY

★ **Asprey.** Created by architect Norman Foster and interior designer David Mlinaric, this "global flagship" store displays exquisite jewelry—as well as silver and leather goods, watches, china, and crystal—in a discreet, very British setting that oozes quality, expensive good taste, and hushed comfort. If you're in the market for an immaculate 1930s cigarette case, a crystal vase, or a pair of pavé diamond and sapphire earrings, you won't be disappointed. And, for the really well-heeled, there's a custom-made jewelry service available as well. ⊠ *167 New Bond St., Mayfair* ☎ *020/7493–6767* ⊕ *www.asprey.com* Ⓜ *Green Park.*

Garrard. Formally known as "Garrard, the Crown Jeweler," this company has been creating royal crowns since Queen Victoria's reign (you can see several on display in the Tower of London). Today the focus is on precious gems in simple, classic settings, along with silver accessories.

Although some collections, such as Entanglement and Wings (minimalist hoop earrings and pendants with a wing motif), are definitely contemporary, many of the designs are traditional and impressive, should you be in the market for an old-school diamond tiara. ✉ *24 Albemarle St., Mayfair* ☎ *020/7518–1070* ⊕ *www.garrard.com* Ⓜ *Green Park.*

SHOES

★ **Beatrix Ong.** This young designer trained under Jimmy Choo, and her collection is just as sexy and bold, with a ready-to-wear collection of strappy sandals and stilettos. Brides-to-be are also well catered for. ✉ *188 Pavillion Rd., Chelsea* ☎ *020/7463–7369* ⊕ *www.beatrixong. com* Ⓜ *Sloane Sq.*

Nicholas Kirkwood. You won't be able to hike in Kirkwood's imaginative, elegant, sky-high stilettos, but you will be able to make quite an entrance. Pick up something from the creative shoemaker's own line, his collaborations with designers Rodarte and Peter Pilotto, or even one of the 12 designs inspired by artist Keith Haring at Kirkwood's first retail boutique. ✉ *5B Mount St., Mayfair* ☎ *020/7499–5781* ⊕ *www. nicholaskirkwood.com* ⊙ *Closed Sun.* Ⓜ *Green Park.*

★ **Rupert Sanderson.** Designed in London and made in Italy, Sanderson's elegant shoes have been a huge hit in fashion circles. Ladylike styles, bright colors, smart details, and a penchant for peep toes are signature elements. Prices reflect the impeccable craftsmanship. There's now a tiny outpost next to Harrods at 2A Hans Road. ✉ *33 Bruton Pl., Mayfair* ☎ *0207/491–2220* ⊕ *www.rupertsanderson.com* ⊙ *Closed Sun.* Ⓜ *Bond St., Green Park.*

ST. JAMES'S

ACCESSORIES: HATS

James Lock & Co. Ltd. Need a silk top hat, a flat-weave Panama, or a traditional tweed flat cap? James Lock of St. James's has been providing hats from this cozy shop since 1676 for customers ranging from Admiral Lord Nelson, Oscar Wilde, and Frank Sinatra to, more recently, Robert Downey Jr. and Guy Ritchie, as well as trendsetting musicians and models. ✉ *6 St. James's St., St. James's* ☎ *020/7930–8884* ⊕ *www. lockhatters.co.uk* ⊙ *Closed Sun.* Ⓜ *Green Park, Piccadilly Circus.*

★ **Swaine Adeney Brigg.** This shop has been selling practical supplies for country pursuits since 1750. Not just for the horsey set, the store carries beautifully crafted umbrellas, walking sticks, and hip flasks, or ingenious combinations of same, such as the umbrella with a slim tipple-holding flask secreted inside the stem. The same level of quality and craftsmanship applies to the store's leather goods, which include attaché cases and wallets. Downstairs you'll find scarves, caps, and the Herbert Johnson "Poet Hat," the iconic headgear (stocked since 1890) worn by Harrison Ford in every Indiana Jones film. ✉ *54 St. James's St., St. James's* ☎ *020/7409–7277* ⊕ *www.swaineadeney.co.uk* ⊙ *Closed Sun.* Ⓜ *Green Park.*

BEAUTY

Fodor's Choice
★

Floris. What do Queen Victoria and Marilyn Monroe have in common? They both used fragrances from Floris, one of the most beautiful shops in London, with gleaming glass-and-Spanish-mahogany showcases salvaged from the Great Exhibition of 1851. In addition to scents for both men and women, Floris makes its own shaving products, reflecting its origins as a barbershop. Other gift possibilities include goose-down powder puffs, cut-glass atomizers, and a famous rose-scented mouthwash, as well as beautifully-packaged soaps and bath essences. ✉ 89 Jermyn St., St. James's ☎ 020/7930–2885 ⊕ www.florislondon.com ⊙ Closed Sun. Ⓜ Piccadilly Circus, Green Park.

BOOKS

Fodor's Choice
★

Hatchards. This is London's oldest bookshop, open since 1797 and beloved by writers themselves (customers have included Oscar Wilde, Rudyard Kipling, and Lord Byron). Despite its wood-paneled, "gentleman's library" atmosphere, and eclectic selection of books, Hatchards is owned by the large Waterstone's chain. Nevertheless, the shop still retains its period charm, aided by the staff's old-fashioned helpfulness and expertise. Look for the substantial number of books signed by notable contemporary authors on the well-stocked shelves. ✉ 187 Piccadilly, St. James's ☎ 020/7439–9921 ⊕ www.hatchards.co.uk Ⓜ Piccadilly Circus.

CLOTHING: MEN

Thomas Pink. This specialist chain is best known for its colorful and stylish formal shirts for both men and women, many in such fine fabrics as Sea Island or Egyptian cotton. More casual shirts are for sale as well, along with ties, boxers, pyjamas, belts, and other accessories, as are dresses, skirts, jackets, and knitwear for women. Bespoke shirts for men can be ordered at the Jermyn Street branch. There are other branches in The City, Chelsea, Canary Wharf, St. Pancras Int'l, and the Westfield shopping center. ✉ 85 Jermyn St., St. James's ☎ 020/7930–6364 ⊕ www.thomaspink.co.uk Ⓜ Green Park, Piccadilly Circus.

★ **Turnbull & Asser.** This is *the* custom shirtmaker, dripping exclusivity from every fiber—after all, Prince Charles is a client and every filmic James Bond has worn shirts from here. At least 15 separate measurements are taken, and the cloth, woven to the company's specifications, comes in 1,000 different patterns—the cottons feel as good as silk. The first order must be for a minimum of six shirts, which start from £195 each. As well as jackets, cashmeres, suits, ties, pajamas, and accessories perfect for the billionaire who has everything, the store also carries less expensive, though still exquisite, ready-to-wear shirts. ✉ 71–72 Jermyn St., St. James's ☎ 020/7808–3000 ⊕ www.turnbullandasser.com ⊙ Closed Sun. Ⓜ Green Park.

FOOD

Berry Bros. & Rudd. Nothing matches Berry Bros. & Rudd for rare offerings and a unique shopping experience. A family-run wine business since 1698, "BBR" stores its vintage bottles and casks in vaulted cellars that are more than 300 years old. The shop has a quirky charm, and the staff is extremely knowledgeable—and not snooty if you're on a budget. ✉ 3 St. James's St., St. James's ☎ 020/7396–9600 ⊕ www.bbr.com ⊙ Closed Sun. Ⓜ Green Park.

Fodor's Choice ★ **Fortnum & Mason.** Although popularly known as the Queen's grocer, and the impeccably mannered staff wear traditional tailcoats, F&M's food hall stocks gifts for all budgets, such as loads of irresistibly packaged luxury foods stamped with the gold "By Appointment" crest for less than £5. Try the teas, preserves (unusual products include rose-petal jelly), condiments, chocolate, tins of pâté, or Gentleman's Relish (anchovy paste). The store's famous hampers are always a welcome gift. The gleaming food hall spans two floors and includes a sleek wine bar designed by David Collins, with the rest of the store devoted to upscale homewares, men and women's gifts, toiletries, and accessories, women's jewelry and cosmetics, and clothing and toys for children. If you start to flag, break for afternoon tea at one of the four other restaurants (one's an indulgent ice-cream parlor)—or a treatment in the Beauty Rooms. ⊠ *181 Piccadilly, St. James's* ☎ *020/7734–8040* ⊕ *www. fortnumandmason.com* Ⓜ *Green Park.*

TOYS
The Armoury of St. James's. The fine toy soldiers and military models in stock here are collectors' items. Painted and mounted knights only 6 inches high can cost up to £1,200 (though figures start at a mere £7.50 for a toy soldier). Besides lead and tin soldiers, the shop has regimental brooches, porcelain figures, military memorabilia, and military antiques. ⊠ *17 Piccadilly Arcade, St. James's* ☎ *020/7493–5082* ⊕ *www.armoury.co.uk* ⊙ *Closed Sun.* Ⓜ *Piccadilly Circus, Green Park.*

SOHO AND COVENT GARDEN

18

COVENT GARDEN

BOOKS AND PRINTS
★ **Grosvenor Prints.** London's largest collection of 17th- to-early 20th-century prints emphasizes views of the city and architecture as well as sporting and decorative motifs. The selection is eclectic, with prices ranging from £5 into the thousands. ⊠ *19 Shelton St., Covent Garden* ☎ *020/7836–1979* ⊕ *www.grosvenorprints.com* ⊙ *Closed Sun.* Ⓜ *Covent Garden, Leicester Sq.*

Fodor's Choice ★ **Stanfords.** When it comes to encyclopedic coverage, there is simply no better travel shop on the planet. Stanfords is packed with a comprehensive selection of maps, guide books, and travel gadgets. Whether you're planning a day trip to Surrey or an adventure to the South Pole, this should be your first stop. Dig the floors here: gigantic blowups of maps. ⊠ *12–14 Long Acre, Covent Garden* ☎ *020/7836–1321* ⊕ *www. stanfords.co.uk* Ⓜ *Covent Garden.*

CLOTHING
★ **Paul Smith.** British classics with an irreverent twist define Paul Smith's collections for women, men, and children. Beautifully tailored men's suits in exceptional fabrics might sport flamboyant linings or unusual detailing. Women's lines tend to take hallmarks of traditional British style and turn them on their heads with humor and color. Gift ideas abound—wallets, scarves, diaries, spectacles, even a soccer ball—all in

Smith's signature rainbow stripes. There are several branches throughout London, in Notting Hill, South Kensington, Chelsea, and Borough Market, plus a vintage furniture shop at 9 Albemarle Street in Mayfair and a shoes and accessories shop on Marylebone High Street. ⊠ *40–44 Floral St., Covent Garden* ☎ *020/7379–7133* ⊕ *www.paulsmith.co.uk* Ⓜ *Covent Garden.*

CLOTHING: WOMEN'S WEAR

Orla Kiely. This Irish designer is probably best known for her appealingly simple retro-tinged prints (based on everyday objects like cars and mugs or more abstract designs), which appear on everything from dresses and raincoats to lamp shades, diaries, towels, sheets, kitchenware, and wallpapers—all showcased in this airy flagship store (there's another branch on King's Road in Chelsea). You can also pick up bags, wallets, radios, and MacBook sleeves bearing her signature leaf print. ⊠ *31 Monmouth St., Covent Garden* ☎ *020/7240–4022* ⊕ *www.orlakiely. com* Ⓜ *Covent Garden.*

Poste Mistress. This boudoir-styled boutique outpost of the Office chain features gorgeous, high-heeled (and pricey) styles from designers like Stella McCartney, Dries van Noten, Miu Miu, as well as the Poste Mistress line. More casual alternatives, such as Vivienne Westwood rubber booties and Converse sneakers, are also available. There's a branch devoted to designer men's shoes on South Moulton Street in Mayfair. ⊠ *61 Monmouth St., Covent Garden* ☎ *020/7379–4040* ⊕ *www.office. co.uk* ⊠ *10 South Molton St., Mayfair* Ⓜ *Covent Garden.*

Fodor's Choice
★

United Nude. Co-created by noted architect Rem D Koolhaas (who also designed this Covent Garden flagship store) and Galahad Clark (of the Clark's shoes dynasty), these distinctive, futuristic designs that use up-to-the-minute techniques such as carbon fiber heels and injection-molded soles are flattering and surprisingly comfortable. There are other branches in Camden, Mayfair, and St. James's. ⊠ *13 Floral St., Covent Garden* ☎ *0207/240–7106* ⊠ *61–63 Monmouth St., Covent Garden* ☎ *020/7379–4040* ⊕ *www.office.co.uk* Ⓜ *Covent Garden.*

HOUSEHOLD

Cath Kidston. If you love chintz and colorful patterns, then stop by Cath Kidston. Her signature look is bright, feminine textiles—ginghams, polka dots, and lots of big, blooming roses—pasted over everything in sight, from ceramics and bed linens to fine china, stationery, and doggie beds. There are several clothing and nightwear lines for women and children, along with handbags, totes, and cosmetic bags. Everything in this shop is basically a canvas for Kidston's ladylike prints. There are branches throughout the city, including ones in Chelsea, Marylebone, and Notting Hill. ⊠ *28–32 Shelton St., Covent Garden* ☎ *020/7836–4803* ⊕ *www.cathkidston.co.uk* Ⓜ *Covent Garden.*

TOYS

Ⓒ
Fodor's Choice
★

Benjamin Pollock's Toyshop. This Covent Garden Piazza shop carries on the tradition of its eponymous founder, who sold miniature theater stages made from richly detailed paper from the late-19th century until his death in 1937. Among his admirers was Robert Louis Stevenson, who wrote, "If you love art, folly, or the bright eyes of children, speed to Pollock's." Today the antique model theaters tend to be expensive, but there are plenty of magical reproductions for under 10 pounds. There's also an extensive selection of new but nostalgic puppets, marionettes, teddy bears, spinning tops, jack-in-the-boxes, and similar traditional children's toys from the days before batteries were required. ⊠ *44 The Market, Covent Garden* ☎ *020/7379–7866* ⊕ *www.pollocks-coventgarden.co.uk* Ⓜ *Covent Garden.*

SOHO

ACCESSORIES

☺ **Peckham Rye.** The epicenter of "Swinging London" in the mid-'60s

Fodor'sChoice has recently undergone a renaissance, particularly in the "Newburgh

★ Quarter," the small cobbled streets leading off Carnaby Street. Here's where you'll find small specialist boutiques such as Peckham Rye, a family-owned business that sells men's accessories—handmade silk and twill ties (the name is Cockney rhyming slang for same), bow ties, and scarves, all using traditional patterns from their archives, plus socks, striped shirts, and hankies. Fans include modern day Beau Brummels like Mark Ronson and David Beckham. ⊠ *11 Newburgh St., Soho* ☎ *0207/734–5181* ⊕ *www.peckhamrye.com* Ⓜ *Oxford Street.*

BOOKS

Fodor'sChoice **Foyles.** Founded in 1903 by the Foyle brothers after they failed the

★ Civil Service exam, the five floors of this quirky, labyrinthine store (still family-owned) carries almost every title imaginable. One of London's best sources for textbooks, Foyles also stocks everything from popular fiction to military history, sheet music, medical tomes, opera scores, and handsome illustrated fine arts books. It also offers the store-within-a-store Ray's Jazz (one of London's better outlets for music), a cool café, and even a piranha tank on the children's floor. Foyles has branches in the Southbank Centre, St. Pancras International train station (the Eurostar's U.K. terminus), and the Westfield shopping centers in Shepherd's Bush and Stratford. ⊠ *113–119 Charing Cross Rd., Soho* ☎ *020/7437–5660* ⊕ *www.foyles.co.uk* Ⓜ *Tottenham Court Rd.* ⊠ *Royal Festival Hall, South Bank* ☎ *020/7437–5660* Ⓜ *Waterloo*

CLOTHING

Aquascutum. Known for offering quintessentially British style at prices that are reasonable for this level of workmanship, Aquascutum carries timeless men's suits and knitwear as well as a surprisingly funky women's collection with a fresh take on items like tunics and jersey dresses. Aquascutum's founder, John Emary, made his name by pioneering a rain-repellent cloth (the name means "water shield" in Latin) and designing a trench coat—as worn by Churchill and Cary Grant—that remains a signature item of the brand to this day. There is a branch at Canary Wharf, plus you'll find Aquascutum concessions within Austin Reed and Jaeger on Regent Street and within several West End department stores. ⊠ *162A Sloane St., Knightsbridge* ☎ *0784/145–2274* ⊕ *www.aquascutum.co.uk* ☉ *Closed Sun.* Ⓜ *Knightsbridge.*

18

CLOTHING: WOMEN'S WEAR

Reiss. With an in-house design team whose experience includes stints at Gucci and Calvin Klein and customers like Beyoncé and the Duchess of Cambridge (formerly Kate Middleton, who wore a Reiss dress for her official engagement picture), this hot chain brings luxury standards of tailoring and details to mass-market women's and menswear. The sleek and contemporary style is not cheap, but does offer value for money. There are branches in Knightsbridge, The City, Covent Garden, Chelsea, Hampstead, Notting Hill, Soho, and basically all over London. ⊠ *10 Barrett St., Fitzrovia* ☎ *020/7486–6557* ⊕ *www.reissonline.com* Ⓜ *Oxford Street.*

Fodor'sChoice **Topshop.** Since its transition from cheesy-but-cheap to genuine fash-
★ ion (but still affordable) hot spot, numerous foreign fashion editors have made Topshop their first port of call when in London. Clothes and accessories are geared to the younger end of the market, although women who are young at heart and girlish of figure can find plenty of wearable items here. However, you will need a high tolerance for loud music and busy dressing rooms. While the main aim is still to produce low-cost copies of runway trends as fast as possible, the store also has its own in-house high-end designer line called Topshop Unique and a vintage department in the basement. As well, each season an ever-changing array of fashion icons such as Kate Moss—along with a roster of emerging designers—create small collections for the in-store boutique. Innovations such as personal style advisers, an on-site nail bar, and a cupcake stand are constantly being introduced. Topman brings the same fast-fashion approach to clothing for men. ■TIP➔ If the crowds become too much, head to one of the numerous smaller Topshops in town, such as the ones on Kensington High Street and in Knightsbridge. ⊠ *214 Oxford St., Oxford Street* ☎ *020/927–7700* ⊕ *www.topshop.com* Ⓜ *Oxford Circus* ⊠ *42–44 Kensington High St., Kensington* ☎ *020/7938–1242* Ⓜ *High Street Kensington.*

MUSIC

BM Soho. House, drum 'n' bass, electro, dubstep—this shop (formerly Blackmarket Records) is London's longest-established dance music store and stocks the hottest club music around. They carry some CDs, but this is really a shop for vinyl lovers. ⊠ *25 D'Arblay St., Soho* ☎ *020/7437–0478* ⊕ *www.bm-soho.com* Ⓜ *Oxford Circus, Tottenham Court Rd.*

TOYS

Ⓒ **Hamleys.** Besieged by pester power? Don't worry, help is at hand—this
Fodor'sChoice London institution has six floors of the latest dolls, soft toys, video
★ games, and technological devices (plus such old-fashioned pleasures as train sets, drum kits, and magic tricks), with every must-have on the pre-teen shopping list. Some may find the offerings to be overly commercialized (it's heavy on movie and TV tie-ins), and the store only got rid of its separate pink and blue floors for girls and boys in 2011 after a protest campaign. Nevertheless, when British children visit London, Hamleys is at the top of their agenda. It's a madhouse at Christmastime, but Santa's grotto is one of the best in town. There's a smaller branch in St. Pancras International train station. ⊠ *188–196 Regent St., Soho* ☎ *0800/280–2444* ⊕ *www.hamleys.com* Ⓜ *Oxford Circus, Piccadilly Circus.*

Side Trips from London

WORD OF MOUTH

"It's perfectly possible to get a HUGE amount out of a 6-hour Oxford stay—especially by following the self-guided tours on the Oxfordshire official tourist site or booking a Blue Badge walking tour at the city's Tourist Information Centre. Or opt to spend a month there. Neither strategy (or anything in between) is self-evidently wrong."

—flanneruk

Updated by
Ellin Stein

Londoners are undeniably lucky. Few urban populations enjoy such glorious—and easily accessible—options for day-tripping. Even if vacationers or travelers have only one day to spare, head out of the city. A train ride past hills dotted with sheep, a stroll through a medieval town, or a visit to one of England's great castles could make you feel as though you've added another week to your vacation.

Not only is England extremely compact, the train and bus networks, although somewhat inefficient and expensive compared with their European counterparts, are extensive and easily booked (though pricing structures can be confusing), making "a brilliant day out" an easy thing to accomplish.

Although you could tackle any one of the towns in this chapter on a frenzied day trip—heavy summer crowds make it difficult to cover the sights in a relaxed manner—consider staying for a day or two. You'd then have time to explore a very different England—one blessed with quiet country pubs, tree-lined lanes, and neatly trimmed fields. No matter where you go, lodging reservations are a good idea from June through September, when foreign visitors saturate the English countryside.

PLANNING

GETTING AROUND
Normally the towns covered in this chapter are best reached by train. Bus travel costs less, but can take twice as long. Wherever you're going, plan ahead: check the latest timetables before you set off, and try to get an early start. ⇨ *Also see the Travel Smart chapter.*

STATION TIPS
You can reach any of London's main-line train stations by Tube. London's bus stations can be confusing for the uninitiated. Here's a quick breakdown:

Green Line Coach Station is on Bulleid Way (in front of the Colonnades Shopping Centre on Buckingham Palace Road) and is the departure point for most Green Line and Megabus services.

Victoria Bus Station is where many of the local London bus services arrive and depart, and is directly outside the main exits of the train and Tube stations.

Victoria Coach Station is on Buckingham Palace Road: it's a five-minute walk from Victoria Tube station. This is where to go for coach departures; arrivals are at a different location, a short walk from here.

TO GET TO . . .

	TAKE THE TRAIN FROM . . .	TAKE THE BUS FROM . . .
Cambridge	King's Cross (47–90 minutes; every 10 or 20 minutes); Liverpool St. (80 minutes; every 30 minutes)	Victoria Coach (about 2.5 hours; every hour–90 minutes)
Oxford	Paddington (55–110 minutes; every 3–20 minutes)	Victoria Coach (100 minutes; every half hour; Oxford Tube, Buckingham Palace Rd. (100 minutes; every 12–20 minutes)
Stratford-upon-Avon	Marylebone (2 hours, 2 minutes to 3 hours, 14 minutes; every 2 hours); or Euston (2 hours, 40 minutes to 3 hours; every 20 or 40 minutes or hourly)	Victoria Coach (3 hours, 25 minutes; about 3 times daily)
Windsor	Paddington (25–50 minutes; every 5–30 minutes) or Waterloo (1 hour, 5 minutes; every half hour)	Green Line Bus Station, Victoria (1 hour, 5 minutes; hourly)

19

CAMBRIDGE

60 miles (97 km) northeast of London.

With the spires of its university buildings framed by towering trees and expansive meadows, its medieval streets and passages enhanced by gardens and riverbanks, the city of Cambridge is among the loveliest in England. The city predates the Roman occupation of Britain, but the university was not founded until the 13th century. There's disagreement about the birth of the university: one story attributes its founding to impoverished students from Oxford, who came in search of eels—a cheap source of nourishment. Today a healthy rivalry persists between the two schools.

This university town may be beautiful, but it's no museum. Even when the students are on vacation, there's a cultural and intellectual buzz here. Well-preserved medieval buildings sit cheek-by-jowl next to the latest in modern architecture (for example the William Gates building,

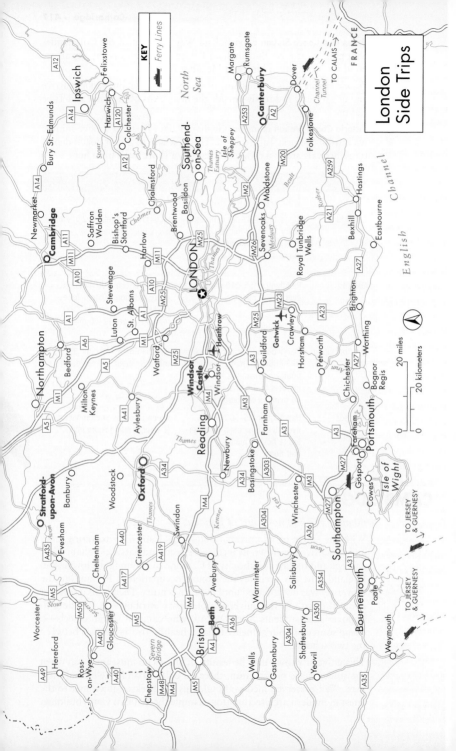

which houses Cambridge University's computer laboratory) in this growing city dominated culturally and architecturally by its famous university (whose students make up around one-fifth of the city's 109,000 inhabitants), and beautified by parks, gardens, and the quietly flowing River Cam. A quintessential Cambridge pursuit is punting on the Cam (one occupant propels the narrow, square-end, flat-bottom boat with a long pole), followed by a stroll along the Backs, the left bank of the river fringed by St. John's, Trinity, Clare, King's, and Queens' colleges, and by Trinity Hall.

VISITING THE COLLEGES

College visits are certainly a highlight of a Cambridge tour, but remember that the colleges are private residences and workplaces, even when school isn't in session. Each is an independent entity within the university; some are closed to the public, but at others you can see the chapels, dining rooms (called halls), and sometimes the libraries, too. Some colleges charge a small fee for the privilege of nosing around. All are closed during exams, usually from mid-April to late June, and the opening hours often vary. Additionally, all are subject to closures at short notice, especially King's; check the websites in advance. For details about visiting specific colleges not listed here, contact **Cambridge University** (☎ *01223/337733* ⊕ *www.cam.ac.uk*).

By far the best way to gain access without annoying anyone is to join a walking tour led by an official Blue Badge guide—in fact, many areas are off-limits unless you do. The two-hour tours (£16) leave from the **Tourist Information Centre.** Hours vary according to the tour, with the earliest leaving at 11 am and the latest at 1 pm in winter, 2 in summer. (✉ *Peas Hill* ☎ *0871/226–8006, 1223/464732 from abroad* ⊕ *www. visitcambridge.org* ⊗ *Apr.–Sept., weekdays 10–5, Sat. 10–5, Sun. 11–3; Oct.–Mar., weekdays 10–5, Sat. 10–5.*)

ESSENTIALS

Visitor Information Cambridge (☎ *0871/226–8006, 1223/464732 from outside U.K.* ⊕ *www.visitcambridge.org*).

19

EXPLORING

In 1284 the Bishop of Ely founded **Peterhouse College,** Cambridge's smallest and oldest college. Take a tranquil walk through its former deer park, by the river side of its ivy-clad buildings; nearby is the Fitzwilliam Museum. ✉ *Trumpington St.* ☎ *01223/338200* ⊕ *www.pet.cam.ac.uk* ⊡ *Free* ⊗ *Daily 9–5 (groups 1–5).*

Fodor's Choice ★ One of England's finest art galleries, the **Fitzwilliam Museum** houses an outstanding collection of art, as well as striking antiquities from ancient Egypt, Greece, and Rome. Highlights include two large Titians, an extensive collection of French impressionist paintings, and many paintings by Matisse and Picasso. The gallery holds occasional free classical music concerts. ✉ *Trumpington St.* ☎ *01223/332900* ⊕ *www. fitzmuseum.cam.ac.uk* ⊡ *Free* ⊗ *Tues.–Sat. 10–5, Sun. noon–5.*

Across from Peterhouse is **Pembroke College** (1347), with delightful gardens and a bowling green. Its chapel, completed in 1665, was the architect Christopher Wren's first commission. ⊠ *Trumpington St.* ☎ *01223/338100* ⊕ *www.pem.cam.ac.uk* ⊑ *Free* ☉ *Daily 9–dusk.*

Head down Pembroke Street to reach **Emmanuel College** (1584), the alma mater of one John Harvard, who gave his books and his name to the American university. A number of the Pilgrims were Emmanuel alumni; they named Cambridge, Massachusetts, after their onetime home. ⊠ *St. Andrew's St.* ☎ *01223/334200* ⊕ *www.emma.cam.ac.uk* ⊑ *Free* ☉ *Daily 9–6.*

Fodor'sChoice
★

Westward from Jesus College is **St. John's College** (1511), the university's largest, which boasts noted alumni (Wordsworth studied here), a series of beautiful courtyards, and two of the finest sights in town: the **School of Pythagoras,** the oldest house in Cambridge; and the 1831 **Bridge of Sighs,** modeled on its Venetian counterpart. The windowed, covered stone bridge reaches across the Cam to the mock-Gothic New Court (1825–31). The New Court cupola's white crenellations have earned it the nickname "the wedding cake." ⊠ *St. John's St.* ☎ *01223/338600* ⊕ *www.joh.cam.ac.uk* ⊑ *£3.20* ☉ *Mar.–Oct., daily 10–5:30; Nov.–Feb., daily 10–3:30.*

Fodor'sChoice
★

Trinity College was founded by Henry VIII in 1546, and has the largest student population of all the colleges. It's also famous for having been attended by Byron, Thackeray, Tennyson, Bertrand Russell, Nabokov, Nehru, and 31 Nobel Prize winners. Many of Trinity's features reflect its status as one of Cambridge's largest colleges, not least its 17th-century "great court," scene of the university race in *Chariots of Fire.* Don't miss the wonderful library by Christopher Wren, where you can see a letter written by alumnus Isaac Newton with early notes on gravity, and A. A. Milne's handwritten manuscript of *The House at Pooh Corner.* ⊠ *Trinity St.* ☎ *01223/338400* ⊕ *www.trin.cam.ac.uk* ⊑ *£3 mid-Mar.–Oct.* ☉ *College daily 10–5; library weekdays noon–2, Sat. in term time 10:30–12:30; hall and chapel open to visitors, but hrs vary.*

Fodor'sChoice
★

South of Trinity College is **King's College** (1441), notable as the site of the world-famous Gothic-style **King's College Chapel** (built 1446–1547). With its great fan-vaulted roof, the largest ever built, supported by a delicate tracery of perpendicular buttresses, it is widely considered to be one of the finest examples of Perpendicular Gothic in Europe. It's the home of the famous King's College Choir, and, to cap it all, Rubens's *Adoration of the Magi* is tucked away behind the altar. The college's Back Lawn leads down to the river, from which the panorama of college and chapel is one of the university's most photographed views. ⊠ *King's Parade* ☎ *01223/331212* ⊕ *www.kings.cam.ac.uk* ⊑ *£7.50* ☉ *Term time, weekdays 9:30–3:30, Sat. 9:30–3:15, Sun. 1:15–2:15; out of term, Mon.–Sat. 9:30–4:30, Sun. 10–5. Hrs may vary, grounds closed during exams; call in advance or see website.*

★

Reached along the Backs and tucked away on Queen's Road is **Queens' College.** Originally established in 1447 as the College of St. Bernard's, one of Cambridge's most eye-catching colleges was re-founded a year later by Margaret of Anjou, queen of Henry VI, and then re-founded again in 1475 by Elizabeth, queen of Edward IV—hence the new name.

Cross over the Cam via the **Wooden Bridge,** also known as the Mathematical Bridge. A popular myth tells of how it was built by Isaac Newton without any binding save gravity, then dismantled by curious scholars eager to learn Sir Isaac's secret. However, the bridge wasn't actually put together until 1749, 22 years after Newton's death. ☒ *Queens' College* ☎ *01223/335511* ⊕ *www.queens.cam.ac.uk* ☒ *£2.50. Free to individuals Nov.–mid-Mar., Oct., weekdays* ☉ *Mid-Mar.–mid-May, daily 10–4:30; mid-June–Sept., daily 10–4:30; Oct., weekdays 2–4, weekends 10–4:30; Nov.–mid-Mar., daily 2–4.*

The only Cambridge College founded by townspeople (in 1352) is **Corpus Christi College,** whose beautiful, serene, 14th-century Old Court is the oldest college quadrangle in Cambridge. The college's Parker Library contains one of the world's finest collections of medieval manuscripts. ☒ *Trumpington St.* ☎ *01223/338000* ⊕ *www.corpus.cam.ac.uk* ☒ *Free* ☉ *Daily 2–4.*

WHERE TO EAT

$ ✗**Fitzbillies.** Usually filled with students' visiting parents, this long-
CAFÉ established café (now under new management) is famous for its exceptionally sticky Chelsea buns (if you don't want to sit down, the bakery next door has the same pastries to take away). It also serves tasty lunches, afternoon teas, and dinners (Friday and Saturday) with Modern British dishes such as chicken wrapped in savoy cabbage, beef and oyster pie, and Seville orange tart. ☒ *52 Trumpington St.* ☎ *01223/ 352500* ⊕ *www.fitzbillies.co.uk.*

$$$$ ✗**Midsummer House.** In fine weather the gray-brick Midsummer House's
ECLECTIC conservatory, beside the River Cam, makes for a memorable lunchtime
★ jaunt. Choose from a selection of innovative French and Mediterranean dishes. You might get braised turbot, pumpkin and cep cannelloni, or slow-cooked duck with beetroot puree. ☒ *Midsummer Common* ☎ *01223/369299* ⊕ *www.midsummerhouse.co.uk* ⌣ *Reservations essential* ☉ *Closed Sun. and Mon. No lunch Tues.*

19

OXFORD

62 miles (100 km) northwest of London.

The university that educated former Prime Minister Tony Blair, former President Bill Clinton, and writers J. R. R. Tolkien, Percy Bysshe Shelley, Oscar Wilde, W. H. Auden, and C. S. Lewis is the heart and soul of the town. Its fabled "dreaming spires" can be seen for miles around, and it's not at all unusual to see robed students rushing to class or harried dons clutching mortarboards as they race to exams on bicycles. Dating from the 12th century, Oxford University is older than Cambridge, and the city is bigger and more cosmopolitan than its competitor to the east. It's satisfyingly filled with hushed quadrangles, chapels, canals, rivers, and vivid gardens. Bikes are inevitably propped against picturesque wrought-iron railings, and students propel flat-bottom boats down the little River Cherwell with long poles. (It's harder than it looks, but you can rent a punt yourself at the foot of Magdalen Bridge.)

In the end, though, central Oxford is also a bit of an illusion. Outside of the eminently photographable university area, it's a major industrial center, with sprawling modern suburbs and large car and steel plants around its fringes.

VISITING THE COLLEGES

The same concerns for people's work and privacy hold here as in Cambridge. Note that many of the colleges and university buildings are closed around Christmas (sometimes Easter, too) and on certain days from April to June for exams and degree ceremonies.

> **HERE'S WHERE**
>
> The Bodleian Library's Divinity School, open to the public, is a superbly vaulted room dating to 1462, which acted as Hogwarts in *Harry Potter and the Sorcerer's Stone.* The dining hall at Christ Church College should look familiar to fans as well—it was used as the model for the Hogwarts dining hall.

If you have limited time, get a detailed map from the tourist office and focus on selected sights. The Oxford University website (⊕ *www.ox.ac.uk*) is a great source of information if you're planning to go it alone.

TOURS

Guided city walking tours (both themed and general) leave the **Oxford Tourist Information Centre** at different times throughout the day. ✉ *15–16 Broad St.* ☎ *01865/252200* ⊕ *www.visitoxfordandoxfordshire.com* ✆ *Tours from £8* ⊘ *Mon.–Sat. 9:30–5, Sun. 10–3.*

Oxford also features the hop-on, hop-off guided bus tours that have been such a hit in major destinations around the world. Operated by City Sightseeing Oxford, the tours last for about an hour, departing every 10–15 minutes in summer and every 30 minutes in winter. Although there are stops throughout the city, the main terminus location is outside the Oxford railway station. ✉ *No.1 Shop, Railway Station, Park End St.* ☎ *01865/790522* ⊕ *www.citysightseeingoxford.com* ✆ *Tours from £13* ⊘ *Daily Mar. and Oct., 9:30–5; Apr.–Sept., 9:30–7; Nov.–Feb., 9:30–4.*

ESSENTIALS

Visitor Information Oxford (☎ *01865/252200* ⊕ *www.visitoxfordandoxfordshire.com*).

EXPLORING

Any Oxford visit should begin at its very center—a pleasant walk of 15 minutes or so east from the train station—with the splendid **University Church of St. Mary the Virgin** (the oldest part of the building dates from 1280). Climb 127 steps to the top of its 14th-century tower for a panoramic view of the city. ✉ *High St.* ☎ *01865/279111* ⊕ *www.university-church.ox.ac.uk* ✆ *Church free, tower £3* ⊘ *Church admission Sept.–June, Mon.–Sat. 9–5, Sun. noon–5; July and Aug., Mon.–Sat. 9–6, Sun. noon–6.*

Fodor's Choice ★ Just north of the St. Mary the Virgin church is one of Oxford's most famous sights, the gorgeous, round **Radcliffe Camera** (1737–49), the most beautiful of its buildings housing the extensive contents of the august

Radcliffe Camera, an unmissable circular library at Oxford University

Bodleian Library. The baroque domed rotunda with an octagonal base sits in a lovely square where your photographic instincts can run riot. Not many of the 6-million-plus volumes are on view to those who aren't dons, but you can see part of the collection if you call ahead to book a guided tour. Note that children under 11 are not allowed on guided tours, though they are on the self-guided audio tour and Divinity School tour. ⊠ *Broad St.* ☎ *01865/277224* ⊕ *www.bodleian.ox.ac.uk* ✉ *Bodleian self-guided audio tour £2.50; 30-min guided tour £4.50, 1-hr guided tour £6.50, extended guided tour £13* ☉ *Weekdays 9–5, Sat. 9–4:30, Sun. 11–5; Divinity School weekdays 9–5, Sat. 9–4:30, Sun. 11–5 (admission £1). Closed for University functions and events (check website).*

★ A minute's stroll from the Radcliff Camera is the **Sheldonian Theatre,** built between 1664 and 1668. This was Sir Christopher Wren's first major work (the chapel at Pembroke College was his first commission). The theater, which he modeled on a Roman amphitheater, made his reputation. It was built as a venue for the university's public ceremonies, and graduations are still held here—entirely in Latin, as befits the building's spirit. Outside is one of Oxford's most striking sights—a boundary wall topped with stone busts of 18 Roman emperors (modern reproductions of the originals, which were eaten away by pollution). ⊠ *Broad St.* ☎ *01865/277299* ⊕ *www.sheldon.ox.ac.uk* ✉ *£3* ☉ *Mar.–Oct., Mon.– Sat. 10–12:30 and 2–4:30; Nov.–Feb., Mon.–Sat. 10–12:30 and 2–3:30. Last admission 30 mins before closing. Closed for 10 days at Christmas and 4 days at Easter and for degree ceremonies and events.*

Broad Street leads into Giles Street and prestigious **Balliol College** (1263). Past the "new" (they're actually Victorian) college gates you can find a cobblestone cross in the sidewalk that marks the spot where Archbishop Cranmer and bishops Latimer and Ridley were burned in 1555 for their Protestant beliefs. The original college gates (rumored to have existed at the time of the scorching) hang in the library passage, between the inner and outer quadrangles. ⊠ *Broad St.* ☎ *01865/277777* ⊕ *www. balliol.ox.ac.uk* ⊠ *£2* ☺ *Daily 10–5, or dusk if earlier.*

★ The **chapel of Trinity College** (1555) is an architectural gem—a tiny place with a delicately painted ceiling, gorgeously tiled floor, and elaborate wood carvings on the pews, pulpit, and walls. Some of the superb carvings were done by Grinling Gibbons, a 17th-century master carver whose work can also be seen in Hampton Court Palace and St. Paul's Cathedral, and who inspired the 18th-century cabinetmaker Thomas Chippendale. ⊠ *Broad St.* ☎ *01865/279900* ⊕ *www.trinity.ox.ac.uk* ⊠ *£2* ☺ *Daily 1:30–4, or dusk if earlier.*

Fodor's Choice Westward from Giles Street, Beaumont Street is the site of the **Ashmolean**
★ **Museum,** founded in 1683, making it Britain's oldest public museum. Some of the world's most precious art objects are stashed here—drawings by Michelangelo and Raphael, European silverware and ceramics, a world-class numismatic collection, and Egyptian, Greek, and Roman artifacts. A renovation by noted architect Rick Mather, creating 39 additional galleries and a rooftop restaurant, opened in November 2009. ⊠ *Beaumont St.* ☎ *01865/278000* ⊕ *www.ashmolean.org* ⊠ *Free* ☺ *Tues.–Sun. 10–6.*

North and across St. Giles Road from the Ashmolean Museum is **St. John's College** (1555), former Prime Minister Tony Blair's alma mater, which is worth a stop for its historic courtyards, world-renowned symmetrical gardens. The library contains some of Jane Austen's letters and an illustrated 1483 edition of *The Canterbury Tales* by the English printer William Caxton, but is not open to the public. ⊠ *St. Giles* ☎ *01865/277300* ⊕ *www.sjc.ox.ac.uk* ⊠ *Free* ☺ *Daily 1–5, 1–dusk in winter. May be closed for functions (call for info).*

College members, but not visitors, can enter the university's largest college via **Tom Gate.** This massive gatehouse is surmounted by Christopher Wren's **Tom Tower,** which contains Great Tom, a giant clock that strikes each hour with high and low notes.

☺ The leading college of the southern half of Oxford is **Christ Church Col-**
★ **lege.** Traditionally called "the House" by its students, Christ Church has the largest quadrangle in town. This is where Charles Dodgson, better known as Lewis Carroll, was a math don; a shop across from the parkland (known as "the meadows") on St. Aldate's was the inspiration for the shop in *Through the Looking Glass.* More recently, various college locations appeared in the Harry Potter films. Don't miss the 800-year-old chapel, or the famous Tudor dining hall, with its portraits of former students—John Wesley, William Penn, and 6 of the 13 prime ministers who attended the college. ⊠ *St. Aldate's* ☎ *01865/276492* ⊕ *www.chch.ox.ac. uk* ⊠ *Apr.–June, £8; July and Aug., £8.50; Sept.–Mar., £7* ☺ *Weekdays 10–11:45 and 2–4:30, weekends 2:30–4:30 during term, 10–4:30 outside of term. Dining hall weekdays 2:30–4:30 during school year.*

WHERE TO EAT

$$
CONTINENTAL
★

✕**Brasserie Blanc.** Raymond Blanc's Conran-designed brasserie is sophisticated even by London standards. The top British chef populates his menu with modern European and regional French dishes: you might see boeuf bourguignon, or a rack of lamb. At £11.50 for two courses or £13.95 for three, the "Dine With Wine" deal, available until 7, is an incredible value (after 7 it's £14 for two courses and £16.45 for three), and well worth the 15-minute walk north of the town center. ✉ *71–72 Walton St.* ☎ *01865/510999* ⊕ *www.brasserieblanc.com* ✐ *Reservations essential.*

$
CAFÉ

✕**Grand Café.** In a lovely 1920s building, this inexpensive café looks as if it should cost the world. Golden tiles, carved columns, and antique marble floor fill the place with charm, and the menu of tasty sandwiches, salads, and tarts, as well as afternoon tea, perfect coffee drinks and desserts, make it a great place for lunch or an afternoon break. At night it puts away its menus and transforms itself into a popular cocktail bar. ✉ *84 High St.* ☎ *01865/204463* ⊕ *www.thegrandcafe.co.uk.*

$
ITALIAN

✕**Pizza Express.** Many people are surprised to discover that this uniquely situated restaurant in the former sitting room of the 15th-century Golden Cross—Shakespeare's stopover lodging on his frequent trips from Stratford to London—is part of a nationwide chain. Creativity is encouraged here, so vegetarians, vegans, and meat eaters alike can enjoy inventing their own dream pizzas. A terrace is open in summer, but be sure to check out the medieval paintings and friezes inside the restaurant before heading out. ✉ *8 The Golden Cross, Cornmarket St.* ☎ *01865/790442* ⊕ *www.pizzaexpress.com.*

STRATFORD-UPON-AVON

19

104 miles (167 km) north of London.

Stratford-upon-Avon has become adept at accommodating the hordes of people who stream in for a glimpse of William Shakespeare's world. Filled with all the distinctive, Tudor half-timber buildings your heart could desire, this is certainly a handsome town. But it can feel, at times, like a literary amusement park, so if you're not a fan of the Bard, you'd probably do better to explore a historic English market town.

TOURS AND TICKETS

It's difficult to avoid feeling like a herd animal as you board the Shakespeare bus, but tours like City Sightseeing's **Stratford and the Shakespeare Story** (✉ *Tourist Information Centre Bridgefort* ☎ *01789/412680* ⊕ *www.city-sightseeing.com* 🎫 *£11.75*), with a hop-on, hop-off route around the five Shakespeare Birthplace Trust properties (two of which are out of town), can make a visit infinitely easier if you don't have a car.

It's worth purchasing a combined ticket to the **Shakespeare's Birthplace Trust properties,** which include Shakespeare's Birthplace Museum, Nash's House and New Place, Hall's Croft, Anne Hathaway's Cottage, and the Shakespeare Countryside Museum. The ticket, which is valid for one year and is available at any of the properties, costs £19.50 for all the sites, or £12.50 for the three in-town properties (not including Anne

Hathaway's Cottage and Mary Arden's House). Note that you cannot buy a ticket for just one of the in-town sites. ☎ *01789/204016* ⊕ *www. shakespeare.org.uk*.

ESSENTIALS

Visitor Information Stratford-upon-Avon (☎ *01789/264293* ⊕ *www. shakespeare-country.co.uk*).

EXPLORING

Most visitors to Stratford start at **Shakespeare's Birthplace.** The half-timber building in which Shakespeare was born in 1564 is a national treasure. It was owned by his descendants until the 19th century, and it became a national memorial in 1847. It's been furnished and decorated with simple whitewashed walls and brightly colored fabrics that were popular in Shakespeare's time. All the textiles have been hand-dyed using period methods. The revamped visitor center tells the story of Shakespeare's life in great detail, which makes a good starting point for any tour of Stratford. ✉ *Henley St.* ☎ *01789/204016* ⊕ *www. shakespeare.org.uk* ✉ *£12.50, includes admission to Nash's House and Hall's Croft* ☉ *Apr., May, Sept., and Oct., daily 9–5; June–Aug., daily 9–6; Nov.–Mar., daily 10–4.*

On High Street, the center road of Stratford, is **Nash's House and New Place,** which contains annually changing exhibitions, against a backdrop of period furniture and tapestries. The main attraction is really the extravagant gardens around the adjacent remains of **New Place,** the home where Shakespeare spent his last years, and where he died in 1616. A gorgeous Elizabethan knot garden, based on drawings of gardens from Shakespeare's time, grows around the remaining foundation of the house, which was destroyed in 1759 by its last owner, the Reverend Francis Gastrell, worn down by tax problems and a constant tide of sightseers. ✉ *Chapel St.* ☎ *01789/204016* ⊕ *www.shakespeare. org.uk* ✉ *£12.50, includes admission to Shakespeare's Birthplace and Hall's Croft* ☉ *Nov.–Mar., daily 11–4; Apr.–June, Sept., and Oct., daily 10–5; July and Aug., daily 10–6.*

★ On the venerable road called Old Town you'll find Stratford's most beautiful Jacobean town house, **Hall's Croft.** This was—almost definitely—the home of Shakespeare's daughter Susanna and her husband, Dr. John Hall. It's outfitted with furniture of the period and the doctor's dispensary. The walled garden is delightful. ✉ *Old Town St.* ☎ *01789/204016* ⊕ *www. shakespeare.org.uk* ✉ *£12.50, includes admission to Shakespeare's Birthplace and Nash's House* ☉ *Nov.–Mar., daily 11–4; Apr.–Oct., daily 10–5.*

WORD OF MOUTH

"We took kids ages 9 and 11 to Warwick Castle and we all loved it. I like history and, once I got over the fact that the interiors were furnished with Victorian (or Edwardian) era items though the castle is much, much older, I truly enjoyed that. And, of course, it is not far from the Cotswolds and Stratford, so you won't be driving far out of the way if you are seeing those places as well."
—LeslieC, Jan 2012

At the end of Old Town is "Shake-speare's church," the 13th-century **Holy Trinity,** which is fronted by a beautiful avenue of lime trees. Shakespeare is buried here, in the chancel. The bust of the Bard is thought to be an authentic likeness, executed a few years after his death. ✉ *Old Town* ☎ *01789/266316* 🎫 *Church free, chancel £2* ⏱ *Mar., Mon.–Sat. 9–5, Sun. noon–5; Apr.–Sept., Mon.–Sat. 8:30–6, Sun. noon–5; Oct., Mon.–Sat. 9–5, Sun. noon–5; Nov.–Feb., Mon.–Sat. 9–4, Sun. noon–5.*

<table>
<tr><td>

FAMILY TREES

Nash's House belonged to Thomas Nash, first husband of Shake-speare's granddaughter Elizabeth Hall: you can see how tenuous the Shakespearean links can get around here.

</td></tr>
</table>

Fodor's Choice
★

Not far from Holy Trinity church is the **Royal Shakespeare Theatre,** famously set on the bank of the Avon and the landmark home of the Royal Shakespeare Company in Stratford. It reopened in late 2010 after massive renovations. Classic productions of the Bard can be seen in the refurbished **Main Theatre,** along with the smaller **Swan Theatre** in the same building. Check the website to see what's going to be on during your visit. It's always best to book in advance, especially now that the renovated theater has garnered its fair share of world headlines; day-of-performance tickets are sometimes available. ✉ *Waterside* ☎ *0844/800–1110 ticket hotline and general information* ⊕ *www.rsc.org.uk.*

STRATFORD ENVIRONS

The two remaining stops on the Shakespeare trail are just outside Stratford.

★ **Anne Hathaway's Cottage,** the early home of the playwright's wife, is perhaps the most picturesque thatched cottage in the world. It has been gorgeously restored to reflect the comfortable middle-class Hath-away life. You can walk here from town—it's just over a mile from central Stratford. ✉ *Cottage La., Shottery* ☎ *01789/204016* ⊕ *www.shakespeare.org.uk* 🎫 *£7.50* ⏱ *Apr.–Oct., daily 9–5; Nov.–Mar., daily 10–4.*

🅒 **Mary Arden's Farm** uses 16th-century methods to grow food on its work-ing farm. This stop is great for kids, who can see the lambs and calves, listen as the farmers explain their work in the fields, and watch the cooks prepare food in the Tudor farmhouse kitchen. This site was for-merly referred to as Mary Arden's House, and believed to be where Shakespeare's mother grew up. In late 2000, research findings based on newly discovered real-estate records revealed that the real **Mary Arden's Farm,** hitherto known as Glebe Farm, was actually nearby and (thank-fully) already owned by the Shakespeare Birthplace Trust. ✉ *Wilmcote* ☎ *01789/204016, 01789/293455 for information on special events* ⊕ *www.shakespeare.org.uk* 🎫 *£9.50; children £5.50* ⏱ *Apr.–Oct., daily 10–5. Closed Nov.–Mar.*

🅒
★ Some 8 miles north of Stratford in the medieval town of Warwick, **War-wick Castle** fulfills the most clichéd Camelot daydreams. This medieval, fortified, much-restored, castellated, moated, landscaped (by Capability

19

Stratford-upon-Avon honors Shakespeare's birthday with an annual procession.

Brown) castle, now under the same management as Madame Tussauds, is a true period museum—complete with dungeons and a torture chamber, state rooms, and the occasional battle reenactment or joust. Note: It gets very crowded in summer, when lines for tickets, as well as food and drink, can be long, so it's not for those looking for a quiet, historic retreat to explore. Tickets are cheaper if purchased in advance on the website (minimum of two days before visit) and you'll also avoid some lines. ⊠ *Castle La. off Mill St., Warwick* ☎ *01926/495421, 0871/265–2000 24-hr information line* ⊕ *www.warwick-castle.co.uk* ☎ *£21.60–£30.60 on the day, £17.28–£24.48 online* ⊙ *Apr.–Sept., daily 10–6; Oct.–Mar., daily 10–5; last admission 30 mins before closing.*

WHERE TO EAT

$
BRITISH
✕ **The Black Swan.** Also known as the Dirty Duck (a nickname bestowed by American GIs who were stationed here during WWII), this is one of Stratford's most celebrated pubs—it has attracted actors since the 18th-century thespian David Garrick's days. A little veranda overlooks the theaters and the river here. Along with a pint of bitter, it's a fine place to enjoy English grill specialties, as well as braised oxtail and honey-roasted duck. You can also choose from an assortment of bar meals. ⊠ *Waterside* ☎ *01789/297312.*

$
BRITISH
✕ **Lambs of Sheep Street.** Sit downstairs to appreciate the hardwood floors and oak beams of this local epicurean favorite; upstairs, the look is more contemporary. The updates of tried-and-true dishes include rib-eye steak with vine tomatoes, and slow-roasted lamb shank. Daily fish specials keep the menu seasonal, and the desserts are fantastic.

A fixed-price menu available until 7 is a good deal at £12.50 for two courses, £16 for three. ⊠ *12 Sheep St.* ☎ *01789/292554* ⊕ *www. lambsrestaurant.co.uk.*

$ ✕ **The Opposition.** Hearty, warming meals are offered at this informal,
BRITISH family-friendly restaurant, more commonly known as the "Oppo," in a 16th-century building on the main dining street near the theaters. The American and Modern British dishes on the menu win praise from the locals. Try the roast chicken with banana. ⊠ *13 Sheep St.* ☎ *01789/ 269980* ⊕ *www.theoppo.co.uk.*

WINDSOR CASTLE

24 miles (39 km) west of London.

The tall turrets of Windsor Castle, believed to be the world's largest inhabited castle, can be seen for miles around. The grand stone building is the star attraction in this quiet town with some remaining medieval elements—though Eton College, England's most famous public school, is also just a lovely walk away across the Thames. The castle is the only royal residence to have been in continuous royal use since the days of William the Conqueror, who chose this site to build a timber stockade soon after his conquest of Britain in 1066. It was Edward III in the 1300s who really founded the castle: he built the Norman gateway, the great Round Tower, and the State Apartments. Charles II restored the State Apartments during the 1600s, and, during the 1820s George IV—with his mania for building—converted what was still essentially a medieval castle into the palace you see today.

ESSENTIALS
Visitor Information Windsor (☎ *01753/743900* ⊕ *www.windsor.gov.uk*).

EXPLORING

19

The massive citadel of **Windsor Castle** occupies 13 acres, but the first part you notice on entering is the **Round Tower,** from the top of which the Standard is flown and at the base of which is the 11th-century Moat Garden. Passing under the portcullis at the Norman Gate, you reach the **Upper Ward,** the quadrangle containing the State Apartments—which you may tour—and the sovereign's Private Apartments. Processions for foreign heads of state and other ceremonies take place here, as does the Changing of the Guard when the Queen is in residence. A short walk takes you to the Lower Ward, where the high point is the magnificent **St. George's Chapel,** home of the Order of the Garter, the highest chivalric order in the land, founded in 1348 by Edward III. Ten sovereigns are buried in the chapel—a fantastic Perpendicular Gothic vision 230 feet long, complete with

DID YOU KNOW?

The Queen uses Windsor often—it's said she likes it much more than Buckingham Palace—spending most weekends here, often joined by family and friends. You know she's in when the Royal Standard is flown above the Round Tower but not in when you see the Union Jack.

gargoyles, buttresses, banners, swords, and choir stalls. This is also where royal weddings take place.

The **State Apartments** are as grand as Buckingham Palace's and have the added attraction of a few gems from the Queen's vast art collection: choice canvases by Rubens, Rembrandt, Van Dyck, Gainsborough, Canaletto, and Holbein; da Vinci drawings; Gobelin tapestries; and lime-wood carvings by Grinling Gibbons. The entrance is through a grand hall holding cases crammed with precious china—some still used for royal banquets. Don't miss the outsize suit of armor, made for Henry VIII, in the armory. Make sure you take in the magnificent views across to Windsor Great Park, which are the remains of a former royal hunting forest.

☺ One unmissable treat is **Queen Mary's Dolls' House,** a 12:1 scale, seven-story palace with electricity, running water, and working elevators, designed in 1924 by Sir Edwin Lutyens. The detail is incredible—even the diminutive wine bottles hold the real thing. ⊠ *Windsor Castle* ☎ *020/7766–7304 tickets, 01753/831118 opening hrs* ⊕ *www.royalcollection.org.uk* ✉ *£17 (£44.75 family ticket) for Precincts, State Apartments, Gallery, St. George's Chapel, Albert Memorial Chapel, and Queen Mary's Dolls' House; £9.30 when State Apartments are closed* ⊘ *Mar.–Oct., daily 9:45–5:15, last admission at 4; Nov.–Feb., daily 9:45–4:15, last admission at 3; St. George's Chapel closed Sun. except to worshippers. Hrs vary; check website.*

★ The splendid redbrick Tudor-style buildings of **Eton College,** founded in 1440 by King Henry VI, border the north end of High Street. During the college semesters, schoolboys dress in their distinctive striped trousers, swallow-tailed coats, and stiff collars to walk to class—it's all terrifically photogenic. The Gothic **Chapel** rivals St. George's at Windsor in size and magnificence, and is both austere and intimate. The **Museum of Eton Life** has displays on the school's history. Admission to the school during term time is with a prebooked guided tour for groups of at least 14 (no children) only, but there are also public tours during school holidays for individuals that don't require prebooking and are open to children. ⊠ *Main entrance off Eton High St.* ☎ *01753/671177* ⊕ *www.etoncollege.com* ✉ *£7 short tour, £10.50 extended tour* ⊘ *Tours mid-Mar.–Oct., Wed.–Fri., weekends at 2 and 3:15. Guided tours mid-Mar.–Oct., daily 10:30–4:30. During term time (Nov.–Feb.) Wed.–Fri., weekends after 1:30. Check website for details.*

WHERE TO EAT

$ ✗ **Two Brewers.** Two small, low-ceiling rooms make up this 17th-century
BRITISH   pub where locals congregate and palace staff unwind after work. Children are not welcome, but adults will find a suitable collection of wine, espresso, and local beer, plus an excellent little tapas-only menu. On Sunday the pub serves a traditional roast. With only nine tables, reservations are essential. ⊠ *34 Park St.* ☎ *01753/855426* ▭ ⊘ *Closed Fri. and Sat. evenings.*

UNDERSTANDING LONDON

LONDON AT-A-GLANCE

FAST FACTS

Type of government: Representative democracy. In 1999 the Greater London Authority Act reestablished a single local governing body for the Greater London area, consisting of an elected mayor and the 25-member London Assembly. Elections, first held in 2000, take place every four years.

Population: Inner city 3 million, Greater London 7.7 million

Population density: 12,331 people per square mi

Median age: 38.4

Infant mortality rate: 5 per 1,000 births

Language: English. More than 300 languages are spoken in London. All city government documents are translated into Arabic, Bengali, Chinese, Greek, Gujurati, Hindi, Punjabi, Turkish, Urdu, and Vietnamese.

Ethnic and racial groups: White British 70%, White Irish 3%, Other White 9%, Indian 6%, Bangladeshi 2%, Pakistani 2%, other Asian 2%, Black African 6%, Black Caribbean 5%, Chinese 1%, Other 3%.

Religion: Christian 58%, nonaffiliated 15%, Muslim 8%, Hindu 4%, Jewish 2%, Sikh 1%, other religion 1%, Buddhist 0.8%.

When a man is tired of London, he is tired of life; for there is in London all that life can afford.

—Samuel Johnson

GEOGRAPHY AND ENVIRONMENT

Latitude: 51° N (same as Calgary, Canada; Kiev, Ukraine; Prague, Czech Republic)

Longitude: 0° (same as Accra, Ghana). A brass line in the ground in Greenwich marks the prime meridian (0° longitude).

Elevation: 49 feet

Land area: City, 67 square mi; metro area, 625 square mi

Terrain: River plain, rolling hills, and parkland

Natural hazards: Drought in warmer summers, minor localized flooding of the Thames caused by surge tides from the North Atlantic

Environmental issues: The city has been improving its air quality, but up to 1,600 people die each year from health problems related to London's polluted air. Only half of London's rivers and canals received passing grades for water quality from 1999 through 2001. More than £12 million ($22 million) is spent annually to ensure the city's food safety.

I'm leaving because the weather is too good. I hate London when it's not raining.

—Groucho Marx

ECONOMY

Workforce: 3.8 million; financial/real estate 28%, health care 10%, manufacturing 4%, education 7%, construction 5%, public administration 5%

Unemployment: 7.2%

Major industries: The arts, banking, government, insurance, tourism

London: a nation, not a city.

—Benjamin Disraeli, Lothair

ENGLISH VOCABULARY

You and a Londoner may speak the same language, but some phrases definitely get lost in translation once they cross the Atlantic.

British English	American English

BASIC TERMS AND EVERYDAY ITEMS

British English	American English
bill	check
flat	apartment
lift	elevator
nappy	diaper
holiday	vacation
note	bill (currency)
plaster	Band-Aid
queue	line
row	argument
rubbish	trash
tin	can
toilet/loo/WC	bathroom

CLOTHING

British English	American English
braces	suspenders
bum bag	fanny pack
dressing gown	robe
jumper	sweater
pants/knickers	underpants/briefs
rucksack	backpack
suspender	garter
tights	pantyhose
trainers	sneakers
trousers	pants
vest	undershirt
waistcoat	vest

TRANSPORTATION

British English	American English
bonnet	hood
boot	trunk

coach	long-distance bus
pavement	sidewalk
petrol	gas
pram	baby carriage
puncture	flat
windscreen	windshield

FOOD

aubergine	eggplant
banger	sausage
biscuit	cookie
chips	fries
courgette	zucchini
crisps	potato chips
jam	jelly
main course (or main)	entrée
pudding	dessert
rocket	arugula
starter	appetizer
sweet	candy
tea	early dinner

SLANG

all right	hi there
cheers	thank you
chuffed	pleased
fit	attractive
geezer	dude
guv'nor, gaffer	boss
hard	tough
mate	buddy
sound	good
ta	thank you

BOOKS AND MOVIES

London has been the focus of countless books and essays. For sonorous eloquence, you still must reach back more than half a century to Henry James's *English Hours* and Virginia Woolf's *The London Scene*. Today most suggested reading lists begin with V.S. Pritchett's *London Perceived* and H.V. Morton's *In Search of London*, both decades old. Four more-up-to-date books with a general compass are Peter Ackroyd's *Thames* and anecdotal *London: The Biography,* which traces the city's growth from the Druids to the 21st century; John Russell's *London,* a sumptuously illustrated art book; and Christopher Hibbert's *In London: The Biography of a City.* Stephen Inwood's *A History of London* explores the city from its Roman roots to its swinging 60s heyday. Piet Schreuders's *The Beatles' London* follows the footsteps of the Fab Four.

That noted, there are books galore on the various facets of the city. *The Art and Architecture of London* by Ann Saunders is fairly comprehensive. *Inside London: Discovering the Classic Interiors of London,* by Joe Friedman and Peter Aprahamian, has magnificent color photographs of hidden and overlooked shops, clubs, and town houses. For a wonderful take on the golden age of the city's regal mansions, see Christopher Simon Sykes's *Private Palaces: Life in the Great London Houses.* For various other aspects of the city, consult Mervyn Blatch's helpful *A Guide to London's Churches,* Andrew Crowe's *The Parks and Woodlands of London,* Sheila Fairfield's *The Streets of London,* Ann Saunders's *Regent's Park,* Ian Norrie's *Hampstead, Highgate Village, and Kenwood,* and Suzanne Ebel's *A Guide to London's Riverside: Hampton Court to Greenwich.* For keen walkers, there are two books by Andrew Duncan: *Secret London* and *Walking Village London. City Secrets: London,* edited by Robert Kahn, is a handsome book of anecdotes from London writers, artists, and historians about their favorite

places in the city. For the last word on just about every subject, see *The London Encyclopaedia,* edited by Ben Weinreb and Christopher Hibbert. HarperCollins's *London Photographic Atlas* has a plethora of bird's-eye images of the capital. For an alternative view of the city, it would be hard to better Iain Sinclair's witty and intelligent *London Orbital: A Walk Around the M25* in which he scrutinizes the history, mythology, and politics of London from the viewpoint of its ugly ring road. Sinclair is also the editor of *London: City of Disappearances,* an anthology exploring what has vanished.

Of course, the history and spirit of the city are also to be found in celebrations of great authors, British heroes, and architects. Peter Ackroyd's massive *Dickens* elucidates how the great author shaped today's view of the city; Martin Gilbert's magisterial, multivolume *Churchill* traces the city through some of its greatest trials; J. Mansbridge's *John Nash* details the London buildings of this great architect. Liza Picard evokes mid-18th-century London in *Dr. Johnson's London.* For musical theater buffs, Mike Leigh's *Gilbert and Sullivan's London* takes a romantic look at the two artists' lives and times in the capital's grand theaters and wild nightspots. *Rodinsky's Room* by Rachel Lichtenstein and Iain Sinclair is a fascinating exploration of East End Jewish London and the mysterious disappearance of one of its occupants.

Maureen Waller's *1700: Scenes from London Life* is a fascinating look at the daily life of Londoners in the 18th century. Nineteenth-century London—the city of Queen Victoria, Tennyson, and Dickens—comes alive through *Mayhew's London,* a massive study of the London poor by Henry Mayhew, and Gustave Doré's *London,* an unforgettable series of engravings of the city (often reprinted in modern editions) that detail its horrifying slums and grand avenues. When it comes to fiction, of course, Dickens's immortal works top the list. Stay-at-home detectives have long walked the streets of London, thanks to great mysteries by Dorothy L. Sayers, Agatha Christie, Ngaio Marsh, and Antonia Fraser. Cops and bad guys wind their way around 1960s London in Jake Arnott's pulp fiction books, *The Long Firm* and *He Kills Coppers*. Martin Amis's *London Fields* tracks a murder mystery through West London. For so-called "tart noir," pick up any Stella Duffy book. Marie Belloc-Lowndes's *The Lodger* is a fictional account of London's most deadly villain, Jack the Ripper. Victorian London was never so salacious as in Sarah Waters's story of a young girl who travels the theaters as a singer, the Soho squares as a male prostitute, and the East End as a communist in *Tipping the Velvet*. Late-20th-century London, with its diverse ethnic makeup, is the star of Zadie Smith's famed novel *White Teeth*. The vibrancy and cultural diversity of London's East End come to life in Monica Ali's *Brick Lane*.

Many films—from *Waterloo Bridge* and *Georgy Girl* to *Secrets and Lies* and *Notting Hill*—have used London as their setting. The great musicals Walt Disney's *Mary Poppins*, George Cukor's *My Fair Lady*, and Sir Carol Reed's *Oliver!* evoke the Hollywood soundstage version of London.

Children of all ages enjoy Stephen Herek's *101 Dalmatians*, with Glenn Close as fashion-savvy Cruella de Vil. King's Cross Station in London was shot to cinematic fame by the movie version of J. K. Rowling's *Harry Potter and the Philosopher's Stone*. Look for cameos by the city in all other *Harry Potter* films.

The swinging 60s are loosely portrayed in M. Jay Roach's *Austin Powers: International Man of Mystery*, full of references to British slang and some great opening scenes in London. For a truer picture of the 60s in London, Michelangelo Antonioni weaves a mystery plot around the world of a London fashion photographer in *Blow-Up*. British gangster films came into their own with Guy Ritchie's amusing tales of London thieves in *Lock, Stock, and Two Smoking Barrels,* filmed almost entirely in London, and the follow-up *Snatch*. More sobering portraits of London criminal life include Neil Jordan's *Mona Lisa*, Paul McGuigan's *Gangster No. 1*, and John Mackenzie's *The Long Good Friday*. Of course, the original tough guy is 007, and his best exploits in London are featured in the introductory chase scene in *The World Is Not Enough*.

Sir Arthur Conan Doyle knew the potential of London as a chilling setting, and John Landis's *An American Werewolf in London* and Hitchcock's *39 Steps* and *The Man Who Knew Too Much* exploit the Gothic and sinister qualities of the city. For a fascinating look at Renaissance London, watch John Madden's *Shakespeare in Love*. Dickens's London is indelibly depicted in David Lean's *Oliver Twist*.

Some modern-day romantic comedies that use London as a backdrop are Peter Howitt's *Sliding Doors* with Gwyneth Paltrow and the screen adaptations of Helen Fielding's *Bridget Jones's Diary* (and its sequel), starring Renée Zellweger, Hugh Grant, and Colin Firth. Glossy London is depicted in Woody Allen's *Match Point,* bohemian London in David Kane's *This Year's Love*, gritty London in Shane Meadow's *Somers Town*, and post-zombie London in Danny Boyle's *28 Days Later*, while Patrick Kellior's *London* offers a uniquely informed, idiosyncratic view of the city.

Travel Smart London

WORD OF MOUTH

"We LOVED the Tube—always amazed at how spotless the cars and stations are kept. What a pleasure!"

—keemick

"Having just got back from London, I'd recommend an Oyster travel card [refillable multi-trip pass on the Tube and buses] to anyone staying more than two days."

—khunwilko

"I keep my Oyster and, before leaving London, I always make sure I have enough money left on it for my next inbound trip from Heathrow into London, so I don't have to wait in line to 'top up'."

—yk

www.fodors.com/community

GETTING HERE AND AROUND

Central London and its surrounding districts are divided into 32 boroughs—33, counting the City of London. More useful for finding your way around, however, are the subdivisions of London into postal districts. Throughout the guide we've given the full postal code for some listings. The first one or two letters give the location: N means north, NW means northwest, and so on. Don't expect the numbering to be logical, however. You won't, for example, find W2 next to W3. The general rule is that the lower numbers, such as W1 or SW1, are closest to Buckingham Palace, but it is not consistent—SE17 is closer to the city center than E4, for example.

■ AIR TRAVEL

Flying time to London is about 6½ hours from New York, 7½ hours from Chicago, 11 hours from San Francisco, and 21½ hours from Sydney.

For flights out of London, the general rule is that you arrive one hour before your scheduled departure time for domestic flights and two hours before international flights for off-peak travel.

Airline Security Issues Transportation Security Administration. ⊕ www.tsa.gov.

AIRPORTS

International flights to London arrive at either Heathrow Airport (LHR), 15 miles west of London, or at Gatwick Airport (LGW), 27 miles south of the capital. Most flights from the United States go to Heathrow, which is the busiest and is divided into five terminals, with Terminals 3, 4, and 5 handling transatlantic flights. Gatwick is London's second gateway. It has grown from a European airport into an airport that also serves dozens of U.S. destinations. A smaller third airport, Stansted (STN), is 35 miles northeast of the city. It handles mainly European and

domestic traffic, although there's also scheduled service from New York. Two smaller airports, Luton (LTN), 30 miles north of town, and business-oriented London City (in East London E16) mainly handle flights to Europe.

Airport Information Gatwick Airport ☎ 0844/892–0322 ⊕ www.gatwickairport.com. **Heathrow Airport** ☎ 0844/335–1801 ⊕ www. heathrowairport.com. **London City Airport** ☎ 020/7646–0088 ⊕ www.londoncityairport. com. **Luton Airport** ☎ 01582/405100 ⊕ www.london-luton.co.uk. **Stansted Airport** ☎ 0844/355–1803 ⊕ www.stanstedairport. com.

GROUND TRANSPORTATION

London has excellent if pricey bus and train connections between its airports and central London. If you're arriving at Heathrow, you can pick up a map and fare schedule at the Transport for London (TfL) Information Centre located in the Underground station serving Terminals 1, 2, and 3. Train service can be quick, but the downside (for trains from all airports) is that you must get yourself and your luggage to the train via a series of escalators and connecting trams. Airport link buses (generally National Express Airport buses) may ease the luggage factor and drop you closer to central hotels, but they're subject to London traffic, which can be horrendous and make the trip drag on for hours. Taxis can be more convenient than buses, but beware that prices can go through the roof. Airport Travel Line has additional transfer information and takes advance booking for transfers between airports and into London. The BAA (British Airport Authority) website is a useful resource, giving all transport options from Gatwick, Heathrow, and Stansted.

FROM HEATHROW TO CENTRAL LONDON		
Travel Mode	Time	Cost
Taxi	1 hour+	£50+
Heathrow Express Train	15 minutes	£16.50 (£32 round-trip) and £26 for first class
Underground	50 minutes	£4.50 one-way (less with Oyster card)
National Express Bus	1 hour	£4 one-way
Hotel by Bus	1 hour+	£22 one-way

Heathrow by Bus: National Express buses take one hour to reach the city center (Victoria) and costs £5 one-way and £10 round-trip. A rival service, easyBus, offers buses from as little as £2. The National Express Hotel Hoppa service runs from all airports to around 20 hotels located near the airport (£4). Alternatively, nearly every hotel in London itself is served by the Hotel By Bus service. Fares to central London average around £22. SkyShuttle also offers a shared minibus service between Heathrow and any London hotel. The N9 night bus runs every half hour from midnight to 5 am to Trafalgar Square; it takes an hour and costs £4.

Heathrow by Train: The cheap, direct route into London is via the Piccadilly line of the Underground (London's extensive subway system, or "Tube"). Trains normally run every four to eight minutes from all terminals from early morning until just before midnight. The 50-minute trip into central London costs £4.50 one-way and connects with other central Tube lines. The Heathrow Express train is comfortable and convenient, if costly, speeding into London's Paddington station in 15 minutes. Standard one-way tickets cost £16.50 (£32 round-trip) and £26 for first class. Book ahead (online is the cheapest option, at a counter/kiosk less so), as tickets are more expensive to

NAVIGATING LONDON

London is a confusing city to navigate, even for people who've visited it a few times. Its streets are arranged in medieval patterns that no longer make much sense, meaning that you can't always use logic to find your way around. A good map is essential, and public transportation can be a lifesaver: buses will take you magically from point A to point B, and the Tube is often the quickest way to reach your destination. Here are some basic tips to help you find your way around:

■ Although free tourist maps can be handy, they're usually quite basic and include only major streets. If you're going to be doing lots of wandering around, buy the pocket-size map book *London A–Z* sold in bookstores and Tube and train stations throughout the city. Its detailed maps are lifesavers.

■ To find your way, look for tall landmarks near where you are headed: the London Eye, for example, or the cross atop St. Paul's Cathedral—or the most obvious of all, Big Ben.

■ If you get properly lost, the best people to ask are the Londoners hustling by you, who know the area like nobody else. The worst people to ask are the people working in souvenir kiosks, and street vendors handing out the local *Evening Standard* newspaper; they're famously rude and unhelpful to lost tourists.

■ The tourist hubs of Soho, Covent Garden, Leicester Square, and Trafalgar Square are separated from one another by only a few blocks. Taking the Tube from one to another actually takes longer than walking.

■ On the other hand, when you're lost, the Tube is often the shortest distance between two points. Don't hesitate to use it.

buy on board. There's daily service from 5:10 am (5:50 am on Sunday) to 11:25 pm (10:50 pm on Sunday), with departures every 15 minutes. The Heathrow Connect service leaves from Paddington station and makes five local stops before arriving at Terminals 1, 3, and 5. At 25 minutes, journey time is only slightly slower than the Express and one-way tickets are £7.90.

Gatwick by Bus: Hourly bus service runs from Gatwick's north and south terminals to Victoria station with stops at Hooley, Coulsdon, Mitcham, Streatham, Stockwell, and Pimlico. The journey takes up to 90 minutes and costs from £4.50 one-way. The easyBus service runs a service to west London (Fulham) from as little as £2; the later the ticket is booked online, the higher the price (up to £10 on board).

Gatwick by Train: The fast, nonstop Gatwick Express leaves for Victoria station every 15 minutes 5:15 am–midnight. The 30-minute trip costs £16.90 one-way, £23 round-trip. Book in advance, as tickets cost more on board. The First Capital Connect rail company's nonexpress services are cheaper; Capital Connect train runs regularly throughout the day until midnight to St. Pancras International, London Bridge, and Blackfriars stations; departures are every 15 to 30 minutes, and the journey takes almost one hour. Tickets are from £8 one-way. FlyBy service to Victoria (£10 single) is not express, but the fare applies only on trains operated by Southern Trains.

Stansted by Bus: Hourly service on National Express Airport bus A6 (24 hours a day) to Victoria Coach station costs from £10 one-way, £17 round-trip, and takes about 1 hour and 40 minutes. Stops include Golders Green, Finchley Road, St. John's Wood, Baker Street, Marble Arch, and Hyde Park Corner. The easyBus service to Victoria via Baker Street costs from £2.

Stansted by Train: The Stansted Express to Liverpool Street station (with a stop at Tottenham Hale) runs every 15 minutes 4:10 am–11:25 pm daily. The 45-minute trip costs £18.80 one-way, £26.70 round-trip if booked online. Tickets cost more when purchased on board.

Luton by Bus and Train: A free airport shuttle runs from Luton Airport to the nearby Luton Airport Parkway station, from which you can take a train or bus into London. From there, the First Capital Connect train service runs to St. Pancras, Farringdon, Blackfriars, and London Bridge. The journey takes about 25 minutes. Trains leave every 10 minutes or so from 5 am until midnight. Single tickets cost £13.50. The Green Line 757 bus service from Luton to Victoria station runs three times an hour, takes about 90 minutes, and costs from £14 (£15 return).

Heathrow, Gatwick, Stansted, and Luton by Taxi: This is an expensive and time-consuming option. The city's congestion charge (£8) may be added to the bill if your hotel is in the charging zone, you run the risk of getting stuck in traffic, and if you take a taxi from the stand, the price will be even more expensive (whereas a minicab booked ahead is a set price). The trip from Heathrow, for example, can take more than an hour and cost more than £50.

TRANSFERS BETWEEN AIRPORTS

Allow at least two to three hours for an interairport transfer. The cheapest option—but most complicated—is public transport: from Gatwick to Stansted, for instance, you can catch the nonexpress commuter train from Gatwick to Victoria station, take the Tube to Liverpool Street station, then catch the train to Stansted from there. To get from Heathrow to Gatwick by public transport, take the Tube to King's Cross, then change to the Victoria line, get to Victoria station, and then take the commuter train to Gatwick.

The National Express Airport bus is the most direct option between Gatwick and Heathrow. Buses pick up passengers every 15 minutes from 5:20 am to 11 pm from both airports. The trip takes around 70 minutes, and the fare is £19.50 one-way. It's advisable to book tickets in advance. National Express buses between Stansted and Gatwick depart every 30 to 45 minutes and take around 3 hours and 45 minutes. The adult single fare is £30.20. Some airlines may offer shuttle services as well—check with your travel agent in advance of your journey.

Contacts BAA ⊕ www.baa.com. **easyBus** ⊕ www.easybus.co.uk. **First Capital Connect** ☎ 0845/0264-700 ⊕ www.firstcapitalconnect. co.uk. **Gatwick Express** ☎ 0845/850-1530 ⊕ www.gatwickexpress.com. **Heathrow Express** ☎ 0845/600-1515 ⊕ www. heathrowexpress.com. **National Express** ☎ 08717/818178 ⊕ www.nationalexpress. com. **SkyShuttle** ☎ 0845/481-0960 ⊕ www. skyshuttle.co.uk.com. **Stansted Express** ☎ 0845/850-0150 ⊕ www.stanstedexpress. com.

Transfer Information Airport Travel Line ☎ 0871/200-2323.

FLIGHTS

British Airways is the national flagship carrier and offers mostly nonstop flights from 16 U.S. cities to Heathrow and Gatwick airports, along with flights to Manchester, Birmingham, and Glasgow. It also offers flights to New York from London City Airport near Docklands.

Airline Contacts American Airlines ☎ 800/433-7300, 0844/499-7300 in London ⊕ www.aa.com. **British Airways.** British Airways to Heathrow, Gatwick. ☎ 800/247-9297, 0844/493-0787 in London ⊕ www. ba.com. **Delta Airlines** ☎ 800/241-4141 for international reservations, 0871/221-1222 in London ⊕ www.delta.com. **United Airlines** ☎ 800/538-2929 for international reservations, 0845/844-4777 in London ⊕ www. united.com. **US Airways** ☎ 800/622-1015 for international reservations, 0845/600-3300 in London ⊕ www.usairways.com. **Virgin Atlantic** ☎ 800/862-8621, 0844/209-7310 in London ⊕ www.virgin-atlantic.com.

▌BUS TRAVEL

ARRIVING AND DEPARTING

National Express is the biggest British coach operator and the nearest equivalent to Greyhound. It's not as fast as traveling by train, but it's comfortable (with washroom facilities on board). Services depart mainly from Victoria Coach station, a well-signposted short walk behind the Victoria mainline rail station. The departures point is on the corner of Buckingham Palace Road; this is also the main information point. The arrivals point is opposite at Elizabeth Bridge. National Express buses travel to all large and midsize cities in southern England and the midlands. Scotland and the north are not as well served. The station is extremely busy around holidays and weekends. Arrive at least 30 minutes before departure so you can find the correct exit gate. Smoking is not permitted on board.

Another bus company, Megabus, has been packing in the budget travelers in recent years, since it offers cross-country fares for as little as £1 per person. The company's single- and double-decker buses serve an extensive array of cities across Great Britain with a cheerful budget attitude. In London, buses for all destinations depart from the Green Line bus stand at Victoria station. Megabus does not accommodate wheelchairs, and the company strictly limits luggage to one piece per person checked, and one piece of hand luggage.

Greyhound itself recently launched a low-cost bus service connecting London Victoria with several destinations on England's south coast, as well as Cardiff and Swansea in Wales.

Green Line serves the counties surrounding London, as well as airports. Bus stops (there's no central bus station) are on Buckingham Palace Road, between the Victoria mainline station and Victoria Coach station.

Tickets on some long-distance routes are cheaper if purchased in advance, and traveling midweek is cheaper than over weekends and at holiday periods.

GETTING AROUND LONDON

Private, as opposed to municipal, buses are known as coaches. Although London is famous for its double-decker buses, long articulated buses (locally known as "bendy buses") replaced the oldest buses—the beloved rattletrap Routemasters, which had the jump-on/off back platforms, under the previous mayor. However, these proved both unpopular and money-losing and are being phased out, to be replaced by a redesigned Routemaster in the near future. Two Routemaster "heritage" routes keep the old familiar double-decker buses working, however: the No. 9 travels through Piccadilly, Trafalgar Square, and Knightsbridge, and the No. 15 travels from Trafalgar Square down Fleet Street and on to St. Paul's Cathedral.

Bus stops are clearly indicated; signs at bus stops feature a red TfL symbol on a plain white background. You must flag the bus down at some stops. Each numbered route is listed on the main stop, and buses have a large number on the front with their end destination. Not all buses run the full route at all times; check with the driver to be sure. You can pick up a free bus guide at a TfL Travel Information Centre (at Euston, Liverpool Street, Piccadilly Circus, King's Cross, and Victoria Tube stations; and at Heathrow Airport).

Buses are a good way of seeing the town, particularly if you plan to hop on and off to cover many sights, but don't take a bus if you're in a hurry, as traffic can really slow them down. To get off, press the red "Stop" buttons mounted on poles near the doors. You will usually see a "Bus Stopping" sign light up. Expect to get very squashed during rush hour, from 8 am to 9:30 am and 4:30 pm to 6:30 pm.

Night buses, denoted by an "N" before their route numbers, run from midnight to 5 am on a more restricted route than day buses. However, some night bus routes should be approached with caution and the top deck avoided. All night buses run by request stop, so flag them down if you're waiting or push the button if you want to alight.

All journeys cost £2, and there are no transfers. If you plan to make a number of journeys in one day, consider buying a Travelcard (⇨ *Underground Travel : The Tube*), good for both Tube and bus travel. Also consider getting a prepaid Oyster card, as single journeys are just over a pound using a prepaid card. Travelcards are also available in one-, three-, or seven-day combinations. Visitor Oyster cards cost £2 and can be topped up. They are available from ticket desks at Gatwick and Stansted airports or at any Tube station and are transferable if you have money left over. Traveling without a valid ticket makes you liable for a fine (£20). Buses are supposed to swing by most stops every five or six minutes, but in reality, you can often expect to wait a bit longer, although those in the center of town are quite reliable.

In central London, if you don't have a prepaid Travel- or Oyster card, you must pay before you board the bus. Automated ticket machines are set up at these bus stops, which are clearly marked with a yellow sign "Buy Tickets Before Boarding." Otherwise, you can buy tickets at most central London Tube stations as well as at newsagents and shops that display the sign "Buy Your TravelCards & Bus Passes Here." Outside the central zone, payment may be made to the driver as you board (exact change is best so as to avoid incurring the driver's wrath).

Bus Information easyBus ⊕ *www.easybus. co.uk.* **Green Line** ☎ *0844/801-7261* ⊕ *www. greenline.co.uk.* **Greyhound UK** ☎ *0900/096- 0000* ⊕ *www.greyhounduk.com.* **Megabus** ☎ *0871/266-3333* ⊕ *www.megabus.com.* **National Express** ☎ *0871/781-8178* ⊕ *www. nationalexpress.com.* **Transport for London** ☎ *0843/222-1234* ⊕ *www.tfl.gov.uk.* **Victoria Coach station** ☎ *020/7027-2520.*

■ CAR TRAVEL

The best advice on driving in London is this: don't. London's streets are a winding mass of chaos, made worse by one-way roads. Parking is also restrictive and expensive, and traffic is tediously slow at most times of the day; during rush hours—from 8 am to 9:30 am and 4:30 pm to 6:30 pm—it often grinds to a standstill, particularly on Friday, when everyone wants to leave town. Avoid city-center shopping areas, including the roads feeding Oxford Street, Kensington, and Knightsbridge. Other main roads into the city center are also busy, such as King's Cross and Euston in the north. Watch out also for cyclists and motorcycle couriers, who weave between cars and pedestrians and seem to come out of nowhere, and you may be fined heavily for straying into a bus lane during its operating hours—check the signs.

If you are staying just in London on this trip, there's virtually no reason to rent a car since the city and its suburbs are widely covered by public transportation. However, you might want a car for day trips to castles or stately homes out in the countryside. Consider renting your car in a medium-size town in the area where you'll be traveling, and then journeying there by train and picking up the car once you arrive. Rental rates are generally reasonable, and insurance costs are lower than in comparable U.S. cities. Rates generally begin at £42 a day for a small economy car (such as a subcompact General Motors Vauxhall, Corsa, or Renault Clio), usually with manual transmission. Air-conditioning and unlimited mileage generally come with the larger-size automatic cars.

In London your U.S. driver's license is acceptable (as long as you are over 23 years old, with no driving convictions). If you have a driver's license from a country other than the United States, it may not be recognized in the United Kingdom. An International Driver's Permit is a good idea no matter what; it's available from the American (AAA) or Canadian Automobile Association and, in the United Kingdom, from the Automobile Association (AA) or Royal Automobile Club (RAC). International permits are universally recognized, and having one may save you a problem with the local authorities.

Remember that Britain drives on the left, and the rest of Europe on the right. Therefore, you may want to leave your rented car in Britain and pick up a left-side drive if you cross the Channel (⇨ *Train Travel*).

CONGESTION CHARGE

Designed to reduce traffic through central London, a congestion charge has been instituted. Vehicles (with some exemptions) entering central London on weekdays from 7 am to 6 pm (excluding public holidays) have to pay an £8 daily fee; it can be paid up to 90 days in advance, on the day of travel, or on the following charging day, when the fee goes up to £10. Day-, month-, and yearlong passes are available on the Congestion Charging page of the Transport for London website, at gas stations, parking lots (car parks), by mail, by phone, and by SMS text message. One day's payment is good for all access into the charging zone on that day. Traffic signs designate the entrance to congestion areas, and cameras read car license plates and send the information to a database. Drivers who don't pay the congestion charge by midnight of the next charging day following the day of driving are penalized £120, which is reduced to £60 if paid within 14 days.

Information Congestion Charge Customer Service ✍ *Box 4782, Worthing BN11 9PS* ☎ *0845/900–1234* ⊕ *www.cclondon.com.* **Transport for London** ⊕ *www.tfl.gov.uk.*

GASOLINE

Gasoline (petrol) is sold in liters and is expensive (at this writing about £1.20 per liter—around $7 per gallon). Unleaded petrol, denoted by green pump lines, is predominant. Premium and Super Premium are the two varieties, and most cars run on regular Premium. Supermarket pumps usually offer the best value. You won't find many service stations in the center of town; these are generally on main, multilane trunk roads out of the center. Service is self-serve, except in small villages, where gas stations are likely to be closed on Sunday and late evening. Most stations accept major credit cards.

PARKING

During the day—and probably at all times—it's safest to believe that you can park nowhere except at a meter, in a pay-and-display bay, in a garage, otherwise, you run the risk of an expensive ticket, plus possibly even more expensive clamping and towing fees (some boroughs are clamp-free). Restrictions are indicated by the "No Waiting" parking signpost on the sidewalk (these restrictions vary from street to street), and restricted areas include single yellow lines or double yellow lines, and Residents' Parking bays. Parking at a bus stop or in a bus lane is also restricted. On Red Routes, indicated by red lines, you are not allowed to park or even stop. It's illegal to park on the sidewalk, across entrances, or on white zigzag lines approaching a pedestrian crossing.

Meters have an insatiable hunger in the inner city—a 20p piece may buy just three minutes—and some will permit only a two-hour stay. Meters take 20p and £1 coins, pay-and-display machines 10p, 20p, 50p, £1, and £2 coins. Some take payment by credit card. In some parts of central London, meters have been almost entirely replaced by pay-and-display machines that require payment by cell phone. You will need to set up an account to do this (⊕ *www.westminster.gov.uk*). Meters are free after 6:30 or 8:30 in the evening, on Sunday, and on holidays. Always check the sign. In the evening, after restrictions end, meter bays are free. After meters are free, you can also park on single yellow lines—but not double yellow lines. In the daytime, take advantage of the many NCP parking lots in the center of town (about £4 per hour, up to eight hours).

Information NCP ☎ *0845/050–7080* ⊕ *www.ncp.co.uk.*

ROADSIDE EMERGENCIES

If your car is stolen, you're in a car accident, or your car breaks down and there's nobody around to help you, contact the police by dialing ☎ 999.

The general procedure for a breakdown is the following: position the red hazard triangle (which should be in the trunk of the car) a few paces away from the rear of the car. Leave the hazard warning lights on. Along highways (motorways), emergency roadside telephone booths are positioned at intervals within walking distance. Contact the car-rental company or an auto club. The main auto clubs in the United Kingdom are the Automobile Association (AA) and the RAC. If you're a member of the American Automobile Association (AAA), check your membership details before you depart for Britain, as, under a reciprocal agreement, roadside assistance in the United Kingdom should cost you nothing. You can join and receive roadside assistance from the AA on the spot, but the charge is higher—around £75—than a simple membership fee.

Emergency Services American Automobile Association ☎ *800/564-6222* ⊕ *www.aaa. com.* **Automobile Association** ☎ *0800/085-2721, 161/333-0004 from outside the U.K., 0800/887766 for emergency roadside assistance from mobile phones* ⊕ *www.theaa. com.* **RAC** ☎ *01922/437000, 0800/828282 for emergency roadside assistance* ⊕ *www.rac. co.uk.*

RULES OF THE ROAD

London is a mass of narrow, one-way roads, and narrow, two-way streets that are no bigger than the one-way roads. If you must risk life and limb and drive in London, note that the speed limit is either 20 or 30 mph—unless you see the large 40 mph signs found only in the suburbs. Speed bumps are sprinkled about with abandon in case you forget. Speed is strictly controlled by cameras mounted on occasional lampposts, which photograph speeders for ticketing.

Medium-size circular intersections are often designed as "roundabouts" (marked by signs in which three arrows curve into a circle). On these, cars travel left in a circle and incoming cars must yield to those already on their way around from the right. Signal when about to leave the roundabout.

Jaywalking is not illegal in London and everybody does it, despite the fact that striped crossings with blinking yellow lights mounted on poles at either end—called "zebra crossings"—give pedestrians the right of way to cross. Cars should treat zebra crossings like stop signs if a pedestrian is waiting to cross or already starting to cross. It's illegal to pass another vehicle at a zebra crossing. At other crossings (including intersections) pedestrians must yield to traffic, but they do have the right-of-way over traffic turning left at controlled crossings—if they have the nerve.

Traffic lights sometimes have arrows directing left or right turns; try to catch a glimpse of the road markings in time, and don't get into the turn lane if you mean to go straight ahead. A right turn is not permitted on a red light. Signs at the beginning and end of designated bus lanes give the time restrictions for use (usually during peak hours); if you're caught driving on bus lanes during restricted hours, you will be fined. By law, seat belts must be worn in the front and back seats. Drunk-driving laws are strictly enforced, and it's safest to avoid alcohol altogether if you'll be driving. The legal limit is 80 milligrams of alcohol per 100 milliliters of blood, which roughly translated means two units of alcohol—two small glasses of wine, one pint of beer, or one glass of whiskey.

DLR: DOCKLANDS LIGHT RAILWAY

For destinations in East London, the quiet, driverless Docklands Light Railway (DLR) is a good alternative, offering interesting views of the area.

The DLR connects with the Tube network at Bank and Tower Hill stations as well as at Canary Wharf. It goes to London City Airport, the Docklands financial district, and Greenwich, running 5:30 am–12:30 am Monday–Saturday, 7 am–11:30 pm Sunday. The DLR takes Oyster cards and Travelcards, and fares are the same as those on the Tube. A £14.50 River Rover ticket combines one-day DLR travel with hop-on, hop-off travel on City Cruises riverboats between Westminster, Waterloo, Tower and Greenwich piers.

Information Transport for London ☎ 0843/222-1234 ⊕ www.tfl.gov.uk.

RIVER BUS

In the run-up to the 2012 Olympics, a new push has been made to develop river travel as part of London's overall public transport system. The service now stops at 10 piers between the London Eye/Waterloo and Greenwich, with peak-time extensions to Putney in the west and Woolwich Arsenal in the east. The Waterloo-Woolwich commuter service runs every 20 minutes from 6 am to 1 am on weekdays, 8:30 am–midnight on weekends. Tickets are £5.30, with a one-third discount for Oyster card and Travelcard holders (full integration into the Oyster-card system is expected in 2012). When there are events at the O2 (North Greenwich Arena), a half-hourly express service runs to and from Waterloo starting three hours before the event. There is also a special Tate-to-Tate express, a 20-minute trip between Tate Modern and Tate Britain that costs £5. Boats run every 40 minutes from 10 to 5. A £12 River Roamer ticket offers unlimited river travel 10–10 weekdays and 8 am–10 pm on weekends.

Contacts Thames Clippers ☎ *020/7001–2200* ⊕ *www.thamesclippers.com.*

▌TAXI

Universally known as "black cabs" (even though many of them now come in other colors), the traditional big black London taxicabs are as much a part of the city's streetscape as red double-decker buses, and for good reason: the unique, spacious taxis easily hold five people, plus luggage. To earn a taxi license, drivers must undergo intensive training on the history and geography of London. The course, and all that the drivers have learned in it, is known simply as "the Knowledge." There's almost nothing your taxi driver won't know about the city.

Hotels and main tourist areas have cabstands (just take the first in line), but you can also flag one down from the roadside. If the yellow "For Hire" sign on the top is lighted, the taxi is available. Cabdrivers often cruise at night with their signs unlighted so that they can choose their passengers and avoid those they think might cause trouble. If you see an unlighted, passengerless cab, hail it: you might be lucky.

Fares start at £2.20 and charge by the minute—a journey of a mile (which might take between 5 and 12 minutes) will cost anything from £4.60 to £8.60 (the fare goes up between 10 pm and 6 am—a system designed to persuade more taxi drivers to work at night). A surcharge of £2 is applied to a telephone booking. At Christmas and New Year, there is an additional surcharge of £4. You can, but do not have to, tip taxi drivers 10% of the tab. Usually passengers round up to the nearest pound.

Minicabs, which operate out of small, curbside offices throughout the city, are generally cheaper than black cabs, but are less reliable and trusted. These are usually unmarked passenger cars, and their drivers are often not native Londoners, and do not have to take or pass "the Knowledge" test. Still, Londoners use them in droves

because they are plentiful and cheap. If you choose to use them, do not ever take an unlicensed cab: anyone who curb-crawls looking for customers is likely to be unlicensed. Unlicensed cabs have been associated with many crimes and can be dangerous. All cab companies with proper dispatch offices are likely to be licensed. Look for a small purple version of the Underground logo on the front or rear windscreen with "private hire" written across it.

There are plenty of trustworthy and licensed minicab firms. For London-wide service try Lady Mini Cabs, which employs only women drivers, or Addison Lee, which uses comfortable minivans but requires that you know the full postal code for both your pickup location and your destination. When using a minicab, always ask the price in advance when you phone for the car, then verify with the driver before the journey begins.

Black Cabs Dial-a-Cab ☎ *020/7253–5000.* **Radio Taxis** ☎ *020/7272–0272.*

Minicabs Addison Lee ☎ *0844/800–6677.* **Lady MiniCabs** ☎ *020/7272–3300.*

▌TRAIN TRAVEL

The National Rail Enquiries website is the clearinghouse for information on train times and fares as well as to book rail journeys around Britain—and the earlier the better. Tickets bought two to three weeks in advance can cost a quarter of the price of tickets bought on the day of travel. However, journeys within commuting distance of city centers are sold at unvarying set prices, and those can be purchased on the day you expect to make your journey without any financial penalty. You may also be able to purchase a PlusBus ticket, which adds unlimited bus travel at your destination. Note that, in busy city centers such as London, all travel costs more during morning rush hour. You can purchase tickets online, by phone, or at any rail station in the United

Kingdom. Check the website or call the National Rail Enquiries line to get details of the train company responsible for your journey and have them give you a breakdown of available ticket prices. Regardless of which train company is involved, many discount passes are available, such as the 16–25 Railcard (for which you must be under 26 and provide a passport-size photo), the Senior Railcard, and the Family & Friends Travelcard, which can be bought from most mainline stations. But if you intend to make several long-distance rail journeys, it can be a good idea to invest in a BritRail Pass (which you must buy in the United States).

You can get a BritRail Pass valid for London and the surrounding counties, for England, for Scotland, or for all of Britain. Discounts (usually 20%–25%) are offered if you're between 16 and 25, over 60, traveling as a family or a group, or accompanied by a British citizen. The pass includes discounts on the Heathrow Express and Eurostar. BritRail Passes come in two basic varieties. The Classic pass allows travel on consecutive days, and the FlexiPass allows a number of travel days within a set period of time. The cost (in U.S. dollars) of a BritRail Consecutive Pass adult ticket for eight days is $359 standard and $509 first-class; for 15 days, $535 and $759; and for a month, $759 and $1,139. The cost of a BritRail FlexiPass adult ticket for four days' travel in two months is $315 standard and $445 first-class; for eight days' travel in two months, $459 and $649; and for 15 days' travel in two months, $689 and $975. Prices drop by about 25% for off-peak travel passes between November and February.

Most long-distance trains have refreshment carriages, called buffet cars. Most trains these days also have "quiet cars" where use of cell phones and music devices is banned, but these rules are not enforced with any enthusiasm. Smoking is forbidden in all rail carriages.

Generally speaking, rail travel in the United Kingdom is expensive: for instance, a round-trip ticket to Bath from London can cost around £143 per person at peak times. The fee drops to around £27 at other times, so it's best to travel before or after the frantic business commuter rush (after 9:30 am and before 4:30 pm). Credit cards are accepted for train fares paid both in person and by phone.

Delays are not uncommon, but they're rarely long. You almost always have to go to the station to find out if there's going to be one (because delays tend to happen at the last minute). Luckily, most stations have coffee shops, restaurants, and pubs where you can cool your heels while you wait for the train to get rolling. National Rail Enquiries provides an up-to-date state-of-the-railways schedule.

Most of the time, first-class train travel in England isn't particularly first-class. Some train companies don't offer at-seat service, so you still have to get up and go to the buffet car for food or drinks. First class is generally booked by business travelers on expense accounts because crying babies and noisy families are quite rare in first class, and quite common in standard class.

Short of flying, taking the Eurostar train through the channel tunnel is the fastest way to reach the continent: 2 hours and 15 minutes from London's St. Pancras International station to Paris's Gare du Nord. The high-speed Eurostar trains use the same tunnels to connect St. Pancras International directly with Midi station in Brussels in around two hours. If purchased in advance, round-trip tickets from London to Belgium or France cost from around £125, cheaper in the very early or very late hours of the day. If you want to bring your car over to France, you can use the Eurotunnel Shuttle, which takes 35 minutes from Folkestone to Calais, plus at least 30 minutes to check in. The Belgian border is just a short drive northeast of Calais.

Information BritRail Travel ☎ 866/938–7245 in U.S. ⊕ www.britrail.com. **Eurostar** ☎ 08432/186186 in London, 123/361–7575 outside U.K. ⊕ www.eurostar.com. **National Rail Inquiries** ☎ 0845/748–4950, 020/7278–5240 outside U.K. ⊕ www.nationalrail.co.uk.

Channel Tunnel Car Transport Eurotunnel ☎ 0844/335–3535 in U.K., 33–321/002061 from outside Europe ⊕ www.eurotunnel.com.

■ UNDERGROUND TRAVEL: THE TUBE

London's extensive Underground train (Tube) system has color-coded routes, clear signage, and many connections. Trains run out into the suburbs, and all stations are marked with the London Underground circular symbol. (Do not be confused by similar-looking signs reading "subway"—in Britain, the word subway means "pedestrian underpass.") Trains are all one class; smoking is *not* allowed on board or in the stations. There is also an Overground network serving the further reaches of Inner London. These now accept Oyster cards.

Some lines have multiple branches (Central, District, Northern, Metropolitan, and Piccadilly), so be sure to note which branch is needed for your particular destination. Do this by noting the end destination on the lighted sign on the platform, which also tells you how long you'll have to wait until the train arrives. Compare that with the end destination of the branch you want. When the two match, that's your train. ■TIP→ Before the 2012 Olympics, service on many Tube lines will be disrupted, especially on weekends, as a widespread improvements program continues. Check the TfL website for up-to-date information.

London is divided into six concentric zones (ask at Underground ticket booths for a map and booklet, which give details of the ticket options), so be sure to buy a ticket for the correct zone or you may be liable for an on-the-spot fine of £20.

Don't panic if you do forget to buy a ticket for the right zone: just tell a station attendant that you need to buy an "extension" to your ticket. Although you're meant to do that in advance, generally if you're an out-of-towner, they don't give you a hard time.

For single fares paid in cash, a flat £4 price per journey now applies across all six zones, whether you're traveling one stop or 12 stops. If you're planning several trips in one day, it's much cheaper to buy a tourist Oyster card or Travelcard, which is good for unrestricted travel on the Tube, buses, and some Overground railways for the day. The off-peak Oyster-card fare for Zones 1–2, for example, is £1.80. Bear in mind that Travelcards cost much more if purchased before the 9:30 am rush-hour threshold. A one-day Travelcard for Zones 1–2 costs £7.20 if purchased before 9:30 am, and £5.60 if bought after 9:30 am. The more zones included in your travel, the more the Travelcard will cost. For example, Kew is Zone 4, and Heathrow is Zone 6. If you're going to be in town for several days, buy a seven-day Travelcard (£25.80 for Zones 1–2, £47.60 for Zones 1–6). Children 11–15 can travel at discounted rates on the Tube and free on buses and trams with an Oyster photocard (order at least four weeks before date of travel), while children under 11 travel free on the Tube if accompanied by an adult or with an Oyster photocard and on buses at all times. Young people 16–18 and students over 18 get discounted Tube fares with an Oyster photocard.

Oyster cards are "smart cards" that can be charged with a cash value and then used for discounted travel throughout the city. Each time you take the Tube or bus, you swipe the blue card across the yellow readers at the entrance and the amount of your fare is deducted. The London mayor is so eager to promote the cards that he set up a system in which those using Oyster cards pay lower rates. Oyster-card Tube fares start at £1.30 and go up depending on the number of zones you're covering, time of day, and whether you're traveling into Zone 1. You can open an Oyster account online or pick up an Oyster card at any London Underground station, and then prepay any amount you wish for your expected travel while in the city. Using an Oyster card, bus fares are £1.20 instead of £2. If you make numerous journeys in a single day, your Oyster-card deductions will always be capped at the standard price of a one-day Travelcard.

Trains begin running just after 5 am Monday–Saturday; the last services leave central London between midnight and 12:30 am. On Sunday, trains start two hours later and finish about an hour earlier. The frequency of trains depends on the route and the time of day, but normally you should not have to wait more than 10 minutes in central areas.

There are TfL Travel Information Centres at the following Tube stations: Euston, Liverpool Street, Piccadilly Circus, King's Cross, and Victoria, open 7:15 am–9:15 pm; and at Heathrow Airport (in Terminals 1, 2, and 3), open 6:30 am–10 pm.

Important Note: as with the Metro system in Paris—and unlike the subway system in New York City—you need to have your ticket (Oyster-card pass or regular ticket) handy in order to exit the turnstiles of the Tube system, not just enter them.

Information Transport for London
☎ 0843/222–1234 ⊕ www.tfl.gov.uk.

ESSENTIALS

▮ BUSINESS SERVICES AND FACILITIES

There are several FedEx Kinko's and Mail Boxes Etc. locations in London to handle your photocopying, next-day mail, and packaging needs. Check their websites for more locations.

Contacts FedEx Kinko's, operating now as "The Color Company" ⊠ *1 Curzon St., Mayfair* ☎ *020/7717–4900* ⊕ *www.color.co.uk.* **Mail Boxes Etc.** ⊠ *19–21 Crawford St., Marylebone* ☎ *020/7224–2666* ⊕ *www.mailboxes-etc.co.uk.*

▮ COMMUNICATIONS

INTERNET

If you're traveling with a laptop, carry a spare battery and adapter: new batteries and replacement adapters are expensive; if you do need to replace them, head to Tottenham Court Road (W1), which is lined with computer specialists. For Macintosh computers, Micro Anvika is a good chain for parts and batteries, and the Apple Stores on Regent Street off Oxford Street and in the Covent Garden Piazza do repairs. John Lewis department store and Selfridges, on Oxford Street (W1), also carry a limited range of computer supplies.

The United Kingdom is finally catching up to the United States in terms of the spread of broadband and Wi-Fi. In London, free Wi-Fi is increasingly available in hotels, pubs, coffee shops—even certain branches of McDonald's—and broadband coverage is widespread; generally speaking, the pricier the hotel, the more likely you are to find Wi-Fi there. To find your nearest free hot spot, see the Wi-Fi FreeSpot website.

Contacts Cybercafes. Cybercafes lists more than 4,000 Internet cafés worldwide. ⊕ *www.cybercafes.com.* **My Hot Spot** ⊕ *www. myhotspots.co.uk.* **FreeSpot** ⊕ *wififreespot. com.*

PHONES

The good news is that you can now make a direct-dial telephone call from virtually any point on Earth. The bad news? You can't always do so cheaply. Calling from a hotel is almost always the most expensive option; hotels usually add huge surcharges to all calls, particularly international ones. Calling cards usually keep costs to a minimum, but only if you purchase them locally. And then there are mobile phones, which are sometimes more prevalent—particularly in the developing world—than landlines; as expensive as mobile phone calls can be, they are still usually a much cheaper option than calling from your hotel.

The minimum charge from a public phone is 60p for a 110-second call. To make cheap calls it's a good idea to pick up an international phone card, available from newsstands, which can be used from residential, hotel, and public pay phones. With these, you can call the United States for as little as 5p per minute.

To dial from the United States or Canada, first dial 011, then Great Britain's country code, 44. Continue with the local area code, dropping the initial "0." The code for London is 020 (so from abroad you'd dial 20), followed by a 7 for numbers in central London, or an 8 for numbers in the Greater London area. Freephone (toll-free) numbers start with 0800, 0500 or 0808; low-cost national information numbers start with 0845 or 0844.

A word of warning: 0870 numbers are *not* toll-free numbers; in fact, numbers beginning with this, 0871, or the 0900 prefix are "premium rate" numbers, and it costs extra to call them. The amount varies and is usually relatively small when dialed from within the country but can be excessive when dialed from outside the United Kingdom.

CALLING WITHIN BRITAIN

There are three types of phones: those that accept (1) only coins, (2) only British Telecom (BT) phone cards, or (3) BT phone cards and credit cards, although with the advent of cells, it's increasingly difficult to find any type of public phone, especially in London.

The coin-operated phones are of the push-button variety; the workings of coin-operated telephones vary, but there are usually instructions on each unit. Most take 10p, 20p, 50p, and £1 coins. Insert the coins *before* dialing (the minimum charge is 10p). If you hear a repeated single tone after dialing, the line is busy; a continual tone means the number is unobtainable (or that you have dialed the wrong—or no—prefix). The indicator panel shows you how much money is left; add more whenever you like. If there is no answer, replace the receiver and your money will be returned.

There are several different directory-assistance providers. For information anywhere in Britain, try dialing 118–888 (49p per call, then 9p per minute) or 118–118 (49p per call, then 14p per minute); you'll need to know the town and the street (or at least the neighborhood) of the person or organization for which you're requesting information. For the operator, dial 100.

You don't have to dial London's central area code (020) if you are calling inside London itself—just the eight-digit telephone number. However, you do need to use it if you're dialing an 0207 (Inner London) number from an 0208 (Outer London) number, and vice versa.

For long-distance calls within Britain, dial the area code (which begins with 01), followed by the number. The area-code prefix is used only when you are dialing from outside the destination. In provincial areas, the dialing codes for nearby towns are often posted in the booth.

CALLING OUTSIDE BRITAIN

For assistance with international calls, dial 155.

To make an international call from London, dial 00, followed by the country code and the local number.

When calling from overseas to access a London telephone number, drop the first 0 from the prefix and dial only 20 (or any other British area code) and then the eight-digit phone number.

The United States country code is 1.

Access Codes AT&T Direct ☎ *0800/800011 in U.K.* **MCI** ☎ *0800/890222 in U.K., 800/888-8000 for U.S. and other areas.* **Sprint International Access** ☎ *0808/234-6616 in U.K..*

CALLING CARDS

Public card phones operate either with cash or with special cards that you can buy from post offices or newsstands. Ideal for longer calls, they are composed of units of 10p, and come in values of £3, £5, £10, and more. To use a card phone, lift the receiver, insert your card, and dial the number. An indicator panel shows the number of units used. At the end of your call, the card will be returned. Where credit cards are taken, slide the card through, as indicated.

MOBILE PHONES

If you have a multiband phone (Britain uses different frequencies from those used in the United States) and your service provider uses the world-standard GSM network (as do T-Mobile, AT&T, and Verizon), you can probably use your phone abroad. Roaming fees can be steep, however: 99¢ a minute is considered reasonable. And overseas you normally pay the toll charges for incoming calls. It's almost always cheaper to send a text message than to make a call, since text messages have a very low set fee (often less than 5¢).

If you just want to make local calls, consider buying a new SIM card (note that your provider may have to unlock your phone for you to use a different SIM card) and a prepaid service plan in London.

You'll then have a local number and can make local calls at local rates. If your trip is extensive, you could also simply buy a new cell phone in your destination, as the initial cost will be offset over time.

■**TIP➔** If you travel internationally frequently, save one of your old mobile phones or buy a cheap one on the Internet; ask your cell phone company to unlock it for you, and take it with you as a travel phone, buying a new SIM card with pay-as-you-go service in each destination.

Any cell phone can be used in Britain if it's tri-band/GSM. Travelers should ask their cell phone company if their phone is tri-band and what network it uses, and make sure it is activated for international calling before leaving their home country.

You can rent a cell phone from most car-rental agencies in London. Some upscale hotels now provide loaner cell phones to their guests. Beware, however, of the per-minute rates charged, as these can be shockingly high.

Contacts Cellular Abroad. Cellular Abroad rents and sells GMS phones and sells SIM cards that work in many countries. ☎ *800/287–5072* ⊕ *www.cellularabroad.com.* **Mobal.** Mobal rents mobiles and sells GSM phones (starting at $49) that will operate in 150 countries. Per-call rates vary throughout the world. ☎ *888/888–9162* ⊕ *www.mobal.com.* **Planet Fone.** Planet Fone rents cell phones, but the per-minute rates are expensive. ☎ *888/988–4777* ⊕ *www.planetfone.com.* **Rent a Mobile Phone.** Rent a Mobile Phone has phones with short contract. ☎ *020/7353–7705* ⊕ *www.rent-mobile-phone.com.*

■ CUSTOMS AND DUTIES

You're always allowed to bring goods of a certain value back home without having to pay any duty or import tax. But there's a limit on the amount of tobacco and liquor you can bring back duty-free, and some countries have separate limits for perfumes; for exact figures, check with your customs department. The values of

so-called "duty-free" goods are included in these amounts. When you shop abroad, save all your receipts, as customs inspectors may ask to see them as well as the items you purchased. If the total value of your goods is more than the duty-free limit, you'll have to pay a tax (most often a flat percentage) on the value of everything beyond that limit.

There are two levels of duty-free allowance for entering Britain: one for goods bought outside the European Union (EU) and the other for goods bought within the EU.

Of goods bought outside the EU you may import the following duty-free: 200 cigarettes or 100 cigarillos or 50 cigars or 250 grams of tobacco; 4 liters of still wine and 16 liters of beer and, in addition, either 1 liter of alcohol over 22% by volume (most spirits), or 2 liters of alcohol under 22% by volume (fortified or sparkling wine or liqueurs).

Of goods bought within the EU, you should not exceed the following (unless you can prove they are for personal use): 3,200 cigarettes, 400 cigarillos, 200 cigars, or 3 kilograms of tobacco, plus 10 liters of spirits, 20 liters of fortified wine such as port or sherry, 90 liters of wine, or 110 liters of beer.

Pets (dogs and cats) can be brought into the United Kingdom from the United States without six months' quarantine, provided that the animal meets all the PETS (Pet Travel Scheme) requirements, including microchipping and vaccination. Other pets have to undergo a lengthy quarantine, and penalties for breaking this law are severe and strictly enforced.

Fresh meats, vegetables, plants, and dairy products may be imported from within the EU. Controlled drugs, flick knives, obscene material, counterfeit or pirated goods, and self-defense sprays may not be brought into the United Kingdom, although firearms (both real and imitation) and ammunition, as well as souvenirs made from endangered plants or animals, are barred except with relevant permits.

Information HM Revenue and Customs ✉ *Crownhill Ct., Tailyour Rd., Plymouth* ☎ *0845/010–9000* ⊕ *www.hmrc.gov.uk.* **U.S. Customs and Border Protection** ⊕ *www. cbp.gov.*

■ ELECTRICITY

The electrical current in London is 220–240 volts (coming into line with the rest of Europe at 230 volts), 50 cycles alternating current (AC); wall outlets take three-pin plugs, and shaver sockets take two round, oversize prongs. For converters, adapters, and advice, stop in one of the many STA Travel shops around London or at Nomad Travel.

Consider making a small investment in a universal adapter, which has several types of plugs in one lightweight, compact unit. Most laptops and mobile phone chargers are dual voltage (i.e., they operate equally well on 110 and 220 volts), and thus require only an adapter. These days the same is true of small appliances such as hair dryers. Always check labels and manufacturer instructions to be sure. Don't use 110-volt outlets marked "For Shavers Only" for high-wattage appliances such as hair dryers.

Contacts Nomad Travel ✉ *43 Bernard St., Bloomsbury* ☎ *020/7833–4114* ⊕ *www. nomadtravel.co.uk* ✉ *52 Grosvenor Gardens, Victoria* ☎ *020/7823–5823.* **STA Travel** ☎ *0871/230–0040* ⊕ *www.statravel.co.uk.* **Steve Kropla's Help for World Travelers.** Steve Kropla's Help for World Travelers has information on electrical and telephone plugs around the world. ⊕ *www.kropla.com.* **Walkabout Travel Gear.** Walkabout Travel Gear offers some helpful advice on electricity under "Adapters." ⊕ *www.walkabouttravelgear.com.*

■ EMERGENCIES

London is a relatively safe city, though crime does happen (even more so than in New York City), especially in areas of built-up social housing or tourist meccas. If you need to report a theft or an attack, head to the nearest police station (listed in the Yellow Pages or the local directory) or dial 999 for police, fire, or ambulance (be prepared to give the telephone number you're calling from). National Health Service hospitals, *several of which are listed below*, give free round-the-clock treatment in Accident and Emergency sections, where waits can be an hour or more. As a non-EU foreign visitor, you will be expected to pay for any treatment you receive before you leave the country. Prescriptions are valid only if made out by doctors registered in the United Kingdom. All branches of Boots are dispensing pharmacies, *and the one listed is open until midnight*.

Doctors and Dentists Dental Emergency Care Service ☎ *020/7748–9365* ⊕ *www.24hour-emergencydentist.co.uk.* **Medical Express Clinic** ✉ *117A Harley St.* ☎ *020/7499–1991 or 0800/980–0700* ⊕ *www. medicalexpressclinic.com.* **UCL Eastman Dental Hospital** ✉ *256 Gray's Inn Rd.* ☎ *023/456–7899* ⊕ *www.uclh.nhs.uk.*

Foreign Embassies U.S. Embassy ✉ *24 Grosvenor Sq., Mayfair* ☎ *020/7499–9000* ✉ *londonpassport@state.gov* ⊕ *www. usembassy.org.uk.*

General Emergency Contacts Ambulance, fire, police ☎ *999.*

Hospitals and Clinics Charing Cross Hospital ✉ *Fulham Palace Rd., Fulham* ☎ *0203/311–1234* ⊕ *www.imperial.nhs.uk/ charingcross.* **Royal Free Hospital** ✉ *Pond St., Hampstead* ☎ *020/7794–0500* ⊕ *www. royalfree.nhs.uk.* **St. Thomas's Hospital** ✉ *Westminster Bridge Rd., Lambeth* ☎ *020/7188–7188* ⊕ *www.guysandstthomas. nhs.uk.* **University College Hospital** ✉ *235 Euston Rd., Bloomsbury* ☎ *0845/155–5000* ⊕ *www.uclh.nhs.uk.*

Hotlines Samaritans. Samaritans for counseling. ☎ *0845/790–9090.*

Pharmacies Boots ✉ *44–46 Regent St., Piccadilly Circus* ☎ *020/7734–6126* ⊕ *www.boots. com.*

▮ HOLIDAYS

Standard holidays are New Year's Day, Good Friday, Easter Monday, May Day (first Monday in May), spring and summer bank holidays (last Monday in May and August, respectively), Christmas, and Boxing Day (December 26). On Christmas Eve and New Year's Eve, some shops, restaurants, and businesses close early. Some museums and tourist attractions may close for at least a week around Christmas, or operate on restricted hours—call to verify.

▮ MAIL

Stamps can be bought from post offices (generally open weekdays 9–5:30, Saturday 9–noon), from stamp machines outside post offices, and from some newsagents and newsstands. Mailboxes are known as postal or letter boxes and are painted bright red; large tubular ones are set on the edge of sidewalks, whereas smaller boxes are set into post-office walls. Allow seven days for a letter to reach the United States. Check the Yellow Pages for a complete list of branches, though you cannot reach individual offices by phone.

Airmail letters up to 10 grams (0.35 ounce) to North America, Australia, and New Zealand cost 67p. Letters under 9.4 inches x 6.4 inches within Britain are from 41p for first class, 32p for second class. Large letters (over 9.4 inches x 6.4 inches, under 13.8 inches x 9.8 inches) cost from 66p first-class, 51p second-class within the United Kingdom, depending on weight. Airmail is assessed by weight alone.

If you're uncertain where you'll be staying, you can have mail sent to you at the London Main Post Office, c/o poste restante. The post office will hold international mail for one month.

Contact Post Office ☎ 08457/223344 ⊕ www.postoffice.co.uk.

Main Branches London Main Post Office 24–28 William IV St., Trafalgar Sq. ⊕ www. postoffice.co.uk ✉ 43–44 Albemarle St., Mayfair ✉ 111 Baker St., Marylebone ✉ 54–56 Great Portland St., Fitzrovia ✉ 181 High Holborn, Holborn.

SHIPPING PACKAGES

Most department stores and retail outlets can ship your goods home. You should check your insurance for coverage of possible damage. Private delivery companies such as DHL, FedEx, and Parcelforce offer two-day delivery service to the United States, but you'll pay a considerable amount for the privilege.

Express Services DHL ☎ 0844/248–0844 ⊕ www.dhl.com. **FedEx** ☎ 0845/607–0809 ⊕ www.fedex.com. **Parcelforce** ☎ 0844/800–4466 ⊕ www.parcelforce.com.

▮ MONEY

No doubt about it, London is one of the most expensive cities in the world: getting around is expensive, eating can be expensive, travel is pricey, and hotels aren't cheap. However, for every yin there's a yang, and travelers do get a break in other places: most museums are free, for example, and Oyster cards help cut the price of travel.

ATMS AND BANKS

Your own bank will probably charge a fee for using ATMs abroad; the foreign bank you use may also charge a fee. Nevertheless, you'll usually get a better rate of exchange at an ATM than you will at a currency-exchange office or even when changing money in a bank. And extracting funds as you need them is a safer option than carrying around a large amount of cash.

▮TIP➔ PIN numbers with more than four digits are not recognized at ATMs in many countries. If yours has five or more, remember to change it before you leave.

Credit cards or debit cards (also known as check cards) will get you cash advances at ATMs, which are widely available in London. To make sure that your Cirrus or Plus card (to cite just two of the leading names) works in European ATMs, have your bank reset it to use a four-digit PIN number before your departure.

CREDIT CARDS

■ **TIP→** Remember to inform your credit-card company before you travel, especially if you're going abroad and don't travel internationally very often. Otherwise, the credit-card company might put a hold on your card owing to unusual activity—not a good thing halfway through your trip. Record all your credit-card numbers—as well as the phone numbers to call if your cards are lost or stolen—in a safe place, so you're prepared should something go wrong. Both MasterCard and Visa have general numbers you can call (collect if you're abroad) if your card is lost, but you're better off calling the number of your issuing bank, since Master-Card and Visa usually just transfer you to your bank; your bank's number is usually printed on your card.

If you plan to use your credit card for cash advances, you'll need to apply for a PIN at least two weeks before your trip. Although it's usually cheaper (and safer) to use a credit card abroad for large purchases (so you can cancel payments or be reimbursed if there's a problem), note that some credit-card companies *and* the banks that issue them add substantial percentages to all foreign transactions, whether they're in a foreign currency or not. Check on these fees before leaving home, so there won't be any surprises when you get the bill.

■ **TIP→** Before you charge something, ask the merchant whether he or she plans to do a dynamic currency conversion (DCC). In such a transaction the credit-card processor (shop, restaurant, or hotel, not Visa or Mas-terCard) converts the currency and charges you in dollars. In most cases you'll pay the merchant a 3% fee for this service in addition to any credit-card company and issuing-bank foreign-transaction surcharges.

Dynamic currency conversion programs are becoming increasingly widespread. Merchants who participate in them are supposed to ask whether you want to be charged in dollars or the local currency, but they don't always do so. And even if they do offer you a choice, they may well avoid mentioning the additional sur-charges. The good news is that you *do* have a choice. And if this practice really gets your goat, you can avoid it entirely thanks to American Express; with its cards, DCC simply isn't an option.

Credit cards are accepted virtually every-where in London.

Reporting Lost Cards American Express ☎ 800/528–4800 in U.S., 01273/696933 in U.K. ⊕ www.americanexpress.com. **Diners Club** ☎ 800/234-6377 in U.S., 702/797-5532 collect from abroad ⊕ www.dinersclub. com. **MasterCard** ☎ 800/627-8372 in U.S., 0800/964767 in U.K. ⊕ www.mastercard.com. **Visa** ☎ 800/847-2911 in U.S., 0800/891725 in U.K. ⊕ www.visa.com.

CURRENCY AND EXCHANGE

The units of currency in Great Britain are the pound sterling (£) and pence (p): £50, £20, £10, and £5 bills (called notes); £2, £1 (100p), 50p, 20p, 10p, 5p, 2p, and 1p coins. At this writing, the exchange rate was about Australian $1.65, Canadian $1.64, New Zealand $2.16, U.S. $1.58, and €1.78 to the pound (also known as quid).

Even if a currency-exchange booth has a sign promising no commission, rest assured that there's some kind of huge, hidden fee. (Oh . . . that's right. The sign didn't say no *fee*.) And as for rates, you're almost always better off getting foreign currency at an ATM or exchanging money at a bank or post office.

■ **TIP→** Banks never have every foreign currency on hand, and it may take as long as a week to order. If you're planning to exchange funds before leaving home, don't wait until the last minute.

Currency Conversion Google. Google does currency conversion. Just type in the amount you want to convert and an explanation of how you want it converted (e.g., "14 British pounds in dollars"), and voilà. ⊕ *www.google.com*. **Oanda.com**. Oanda.com allows you to print out a handy table with the current day's conversion rates. ⊕ *www.oanda.com*. **XE.com**. XE.com is another good currency conversion website. ⊕ *www.xe.com*.

▌PACKING

London's weather is unpredictable. It can be cool, damp, and overcast, even in summer, but the odd summer day can be uncomfortable, as not very many public venues, theaters, or the Tube are air-conditioned. In general, you'll need a heavy coat for winter and light clothes for summer, along with a lightweight coat or jacket. Always pack a small umbrella that you can easily carry around with you. Pack as you would for any American city: jackets and ties for expensive restaurants and nightspots, casual clothes elsewhere. Jeans are popular in London and are perfectly acceptable for sightseeing and informal dining. Sports jackets are popular with men. In five-star hotels men can expect to be asked to wear a jacket and tie in the restaurant and bar, and women might feel out of place unless they're in smart clothes. Otherwise, for women, ordinary dress is acceptable just about everywhere.

▌PASSPORTS AND VISAS

U.S. citizens need only a valid passport to enter Great Britain for stays of up to six months. If you're within six months of your passport's expiration date, renew it before you leave—nearly extinct passports are not strictly banned, but they make immigration officials anxious, and may cause you problems.

PASSPORTS

We're always surprised at how few Americans have passports—only 25% at this writing. This number is expected to grow now that it is impossible to reenter the United States from trips to neighboring Canada or Mexico without one.

Remember this: A passport verifies both your identity and nationality—a great reason to have one.

U.S. passports are valid for 10 years. You must apply in person if you're getting a passport for the first time; if your previous passport was lost, stolen, or damaged; or if your previous passport has expired and was issued more than 15 years ago or when you were under 16. All children under 18 must appear in person to apply for or renew a passport. Both parents must accompany any child under 14 (or send a notarized statement with their permission) and provide proof of their relationship to the child.

There are 24 regional passport offices, as well as 7,000 passport acceptance facilities in post offices, public libraries, and other governmental offices. If you're renewing a passport, you can do so by mail. Forms are available at passport acceptance facilities and online.

The cost to apply for a new passport is $110 for adults, $80 for children under 16; renewals are $110. There is an additional "execution fee" of $25. Allow six weeks for processing, both for first-time passports and renewals. For an expediting fee of $60 you can reduce this time to about two weeks. If your trip is less than two weeks away, you can get a passport even more rapidly by going to a passport office with the necessary documentation. Private expediters can get things done in as little as 48 hours, but charge hefty fees for their services.

▌**TIP➜** Before your trip, make two copies of your passport's data page (one for someone at home and another for you to carry separately). Or scan the page and email it to someone at home and/or yourself.

VISAS

A visa is essentially formal permission to enter a country. Visas allow countries to keep track of you and other visitors—and generate revenue (from application fees). You *always* need a visa to enter a foreign country; however, many countries routinely issue tourist visas on arrival, particularly to U.S. citizens. When your passport is stamped or scanned in the immigration line, you're actually being issued a visa. Sometimes you have to stand in a separate line and pay a small fee to get your stamp before going through immigration, but you can still do this at the airport on arrival. Getting a visa isn't always that easy. Some countries require that you arrange for one in advance of your trip. There's usually—but not always—a fee involved, and said fee may be nominal ($10 or less) or substantial ($100 or more).

If you must apply for a visa in advance, you can usually do it in person or by mail. When you apply by mail, you send your passport to a designated consulate, where your passport will be examined and the visa issued. Expediters—usually the same ones who handle expedited passport applications—can do all the work of obtaining your visa for you; however, there's always an additional cost (often more than $50 per visa).

Most visas limit you to a single trip—basically during the actual dates of your planned vacation. Other visas allow you to visit as many times as you wish for a specific period of time. Remember that requirements change, sometimes at the drop of a hat, and the burden is on you to make sure that you have the appropriate visas. Otherwise, you'll be turned away at the airport or, worse, deported after you arrive in the country. No company or travel insurer gives refunds if your travel plans are disrupted because you didn't have the correct visa.

U.S. Passport Information U.S. Department of State ☎ 877/487–2778 ⊕ travel.state.gov/passport.

U.S. Passport and Visa Expediters A. Briggs Passport & Visa Expeditors ☎ 800/806–0581 or 202/388–0111 ⊕ www.abriggs.com. **American Passport Express** ☎ 800/455–5166 ⊕ www.americanpassport.com. **Passport Express** ☎ 800/362–8196 ⊕ www.passportexpress.com. **Travel Document Systems** ☎ 800/874–5100 or 202/638–3800 ⊕ www.traveldocs.com. **Travel the World Visas** ☎ 866/886–8472 ⊕ www.world-visa.com.

▌SAFETY

The rules for safety in London are the same as in New York or any big city. If you're carrying a considerable amount of cash and do not have a safe in your hotel room, it's a good idea to keep it in something like a money belt, but don't get cash out of it in public. Keep a small amount of cash for immediate purchases in your pocket or handbag.

Beyond that, use common sense. In central London, nobody will raise an eyebrow at tourists studying maps on street corners, and don't hesitate to ask for directions. However, outside of the center, exercise general caution about the neighborhoods you walk in: if they don't look safe, take a cab. After midnight, outside of the center, take cabs rather than waiting for a night bus. Although London has plenty of so-called "minicabs"—normal cars driven by self-employed drivers in a cab service—don't ever get into an unmarked car that pulls up offering you "cab service." Take a licensed minicab only from a cab office, or, preferably, a normal London "black cab," which you flag down on the street. Unlicensed minicab drivers have been associated with a slate of violent crimes in recent years.

If you carry a purse, keep a firm grip on it (or even disguise it in a local shopping bag). Store only enough money in the purse to cover casual spending. Distribute the rest of your cash and any valuables among deep front pockets, inside jacket or vest pockets, and a concealed money pouch. Some pubs and bars have "Chelsea clips" under the tables where you can hang your handbag at your knee. Never leave your bag beside your chair or hanging from the back of your chair. Be careful with backpacks, as pickpockets can unzip them on the Tube, or even as you're traveling up an escalator.

■ **TIP**➜ Distribute your cash, credit cards, IDs, and other valuables between a deep front pocket, an inside jacket or vest pocket, and a hidden money pouch. Don't reach for the money pouch once you're in public.

Advisories U.S. Department of State. U.S. Department of State ⊕ *travel.state.gov.*

■ TAXES

Departure taxes are divided into four bands, depending on destination. The Band A tax on a per-person Economy fare is £12, Band B is £60, Band C is £75, and Band D is £85. The fee is subject to government tax increases.

The British sales tax (V.A.T., value-added tax) is 20%. The tax is almost always included in quoted prices in shops, hotels, and restaurants.

Most travelers can get a V.A.T. refund by either the Retail Export or the more cumbersome Direct Export method. Many, but not all, large stores provide these services, but only if you request them; they will handle the paperwork. For the Retail Export method, you must ask the store for Form VAT 407 when making a purchase (you must have identification—passports are best). Some retailers will refund the amount on the spot, but others will use a refund company or the refund booth at the point when you leave the country. For the latter, have the form stamped like any customs form by U.K. customs officials when you leave the country, or, if you're visiting several European Union countries, when you leave the EU. After you're through passport control, take the form to a refund-service counter for an on-the-spot refund (which is usually the quickest and easiest option), or mail it to the address on the form (or the envelope with it) after you arrive home. You receive the total refund stated on the form (the retailer or refund company may deduct a handling fee), but the processing time can be long, especially if you request a credit-card adjustment. This may be preferable to a check, however, as U.S. banks will charge a fee for depositing a check in a foreign currency.

With the Direct Export method, the goods are shipped directly to your home. You must have a Form VAT 407 certified by customs, the police, or a notary public when you get home and then send it back to the store, which will refund your money. For inquiries, contact Her Majesty's Customs & Excise office.

Global Refund is a worldwide service with 240,000 affiliated stores and more than 200 Refund Offices. Its refund form, called a Tax Free Check, is the most common across the European continent. The service issues refunds in the form of cash, check, or credit-card adjustment. Again, the cost of cashing a foreign currency check may exceed the amount of the refund.

V.A.T. Refunds Global Refund ☎ *866/706–6090 in U.S., 800/321–1111 in U.K.* ⊕ *www.globalrefund.com.* **Her Majesty's Revenue & Customs** ☎ *0845/010–9000 within U.K., 292/050–1261 from outside U.K.* ⊕ *www.hmrc.gov.uk/vat.*

■ TIME

London is five hours ahead of New York City. In other words, when it's 3 pm in New York (or noon in Los Angeles), it's 8 pm in London. Note that Great Britain and most European countries also move their clocks ahead for the one-hour differential when daylight saving time goes into effect (although they make the changeover several weeks after the United States).

Time Zones Timeanddate.com. Timeanddate.com can help you figure out the correct time anywhere in the world. ⊕ *www.timeanddate.com/worldclock.*

■ TIPPING

Tipping is done in Britain just as in the United States, but at a lower level. So, although it might make you uncomfortable, tipping less than you would back home in restaurants—and not tipping at all in pubs—is not only accepted, but standard. Tipping more can look like you're showing off. Do not tip movie or theater ushers, elevator operators, or bar staff in pubs—although you can always offer to buy them a drink.

TIPPING GUIDELINES FOR LONDON	
Bartender	In cocktail bars, on the other hand, if you see a tip plate, it's fine to leave £1 or £2. For table service, tip 10% of the cost of the bill. However, the gratuity is often included in the check at more expensive bars.
Bellhop	£1 per bag, depending on the level of the hotel.
Hotel Concierge	£5 or more, if a service is performed for you.
Hotel Doorman	£1 for hailing taxis or carrying bags to check-in desk.
Hotel Maid	It's extremely rare for hotel maids to be tipped; £1 or £2 would be generous.
Porter at Airport or Train Station	£1 per bag
Skycap at Airport	£1–£3 per bag
Taxi Driver	Optional 10%–12%, perhaps a little more for a short ride.
Tour Guide	Tipping optional; £1 or £2 would be generous.
Waiter	10%–15%, with 15% being the norm at high-end restaurants; nothing additional if a service charge is added to the bill.
Other	Restroom attendants in expensive restaurants expect some small change (50p or so). Tip coat-check personnel £1 unless there is a fee (then nothing). Hairdresser and barbers get 10%–15%.

▌ TOURS

BIKE TOURS

London's mayor, Boris Johnson, is a real cycling enthusiast and keen to make the capital more bike-friendly. A 24-hour cycle-for-hire scheme, the Barclays Cycle Hire, was introduced in 2010 to enable Londoners to pick up a bicycle at one of more than 400 docking stations and return it at another. *You can find a map of docking stations at the website below.* The first 30 minutes are free. After that, charges rise incrementally from £1 for one hour up to £50 for the entire 24 hours. There is also a £1 per-day access charge. Fees are payable online, by phone or at docking stations, by credit or debit cards only—cash is not accepted. To sign up, a user goes to the TfL (Transport for London) website and then receives a bike key in the mail, so this scheme is really meant for locals, not tourists. But whether you join the Barclays Cycle Hire scheme or just, per usual, hire a bike for rent from a rental shop, remember that London is still a busy metropolis: unless you're familiar with riding in London traffic, the best way to see it on two wheels is probably to contact one of the excellent cycle tour companies that aim to take you around town, avoiding all the busy routes and traveling along cycle lanes and river paths, down quiet backstreets and through parks.

Tour Operators Barclays Cycle Hire. Barclays Cycle Hire ☎ *0845/026–3630 within U.K., 208/216–6666 from outside U.K.* ⊕ *www.tfl. gov.uk/roadusers/cycling/14808.aspx.* **Cycle Tours of London** ☎ *0778/899–4430* ⊕ *www. biketoursoflondon.com.* **Fat Tire Bike Tours** ☎ *0788/238779 within U.K., 0788/238–8779 from outside U.K.* ⊕ *www.fattirebiketours.com.* **London Bicycle Tour Company** ☎ *020/7928– 6838* ⊕ *www.londonbicycle.com.*

BOAT TOURS

Year-round, but more frequently from April to October, boats cruise the Thames, offering a different view of the London skyline. Most leave from Westminster Pier, Charing Cross Pier, and Tower Pier.

Downstream routes go to the Tower of London, Greenwich, and the Thames Barrier via Canary Wharf. Upstream destinations include Kew, Richmond, and Hampton Court (mainly in summer). Most of the launches seat between 100 and 250 passengers, have a public-address system, and provide a running commentary on passing points of interest. Some include musical entertainment. Depending upon the destination, river trips may last from one to four hours.

Details on all other operators are available as a PDF from Transport for London's River Services page. ⊕ *www.tfl.gov. uk*

River Cruise Operators Bateaux London ☎ *020/7695–1800* ⊕ *www.bateauxlondon. com.* **London Duck Tours** ☎ *020/7928–3132* ⊕ *www.londonducktours.co.uk.* **Thames Cruises** ☎ *020/7928–9009* ⊕ *www. thamescruises.com.* **Thames River Boats** ☎ *020/7930–2062* ⊕ *www.wpsa.co.uk.* **Thames River Services** ☎ *020/930–4097* ⊕ *www.thamesriverservices.co.uk.*

BUS, COACH, AND TAXI TOURS

Guided sightseeing tours from the top of double-decker buses, which are open-top in summer, are a good introduction to the city, as they cover all the main central sights. Numerous companies run daily bus tours that depart (usually between 8:30 and 9 am) from central points. In hop-on, hop-off fashion, you may board or alight at any of the numerous stops to view the sights, and reboard on the next bus. Most companies offer this hop-on, hop-off feature but others, such as Best Value, remain guided tours in traditional coach buses. Tickets can be bought from the driver and are good all day. Prices vary according to the type of tour, although £20 is the benchmark. For that more personal touch, try out a tour in a guided taxi. Other guided bus tours, like those offered by Golden, are not open-top or hop-on, hop-off, but enclosed (and more expensive) coach bus versions.

Bus Tour Operators Best Value Tours ☎ *020/8133–8375* ⊕ *www.bestvaluetours. co.uk.* **Big Bus Tours** ☎ *020/7233–9533* ⊕ *www.bigbustours.com.* **Black Taxi Tour of London** ☎ *020/7935–9363* ⊕ *www. blacktaxitours.co.uk.* **Golden Tours** ☎ *0844/880–5050 in U.K., 800/509–2507 in U.S.* ⊕ *www.goldentours.co.uk.* **Original London Sightseeing Tour** ☎ *020/8877–1722* ⊕ *www.theoriginaltour.com.* **Premium Tours** ☎ *020/7713–1311* ⊕ *www.premiumtours.co.uk.*

CANAL TOURS

The tranquil side of London can be found on narrow boats that cruise the city's two canals, the Grand Union and Regent's Canal; most vessels operate on the latter, which runs between Little Venice in the west (nearest Tube: Warwick Avenue on the Bakerloo line) and Camden Lock (about 200 yards north of Camden Town Tube station). Fares start at about £8.50 for 1½-hour round-trip cruises.

Canal Tour Operators Canal Cruises ☎ *020/8440–8962* ⊕ *www.londoncanalcruises. com.* **Jason's Trip** ☎ *020/7286–3428* ⊕ *www. jasons.co.uk.* **London Waterbus Company** ☎ *020/7482–2550* ⊕ *www.londonwaterbus. co.uk.*

EXCURSIONS

Evan Evans, Green Line, and National Express all offer day excursions by bus to places within easy reach of London, such as Hampton Court, Oxford, Stratford, and Bath.

Tour Operators Evan Evans ☎ *020/7950– 1777, 800/422–9022 in U.S.* ⊕ *www. evanevanstours.co.uk.* **Green Line** ☎ *0844/801–7261* ⊕ *www.greenline.co.uk.* **National Express** ☎ *0871/781–8178* ⊕ *www. nationalexpress.com.*

WALKING TOURS

One of the best ways to get to know London is on foot, and there are many guided and themed walking tours from which to choose. Richard Jones's London Walking Tours includes the Jack the Ripper Walk following in the footsteps of the titular killer, as does the Blood and Tears

Walk. Other tours include Secret London, the West End with Dickens, and Hampstead—A Country Village. Context London's expert docents lead small groups on walks with art, architecture, and similar themes. The London Walks Company hosts more than 100 walks every week on a variety of themes, including a Thames pub walk, Literary Bloomsbury, and Spies and Spycatchers. For more options, pick up a copy of *Time Out* magazine and check the weekly listings for upcoming one-off tours.

Walking Tour Operators Blood and Tears Walk ☎ *07905/746733* ⊕ *www. shockinglondon.com.* **Blue Badge** ☎ *020/7403-1115* ⊕ *www.blue-badge-guides. com.* **Context London** ☎ *0203/318-5637, 800/691-6036 in U.S.* ⊕ *www.contexttravel. com/london.* **London Walks** ☎ *020/7624-3978* ⊕ *www.walks.com.* **Richard Jones's London Walking Tours** ☎ *020/8530-8443* ⊕ *www.walksoflondon.co.uk.* **Shakespeare City Walk** ☎ *07905/746733* ⊕ *www. shakespeareguide.com.*

∎ VISITOR INFORMATION

When you arrive in London, you can get good information at the Travel Information Centre near the Eurostar arrivals area at St. Pancras International train station and at Victoria and Liverpool Street stations. These are helpful if you're looking for brochures for London sights, or if something's gone horribly wrong with your hotel reservation—if, for example, you don't have one—as they have a useful reservations service. The Victoria station center, opposite Platform 8, is open Monday–Saturday 7:15 am–9:15 pm, Sunday 8:15 am–8:15 pm, as are the St. Pancras and Liverpool Street centers. A Travel Information Centre at Euston station has the same hours but closes Saturday at 6:15 pm, while one at the Piccadilly Circus Tube station is open daily 9:15 am–7 pm. The Travel Information Centre at Heathrow is open daily 7:15 am–9 pm, while the Britain and London Visitor Centre on Lower Regent Street is a worthwhile stop for travel, hotel, and entertainment information; it's open Monday 9:30–6 October–March and 9:30–6:30 April–September, Tuesday–Saturday 9–6 October–March and 9–6:30 during April–September, and weekends and public holidays 10–4. There are also London Tourist Information Centres in Greenwich and some other Outer London locations.

Official Websites ⊕ *www.visitbritain.com,* ⊕ *www.visitlondon.com.*

Other Websites ⊕ *www.londontown.com,* the *Evening Standard*'s online ⊕ *www.thisislondon. com,* No. 10 Downing Street ⊕ *www. number-10.gov.uk,* and the BBC ⊕ *www.bbc. co.uk.*

Entertainment Information ⊕ *www.timeout. com/london,* ⊕ *www.officiallondontheatre. co.uk,* and ⊕ *www.kidslovelondon.com.*

INDEX

PHOTO CREDITS

1, Sylvain Grandadam / age fotostock. 3, Rich B-S/Flickr. Chapter 1: Experience: 6-7, William Helsel/ age fotostock. 8, Angelina Dimitrova/Shutterstock. 9 (left), British Tourist Authority. 9 (right), PCL/ Alamy. 10, gary718/Shutterstock. 11 (left), Pres Panayotov/Shutterstock. 11 (right), Kathy deWitt/ Alamy. 12, Jan Kranendonk/Shutterstock. 13 (left), Dominic Burke/Alamy. 13 (right), Doug Scott/age fotostock. 15, Marc Pinter/Shutterstock. 16 (left), Sean Nel/Shutterstock. 16 (top center), Vinicius Tupinamba/Shutterstock. 16 (bottom center), WH Chow/Shutterstock. 16 (top right), Jan Kranendonk/ iStockphoto. 16 (bottom right), Thomas Sztanek/Shutterstock. 17 (top left), Bob Masters/Alamy. 17 (bottom left), Andrew Ward/Life File/Photodisc. 17 (top center), Jack Sullivan/Alamy. 17 (bottom center), Dominic Burke/Alamy. 17 (right), Walter Bibikow/viestiphoto.com. 18 (left), wikipedia.org. 18 (top center), The Print Collector/Alamy. 18 (bottom center and top right), wikipedia.org. 18 (bottom right), www.wga.hu. 19 (top left, bottom left, and right), wikipedia.org. 19 (top center), newsphoto / Alamy. 21 (left and right), British Tourist Authority. 23 (left), Lebrecht Music and Arts Photo Library/ Alamy. 23 (right), Visit London. 26, London 2012. 27, Sylvain Grandadam/age fotostock. 28, British Tourist Authority. 29, David Peta/Shutterstock. 30 (top left), UK21/Alamy. 30 (bottom left), wikipedia. org. 30 (right), Kobby Dagan/Shutterstock. 31 (left), Mike Booth/Alamy. 31 (top right), wikipedia.org. 31 (bottom right), INTERFOTO Pressebildagentur/Alamy. 32 (top left), Robert Stainforth/Alamy. 32 (bottom left), Jeffrey Blackler/Alamy. 32 (right), Andrew Dunn/wikipedia.org. 33 (left), Eric Nathan/ Alamy. 33 (right), Chris Batson/Alamy. 34 (left), Directphoto.org/Alamy. 34 (top right), Zaha Hadid/ wikipedia.org. 34 (bottom right), Nigel Young/British Museum. Chapter 2: Westminster & Royal London: 35, British Tourist Authority. 37, Eric Nathan/ britainonview.com. 38, Peter Adams/age fotostock. 41, ktylerconk/Flickr. 42, Mark William Richardson/Shutterstock. 45, Pres Panayotov/Shutterstock. 48-49, Doug Pearson/age fotostock. 50, British Tourist Authority. 52, John Sturrock/Alamy. 55, Sean Nel/Shutterstock. 59 (left), F. Monheim/R. von Göt/Bildarchiv Monheim/age fotostock. 59 (top right), Dean and Chapter of Westminster. 59 (center right), Mark Thomas/Alamy. 59 (bottom right and 61, Dean and Chapter of Westminster. 63, British Tourist Authority.Chapter 3: St. James's & Mayfair: 65, Roberto Herrett / age fotostock. 67, British Tourist Authority. 68, David Noton Photography/Alamy. 70, Tibor Bognar / age fotostock. 71, Jess Moss. 73, Pawel Libera/Alamy. 74, Derek Croucher/Alamy. 77, Matthew Mawson/Alamy. Chapter 4: Soho & Covent Garden: 79, 81 and 82, British Tourist Authority. 83, Julian Love/John Warburton-Lee Photography/photolibrary.com. 84, Jon Arnold/age fotostock. 86, Ann Steer/iStockphoto. 89, British Tourist Authority. Chapter 5: Bloomsbury & Holborn: 91, Michael Jenner/Alamy. 93 and 94, British Tourist Authority. 96, Jarno Gonzalez Zarraonandia/Shutterstock. 97 and 98 (top), British Museum. 98 (bottom), Grant Rooney/Alamy. 100, British Museum. 101, James McCormick/britainonview.com. 102, Eric Nathan/Alamy. Chapter 6: The City: 107, PSL Images/Alamy. 109, Ryan Fox/age fotostock. 110-11, Jason Hawkes. 112, Jerry Millevoi/age fotostock. 115 (left), F. Monheim/R. von Göt/Bildarchiv Monheim/age fotostock. 115 (top right), Jeff Gynane/Shutterstock. 115 (center right), Ken Ross/viestiphoto.com. 115 (bottom right), Marcin Stalmach/iStockphoto. 117, Rene Ramos/Shutterstock. 119, Russ Merne/Alamy. 121, Imagestate/age fotostock.com. 123, iStockphoto. 125 (left), Walter Bibikow/viestiphoto.com. 125 (right), Tom Hanley/ Alamy. 126 (top), Natasha Marie Brown/HRP/newsteam.co.uk. 127, Peter Phipp/Peter Phipp/age fotostock. 128 (left), Mary Evans Picture Library/Alamy. 128 (center), Reflex Picture Library/Alamy. 128 (right), Classic Image/Alamy. 129, Jan Kranendonk/iStockphoto. Chapter 7: The East End: 131, Janine Wiedel Photolibrary/Alamy. 133, Neil Setchfield/Alamy. 134, foybles/Alamy. 137, Jon Arnold/age fotostock. 140, Elly Godfroy/Alamy. Chapter 8: The South Bank: 143, Mike Peel/wikipedia/org. 145, Eric Nathan/britainonview.com. 146, PCL/Alamy. 149 (top), Shutterstock. 149 (bottom), Duncan Soar/ Alamy. 150, Vehbi Koca/Alamy. 151 (top), Lebrecht Music and Arts Photo Library/Alamy. 151 (bottom), Eric Nathan/britainonview.com. 153, AA World Travel Library/Alamy. 154, Terry Walsh/Shutterstock. 155, Jess Moss. 156, David Pearson / Alamy. Chapter 9: Kensington, Chelsea & Knightsbridge: 159, Cahir Davitt/age fotostock. 161, British Tourist Authority. 162, Robert Harding Picture Library Ltd/Alamy. 165, John Warburton-Lee Photography/Alamy. 166, Londonstills.com/Alamy. 167, British Tourist Authority. 170, Ant Clausen/Shutterstock. 171, PCL/Alamy. Chapter 10: Notting Hill & Bayswater: 173, Roger Cracknell 01/classic / Alamy. 175, Doug Scott/age fotostock. 176, David H. Wells/ age fotostock. 178, Peter Cook/age fotostock. 179, Corbis. 181, Joe Viesti/viestiphoto.com. 182, TNT MAGAZINE/Alamy. 183 (left), Andrew Holt/Alamy. 183 (top right), Dominic Burke/Alamy. 183 (bottom right), David Berry/Shutterstock. Chapter 11: Regent's Park & Hampstead: 185, Earl Patrick Lichfield/britainonview.com. 187, British Tourist Authority. 188, Bildarchiv Monheim GmbH/Alamy. 192, ARCO/R. Kiedrowski/age fotostock. 194, PCL/Alamy. 197, Pictorial Press Ltd/Alamy. 199, PCL/ Alamy. Chapter 12: Greenwich: 201, Michael Booth/Alamy. 203, Visit London. 204, one-image photography/Alamy. 206, Bartlomiej K. Kwieciszewski/Shutterstock. 207, Jon Arnold Images Ltd/Alamy.

209, Mcginnly/wikipedia.org. 210, Visit London. Chapter 13: The Thames Upstream: 213, britainonview.com. 215 and 216, Danilo Donadoni/Marka/age fotostock. 219 and 221, britainonview.com. 223, Rich B-S/Flickr. 224, Rafael Campillo/age fotostock. 225 (left), British Tourist Authority. 225 (right), Danilo Donadoni/Marka/age fotostock. 226, photogl/Shutterstock. 227 (top left), Roger Hutchings/Alamy. 227 (top right), Corbis. 227 (bottom), Lyndon Giffard/Alamy. 228 (top), Mike Booth/Alamy. 228 (bottom), Danilo Donadoni/Marka/age fotostock. 229, wikipedia.org. Chapter 14: Where to Eat: 231, Alain Schroeder / age footstock . 232, Damian Russell. 238, Atlantide S.N.C./age fotostock. 239 (top), Ladurée macaroon by Ewan Munro www.flickr.com/photos/55935853@N00/3911502465/ Attribution ShareAlike License. 239 (bottom), Hix Oyster and Chop House, Smithfield, London by Ewan Munro www.flickr.com/photos/55935853@N00/4337483788/ Attribution ShareAlike License. 240, Gay Hussar. 241 (top), Mowie Kay (www.mowielicious.com). 241 (bottom), Herbert Ypma. 242, Duncan Hale-Sutton / Alamy. 243 (top), Bea's of Bloomsbury by Melanie Seasons www.flickr.com/photos/melanieseasons/5214233876/ Attribution-ShareAlike License. 243 (bottom), Fino. 244, British Tourist Authority. 245 (top), Alexandr Shebanov/Shutterstock. 245 (bottom), Kathy de Witt/britainonview.com. 246, The Berkeley. 247 (top), Dorota Kleina. 247 (bottom), Braised salmon skin and fried aubergine by Ross Bruniges www.flickr.com/photos/thecssdiv/5263440054/Attribution License. 248, Ken Ross/viestiphoto.com. 249 (top), John Carey. 249 (bottom), Four Seasons. 252, Goodman, Mayfair, London by Ewan Munro www.flickr.com/photos/55935853@N00/4476609453/ Attribution ShareAlike License. 257, Jason Lowe Ltd. 266, Harwood Arms. 271, The Orange. Chapter 15: Where to Stay: 289, Danita Delimont/Alamy. 290, City Inn Westminster. 299 (top left), Claridges's Hotel. 299 (bottom left), the Dorchester. 299 (top right), Damian Russell. 299 (bottom right), The Stafford. 309 (top), Marriott International. 309 (bottom left), Leading Hotels of the World. 309(bottom right), Generator Hostel London. 314 (top left), Mandarin Oriental. 314 (top right), Church Street Hotel. 314 (center left), The Hoxton. 314 (center right), Firmdale Hotels. 314 (bottom left), VIEW Pictures Ltd/Alamy. 314 (bottom right), gorehotel.com.uk. Chapter 16: Pubs & Nightlife: 325, Jess Moss. 326, Everynight Images/Alamy. 330, Jess Moss. 335, Phillie Casablanca/Flickr. 341, Phillie Casablanca/Flickr. 342, British Tourist Authority. Chapter 17: Arts & Entertainment: 349, James McCormick/British Tourist Authority. 350, Grant Pritchard/British Tourist Authority. 352, Hugo Glendinning. 354, Bettina Strenske / age fotostock. 362, Lebrecht Music and Arts Photo Library/Alamy. 366, Tate Photography. Chapter 18: Shopping: 369, Tibor Bognar / age fotostock. 372, Heeb Christian/age fotostock. 373, Andrew Parker/Alamy. 374, Jim Batty/Alamy. 375, Phil O'Connor/age fotostock. 376, Ming Tang-Evans. 377, www.kohsamui.co.uk. 387 and 388, British Tourist Authority. 389 and 390, Ingrid Rasmussen/ British Tourist Authority. 391 (top), Nigel.Hicks/britainonview.com. 391 (bottom), and 392 (top and bottom), British Tourist Authority. Chapter 19: Side Trips from London: 415, Andrew Holt/Alamy. 416, Mark Sunderland/Alamy. 423, Daniel Bosworth/Tourism South East /British Tourist Authority. 428, John Martin/Alamy.

NOTES

NOTES

NOTES

NOTES

ABOUT OUR WRITERS

Julius Honnor has lived in, and written about, London for 12 years. Though he is often disappearing off to write and take photographs for guidebooks to places such as Morocco, Italy, and Bolivia, he always hurries home to a fine pint of ale in one of his favorite pubs. Not surprisingly, for this edition, he updated our Pubs and Nightlife chapter along with our Arts and Entertainment chapter, plus our Soho chapter.

A Londoner since public transport was cheap, **Jack Jewers** updated our Experience London and Where to Stay chapters, along with our neighborhood chapters on Notting Hill, Regent's Park, Greenwich, and the Thames Upstream. An ancestor of his was a notorious pirate who was hanged at Tyburn (now a corner of Oxford Street). As London-related jobs go, Jack's may be somewhat less glamorous, but at least his career trajectory is better: he makes independent films, the latest of which, Shalom Kabul, is about the last two Jews of Afghanistan.

James O'Neill loves London and—as his work updating our chapters on Westminster and Royal London, St. James and Mayfair, Bloomsbury and Holborn, The City, and Travel Smart for this edition proves—loves re-discovering it, too. Although originally from Ireland, he's lived in this "quirky, fresh, ever-changing" place (to quote the man himself) for almost twenty years—and still loves it just as much now as he did back then. Over the past 15 years, he has written extensively for TV & radio (mainly for the BBC and Channel 4), the stage, and the page. He is currently finishing his debut novel which is set in—where else?—London.

Ellin Stein has written for publications on both sides of the Atlantic, including the *New York Times, the Times [London], the Guardian, the Telegraph, Variety, People,* and *InStyle,* for whom she was European correspondent. Her new hardcover, *That's Not Funny, That's Sick: The National Lampoon and the Comedy Insurgents Who Captured the Mainstream,* was published by W. W. Norton & Co. in March 2013. Originally from Manhattan, she has lived in London for two decades and is married to a native. For this edition, she updated our Kensington, East End, South Bank, Shopping, and Side Trips from London chapters.

By day, Londoner **Alex Wijeratna** works as a research director for ActionAid: at all other times, he hunts down the best food in town. With his mixed roots, Alex is well aware that London's restaurant boom is built in ethnic diversity. He's written for the *Times, Guardian, Independent* and the *Daily Mail,* and for this edition, Alex updated the Where to Eat chapter.

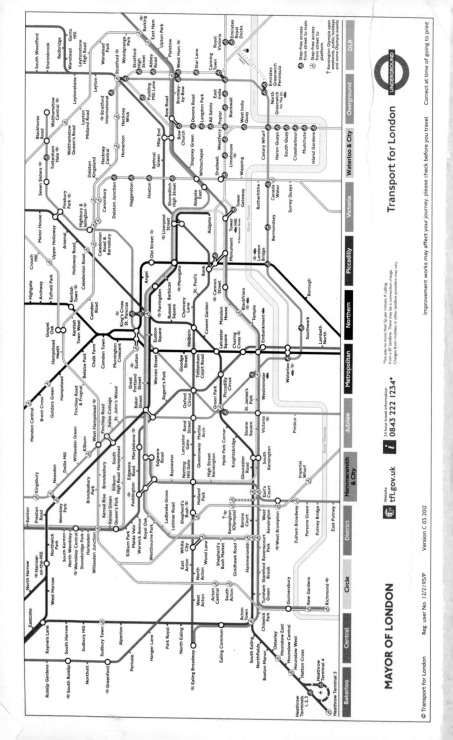